International Logistics

The Management of International Trade
Operations

Pierre A. David
Baldwin Wallace University

June 2017

Cicero Books, www.cicerobooks.com

International Logistics: The Management of International Trade Operations, 5e

Pierre A. David, PhD

Cover image:
Photo © José Lledo/
Shutterstock
used with permission

Cover art:
Daisy Krokos

For product information and technology assistance, please contact us at info@cicerobooks.com or 440.212.5659.
For permission to use material from this book, submit all requests to info@cicerobooks.com.

Library of Congress Control Number: 2017907323

BOOK ISBN-13: 978-0-9894906-4-1
BOOK ISBN-10: 0989490645

Cicero Books LLC
1060 West Bagley Road
Suite 103-B
Berea, OH 44017
440.212.5659

Printed in the United States of America
2 3 4 5 6 7 8 9 10

To my parents, Jack and Eliane

Contents

List of Figures

List of Tables

Preface

A User's Perspective

The content of this textbook has been compiled with the users of international logistics services in mind. It covers all of the concepts that are important to managers who are actively exporting or importing goods, or are otherwise involved in international trade operations. All of the relevant issues are thoroughly explained, including documentation, terms of payment, terms of trade (Incoterms® rules), exchange rate exposure, international insurance, customs clearance, agency and distributorship sales contracts, packaging, transportation, security issues, warehousing, inventory, and quality management.

The book is accessible to the reader: the concepts are clearly and accurately portrayed and the vocabulary is precise, which makes it an easy read for all, including non-native speakers of English. The presentation of the material is logical and the reader can understand a concept without having to refer to material that is presented later in the book. Nevertheless, the interested reader should attempt to read the book "quickly" once, before delving into some of its finer details, in order to get an indication of the interdependencies of the concepts presented.

Since the book introduces topics that tend to be technical or unfamiliar to many readers, there are more than two hundred and forty color illustrations, tables, and figures in the text to support the core content. All were chosen carefully to accurately depict the concepts presented in the text.

This textbook has been adopted by most of the logistics programs in the United States and many abroad. It is the official reference textbook for the international portion of the Certification in Transportation and Logistics offered by the American Society of Transportation and Logistics, and is recommended for the Certified Global Business Professional examination of the North American Small Business International Trade Educators.

What's New in this Edition

The fifth edition includes many changes, the most obvious being that there are now three additional chapters: warehousing, supply chain operations: inventory control, and supply chain operations: quality. The warehousing chapter is a necessary addition for those survey courses that attempt to cover all aspects of international logistics, and several faculty members had requested that it be added. I hope that it meets their expectations. The operations chapters are more technical and are better suited for those courses that are managerial in their focus. Several faculty members had also requested this addition, and I hope that they meet their expectations. These two chapters require that the students be somewhat familiar with statistical concepts before they can be understood.

I am pleased that the book is still published by Cicero Books, a publisher that is committed to offering this book at an affordable price. The publisher accepted to publish all illustrations in color, which makes the concepts of international logistics more vivid and attractive.

As for previous editions, the remainder of the text has been completely updated, with new tables, new examples, and new photographs.

Electronic and Print Versions

International Logistics: The Management of International Trade Operations, Fifth Edition, is available electronically, in a Kindle and a Javelin (secure pdf) version, as well as in print. Students who purchase the book directly from Cicero Books— in either version at the publisher's website, www.cicerobooks.com—have access to the Powerpoint presentations accompanying each chapter. They do not need to be online to read it, and the book is permanently stored on their computer, tablet, or phone.

Instructors' Supplements

Powerpoint presentations are provided with each chapter, which can be freely edited to reflect a particular pedagogical style. There are two versions of the slides: one is in full color for direct classroom use, and the other is basic so it can be imported in a professor's own presentation template.

A **test bank** is available as well, written in Microsoft Word, so the questions can be edited to reflect the style of the faculty member and the level of instruction. It can also be imported directly into Blackboard or Moodle.

A brief **instructor's manual** offers sample syllabi and other suggestions to suit a particular academic emphasis.

Finally, there is a free **USB card of videos and photographs** that complement the materials in this book. They are available to faculty members upon request, by contacting the author at pdavid@bw.edu.

Acknowledgements

This book is the result of the influence of many: Richard Stewart, of the University of Wisconsin-Superior, who was my co-author for the second and third edition, and whose contributions are most present in Chapter 11; Robert Materna, of Embry-Riddle Aeronautical University Worldwide, who was instrumental on a revision of Chapter 12 in the third edition; and Earl Peck, professor *emeritus* at Baldwin Wallace University, who provided much material for Chapter 8. Finally, the influence of my mentors at Kent State University, J. Randall Brown and Milton Harvey, is evident throughout the book, as they taught me this writing style.

I am also thankful for all of the suggestions I received from many colleagues: Hans-Joachim Schramm (Wirtschaftsuniversität Wien), Ephrem Eyob (Virginia State University), Bruce Arntzen (Massachusetts Institute of Technology), Helmut Kellerman (Tacoma Community College), William Borden (John Carroll University), Bud Cohan (Columbus State Community College), Jim Chester (Baylor Law School), Frank W. Davis (University of Tennessee-Knoxville), Charles Kerr (Long Beach City College), Jeanne Lawrence (East Carolina University), Edison Moura (Sul Ross State University-Rio Grande College Del Rio), MyongSop Pak (Sungkyunkwan University), Stephen Hays Russell (Weber State University), Yavuz Agan (Western Illinois University), Syed Tariq Anwar (West Texas A&M University), Angelica Cortes (University of Texas-Pan American), Stanley Flax (St. Thomas University), Mary Jo Geyer (Robert Morris University), Tom Grooms (Northwood University), Jon Helmick (United States Merchant Marine Academy), Thuong T. Le (University of Toledo), Larry LeBlanc (Vanderbilt University), Michael Munro (Florida International University), Steve Swartz (University of North Texas), Evelyn Thomchick (The Pennsylvania State University), and Peter Weaver (Ferris State University).

Many students also helped me make this book a reality: I would like to recognize George Iskandar, Mark Forquer, Jeffrey Halaparda, Jamie Serenko, Elise Wallis, Andrew Ghanem, Patrick LaGuardia, Clay Gillman, and Daisy Krokos (all of Baldwin Wallace University).

I am also indebted to Steve Scoble, Kendra Leonard, and Matt Walker at Atomic Dog-Thomson Publishing, as well as Sarah Blasco and Greg Albert at Cengage for their help with prior editions. This edition was edited by Kristina Stiffler, of Commercial Writing Solutions, LLC, with whom I have worked on many projects for the Accenture Supply Chain Academy and the Accenture Finance Academy.

Finally, I must thank my wife Beth and our children Natalie, Caroline, and Timothy for their help and support in getting this fifth edition together. I could not have done it without your continued patience and understanding.

Thank you.

About the Author

Pierre A. David, Ph.D.
Baldwin Wallace University

Pierre David is a Professor of Business Administration at Baldwin Wallace University, a private liberal-arts institution located in Berea, Ohio. His teaching interests are in marketing and operations management, particularly as these disciplines are applied to an international environment: his primary teaching focus are the courses in international logistics and international market research. His regular teaching schedule also includes courses in international marketing, market research, and operations management at the graduate and undergraduate levels. Based upon student recommendations, he has received the Bechberger Award for Excellence in Teaching.

He has been a course developer for the Accenture Supply Chain Academy and the Accenture Finance Academy since 2008, for which he has written more than fifteen courses on topics related to international logistics and the management of the international supply chain.

He earned a PhD from Kent State University, an MBA from the University of Pittsburgh, and an MBA from l'École de Hautes Études Commerciales du Nord in Lille, France, all of which were in marketing and operations management. His French *baccalauréat* is in mathematics and physics.

Pierre has had the opportunity to conduct international logistics training sessions in the United States, France, Turkey, China, and Brazil. He has lived in four different countries (Tunisia, Switzerland, France, and the United States) and visited a dozen more.

Chapter 1

International Trade

international trade
The sale of goods and
services across
international borders.

Since World War II the world has seen an unprecedented increase in international trade and a parallel improvement in the economic development of most nations. Countries that could barely feed their population sixty years ago are now economic powerhouses where inhabitants enjoy a modern standard of living and where many companies trade internationally. In most developing countries, governments are no longer addressing famine and abject poverty. Their concerns are now similar to those of other developed countries: pollution and urban gridlock.

constant dollars
Dollars adjusted for
inflation so that it is
possible to compare dollar
values from one period to
another.

This increase in international trade was triggered by the realization that countries' economies benefit from international trade and that trade increases the well-being of the world's population. Figure 1.1 shows how much international trade has grown in constant dollars. It also shows the respective shares of international trade that the twenty-eight European Union countries, the United States, Japan, China, and the remainder of the world represented from 1950 until 2015.[1] Although the economic crisis of 2008-2009 reduced the overall volume of international trade, this decrease was temporary. As people's standards of living increase worldwide, so does their ability to purchase goods, and therefore international trade also increases.

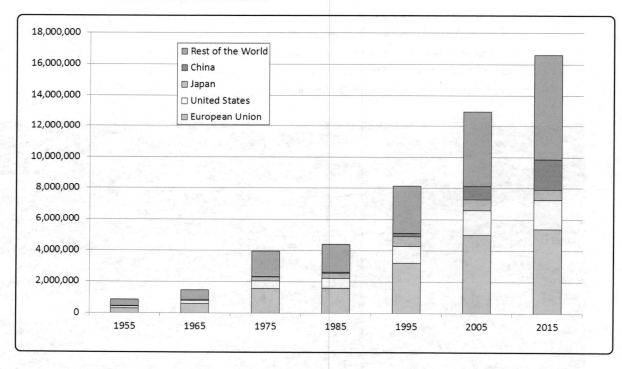

Figure 1.1: Growth in International Merchandise Trade and Share of Selected Countries (in constant [2015] US$ millions)
World Trade Organization.

International-logistics professionals have been the main facilitators of international-trade growth. They have been the managers responsible for the safe and timely deliveries of these billions of dollars of goods. They are responsible for:

- arranging the transportation of goods over thousands of miles,

- understanding the trade-offs between the different modes of transportation,

- choosing the right carrier,

- making sure that the goods are packaged properly for their journey,

- understanding the risks the goods face while in transit, and insuring against these risks appropriately,

- minimizing the risks associated with international payments by selecting the right payment currency and the right hedging strategy,

- making sure that the goods are accompanied by the proper documentation so that they can clear customs in the country of destination,

- defining who, whether themselves or their foreign counterparts, is responsible for each aspect of the voyage and related documents,

- determining which payment method is most suitable between the exporter and the importer,

- following the security measures designed to prevent damage to the goods while they are in transit, as well as following regulations imposed by the governments of importing countries and international organizations,

- storing the goods in appropriate warehouses and distribution centers when they are not in transit,

- ensuring that the inventory levels of the goods in the supply chain are sufficient to meet customer demand,

- verifying that the quality standards specified by customers are appropriately followed,

- following the best sustainability practices in shipping, packaging, and storing goods, and

- providing information to all the parties involved in an international transaction, so that these parties can determine where the goods are located at any time.

While the responsibilities of an international logistics manager will be covered throughout this textbook, this chapter reviews the extent of international trade, the economic theories of international trade, and the difficulties associated with conducting business in an international environment.

Figure 1.2: The Boeing 787 Dreamliner
Photo ©Philip Pilosian/Shutterstock. Used with permission.

The Boeing 787 Dreamliner

The Boeing Company introduced its Boeing 787 model in 2007, and its first commercial flight was in early 2012 with All Nippon Airways. By all accounts, the 787 aircraft is a commercial success; by the end of February 2017, the company had delivered more than 500 aircrafts to 43 different airlines,[2] in more than 20 countries, at an approximate cost of US$ 250 million each.[3] The company had orders for more than 700 additional aircrafts from more than 20 other companies. There are at least 120 airports in 100 countries in which this aircraft operates.

Ethiopian Airlines has ordered 16 of these airplanes, and has taken possession of 13 of them. Figure 1.2 shows one of them taking off from Los Angeles airport.

When designing its 787 new aircraft, Boeing changed two of its past practices. First, the aircraft is made of composite materials rather than aluminum, which makes it lighter and more efficient to operate. The company also decided to build this aircraft by outsourcing many of its components to foreign and domestic suppliers, rather than build it mostly in-house, as it had for previous models; engines can be supplied by General Electric in the United States or Rolls-Royce in Great Britain, wings are made by Mitsubishi in Japan, the wingtips by KAA in Korea, the forward fuselage by Kawasaki in Japan, the center fuselage by Alenia in Italy, and the rear fuselage by Boeing in the United States. Passenger doors are made by Latécoère in France, and the cargo doors by Saab in Sweden. The landing gears are made by Messier-Dowty in Great Britain, and the landing gear doors by Boeing in Canada.

All in all, Boeing, the largest exporter in the United States—it accounts for roughly 2 percent of the total U.S. exports[4]—exports to dozens of countries and imports from many others. The Boeing 787, although it is an American plane designed by an American company, is truly characteristic of the world economy in which international logisticians operate; an international supply chain.

1.1   International Trade Growth

In current U.S. dollars (that is, not corrected for inflation), international trade in merchandise has grown 27,600 percent between 1948 and 2015.[5] That is, international trade is 277 times larger in 2015 than in 1948, which equates to an average annual growth rate of 8.62 percent. In constant US dollars (that is, corrected for inflation, and expressed in 2015 dollars), the growth was 2,714 percent for the same period. International trade is 28.1 times larger in 2015 than it was in 1948, which equates to an average annual growth rate of 5.03 percent.

In constant US dollars (2015 dollars), international trade in merchandise and services has almost tripled since 1990, an increase that equates an average annual growth rate of about 4 percent. Tables 1.1[6], 1.2[7], and 1.3[8] show the World Trade Organization's data for the value of international trade in merchandise, services, and both, for the years for which it has collected that information.

The tables show modest growth between 2010 and 2015. However, this is somewhat misleading: international trade actually grew substantially during this period. The total value of world trade (merchandise and services) in 2014—a value not displayed on Table 1.3—was US$ 24,089 billion for exports, and US$ 24,048 billion for imports. The sharp decrease from 2014 to 2015—to US$ 21,236 billion and US$ 21,337 billion respectively, as shown on the Table—does not correspond to an actual decrease in international trade, but is due to the data being tabulated in United States dollars: international trade decreased 12 percent in U.S. dollars from 2014 to 2015, despite a 2.8 percent increase in volume,[9] because the value of the dollar increased substantially against other currencies during that period. As the value of the dollar increases, transactions that take place in other currencies (euros, pounds, yen, yuan, . . . etc.) are recorded at a lower value. International trade volume is expected to grow approximately 2.8 percent in 2016, and 4 percent in 2017.[10]

current dollars
Dollars not adjusted for inflation. Their value is determined by the year they were actually received or paid.

constant dollars
Dollars adjusted for inflation so that it is possible to compare dollar values from one period to another.

International Trade Volume in Merchandise in US$ billions

Year	Current US dollars		2015 Constant US dollars	
	Exports	Imports	Exports	Imports
1955	95	99	840	875
1960	130	137	1,041	1,097
1965	190	199	1,430	1,497
1970	317	329	1,936	2,010
1975	877	912	3,863	4,018
1980	2,036	2,077	5,856	5,974
1985	1,953	2,016	4,302	4,440
1990	3,490	3,600	6,328	6,528
1995	5,168	5,285	8,037	8,219
2000	6,458	6,725	8,888	9,256
2005	10,509	10,870	12,753	13,191
2010	15,301	15,511	16,635	16,863
2015	16,482	16,725	16,482	16,725

Table 1.1: International Trade Volume in Merchandise in US$ billions
World Trade Organization.

International Trade Volume in Services in US$ billions

Year	Current US dollars		2015 Constant US dollars	
	Exports	Imports	Exports	Imports
1980	396	448	1,138	1,288
1985	411	444	906	977
1990	831	875	1,507	1,587
1995	1,222	1,241	1,901	1,930
2000	1,522	1,519	2,095	2,091
2005	2,573	2,472	3,123	3,000
2010	3,896	3,739	4,236	4,065
2015	4,754	4,612	4,754	4,612

Table 1.2: International Trade Volume in Services in US$ billions
World Trade Organization.

In addition, even though the total value of exports and total value of imports should be identical, they are slightly different because of the different ways in which these values are calculated.[11] For 2015, merchandise import values are roughly U.S.$ 250 billion higher than merchandise export values because, in some countries, import values include the value of international shipping and insurance, and export values do not. In other countries, exports and imports are valued identically. For services, exports include the value of assists, which are items such as patents and copyrights, and manufacturing assistance, such as machine molds. They are not counted as services when they are imported, but are counted as part of the value of the merchandises that they help manufacture. Overall, though, the differences between these two numbers are mostly due to technical accounting differences.

assist
An item provided by the importer to the exporter so that the exporter can manufacture the imported goods. The value of the assist should be included in the valuation of the imported goods.

Total International Trade Volume in US$ billions

Year	Current US dollars		2015 Constant US dollars	
	Exports	Imports	Exports	Imports
1980	2,432	2,525	6,994	7,262
1985	2,364	2,460	5,207	5,418
1990	4,321	4,475	7,836	8,115
1995	6,390	6,526	9,938	10,149
2000	7,980	8,244	10,983	11,347
2005	13,082	13,342	15,876	16,191
2010	19,197	19,250	20,870	20,928
2015	21,236	21,337	21,236	21,337

Table 1.3: Total International Trade in Merchandise and Services in US$ billions
World Trade Organization.

The increase in international trade over the last six and a half decades was triggered by a massive liberalization of international commerce following World War II. It was also enabled by the creation of a number of international organizations designed to facilitate international commerce, and a significant decrease in transportation costs and transit times. During this period, a greater consumer acceptance of things "foreign," from food to automobiles, allowed an increasing number of companies to expand sales beyond their domestic borders.

1.2   International Trade Milestones

The development of international trade has been fostered by many critical milestones, the ratification of several key international treaties, and the establishment of international organizations designed to facilitate and support international trade activities. These include the Bretton-Woods Conference, the creation of the World Trade Organization, the ratification of the Treaty of Rome, the creation of the European Union, the introduction of the euro, and the adoption of many other economic agreements.

1.2.1   The Bretton-Woods Conference

Bretton-Woods
A 1944 conference at which many of the international institutions were created.

In July 1944, world leaders of the Allied nations met in the resort town of Bretton-Woods in New Hampshire in the United States. The Bretton-Woods Conference led to the creation of several international institutions, two of which were specifically designed to facilitate world trade:

International Monetary Fund
The international organization created in 1945 to oversee exchange rates and develop an international system of payments.

- The International Monetary Fund (IMF) established an international system of payment and introduced stable currency exchange rates. It was created on December 27, 1945.

General Agreement on Tariffs and Trade
An agreement between countries to lower tariffs and trade barriers.

tariff
A tax collected by an importing country on the value of imported goods.

- The General Agreement on Tariffs and Trade (GATT), which through multiple negotiation periods (in Geneva [1948], Annecy [1949], Torquay [1951], Geneva [1956], the Dillon Round [1960-61], the Kennedy Round [1964-67], the Tokyo Round [1973-79], and the Uruguay Round [1986-94]), led to a decrease of duty rate from an average of over 40 percent in 1947 to an average slightly above 4 percent in 2015.[12]

1.2.2   The World Trade Organization

World Trade Organization
The international organization responsible for enforcing international trade agreements and for ensuring that countries deal fairly with one another.

The World Trade Organization (WTO) was officially created on January 1, 1995.[13] The WTO replaced the GATT and it is the organization in charge of enforcing free trade. From 2001 to 2008, the WTO worked on the Doha Developmental Round of multilateral negotiations. The goal of these negotiations was to improve trade in agricultural commodities, which is impeded by several non-tariff barriers, and replete with agricultural subsidies in developed countries. The Doha Developmental Round stalled in July 2008, and no progress has been made since then. In April 2011, Pascal Lamy, the Director-General of the WTO, urged world leaders to resume the negotiations, but recognized that there were major remaining obstacles.[14] The main point of dissension is that developed countries, specifically the United States, Japan, and the European Union countries, continue to grant agricultural subsidies to their farmers. The developing countries regard these subsidies as trade barriers that prevent their lower-priced commodities from competing. As of September 2016, the Doha Developmental Round seemed to be stalled with no clear possibility of resuming.[15]

1.2.3 The Treaty of Rome and the European Union

The Treaty of Rome was signed in 1957 between Belgium, France, Germany, Italy, Luxembourg, and the Netherlands. This treaty led to the eventual creation of the European Union by these six European countries and it was emulated by countless other groups of countries that were more or less successful in designing their own common markets. The European Union expanded in 1973 (Denmark, Ireland, and the United Kingdom), in 1981 (Greece), in 1986 (Spain and Portugal), in 1995 (Austria, Finland, and Sweden), in 2004 (Cyprus, Czech Republic, Estonia, Hungary, Latvia, Lithuania, Malta, Poland, Slovakia, and Slovenia), in 2007 (Bulgaria and Romania), and in 2013 (Croatia). The European Union includes twenty eight countries as of September 2016. The Treaty of Rome established the groundwork for the creation of the European Union. It was extended by the Maastricht Treaty (1992), which created the euro. It was extended again by the Treaty of Lisbon (2009), which modified the governmental processes of the Union to allow a simple majority of member countries to rule, rather than the unanimity that had been required originally.

Treaty of Rome
The treaty between six countries that started the European Union.

In June 2016, the United Kingdom held a referendum in which voters decided to leave the European Union. The decision to leave, nicknamed Brexit—a contraction for British exit—, was controversial in that some British voters understood the referendum as a vote of non-support for David Cameron, the Prime Minister.[16] The referendum was also analyzed as a vote of frustration against immigration in Britain, which many blamed on the European Union's policies,[17] and as a clash between older voters, who wanted to leave, and younger ones, who wanted to stay.[18] It is unclear how the United Kingdom will leave the Union, and businesses and world leaders are uncertain about the impact of this decision. All agree, though, that the decision by Britain to leave the Union was a setback to the progress of globalization and international trade.[19]

Maastricht Treaty
A 1992 Treaty between the European Union countries in which a number of standards were adopted, including a standard currency.

1.2.4 Other Economic Agreements

The creation and success of the European Union triggered the formation of several other regional economic groups.

The first step[20] in creating of an economic group is establishing a free-trade agreement. These agreements can be bilateral, involving only two countries, or multilateral, involving multiple countries. In a free-trade agreement, the signatory countries eliminate tariffs for goods sold among themselves. The North American Free Trade Area, created in 1994 between the United States, Canada, and Mexico is a free-trade agreement. The Trans-Pacific Partnership (TPP) extends the trade area to countries with which the United States already had bilateral free-trade agreements, such as Australia and Chile, and some with which it did not. The TPP includes twelve countries around the Pacific (see Table 1.4 on the next page), but excludes China. Donald Trump, President of the United States, pulled the United States out of the TPP in January 2017.[21] In the spring of 2017, it was unclear whether the agreement would survive the withdrawal of the largest trade entity in the group.

Economic Group	Current Membership (2016)
Moving toward an Economic and Political Union	
European Union	Austria, Belgium, Bulgaria, Cyprus, Czech Republic, Croatia, Denmark, Estonia, Finland, France, Germany, Greece, Hungary, Ireland, Italy, Latvia, Lithuania, Luxembourg, Malta, the Netherlands, Poland, Portugal, Romania, Slovakia, Slovenia, Spain, Sweden, (the United Kingdom).
Moving toward a Common Market	
Association of South East Asian Nations (ASEAN)	Brunei, Cambodia, Indonesia, Laos, Malaysia, Myanmar, Philippines, Singapore, Thailand, Vietnam.
Gulf Cooperation Council (GCC)	Bahrain, Kuwait, Oman, Qatar, Saudi Arabia, United Arab Emirates.
Eurasian Economic Union (EEU)	Armenia, Belarus, Kazakhstan, Kyrgyzstan, Russia.
Having Established a Customs Union	
Central American Integration System (SICA)	Belize, Costa Rica, El Salvador, Guatemala, Honduras, Nicaragua, Panama.
Andean Community	Bolivia, Colombia, Ecuador, Peru.
Southern Common Market ((Mercosur/Mercosul)	Argentina, Brazil, Paraguay, Uruguay, Venezuela
South African Customs Union	Botswana, Lesotho, Namibia, Swaziland, South Africa.
Having Established a Free-Trade Area	
North American Free-Trade Area (NAFTA)	Canada, Mexico, United States.
East African Community	Burundi, Kenya, Rwanda, South Sudan, Tanzania, Uganda.
Trans-Pacific Partnership (TPP)	Australia, Brunei, Canada, Chile, Japan, Malaysia, Mexico, New Zealand, Peru, Singapore, Vietnam.
Having Establishing a Cooperation Group	
Caribbean Community (Caricom)	Antigua and Barbuda, Bahamas, Barbados, Belize, Dominica, Grenada, Guyana, Haiti, Jamaica, Montserrat, Saint Kitts and Nevis, Saint Lucia, Saint Vincent and the Grenadines, Suriname, Trinidad and Tobago.
Economic Community of Community of Western African States (ECOWAS)	Benin, Burkina Faso, Cape Verde, Côte d'Ivoire, Gambia, Ghana, Guinea, Guinea-Bissau, Liberia, Mali, Niger, Nigeria, Senegal, Sierra Leone, Togo.
Economic Community of Central African States (ECCAS)	Angola, Burundi, Cameroon, Central African Republic, Chad, Democratic Republic of the Congo, Republic of the Congo, Equatorial Guinea, Gabon, Rwanda, São Tomé and Príncipe.

Table 1.4: Economic Trade Blocs

The next step in creating an economic group is to establish a customs union, in which member countries agree to implement a common external trade policy. This policy includes charging the same tariff for goods imported in the member countries. The Southern Common Market (Mercosur in Spanish, Mercosul in Portuguese), the Central American Integration System (SICA), and the South African Customs Union have all created customs unions. Table 1.4 lists these groups' memberships. Once a group of countries adopts a common economic policy, the group is generally recognized as a trade bloc, or a single economic entity rather than a group of individual countries.

Trade blocs become common markets when they allow the free circulation of goods, people, and capital among member countries. Citizens of one member country can freely work in another member country, for example. The Association of South East Asian Nations (ASEAN), the Gulf Cooperation Council (GCC), and the Eurasian Economic Union (EEU), have achieved some of these objectives. ASEAN allows professionals, such as physicians and engineers, to work in any of the group's countries, but not all workers. The GCC allows the free flow of capital and workers, but some barriers remain in the flow of goods and services.[22] The EEU has achieved the free movement of most services, but air services are still purely national.[23]

The next step is to create an economic union, in which member countries establish common economic strategies, including fiscal and monetary policies. The European Union has achieved a common monetary policy with the creation of the European Central Bank. However, the Union has struggled with fiscal policy, with some countries exercising fiscal control and restraints, and others being more profligate. The EU has also had difficulties in implementing a common agricultural policy that would eliminate the various subsidies granted to some farmers.[24]

Finally, a group of countries can become a political union when it centralizes its government. The European Union has a European Parliament as well as a European Court system, but does not have a single executive decision body. There are no groups of countries that have achieved a political union, although it is possible to consider the United States, with fifty states but a single central government, and Switzerland, a Confederation of twenty six *cantons*, as political unions.

1.2.5 The Creation of the Euro

The euro is the European currency introduced in 1999 and put into circulation on January 1, 2002 in twelve of the fifteen countries of the European Union (Austria, Belgium, Finland, France, Germany, Greece, Italy, Ireland, Luxembourg, the Netherlands, Portugal, and Spain). The adoption of the euro was extended to Slovenia in 2007, to Cyprus and Malta in 2008, to Slovakia in 2009, to Estonia in 2011, to Latvia in 2014, and to Lithuania in 2015.

The euro has become the currency of several smaller countries not part of the European Union (Andorra, the Holy See—Vatican City—, Kosovo, Monaco, Montenegro, and San Marino), as well as the currency to which many other countries

euro
The common currency of 19 of the 28 countries of the European Union.

have pegged their currencies: Tunisia, Bulgaria, Macedonia, as well as Bosnia and Herzegovina, use currencies that have a fixed exchange rate with the euro. The Communité Française Africaine (Benin, Burkina Faso, Cameroon, Central African Republic, Chad Equatorial Guinea, Gabon, Guinea-Bissau, Ivory Coast, Mali, Niger, Republic of the Congo—Brazzaville—, Senegal, Togo) is also a group of countries whose currencies are pegged to the euro.

Figure 1.3: The European Currency since 2001, the Euro
Photo ©Billion Photos/Shutterstock. Used with permission.

Before the euro was created, the European Union member nations had agreed to keep the values of their currencies within a few percentage points of one another, with the objective of preparing for a single currency. This system was called the Exchange Rate Mechanism. Of the countries that initially signed the Maastricht Treaty in 1992, three did adopt the euro. Denmark is the only member country that has kept its currency in the Exchange Rate Mechanism: the krone's exchange rate must remain within ±2.25 percent of the euro's value. The United Kingdom and Sweden have currencies (the pound and the krona) that float freely against the euro; their values are determine by the supply and demand of these currencies. All of the countries that adopt the euro have to successfully participate in the ERM for a minimum of two years in preparation for the adoption of the euro: Bulgaria, Croatia, the Czech Republic, Hungary, Poland, and Romania are EU members that are planning to eventually use the euro. Bulgaria's currency (lev) is pegged to the euro, but the country has not set a date for the adoption of the common currency. The Czech Republic (koruna) intends to adopt the euro by 2020, and so do Hungary (forint), and Romania (leu). They will therefore have to join the ERM by 2018. Croatia (kuna) admits its economy is not ready for the change, and Poland (zloty) has made no decision in view of some political opposition to the move.

The euro was the first multinational effort at replacing eleven strong legacy currencies (the twelfth, the Greek drachma, was added in 2001, just before the introduction of the euro), and it has become the second most widely-traded currency in the world, after the U.S. dollar. Of all international transactions conducted in the world, the U.S. dollar represents 87 percent, and the euro represent 33 percent (all currency transactions add to 200 percent since two currencies are involved in each transaction).[25]

1.3 Largest Exporting and Importing Countries

Figures 1.4 on the following page[26] and 1.5 on page 15[27] show the fifteen largest exporting and importing countries for 2015 according to the World Trade Organization.

Most of these countries have liberal trading policies and multiple free-trade agreements, confirming that liberal trade policies encourage economic growth and development; more specific information about these countries' general trade policies can be found in the World Bank's "Doing Business" database.[28]

There are nevertheless substantial differences in the ratio of exports to imports for the largest exporting countries. For example, three countries run large trade deficits; the United States, with a deficit of U.S.$ 803 billion, imports about 53 percent more than it exports. The United Kingdom imports U.S.$ 166 billion more than it exports—or 36 percent of its exports—and India imports U.S.$ 125 billion more than it exports—or 47 percent of its exports.

trade deficit
A situation where the total exports of a country are worth less than its total imports.

In contrast, China runs a trade surplus of U.S.$ 593 billion, importing only 74 percent of what it exports. Germany runs a trade surplus of U.S.$ 279 billion—and imports only 79 percent of what it exports. The Netherlands and Belgium also show a trade surplus with imports representing only 89 and 78 percent of their exports, respectively. Although China's surplus is due to its low manufacturing labor costs, Germany, the Netherlands and Belgium experience some of the highest manufacturing labor costs in the world; Belgium's hourly manufacturing labor costs are 50 percent higher than those of the United States, for example.[29] Their export success is due to their unrelenting efforts at securing international sales for their innovative products.

trade surplus
A situation where the total exports of a country are worth more than its total imports.

Some countries are extremely dependent on world trade and export a substantial percentage of their GDP. Belgium exports 84 percent of what it produces, the Netherlands exports 83 percent, and Germany exports 47 percent. In contrast, the United States exports only 13 percent of its GDP, and Japan exports only 18 percent. China, the largest exporter in the world, exports 22 percent of its GDP.[30]

Finally, all of the countries on these lists export—and import—mostly manufactured goods, rather than raw materials or agricultural products.

Rank	Exporting Country	Exports	Share
1	China	2,275	13.8%
2	United States	1,505	9.1%
3	Germany	1,329	8.1%
4	Japan	625	3.8%
5	The Netherlands	567	3.4%
6	Republic of Korea	527	3.2%
7	Hong Kong, China	511	3.1%
8	France	506	3.1%
9	United Kingdom	460	2.8%
10	Italy	459	2.8%
11	Canada	408	2.5%
12	Belgium	398	2.4%
13	Mexico	381	2.3%
14	Singapore	351	2.1%
15	Russian Federation	340	2.1%
	Top fifteen exporters	10,643	64.6%
	Rest of the World	5,839	35.4%
	Total	16,482	100%

Figure 1.4: Largest Merchandise Exporting Countries (2015) in U.S.$ billions
World Trade Organization.

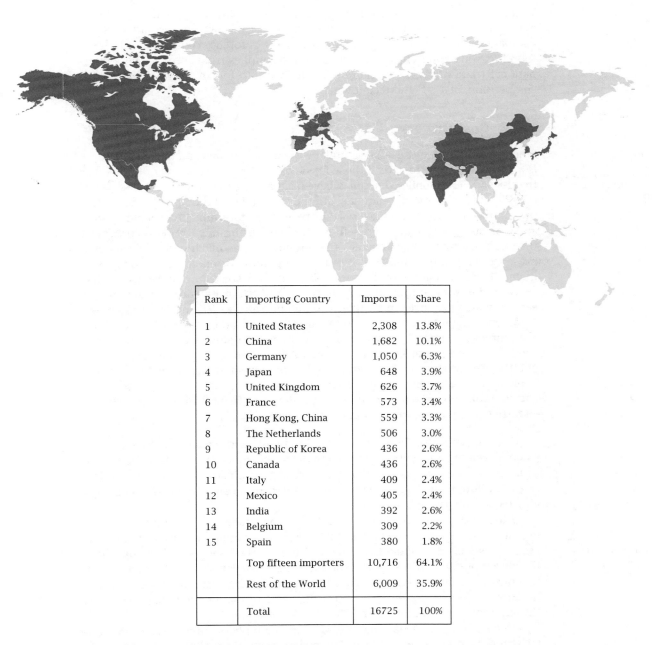

Rank	Importing Country	Imports	Share
1	United States	2,308	13.8%
2	China	1,682	10.1%
3	Germany	1,050	6.3%
4	Japan	648	3.9%
5	United Kingdom	626	3.7%
6	France	573	3.4%
7	Hong Kong, China	559	3.3%
8	The Netherlands	506	3.0%
9	Republic of Korea	436	2.6%
10	Canada	436	2.6%
11	Italy	409	2.4%
12	Mexico	405	2.4%
13	India	392	2.6%
14	Belgium	309	2.2%
15	Spain	380	1.8%
	Top fifteen importers	10,716	64.1%
	Rest of the World	6,009	35.9%
	Total	16725	100%

Figure 1.5: Largest Merchandise Importing Countries (2015) in U.S.$ billions
World Trade Organization.

1.4   International Trade Drivers

There are several international trade drivers that have created the enormous surge in international trade in the second half of the twentieth century. Some companies found reasons to expand their sales in foreign countries, and others found reasons to purchase raw materials and supplies from abroad. These international trade drivers can generally be divided into four main categories: cost, competition, market, and technology.

1.4.1   Cost Drivers

cost driver
One reason a firm may go international is to spread its costs over a large number of units.

When companies require large capital investments in plants and machinery, there is a strong incentive to spread those fixed costs over a large number of units. For that reason, automobile companies have been among the first to seek customers outside of their domestic markets, and the companies that dominate that industry are present in just about every country: Ford Motor Company, Toyota Motors, and Volkswagen produce and sell automobiles in the most remote corners of the world. Automobile companies that do not have as much of an international presence tend to be purchased by their competitors or enter partnerships with them. The consolidation of the automobile industry started in the 1970s and has evolved to include approximately fourteen multinational manufacturing groups, each of which produces more than two million vehicles: the newcomers are the automobile manufactures from India and China, and these manufacturers have also purchased assets worldwide. For example, Tata Motors of India purchased Land Rover and Jaguar in 2008, and Geely Automobile of China purchased Volvo in 2010. The worldwide consolidation of automobile manufacturing is evident in Table 1.5 on the facing page, that shows the world's largest automobiles groups,[31] and in Table 1.6 on page 18, that shows the top fifteen vehicle-manufacturing countries (automobiles and commercial vehicles).[32]

However, cost drivers are not limited to plants and machinery. In industries where developmental costs are high and the costs of manufacturing are low, such as in the software industry, companies are eager to increase their international sales to dilute their developmental costs; Microsoft is an example of a company affected by this type of cost driver.

outsourcing
A practice that consists of a business contracting with other businesses to have them perform some of the operations it used to handle in-house.

Other cost drivers that increase international trade are found on the sourcing side; for example, companies that assemble products from parts and sub-assemblies (called Original Equipment Manufacturers) seek suppliers that have the lowest possible prices. These suppliers, in turn, seek to consolidate their operations through mergers and acquisitions, so that they can lower their costs to the greatest extent possible. In 2015, the value of mergers and acquisitions in the automotive parts industry reached U.S.$ 38 billion.[33]

Original Equipment Manufacturers and their suppliers purchase parts in countries that have low labor costs or low energy costs. This purchasing pattern is called outsourcing. For example, Royal Appliance Manufacturing, a producer of vacuum cleaners under the brand Dirt Devil, used to manufacture all of its prod-

Top Twenty Five Vehicle Manufacturers (2014)

	Automobile Group	Units sold worldwide	Brands
1	Toyota Motors Corporation	10,475,000	Lexus, Scion, Daihatsu, Hino, Toyota
2	Volkswagen Group AG	9,895,000	Volkswagen, Audi, Porsche, Škoda, Scania, SEAT, MAN
3	General Motors Corporation	9,609,000	Cadillac, GMC, Buick, Chevrolet, Opel, Vauxhall, Holden
4	Hyundai Motor Group	8,009,000	Hyundai, Kia
5	Ford Motor Company	5,970,000	Ford, Lincoln, Troller, Bedford
6	Nissan	5,098,000	Nissan, Dacia, Infiniti, Datsun
7	Fiat Chrysler Automobiles	4,866,000	Fiat, Chrysler, Dodge, Alfa-Romeo, Ram, Ferrari
8	Honda Motors	4,514,000	Honda, Acura
9	Suzuki	3,017,000	Suzuki, Maruti
10	Peugeot-Citroën SA	2,917,000	Peugeot, Citroën
11	Renault	2,762,000	Renault
12	BMW AG	2,166,000	BMW, Mini, Rolls-Royce
13	SAIC Motors	2,088,000	Wuling, Baojun
14	Daimler AG	1,973,000	Mercedes-Benz, Mitsubishi-Fuso, Setra, Smart, Freightliner
15	Chang'an	1,447,000	Chang'an, Chana
16	Mazda Motors	1,328,000	Mazda
17	DongFeng Motors	1,302,000	Dongfeng, Fengshen
18	Mitsubishi	1,262,000	Mitsubishi
19	Beijing Automotive Group	1,116,000	BAIC, BAW, Foton
20	Tata	945,000	Tata, Jaguar, Land-Rover
21	Geely	891,000	Geely, Emgrand, Englon, Gleagle, Shanghai Maple
22	Fuji	889,000	Subaru
23	Great Wall	731,000	Great Wall, Haval
24	FAW	624,000	FAW, Besturn, Hong Qi, Jilin
25	Iran Khodro	587,000	IKCO, Peugeot, Renault, Suzuki
	Rest of the world	6,236,000	
	Total worldwide production	90,717,000	

Table 1.5: Top Twenty Five Vehicle Manufacturers in 2014
International Organization of Motor Vehicle Manufacturers.

ucts in the United States. By 2006, it produced none in the United States, having outsourced all of its production.

This outsourcing phenomenon is called the "Walmart effect" in the United States. Manufacturers are asked to provide products at certain prices, called "price points," and there is an unrelenting pressure to make these price points lower every year, in response to consumer preferences. Manufacturers then

Top Fifteen Countries in Vehicle Production (2015)

	Country	Vehicles Produced
1	China	24,503,000
2	United States	12,100,000
3	Japan	9,278,000
4	Germany	6,033,000
5	South Korea	4,556,000
6	India	4,126,000
7	Mexico	3,565,000
8	Spain	2,733,000
9	Brazil	2,429,000
10	Canada	2,283,000
11	France	1,970,000
12	Thailand	1,915,000
13	United Kingdom	1,464,000
14	Russia	1,458,000
15	Turkey	1,359,000
	Rest of the World	10,862,000
	Total	90,781,000

Table 1.6: Top Fifteen Countries in Total Vehicle Production (Automobiles and Trucks) for 2015
International Organization of Motor Vehicle Manufacturers.

seek the lowest-cost suppliers, invariably abroad. In essence, price-sensitive consumers who shop at Walmart because of its relentless efforts to keep goods affordable are also those likely to be employed in low-pay positions that are most vulnerable to outsourcing.[34] The pursuit of the lowest manufacturing costs has caused a substantial outsourcing shift in many industries, notably those industries that manufacture products that are sold to consumers at retail: textiles, toys, housewares, and so on.

reshoring
The practice of returning to the home country the manufacturing processes that had been outsourced abroad.

However, many companies have recently faced increased manufacturing costs abroad, particularly in China, as labor costs have increased and the Chinese currency, the yuan, has appreciated.[35] As a result, since 2010, some companies are bringing product manufacturing back to their home countries, a trend called reshoring.[36] Other companies choose to manufacture in Mexico, a practice called near-shoring.[37] North American labor costs are higher than those in China, but manufacturers are able to respond more quickly to their customers' requests and save on transportation costs.[38]

1.4.2   Competition Drivers

In some cases, competition drivers cause companies to expand overseas. For example, a company's domestic competitors may venture into a particular country and the company feels compelled to follow, so as to not lose overall market share. Examples of such competitive behavior are more common in industrial goods than they are in consumer goods; however, this is the drive for the intense competition between the two largest retailers in the world. Carrefour of France and Walmart of the United States compete in many different countries; as soon as one enters a foreign market, the other feels compelled to follow suit.

In other cases, companies expand their sales abroad in response to a competitor moving into the company's home market. When a new overseas competitor enters a company's home market, the company retaliates by going overseas and competing in that newcomer's home market. An example of such behavior is The Gap entering the Italian market after Benetton started competing in the United States.

Competition drivers also exist on the sourcing side. If a competitor starts offering an entry-level product targeted at price-conscious consumers, a company may retaliate by offering a similar product in order to maintain its market share. Because the competitor's entry-level product tends to be manufactured in a low-cost country, the company has little choice but to source overseas as well.

competition driver
One reason a firm may go international is to compete more aggressively against its foreign competitors.

1.4.3   Market Drivers

As international tourism exploded, consumers became increasingly global in their interests, and their tastes and preferences have become almost uniform worldwide. This phenomenon was originally observed for products that reflected consumer mobility, such as camera film and hotel rooms. Should a consumer want film in any country, there were essentially only three choices everywhere (Kodak, Agfa, and Fuji), but they were easy to purchase with identical sizes, sensitivities, and processing technologies. For hotel rooms, the number of alternative brands is much greater, but the uniformity of choices is similar.

Thus, firms faced with consumers who wanted to find their products everywhere had to expand overseas. In the 1970s, McDonald's restaurants in Germany, Great Britain, and France were mostly patronized by foreigners looking for an experience with which they were familiar. Although foreigners still represent a sizable portion of current sales, McDonald's restaurants now cater mostly to domestic consumers who have come to appreciate the convenience of fast food. This phenomenon of standardization of tastes is everywhere: television shows, clothing, books, music, food, sports, and so on.

Finally, as consumers become increasingly knowledgeable about the products they consume, they are more likely to purchase unfamiliar products. The wine industry is a typical example of this phenomenon. French and Italian wines once dominated the higher segments of the market, but the way they were marketed demanded that consumers learn a complex system of classification. When United States vintners simplified the wine industry by labeling the bottles with the name

market driver
One reason a firm may go international is to follow its customers when they travel abroad.

of the grape variety they used, it expanded the market by making it less intimidating to buy wine. Consumers were less likely to make mistakes and more likely to enjoy their wines. An unintended consequence of this simplification was a substantial increase in the sales of wines from countries that traditionally had sold only domestically; Chile, South Africa, and New Zealand, for example.

1.4.4   Technology Drivers

technology driver
One reason a firm may go international is to respond to technologically savvy customers who buy products worldwide.

The diffusion of information has also increased people's familiarity with products. Anyone with an internet connection can quickly access Wikipedia or any other informational website. Consumers can conveniently purchase products everywhere, and it is just as convenient to purchase from overseas as it is to purchase locally. Companies that have an internet presence are enticing consumers everywhere to purchase their products—and, by extension, are competing with companies worldwide. Expanding on this concept of worldwide competition between companies, Thomas Friedman argues that the world has become flat, and that individuals are now competing with each other on a worldwide scale for jobs: easy communications and transfer of information have made a person's location irrelevant.[39]

An easy example of the worldwide availability and sharing of information is this textbook; in order to find good illustrations of certain concepts, the author searched for relevant photographs on an internet site offering royalty-free photographs and artwork. Eighty-six different photographers from twenty-four different countries provided the illustrations for this textbook. All of the photographers were easily contacted to request their authorization to use their work. Similarly, companies can easily find suppliers for almost any product on the internet, using search engines such as the Hong Kong-based alibaba.com.[40]

1.5   International Trade Theories

On a formal level, economists have developed several theories to explain why countries trade, and all have empirical support. Four theories are commonly used to explain bilateral trade between two countries: Smith's Theory of Absolute Advantage, Ricardo's Theory of Comparative Advantage, Heckscher and Olin's Factor-Endowment Theory, and Vernon's International Product Life Cycle Theory. Two additional theories, Porter's Cluster Theory and Sheffi's Logistics Cluster Theory, are presented in this section, to explain why certain areas of the world develop a trade advantage over others.

1.5.1   Smith's Theory of Absolute Advantage

Adam Smith defined his Theory of Absolute Advantage in *The Wealth of Nations* in 1776: "If a foreign country can supply us with a commodity cheaper than we ourselves can make it, better buy it of them with some part of the produce of our own industry, employed in a way in which we have some advantage."[41]

The principle of absolute advantage is easy to understand. Suppose companies, located in France, can produce 20,000 liters of wine for each year of labor they employ, and, also using a year of labor, can produce two units of machinery. Suppose companies in Germany produce, with the same amount of labor, 15,000 liters of wine or three units of machinery. It is clear that the French enjoy an absolute advantage in making wine, producing 20,000 liters of wine to Germany's 15,000 liters, and that the Germans have an absolute advantage in making machinery, producing three machines when the French only produce two. Therefore, it is in the best interest of both France and Germany to have the French companies produce wine and the German companies make machinery.

absolute advantage
An economic theory that holds that when a nation can produce a certain type of product more efficiently than other countries, it will trade with countries that produce other goods more efficiently.

Production before Trading

	France	Germany	Combined Output
Wine	20,000 liters	15,000 liters	35,000 liters
Machinery	2 units	3 units	5 units

Production after Trading

	France	Germany	Combined Output
Wine	40,000 liters	0 liters	40,000 liters
Machinery	0 units	6 units	6 units

Consumption after Trading

	France	Germany	Combined Consumption
Wine	20,000 liters	20,000 liters	40,000 liters
Machinery	3 units	3 units	6 units

Table 1.7: A numerical example of the Theory of Absolute Advantage

Table 1.7 illustrates the Theory of Absolute Advantage. Before trading, both France and Germany use their respective resources to make wine and machinery. France produces 20,000 liters of wine and 2 units of machinery, while Germany produces 15,000 liters of wine and 3 units of machinery. If the two countries trade and use their respective absolute advantages, France takes all of the resources it had been using to make two units of machinery and divert them to make 20,000 additional liters of wine. Germany also shifts its resources and, instead of making 15,000 liters of wine, it makes three additional units of machinery.

France can then buy 3 units of machinery from Germany, which is more than it produced on its own. France is willing to pay as much as 30,000 liters of wine for those 3 units, as this is what it has to give up in order to make these units. Germany, reciprocally, buys 20,000 liters of wine. Germany is willing to pay up to 4 units of machinery, as this is what Germany has to give up to make those

20,000 liters. Overall production, consumption and satisfaction are higher in both countries as a result of the trade.

The theory of absolute advantage does not concentrate on labor alone, but on the sum of all resources that are needed to make the product. A country or company has an absolute advantage if it produces more goods than another, using the same amount of input; in other words, a country or company enjoys an absolute advantage if it is more efficient.

There are many examples of absolute advantage in international trade; countries specialize in specific crops or types of manufactured products because they enjoy a worldwide absolute advantage over all other countries. For example, Kuwait produces crude oil less expensively than any other country and imports most everything else its economy needs. Taiwan produces most of the world's supply of random access memory (RAM) chips, and uses the proceeds from exporting these chips to import other products and goods it cannot produce as efficiently, such as soybeans from Brazil.

1.5.2   Ricardo's Theory of Comparative Advantage

comparative advantage
An economic theory that holds that nations will trade with one another as long as they can produce certain goods relatively more efficiently than one another.

The Theory of Comparative Advantage is most frequently attributed to David Ricardo, but it was first outlined by Robert Torrens in his *Essay on the External Corn Trade* published in 1815.[42] However, in 1817 Ricardo illustrated this theory with a numerical example in *On the Principles of Political Economy and Taxation*[43] and is responsible for the theory's great acceptance. The principle of comparative advantage is more complex than the theory of absolute advantage.

Suppose that companies in Great Britain can manufacture, using one year of labor, five units of machinery and one hundred tons of wheat. By contrast, companies in Brazil can manufacture, using the same input of labor, three units of machinery and ninety tons of wheat. In this case, Great Britain enjoys an absolute advantage in the production of both machinery and wheat, and therefore, according to the Theory of Absolute Advantage, the two countries will not trade.

However, Great Britain enjoys a comparative advantage in producing machinery and Brazil enjoys a comparative advantage in producing wheat. For Great Britain to manufacture one hundred tons of wheat, it has to give up five units of machinery; in other words, the cost of one piece of machinery is twenty tons of wheat. For Brazil, to produce ninety tons of wheat, it has to give up three units of machinery. The cost to Brazil of producing one unit of machinery is therefore thirty tons of wheat. Thus, it makes sense for both countries to trade; Great Britain can sell units of machinery in exchange for wheat from Brazil. If the agreed-upon price is between the British value of twenty tons of wheat for each unit of machinery and the Brazilian value of thirty tons of wheat for each unit of machinery, both countries will find it beneficial to trade. Assuming a market price of twenty-five tons of wheat for each piece of machinery, Great Britain is better off making machinery than growing wheat, and Brazil is better off growing wheat than making machinery.

Table 1.8 illustrates this example of a comparative advantage. Before trading, both countries use their respective resources to make wheat and machinery.

Production before Trading

	Great Britain	Brazil	Combined Output
Wheat	100 tons	90 tons	190 tons
Machinery	5 units	3 units	8 units

Production after Trading

	Great Britain	Brazil	Combined Output
Wheat	80 tons	120 tons	200 tons
Machinery	6 units	2 units	8 units

Consumption after Trading

	Great Britain	Brazil	Combined Consumption
Wheat	105 tons	95 tons	200 tons
Machinery	5 units	3 units	8 units

Table 1.8: A numerical example of the Theory of Comparative Advantage

Great Britain produces a hundred tons of wheat and five units of machinery, while Brazil produces ninety tons of wheat and three units of machinery. If the two countries trade and use their respective comparative advantages, Great Britain can take the resources it had been using to produce wheat and use them to make more units of machinery.

Great Britain thus decreases its production of wheat by twenty tons and increases its production of machinery by one unit. Brazil decreases its production of machinery by one unit, and increases its production of wheat by thirty tons. Using a market price of twenty-five tons of wheat for each unit of machinery, Great Britain then buys twenty-five tons of wheat from Brazil in exchange for one unit of machinery. Brazil, reciprocally, buys this unit of machinery by selling twenty-five tons of wheat. British companies now have one hundred-and-five tons of wheat available for consumption and Brazil has ninety-five tons. Overall, production, consumption and satisfaction are higher in both countries.

The Theory of Comparative Advantage is present in most of the exchanges that companies make internationally. Most firms specialize in making certain products efficiently and these specializations give them a comparative advantage over other companies. At one point in its history, the Ford Motor Company built the River Rouge plant where, at one end, iron ore and coal were delivered, and at the other, finished automobiles rolled off the assembly line. Today, Ford has a comparative advantage in designing and assembling automobiles and countless suppliers have made a business out of their own comparative advantage; Mittal Steel (India) in sheet metal, Alcan in aluminum products, TRW in airbags, and so on. Even though the Ford Motor Company is capable of producing these products, it chooses not to, instead buying them from companies that can produce them more efficiently than it can.

1.5.3   Heckscher-Ohlin Factor Endowment Theory

factor endowment
An economic theory that holds that a nation will have a comparative advantage over other countries if it is naturally endowed with a greater abundance of one of the factors of economic production.

Eli Heckscher and Bertil Ohlin developed the Factor Endowment Theory in 1933[44] by building on Ricardo's comparative advantage concept. Ricardo explained factor endowment by comparing the effectiveness of a country at using its labor to produce goods, and this comparison assumed different levels of technology to account for the differences in the countries' ability to manufacture goods.

The Heckscher-Ohlin Theory extends this idea by assuming that, even when technology is identical, some countries have a comparative advantage over others because they are endowed with a greater abundance of a particular factor of production. Since economists consider that there are four factors of production—land, labor, capital, and entrepreneurship—countries with more one of these factors have an advantage over others.

A country may have a relative abundance of capital and relatively scarce labor resources. Because capital is plentiful, it is inexpensive, and therefore the products made by industries that require a lot of capital tend to have a relatively low production cost when compared to products made by industries that require a lot of labor, since labor is relatively scarce and therefore expensive.[45]

For example, Japan has a relative abundance of capital, and therefore Japanese companies can manufacture products such as precision machinery, that are capital-intensive at a relatively low cost. Japan has a heavily-subsidized agriculture, but it still produces rice at a high unit cost. There are two reasons for that high production cost; Japan has a relative scarcity of land (only about 12 percent of its land is arable) and of labor (it has a very low unemployment rate due to a decreasing labor force caused by a declining overall population and an aging workforce). By contrast, Indonesia has an abundance of young labor and much agricultural land, and Indonesian farmers can therefore produce rice at a very low cost. However, capital is relatively scarce in Indonesia, and therefore manufacturing costs are high, and few companies are producing precision machinery. Because Japanese companies enjoy an abundance of capital, their output is much greater than the output of Indonesian companies. Similarly, because Indonesian farmers have access to more labor and land, their production of rice is much greater than the output of Japanese farmers.

Table 1.9 illustrates this example more precisely and the figures are based on actual data.[46,47,48,49] In 1978, Japan produced 6 million cars and 16 million tons of rice. Japan's automobile industry used abundant capital, and therefore had relatively low production costs. On the other hand, rice was produced using high priced labor and scarce land, and therefore it was a high-cost commodity. In Indonesia, the situation was reversed; the country produced fewer than 20,000 automobiles, because such production demanded a large amount of capital, which was scarce in Indonesia. However the country produced 26 million tons of rice because of its abundant labor and agricultural land. Despite these factors, in 1978, there was relatively little trade between the two countries.

Total Country Output before Trading (1978)

	Japan	Indonesia	Combined Output
Automobiles	6 million cars	0.02 million cars	6.02 million cars
Rice	16 million tons	26 million tons	42 million tons

Production after Trading (2010)

	Japan	Indonesia	Combined Output
Automobiles	8.4 million cars	0.8 million cars	9.2 million cars
Rice	10.6 million tons	66.5 million tons	77.1 million tons

Table 1.9: A numerical example of the Heckscher-Ohlin Theory (based on actual data)

In 2010, Japan produced only 10.6 million tons of rice, a decrease of more than 30 percent, but Indonesia's rice production reached a record 66.5 million tons, more than twice what it was in 1978. Japanese companies used their capital to expand production to satisfy the automobile needs of the Indonesian population, producing a total of 10 million vehicles. However, they also made capital investments in Indonesia; automobile production in Indonesia soared to about 838,000 vehicles in 2011, and many of these automobiles were made in plants owned by Japanese, European or U.S. manufacturers. Four distributors dominate the Indonesian market: P.T. Astra that sells Toyota, Daihatsu, Peugeot, BMW, and Lexus; P.T. Indomobil that sells Nissan, Volvo, Volkswagen, Audi, Renault, and Infiniti; P.T. Ford Motor that sells Ford products only; and P.T. GM Auto World Indonesia that sells General Motors products.[50]

The Factor Endowment Theory explains why certain countries specialize in the production of certain products. Argentina has abundant grazing land, and therefore enjoys a comparative advantage over other countries in beef production. India has abundant educated labor, and therefore enjoys a comparative advantage in the staffing of call centers. The United States has an economic system in which entrepreneurship is handsomely rewarded, and it enjoys a comparative advantage in innovation and the development of intellectual property.

1.5.4   International Product Life Cycle

Raymond Vernon developed the International Product Life Cycle Theory in 1966.[51] The International Product Life Cycle Theory explains the development of international trade in three stages. Figure 1.6 illustrates the theory's three stages.

In the first stage, a company creates a new product to satisfy a market need. This generally takes place in a developed country, as the critical number of customers necessary for a new product launch is often only found in such countries. The product may also use proprietary technology that is   only   available in that

international product life cycle
An economic theory that holds that, over its life cycle, a product will be manufactured in different countries.

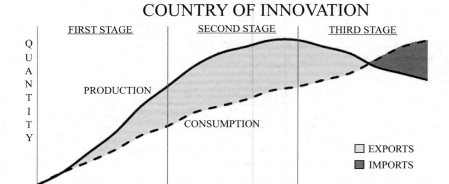

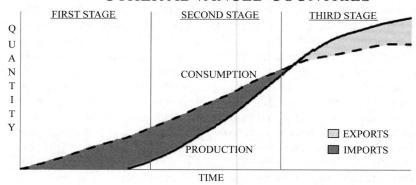

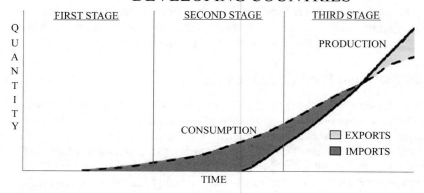

Figure 1.6: The International Product Life Cycle Theory
Adapted by Daisy Krokos. Used with permission.

country. The company manufactures the product in the country of innovation because it needs to be able to monitor the manufacturing process carefully, since there are always unexpected problems in manufacturing a new product. As the product gains acceptance, the company exports the product to other developed countries, where similar markets start to emerge.

In the second stage, sales in other developed countries start to grow and local competitors see that there are enough customers to justify producing products that imitate the original product. Alternative processes or patents are developed. Sales grow further and the product manufacturing process becomes better controlled and somewhat standardized, so that many companies can master the intricacies of making that product. At the same time, the higher-income segments of developing countries' markets import the product from developed countries, and a market in those countries emerges.

In the third stage, the manufacturing process has become completely standardized and almost routine. Companies now face pressures to lower production costs. At the same time, the markets in developing countries become large enough that entrepreneurs in these countries start to produce the products, frequently under contract from companies in developed countries.

Because the manufacturing costs of a mature product tend to be mostly labor related, companies from developing countries start to export massively toward developed countries, slowly replacing all of the manufacturing capacity in those markets.

A lot of empirical evidence supports the International Product Life Cycle Theory. The first televisions were manufactured and sold in Great Britain. They then were manufactured in other developed countries in Europe, North America, Japan, Australia, and New Zealand. As the televisions' popularity increased, all of the manufacturing facilities in those developed countries were eventually replaced by manufacturing facilities in developing countries in Southeast Asia.[52] As of 2003, there were no longer any television manufacturing facilities in the United States.

1.5.5 Porter's Cluster Theory

Michael Porter developed the Cluster Theory in 1990.[53] The Cluster Theory is not a theory of international trade, but an explanation of the success of certain regions in developing a worldwide absolute (or comparative) advantage in a particular technology or product—despite having no particular advantage in any specific factor of production.

cluster
An observation that a firm can develop a substantial competitive advantage in manufacturing certain goods when a large number of its competitors and suppliers are located in close proximity.

The cluster theory argues that, to create an advantage, it is critical to have a cluster of companies and their suppliers, concentrated in one geographic area and serving the same industry. The companies feed on each other's knowledge, and their competitiveness pushes them to innovate faster. In addition, when a cluster exists, the best and brightest employees are eager to move to that location, as they know that they will easily find employment. In addition, as employees move from company to company, they take with them the knowledge they acquired with their previous employers. Thus, innovation travels between companies. In some cases, these employees develop technologies and ideas that their employers may not want to pursue further, and the employees then start a company to exploit these ideas. The result is that innovation flourishes within the cluster's geographic area.

There are several areas of the world where clusters of companies serving the same industry can be found. The most commonly mentioned location is Silicon Valley in California, where most of the innovation in computer technology took place in the latter part of the twentieth century. However, Porter studied the cluster of Sassuolo in Italy, which specializes in ceramic tiles. This cluster produces more than 30 percent of the world's ceramic tiles, and exports more than 70 percent of that production.[54] Another well-known cluster is located in the area around the Jura mountains in France and Switzerland. From the late eighteenth century until the mid-twentieth century, this cluster produced most of the mechanical watches that were made worldwide.[55] The cluster lost its hegemony when the companies in that region did not embrace the quartz technology that was developed by Bell Laboratories in the United States and commercialized by Seiko in Japan.

1.5.6   Sheffi's Logistics Cluster Theory

In 2012 Yossi Sheffi extended Michael Porter's Cluster Theory to the logistics industry.[56] Sheffi observed that some locations can develop into economic powerhouses because multiple providers of logistical services are located within that area. Such a situation attracts manufacturers as they can easily obtain raw materials and ship goods in the most cost-effective way possible. Some regions, such as Singapore, are poor in natural resources, yet develop into international hubs because of the concentration of logistical service providers within the area.[57] Sheffi emphasizes that local governments and chambers of commerce can be instrumental in developing such clusters by facilitating the concentration of logistical services in one area. Sheffi was particularly impressed with the Zaragoza cluster, called PLAZA—*Platforma Logística de Zaragoza*—located in an area roughly equidistant from all of the manufacturing and population centers of Spain. PLAZA has attracted multiple logistical companies, and it has become the transportation hub of Spain.[58] The area around Montevideo, in Uruguay, is also a cluster of free-trade zones, and it has attracted a large number of companies doing business all over South America.

1.6   The International Business Environment

On a more practical level, the international logistics professional should have some knowledge of the particularities of the international business environment. While it is impossible to replace experience in working with people from different countries, it is often useful to identify the relevant issues. These paragraphs are no substitute for classes in international marketing, intercultural communication, international finance, and international economics, but neither are these classes substitutes for experience in world travel, frequent contact with people from different countries, and the extensive study of a foreign language.

The international environment is often first described by differences in culture, a term that encompasses the entire heritage of the people living in a particular country or geographical area; their language, their customs, their traditions, their morals, their beliefs, and their relationships with one another. If there is one aspect of international business about which it is difficult to generalize, it is culture. Not only are there differences between countries, but there are often differences between regions of a country (in the United States, consider the differences between New York and Hawaii, or between Minnesota and New Orleans), between industries within a country (the bio-tech industry and the auto industry), and often between companies within an industry (IBM versus Apple). Therefore, stating that the normal business attire in the United States is a pin-striped suit, a white shirt, and a conservative tie is correct, but only in a certain industry, in a certain geographic location, and in a particular company. In a different company, in a different industry, and in a different location, a colorful shirt, shorts, and sandals would be perfectly acceptable. Making similar generalizations about other countries is just as incorrect.

The best strategy for someone interested in a career in international business is to become familiar with techniques developed in intercultural communications. A number of excellent textbooks have been written in this field.[59,60,61] For someone interested in conducting business with a firm in the United States, there are books describing the American business culture.[62] For managers interested in a specific country, Brigham Young University publishes the *Culturegrams*, which are an excellent synopsis (a few pages) of a particular country's culture.[63] Despite all of these tools, culture and cultural misunderstandings are often the greatest sources of frustration for managers involved in international business. Several tools are presented in Chapter 20 to prevent some of these problems, but the best strategy is to be both flexible and sensitive to other people's reactions.

The remainder of the international environment is easier to understand; countries have different approaches to their legal system, to the way they run their governments, and to the way their economies function. Most such information about a country can easily be found in the World FactBook published by the Central Intelligence Agency,[64] in the Country Commercial Guides published by the United States Department of Commerce,[65] in the Country Profiles and Country Reports published by The Economist's Intelligence Unit,[66] and in the Business Planet database of the World Bank.[67]

Further information on countries can be found in other sources: the Culturegrams of Brigham Young University give excellent insights on the cultures of 190 countries in the world, as well as the 50 U.S. states and 13 Canadian provinces. The United Nations' Human Development Report[68] provides a composite perspective on the quality of life in most countries.

Finally, and this is a "must see," data on multiple countries are vividly illustrated by Gapminder,[69] a website dedicated to illustrating data in graphic and dynamic form. This website is the result of a phenomenal effort undertaken by the late Hans Rosling of Sweden, his son Ola Rosling and his daughter-in-law

Anna Rosling Rönnlund who created a software that makes data literally "come alive." The software was purchased by Google in 2007.

Review and Discussion Questions

1. Given the total volume and importance of international trade and international exchanges, describe the implications to someone's career in business, and to your education in particular.

2. Consider two countries: Country A can produce six automobiles or twelve movies with the same amount of resources. Country B can produce five automobiles or eight movies with the same amount of resources. Using Ricardo's Theory of Comparative Advantage, determine which country will produce automobiles, which will produce movies, and the range of relative prices for these products within which these countries trade.

3. Walmart is famous for requesting ever decreasing price points from its suppliers: if a supplier offers a product for $45.00, Walmart will ask the supplier to consider introducing a similar product for $39.00. According to the Heckscher-Ohlin Factor Theory, what consequences do such requests have?

4. In addition to the clusters of Silicon Valley and Sassuolo, Michael Porter identified a cluster for printing presses in Heidelberg, Germany, and others have written about clusters in Limoges, France, for porcelain and in Valenza Po, Italy, for gold jewelry. What characteristics do industrial clusters have that other cities do not have? Can you think of another cluster in the world?

Notes

[1] World Trade Organization Statistical Database, http://stat.wto.org/StatisticalProgram/WSDBStat-ProgramSeries.aspx?Language=E, retrieved August 28, 2016.

[2] Boeing Company, "787 Model Summary," http://active.boeing.com/commercial/orders/display-standardreport.cfm?cboCurrentModel=787optReportType=AllModels&cboAllModel=787&ViewReport-F=View+Report, retrieved March 5, 2017.

[3] Ausick, Paul, "What Does Boeing 787 Cost?", *24/7 Wall Street*, July 26, 2015, http://247wallst.com-/aerospace-defense/2015/07/26/what-does-boeing-787-dreamliner-cost, retrieved March 5, 2017.

[4] White, Martha, "The Boeing Company", *Slate*, November 2010, http://www.slate.com/articles/business/exports/2010/11/the_boeing_co.html, retrieved March 5, 2017.

[5] World Trade Organization Statistical Database, http://stat.wto.org/StatisticalProgram/WSDBStat-ProgramSeries.aspx?Language=E, retrieved August 28, 2016.

[6] *Ibid.*

[7] *Ibid.*

[8] *Ibid.*

[9] World Trade Organization, "Trade growth to remain subdued in 2016 as uncertainties weigh on global demand," Press release, April 7, 2016. https://www.wto.org/english/news_e/pres16_e/pr768-_e.htm, retrieved September 6, 2016.

[10] *Ibid.*

[11] C.W., "Global trade imbalances: fiddling the data," *The Economist*, September 27, 2013, www.economist.com/node/21586929, retrieved March 4, 2015.

[12] "WTO Tariff Analysis Online,http://tao.wto.org/report/TariffAverages.aspx, retrieved September 6, 2016.

[13] "The WTO in brief: history," http://www.wto.org/english/thewto_e/ whatis_e/inbrief_e/inbr00_e.-htm, retrieved April 13, 2009.

[14] "Documents from the negotiating chairs, 21 April 2011," http://www. wto.org/english/tratop_e/-dda_e/chair_texts11_e/chair_texts11_e.htm,
retrieved August 18, 2012.

[15] World Trade Organization, "Domestic subsidies a priority in farm talks," 2016 News Item, https://www.wto.org/english/news_e/news16_e/agng_13may16_e.htm, May 13, 2016, retrieved July 17, 2016.

[16] Castle, Stephen, and Sewell Chan, "Bitter 'Brexit' campaign could turn on record number of voters," *The New York Times*, June 22, 2016.

[17] Taub, Amanda, "A lesson From 'Brexit': on immigration, feelings trump facts," *The New York Times*, June 26, 2016.

[18] Bittner, Jochen, "Brexit and Europe's angry old men," *The New York Times*, June 24, 2016.

[19] Schwartz, Nelson, and Patricia Cohen, " 'Brexit' in America: a warning shot against globalization," *The New York Times*, June 25, 2016.

[20] Hill, Charles W., *International Business: competing in the global market place*, 2015, Tenth Edition, McGraw-Hill, New York, New York.

[21] Baker, Peter, "Trump Abandons Trans-Pacific Partnership, Obama's Signature Trade Deal," *The New York Times*, January 23, 2017.

[22] "GCC 'common market achieves most goals'," *The Peninsula*, January 9, 2015, http://thepeninsula-qatar.com/news/qatar/315593/gcc-common-market-achieves-most-goals, retrieved September 9, 2016.

[23] Astana, "Russia, Kazakhstan, Belarus developing single Eurasian Sky program", B-News KZ, http://bnews.kz/en/news/tamojennyi_soyuz/astana/spetsproekti/tamojennyi_soyuz/russia-kazakhstan--belarus-developing-single-eurasian-sky-program-2014_05_23-924521, retrieved September 10, 2016.

[24] *The Common Agricultural Policy: a story to be continued*, 2012, Publications of the European Union, http://ec.europa.eu/agriculture/50-years-of-cap/files/history/history_book_lr_en.pdf, retrieved September 9, 2016.

[25] Bank for International Settlements, *Triennial Central Bank Survey: foreign exchange turnover in April 2013*, September 2013, http://www.bis.org/publ/rpfx13fx.pdf, retrieved August 4, 2016.

[26] World Trade Organization Statistical Database, http://stat.wto.org/StatisticalProgram/WSDBStatProgramSeries.aspx?Language=E, retrieved August 28, 2016.

[27] *Ibid.*

[28] Doing Business Database, The World Bank Group, 1818 H Street NW, Washington, DC 20433, http://www.doingbusiness.org/data, retrieved September 10, 2016.

[29] The Conference Board, "Manufacturing hourly compensation costs—2015," https://www.conference-board.org/ilcprogram/, retrieved September 10, 2016.

[30] World Bank, "Exports of goods and services (% of GDP)," 2015, http://data.worldbank.org/indicator/NE.EXP.GNFS.ZS?locations=DO&year_high_desc=true, retrieved September 10, 2016.

[31] "World motor vehicle production," International Organization of Motor Vehicles Manufacturers—Organization Internationale des Constructeurs Automobiles, 4 rue de Berri, 75008 Paris, France, http://oica.net/wp-content/uploads/ranking-2010.pdf, retrieved August 27, 2016.

[32] Motor vehicle production statistics, International Organization of Motor Vehicles Manufacturers—Organization Internationale des Constructeurs Automobiles, 4 rue de Berri, 75008 Paris, France, http://www.oica.net/category/production-statistics/, retrieved September 7, 2016.

[33] Ostermann, Dietman, Doug Harvey, Jan Hesse, and Shan Haque, *M&A in the global automotive supply industry: study finds a bull market with room to grow*, Strategy&, January 14, 2016, http://www.strategyand.pwc.com/reports/mergers-acquisitions-auto-industry, retrieved September 9, 2016.

[34] Fishman, Charles, *The Wal-Mart effect*, 2006, Penguin Books, New York.

[35] Sirkin, Harold L., Michael Zinser, and Justin Rose, "Manufacturing in America: the pendulum swings back," *Distribution Business Management Journal*, **16**:2013, pp.10-13.

[36] Speed, Vicki, "Are manufacturers ready to reshore? The answer is yes…and no," *Inbound Logistics*, January 2016, pp.217-224.

[37] Trunick, Perry A., and Paul Dittman, "Nearshoring on the rise," *World Trade*, July 2014, pp.22-26.

[38] Buxbaum, Peter, "Repatriating your supply chain," *Global Trade*, November-December 2014, pp.42-44.

[39] Friedman, Thomas, *The World is flat: a brief history of the twenty-first century*, Farrar, Strauss and Giroux, New York, New York, 2005.

[40] www.alibaba.com

[41] Smith, Adam, *An inquiry into the nature and causes of the wealth of nations*, Bantam Classics, 2003.

[42] Torrens, Robert, The budget: On commercial and colonial policy, London, Smith, Elder, 1840.

[43] Ricardo, David, On the principles of political economy and taxation, Dover Publications, 2004.

[44] Ohlin, Bertil, *Interregional and international trade*, 1933, reproduced in Samuelson, Paul A., *Heckscher-Ohlin international trade theory*, MIT Press, 1991.

[45] Suranovic, Steven M., "The Heckscher-Ohlin Model overview," *International Trade Theory and Policy*, http://www.internationalecon.com/ Trade/Tch60/T60-0.php, April 14, 2009.

[46]Paddy rice production, by country and geographical region, 1961-2007, Food and Agriculture Organization, http://beta.irri.org/solutions/ index.php?option=com_content&task=view&id=250, retrieved April 19, 2009.

[47]Paddy rice production, by country, 2010, Food and Agricultural Organization, http://faostat.fao.org/site/339/default.aspx, retrieved August 19, 2012.

[48]Fuss, Melvyn A. and Leonard Waverman, "Passenger car production 1961-1984," *Cost and Productivity in Japanese Production: The Challenge of Japanese Efficiency*, Cambridge University Press, 1992.

[49]Motor Vehicle Production Statistics, International Organization of Motor Vehicles Manufacturers— Organization Internationale des Constructeurs Automobiles, 4 rue de Berri, 75008 Paris, France, http:// oica.net/category/production-statistics, retrieved August 18, 2012.

[50]Overview of automobile industry in Indonesia, Indonesian Commercial Newsletter, April 2011, http://www.datacon.co.id/Automotive-2011Industry.html, retrieved August 19, 2012.

[51]Vernon, Raymond, "International investment and international trade in the Product Life Cycle," *Quarterly Journal of Economics*, May 1966, 80(2), pp. 190-207.

[52]Gao, Zhicun, and Clem Tisdell, "Television production: its changing global location, the product cycle and China," *Economic Theory, Applications and Issues*, Working Paper No. 26, University of Queensland, http://ageconsearch.umn.edu/bitstream/90530/2/WP%2026.pdf, retrieved April 19, 2009.

[53]Porter, Michael E., *The competitive advantage of nations* , The Free Press, New York, New York, 1990.

[54]"Sassuolo cluster profile," United Nations Industrial Development Organization, http://www.unido.org/doc/4309, August 10, 2006.

[55]Glasmeier, Amy, "Why Switzerland?," *Manufacturing Time; Global Competition in the Watch Industry: 1790-2000*, Guilford Press, New York, New York, 2000.

[56]Sheffi, Yossi, *Logistics clusters: delivering value and driving growth*, MIT Press, Cambridge, Massachusetts, 2012.

[57]Kulish, Eric, "Logistics clusters," *American Shipper*, November 2012, pp.14-15.

[58]Bradley, Peter,"Logistics clusters as drivers of growth: interview with Yossi Sheffi," *DC Velocity*, December 2012, pp. 38-40.

[59]Lustig, Myron W. and Jolene Koester, *Intercultural competence: interpersonal communication across cultures*, 2012, Seventh Edition, Allyn and Bacon, Boston, Massachusetts.

[60]Beamer, Linda and Iris Varner, *Intercultural communication in the global workplace*, 2010, Fifth Edition, McGraw-Hill-Irwin, Boston, Massachusetts.

[61]Klopf, Donald W. and James McCroskey, *Intercultural communication encounters*, 2006, Fifth Edition, Allyn and Bacon, Boston, Massachusetts.

[62]Robinson, David, *Business protocol*, 2009, Third Edition, Atomic Dog Publishing, Cincinnati, Ohio.

[63]Culturegrams, Pro-Quest and Brigham Young University, http://www.culturegrams.com, retrieved May 10, 2017.

[64]*The World Factbook*, Central Intelligence Agency, https://www.cia.gov/library/publications/the-world-factbook, retrieved May 10, 2017.

[65]Country commercial guides, United States Department of Commerce, http://www.state.gov/e/eb/rls/rpts/ccg.

[66]The Economist's Intelligence Unit, http://www.eiu.com/site_info.asp?info_name=about_eiu.

[67]Business Planet: Mapping the Business Environment, The World Bank Group, http://rru.worldbank.org, accessed May 10, 2017.

[68]United Nations Development Programme, Human Development Reports, http://hdr.undp.org/en/

statistics, accessed May 10, 2017.

[69]Rosling, Ola, Anna Rosling Rönnlund and Hans Rosling, Gapminder: unveiling the beauty of statistics for a fact-based worldview, http://www.gapminder.org.

Chapter 2

International Supply Chain Management

Before presenting the different aspects of international logistics, it is useful to recognize how this function is currently included in the management of a firm engaged in international business. It is essential for the international logistician to determine the responsibilities of that profession and the interactions that this function has with a firm's other operational functions, such as marketing, finance, and production.

The responsibilities of an international logistics manager have evolved substantially. This chapter introduces a brief history of the profession of international logistician, the evolution of the activities that have become his or her responsibility, and the current status of this managerial position. The responsibilities of an international logistician are still changing; it is not known whether the profession will eventually include a greater number of activities or whether its responsibilities will be curtailed.

2.1   Historical Development

2.1.1   The Early, "Slow" Days

international trade
The sale of goods and services across international borders.

The globalization of markets is generally understood to be a recent phenomenon, triggered by the explosion of economic development after World War II; however, while international trade increased dramatically in the second half of the last century, nations have engaged in international trade for centuries.[1] However, before the advent of modern transportation, trade between nations relied on courageous traders who ventured into faraway places in the hope of earning a living. The spice trade was well established in Roman times, and flourished during the Middle Ages,[2] bringing many different products to European consumers. For example, at the beginning of the fifteenth century, a Florentine merchant listed 288 different spices that it could procure. These goods moved either by sea or by caravans of pack animals, "with many trans-shipments, many tolls, and much danger of loss."[3]

The adventurers/logisticians of that period determined what goods they should take as payment for the goods they hoped to bring back, negotiated with foreigners with whom they did not share a language, and arranged for the transportation and safekeeping of the goods while in transit. They were exposed to the risks of international travel, market preferences, and political instability. They were pioneers.

Can these early traders be considered to be the first people involved in international logistics? Undoubtedly. The word "logistics" comes from the Greek *logistike*, which translates as "the art of calculating"[4] using concrete items, in contrast with *arithmetike*, which was the art of calculating using abstract concepts.*

---

*This interpretation may not be shared by all readers of Klein's work: the distinction is not very accessible.

The latter evolved into the modern concepts of arithmetic and algebra. The former gave birth to the modern term "logistics," which has evolved into the art and science of determining eminently concrete aspects of business management, from transportation and packaging to warehousing and inventory management.

The first international traders were involved in logistics; they calculated how much their ships—or beasts—could carry, how much food to bring, and how best to package the goods while in transit. These decisions parallel what modern logistics managers do when considering how many units to place in a container, how to balance the load, and how to protect the goods for an international voyage. Early traders decided which payment method was most appropriate, just as a modern exporter must determine the best way to ensure it will get paid. While many aspects of international logistics have changed, the main concerns of the people involved in this field are similar; they must ensure that goods manufactured in one part of the world arrive safely at their destination.

The modern interpretation of the term "logistics" has its origins in the military, where it was used to describe the activities related to the procurement of ammunitions and essential supplies for troops located at the front. The term gave birth to the title of *Maréchal des Logis* in the French military, which is given to a sergeant in charge of a unit's supplies and housing. However, when the term applies to the branch of the military overseeing logistics on a large scale, the modern French military uses a different word, "*le train*," which refers to all activities that support the combat branches of the military.

Initially, logistics was defined as "physical distribution," and was based on the military concept encompassing the physical movement of goods. The first author to expand logistics beyond this early interpretation was Shaw,[5] in 1915, who incorporated into the concept the remainder of distribution activities, such as inventory and the selection of distribution intermediaries. In 1933, Lewis added the purchasing function to the physical-distribution classes he taught in the marketing department.[6] Today, the term is much broader and includes not only all the activities related to the physical movement of goods, both upstream (procurement) and downstream (sales) activities, but also the management of supplier and customer relationships.

Over the last thirty years, the focus of logistics has evolved substantially: until the mid-1980s, the main concern of logistics managers and specifically of international logistics managers, was to ensure that the goods arrived at their destination in good condition and at the lowest possible cost. Shorter transit times were considered, but only when the goods were perishable or when the goods were so urgently needed that the additional costs were justified; for most goods, however, long transit times were considered normal. Since then, a transition to shorter transit times has been made to better respond to customers' needs.

2.1.2 The Move Toward Speed

Containers—"boxes" in the logisticians' vernacular—changed the focus of international logistics. Though they were introduced in 1956, containers did not have

container
A large metallic box used in international trade that can be loaded directly onto a truck, a railroad car or an ocean-going vessel. The most common dimensions of a container are $8 \times 8.5 \times 20$ feet and $8 \times 8.5 \times 40$ feet.

longshoreman
A person who performs manual labor in a port.

a significant impact on international trade until the early 1970s.

Before containers, the process of shipping internationally by ocean was cumbersome, labor intensive, and time consuming. The traditional method was to first pack the goods into a truck or railroad car for their inland trip to the port. The goods were then unloaded in the port and transferred onto a ship using cranes and slings, as well as several longshoremen who stowed them appropriately for their ocean voyage. The goods were then unloaded from the ship in the port of arrival, placed in a truck or railroad car for their inland trip, and finally unloaded at their destination. Packages had to be small and light enough to be handled by humans in the ship's holds, and sturdy enough to withstand being handled numerous times. A transatlantic shipment took over one month, with most of that time spent with the cargo delayed in the ports.

Stevedores

Before the use of containers, stevedoring was back-breaking work. The goods being shipped abroad arrived to the port in trucks or railroad cars and in small packages or in pallets. They were then unloaded and counted in a warehouse located alongside the pier. When the ship arrived, it first had to be completely emptied and that merchandise removed from the pier before any loading could start. The merchandise to be loaded was then moved from the warehouse to the quay and counted again. A loading plan determined what should be loaded first (the heavier, more resilient items), and what should be loaded last.

Longshoremen then assembled the goods into "drafts," which were larger parcels that could be loaded onto the ship by cranes. The longshoremen assembled the drafts by hand, carrying, dragging, and rolling the merchandise to a location where the crane could lift them; longshoremen placed slings under each draft before it was loaded. The cranes then lifted the merchandise onto the ship where another gang of longshoremen unpacked the drafts, counted the goods once again, and positioned them into the holds of the ship (still using muscle power), making sure that every piece of cargo was tightly braced against the others so that it would not shift during the voyage.

Many goods were not packaged to be handled easily; some bags of grain weighed as much as 100kg (220 lbs.) and bags of sugar weighed 60kg (132 lbs.). A single longshoreman generally could carry a bag of sugar, but two shared the work of moving a bag of grain. Bananas were regularly unloaded by walking down a gangplank on the side of the ship rather than by crane. Each weighed about 80kg (176 lbs.). With such working conditions, in addition to the hazards of working around cranes and trucks, longshoremen accidents were common; every year, one in six was injured. Between 1947 and 1957, forty-seven longshoremen were killed in the port of Marseille.[7]

Unloading was not much different. The result of such labor-intensive work was millions of longshoremen employed worldwide. Just in the ports of New York, London, and Marseille, there were as many as 50,000 stevedores. Smaller ports still had thousands. Most of these men—they were all men—were employed only part-time, working whenever there was a ship, idle when there were none, and competing for work when a ship was scheduled to arrive in port. They toiled in all sorts of weather, and had to learn to move anything; one day they would load and unload delicate goods, and the next, heavy, dirty, smelly bags.[8] On other days, they maneuvered heavy barrels or drums on steep inclines, as shown in Figure 2.1.

All this changed with the advent of containers, which allowed the loading and unloading of ships to be mechanized. A stevedore's work became much less physical; although some dockworkers still need to be aboard the ship to position the twist locks that tie the containers to one another, and lash down the two lower containers in a stack, many stevedores drive trucks to pick up or position containers alongside the ship, or operate a gantry crane.[9,10,11]

Figure 2.1: Traditional stevedores in the Port of New Orleans
Photo ©Russell Lee, U.S. Farm Security Administration. Used with permission.

stevedore
A person who loads and
unloads goods from a
vessel in a port.

With the advent of containers, shipments also began to speed up. Instead of loading and unloading the goods several times, containers were loaded only once, in the shipper's plant, and unloaded only once, at the customer's facility. Packaging did not have to be as sturdy. In addition, ship loading and unloading operations went much faster. Ships no longer had to be completely empty to load new cargo; as soon as a stack of containers was empty, a new set of containers could be loaded in that space. The crane that was unloading containers from the ship did not have to return empty to the ship; it could immediately pick up another container to be loaded onto the vessel. This single difference doubled the productivity of crane operators. Due to these improvements, the costs of ocean shipping came down: port labor costs decreased, ships' productivity increased because less time was spent idling in ports, and significant investments were made in container ships that became ever more efficient.

Figure 2.2: Thousands of Containers in the Port of Barcelona, Spain
Photo ©Sergio Morchon, courtesy of flickr.com. Used with permission.

Only a few years later, in the late 1970s and early 1980s, there was an explosion in the number of international air shipments. Even though DHL was founded in 1969 and Federal Express in 1973, neither service provided much international coverage: DHL was strictly a San Francisco-Honolulu service until 1974, and Federal Express had only twenty-five domestic destinations until 1979. However, Federal Express sales rose quickly, and by 1983 it had become a billion-dollar corporation strictly based on domestic shipments. Federal Express started international operations in 1984, and, by 2005, it had changed its name to FedEx, and become a $30 billion corporation. In the United States, the term "fedex" is a verb. For its fiscal year 2016, FedEx reported global sales of $50 billion.[12]

The costs of air shipments also declined considerably during this period. In the beginning, Federal Express operated with Dassault Falcon jets, which have limited cargo capacity. By the end of the 1970s, after a partial deregulation of the airline industry, Federal Express had acquired Boeing 727s and McDonnell-Douglas DC10s, both of which have much greater cargo capacity. Further deregulation in the 1980s and open-sky agreements in the 1990s increased the number of aircrafts dedicated to freight, and air shipments became increasingly cost competitive with surface alternatives.

As customers' expectations of speedy delivery increased, it became clear that delivery speed had become one of the salient criteria in selecting a supplier. David Hummels estimated that "each additional day spent in transport reduces the probability that [a company] will source from that country by 1 to 1.5 percent."[13]

Malcom McLean

Today, anyone observing one of the world's ports would see a constellation of containers (see Figure 2.2 on the facing page). This constellation includes containers being hoisted off ships and onto trucks or trains, others being loaded onto ships, and still hundreds of others stacked and waiting to be moved. Other than these boxes, there are no goods to be seen, and observers have no way of knowing what goods are coming and going. Inside the boxes could be televisions or shampoo, computers or recycled paper. The scene at these same ports just a few decades ago would have been very different.

The idea of one man, Malcom McLean, changed all that.

Before containerization, goods were delivered to the waterfront as separate pieces by truck or train. From there they were manually taken to a storage shed to wait for longshoremen to load them onto a ship. The longshoremen then took each piece and manually placed it in the cargo hold. Loading thousands of goods onto a ship could take days and the process had to be reversed to unload the ship when it reached its destination.[14]

Those wishing to export merchandise typically had to arrive days or even weeks before the ship was to set sail to ensure the goods would be loaded. "Ships remained in port for days while longshoremen wrestled individual boxes, barrels and bales into and out of tight spaces below deck. Damage was frequent and expensive, as were losses from pilferage."[15] This process was terribly inefficient and slow, and was a major deterrent for many manufacturers considering transporting their goods overseas or even to other parts of the country.

This was the scene in 1937 when Malcom McLean drove a truck loaded

Figure 2.3: Malcom McLean's First Containership, the Ideal X
Photo ©the Port Authority of New York and New Jersey. Used with permission.

with cotton intended for export to a port in New Jersey. After waiting for days for longshoremen to load his cotton, McLean figured there had to be a better way. McLean owned a small trucking company in North Carolina. After his experience in New Jersey he worked on building a better system of shipping that could grow his company into an efficient competitor in the shipping industry.

McLean hired as many experts in containerization as he could find and learned everything he could about the field. He considered driving truck trailers onto ships but found the idea impractical. Eventually McLean and one of his engineers decided to use "containers thirty-three feet long, a length chosen because the available deck space aboard the T-2 tankers was divisible by thirty-three."[16] The containers were much larger than anything seen before and were loaded onto tanker ships by cranes. The tankers had specially designed on-deck frames to hold the containers in place.

McLean tested his idea on April 26, 1956, when the converted tanker ship *Ideal X* set sail from Newark. McLean and his team watched a crane load fifty-eight containers onto the ship, one every seven minutes. What previously had taken days now took only hours. The ship left the Port of Newark destined for Houston, trailed the entire way by the Coast Guard to ensure its safety. Six days later the team watched the *Ideal X* come into port in Houston with all fifty-eight containers still safely aboard. This first test was a complete success.

When the transit costs of the journey were calculated, McLean knew he had a real winner. Traditional shipping costs of loose cargo at the time were about "$ 5.83 per ton" while shipping costs on the *Ideal X* container ship cost only "$ 0.158 per ton."[17] These dramatically reduced costs drove the development of container shipping and an infrastructure was built to handle containers at ports around the world. McLean's company grew along with many competitors and new technologies were developed to make containerization even more cost effective. Larger ships that could handle more contain-ers were built and the trend continues today as bigger ships are constantly in development. Despite the protests of longshoremen, the old way of loading ships was quickly abandoned and containerization was embraced. This encouraged more businesses to ship their products longer distances creating new markets. It also allowed new foods and other goods to be sent around the world to places where they had never been seen before.

The idea of containerization fueled the spread of globalization.

2.1.3   The Emphasis on Customer Satisfaction

By the early 1990s, the increased speed of ocean shipments and the availability of affordable airfreight services changed the focus of logistics managers: they began to consider the shortest reasonable transit time in response to customers' request for speedy deliveries. Although it was still fundamental to make sure that the goods arrived in good condition and at the lowest possible cost, the managers' focus had shifted from these process-oriented concerns to satisfying customers' requirements.

The major reason behind the requirements for shorter delivery times was the increased focus by large manufacturers on the reduction of inventories during the 1980s. Starting in the mid-1970s, but culminating in the early 1980s, interest rates increased to unprecedented levels, triggering concerns about the money immobilized in inventory. In the 1980s, companies emphasized reducing heir "static" inventories, or the goods they kept in their warehouses or plants. By the early 1990s, companies shifted their attentions to their "mobile" inventories, or the goods that were in transit between two of their plants or between their suppliers and their plants. The tools they used were Materials Requirement Planning (MRP) and Manufacturing Resource Planning (MRP II), which allowed them to create Just-In-Time manufacturing processes (see Chapter 18). In turn, these processes created requirements for "time-definite" deliveries of assembly parts; most plants demanded to have parts delivered just before they were used on the assembly line, and not earlier or later. That allowed companies to avoid holding any inventory in their building. The number of "in transit" goods had to be curtailed as well.

By the mid-1990s, all manufacturers had adopted these techniques and were requiring suppliers to ship just-in-time. At the same time, large retailers and other distributors adopted techniques derived from MRP and MRP II, which they

Materials Requirement Planning [MRP]
A management tool that allows a manufacturer to determine what to produce and in which quantity, in function of what it sells to its customers.

just-in-time
A management philosophy that consists of planning the manufacturing of goods in such a way that they are produced just before they are needed in the next step of the assembly process.

Distribution Resource Planning (DRP)
A management tool that allows a retail firm to determine what to order from its suppliers and in which quantity, in function of what it sells to its customers.

called Distribution Resource Planning (DRP) techniques, which used final consumer sales data to pull products through the distribution channel. Consumer sales data were collected through point-of-sale (POS) scanners. If products sold well, then the DRP program reordered the goods and had them delivered just-in-time to the appropriate warehouse or retail store. If a product did not sell well, none were re-ordered. This strategy forced logistics managers to focus on transit times and adapt to frequent changes in their work. This came to be known as "agile logistics."

Today, most manufacturers and large retail chains financially penalize suppliers that do not deliver on time (both too early and too late) by withholding a portion of the invoice at the time of payment.

It is fair to say that customer satisfaction is now logisticians' primary concern: not only does the shipment have to be accurate (the right parts, in the right quantity), complete (no back-ordered parts), and the packaging appropriate so that the goods arrive undamaged and ready to be sold, but it must also be delivered within a very specific time frame.

While international logisticians must ensure that the shipment is accurate, complete, and on time, they also have many additional responsibilities. Logisticians must make certain that their shipment's paperwork is in perfect order so that it can clear customs without delay. They must make sure that the packaging is sufficient to protect the goods during their long (and often eventful) international voyage. They must comply with a myriad of security requirements and manage transactions involving different currencies and different laws. They must choose the right mode of transportation and ensure that the goods are properly insured. In short, logisticians have many challenges with which to contend for each shipment.

2.1.4   The Transformation into a Strategic Advantage

The 1990s saw logistics integrated into supply chain management, and the early 2000s saw supply chain management emerge as a strategic tool; by the 2010s, supply chain management had clearly become a means by which corporations sought a competitive advantage, and it now commanded the attention of top managers, often with the creation of the position of Chief Supply Chain Management Officer.

The emphasis of logistics managers also shifted to securing a differential advantage over competitors by providing better customer service, by offering better delivery terms, by working with suppliers and customers to offer greater flexibility, and by making the processes as seamless as possible. These tasks were particularly challenging as the complexity of the global supply chain increased drastically during the same period: from 1995 to 2015, the number of companies operating in multiple countries (which the United Nations calls "transnational companies") increased from 38,000 to 320,000, and the number of foreign subsidiaries increased from 265,000 to 774,000.[18] The number of people employed by the foreign affiliates of these transnational companies represented 79,505,000 people.[19]

A study of Chief Supply Chain Officers conducted by the Aberdeen Group in 2013[20] identified the three greatest challenges faced by companies involved in international trade:

- Rising supply chain management costs, including total landed costs, fuel costs, and labor costs.

- Escalating demand for service from customers, including delivery performance, information availability, and levels of service.

- Growing complexity of global operations, including increasing number of suppliers, partners, carriers, customers, countries, and logistics channels.

Over the past ten years, companies involved in international trade have implemented tools and methods to help them face these challenges, under the umbrella of a comprehensive product called Global Trade Management software.

2.1.5 The Current State of Affairs: Global Trade Management

To manage the increased complexity of international trade, companies are implementing Global Trade Management software (GTM) to automate their international-trade operations, optimize their supply chain decisions, and monitor their transactions with all their trading partners and service providers.[21]

GTM software is complex, as it attempts to manage all of a company's international-supply-chain decisions, while interacting with the ERP system with which the company runs its internal operations. GTM software has several benefits, but its primary advantages are in compliance, visibility, and optimization.

Compliance

A complex aspect of international logistics is the number of different rules and regulations with which companies must comply to ship goods internationally.

All countries have import regulations, import quotas, and duty rates, many of which change frequently. For example, in the summer of 2016, China implemented a fumigation requirement for all goods originating in countries that were affected by the zika virus, and the list of countries to which this requirement applied changed frequently as the number of virus-affected countries increased. In August 2016, China had applied that requirement to sixty countries.[22]

Countries also enter into bilateral and multilateral free-trade agreements that have different country-of-origin requirements. The criteria that determine a good's country of origin, that is where it is considered "made," can vary considerably. For example, a product needs 35 percent Israeli content to enter the United States duty free under the Israel Free-Trade Agreement,[23] but it needs 50 percent content from Canada and Mexico to enter duty free under the North American Free Trade Agreement.[24] These agreements also have different computing methods to determine the percentage of a product that has a particular country of origin.

Some countries have export regulations, export taxes, or export quotas, all of which must be respected to avoid shipping delays and fines. The United States enforces several rules regarding exports, and violations include prison times and large fines. For example, Schlumberger Oilfield Holdings Ltd., despite having "policies and procedures designed to ensure that [it] did not violate U.S. sanctions," was fined $ 233 million for "providing certain technical services and expertise in order to troubleshoot mechanical failures [of] drilling tools and related equipment in Iran and Sudan."[25]

Ocean carriers, airlines, railroads, and trucking companies have different packaging requirements, size limitations, and labeling requirements. For example, the International Maritime Organization requires certification of container weight before the containers are loaded onto a ship, but different ports have different ways of ensuring that shippers comply, and some do not accept another port's certification.[26]

GTM software allows companies to comply with these many regulations and rules.[27]

Visibility

As supply chains grow in length and in complexity, and use more intermediaries, it is more difficult for companies to determine the location of goods, and manage problems before they arise.

Companies and their customers seek to determine the location of their shipments.[28] They want to determine whether their goods are on their way, whether the goods have been delayed, or whether they are affected by a strike or other natural disaster. When a tsunami struck the Japanese coast in 2011, many companies did not realize that their supply chain had been affected until several days later. That event triggered a need for companies to determine the geographical origin of the goods they purchase. Companies knew their supplier was Japanese—or French or German—, but they did not know the geographical location of that supplier's plant. When an earthquake hit southern Japan in 2016, companies that had implemented a GTM program were able to react quickly to the supply-chain disruption, and plan alternative means to obtain goods to maintain operations.[29]

For companies with fragile or perishable cargo, it is important to know whether a transportation disruption caused the temperature of the goods to go above what was planned, or whether they were exposed to rough handling or bad weather. Information gathered from a "smart" container's recording device,[30] and transmitted to the shipper's GTM system, allows companies to reach better decisions regarding that shipment, file appropriate insurance claims, and use a different route for future shipments.

Optimization

The information gathered from GTM software can lead a company to better decisions regarding its supply chain. If goods are regularly delayed in a particular port, or if a carrier is having difficulties in handling the goods carefully, it is possible to choose a different itinerary or supplier. If a strike is anticipated in a transit port, goods can be re-routed to avoid that disruption.[31]

By accumulating data on the movement of goods through the supply chain, companies can make better decisions, and improve customer service and on-time deliveries.

2.2 Logistics and Supply Chain Management

As the fields of logistics and international logistics evolved, the managers working in those fields changed the definitions that they used to describe their profession. Though "logistics" was the most commonly accepted term for the activities in which theses managers engaged, the term was broadened in the mid-1980s to include additional activities; eventually, the profession was renamed "supply chain management" in the 1990s. Today, the term "logistics" encompasses several activities that are a subset of the activities that constitute Supply Chain Management.

2.2.1 Logistics

Today, professionals in the field define the term "logistics" in the following manner:

> Logistics is that part of the supply chain process that plans, implements, and controls the efficient, effective forward and reverse flow and storage of goods, services, and related information between the point of origin and the point of consumption in order to meet customers' requirements.[32]

From this definition, it is clear that logistics managers see the focus of their profession as those activities that are related to the physical movement of goods from supplier to customer. Logisticians are mostly concerned about transporting, packaging, warehousing, securing, and handling goods that their firm purchases or sells. Logisticians also interact daily with other managers who hold responsibilities closely related to moving these goods, such as manufacturing and production, purchasing and procurement, marketing, inventory management, finance, customer service, and so on.

Figure 2.4 summarizes a slightly different opinion of the evolution of logistics, as seen by Alfred Battaglia.[33] In his view, a company's logistical function came to include the management of materials and manufacturing somewhat earlier than the 1990s. What is clear is that most logistics professionals referred to their profession as "supply chain management" by the early 2000s, and all did by 2010.

2.2.2 Supply Chain Management

In an international survey of logistics educators that was conducted in 2001, Larson and Halldorsson[34] found several viewpoints regarding the relationship

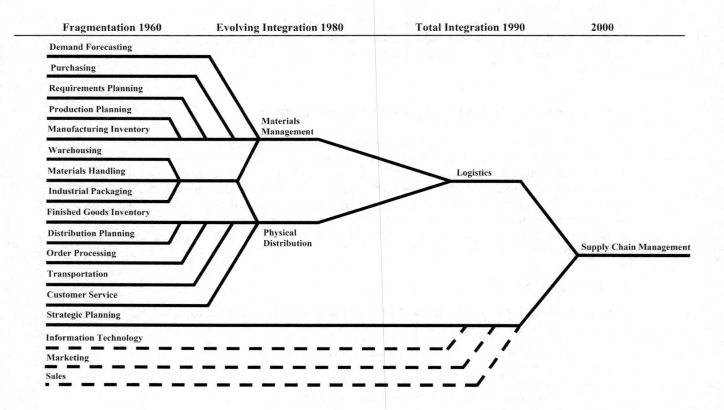

| Fragmentation 1960 | Evolving Integration 1980 | Total Integration 1990 | 2000 |

Figure 2.4: The Evolution of Logistics
Adapted from Alfred J. Battaglia. Reproduced by Natalie David.

between logistics and supply chain management,. However, by 2004, the point of view that logistics management was part of supply-chain management had prevailed, as the Council of Logistics Management changed its name to the Council of Supply Chain Management Professionals (CSCMP) to reflect the perceived broader nature of the field. It also produced this definition:

> Supply Chain Management encompasses the planning and management of all activities involved in sourcing and procurement, conversion, and all Logistics Management activities. Importantly, it also includes coordination and collaboration with channel partners, which can be suppliers, intermediaries, third-party service providers, and customers. In essence, Supply Chain Management integrates supply and demand management within and across companies.[35]

In the view of the CSCMP, shifting from logistics to supply chain management reflected moving from an internal focus on the company's own processes to an external focus that includes all of the firm's partners. The scope of supply chain management is therefore much broader than the scope of logistics; not only does supply chain management include all of the tactical and managerial decisions on which logistics and operations managers tend to focus, but it also includes strategic issues that are more traditionally the domain of the managers in those top management positions that are colloquially referred to as C-level positions (CEO, Chief Executive Officer, CFO, Chief Financial Officer, COO, Chief Operations Officer, and so on). Ten years ago, several companies created positions of Chief Supply Chain Officers, and by 2016, these positions had become prevalent in most large international organizations.[36]

2.2.3 International Logistics

The role of international logistics in the global supply chain mirrors that of logistics in the domestic environment: international logistics professionals focus on the tactical aspects of the global supply chain, activities that are inherent to the movement of goods and paperwork from one country to another, and activities that constitute the basis for export and import operations.

The definition of logistics provided by the Council of Supply Chain Management Professionals can therefore be logically modified to define international logistics by including elements of the international environment:

> International logistics is the process of planning, implementing, and controlling the flow and storage of goods, services, and related information from a point of origin to a point of consumption located in a different country.

The emphasis of international logistics is therefore on the creation of internal processes and strategies. These processes and activities are the focus of this textbook.

2.2.4 International Supply Chain Management

Supply chain management is inherently global; nearly every company outsources some percentage of its production abroad or sells to customers that are located abroad. If the company does not, its suppliers or customers do. In many instances, the product's brand nationality gives little indication of the country in which the product was made. In 2016, the cars.com website created the American-Made Index, and found only eight cars sold in the United States that had U.S. content in excess of 75 percent. The Toyota Camry, a Japanese sedan sold in the United States, was the highest ranked vehicle, followed by the Honda Accord, another Japanese sedan, and the Toyota Sienna, a Japanese minivan. The highest ranked American-brand vehicle was the Chevrolet Traverse, in sixth position. The best-selling American product, the Ford F-150 pickup truck, did not meet the threshold of 75 percent American content.[37]

It is not clear why the Council of Supply Chain Management Professionals did not include this global aspect of supply chain management in its definition. The Council's definition should more accurately read:

> Supply Chain Management encompasses the planning and management of all activities involved in sourcing and procurement, conversion, and all Logistics Management activities. Importantly, it also includes coordination and collaboration with channel partners, which can be suppliers, intermediaries, third-party service providers, and customers, whether they are located in the United States or abroad. In essence, Supply Chain Management integrates supply and demand management within and across companies.

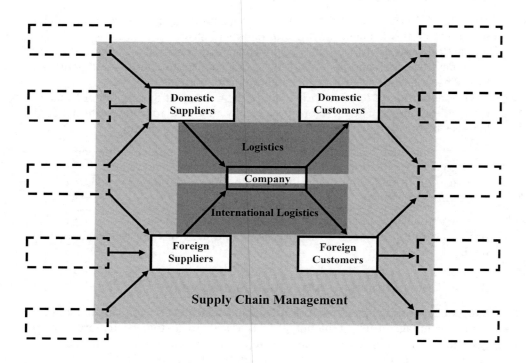

Figure 2.5: Logistics, International Logistics, and Supply Chain Management
Diagram by Pierre David. Reproduced by Natalie David.

Figure 2.5 outlines the relationships between logistics, international logistics, and supply chain management as of 2016. The activities included in the logistics function include physically transporting the goods from the supplier(s) to the company and from the company to its customer(s). Logistics also includes warehousing and other inventory functions within the company that involve the goods it purchases, manufactures, and sells.

International logistics works in a parallel form for foreign suppliers and customers. It includes additional activities, such as customs clearance, documents handling, and international packaging; however, international logistics focuses on the physical movement of goods from suppliers to the company and from the company to its customers. The fact that the movement occurs in an international arena makes fulfilling these activities more complex. Supply chain management is a much broader term; it includes both domestic and international logistics functions, and also encompasses managing the relationships with suppliers and customers (domestic or foreign) and, to some degree, of their relationships with their suppliers and customers. Supply chain management deals with the entire supply chain, attempting to manage a smooth flow of goods from the first supplier to the end customer. A possible example of a supply chain management activity is the management of quality by the large U.S. Original Equipment Manufacturers (General Motors, Ford Motor Company, and Daimler-Chrysler), that implemented QS-9000, which includes a process by which they certify the quality function of their direct suppliers (called tier-one suppliers), of these suppliers' suppliers (called tier-two), and of these firms' suppliers (called tier-three). Chapter 19 has more details on these points.

2.3   Elements of International Logistics

Only a few activities are exclusive to international logistics; however, traditional logistical activities are managed differently in an international environment than they are in a domestic environment.

- The environment involved in international logistics is important. While there is the obvious issue of language and culture—neither of which should be underestimated, but are better covered in an intercultural management textbook—the physical environment of international logistics is distinct. The differences in the infrastructure of international logistics and the related challenges they represent are covered in Chapter 3.

- International transportation decisions are eminently more complicated. Because of the distances involved, there are different modes of transportation, different carriers, different transportation documents, and much greater transit times. Chapters 11, 12, and 13 identify these transportation alternatives.

- A larger number of intermediaries are involved. Banks, insurance companies, freight forwarders, and the governments of the exporting country and of the importing country, have different paperwork requirements. Chapter 9 lists the multitude of documents that are utilized in international trade.

- The inherent risks and hazards of international transportation are much more significant. To protect the goods while they are in transit, the logistics manager must have a complete understanding of the available packaging options. Chapter 14 details the choices and decisions surrounding packing for international transport. Chapter 16 reviews the management of security issues in international trade.

- International insurance is much more complex. Contracts are sometimes written using archaic language and terminology with meaning that varies based on the country in which the insurance contract is drawn. Chapter 10 presents the different types of insurance coverage available in an international environment.

- International payments are more involved. The risks of nonpayment and currency fluctuations call for specific strategies that are never used in domestic transactions. Chapter 7 presents various means of international payment and Chapter 8 explains the methods used by international traders to protect themselves against the risks created by currency fluctuations.

- Terms of trade are much more complicated, as a greater number of nodes and links increases the number of possible alternatives for transfer of responsibility and ownership. The terms of trade used in international sales—the Incoterms© Rules of the International Chamber of Commerce— are thoroughly reviewed in Chapter 6.

- Crossing borders creates specific challenges. Products sold abroad or purchased from abroad must go through customs, a complicated and paper-intensive process in most countries. The procedures involved in such a process are described in Chapter 17. In addition, when conducting business with foreign firms, issues arise in the contracts of sale, distribution agreements, and other legal documents. Chapters 4 and 5 list the options available to a firm engaged in international trade.

- Inventory is managed differently, as the risks of delays and variations in shipping times increase the challenges of determining order sizes and lot sizes, especially when they are linked to Just-in-Time production. Safety stocks are calculated using slightly more complicated algorithms. A good primer on such methods can be found in Chapter 18.

- Warehousing and distribution centers are created and managed differently, as the challenges of operating in an international environment are more significant. Chapter 15 presents an overview of these challenges.

- Quality issues must be monitored as carefully as they are in a domestic environment. However, the length of international supply chain channels, and the potential delays caused by non-conforming products, call for a review of the techniques of quality control and quality acceptance, and Chapter 19 covers these points.

- Supply chain managers are becoming more conscious of sustainability issues, and are therefore making decisions that reduce the energy and the resources used in manufacturing, packaging and shipping goods across borders. Each chapter of this textbook, when appropriate, includes sustainability issues that are relevant to the chapter's topic.

2.4 The Economic Importance of Logistics

Logistical activities represent a substantial proportion of the economic activity of the world economy.

2.4.1 Logistics in the United States

In a yearly study of domestic logistics, started by Bob Delaney, continued by Rosalyn Wilson, and now written by the A.T. Kearney consulting firm, the percentage of the United States' Gross Domestic Product (GDP) that is spent on logistical activities (transportation, inventory, and other administrative costs linked to logistical activities) stood at 8.5 percent in 2003. This percentage increased to 9.9 percent in 2007 due to rising energy costs, but then continued on the downward trend started in 1960 and decreased to 8.3 percent in 2015,[38] as shown in Figure 2.6.

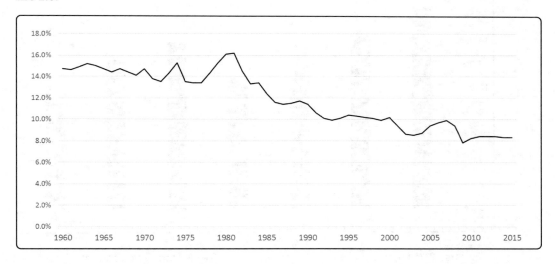

Figure 2.6: Logistics Costs (Percentage of U.S. Gross Domestic Product)
Annual State of Logistics Reports, 2000-2016.

This decrease is mostly due to corporations becoming more efficient in their use of inventory. The advent of Just-in-Time, Manufacturing Resources Planning, and their derivatives have decreased inventory levels from 24 percent of the United States' GDP in 1981 to a near-record low of 14 percent in 2015.[39] Inventory holding costs contribute to approximately one third of total logistics costs in the United States.

Some of the decrease in logistics spending can also be attributed to more efficient means of transportation—for example, the increased use of containers—and to the deregulation of the U.S. transportation industry, especially during the 1980s and early 1990s. Collectively, American businesses spend almost U.S. $1.48 trillion on domestic logistics activities,[40] including U.S. $934 billion on transportation services in 2015,[41] or about 3 percent of the United States' GDP.

2.4.2 Logistics in Other Countries

The logistics functions of United States companies appear to be much more efficient than the logistics functions of many of its trade partners' companies.

In 2013, the China Federation of Logistics and Purchasing estimated that logistics costs were 20 percent of the Chinese GDP in 2000, and that these costs had only decreased to 18 percent by 2012.[42] This decrease was due to improvements in infrastructure and the adoption of better inventory management techniques; nevertheless, they are still more than twice the relative weight of logistics costs in the U.S.

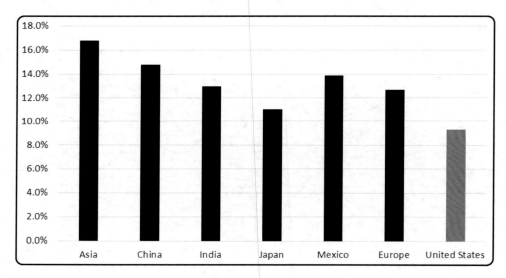

Figure 2.7: Logistics Costs as a Percentage of Gross Domestic Product
SupplyChainDigest, June 2013.

Worldwide, logistics activities are estimated to total U.S.$ 8 trillion.[43] Figure 2.7 shows an estimate of the percentages of several regions' GDP spent on domestic logistics. Since the total world output is estimated at U.S. $76.7 trillion,[44] logistical activities can be estimated to represent about 10.4 percent of the world's economy.

It is difficult to compare logistics costs between countries, as there is no standard method by which these costs are calculated; one country's costs may be higher simply because the methodology used to calculate logistics costs in that country differs from the methodology used in another. The three sources used in this section provide data that clearly uses different calculation methodologies. Nevertheless, it can be inferred that logistics costs in most countries represent at least 10 to 15 percent of the country's GDP.

2.4.3 International Logistics

While there is no comprehensive data illustrating the total value of international logistics activities—logistics activities related to trade between nations—it can be conservatively estimated that the percentage spent on international logistics activities is approximately 15 percent of the total volume of international trade. Because the total value of the world's merchandise trade in 2014 was U.S. $19 trillion, the total expenditures on international logistics for that same year was approximately U.S. $2.85 trillion. This estimate considers that international logistics activities are typically more costly due to more complex procedures, inefficient infrastructures, and longer distances.

However, there is one aspect of international logistics that distinguishes it from domestic logistics in terms of its impact on the world's economy; not only are the profits of corporations involved in logistics taxed by their respective governments, but international trade also generates a considerable amount of additional government revenue, as most imports are subject to tariffs. A conservative estimate of the "value" of duty collection and other taxes directly linked to international trade is approximately 5 percent[45] of the world's merchandise trade. International logistic activities therefore generate about U.S. $1 trillion in additional government revenue, or the equivalent of the entire GDP of Mexico, Indonesia, or the Netherlands.

2.5 International Reverse Logistics

A recent development in logistics is the introduction of reverse logistics, or the management of products and packaging returned by customers. More broadly, reverse logistics involves managing the handling of goods after they have been sold to the final consumer or customer. Reverse logistics is the "process of planning, implementing, and controlling the efficient, cost effective flow of raw materials, in-process inventory, finished goods and related information from the point of consumption to the point of origin for the purpose of recapturing value or proper disposal."[46] Essentially, reverse logistics activities are the same as those of traditional logistics, except in "reverse."

Goods are returned to the manufacturer for many reasons, including:

- The goods have completed their useful life for the consumer or customer and are returned because they can be remanufactured or refurbished. There are multiple incentives for both the customer and the manufacturer to do

this; either there are sustainability incentives to the consumer (laws to encourage the return of obsolete or depleted goods), or the costs of returning
the goods are lower than the disposal costs for the customer, or the return
and reuse costs for the manufacturer are lower than the costs of manufacturing new parts.

• The goods are returned because the consumer needs them to be repaired
under warranty, or the goods do not meet the customer's expectations.

• The goods are defective and the manufacturer issues a recall of the goods,
so that they can be repaired or made conform to market requirements.

• The packaging that was used to ship the goods from the manufacturer's
plant to the customer's facilities can be reused for another shipment.

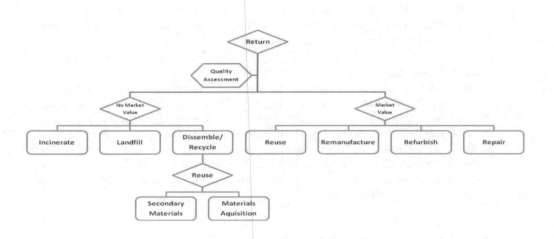

Figure 2.8: Typical Flow Diagram of a Reverse Logistics System
Lora Skarman. Used with permission.

Many companies are now realizing that a reverse logistics system combined
with source-reduction processes can be used to gain competitive advantage through
value creation.[47] Specific examples come from Kodak, Estée Lauder and Caterpillar. Kodak started a campaign in 1990 to take back, reuse, and recycle its
single-use cameras, originally designed as disposables. In 1990 Kodak collected
0.9 million cameras and by 1998 that figure had jumped to 61 million units. In
2008, Kodak had multiple recycling facilities where up to 86 percent of camera
parts were reused to manufacture new cameras.

Estée Lauder used to dump $60 million of its products into landfills annually.
In the first year of its reverse logistics program, after an initial investment of
$1.3 million, Estée Lauder increased the number of returned products by twenty-
four percent, reduced the number of destroyed products from 37 percent to 27

percent of returned products and saved $0.5 million in labor costs. Estée Lauder has since created a $250 million product line from its return flows, the third most profitable product line in the company.

Caterpillar, operates fourteen remanufacturing plants worldwide. The plants can disassemble and rebuild diesel engines—cleaning, inspecting, and repairing as many as 20,000 parts as they do this. Caterpillar's remanufacturing division is its fastest growing division, at a rate of twenty percent per year, and annual revenues exceed $1 billion.[48]

In all cases, especially in an international environment, the process of getting the goods from the customer or consumer to the manufacturer involves the intermediaries that were present at the time of the original sale, making it somewhat cumbersome to import products that had originally been exported.[49] However, small-package shippers, such as United Parcel Service, have implemented processes to help exporters handle goods that are returned by their international customers.[50]

Many companies are implementing a "cradle to cradle" manufacturing system, in which the product is manufactured, used by consumers, recovered after use, and then reused, refurbished, resold or some combination of these activities, to put the product back into circulation. Figure 2.8 on the preceding page shows the flows in a typical reverse logistics system from "cradle to cradle." [51]

Two Different Reverse Logistics Programs

In 1991, the German government passed a law requiring all consumer packaged goods manufacturers to take back the packaging that the manufacturers used to ship their goods, including the final consumer containers. This law created a dual refuse collection system, ubiquitous in the country, called *Der Grüne Punkt*—The Green Dot—designed to collect and return all consumer packaging materials to manufacturers.

Set up by the industry, this secondary garbage collection system is made up of yellow collection bins located near retail centers and of yellow plastic bags used by households on garbage collection days, that are designed to collect used consumer packages. The materials collected are then sorted, recycled or re-used. The entire system is funded by the industry.

By 2009, German consumers recycled more than 88 percent of their packaging materials,[52] and German municipal household waste was 48 percent recycled and 18 percent composted, the highest percentage in the world.[53]

The city of Curitiba, Brazil, has implemented its recycling program in a completely different manner. Curitiba has placed recycling containers throughout the city, and encouraged families to sort their household waste. It is an entirely voluntary program, but the city has managed to recycle more than two-thirds of its household refuse.[54]

The city hires homeless and very low income residents to collect recyclable items and exchanges what they collect for food and money. The city even has a "green exchange" program through which residents of the *favelas* that surround the city can take the household trash that they have collected and exchange it for food. This has the effect of keeping the slums cleaner, and improving the nutrition and income of its poorest residents.

Whether compulsory or voluntary, several other recycling programs are in place in many other countries. As countries become more urbanized, such programs are likely to become more common.

Figure 2.9: The Colorful Recycling Bins of Curitiba, Brazil
Photo ©Ricardo de Paula Ferreira/Shutterstock. Used with permission.

Manufacturers, especially in the United States, have not typically designed products for repair, reuse or recovery. There is a strong sentiment worldwide to change that business model by introducing extended producer responsibility laws. European environmental laws have been introduced with the intent of extending producer responsibility for everything from the products themselves to packaging materials. Many firms are now realizing that designing products for not only the first use, but also subsequent use provides a cost advantage because these products can be sold in secondary markets with minimal work after recovery. The cost of raw materials, transportation, storage, and other supply chain components as well as regulations will drive international logistics professionals to get the most out of their product's life cycle.

Review and Discussion Questions

1. What elements differentiate international logistics from domestic logistics?

2. What are the principal distinct components of international logistics?

3. What are the major costs of international logistics? Given what you read in Chapter 1 about the World Trade Organization, what trend do you expect these costs to follow?

4. MRP and DRP have allowed manufacturers and retailers to carry less and less inventory. What consequences would a major snowstorm or transportation disruption have on Just-In-Time management systems?

5. Describe the impact of international trade on your own life, using the products that you own or have purchased in the recent past.

Notes

[1] Pomerantz, Kenneth, and Steven Topik, *The world that trade created*, 2013, M.E. Sharpe, Armonk, New York, 2013.

[2] Turner, Jack, *Spice: The History of a Temptation*, Vintage Books, Random House, New York, New York, 2005.

[3] Gies, Frances and Joseph, *Cathedral, Forge and Waterwheel; Technology and Invention in the Middle Ages*, Harper-Collins Publishers, New York, New York, USA, 1995.

[4] Klein, Jacob, *Greek Mathematical Thought and the Origin of Algebra*, translated by Eva Brann, Dover Publications, Mineola, New York, USA, reprinted October 1992. Original publication by MIT Press, Cambridge, Massachusetts, USA, 1968.

[5] Shaw, Arch Wilkinson, *Some Problems in Market Distribution*, Harvard University Press, Cambridge, MA, 1915.

[6] Lewis, Howard, *Industrial Purchasing*, Prentice-Hall, Inc., 1933

[7] Pacini, Alfred and Dominique Pons, *Docker à Marseille, Récits de vie*, Payot, T.S. Simey, editeurs, Paris, 1996.

[8] Levinson, Marc, *The box; how the shipping container made the world smaller and the world economy bigger*, Princeton University Press, Princeton, New Jersey, 2006.

[9] *Ibid.*

[10] Cudahy, Brian J., *Box boats: How containerships changed the world*, Fordham University Press, New York, New York, 2006.

[11] Donovan, Arthur, and Joseph Bonney, "The box that changed the world," *The Journal of Commerce*, Commonwealth Business Media, New York, New York, 2006.

[12] Fedex Annual Report, http://annualreport.van.fedex.com/2016/docs/FedEx_2016_Annual_Report.pdf, May 31, 2016.

[13] Hummels, David, "Time as a Trade Barrier," Purdue University working paper, July 2001, http://www.unc.edu/depts/econ/seminars/hummels.pdf, January 21, 2009.

[14] Levinson, Marc, *The box; how the shipping container made the world smaller and the world economy bigger*, Princeton University Press, Princeton, New Jersey, 2006.

[15] Donovan, Arthur, and Joseph Bonney, "The box that changed the world," *The Journal of Commerce*, Commonwealth Business Media, New York, New York, 2006.

[16] Levinson, Marc, *The box; how the shipping container made the world smaller and the world economy bigger*, Princeton University Press, Princeton, New Jersey, 2006.

[17] *Ibid.*

[18] *World Investment Report 1996: Investment, Trade, and International Policy Agreements*, United Nations, August 1996, and *World Investment Report 2016—Investor nationality: policy challenges*, United Nations, June 21, 2016, http://unctad.org/en/PublicationsLibrary/wir2016_en.pdf, retrieved September 14, 2016.

[19] *Ibid.*

[20] *CSCO 2014: Top Three Supply Chain Execution Priorities*, December 2013, Aberdeen Group, 451 D Street, Suite 700, Boston, MA 02210, http://v1.aberdeen.com/launch/report/perspective/8757-AI-supply-chain-priorities.asp, retrieved February 23, 2016.

[21] Douglas, Merrill, "Global trade in the key of GTM," *Inbound Logistics*, March 2014, pp.46-51.

[22] Paris, Costas, "China's zika move makes waves for shippers," *The Wall Street Journal*, August 26, 2016, p. B1.

[23] Israel Free Trade Agreement, August 19, 1985, http://tcc.export.gov/trade_agreements/all_trade_-agreements/exp_005439.asp, retrieved September 18, 2016.

[24] North American Free Trade Agreement, Chapter 4: Rules of Origin, January 1, 1994, http://www.sice.oas.org/trade/nafta/chap-041.asp, retrieved September 18, 2015.

[25] Bureau of Industry and Security, Export Enforcement, *Don't let this happen to you*, July 2015 edition, http://www.bis.doc.gov/index.php/forms-documents/doc_view/1005-don-t-let-this-happen-to-you-071814, retrieved September 18, 2016.

[26] Chao, Loretta, Erica Phillips, and Joanne Chiu, "Shippers brace for new weight-data rule," *the Wall Street Journal*, July 1, 2016, p. B3.

[27] SCM World, *Managing global trade: rising importance but lagging execution*, July 31, 2013, https://content.scmworld.com/research/reports/managing-global-trade–rising-importance-but-lagging-execution/, retrieved August 30, 2013.

[28] Terry, Lisa, "Supply chain visibility: chasing the big picture," *Inbound Logistics*, July 2015, pp. 144-150.

[29] Reuters, "Toyota, other major Japanese firms hit by quake damage, supply disruptions," *Forbes*, April 17, 2016.

[30] O'Reilly, Joseph, "Ocean containers talk back," *Inbound Logistics*, October 2015, p. 27.

[31] Johnson, Eric, "Global TMS comes of age," *American Shipper*, May 2016, pp. 10-16.

[32] Council of Supply Chain Management Professionals, "Bylaws of CSCMP," July 15, 2015, https://cscmp.org/sites/default/files/user_uploads/footer/downloads/bylaws/cscmp-bylaws-i.pdf, retrieved September 18, 2016.

[33] Battaglia, Alfred J., "Beyond Logistics: Supply Chain Management (Operations)," *Chief Executive*, Nov-Dec 1994, pp. 48-50.

[34] Larson, Paul D. and Arni Halldorsson, "Logistics vs. Supply Chain Management: An International Survey," *Journal of Supply Chain Management*, March 2004, pp. 17-31.

[35] Council of Supply Chain Management Professionals, "Bylaws of CSCMP," July 15, 2015, https://cscmp.org/sites/default/files/user_uploads/footer/downloads/bylaws/cscmp-bylaws-i.pdf, retrieved September 18, 2016.

[36] Thalbauer, Hans, "Is Chief Supply Chain Officer most important role In executive suite?," *Forbes*, March 25, 2016, and "The growing role of the Chief Supply Chain Officer," *SupplyChainBrain*, September 11, 2014.

[37] Mays, Kelsey, "The 2016 Cars.com American-Made Index," June 28, 2016, https://www.cars.com/articles/the-2016-carscom-american-made-index-1420684865874/, retrieved September 14, 2016.

[38] Kearney, A.T., *Twenty-seventh Annual State of Logistics Report: Logistics in transition. New drivers at the wheel*, Council of Logistics Management, June 21, 2016, https://cscmp.org/member-benefits/state-of-logistics, retrieved July 1, 2016.

[39] Cassidy, William, and Reynolds Hutchins, "High US inventories could be the new normal," *JOC.com*, June 29, 2016, http://www.joc.com/economy-watch/us-economy-news/some-signs-indicate-long-awaited-destocking-under-way_20160629.html, retrieved September 18, 2016.

[40] Kearney, A.T., *Twenty-seventh Annual State of Logistics Report: Logistics in transition. New drivers at the wheel*, Council of Logistics Management, June 21, 2016, https://cscmp.org/member-benefits/state-of-logistics, retrieved July 1, 2016.

[41] Trading Economics, "United States GDP from transportation and warehousing," http://www.trading-economics.com/united-states/gdp-from-transport, retrieved September 18, 2016.

[42] China Federation of Logistics and Purchasing, "Review of China's Logistics Industry Development in 2012 and Prospect in 2013 (Foreword)," http://www.chinawuliu.com.cn/english/201406/16/290820.-shtml, retrieved September 19, 2016.

[43] Armstrong, Richard, "There Could be a great 3PL in your Future," *SupplyChainBrain*, March-April

2012, pp. 48-50.

[44]World Development Indicators: Size of the Economy, World Bank, 10 August 2016, http://wdi.-worldbank.org/table/1.1, retrieved September 23, 2016.

[45]Tariffs and Import Fees, U.S. Department of Commerce International Trade Administration, http://export.gov/logistics/eg_main_018130.asp, November 1, 2012.

[46]Hawks, Karen, "What is Reverse Logistics?," *Reverse Logistics Magazine*, Winter-Spring 2006, pp.12-13.

[47]Jayaraman, Vaidyanathan, and Yadong Luo, "Creating Competitive Advantages Through New Value Creation: A Reverse Logistics Perspective," *Academy of Management Perspectives*, May 2007, pp. 56-73.

[48]*Ibid.*

[49]Stanton, Tom, "Avoiding the Pitfalls of International Returns," *Reverse Logistics Magazine*, June 2010, pp. 42-43 (part I), August 2010, pp. 39-42 (part II), and October 2010, pp.42-44 (part III).

[50]United Parcel Service, "International Returns Made Easy," advertorial, *DC Velocity*, April 2013, p.54.

[51]Stock, James R., *Development and Implementation of Reverse Logistics Processes*, Council of Logistics Management, 1998.

[52]"Trash Planet: Germany," *Earth911.com*, http://earth911.com/news/2009/07/13/trash-planet-germany, November 10, 2012.

[53]"German recycling system gets an overhaul," *The Local*, May 3, 2011, http://www.thelocal.de/society/20110503-34757.html, November 10, 2012.

[54]Alvarado, Paula, "Jaime Lerner and Sustainability in Curitiba and 'Urban Acupuncture'," November 12, 2007, http://www.treehugger.com/files/2007/11/jaime_lerner_interview_planeta_sustentavel-.php, November 1, 2012.

Chapter 3

International Infrastructure

For an international logistics manager, it is important to recognize the challenges presented by the different levels of infrastructure found abroad. One of the first problems encountered by an international manager is that things don't work abroad like they do at "home." There are different standards, there are different performance expectations, there are things that work much better, and there are things that do not work as well—in some cases, not at all. Adapting to these differences, and anticipating problems before they arise, are part of the attributes of an experienced international logistics manager.

infrastructure
A term that refers to all the public and private goods that facilitate transportation, communication, and business exchanges.

The issue with managing these infrastructure differences is that they are difficult to generalize in one comment or statement. Most infrastructure challenges tend to be concentrated in small geographic areas and, in most cases, are limited to a single location: a specific port is not equipped with sufficient cold-storage warehousing space, does not have an appropriately-sized crane, or is experiencing delays in getting the goods from the port to the remainder of the country; a road is congested, a specific tunnel has recently closed, or a railroad is experiencing shortages of appropriate cars. These challenges force the international logistics manager to recognize the possibility of serious problems. The purpose of this chapter is to present enough information and examples to encourage him or her to ask questions at the onset of a transaction, so that there are no discrepancies between the expectations of the company and what can be achieved.

3.1 Definitions

First, it is useful to identify what is meant by infrastructure in the context of international logistics. A few dictionary definitions would provide a good start:

> The American Heritage Dictionary defines infrastructure in the broadest terms: "The basic facilities, services, and installations needed for the functioning of a community or society, such as transportation and communications systems, water and power lines, and public institutions including schools, post offices, and prisons."[1]
>
> The Oxford English Dictionary defines infrastructure more narrowly, using its military origins: "A collective term for the subordinate parts of an undertaking; substructure, foundation. The permanent installations forming a basis for military operations, as airfields, naval bases, training establishments, ... etc."[2]
>
> Merriam-Webster's definition of infrastructure is the most succinct with "the system of public works of a country, state, or region,"[3] and ignores the privately owned elements of infrastructure.

In logistics, the definition of infrastructure must be broad: it is a collective term that refers to all the elements in place (publicly or privately owned goods) that facilitate transportation, communication, and business exchanges. Infrastructure therefore includes not only transportation and communication elements, but also the existence and quality of public utilities, banking services, and retail distribution channels. It also makes sense to add the existence and quality of the court system, the defense of intellectual property rights, and the existence of national standards. As these concepts are introduced in this chapter, their inclusion into the concept of infrastructure will become more evident.

The study of infrastructure is important because the movement of goods and documents, as well as the movement of money and information, depends on these infrastructure components.

3.2 Transportation Infrastructure

The infrastructure that most obviously affects the movement of goods internationally is the transportation infrastructure. Without a good understanding of the transportation infrastructure that a shipment will face, a manager may package a product inappropriately, incur delays, or even receive unexpectedly damaged merchandise.

3.2.1 Port Infrastructure

Port infrastructure is made up of several items, most of which are interconnected, and affect the type of ships that can call a given port, as well as the type of merchandise that can transit through it.

Until the late 1990s, the largest containerships that called on ports were ships called Panamax ships. These ships were as large as they could be and still fit through the locks of the Panama Canal. However, several shipping lines started building larger ships, called post-Panamax ships, in the early 1990s to serve the Asia-United States and the Asia-Europe trade routes. Ports were then faced with many challenges: the size of post-Panamax ships stretched the capabilities of the ports, as the ships were much wider, longer, higher above the water, and had a much deeper draft.

Panamax ship
A ship of the maximum size that can enter the locks of the Panama Canal.

post-Panamax ship
A ship whose size is too large to enter the locks of the Panama Canal.

The 2000s and 2010s saw an explosion in the size of post-Panamax containerships. While the first ones were designed to hold 6,000 TEUs—twenty-foot equivalent units or twenty-foot containers—the ones built in the 2000s had capacities in the 10,000-TEU range, and the ones built in the 2010s were almost twice that size. There were 47 containerships with a capacity greater than 18,000 TEUs in operation as of January 2017, and another 58 ordered, with expected deliveries in 2017 and 2018 (see Table 3.1 on the following page). Altogether, these 105 mega-ships—representing less than 2 percent of the total containership fleet—will eventually represent 8.6 percent of the world's total container-carrying capacity.[4,5]

Containerships in Operation

TEU size range	Number of Ships	Percentage of Ships in Use	Capacity (in TEUs)	Percentage of Capacity
100-499	187	3.7%	60,649	0.3%
500-999	753	14.7%	560,370	2.8%
1,000-1,499	699	13.7%	807,654	4.0%
1,500-1,999	590	11.5%	1,008,445	5.0%
2,000-2,999	621	12.1%	1,571,908	7.8%
3,000-3,999	249	4.9%	864,922	4.3%
4,000-5,099	**679**	**13.3%**	**3,077,443**	**15.2%**
5,100-7,499	471	9.7%	2,911,464	14.4%
7,500-9,999	475	6.9%	4,176,453	20.6%
10,000-13,299	**215**	**3.5%**	**2,511,886**	**12.4%**
13,300-17,999	126	3.5%	1,829,534	9.0%
18,000-21,000	47	3.5%	890,497	4.4%
	5,112		20,271,225	

Containerships on Order

TEU size range	Number of Ships	Percentage of Ships on Order	Capacity (in TEUs)	Percentage of Capacity
100-499	9	2.2%	2,998	0.1%
500-999	6	1.5%	3,903	0.1%
1,000-1,499	44	10.7%	52,402	1.6%
1,500-1,999	59	14.4%	106,242	3.3%
2,000-2,999	74	18.0%	193,309	6.0%
3,000-3,999	30	7.3%	106,439	3.3%
4,000-5,099	**4**	**1.0%**	**16,022**	**15.2%**
5,100-7,499	5	1.2%	28,062	0.9%
7,500-9,999	7	1.7%	64,592	2.0%
10,000-13,299	**68**	**16.5%**	**807,833**	**25.3%**
13,300-17,999	47	11.4%	670,998	21.0%
18,000-21,000	58	14.1%	1,135,887	35.6%
	411		3,188,687	

Table 3.1: Containerships in Operation and on Order as of January 2017
Alphaliner. (Panamax and Neo-Panamax in bold)

The Panamax designation is now partially obsolete as the Panama Canal Authority built another set of locks that run parallel to the older ones. Ships that can fit through these locks are called Neo-Panamax or New Panamax. The Neo-Panamax ships can hold as many as 13,300 TEUs.

Neo-Panamax and larger ships represent most of the new containership orders, as shown in Table 3.1. There were 173 to be built and delivered before 2019 (see Table 3.1 on the preceding page), representing almost half of all ships ordered for that period,[6] and more than 80 percent of the capacity being built. Most of these ships operate on the routes between Asia and Western Europe, and between Asia and North America. Such large ships mean that as many as 5,000 forty-foot containers need to be unloaded and 5,000 loaded in a single port.[7]

neo-Panamax ship
A ship whose size allows it to enter the newest locks of the Panama Canal.

Depth of Water

The first issue is the depth of water in a port, which has to be sufficient to accommodate the draft of the ships that call that port. In many ports, the depth of the channels and of the berths, which had been sufficient to accommodate Panamax ships, is not sufficient to accommodate the newer, larger ships. Therefore, in many ports, the port authorities have engaged in dredging activities to allow ships with drafts exceeding 13.5 meters [40 feet] to access the port. Only a few ports with naturally deep channels have been exempt from this activity.

draft
The minimum depth of water that a ship needs in order to float.
berth
In a port, the location at which a ship can load and unload its cargo.

Despite the fact that dredging channels and ports can be exceedingly expensive, port authorities have little alternative but to undertake this improvement of their port capabilities. One port that has benefited from its natural deep waters is the Port of Prince Rupert in British Columbia, Canada, which started handling container freight in the autumn of 2007. The port enjoys terminals with a natural draft of 20 meters [67 feet], as well as a Canadian National Railroad terminal, giving it a direct link to the North American continent. Since Prince Rupert is also the North American port closest to the Asian Pacific Rim ports, it is attempting to divert some of the traffic that traditionally called on West Coast ports in the United States; it can shorten transit times from China to Chicago by as many as 60 hours.[8] However, Prince Rupert has so far diverted only a small fraction of the cargo discharged on the West Coast of North America, handling a total of 776,000 TEUs in 2015,[9] or about 5 percent of what is handled by the ports of Los Angeles and Long Beach.[10]

dredging
The removal of sediments or soil from the bottom of a water channel to increase its depth.

In a parallel fashion, longer ships require longer turning circles, and therefore a redesign—and dredging—of different access channels. As ships become yet longer, wider, and heavier, the challenge for the port authorities will be to adapt to these ships' requirements.

Bridge Clearance

Another important factor is the clearance under waterway bridges leading to the port; the ships that call on a port have an air draft which dictates the minimum space that the ship needs under a port's waterway bridges. In many older ports, the bridges are too close to the water, leaving very little clearance for tall ships or

air draft
The distance between the
water level at high tide and
the lowest point on a
bridge.

ships carrying oversized cargo. To access the Port of New York-New Jersey, ships had to be modified or designed so that they could clear the Bayonne Bridge's low clearance: 45 meters [151 feet] above the water at high tide.[11] In 2013, the Port Authority of New York and New Jersey awarded a contract to lift the Bayonne Bridge roadway to reach 65 meters [215 feet] above water, to be completed by the end of 2019.[12]

Factors such as the depth of channels and berths, as well as bridge clearance, are likely to affect how ports are used in the future. There is a strong probability that some ports will be unable to make the necessary infrastructure investments to accommodate the largest ships and that large port hubs will need to be created to handle mega-containerships. Smaller ports can then be served by smaller "feeder" ships that do not tax the ports' infrastructure beyond their capacity. Such large port hubs were created in the 1990s in the Mediterranean Sea: Marsaxlokk in Malta and Cagliari in Sardinia (Italy) serve as trans-shipment ports, loading and unloading large containerships in a deep-water port and using feeder ships to serve the local markets and shallower ports of France, Italy, and Spain.[13]

China's most noticeable response to the increase in the number of mega-containerships was the construction of the deep-water port of Yangshan (see Figure 3.1), part of the Port of Shanghai, in China. As the port of Shanghai became congested, and since it is relatively shallow and would have required a lot of dredging, the government of China decided to build a deep-water port in the

Figure 3.1: The Largest Port in the World: Yangshan-Shanghai, China
Photo ©Prasit Rodphan/Shutterstock. Used with permission.

Hangzhou Bay, just south of the city of Shanghai. The port was built on a large landfill between two uninhabited islands, and is linked to the mainland by the Donghai Bridge, a 32-kilometer-long (20-mile) bridge, most of which is above water.

The combined ports of Shanghai and Yangshan constitute the largest port in the world; in 2012, these two ports, combined, moved ahead of the two ports that had dominated the list for the first decade of the twenty-first century: Singapore and Hong Kong. Shenzen and Ningbo, two other Chinese ports, eventually surpassed Hong Kong in 2014. In 2015, Shanghai handled 36.5 million TEUs, with Singapore and Hong Kong at 30.9 and 20.0 million TEUs respectively. [14] As of 2017, the Port of Yangshan can handle 14 million TEUs with 22 berths. When it is completed in 2020, it will have 30 berths and will be able to handle 15 million TEUs.[15] For a sense of perspective, Table 3.2[16] lists the twenty five largest container-handling ports in the world. The largest European port is Rotterdam with 12.2 millon TEUs, and the largest North American port is Los Angeles, with 8.1 million TEUs. Even with its sister port in Long Beach, the two ports' combined volume was "only" 15.3 million TEUs, or less than half of Shanghai-Yangshan.

Largest Container Ports of the World (in millions of TEUs)

Rank	Port	TEUs	Rank	Port	TEUs
1	Shanghai, CN	36.54	14	Antwerp, BE	9.65
2	Singapore, SG	30.92	15	Dalian, CN	9.45
3	Shenzhen, CN	24.20	16	Xiamen, CN	9.18
4	Ningbo, CN	20.63	17	Tanjung Pelepas, MY	9.10
5	Hong Kong , HK	20.07	18	Hamburg, DE,	8.82
6	Pusan, KR	19.45	19	Los Angeles, US	8.16
7	Qingdao, CN	17.47	20	Keihin Ports, JP	7.52
8	Guangzhou, CN	17.22	21	Long Beach, US	7.19
9	Dubai, UAE	15.60	22	Laem Chabang, TH	6.82
10	Tianjin, CN	14.11	23	New York-New Jersey, US	6.37
11	Rotterdam, NL	12.23	24	Yingkou, CN	5.92
12	Port Klang, MY	11.89	25	Bremerhaven, DE	5.48
13	Kaohsiung, TW	10.26			

Table 3.2: 2015 World's Largest Container Ports (in millions of TEU movements)
World Shipping Council.

Cranes

In port terminals, the width and height of post-Panamax ships can be a challenge for the cranes. Traditional Panamax ships can be loaded with up to thirteen containers in the width of a ship, and no more than six stacked on top of one another above deck (see Figure 11.2 on page 387). The largest post-Panamax ships can be loaded with as many as twenty-three containers side-by-side[17] and nine stacked on top of one another (Figure 3.2 shows a 14,000-TEU ship with 20 containers abreast). This presents a problem for ports in which the cranes cannot reach the far side of the larger ships. Early on, ports managed the lack of crane capacity by loading ships from one side, turning the ships around, and then loading the remainder of the containers. The problem then became one of balance, as the ships list if they are heavier on one side. Today's ports have made considerable investments in new large-capacity cranes that can load larger ships and ports that have not are at a competitive disadvantage, as modern ships have become much larger.

Figure 3.2: A 14,000-TEU Containership in the Port of Hamburg, Germany
Photo ©Olaf Schulz/Shutterstock. Used with permission.

Existing cranes had to be modified or replaced to reach higher and farther. These modifications can be expensive for a port and new cranes capable of serving large ships can cost U.S.\$ 12 million.[18] Another alternative, chosen by the Amsterdam Container Terminals at the Paragon Terminal, is to create an indented berth to allow the ship to be loaded from both sides. An advantage of this configuration is that it allows the ship to be loaded with up to twelve cranes rather than the maximum of six in a traditional port. This alternative speeds up the loading of the ship, from a maximum of 160 containers per hour (the world record held by the Port of Singapore for a traditional berth) to up to 300 containers per hour,

Port of Gibraltar

Latitude	36° 8'13" N	Longitude	5° 21'41" W

Water Depth

Channel	12.5-13.7 m	Anchorage	18.6-19.8 m
	(41-45 ft)		(61-65 ft)
Cargo Pier	7.1-9.1 m	Oil Terminal	6.4-7.6 m
	(26-30 ft)		(21-25 ft)
Tide	0.3 m (1 ft)		

Entrance Restrictions

Tide	no	Overhead Limit	no
Ice	no	Swell	yes

Pilotage

Compulsory	yes	Advisable	yes
Available	yes		

Cranes

100+ ton		Fixed cranes	yes
50-100 ton		Mobile cranes	yes
25-49 ton	yes	Floating cranes	
0-24 ton	yes		

Table 3.3: Excerpts from a Port-of-Call Entry on *World Port Source* Website
World Port Source.

decreasing the time that a ship spends in port and therefore increasing its profitability.[19] The Paragon terminal is still the only container terminal in the world to have adopted this configuration.

Container crane productivity is important to shipping lines; the faster a ship can be loaded and unloaded, the less time it spends in ports, and the more revenue it can generate. Each individual port crane can move approximately 25 to 40 containers per hour. Port productivity is therefore a function of the number of cranes that a terminal can allocate to a ship; ports can allocate as many as seven cranes to a post-Panamax ship, and as few as four to a Panamax ship. The most productive Asian port, the Port of Tianjin, had an average of 130 container moves per hour per berth (for all ship sizes) in 2013. The most productive European ports were the ports of Bremerhaven and Rotterdam with 86 moves, and the most productive in the Americas was the Port of Balboa in Panama, with 91 moves per hour. The ports of Long Beach and Los Angeles were in the high 80s, and New York-New Jersey was at 78.[20]

For shippers handling non-containerized cargo, the cranes' capacity is a major factor in deciding through which port to send specific cargo. Fortunately, the website *World Port Source*[21] provides an excellent database about most ports in the world, based on the data contained in the World Port Index compiled by the National Geospatial Intelligence Agency. Table 3.3 shows an excerpt of the information included in the World Port Source database for the Port of Gibraltar.

From a shipper's standpoint, it should be obvious that the crane at the port of destination should have at least the same capacity as the one that was used to load the cargo. Failure to pay attention to crane capacity is likely to lead to a dismantling of the cargo or to the use of an overloaded crane, both of which can place the cargo in jeopardy.

Port Operations

Another issue in ports is the way the port is managed, particularly its work rules, which are often dictated by strong unions. Some ports, such as the Port of Long Beach on the Pacific Coast of the United States, used to only operate eight hours a day[22] instead of the more efficient twenty-four hours a day, seven days a week of most Asian Pacific Rim ports. Today, the port stevedores will load and unload a ship at any time, but the terminals' truck gates are only open from 7:00 am until 5:00 pm, and only on weekdays, ostensibly to accommodate the work hours

Figure 3.3: Automated Guided Vehicle in the Port of Rotterdam, the Netherlands
Photo ©VanderWolff Images/Shutterstock. Used with permission.

of the businesses shipping goods to and from the port.[23] Nevertheless, since the majority of the goods transiting through the Ports of Long Beach and Los Angeles are destined for areas beyond Southern California, the rule is very constraining.

Work rules can also be complex and hamper the efficiency of ports to the point where they are less and less competitive: in the 1950s, unions dominating the ports of South America refused to unload containers, for example.[24] When there are attempts to modify these rules, strikes are common: some Japanese and European ports are plagued with recurring work stoppages. Finally, the issue of productivity is often linked to labor practices; while Japanese ports routinely handle 45 container movements per hour per crane, most United States ports are stagnating at 25 movements per hour.[25] As port productivity increases, the need for additional capital expenditures decreases; for many ports, physically constrained by the sea on one side and a large city on the other, increases in productivity are the only possible avenues for handling the growth in cargo volume.

Port operations' productivity depends on the availability of port vehicles to move the containers from the yard to the crane, and from the crane to the yard. Ports can do that with stevedores driving a truck pulling a trailer—called a chassis in port vernacular—or by using port automated guided vehicles (AGVs) (see Figure 3.3).

Warehousing and Storage Space

The amount of warehouse storage space in the port is also important for a shipper considering having merchandise transit through a port. In most instances, it is necessary for breakbulk merchandise to be placed in a storage area that is protected from the elements, specifically rain and sun. If these storage areas are not available or are overcrowded, then it's likely that cargo will be left exposed, leading to possible damage.

Ports are dusty by nature, because some of the cargo they handle is dry bulk, such as grain, coal, minerals, and fertilizers, which eventually cover everything with a fine coat of particles. Car finishes are sensitive to this exposure if they are left for much more than a few hours in the open (see Figure 3.4). It is therefore best to select ports in which the car-transit area is away from the breakbulk area, although that is not always possible to achieve.

Similarly, the shipper should consider the amount of space available in the port to store containers before and after their ocean voyage; the smaller the space, the greater the probability that the container will be moved multiple times, or that it will be stored in an inappropriate location. Even if the cargo can tolerate being left exposed to the elements, another concern is the possibility of flooding in the container—or cargo—staging area. It is not unusual, when bad weather strikes, to see a port's container yard flood, and the containers at the bottom of a stack partially immersed, even in a modern port. During the floods that devastated southern Brazil in 2008, hundreds of containers were affected by the water surge in the ports of Paranaguá, Itajaí and São Francisco do Sul.

For shippers involved with refrigerated cargo, storage issues are compounded with the need for reliable power supply, as well as proper reefer storage areas,

Figure 3.4: Cars Covered in Dust in the Port of Eilat, Israel
Photo ©Vicspacewalker/Shutterstock. Used with permission.

equipped with power outlets and personnel competent enough to monitor the temperature charts of the refrigerated containers.

Connection with Land-Based Transportation Services

Yet another issue is the port's connection to the remainder of the country's transportation infrastructure, such as rail and road access. In some cases, there is so much congestion in the access roads to port terminals that cargo can be delayed substantially. This is a major issue in just about every port in the world, but particularly in North and South America and in China.[26] Most ports are obviously located near the ocean, and the cities that developed around these ports are located between the port and the hinterlands, where the cargo eventually must go. Therefore, every piece of cargo that is shipped through the port must travel through the city, which creates a serious strain on road and railroad infrastructures to the port, and engenders serious traffic jams and the resentment of the local population. Ports are actively looking at overcoming these bottlenecks.[27]

In 2002, the Ports of Los Angeles and Long Beach inaugurated the Alameda Corridor, a north-south, twenty-mile rail link between the ports and the transcontinental rail yards on the eastern edge of the city of Los Angeles. The Corridor is a thirty-three-feet deep trench that cuts through the city's neighborhoods and is uninterrupted by road traffic.[28] A competitive advantage can be obtained by ports that have a direct connection with the railroad or road network of a country, such as the Port of Prince Rupert, in Canada, or the Port of Yangshan in China. Another port that was updated in order to allow shippers to bypass the congestion of Los Angeles-Long Beach is the Port of Lázaro Cárdenas, in Mexico, with a direct rail connection to the United States through the Kansas City Southern rail network.[29]

Figure 3.5: The Port of Prince Rupert, Canada
Photo ©BG Smith/Shutterstock. Used with permission.

Port Capacity

Yet another issue in ocean transportation is the strained port capacity, as many ports are operating at capacity or very near their capacity. Because ports tend to be physically located between an ocean and a city, there are limits in the ways that they can expand as traffic increases. Many ports add capacity by gaining on the sea with landfills or by purchasing city real estate that is then transformed into port terminals; however, both solutions are expensive. For example, the port of Santos in Brazil is located on a river that stretches between an island and the main land. The older port is located on the island, and it cannot expand because it is constrained by the city of Santos on one side and the river, which cannot be made narrower through landfills, on the other side. All the port expansions to date have been on the other side of the river, but, there again, expansion is limited by the river and suburbs that are now growing with the city.

In the United States, there is an increasing need for additional capacity in container terminals on the Pacific Coast, and this capacity cannot come from expanding the ports; it has to come from increases in productivity, which are difficult to achieve, or from the addition of new ports. The creation of the Port of Prince Rupert (see Figure 3.5 on the previous page), in a city of 14,000 inhabitants unconstrained by urban sprawl, with a strong rail connection to the hinterlands and a deep natural harbor, is a harbinger of what is to come.

The Panama Canal

On August 15, 1914 the *Ancon* became the first ship to officially pass through the Panama Canal. This unprecedented voyage ushered in a new era of shipping and international trade. The Panama Canal allowed ships to make the trans-Pacific voyage from Asia to the Americas quickly and safely. With a construction cost of three hundred seventy-five million dollars (and twenty-five thousand lives), the Canal immediately put Panama at the center of global trade.[30]

Today, more than one hundred years later, the canal is as important as ever, and as much as five percent of world trade's cargo transits through it. However, in the late 1990s, the canal was reaching its capacity, with some ships waiting several days to cross,[31] and the newly built giant containerships too large to fit through the canal's locks. The increasing number of giant ships meant capacity had become a major issue, and the Panama Canal Authority was faced with either improving the canal or watching it become outdated. After years of planning, the Canal Authority decided to create a new set of locks, parallel to the historical ones, to allow larger ships to transit.

The Panama Canal Authority spent $5.5 billion to double the canal's capacity. The first ship to use the new locks was the Cosco *Panama* on June 26, 2016. The new locks were a massive engineering project that leveraged techniques learned in building the original canal and implemented new methods to build the new canal faster and make it more efficient. One major obstacle the engineers struggled with was getting access to enough water to supply the locks, which requires two billion gallons per day. They solved this problem by implementing a system that reuses sixty percent of the water flushed out during each ship's passing. This means that although the new canal locks hold sixty-five percent more water than the old ones, they use seven percent less water.[32]

Figure 3.6: The Gigantic New Panama Canal Locks When Under Construction
Photo ©Abner Veltier/Shutterstock. Used with permission.

3.2.2   Canals and Waterways Infrastructure

Maritime transportation also depends on the existence and proper maintenance of canals and other maritime channels. Channel and lock sizes have a great influence on international trade. For example, ships sized to get through the Suez Canal are called Suez-Max ships. From an international logistics standpoint, several waterways are fundamentally and strategically important.

- The **Panama Canal** allows ships to avoid traveling around South America. However, the Canal is remarkably "slow," because it is running at its maximum capacity. Wait times to enter the Canal average two days, but can extend to five or six days for ships that are required to cross during daylight hours.[33] However, despite the emergence of land bridges in the United States, the Canal still retains its commercial importance even though its tolls are expensive. For a 5,000-TEU fully laden Panamax containership, for example, a passage costs U.S.$ 485,000.[34]

- The **Bosporus Strait** in Turkey (see Figure 3.7) joins the Black Sea to the Mediterranean Sea. It is the only water link between the Black Sea and the oceans. A large percentage of the merchandise trade between Russia and the rest of the world transits through the Strait, creating severe congestion and raising safety concerns for the city of Istanbul, which is built on both sides of the Strait. Several efforts have been made to convert some of that ship traffic to a network of pipelines, but none have yet been built. A rail tunnel, called Marmaray, has been built under the Bosporus to connect the European side and the Asian side of the country, and it opened in 2013, but only to passenger traffic. As of 2017, there were no plans to open the tunnel to freight traffic. A canal parallel to the Bosporus has been considered, but no specific plans have been drawn.[35]

- The **Suez Canal** cuts through the Sinai Desert (see Figure 3.8 on the facing page) and allows ships to avoid traveling around the entire continent of Africa when they are going from the Persian Gulf to Europe. When it was closed after the Six-Day War in 1967, oil companies started to build much larger oil tankers, to make the voyage around the Cape (South Africa) more

Figure 3.7: A Containership in the Bosporus Strait, Turkey
Photo ©Mehmet Cetin/Shutterstock. Used with permission.

cost-effective. Since its reopening in 1975, the Canal has recaptured some of the traffic it had lost, by widening and deepening the Canal. However, the Canal is still too shallow for many ships, and its tolls are prohibitive. The cost of a single trip for a fully laden VLCC—very large crude carrier—through the Canal can exceed U.S.$750,000.[36]

Figure 3.8: A Containership on the Suez Canal
Photo ©Don Victorio/Shutterstock. Used with permission.

- The **Saint Lawrence Seaway** links the Great Lakes to the St. Lawrence River and the Atlantic Ocean. Unfortunately, the Seaway is narrow, and few ships can pass through its locks. It is also plagued by ice, and the Welland Canal—which links Lake Erie to Lake Ontario and bypasses the Niagara Falls—closes from January to March. This has forced companies to find alternative means of transportation, and the traffic through the Seaway is down 45 percent from what it was twenty-five years ago.

- The **Strait of Malacca** links the Indian Ocean to the South China Sea. The Strait is a long and narrow stretch of water between the island of Sumatra, in Indonesia, and the Malaysian Peninsula. It leads to the Port of Singapore. In 2016, the Strait of Malacca was used by 122,000 ships annually, and it is an important link between Asian ports and European ports. However, the Strait is still infested with pirates who attack ships while they are in transit through it.

- The **Strait of Hormuz** links the Persian Gulf to the Indian Ocean. The Strait is vitally important to the oil trade, as 17 million barrels transits through it every day, representing approximately one third of all of the petroleum used in the world, and as much as 85 percent of the petroleum going to Asian ports.[37] At its narrowest, the Strait is less than 40 miles wide.

- The **Strait of Dover** is the narrow point in the English Channel that links the Atlantic Ocean to the North Sea. Every day, more than 400 ships cross the Strait, and it is dangerous due to the amount of traffic going across the sea lanes, as ferries link France to Great Britain. Although the number of collisions has significantly declined, there are still one or two every year.

- The **Corinth Canal** connects two parts of the Mediterranean Sea, the Ionian Sea and the Aegean Sea, by making a spectacular cut through the Isthmus of Corinth, between the Peloponnese peninsula and the remainder of Greece. Designed by the Ancient Greeks and started by the Roman Emperor Nero, the Corinth Canal was only completed at the end of the nineteenth century. It is mainly used by local traffic and tourist ships.

The absence of certain waterways is also detrimental to international trade and the efficient movement of goods. For example, there has been considerable talk about a canal through Nicaragua that would run "parallel" to the Panama Canal and be free of locks, an advantage that would speed up transit time considerably. In addition, the canal would be several hundred miles further North, which would also reduce transit times.[38] A railroad "dry canal" was also once proposed for the same region, with two options. One option suggested transporting ships—without unloading them—from one ocean to the other by carrying the ships on a railroad cradle. The other option was more conventional and simply proposed a double-decker container service on railroad cars.[39] However, all of these projects have been abandoned or placed on hold, and the Panama Canal is, for the foreseeable future, the only connection between the Atlantic and the Pacific.

A canal through the Isthmus of Kra in Thailand—the Malay Peninsula—which would bypass the Strait of Malacca and the Port of Singapore would speed up the transit time between Europe and the Far East as well. This project has been in the planning stages on and off in the past decades within the Thai government, and there is increased interest on the part of Malaysia, Indonesia, and particularly China.[40] No decision had been made by spring 2017.

The same lack of infrastructure is found in freshwater passages. After the War in the Balkans, there was a period during which there was no freshwater communication between the Black Sea and Northern Europe, as many bridges were demolished on the Danube River[41] and barges could not pass. There is still no large-capacity freshwater communication between the Mediterranean Sea and Northern Europe, as the expansion of an eighteenth-century canal between the Rhône River and the Rhine River is still being debated; however, the Europakanal, a canal between the Rhine and the Danube, was completed in 1992, and is heavily traveled.

3.2.3   Airport Infrastructure

Airports are also a fundamental part of the transportation infrastructure. There are fewer critical issues for international logisticians in using an international airport than there are in a port, but the issues can be just as constraining.

Runways

An airport's runways determine the type of aircraft that it can serve. Runway lengths are particularly relevant, as the lengths determine whether the airport can support direct flights to faraway places, as airplanes leaving for distant destinations must carry additional fuel and need longer runways. Many airports in the world cannot accommodate the large jumbo jets that serve international destinations because the runways were designed for the smaller aircraft of the 1950s and 1960s. As the cities around the airports grew, the airports became landlocked, unable to extend their runways. A plan by the Port Authority of New York and New Jersey to accommodate additional traffic at the JFK International airport included razing terminals and building on a land-fill in a portion of the Jamaica Bay.[42]

Several cities have had to build airports far from their city centers so that they could accommodate international flights. Whereas Charles de Gaulle Airport in Paris, France, and Heathrow Airport in London, UK, (both built in the 1970s) are about twenty-five kilometers (fifteen miles) from the cities they serve, the airports built in the 1990s are much further away: Denver International is thirty-seven kilometers (twenty-three miles) from the city and Malpensa in Milan, Italy, is forty-eight kilometers (thirty miles) away.

Island Airports

Japan is an island country that has very little land that is not mountainous. The few flat areas are mostly urbanized, with a high habitation density. It is therefore difficult to build large airports since they would encroach on urban areas. In 1971, when the Narita Airport in Tokyo could no longer accommodate the international traffic it generated, it tried to expand. However, the process involved purchasing privately owned land, and Japanese law does not include a provision for "eminent domain."[43] Over the protests of landowners, the airport nevertheless managed to acquire enough land to build a second runway, but it was much shorter than originally planned.[44]

When it was time to expand the Nagasaki Airport, the Japanese solved this dilemma in a creative way. Rather than build on existing land, the airport was built on an artificial island, a few hundred meters from the shore. Although the cost was enormous, it allowed the city to circumvent the opposition that a significant land purchase would have likely generated.

Soon after, the Kansai International Airport (near the city of Osaka) and then the Kobe airports were also built on artificial islands (see Figure 3.9). Hong Kong faced a similar situation; it is an island nation that is entirely built up, and its Kai Tak Airport was literally built in the middle of the city; as the airplanes landed, they flew a few hundred feet away from the high rises and the hills that surrounded the airport. It was an uncomfortable experience for many passengers.

In 1998, Kai Tak's replacement, Chek Lap Kok Airport, was built. Dubbed the most expensive construction project in the world at U.S.$20 billion—the Chunnel under the English Channel cost "only" U.S.$15 billion—Chek Lap Kok is an artificial island on the outskirts of the city, with its own dedicated tunnel, its own suspension bridge, its own commuter railroad, and the largest cargo facility in the world. It operates twenty-four hours a day, a boon for cargo shippers involved in the South-East Asian market, because Kai Tak closed at night.

The new airport has become the busiest international cargo airport in the world, handling more than 4.4 million tons in 2016.[45]

Figure 3.9: The Kobe Airport on an Artificial Island in Japan
Photo ©Cowardlion/Shutterstock. Used with permission.

A second concern is the number of runways, which determines the airport's capacity. Most airports have more than one runway. The busiest airports in the world—in number of passengers—are Hatfield Airport in Atlanta with four runways, Beijing International with three runways, Dubai International with two runways, Los Angeles with four runways, and Tokyo Haneda Airport with four runways. However, both Chicago O'Hare and Dallas-Fort Worth International have seven. An airport can be constrained by its lack of runways; for years, Narita Airport in Tokyo had only one runway to accommodate its traffic. The airport was stretched to capacity, and there was no way to build a second runway as several small farmers refused to sell their land to the airport. The airport could not build the runway on the farmers' land, and travelers and cargo shippers were inconvenienced as the number of flights in and out of Narita was limited, increasing the landing fees. It was not until 2009 that Narita was able to add a second runway, long enough to accommodate international flights.[46]

A single runway, or runways that intersect one another, also increase the probability of delays as the slightest accident or malfunction will immobilize the entire airport.

Hours of Operation

Another concern of importance is the airport's hours of operation. Because most airports are geographically close to large cities, their hours of operation are frequently limited by noise constraints, and therefore they can operate only during limited hours. Because cargo tends to fly at night, cargo airlines try to operate in airports that are located outside of large cities and can operate twenty-four hours a day, seven days a week. This is one of the main reasons FedEx chose the Memphis airport, which has become the largest cargo airport in North America—and the second largest cargo airport in the world—with 4.3 million tons of freight in 2015,[47] even though it is not located near a large metropolitan center. The Chet Lap Kok Airport in Hong Kong was also built away from the city, with the idea that it would operate 24 hours a day.

Warehousing Space

Another concern of importance for cargo shippers is whether the airport has appropriate warehouse space; cargo should be protected while it is in transit, and not left to the elements. This is particularly important as air cargo tends to be—sometimes erroneously—not as well packaged as cargo destined for ocean shipping. The problem is more severe for refrigerated warehouse space, which can be in very short supply.

3.2.4 Rail Infrastructure

Another element of a country's transportation infrastructure is its railroad network. In the eighteenth and early nineteenth centuries, railroads were the most important means of long-distance land transportation. In Europe, the United

railroad gauge
The distance between the rails on a railroad.

States, India, Africa, and Asia, a dense network of railroads was built, sometimes under the impetus of colonizing forces who wanted to be able to move troops quickly. The historical development of railroad for troop use led to decisions that are causing significant problems a century and a half later. For example, to prevent possible invaders from using their railroad infrastructures, Spain, Brazil, and Russia developed railroad gauges (the width between the rails) that were incompatible with the rest of Europe. While using incompatible gauges did prevent military troops from using the railroad network, this decision is still causing trouble for any rail transportation between these countries and their neighbors. For example, most trains stop at the French-Spanish border so that cargo can be shifted to railcars that are appropriate for the gauge used in the other country; others—including passenger trains—slow to a crawl while specially designed axles expand or contract to the appropriate width.[48] In Brazil, the cost of rolling stock is substantially higher as every car and locomotive must be adapted to Brazil's unusual gauge size, whether they are purchased new or used. In addition, trains have to travel slower because the cars and locomotives, designed for a traditional gauge, are wider than what the railroad can handle and therefore are less stable on curves.

Most countries updated their railroad infrastructure as their economies grew. However, in a few countries, the economy has rapidly and the infrastructure has not kept pace. Such is the case in China, where rail-transportation demand far outstrips supply. The Chinese government has spent billions of yuans to develop its rail infrastructure, including a large network of high-speed rail lines, as well as to expand its road network. The Chinese government is spending CN¥700 billion—U.S.\$ 122 billion—per *year* to develop its railroad infrastructure between 2012 and 2020.[49] Such an investment is considerable. India is similarly making significant investments in its infrastructure, spending more than U.S.\$ 12 billion per year,[50] though most of that money is going to roads and not railroads.

The United States has an atypical railroad infrastructure; all railroads are privately owned, and that limits the investment that can be spent on improving the country's overall rail infrastructure. In addition, the geography of the United States presents several large obstacles; in particular, the Rocky Mountains present challenges because of their size and climate; the amount of snow that falls in the Rockies routinely exceeds 500 centimeters (200 inches). Because these challenges make it expensive to build and maintain tracks, there are several miles of important East-West railroad connections in the United States that are still "single track," that is, traffic in both directions uses the same set of tracks. Since doubling the track often involves blasting rocks near the existing railroad, progress is time consuming and expensive. The trans-continental railway of the BNSF company was almost completely double-tracked by the end of 2016, except for a small 4-mile section.[51] Double-tracking increases a rail segment's capacity by 500 to 600 percent.

In many countries, though, the railroads gradually lost focus on shipping merchandise and shifted efforts to high-speed passenger transportation. Such is the case in Europe, where most merchandise is transported by means other than railroad, but where intercity rail passenger transportation is commonplace, convenient, fast, and competes with airlines over small distances. The best examples are the French (now European) Trains à Grande Vitesse (TGV), which connect Paris to London in two hours (dubbed the Eurostar) and Paris to Brussels in an hour and a half (the Thalys). There is only one TGV dedicated to merchandise transport, and it is used by the French Postal Service (La Poste) exclusively for mail transportation (see Figure 3.10). A similar switch from merchandise to high-speed passenger transport occurred in Japan; the Shinkansen train covers the 192 kilometers (120 miles) between Hiroshima and Kokura in less than forty-five minutes. These high-speed trains run on dedicated tracks that are separate from the remainder of the slower rail infrastructure.

Figure 3.10: The Only Merchandise High-Speed Train, Used by the French *La Poste*
Photo ©Mecdepaname. Used with permission.

Multi-Modal Emphasis

In the last two decades, three factors have contributed to increased merchandise traffic on railroads: road congestion has worsened, concerns about pollution and noise have increased, and the creation of the multi-modal container has eliminated the need to load and unload merchandise from traditional boxcars.

In the United States, railroads have invested heavily in the modernization of rolling stock; they have shifted from boxcars to piggy-back cars—allowing them to carry truck trailers—and container cars. At the same time, the railroads have improved their infrastructure by increasing the height clearances in tunnels and other areas, allowing trains to transport containers "double-stacked" (*i.e.*, twice as many containers as a single-stack train would). Figures 13.7 on page 457 and 13.8 on page 458 illustrate these concepts. American trains tend to be very long, with as many as 100 cars, allowing a crew of a few individuals to move more than 200 containers or truck trailers, making the trains particularly cost-effective both in labor and energy. In addition, because passenger rail transport is almost nonexistent in the United States—with the exception of the northeastern part of the country—cargo trains have priority on the rail network and tend to be relatively fast. The average speed of cargo trains in the United States is now approximately 24 miles per hour (38 km/h).[52]

Unfortunately, such improvements have not yet been made to the European rail infrastructure, which still consists mostly of aging boxcars. Moreover, the emphasis on passenger transportation gives priority to passenger trains, and relegates cargo trains to second-class status, making them slow and inefficient cargo movers. Multiple attempts to create high-speed cargo railroad links from ports in Northern Europe to ports in the Mediterranean have been made, but politics and administrative delays are unlikely to make this corridor a reality for some years.[53]

Land Bridges

A consequence of the increased efficiency of railroads in the United States has been the creation of land bridges. The concept of a land bridge is based on the idea that containerized ocean cargo can reach its destination faster and at a lower cost by crossing a landmass. Consider, for example, cargo from South-East Asia to Europe that has four alternative means of reaching its destination. It can be shipped through the Pacific Ocean, unloaded in a West-Coast port, cross the North American continent by rail, be reloaded on a cargo ship in an East-Coast port, and then continue on its way to Europe by crossing the Atlantic Ocean. The alternative is to take the Panama Canal; however, it is a fairly long voyage south in the Pacific to reach Balboa, a four-day wait to cross the Panama Canal, a one-day crossing of the canal, and finally a fairly long voyage north from Colón onto Europe in the Caribbean Sea and the North Atlantic. Another alternative for this South-East Asia-to-Europe cargo is to travel around India and through the Suez Canal, which is inconvenient and expensive. The latest consideration consists of shipping the goods *via* the Northwest Passage, through the Arctic Ocean, which is slowly becoming ice-free with climate change, bringing a host of issues, from pollution to government control over those waters.[54]

The alternative encouraged by U.S. railroads is to cross North America on a land bridge; the cargo is unloaded from a large containership on the West Coast of the United States or Canada, and shipped by double-stack container train to the East Coast. The journey is faster and cheaper than by ocean and the Panama Canal. In addition, it allows shipping lines to use post-Panamax ships on their trans-Pacific and trans-Atlantic routes, which is also more efficient. A conse-

single stack
The practice of placing containers on a railroad car on only one height. It contrasts with the practice of placing them two high.

double-stack
The practice of placing containers on a railroad car on top of one another.

land bridge
A term coined to describe the practice of shipping goods from Asia to Europe through the United States by using railroads.

quence of this trend is that cargo going from Taipei to Barcelona is going to transit through Chicago. Such variations from the traditional itinerary of Taipei-Panama-Barcelona are said to be "transparent" to the shipper, which means that the shipper is unaware of them. However, such a transparent voyage may expose the shipment to lower temperatures than those the shipper expected and a shipment may not be protected adequately enough for the extremes in temperature, from the tropical climate of Taipei to the sub-freezing temperatures of the Midwest of the United States.

3.2.5 Road Infrastructure

In addition to the infrastructure of ports, airports, and railroads, a great amount of shipping moves by road, especially on the last portion of the journey, from the port, airport, or rail terminal to its final destination. This part of the on-carriage is often called the "last mile."

A country's road infrastructure is evaluated somewhat differently than the rest of its transportation infrastructure. In almost no country is there a shortage of roads. One exception is Russia, which still does not have a trans-Siberian road connection between the Western and Eastern parts of the country. Russians refer to a large percentage of their country's territory as *bezdorozhye*, or "place without roads."[55] However, Russia is the exception, and for all other countries, road infrastructure issues are the quality and maintenance of the network, its congestion, as well as the existence of high-speed links between major metropolitan areas. The concern therefore is not one of existence, but one of usability and density.

Quality

A country's road infrastructure is generally described in documents such as the U.S. Department of Commerce's Country Commercial Guides[56] or the CIA's World Factbook.[57] Such documents list the total miles of road, and of the percentage of these roads that are paved. For example, Argentina is listed as having 231,374 kilometers (143,800 miles) of roads, of which 69,412 kilometers (43,140 miles)—30 percent—are paved.[58] In the United States, paved roads only represent 65 percent of the road infrastructure,[59] but they represent 100 percent of the network in France, Switzerland, and Germany.[60]

However, the paved percentages are somewhat misleading, as most traffic utilizes paved roads, and unpaved roads serve only remote rural areas. In addition, the condition of a paved road makes a substantial difference in its usefulness; an overcrowded, two-lane highway riddled with potholes is not conducive to the safe transportation of cargo. Such is the case with the roads in the countries of Belarus, Albania, Romania, Lithuania, and Latvia. The government of Poland estimated once that 80 percent of its roads were in unsatisfactory or bad condition, and that only 63 percent of its 800 kilometers of national highways were in good condition.[61] India[62] and China also suffer from a lack of quality road infrastructure, although both countries are spending considerable amounts of money to improve it.[63] Unfortunately, there is no statistical source that indicates the condition of the roads in a country, and because there are substantial variations from one region of a country to another, road quality is even more difficult to evaluate. The United States' road infrastructure received a grade of "D+" by the American Society of Civil Engineers.[64] Mostly, the U.S. infrastructure is not sufficiently well maintained for the traffic that it sustains, and delays cost U.S. businesses considerable amounts, not withstanding the dangers of poorly maintained roads and bridges.[65]

Density

Another concern in road networks that have been recently built (primarily the ones in the Western Hemisphere, Australia, and Africa) is that there is little density. In many cases, there is a road that links two major cities—in the United States, Denver to Kansas City, and in Australia, Sydney to Melbourne—but in others, there is no road linking major cities, necessitating a costly detour through a less direct route: in the United States, for example, there is no direct road link between Denver and Dallas, and in Australia, there is no link between Sydney and Adelaide.[66] This lack of density is not found in Western Europe, where there are direct roads between all major cities.

This lack of density also affects transportation in other ways. Since there is no redundancy, should the primary road be affected by an accident, there is frequently no convenient alternative means for trucks to reach their destination. In some cases, there may not even be secondary-road alternatives; for example, the only bridge that crosses the Congo River for most of its 2,000-mile length is in Matadi, in the Democratic Republic of Congo. In Europe, there is no bridge on the Danube River for the entire length of the Ukraine-Romania border, there are two bridges for the portion of the Danube that forms the Romania-Bulgaria border, and only two bridges for the entire length of the river that meanders through Romania.[67]

Congestion

Congestion of the road infrastructure is also endemic to certain cities: there are too many cars, trucks, and other vehicles for the available roads, and deliveries are difficult to make (see Figure 3.11 on the facing page). In Calcutta, India, the traffic is so congested that the average speed in the city is eight km/h (five mph), and many people travel by rickshaw or by public transportation rather than by car. In New Delhi, the government has created a category of vehicles, called VVIP—Very Very Important Persons—that are allowed to zip through traffic with blaring sirens and flashing lights. The traffic in Beijing is notorious for being at a standstill for a large percentage of the day.[68] To resolve congestion, many developing countries' cities have instituted a system of alternating days for traffic; vehicles with odd-numbered license plates are only allowed to travel on odd-numbered days and vehicles with even-numbered license plates can only travel on even-numbered days. Such is the case in Lagos, Nigeria, for example.

Figure 3.11: Traffic Congestion on Access Road to the Port in Karachi, Pakistan
Photo ©Asianet-Pakistan/Shuterstock. Used with permission.

The congestion is not resolved, however, as resourceful Nigerians obtain two license plates for every vehicle from corrupt civil authorities, and change the plates every morning. Beijing, Jakarta, Bogotá, and likely other cities have implemented the same system to mixed results.[69]

Although congestion is a problem that is extreme in developing countries, it is also present in large metropolitan areas in Europe, Japan, and the United States. As the number of automobiles increases, congestion will worsen further and make deliveries to customers more problematic and inefficient. Many delivery firms are now using motorcycles and mopeds, which are more maneuverable in large cities. London enacted an effective tax system to prevent vehicles from entering the heart of the city; vehicles' license plates are monitored and recorded through a closed-circuit television system and commuters are charged £ 11.50 for each day they travel into the city. Residents receive a 90 percent discount on this daily rate. Fines for non-compliance are substantial. After the tax was enacted in February 2003, the program was judged so successful in downtown London (traffic decreased approximately 15 percent)[70] that it was expanded to a larger portion of the city in February 2007. Other cities are considering adopting a similar system, including Stockholm, Manchester, Singapore, Milan, San Francisco and New York.

Yet another issue in cities is the confusion generated by a lack of signage and a different addressing system. While most North American cities are built on a grid of east-west and north-south streets, with a fairly logical numbering sequence of streets and buildings, European cities are plagued with a maze of different streets that change names at each—or so it seems—intersection. Mexico City has an extraordinarily confusing system of streets; there are nearly 800 streets named after Benito Juárez, 760 named for Miguel Hidalgo, and 300 streets renamed every year. To make things more confusing, 80,000 city blocks have no signage at all.[71] Japan has the tradition of numbering buildings on a street in the order in which they were built, rather than in a sequential order based on location. Most of Bombay's addresses are not based on street names, but defined by a succession of smaller and smaller areas: a person's address will include the name of the house, the name of the street, the name of the block, the name of the city, and the city code. In addition, there will be an east or a west, depending on which side of the railroad track the block is located, with parallel structures on either side. Such systems make it challenging to deliver goods to a new customer. The worst situation from this perspective is on the island of Saipan in the Northern Mariana Islands, with a population of 70,000, which has no address system at all.[72]

To decrease the congestion in cities, countries have built a network of high-speed links that avoid smaller cities while connecting the larger ones. These limited access highways speed up the transportation of goods between cities. Nevertheless, these highways are subject to several rules and regulations, some of which limit the size of the trucks that can travel on them and the speed at which they can travel. Because these rules vary from country to country, it can be a challenge to arrange international truck transportation of merchandise. In addition, in many countries, access to high-speed highways is limited to vehicles that pay a toll, making such roads an expensive alternative. In Germany, for example, the high-speed highway system charges approximately € 0.22 per kilometer (U.S. $ 0.36 per mile) for semi-trucks, but this charge can be reduced if the vehicle is equipped with modern pollution-control devices.[73]

Civil Engineering Structures (Ouvrages d'Art)

ouvrage d'art
A French term describing an engineering structure that eliminates a landscape constraint. A bridge, a tunnel, or a canal lock.

If a country is mountainous, high-speed thoroughfares are built with numerous bridges and tunnels designed to eliminate the constraints of the landscape. A perfect example of such a highway is the Italian Autostrade, which runs along the Appennine Chain and seems to be an unending succession of tunnels and bridges (see Figure 3.12 on the next page). Such engineering structures are called collectively (in French) *ouvrages d'art*—art structures—and it is an apt moniker; unfortunately, there is no English equivalent, so the French term will be used.

The dependence of international trade on such ouvrages d'art cannot be underestimated: most natural borders are either water (oceans or lakes) or mountains at the watershed separation. To cross these natural borders, bridges or tunnels have to be built. The Chunnel—the tunnel built under the English Chan-

Figure 3.12: Succession of Bridges and Tunnels on the Italian Autostrade
Photo ©Tsepova Ekaterina/Shutterstock. Used with permission.

nel, between France and Great Britain—is a case in point. Until the Chunnel's opening in 1994, shipping goods from the continent to Great Britain was delayed by a lengthy ferry voyage, which sometimes could be delayed or canceled due to bad weather. The Chunnel has substantially shortened shipping times between the two countries, although it is quite expensive; for private automobiles, the cost is £ 79, and it can reach £ 500 for semi-trucks.[74]

Another international route that has been radically changed by ouvrages d'art is the trade between Western Europe and the Middle East, with the opening of two suspension bridges in Istanbul, one in 1973 (Bogaziçi Bridge), the other in 1988 (Fatih Sultan Mehmet Bridge). These are the only two bridges that allow road transportation between Europe and Asia, save for an itinerary north of the Black Sea, through Bulgaria, Romania, the Ukraine and Russia. To date (2017), there is no cargo rail link from Southern Europe to Asia—although a passenger rail tunnel opened at the end of 2013.

The so-called Øresund Fixed Link between Copenhagen, Denmark, and Malmö, Sweden, is another example of an ouvrage d'art that has significantly altered the transportation landscape of an international border: the Øresund Fixed Link is a succession of three bridges and a tunnel, with a switchover on an artificial island in the middle of Flinte Channel. It is the first terrestrial communication between Denmark and Sweden, and it replaces a forty-five minute ferry ride with an eight-minute drive. More importantly, it is the first land link between Western Europe and the Scandinavian countries.

The Millau Bridge in southern France opened in 2004 and is another highway bridge that significantly reduces transportation times. It links two high plateaus that are separated by a deep river gorge, for which the only crossing was in the middle of the small town of Millau. Before the construction of the bridge, vehicles had to travel down approximately 300 meters (1,000 feet) through a series of hairpin turns to the city, cross the river, and then climb up the same distance to the other plateau. The town was infamous for its traffic jam, and it was common to spend two hours going from one plateau to the other. With the bridge, the same journey takes less than one minute. The bridge is 345 meters above the river (1,150 feet), about twenty meters higher than the Eiffel Tower, and was built in a little over three years.[75]

Some bridges are less architecturally noticeable but no less important to the economies of the countries they link. For example, the United States and Canada, the two largest trade partners in the world, are only connected by one bridge and a tunnel between Detroit, Michigan and Windsor, Ontario, one bridge in Port Huron, Michigan, and two bridges near Buffalo, New York, for a significant portion of their common border. At least one of those bridges, the Ambassador Bridge between Detroit and Windsor, owned by a private company, has not been updated in 50 years; it is only a four-lane bridge and carries 3.3 million trucks every year. Similarly, the Peace Bridge between Buffalo and Fort Erie, Ontario, is used at its maximum capacity and has not been expanded since 1927. A new bridge between Detroit and Windsor was in the planning stage in 2017, called the Gordie Howe Bridge, entirely financed by the Canadian government, but the Detroit-based owner of the Ambassador Bridge ran a political campaign to prevent its construction. It was defeated.[76] The owner is currently fighting the bridge's construction through legal means, having purchased some of the land on the U.S. side that is needed in order to complete the bridge.[77]

3.2.6   Warehousing Infrastructure

Transportation depends on an infrastructure that allows the movement of goods. However, it is equally important to recognize that cargo is often stationary while it waits for the next transportation alternative to be available. Therefore, a shipper must obtain information about the warehousing infrastructure of the locations where a shipment will be in layover.

The issues regarding warehousing infrastructure concern the protection of the goods while they are waiting during transit. Will they be protected from rain? From the sun? From possible floods? From (unusual) cold? A savvy international logistics manager should attempt to determine the conditions under which the goods will be kept, and will then determine whether the goods are correctly packaged, or whether they need to be shipped through a different itinerary. With the disappearance of the The Cigna Insurance Company's *Ports of the World* booklet, there has not been a comprehensive source of the warehouse space available in each port; the World Port Source website (see Table 3.3 on page 71) has limited information on the warehousing space available in a port. It is therefore necessary to investigate each port's website for information prior to confirming an itinerary.

In many cases, shippers use public warehouses for storage purposes, to deliver goods to their customers without having to resort to an international shipment. This enables the company to provide better customer service by delivering goods with a shorter lead time.

Unfortunately, a country's warehousing infrastructure is difficult to evaluate, as there are no general sources of information on the availability and quality of public warehouses. Therefore, in cases where a company is considering using a public warehouse to serve its customers, it is best to plan a visit to the location considered, as the standards used in public warehousing management may be quite different than the ones expected.

3.3   Communication Infrastructure

In addition to the transportation infrastructure, the communication infrastructure is also of substantial importance to international logisticians. The ability to communicate with customers and suppliers, by mail, by phone, or through other electronic media, is critical to the smooth operation of an international transaction. Unfortunately, there are different expectations of service and performance in communication infrastructure from country to country.

3.3.1   Mail Services

The ability of the postal services to deliver mail on time and reliably should be a given in most developed countries. However, there is ample anecdotal evidence that this is not the case everywhere. On many occasions, there are unacceptable delays and errors: while the European Union countries strive to deliver letters sent to a national address on the day after it is mailed—a so-called D+1 policy— and on the second day if it is international mail within the European community, this is a difficult standard to achieve. Italy, especially before its national postal service was privatized, was notoriously unreliable. France has periodic strikes of its mail service and of its national railway service, both of which can substantially delay mail delivery. In South Africa, the mail service has become so unreliable that businesses and individuals no longer trust it enough to send payments, forcing them to make payments in person or through banks.

Another issue is mail safety: will a letter or package make it to its destination, or will it be lost, damaged, or stolen in transit? Because postal services tend to be large employers, it is difficult to screen all employees effectively. There have been countless documented instances of postal employees stealing the contents of parcels and removing the contents of letters—especially cash and checks—before they reach their destination. Developing countries have an even greater postal-theft problem, as public employees' wages tend to be modest. In some parts of the world, mail service is so unreliable that emigrants sending part of their paychecks to their relatives use parallel services, such as the traditional *hawala* in the Middle East and North Africa, *fei-ch'ien* in China, *padala* in the Philippines, *hui kuan* in Hong Kong, and *hundi* in India,[78] as well as similar parallel systems in Brazil.[79]

Many firms intent on ensuring that postal communications are safely delivered have switched, especially for international documents' exchanges, to private services such as DHL or FedEx. While the cost of private services is much higher than the costs of traditional postal services, these small-packet companies have gained a significant share of the document-delivery market, thanks to their reputation for greater reliability. In particular, the customers' ability to track packages and documents online has increased this perception. This tracking ability is now available for many postal services' products, but it is not available worldwide.

Another phenomenon is the exploitation (arbitrage) of the differences in prices and mail categories for international mail from one country to another. A direct marketer sending a substantial number of identical mail pieces internationally determines in which country the mailing is going to cost the least amount; the marketer then bulk ships the mailing materials to a company operating a re-mailing service in that country. The re-mailer then places the individual items in the mail and lowers the overall mailing costs to the marketer. Commercial materials emanating from France have come to the author from Denmark, Great Britain, and the Netherlands; the lowest cost country was probably determined by the weight of the materials being sent, which placed them in different price categories in different countries.

3.3.2   Telecommunications Services

Telecommunication services face slightly different issues; not only has the demand for voice telecommunication increased about 10 percent a year, but the demand for data telecommunication has essentially doubled every year for the past ten years, and it shows no sign of slowing down. Some countries have built a sufficiently large domestic infrastructure to carry this increased load, often by using their already existing other-goods infrastructure. For example, many gas and oil pipelines have been given the added responsibility of transmitting data through a fiber-optic line laid in their midst. Many countries, though, have not kept up with such growth, and telecommunications in those countries are slow and unreliable.

Reliability is the primary concern in several countries where the economy has grown quickly; the domestic communication infrastructure did not follow. Phone service is notoriously unreliable, with phone conversations disconnected, phone calls regularly connected to wrong numbers, and dial tones all but absent. Table 3.4 on the next page shows the penetration rate of land-line phones for countries in which the population exceeds one million people; it is calculated by dividing the total number of land-line phones by the population.[80] It does not refer to the percentage of the population with access to a land-line phone, because many of these phones are shared by a household.

Fortunately, in some of these countries, a phenomenon known as leap frogging has taken place. Because the "old" land-based telephone infrastructure is not

Landlines *per capita* (2016)

Rank	Country		Rank	Country	
1	Hong Kong	61.8%	11	Canada	46.9%
2	Taiwan	59.8%	12	Portugal	42.4%
3	Germany	58.2%	13	The Netherlands	41.9%
4	France	58.1%	14	New Zealand	41.3%
5	Korea, South	57.9%	15	Belgium	41.2%
6	Switzerland	53.4%	16	Ireland	40.8%
7	United Kingdom	51.6%	17	Serbia	40.0%
8	Japan	50.2%	18	Australia	40.0%
9	Greece	48.5%	19	United States	39.9%
10	Belarus	47.0%	20	Spain	39.3%

Table 3.4: Percentage of Population with a Landline, by Country
CIA's World Factbook.

working properly, people have quickly switched to cellular phones and bypassed the land-line-based system. This switch to cellular is facilitated by the fact that many countries quickly adopted a single operating standard (Global System for Mobile Communications, or GSM), which enables easy portability and increased convenience. As of 2016, there were more than 120 countries in which the penetration rate for cellular phones was greater than 100 percent. Table 3.5 on the following page highlights the penetration rates for cellular telephones in countries where the population exceeds one million people.[81] Since the percentage is calculated as the number of cellular phones divided by the population size, the rate corresponds, roughly, to the number of cell phones that an average individual owns. Only one country (Hong Kong) is listed in both Table 3.4 and Table 3.5 in the top twenty.

In China, there are nearly five times the number of cellular phones (1.3 billion) than there are land-based phones (249.4 million), and the number of cellular phones is growing while the number of traditional landline phones is declining. Countries such as the United States, which have a strong land-based infrastructure, have been much slower at switching to cellular phone usage. As of 2016, the United States was barely in the top 100 countries in the world when ranked by the percentage of the population that owned a cellular telephone. Although this ranking was due to the quality of the land-based infrastructure (and people have much less of an incentive to switch), it is also due to the fact that there are four different operating technologies competing for cellular phone customers, and therefore that there are four times as many towers to be built (and paid for), making cellular phone service particularly expensive.

Internationally, telecommunications depends on a network of underwater cables that run across the Atlantic, the Pacific, the Mediterranean Sea, or other large bodies of water. As telecommunication traffic has increased, the capacity of these

Cellular Telephones *per capita* (2016)

Rank	Country		Rank	Country	
1	United Arab Emirates	283.4%	14	Libya	154.4%
2	Kuwait	268.3%	15	Lithuania	154.2%
3	Hong Kong	242.8%	16	Botswana	153.9%
4	Gabon	207.1%	17	Kazakhstan	152.5%
5	Saudi Arabia	187.1%	18	Italy	151.9%
6	Oman	184.8%	19	Argentina	151.3%
7	Panama	167.3%	20	Singapore	150.5%
8	Estonia	166.9%			
9	Bahrain	166.8%	44	Taiwan	129.6%
10	Uruguay	164.1%	51	Germany	123.3%
11	Trinidad and Tobago	163.9%	53	Japan	120.5%
12	Russia	155.2%	96	United States	98.0%
13	Poland	155.2%	98	France	97.1%

Table 3.5: Percentage of the Population with a Cellular Telephone, by Country
CIA's World Factbook.

cables has also increased dramatically. However, there are still very few cables (only seven cross the Northern Atlantic), and their vulnerability is extraordinary. Although the cables are buried on the portion of their route that is located in shallow water, they are for the most part simply laid on the floor of the oceans, and at the risk of being snagged by fishermen's nets and boat anchors.[82] When these cables cross land, they are just as vulnerable and at the mercy of a careless backhoe operator or other accident. Whenever a cable is snagged or damaged, traffic on that cable ceases until it is repaired. In an outstanding article in *Wired* magazine, Neal Stephenson followed the construction of the FLAG—Fiber-optic Link Around the Globe—and reported on the vulnerability of this network: for example, five of the major worldwide cables are routed through a single building in Alexandria, Egypt.[83]

Satellite telecommunications are no less dependent on a limited number of alternatives and therefore are just as vulnerable; because satellites are increasingly used for communications such as television programs, their capacity is entirely used, and the failure of a single satellite can wreak havoc on telecommunications. Other telecommunication infrastructures are vulnerable; the internet, although touted as robust, depends on root-servers that keep the list of internet addresses.

3.3.3   Internet Access

As the world economy relies more on the internet for commerce and communication, it is interesting to note that only 11.4 percent of the world's population has

Internet Access *per capita* (2016)

Rank	Country		Rank	Country	
1	Denmark	96.5%	11	Sweden	88.1%
2	The Netherlands	95.2%	12	Australia	87.9%
3	Bahrain	94.3%	13	United Arab Emirates	87.7%
4	Norway	93.1%	14	Germany	87.1%
5	Qatar	93.0%	15	Switzerland	86.8%
6	Finland	92.8%	16	Japan	86.3%
7	Canada	91.6%	17	United States	85.4%
8	New Zealand	89.4%	18	France	85.0%
9	United Kingdom	88.9%	19	Kuwait	84.7%
10	Korea, South	88.2%	20	Belgium	83.3%

Table 3.6: Percentage of Population with Internet Access, by Country
CIA's World Factbook.

broadband internet access, with a digital subscriber line, cable modem, or other high-speed technology.[84] Table 3.6 lists the top 20 countries in their population's access to the internet.[85]

3.4 Utilities Infrastructure

Another area of concern for a manager involved in international logistics is the utilities infrastructure. While it is generally taken for granted that all utilities—electricity, water, sewage, gas—are available in most countries, experience shows that there is often a shortage of one or more of these commodities in many countries—including developed countries. While utilities are not directly an issue in transportation, they can become critically important when a company is considering operating a warehouse or establishing a corporate office.

3.4.1 Electricity

The most common problem with utilities is the availability and reliability of electrical power. It is common to have blackouts for part of the day or frequent interruptions in countries where economic growth outpaces growth in electricity production. This situation is endemic in sub-Sahara Africa, where there are scheduled blackouts because electricity production is much lower than the demand for it; households and businesses therefore plan their days around the availability of electricity. India and China are also affected by recurring blackouts, and so is Saudi Arabia. China has invested considerable amounts in electrical generation infrastructure, including the Three River Gorge Dam, which came on-line in 2008, and will eventually produce more than 10 percent of the coun-

Figure 3.13: The 144-MW Wind Farm of Noordoostpolder, in the Netherlands
Photo ©Aerovista Luchtfotografie/Shutterstock. Used with permission.

try's electricity. However, there are still some disruptions in multiple areas of the country.

Electricity service is disrupted in many countries, as the problems tend to be regional as well as national. On the other hand, some countries have abundant electrical resources: Brazil and Paraguay share the Itaipu Dam which provides 82 percent of Paraguay's electrical needs and 26 percent of Brazil's. Nevertheless, for those areas of Brazil that are geographically far from Itaipu, there are still power shortages and temporary blackouts. The transition from fossil-fuel plants to renewable-energy plants, such as the wind farms of Northern Europe (see Figure 3.13) also present challenges as the high-voltage wire network has to be modified to accommodate a less consistent production flow.

In addition to production problems, the electric utilities are sometimes the victims of theft; households and businesses bypass their meters or tap directly in the grid without the "inconvenience" of a meter, preventing utilities from collecting enough income to be able to invest in additional capacity. A World Bank loan to India to build additional power plants was made conditional on the utility getting paid for a greater percentage of its production.[86] In Russia, an endemic problem is the theft of electrical wires for scrap, an activity that kills more than 500 thieves each year, and forces the Russian government to replace miles of high-tension wires, without mention of the disruptions to businesses and individuals.

3.4.2 Water and Sewer

Water supply is also a concern in many countries, leading to interruptions, rationing, and recurring water shortages. It is typical for cities to ration water in the middle of a drought period, on some occasions reducing the availability of water to a few hours a day or a few days a week. As city populations increase, the infrastructure delivering water to the cities is often overtaxed, which can lead to potentially catastrophic problems, especially in cities with aging infrastructures. For example, New York City gets most of its water from reservoirs 125 miles away, and the water is delivered through two tunnels that were built in 1917 and 1937. Neither of these tunnels has ever been shut down for repairs, as the city would not be able to function without the water they deliver. A new water tunnel is currently under construction and is scheduled to be fully operational in 2021.[87] Many cities have leaky pipes and lose a portion of their water supply to those leaks; the city of Manila, in the Philippines, estimates it loses half of its water production through leaks and illegal water siphoning by households and businesses.

Water quality is also a concern: in many cities, the water delivery infrastructure is not well protected, leaving a strong possibility of bacterial contamination, and forcing users to boil the water before use. This procedure is a common recommendation given to international travelers. The World Bank estimates that no more than 85 percent of the rural world population and 96.5 percent of urban dwellers have "reasonable access" to clean water, defined as access within one kilometer (0.62 miles) of the house.[88] For many people, that is a considerable distance.

The infrastructure designed to remove used water is also critical. Many countries have inadequate or overburdened sewer treatment facilities, resulting in the pollution of water tables and adjacent bodies of water, or problems with sewer backups during heavy rains, even in developed countries.[89] While less critical than water availability to the proper operation of a warehouse or distribution center, sewer service is still important as it can be a nuisance to have employees deal with stench or frequent cleanups. The World Bank estimates that only a little over two thirds (67.5 percent) of the world population has access to adequate sanitation.[90]

Similar observations can be made about refuse removal, a service generally provided by the municipalities, but which can be unreliable; strikes of municipal workers can take several days, during which no pickup is conducted, resulting in a problem in the operation of any type of business.

3.4.3 Energy Pipelines

The infrastructure of access to energy is also important. As most of the easily accessible oil and gas fields are near the end of their life expectancies, energy resources now come from remote areas where it is difficult to operate and from where it is difficult to ship. Building energy pipelines from those areas is a challenge, and the obstacles include weather, natural barriers, political issues, environmental challenges, and bickering between the oil companies and the governments of the countries in which they are building.

Nevertheless, the pipeline infrastructure is growing and allows an ever-greater percentage of the energy needs of the world to no longer be transported by ships, trucks, and railroads.

3.5   Services Infrastructure

In addition to a transportation, communication, and utilities infrastructure, businesses need a commercial support services infrastructure to operate efficiently.

3.5.1   Banking Infrastructure

The banking infrastructure allows businesses to transfer funds, obtain foreign currency, move documents both domestically and internationally, and process consumer payments efficiently. This requires a network of bank branches and well-trained employees in multiple countries. In most parts of the world, the banking infrastructure is dominated by domestic banks, with no easy access to international banks. The only exceptions are in large metropolitan areas, such as New York, Tokyo, or Paris, and in large financial centers, such as Hong Kong, London, or Singapore, where most multinational banks have offices. The absence of a knowledgeable banking infrastructure can be a serious impediment to a firm operating in an area other than a major city.

Since the beginning of the twenty-first century, this traditional banking model has changed, mostly under the impetus of one bank, HSBC, that has opened branches in many smaller business centers, beyond the capital cities of most countries. The traditional model of international banks was to be present in large cities only, and develop a network of correspondent banks to serve their international customers in smaller cities. Several other banks have now followed HSBC's lead, and it is not unusual to find multiple international banks in a medium-sized city. This is an excellent development for international logisticians, as they need this banking infrastructure to process foreign-currency payments and handle the documents linked to an international transaction.

Non-banks have also helped develop a system that can assist companies engaged in international business; Paypal, for example, allows companies to process customer payments and move funds internationally at affordable rates, much lower than those of a traditional bank.

3.5.2   Logistics Support Infrastructure

In addition to banking services, international logisticians need to have easy access to professionals in several fields: freight forwarders, couriers, carriers, delivery services, packing services, order fulfillment centers, and other third-party logistics service providers, are critical to the smooth operations of an international logistics department. The success of a logistics cluster is due primarily to the existence of many different services that can support a company involved in international trade, so that the company can find those services quickly and at competitive prices.

Yossi Sheffi makes that point abundantly clear; the reason that many companies settled in the PLAZA—*Plataforma Logística de Zaragoza*—logistical cluster in Spain is because there was a conscious effort on the part of its owner, the Aragon Region government, to provide all sorts of logistical support services in one area. The park now covers 1,200 hectares (3,000 acres), and is expanding.[91] It has attracted all sorts of logistics activities, including the creation of the Zaragoza Logistics Center, a joint venture of the Massachusetts Institute of Technology and the University of Zaragoza.

3.6   Legal and Regulatory Infrastructure

3.6.1   Court Infrastructure

A country's court infrastructure allows businesses to settle disputes quickly and fairly. Court infrastructure must include not only an efficient court system, but also a network of mediators and arbitrators, many competent lawyers, and the existence of clear jurisprudence. In many countries, if not most, the court infrastructure is slow, cumbersome, and inefficient.

The World Bank publishes a *Doing Business* database, that lists how many days it takes to resolve a contract dispute in the court system of all countries in the world, as well as the costs of resolving that dispute and the number of procedural steps that must be taken. The range is considerable. Whereas the average contract dispute is resolved in 164 days in the courts of Singapore, it takes an average of 553 days in OECD countries, and as many as 1,420 days in India and 1,580 days in Greece. The costs also vary dramatically. The average cost of resolving a contractual dispute in the lowest-cost country, Iceland, is 9 percent of the disputed amount. For OECD countries, the average is 21.3 percent. For the highest-cost countries, such as Indonesia, the costs can exceed the amount of the dispute.[92]

When the court system does not operate efficiently, businesses turn to mediators and arbitrators to resolve disputes. It is much more difficult to find aggregate information on the effectiveness of arbitration. However, most arbitrators and mediators operate in multiple countries, unaffected by the local situation, and are generally more efficient and less expensive than litigation.

3.6.2   Intellectual-Property Infrastructure

The intellectual-property infrastructure allows businesses to protect intellectual property, such as copyrights, patents, and trademarks, with law enforcement services intent on enforcing intellectual property laws. In most developed countries, there is an effective way to handle intellectual property, but in some newly industrialized countries, that is not the case. Most notorious are China, Nigeria, and

India, where intellectual property is frequently not respected, and where law enforcement officials and the court system do not enforce the rights of intellectual-property owners.[93]

In many countries, there have been considerable efforts to protect international intellectual-property rights, but intellectual-property infringement and theft are still major issues. Of course, there is a priority aspect to this problem; countries in which there is widespread poverty or substantial economic inequalities, or crime, are not going to allocate resources to a problem that is perceived as not urgent. However, there is also a cultural aspect that hinders the defense of intellectual-property rights; it is politically difficult to favor a large foreign corporation over a local small-business owner who is struggling to survive and whose customers want an affordable alternative to the foreign company's product.

It is likely that intellectual-property issues will eventually be resolved. Intellectual-property rights are always part of the negotiations when heads of state meet, and this issue has very high visibility. The current situation in developing countries is actually fairly similar to the situation in which high-income countries were in the 1980s and 1990s, with widespread copying of software, music, and movies. As intellectual-property companies became aggressive defending these rights, the problem slowly abated.

3.6.3   Standards Infrastructure

The standards infrastructure allows businesses to determine the requirements that their products and operations must meet to be successful in a particular market. These requirements include safety, design, and performance standards. For a company involved in multiple countries, the preference is always for a unified national standard that is clear and widely available. It is much more difficult to sell a product when a country has multiple regional standards, or when the standards are not delineated clearly.

The United States often stands at odds with the remainder of the world when it comes to standards. Not only is the country still operating on a non-metric system, but it often has multiple standards that are state specific. This characteristic makes the U.S. market one of the more challenging markets for a company. However, it also makes it difficult for U.S. exporters, as they must adapt to an unfamiliar environment.

Review and Discussion Questions

1. What are the main elements of the maritime transportation infrastructure? How does the quality and dependability of the maritime transportation infrastructure affect an international shipment?

2. What are the main elements of the air transportation infrastructure? How does the quality and dependability of the air transportation infrastructure affect an international shipment?

3. What are the main elements of the land transportation and warehousing infrastructure? How does the quality and dependability of these infrastructures affect an international shipment?

4. What are the main elements of the communication and utilities infrastructure? How does the quality and dependability of these infrastructures affect an international shipment?

Notes

[1] American Heritage Dictionary, Fifth Edition, https://ahdictionary.com/word/search.html?q=infrastructure, retrieved March 31, 2017.

[2] Oxford English Dictionary, online edition, http://www.oed.com/view/Entry/95624?redirectedFrom=infrastructure#eid, retrieved March 31, 2017.

[3] Merriam-Webster Dictionary, https://www.merriam-webster.com/dictionary/infrastructure, retrieved March 31, 2017.

[4] "Cellular Fleet at 1st January 2017," Alphaliner, http://www.alphaliner.com/liner2/research_files/liner_studies/nofleet/Alphaliner-FleetMthly-2017-01.pdf, retrieved March 31, 2017.

[5] "Cellular Fleet Forecast," Alphaliner, http://www.alphaliner.com/liner2/research_files/liner_studies/nofleet/Alphaliner-FleetForecast-2017-01.pdf, retrieved March 31, 2017.

[6] *Ibid.*

[7] Tirschwell, Peter, "Berth Productivity: the Trends, Outlook and Market Forecasts Impacting Ship Turnaround Times," *JOC, Journal of Commerce*, July 2014, http://www.joc.com/whitepaper/berth-productivity-trends-outlook-and-market-forces-impacting-ship-turnaround-times-0, retrieved April 4, 2017.

[8] Whitman, Reg, "The Port of Prince Rupert—North America's Jewel of the Northwest," *Logistics Quarterly*, 14:5, 2008, pp. 48-49.

[9] "2015 Annual Report," Port of Prince Rupert, http://2015.rupertport.com/, retrieved April 2, 2017.

[10] "Top 50 World Container Ports," World Shipping Council, http://www.worldshipping.org/about-the-industry/global-trade/top-50-world-container-ports, retrieved April 2, 2017.

[11] Leach, Peter, "A bridge too low," *The Journal of Commerce*, June 5, 2006, pp. 30-31.

[12] "Bayonne Bridge Navigational Clearance Project," Port Authority of New York and New Jersey, http://www.panynj.gov/bridges-tunnels/bayonne-navigational-clearance-project.html, retrieved April 3, 2017.

[13] Port of Marsaxlokk, Association of Ship Agents, /http://www.malta shipagents.org/port-of-marsaxlokk, retrieved May 31, 2013.

[14] "Top 50 World Container Ports," World Shipping Council, http://www.worldshipping.org/about-the-industry/global-trade/top-50-world-container-ports, retrieved April 2, 2017.

[15] Zhang, Lilian, "Further 20-billion yuan expansion of Yangshan port in pipeline," *South China Morning Post*, April 4, 2012.

[16] "Top 50 World Container Ports," World Shipping Council, http://www.worldshipping.org/about-the-industry/global-trade/top-50-world-container-ports, retrieved April 2, 2017.

[17] Tirschwell, Peter, "Berth Productivity: the Trends, Outlook and Market Forecasts Impacting Ship Turnaround Times," *JOC, Journal of Commerce*, July 2014, http://www.joc.com/whitepaper/berth-productivity-trends-outlook-and-market-forces-impacting-ship-turnaround-times-0, retrieved April 4, 2017.

[18] Mongelluzzo, Bill, "US shippers should expect higher terminal fees as ship sizes increase," *The Journal of Commerce*, September 30, 2016, http://www.joc.com/port-news/port-productivity/us-shippers-should-expect-higher-terminal-fees-ship-sizes-increase_20160930.html, retrieved April 3, 2017.

[19] Bonney, Joseph, "Cranes to Work from Both Sides," *The Journal of Commerce*, August 25, 1999, p. 1.

[20] Tirschwell, Peter, "Berth Productivity: the Trends, Outlook and Market Forecasts Impacting Ship Turnaround Times," *JOC, Journal of Commerce*, July 2014, http://www.joc.com/whitepaper/berth-productivity-trends-outlook-and-market-forces-impacting-ship-turnaround-times-0, retrieved April 4,

2017.

[21] http://www.worldportsource.com, accessed April 3, 2017

[22] Mongelluzzo, Bill, "Extending Terminal Hours," *The Journal of Commerce*, March 5, 1997, p. 1B.

[23] "How successful is the effort to expand the hours of operations at Port shipping terminals?," FAQ page, The Port of Long Beach, http://polb.com/qc.asp#474, accessed April 3, 2017.

[24] Davies, John, "Slow Passage to Progress," *International Business*, December 1996-January 1997, pp. 14-17.

[25] Casper, Bill, "The 30-Container-per-Hour barrier," *Cargo Business News*, August 2008, pp. 24-25.

[26] Oster, Shai, "China's Boom Snarls Traffic in 60-mile Jam," *The Wall Street Journal*, August 25, 2010, p. A7.

[27] McCue, Dan, "Infrastructure can slow Emerging Markets," *World Trade*, April 2013, pp. 32-39.

[28] Fortner, Brian, "The Train Lane," *Civil Engineering*, 72(9), September 2002, pp.52-61.

[29] Whelan, Robbie, "Trump's Trade Plans Spell Uncertainty for Mexican Port," *The Wall Street Journal*, April 16, 2017, p. B3.

[30] Beatty, Andrew, "Work stars on biggest-ever Panama canal overhaul," Reuters, September 4, 2007.

[31] Reagan, Brad, "The Panama Canal's Ultimate Upgrade," *Popular Mechanics*, February 2007, pp. 63-68.

[32] Bussey, John, "Ripples Likely from Wider Canal," *The Wall Street Journal*, November 11, 2011, p. B1.

[33] Dupin, Chris, "Panama Canal wait times 'back to normal' ", *American Shipper*, December 2, 2015.

[34] Panama Canal Toll Calculator, Wilhelmsen Lines, http://www.wilhelmsen.com/tollcalculators/panama-toll-calculator, accessed April 4, 2017.

[35] Champion, Marc, "Turkey Plans Own 'Panama Canal'," *The Wall Street Journal*, April 28, 2011, p.A12.

[36] Suez Canal Toll Calculator, Wilhelmsen Lines, http://www.wilhelmsen.com/tollcalculators/suez-toll-calculator, accessed April 4, 2017.

[37] Bender, Jeremy, "These 8 Narrow Chokepoints are Critical to the World's Oil Trade," *Business Insider*, April 1, 2015, http://www.businessinsider.com/worlds-eight-oil-chokepoints-2015-4, retrieved April 4, 2017.

[38] Daley, Suzanne, "Lost in Nicaragua, a Chinese Tycoon's Project," *The New York Times*, April 3, 2016, https://www.nytimes.com/2016/04/04/world/americas/nicaragua-canal-chinese-tycoon.html?_r=0, retrieved April 4, 2017.

[39] Rogers, Tim, "Is Russia eyeing Dry Canal?", *Nicaragua Dispatch*, February 6, 2012, http://www.nicaraguadispatch.com/news/2012/02/ will-russia-get-the-trains-rolling-again/2084, retrieved June 4, 2013.

[40] Maverick, Tim, "A Thai Canal to Be Part of Chinaš́s Silk Road," *Wall Street Today*, January 27, 2016, https://www.wallstreetdaily.com/2016/01/27/thailand-kra-canal-china-silk-road/, retrieved April 4, 2017.

[41] Kim, Lucian, "Danube Trade Blocked by Bridges," *Christian Science Monitor*, October 6, 1999, p. 6.

[42] McGeehan, Patrick, "To Expand, Airports May Need Radical Alterations, Report Says," *The New York Times*, January 27, 2011, p.A23.

[43] Kanner, Gideon, "Eminent Domain in Japan," *Gideon's Trumpet*, September 11, 2010, http://gideonstrumpet.info/2010/09/eminent-domain-in-japan/, retrieved April 4, 2017.

[44] Iok-sin, Lao, "Japanese Still Battle Land Seizures at Narita Airport," *Taipei Times*, July 18, 2014, http://www.taipeitimes.com/News/taiwan/archives/2014/07/18/2003595397, retrieved April 4, 2017.

[45]"Top 40 Airport Rankings," *Air Cargo World*, October 25, 2016, http://aircargoworld.com/top-40-airport-rankings-total-cargo-2015/, retrieved April 4, 2017.

[46]"Runway extension at Narita finally opens," *Japan Times*, October 23, 2009, http://www.japantimes.co.jp/news/2009/10/23/news/runway-extension-at-narita-finally-opens/#.Uc1_Ntjxn4s, retrieved June 28, 2013.

[47]"Top 40 Airport Rankings," *Air Cargo World*, October 25, 2016, http://aircargoworld.com/top-40-airport-rankings-total-cargo-2015/, retrieved April 4, 2017.

[48]"Three Routes Lead to Iberia," *SBB Cargo*, http://www.sbbcargo.ch/en/index/sbbcargo_magazine-/00_03/03_00_1.html, March 15, 2001.

[49]Fu, Bill, Brooks Bentz, and Mark McCalla, "Logistics in China: Thinking Ahead," *Logistics Management*, October 2011, pp. 36-40.

[50]Frentzel, David, "The Bright side of Logistics in India," *Inbound Logistics*, September 2011, pp.87-91.

[51]Dupin, Chris, "BNSF CEO: Railroad Regulators Need to Recognize Dip in Coal Traffic," *American Shipper*, September 25, 2016, http://www.americanshipper.com/main/news/bnsf-ceo-railroad-regulators-need-to-recognize-dip-65473.aspx#hide, retrieved April 5, 2017.

[52]Ziobro, Paul, Jacquie McNish, and David George-Kosh, "Railroad Veteran Faces Challenges in U.S.," *The Wall Street Journal*, February 10, 2017, p. B1.

[53]"The European Rail Network for Competitive Freight," European Commission, http://ec.europa.eu-/transport/modes/rail/infrastructures/rail_freight_oriented_network_en.htm, retrieved June 5, 2013.

[54]Schuetze, Christopher, "Deciding the Future of the Arctic," *The New York Times*, May 20, 2013.

[55]Blakely, Alexander, "The place without Roads; Russia paves the Trans-Siberian Gap," *Harper's*, December 2003, pp. 57-63.

[56]Country Commercial Guides, U.S. Department of Commerce, http://www.state.gov/e/eb/rls/rpts-/ccg/, accessed April 5, 2017.

[57]*World Factbook*, Central Intelligence Agency, https://www.cia.gov/library/publications/the-world-factbook/, accessed April 5, 2017.

[58]Argentina, *World Factbook*, Central Intelligence Agency, https://www.cia.gov/library/publications-/the-world-factbook/geos/ar.html, retrieved April 5, 2017.

[59]United States, *World Factbook*, https://www.cia.gov/library/publications/the-world-factbook/geos-/us.html, retrieved March 5, 2017.

[60]*Ibid.*

[61]*Road building in Poland: The Facts and the Myths, Experience and Perspectives*, Price-Waterhouse-Cooper, February 2016, http://pzpb.com.pl/wp-content/uploads/2016/02/Road-building-in-Poland-_ver_ang.pdf, retrieved April 5, 2017.

[62]Bajaj, Vikas, "A High-Tech Titan Plagued by Potholes," *The New York Times*, August 26, 2010, p.B1.

[63]Fu, Bill, Brooks Bentz, and Mark McCalla, "Logistics in China: Thinking Ahead," *Logistics Management*, October 2011, pp. 36-40.

[64]McWhirther, Cameron, "Infrastructure Grade: D+," *The Wall Street Journal*, March 10, 2017, p. A3.

[65]Millman, Joel, Zusha Elinson, and Jim Carlton, "One Link Proves a Bridge's Undoing," *The Wall Street Journal*, May 25-26, 2013, p. A3.

[66]www.google.com/maps.

[67]www.google.com/maps

[68]"Drone Footage Showing Extent of Smog-stricken Beijing's Traffic Jams Leaves Viewers Gasping,"

South China Morning Post, January 3, 2017, http://www.scmp.com/news/china/society/article/20589-26/drone-footage-beijing-smog-traffic-jams-leaves-internet-viewers, retrieved April 5, 2017.

[69]Li, Ruimin, and Min Guo, "Effects of Odd⁄Even Traffic Testriction on Travel Speed and Traffic Volume: Evidence from Beijing Olympic Games," *Journal of Traffic and Transportation Engineering*, February 2016, **3**:1, pp. 71-81.

[70]Timms, Claire, "Has London's Congestion Charge Worked?," *BBC News*, February 15, 2013.

[71]Dillon, Sam, "Can't Find Juárez Street? There are Hundreds!", *The New York Times*, January 12, 2000.

[72]Faison, Seth, "Palm Trees and Sun (and Who Needs an Address)," *The New York Times*, February 23, 1999.

[73]"Toll rates," Toll Collect, https://www.toll-collect.de/en/toll_collect/rund_um_die_maut/maut_tarife-/maut_tarife.html, accessed April 5, 2017.

[74]"Fares," Eurotunnel Freight, http://www.eurotunnelfreight.com/uk/bookings/fares/, accessed April 5, 2017.

[75]Sciolino, Elaine, "A Soaring Bridge puts an Ancien Town on the Map," *The New York Times*, July 17, 2005.

[76]"Michigan Vote Means new Canadian-Financed Detroit-Windsor Bridge one Step Closer," *National Post*, November 7, 2012.

[77]Witsil, Frank, "Moroun Family's Lawsuit Aims to Block Building New Bridge to Canada," *Detroit Free Press*, January 6, 2017, http://www.freep.com/story/money/business/michigan/2017/01/06/gor-die-howe-bridge-matty-moroun/96244910/, retrieved April 5, 2017.

[78]Al-Khalifa, Abdulrahman, "The Use of Hawala as a Remittance System," traccc.gmu.edu/pdfs/stud-ent_research/Hawala_AR.pdf, retrieved June 3, 2013.

[79]Cuevas-Mohr, Hugo, "An Introduction to Understanding The Gray Market Real Exchange in Brazil," International Money Transfer Conference, January 15, 2012.

[80]*World Factbook*, Central Intelligence Agency, https://www.cia.gov/library/publications/the-world-factbook/, retrieved April 1, 2017.

[81]*Ibid.*

[82]Moore, Solomon, "Ships Sever Data Cables, Cutting East Africa Links," *The Wall Street Journal*, February 28, 2012, p. B3.

[83]Stephenson, Neal, "Mother Earth, Mother Board," *Wired*, December 1996, pp. 97-160.

[84]The World Bank, "Fixed broadband Subscriptions," http://data.worldbank.org/indicator/IT.NET.-BBND.P2?end=2015&start=2001, retrieved April 6, 2017.

[85]*World Factbook*, Central Intelligence Agency, https://www.cia.gov/library/publications/the-world-factbook/, retrieved April 1, 2017.

[86]Dugger, Celia W., "India Tries to Plug a Cash Drain: Its Power System," *The New York Times*, February 6, 2000.

[87]Dwyer, Jim, "De Blasio Postpones Work on Crucial Water Tunnel," *The New York Times*, April 5, 2016, p. A1.

[88]The World Bank, "World Development Indicators: Freshwater," http://wdi.worldbank.org/table/3.5, retrieved April 6, 2017.

[89]Schwirtz, Michael, "Report Cites Large Release of Sewage From Hurricane Sandy," *The New York Times*, April 30, 2013.

[90]The World Bank, "Improved Sanitation Facilities," http://data.worldbank.org/indicator/SH.STA.ACSN, retrieved April 6, 2017.

[91]Sheffi, Yossi, *Logistics Clusters: Delivering Value and Driving Growth*, MIT Press, Cambridge,

Massachusetts, 2012.

[92] "Enforcing Contracts," The World Bank, http://www.doingbusiness.org/data/exploretopics/enforcing-contracts, retrieved April 6, 2017.

[93] Wong, Edward, and Didi Kirsten Tatlow, "China Seen in Push to Gain Technology Insights," *The New York Times*, June 5, 2013.

Chapter 4

International Methods of Entry

The first venture of most firms into the international arena is often the result of serendipity rather than of careful planning and thoughtful strategic thinking. The first few sales abroad emerge from a chance contact made at a trade show, an unexpected fax sent from a prospect who viewed a domestic sales brochure, or a sales inquiry due to a trade magazine advertisement. After a few of these haphazard transactions, the firm realizes that there may be a substantial market—at least large enough to warrant further consideration—for its products outside the domestic market, and management considers selling on a more systematic basis abroad. The pitfalls usually start at this point. Firms must correctly assess the market's characteristics, its potential, and, particularly, the advantages and disadvantages of a given method of entry. Market entry must be based on a strategy rather than a chance encounter at a trade show with a foreign agent or distributor, or entering a joint venture with a partner met through casual business acquaintances. Countless headaches can be avoided if the correct entry strategy is determined early on, using as much information as possible.

4.1   Entry Strategy Factors

Many factors influence a company's entry strategy into a foreign market. Some of these factors are related to the characteristics of the market that the firm is targeting, and other factors are related to the characteristics of the product and of the exporter.

Specifically, the exporter should analyze carefully the following determinant factors:

- **The size of the market.** While there is no easy rule, the method of entry differs for a market in which combined sales amount to € 10,000,000 (U.S. $11,000,000) per year and a market that exhibits annual sales in billions of euros.

- **The growth of the market.** A stable market, growing at a moderate rate, calls for a different entry strategy than one in which there is a substantial potential for growth.

- **The potential market share of the exporter.** A market in which the exporter can become a major player calls for a different strategy than one in which the exporter has little chance of being more than a niche player.

- **The type of product.** Products with technology and a need for after-sale service and parts require a different entry strategy than a disposable consumer good.

- **The market strategy of the firm.** Although self-evident, a firm whose strategy is to provide a top-of-the-line product should have a different entry strategy than a firm that has chosen to be the lowest cost provider.

- **The willingness of the firm to get involved.** Firms that actively want to develop foreign markets should have a different entry strategy than firms that focus on their domestic market and consider foreign sales as "secondary."

- **The characteristics of the country considered.** The level of development, the country's infrastructure, the business sophistication of potential trade partners, the overall climate under which business is conducted, the culture of the market, and the culture of customers should all be considered when determining an entry strategy.

- **The time horizon considered.** Products that have a short life cycle, or products that are likely to generate a lot of "me-too" competitors, demand a different entry strategy than products that are protected by a patent, or are likely to have a long life cycle, or engender a long line of complementary products.

Only after all factors are evaluated can a firm decide appropriately which market entry strategy to pursue. Overall, companies should exercise great caution when deciding market-entry strategies. Among all decisions made by marketers regarding the marketing mix, the distribution decision has the longest time horizon, and is the least likely to be quickly adjusted. Not that product, promotion, and price can be easily adjusted, but a distribution change can be quite an undertaking, leading to hurt feelings and lawsuits, and therefore the need for a correct initial market-entry decision is more critical.

The entry strategies available to a casual exporter are presented first, followed by those strategies available to an active exporter, and then the strategies available to a company willing to manufacture abroad.

4.2   Indirect Exporting

Some firms are unwilling exporters in that they prefer to focus on their domestic markets and consider any foreign inquiry as a difficult sale. Such companies do not like to handle foreign sales. Under this banner of indirect exporting, several alternatives are possible, from the lowest level of involvement to some very moderate involvement.

4.2.1   Export Trading Company (ETC)

When a company is unwilling to undertake any of the activities of marketing abroad, using an export trading company is the simplest solution. An export trading company (ETC) is an intermediary that purchases the goods in the exporting country and resells them to a customer in a foreign country.

export trading company
A company that purchases goods in one country for the purpose of reselling them in another country at a profit.

The dominant ETCs are very large firms, with local offices in many countries. The trading companies operate in the following fashion: they take title to the goods in the exporting country, making this transaction a domestic transaction for the exporter. They then transfer title to the importer in the importing country, making that transaction a domestic transaction as well. As far as the parties dealing with the trading company are concerned, the product is seemingly handled by a domestic company. The product's foreign origin is not a concern for the buyer, and its sale abroad is not an issue for the seller.

Trading companies were first created in the Netherlands, France, and Britain for trade with India and Indochina. As these trade routes disappeared, new trading companies were founded in Spain and Portugal for commerce with South America. These trade routes also eventually disappeared in the late nineteenth century. In the twentieth century, trading companies were resurrected in Japan to handle Japan's export efforts after World War II.[1] These so-called *sogo shosha* now dominate the export trading business: Mitsubishi, Mitsui, Itochu, Marubeni, and Sumitomo. All have sales in the trillions of yen, and trade in many types of goods. Mitsui claims to be involved from "noodles to missiles." Because of their presence in all countries of the world, these trading companies have acquired a wealth of information on potential sellers and buyers, and they leverage this knowledge into sales. The trading companies contact sellers when they are aware of a buyer in some foreign country, and contact buyers when they become aware of a motivated seller. In addition, these trading companies have come to offer a complete package of international logistical services; they ship, insure, and finance international trade. In some cases, sophisticated traders rely on the services of these trading companies for complex transactions rather than handle them themselves: the expertise of the trading companies in handling international transactions is unmatched.

sogo shosha
The Japanese term for a trading company.

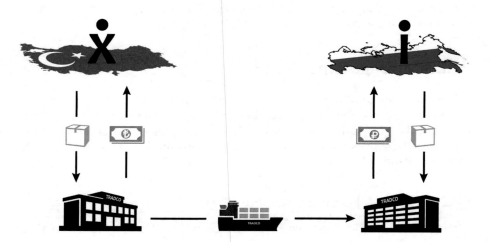

Figure 4.1: A Trading Company

In Figure 4.1, the Turkish office of Tradco, a trading company, first purchases glazed ceramics from a Turkish company. After the companies agree on a price, the transaction takes place in Turkish liras. Tradco then transports the ceramics onboard its own ships to Russia, where its office in that country sells it to a Russian customer. That transaction takes place in rubles. As far as the Turkish seller is concerned, the sale is a domestic transaction with a Turkish customer. As far as the Russian buyer is concerned, the purchase is a domestic transaction with a Russian supplier. The trading company is responsible for all international aspects of the transaction.

Smaller ETCs exist, but they tend to specialize in one geographical area or one product line. However, theses ETCs still offer the breadth of services that a *sogo shosha* offers to an exporter; in particular, ETCs take title to the goods in the exporting country. In the United States, the passage of the Export Trading Companies Act in 1982 spurred the creation of several firms, but all operate on a small scale. The law also created ETC cooperatives that allow trade associations to offer export services to competing companies. Most of these ETC cooperatives are involved in exports of agricultural goods.[2]

Using an ETC makes great sense for a novice exporter or a company unwilling or unable to dabble in the complexities of an occasional international transaction. However, if the company decide to become more involved in the long term, choosing an ETC is a poor strategy, as the customers abroad are not customers of the exporter but those of the ETC, and may not be known to the exporter. It is unlikely that the ETC will relinquish this information if it is no longer profiting from its efforts at developing the market for the exporter's products; it is equally unlikely that the exporter could benefit from the goodwill created by the ETC with its foreign customers.

4.2.2 Export Management Corporation (EMC)

Despite the similarity in name, an export management corporation (EMC) is a different type of intermediary. An EMC is typically located in the exporting country and operates as an export-oriented manufacturer's representative for the exporter. An EMC does not take title to the goods but earns a commission on the sale.

export management corporation
A company that puts suppliers in touch with potential buyers, and earns a commission if a sale is completed.

Most EMCs are small firms, typically with fewer than fifteen employees. The firms rarely have an office abroad, although they do have contacts with many potential importers, and regularly send employees—or, more likely, the owner of the agency—abroad to visit customers and actively attend trade shows and other promotional activities. EMCs tend to restrict sales efforts to potential customers in one country and often specialize in selling one line of products in that country. Most of them represent more than one manufacturer abroad, usually in complementary lines.[3,4]

Because an EMC acts as an agent, the exporter is slightly more involved in the foreign sale than with an ETC. For example, the exporter is responsible for shipping the goods, invoicing the importer, and collecting payment. The degree to which the EMC helps the exporter depends on their relationship and the exporter's level of sophistication. In general, an EMC helps a lot rather than a little: it acts as the export department of the seller, handling every detail of the transaction, from freight forwarding to insurance to invoicing to collection. The com-

agent
The overseas representative of a manufacturer. The agent represents the manufacturer in sales negotiations.

pensation of the EMC therefore varies based on its involvement: it either earns a higher commission for handling all the details of the sale or earns a commission on the sale and fixed fees for the remainder of its efforts. The range of alternative arrangements is such that it is difficult to generalize.

Figure 4.2: An Export Management Corporation

In Figure 4.2, an American export management corporation, Expotech, becomes aware that a company in South Africa needs a forklift truck. Expotech contacts a U.S. manufacturer of handling equipment, which agrees to sell the product to the South African customer if Expotech handles all aspects of the international transaction for a 5-percent commission. The U.S. company ships the forklift to the customer in South Africa and sends him an invoice. When the manufacturer is paid, it sends the commission to Expotech.

Using an EMC makes great sense for a novice exporter; by working with an EMC, and by at least partially managing its foreign accounts, a firm gains substantial insights, which will become quite valuable if the company decides to become further involved in export sales. In practice, though, because the EMC is a small firm and has valuable contacts abroad, it is often absorbed—at least partially—and transformed into the export department of the exporter. This allows the firm to capitalize on the talent of the personnel of the EMC and the goodwill it generated abroad.

African Export Ventures

In a few areas in sub-Sahara Africa, local EMCs, such as Getrade FPS and Fritete African Art Works in Ghana, are spurring the development of an export-led economy. These companies established contacts with importers in the United States and negotiated large purchases of local African artifacts for such companies as Pier 1 Imports, Cost Plus World Market, and Wayfair. None of the local artifact manufacturers had the capacity to handle large orders, so the EMCs coordinated the efforts of hundreds of small artisans,[5] and, after some initial difficulties, procured most of the orders placed by the U.S. firms. As the artisans realized the profitability of such export sales, they started accepting orders for artifacts that were non-traditional in their colors or shapes, to accommodate the customers' requests, creating a perfect example of international marketing. Stay Awake Arts & Carving Co. promises to "carve any animal of your choice," and Joennafrica Handicraft Co. Ltd advertises that its products are made to "customer specification." [6] In addition, as most small businesses in sub-Sahara Africa suffer from a lack of capitalization, the EMCs also brought in "micro-lenders," charitable organizations that will make very small loans (US$500 to $3,000) to help entrepreneurs purchase machinery or obtain working capital. As these loans allow small businesses to grow, it is expected that a business infrastructure will also grow, allowing greater access to financing and triggering further business development. Such micro-lending efforts, pioneered by Muhammad Yunus when he created the Grameem Bank (literally translated as "rural bank" from his native Bengali language), have lifted many local economies out of abject poverty. His efforts earned him the Nobel Prize in Economics in 2006.[7] The United States African Growth and Opportunity Act (AGOA), passed in 2000 and renewed in 2004, allows duty-free access to the U.S. market for goods made in most sub-Sahara African countries, creating additional export growth opportunities for entrepreneurs in that part of the world.[8]

4.2.3 Piggy-Backing

piggy-backing
When a manufacturer goes
overseas and asks its
suppliers to continue doing
business abroad with him,
the suppliers are said to be
piggy backing on that
customer's efforts.

A third alternative choice exists for a reluctant exporter: it is called piggy-backing and can refer to one of two possible situations:

1. A firm's customer enters a foreign market by setting up a manufacturing facility. The customer tells its suppliers that they need to supply parts for assembly and spare parts for customer service. The suppliers therefore also sell their product abroad, piggy-backing on the strategy of an existing customer. In some cases, the suppliers develop independent sales in that market. This piggy-backing also happens with franchised businesses, which require that franchises established overseas be equipped with the same machinery and utilize the same supplies worldwide.

2. A successful exporter involves one of its suppliers—or a company that makes a complementary product—in the markets that the exporter has developed. This form of piggy-backing is sometimes called collaborative exporting; nevertheless, there is certainly an imbalance in the ability of the two partners, with one who is particularly competent and the other who is a novice.

Piggy-backing can sometimes be seen as a passive arrangement (triggered by another firm), making it difficult to call it a strategy. Nevertheless, should the opportunity arise, it makes perfect sense for a company to seize it and acquire some knowledge about selling abroad. If piggy-backing is initiated by a firm eager to develop its own sales in foreign markets, it is quite an appropriate strategy, as the experience gained from the experienced exporter can eventually develop into a solid export strategy with the use of agents, distributors, or even sales subsidiaries.

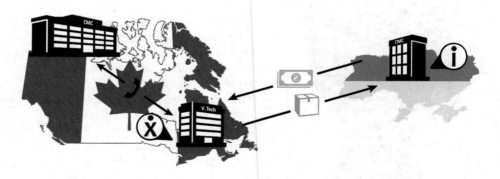

Figure 4.3: Piggy-backing

In Figure 4.3, a large Canadian manufacturer of automobile motors, CMC (Canadian Motors Corp.), announces to its Canadian supplier, V-Tech, that it needs to provide engine valves to the new plant that CMC just built in Ukraine.

V-Tech now supplies valves to the CMC plant in Canada as well as in Ukraine, a country to which it would not have exported without CMC's request.

4.3 Active Exporting

Once a firm wants to exploit the possibilities that sales abroad can bring and decides to become involved in export activities, several alternatives become available. These alternatives differ not only in the level of involvement of the exporter, but also in the strategies pursued by the exporter.[9]

4.3.1 Agent

An agent is usually a small firm or an individual located in the importing country who acts as a manufacturer's representative for the exporter. The agent sells the manufacturer's products to customers in the importing country, using the terms of sale—price, delivery, discounts—determined by the exporter. An agent does do not buy product, but arranges sales directly from the principal to the customers. For this work, an agent is paid a commission, calculated as a percentage of the product's sale price to the customer, and collected after the customer has paid the principal.

agent
The overseas representative of a manufacturer. The agent represents the manufacturer in sales negotiations.

principal
The manufacturer represented by an agent.

An agent often has several principals, and generally sells a group of complementary products rather than products that compete directly with one another. The agent handles all the sales functions for the exporter, from the initial prospecting for customers to the close. The agent is usually given varying support by the exporter: some exporters provide only the bare minimum of a sales brochure and a price list, while more experienced exporters provide training on the product's characteristics, analysis on the competitors' products, information on the company's sales and service philosophy, sales support in the form of samples, catalogs (translated or adapted), trade advertising and financial support to attend trade shows, technical visits by corporate engineers, participation in sales incentive programs, and so on.

Agents typically like to keep control over their schedule and over their sales approach, but the exporter's support of their efforts is critical to their success and to the extent to which they expend effort selling the exporter's product. In particular, requests for quotes and *pro forma* invoices should be handled promptly by the exporter, and negotiations on price and delivery done diligently, so as to avoid delaying the agent's sales efforts; time-zone differences sometimes exacerbate the perception of a lack of responsiveness on the part of the exporter.

Sometimes, there is the suggestion that, given a set of guidelines, the agent can be trusted to reach decisions and negotiate with the customer on critical aspects of the sale: price, delivery, terms of trade (see Chapter 6), terms of sale (see Chapter 7), and collection. However, it is critical that all such negotiations be handled exclusively by the principal, with the agent acting as an intermediary between the exporter and the importer. If the agent is allowed to negotiate

binding agent
An agent who is allowed to make decisions that are binding on the principal. The principal must abide by whatever statements the agent has made.

permanent establishment
A fixed place of business abroad that subjects the exporter to tax liability in the importing country.

directly with the importer, then the agent is considered by many countries' governments as a binding agent, and the exporter is considered to have a permanent establishment in the country of import. This determination has significant taxation implications; the profits realized on the sales made in that country are now considered taxable by the country of import. If there is no permanent establishment, the profits are not taxable in the country of import, although they are obviously taxable in the country of export.

After the sale is concluded between the agent and the importer, all of the other aspects of the transaction, from the *pro forma* invoice to the actual collection of payment, from packaging to shipping the goods, are handled directly and solely by the exporter. Finally, the agent does not get paid until after the exporter has been paid by the importer.

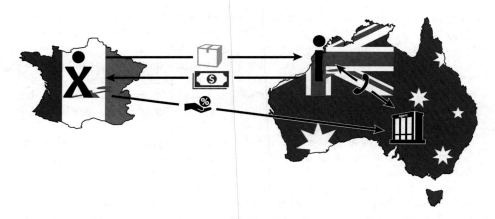

Figure 4.4: An Agent

In Figure 4.4, a French manufacturer of industrial machinery hires an agent in Australia to sell its products and represent the exporter in that market. Whenever the agent finds an Australian customer, the transaction is conducted between the exporter in France and the importer in Australia. When the exporter is paid by the importer, he then sends the agent a commission.

The choice of an agent should be made on several criteria: the agent's ability to represent the exporter and its product accurately, the agent's ability to sell, its contacts, its knowledge of the industry that the exporter wants to target, the compatibility of the agent's objectives with those of the exporter, and so on. Moreover, the choice of an agent is a long-term commitment; although the contract is often based on one-year increments, the duration of an effective relationship between an exporter and its agents is much longer.

There are several ways to find agents in foreign countries; among the most commonly used methods are contacts made at trade shows, participations in trade missions, inquiries with the commercial attachés of the exporter's country's consulates, and contacts with other successful exporters.

Using an agent is generally driven by several factors, one or more of which can be enough to trigger this strategic decision:

1. When the firm estimates that its potential sales in that market are small (perhaps no more than 5 or 10 percent of its domestic sales), with moderate or no growth potential

2. When the product is not a stock item, but a product specifically designed and made for a particular customer

3. When the product is a very expensive item, such as operating machinery

4. When the company expects a short product life cycle

5. When the product does not require frequent after-sale service

6. When the exporter is unlikely to ever become one of the dominant players in the market and will remain a niche player

7. When the company is reasonably well equipped to handle export sales

8. When the company is not pursuing a top-of-the-line strategy and does not attempt to collect premium prices

9. When the company wants to keep a reasonable amount of control over its prices and delivery policies

4.3.2 Distributor

Another entry strategy is to use a firm located in the importing country—or, sometimes, in a neighboring country—that buys the goods from the exporter. Such an intermediary is called a distributor. A distributor takes title to the goods, sells them, and earns a profit on the sales it makes. What characterizes a relationship with a distributor is that there are two sets of invoices: one set of international invoices between the exporter and the distributor, who is also the importer of record; and a set of domestic invoices between the distributor and its customers, who see these transactions as domestic sales of a foreign product. A distributor is therefore carrying inventory of the exporter's goods, and it also often carries inventory of spare parts and provides after-sale service. A distributor often carries complementary products but also may carry products that compete directly with those of the exporter.

distributor
An overseas company that purchases a manufacturer's products with the goal of reselling them at a profit.

A distributor takes much more risk in its relationship with the exporter than does an agent, and experiences much higher costs. The distributor carries the traditional risks associated with inventory and invests a considerable sum of money in the inventory; should the goods not sell well, the distributor is saddled with the unsold or obsolete goods. In addition, it is traditional for a distributor to participate in the costs of advertising, trade show attendance, and so on. In exchange, the distributor has much more freedom in setting prices, negotiating terms with customers, and managing all matters not directly related to the exporter's trademarks or copyrights. However, many exporting firms attempt to limit these freedoms, specifically on price, to maintain a standard strategy from country to country and to eliminate or reduce "parallel imports" (see Section 4.5 on page 137).

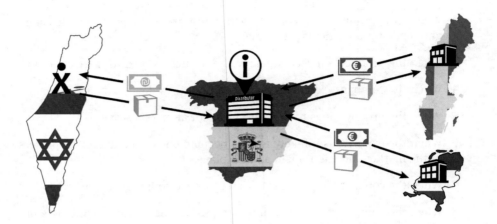

Figure 4.5: A Distributor

In Figure 4.5, an Israeli manufacturer of irrigation equipment, Irridim, enters a contract with a Spanish distributor to sell its products in Western Europe. The Spanish distributor purchases the parts from the Israeli manufacturer and places them in inventory. The Spanish distributor then sells them to its own customers all over Europe.

A distributor should also be considered a long-term partner. Because the distributor makes a substantial investment in inventory and in the training of its employees, the distributor considers itself involved for a long period of time, and great care should be taken in finding the right partner. The choice of a distributor should be made on several criteria: the distributor's ability to represent the exporter and its product accurately, its ability to invest in the exporter's products, to sell them, and to provide after-sale service, as well as the distributor's employees, their contacts, their knowledge of the industry, the compatibility of the distributor's objectives with those of the exporter, and so on.

There are several ways to identify potential distributors in foreign countries; among the most commonly used methods are trade shows, trade missions, the commercial attachés of the exporter's country's consulates, and contacts with other successful exporters.

Using a distributor is generally driven by several factors,[10] one or more of which can be enough to trigger this strategic decision:

1. When the firm estimates that the market is substantial (perhaps 20 or 25 percent of its domestic sales), or when it estimates that there is substantial growth potential

2. When the product is a stock item, and generally not tailored to the needs of a specific customer

3. When the product is a rather moderately priced item

4. When the company expects a fairly long product life cycle

5. When the product requires (frequent) after-sale service and/or maintenance parts

6. When the company estimates it will not become much more than a minor player in the market

7. When the company prefers to handle export sales with only one customer

8. When the company is not pursuing a prestige pricing strategy with premium prices and service

9. When the company is comfortable relinquishing control of its price and delivery terms.

4.3.3 Additional Issues in the Agent-Distributorship Decision

There are two other issues to consider when determining whether an agent or a distributor would be the most appropriate partner—both issues are legal in nature.

First, some countries do not allow agents at all, or do not allow agents to represent foreign manufacturers, or mandate a physical after-sale service presence on the country's soil. All these requirements mandate the use of a distributor.

The second issue is more complicated: many governments make a substantive differentiation in the way agents and distributors are considered by their judicial systems. Because agents tend to be individuals or small firms, many countries have placed them under the protection of labor law, the code of laws that defines the relationships between employers and employees (see Section 5.3.1 on page 154). In many countries, notably in Europe, labor law tends to restrict what an employer can and cannot impose on an employee and, in those countries in which labor law applies to agents, what an exporter can and cannot require of an agent. For example, even though the principal-agent contract may call for a termination notice of thirty days and no compensation, labor law may call for a six-month notice and six-month loss-of-income compensation, overruling the terms of the contract. There are similar restrictions on the number of hours worked, the payment of taxes, the legal requirements of certifications, licenses, and so on.

labor law
A set of laws that govern relationships between employees and employers.

In contrast, because distributors tend to be larger and are assumed to be more sophisticated, their relationships with exporters are covered in almost all countries by contract law. Contract law is much less restrictive, and courts tend to render judgments based upon the terms of the contract. Restrictions are limited

contract law
A set of laws that govern relationships established by contracts between two parties.

to contracts that are obviously biased or coerced, a situation unlikely to be observed if one of the International Chamber of Commerce model contracts or an equivalent is used.

There is another distinction that is often made between an agent and a distributor that presents some potential for misunderstandings; it is often said that a distributor has risks (it invests in inventory), whereas the agent does not. While this is a useful distinction, it is incomplete. The distributor does have substantial financial risks, because it invests in inventory and is faced with the possibility of unsold inventory. However, the agent often has considerable risks as well. The agent invests time and effort in obtaining a sale for which it will not be compensated until after the product is delivered and the importer has paid. In some cases, especially if the product is custom-made for the importer, there may be a lag of several months between the sale and the receipt of the commission check. While it is waiting to be paid, the agent has to maintain its commercial operations.

4.3.4 Marketing Subsidiary

marketing subsidiary
An overseas firm owned by an exporter that is responsible for selling the exporter's products in a foreign market.

Finally, rather than employ an agent or a distributor (over neither of which an exporter has much control), a company may decide to create its own sales or marketing subsidiary in a foreign country.

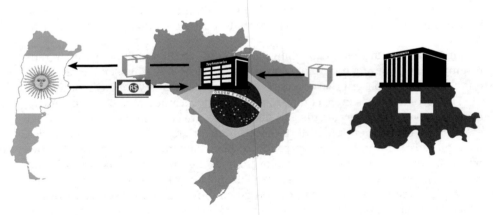

Figure 4.6: A Marketing Subsidiary

In Figure 4.6, a Swiss manufacturer of precision machinery, TechnoSwiss, establishes a marketing subsidiary in Brazil, hiring several employees whose role is to sell Technoswiss products to the South American continent.

A marketing subsidiary is a foreign office staffed by employees of the exporting firm who sell its goods in the foreign market. A subsidiary is legally incorporated in the foreign market, so it is the importer of record as far as the foreign government is concerned, and the "export" takes place between two legal entities that are part of the same company, at a transfer price. Although transfer prices can sometimes create problems when clearing customs, the process is smooth overall, as the traditional concerns of payment, terms of sale, and terms of trade are eliminated. All sales made by the foreign subsidiary to its customers are domestic sales, and therefore are simpler to manage. All profits earned in the importing country are taxable to the importing country's government.

The costs of a marketing subsidiary are higher, and many of them are fixed: a building must be rented, an inventory built, and employees hired and trained before measurable sales can offset these expenses. This is in stark contrast with sales through an agent, which are variable-cost sales (the commission is paid only if the agent sells) or sales through a distributor, where that distributor bears the costs of establishing the business in the foreign market. Investments in a marketing subsidiary obviously also require a long-term commitment on the part of the exporting firm.

The choice of a sales or marketing subsidiary is made when the company wants to retain control over its sales in that country, usually when the company is faced with one or more of the following situations:

1. When the firm estimates that the market potential is considerable (more than 25 percent of its domestic sales) or when it estimates that there is substantial growth potential or substantial profits to be made

2. When the product is technology driven, with substantial intellectual property content

3. When the product is complicated to sell

4. When the company expects to be involved for the long term, with additional products to be introduced later on

5. When the product requires sophisticated after-sale service and/or maintenance parts

6. When the company expects to become one of the major players in the market

7. When the company is exacting premium prices from customers

8. When the company is uncomfortable relinquishing control of its products and prices.

4.3.5 Coordinating Direct Export Strategies

Two types of factors should be considered in the entry decision for an exporter: those factors that are market-driven, and those that are company- or product-driven. Consequently, some firms always follow a strategy driven by their product line and always use a sales subsidiary or a distributor or an agent. However, some firms decide on a country-by-country basis which strategy is the most appropriate, and juggle a combination of agents, distributors, and marketing subsidiaries. Each of these overall strategies has advantages and disadvantages.

When a company chooses to have the same entry strategy in all its export markets, it simplifies the management of the company's exports and presents a unified front to its customers on all aspects of its marketing. In particular, if the firm uses agents or sales subsidiaries in all countries, its prices are likely well coordinated and its after-sale policies clearly controlled. Any discrepancies are known to the firm and can be clearly managed and understood. A firm using distributors in all its markets can exercise the same level of control by using contracts that specify which prices distributors can charge—a practice that is generally legal or, at least, tolerated—and which after-sale services distributors must provide. However, there are problems with this "fit-all" strategy, as inappropriate strategies may lead to a poor match with the market: a potentially lucrative market may be given away to an agent, or a sales subsidiary may have to be established in a small market. Moreover, a firm may have to postpone entry into a lucrative market because of a lack of resources if it adheres to a strategy of building only subsidiaries.

When a firm chooses to have different entry strategies in different countries, or when it decides to sell through a series of independent distributors, coordinating prices and after-sale service is more difficult, and the possibility of parallel imports (see Section 4.5 on page 137) looms. However, the most appropriate strategy is chosen for each country, and, generally, the greatest profits can be extracted from the foreign markets. For a firm, the decision to have a coordinated entry strategy is based on criteria that can be interpreted differently by different management teams.

However, a significant issue to consider once a choice has been made is the cost of changing from one entry strategy to another. For example, if an exporter uses agents or distributors and then changes to a strategy based upon sales subsidiaries, this move can take a significant toll on all involved parties. The agents and distributors have generally invested considerable time, money, and talent into building a significant market for the exporter's products, for which they are rightfully compensated according to the terms of the original contract. If agents and distributors are very successful, the exporter is often tempted to recover these expenses (the commissions paid to the agents or the profit opportunities given to the distributor) by establishing a sales subsidiary. This change of strategy should be avoided as much as possible, as it is traumatic for all involved parties and often results in reduced sales and profits for several years. This is because the customers' loyalties usually lie with the agent or the distributor rather than with the exporter, and regaining the customers' confidence can take considerable effort. The slighted distributor can also be tempted to counterattack, in court or otherwise: some companies can suffer greatly from this change in strategy if the courts are sympathetic to the plight of the local firm,[11] as they often are.

Appropriate Entry Strategy

Criteria	Agent	Distributor	Subsidiary
The company expects a short product life cycle.	X	X	
The product is a stock item.		X	X
The product is custom-made for customers.	X		X
The product is an expensive capital-good item.	X		X
The expected sales are modest.	X	X	
The company pursues a top-of-the-line strategy.			X
The product is moderately priced.		X	X
The product requires after-sale service		X	X
The product has substantial intellectual-property content.			X
The company expects to become a major player in the market.			X
The company anticipates a small market share.	X	X	

Table 4.1: Criteria for Active Exporting Choices

4.4 Production Abroad

A company can also start operations abroad rather than export. This strategy is followed, for example, when manufacturing costs are lower abroad, or when shipping costs are prohibitive, or when domestic manufacturing capacity is reached, or when the product has a significant intangible content, such as in services. Here again, the order in which the alternatives are introduced represents an increasing level of involvement for the company interested in penetrating a foreign market.

4.4.1 Contract Manufacturing/Subcontracting

The first alternative is contract manufacturing—also called subcontracting—which occurs when a company enters an agreement with a producer in the foreign market to manufacture its goods. For example, a publishing firm may contract with a printing facility to publish its books, rather than ship them from its home printing plant. Another example is a cement manufacturer contracting with local producers to make and package cement under its brand. Yet another is a supplier to an automobile manufacturer (called an Original Equipment Manufacturer, or an OEM) that contracts with a company to provide sub-assemblies for that manufacturer's plant in a foreign country.

Contract manufacturing is not truly a method of entry. It is a way to get the product manufactured in a foreign country, while the marketing and distribution of the product still needs to be organized. This distribution can be achieved through a distributor or a marketing subsidiary or, rarely, through the marketing channels used by the local contractor.

contract manufacturing
An arrangement between two companies where one manufactures goods for the other.

Finally, contract manufacturing is often sought as a strategy to enter a market in which there are significant barriers to entry, such as high tariffs and quotas, but there is always great difficulty finding a suitable manufacturing facility in such a country: if the country has a protectionist streak, it is unlikely to have domestic firms that are operating at world standards.

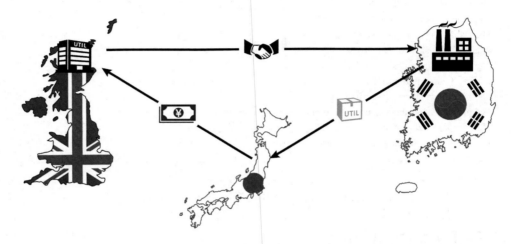

Figure 4.7: A Contract Manufacturing Agreement

In Figure 4.7, Util, a British manufacturer of home appliances, enters a contract with a manufacturer in Korea. The Korean company produces the appliances for the British company, and the British company is responsible for marketing them worldwide, including in Japan.

The "Pet Shop" bags

Firms frequently contract abroad to have a product manufactured and re-imported into their home country, taking advantage of lower production costs than at home. Nothing is particularly special about this. However, the case of the Scottish Pet Shop bags illustrates the possible unintended consequences of such an arrangement.

In 1990, the Pet Shop in Glasgow, Scotland, decided to have shopping bags printed in China. In many ways, the bags were traditional, with the name of the store and its address appearing on them; however, they were also adorned with a drawing of a red parrot. For some unknown reason, the printing plant where the pet store owner had the bags printed decided to print millions more, and these additional bags found their way throughout Central Asia. They have been found by tourists and diplomats in Pakistan, China, Uzbekistan, Russia, and Kyrgyzstan. Curious about the provenance of the bags, they sometimes contact the pet store in Glasgow to inquire about the mystery. The shop owner is as baffled as they are.

Eventually, knock-offs of the Pet Shop bags started emerging in these countries as well, some with two parrots, some with made-up names, or some with the peculiar English found on counterfeit goods all over China, to which my Chinese students refer colloquially as Chenglish: "The Plastic Bag Shop. Welcome Patronage."[12] While it is difficult to argue that there was much intellectual property in the design of a simple shopping bag, and that the pet store lost much in the process—actually, this notoriety may have increased its sales—this example makes it evident that it is difficult to control what a contract manufacturer will do after the initial order is completed.

4.4.2 Licensing

Licensing grants rights to intellectual property owned by a company to another company for a fee. The intellectual property is either a patent on a specific technology, process, design, or product; a trademark; a brand; a copyright; a trade secret or other know-how, and it remains the property of the licensor—the firm granting the license. The company using the intellectual property—the licensee—has the right to use the property for a fee, or royalty, that it must pay for each use. The use of the intellectual property is also constrained by many guidelines, such as the number of times, the products, and the markets in which it can be used. Licensing is quite common in manufacturing, where companies license processes they have developed to other firms, or products such as chemical compounds and molecules.

In an international environment, the licensor is the exporting company and the licensee is the foreign company, and the range of intellectual property commonly licensed in an international agreement is greater than in a domestic agreement; several companies agree to license their more visible intellectual property—trademarks, copyrights, or designs—to foreign firms. This strategy is followed when market access is limited by high tariffs or non-tariff barriers, when shipping costs are prohibitive, or when the licensor is uninterested in actively pursuing the market.

In Figure 4.8 on the next page, Cicero Books, the United States publisher of the book you are reading, enters a licensing agreement with Tsinghua University Press in China. Cicero Books allows Tsinghua to publish this *International Logistics* book in the Chinese market. In exchange, Tsinghua University Press pays a royalty to Cicero Books.

Licensing, as a strategy, can be beneficial to a firm. The company does not have to invest any capital and can generate worldwide income from its intellectual property rapidly. The downside is that intellectual property is not well protected in some countries, that piracy is rampant in several others, and that these risks

licensing
An arrangement between two companies where one uses the other's intellectual property in exchange for a royalty.

royalty
The fee paid by a company so that it can use another party's intellectual property.

licensor
The company that grants to another company, the licensee, the right to use its intellectual property.

licensee
The company that obtains the right to use the licensor's intellectual property.

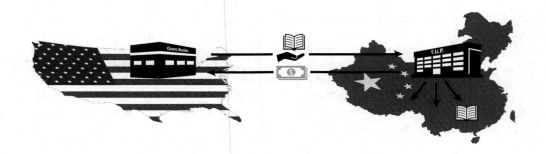

Figure 4.8: A License Agreement

can be perceived as major deterrents for the owners of intellectual property. However, these are danger associated more with the ownership of intellectual property than with the strategy of licensing. An individual who decides to violate a patent or infringe a copyright does not need a licensing agreement to start: patent information is available from all patent offices as a matter of course— the U.S. Patent Office has most of its seven million patents available online—and copyrights are by definition protecting publicly available products, such as this book or computer software, which can be easily purchased. To a certain extent, it is better to have a local firm enforce its license of a copyright than to attempt to enforce the copyright from abroad.

4.4.3   Franchising

franchising
An arrangement between two companies where one licenses an array of related intellectual property items.

franchisor
The company that owns an array of related intellectual property items and lets another firm use them in exchange for a royalty.

franchisee
The company granted the right to use an array of related intellectual property items owned by the franchisor in exchange for a royalty.

Franchising is conceptually quite similar to licensing, except that the franchisor is granting the rights to several intellectual property items at once, all bundled into a business package, to a franchisee who pays royalties for using this business model. The business model includes trademarks, copyrights, and patents, as well as know-how, training, and methods of operation. Most franchises tend to be retail establishments, because consumers tend to value a uniform product and service, and like to find retail names with which they are familiar.

In Figure 4.9, Ace Carwash, a British chain of do-it-yourself car washes, enters a franchising agreement with Australian investors. Ace allows the Australian investors to use its name, designs, and brands, in exchange for the payment of a royalty.

Entrepreneurs abroad like to invest in a business concept with a proven track record, which most franchised businesses have. At the same time, franchisors can gain market share without investing any capital. Franchising has proven to be a fairly popular means of expansion both domestically and abroad.

Franchising is an excellent option for many businesses seeking expansion abroad, but it is also inappropriate for many. Businesses that can enter a market successfully are retail operations that involve a service requiring low-level

Figure 4.9: A Franchise

employee skills, such as fast-food restaurants, car-repair shops, hotels, and car-rental outlets. Franchising is inappropriate for high-skill consulting or advertising services, and nearly impossible for manufactured goods.

One of the consequences of the franchising strategy is that it generates significant piggy-back exporting: the franchisors demand that the franchisees use exactly the same equipment worldwide, so the suppliers of those pieces of equipment end up selling worldwide as well. This is also true for items such as signage, furniture, and, in some cases, consumables: in 1997, it was estimated that, for every dollar earned by franchisors in foreign franchising fees, $15 was spent on U.S. products by the franchisees to set up and run their franchised operations.[13] The proportion today is unlikely to be much different.

4.4.4 Joint Venture

With a joint venture (JV), the exporter invests in a facility abroad, but finds one or more partners with which to share the costs of the venture. A joint venture is characterized by the creation of a new corporation in a foreign country, jointly owned by the venture partners in any combination of ownership percentages; most JVs involve two partners and are owned 50 percent-50 percent or 51 percent-49 percent,[14] but they can be held 97 percent-3 percent. Some JVs include three or more partners, but these are less common.

joint venture
An overseas company that is jointly owned by two or more companies.

Entry strategies using JVs are generally created for one of several reasons:

1. The firm feels compelled to minimize its exposure in a foreign investment (*i.e.*, the amount of money it has at stake in a foreign country), and it achieves this objective by lowering the investment costs by half or two-thirds.

McDonald's Franchising

McDonald's Restaurants has used franchising as the corporation's main method of expansion in the United States and abroad. As of December 2016, McDonald's had 12,978 franchised restaurants in the United States,[15] owned by about 2,400 independent franchisees. Abroad, the company has also followed an aggressive development policy by using franchises. There were 17,389 franchised McDonald's restaurants in 94 countries,[16] (some sources[17] list 121 countries but erroneously count Puerto Rico, Martinique, and Jersey as separate countries, which they are not). Several countries have more than 1,000 restaurants (Japan, China, Brazil, Germany, the United Kingdom, and France). More than 83 percent of these 36,504 McDonald's restaurants are franchised. Worldwide, there were "only" 6,137 restaurants owned by the corporation.

This foreign growth was not without problems; for example, in 1967, McDonald's Corporation divided Canada into two franchising territories, which it licensed to two individuals, George Tidball (Western Canada) and George Cohon (Eastern Canada). Realizing that this large market's potential could not be exploited fully by only two franchisees, McDonald's Corporation purchased these franchises in 1970 and 1971.[18]

The company is intent on expanding the percentage of its restaurants owned by franchisees, as it believes that franchise owners are best at gauging their local markets and key to the company's success: "[McDonald's Corporation sees itself] as a franchisor and believe[s] that franchising is important to delivering great, locally-relevant customer experiences and driving profitability."[19] McDonald's allows its franchisees to adapt its business model to the characteristics of the country. For example, McDonald's serves beer and wine in France and Germany, and it makes scooter deliveries in China (see Figure 4.10 on the facing page).

The franchisees have been one of the greatest strengths of McDonald's development: several of the company's best-selling sandwiches were developed by franchisees, notably the Big Mac (1968) and the Egg McMuffin (1973). The same is true internationally. The former franchisee in Canada, George Cohon, now head of the corporate McDonald's Restaurants of Canada, opened the first restaurant in Moscow, on Pushkin Square, in January 1990. After selling more than 30,000 meals on its first day, this restaurant was still the busiest McDonald's in the world twenty years later, and was only temporarily relegated to second-busiest after the McDonald's restaurant that served the London

Olympic Park operated in the Summer of 2012.[20] As of December 2016, there were 553 McDonald's restaurants in Russia.

In Japan, McDonald's used a slightly different entry strategy: it formed a 50-50 joint venture with Den Fujita in 1970, and soon opened its first restaurant on the glamorous Ginza in Tokyo.

Most of Japan's 2,975 McDonald's restaurants are owned by the joint venture, but eventually McDonald's added franchised operations, and today 22 percent of the restaurants are franchises. Worldwide, McDonald's restaurants' sales are U.S. $82,714 million (2015), approximately 46 percent of which is generated by franchisees in foreign countries. Each of the franchised restaurants grosses an average of just over U.S. $2,200,000 in annual sales, and each of the corporate-owned restaurant generates a little over U.S. $2,500,000 annually.[21]

Figure 4.10: McDonald's delivery scooter in Beijing, China
Photo ©Tony Vingerhoets/Shutterstock. Used with permission.

2. The firm finds a partner with a complementary line of products to offer to the same market. Both partners feel that a joint effort, with a complete line, is the better strategy, and neither is ready to enter the market alone.

3. The firm wants a minority local partner to teach it the local ways of business and help smooth out the many obstacles that a firm can experience in a foreign venture.

4. The firm is legally required to find a local partner by the host government. This requirement was popular until the mid-1990s, and has become less of an issue in the last two decades. Generally, the local partner was a politically connected individual, rather than a partner who brought in additional capital.

The JV strategy was frequently used until the early 1990s for several reasons. First and foremost, this strategy lowered the exposure of firms to the political risk presented by some countries. As early as the 1950s, some developing countries' governments decided that a good way to obtain means of production and create investment capital was to nationalize plants owned by foreign investors. This policy also looked attractive politically, because the local perception was that the natural resources of a country should be managed and owned by its people. Libya, Egypt, Venezuela, and numerous others decided to seize, without compensation to their owners, all the petroleum production facilities within their borders. Several other countries followed the same policy, nationalizing any foreign-owned facility, until the late 1970s; some did it with some form of compensation, most without. The result of these expropriation policies is clear: not only did the countries have difficulties in running plants without the expatriate technicians who had been employed in the facility before it was nationalized, but they also scared away new foreign investors for decades. To minimize the impact of a possible nationalization, foreign firms created joint ventures with a politically well-connected local partner.

In Figure 4.11, a Swiss pharmaceutical company creates a joint venture with a local chemical manufacturer in India to produce a drug with substantial market potential on the Indian market. The Swiss manufacturer chose its partner because the Indian management team had much experience navigating the country's complex regulatory environment.

Countries that still wanted to create local ownership of capital, but did not practice nationalization found another effective strategy: their governments asked foreign enterprises that wanted to invest in their countries to take on local businessmen as JV partners. These local businessmen were always well connected but often under-capitalized and therefore did not bring much beyond their contacts to the venture. In effect, the requirement was a partial nationalization, as the 100 percent investment that the foreign corporation made was quickly diluted to a 50-percent ownership of the JV. Some of these partnerships ended up being extreme examples of nepotism, such as in Indonesia, where President Suharto's relatives were the only possible JV partners.[22] In other cases, the political partners were more of a hindrance than a help, even in dealing with the government, because

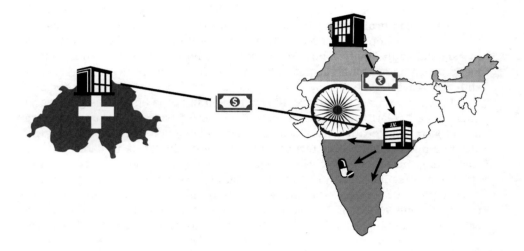

Figure 4.11: A Joint Venture

they had been chosen for their contacts rather than for their business acumen, and some ended up being dishonest; such was the case for the respective partners in China of Kimberly-Clark, Borg-Warner, BASF, Potain, and countless others.[23]

However, the greatest problem with joint ventures, and the reason a majority of them are unsuccessful, is that they are like marriages in which the spouses change over time. When the JV is first created, there is a good fit between both partners' goals and strategies, and most JVs start well. However, over time, the original management on each side changes. Some managers might retire or change positions within the firm, one of the original partners may be purchased by a conglomerate, corporate strategies can change, and gradually, the strategic match that had created the JV is gone and partners squabble over the JV's objectives. Eventually, they accuse each other of all ills. The JV between Ford and Volkswagen in Argentina—named Autolatina—failed because the partners' objectives changed as the venture progressed.[24]

Because of these problems, the strategy of creating joint ventures has become less and less attractive to foreign investors. Some countries have retreated and no longer require foreign investors to create a JV with a local partner, at least partly because the existence of these policies deterred some highly sought investors from entering their markets: for example, Pepsico in India and 3M in China. These countries now routinely allow 100 percent ownership by a foreign entity.

4.4.5 Subsidiary

A subsidiary, also called a wholly owned foreign enterprise (WOFE, pronounced "WOO-fee"), is a 100-percent investment in a foreign venture by a firm. This strategy is followed by firms that want total control of an investment, and are

subsidiary
A company entirely owned by another company.

wholly-owned foreign enterprise
Another term for a subsidiary.

willing to take the risk of such a venture. A WOFE is either a green-field operation, where a foreign firm builds a brand-new facility, or an acquisition of an existing firm. Greenfield operations represent more than 90 percent of all investments in Asia and Latin America, but the preferred method of entry in most European markets is a merger or an acquisition, which represent more than 80 percent of all foreign investments.[25]

There is another alternative, which is limited in scope but that is growing in interest, particularly in developing countries' markets: a firm relocates an entire plant to a foreign location, usually to use cheaper labor and forgo the higher costs of a brand-new facility. The technology may not be the latest available, but the cost savings may be significant, especially if the old plant no longer meets the environmental regulations of the exporting country. As the United States does not track export sales of used equipment—the Electronic Export Information submitted to customs at export (see Section 9.3.1 on page 287) does not distinguish between old and new equipment—the extent of this practice is not fully known, but anecdotal evidence abounds.

The WOFE strategy allows the firm to retain complete control over its investment, which has become the main reason for a firm to choose this form of entry. The firm does not have to share its trade secrets or know-how, and no one is privy to any of its strategies or policies. The firm does not have to share its profits, does not have to rely on outside resources for information on its customers, is free to exit from a given market if the prospective sales do not materialize, and so forth.

The WOFE strategy is also often beneficial to the host country—it creates jobs, for one—and many countries offer substantial incentives to foreign companies willing to establish a facility within their borders: free land, tax abatements, training programs, and infrastructure improvements. If the foreign firm considering the investment is willing to establish itself in a rural or economically depressed area, the incentives can make a WOFE extremely attractive. For example, Ireland established an extensive panoply of tax incentives in the 1980s and achieved unprecedented growth and employment in the following decade. Today, Ireland is no longer perceived as an essentially rural country, but as a booming, economically prosperous country with access to the entire European market; its incentive program convinced dozens of firms to invest there. The southern states of the United States followed a similar strategy in the 1990s and 2000s. The results of these strategies paid off quickly: BMW built in South Carolina, Mercedes-Benz and Honda in Alabama, Nissan in Mississippi, and Volkswagen in Tennessee.

In Figure 4.12, an Italian manufacturer of appliance parts purchases an existing appliance-part company and its plants in Argentina, in order to manufacture parts for the South American market.

The drawbacks of a subsidiary strategy are that there is a high cost of setting up a facility abroad, and all of the costs are borne by a single firm. However, the firm can use this facility to manufacture goods to be shipped back to the home country or to other markets; for example, having a facility within the European Union gives a firm duty-free access to the entire western European market, and more favorable duty rates in eastern Europe than a facility in the United States.

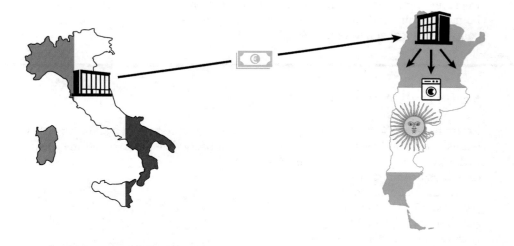

Figure 4.12: A Subsidiary

The costs can therefore be recovered quickly. Similarly, a Japanese firm can get duty-free access to the United States and Canada by setting up a facility in Mexico, which also enjoys low labor costs.

A wholly owned subsidiary exposes the firm to the risks of investments, although the risks that make a management team worry about its investments abroad are in decline: political risks are becoming less prominent, with more countries solidly in the democratic camp, and the economic risks are in decline as well. Except for countries in which there is no real market for many products, the prospects for a stable economy, a stable government, or at least a stable transition to a new government, are very good.

A WOFE also faces relocation costs if the production facility is moved to another country. Costs may include significant compensation to employees who will be laid off during the relocation process. These expenses vary by country, and must be considered in the relocation analysis. In 2006, Kraft Foods decided to move its subsidiary from Australia to China, and this decision resulted in significant costs (see Vignette on the next page).

Finally, a WOFE presents the disadvantage of having to manage in a foreign country without a very good understanding of local customs and regulations. As a firm invests in a foreign country, it oftentimes chooses to have an expatriate manager at its helm; this manager often runs into difficulties that may have been avoided, had the firm elected to have a local partner. For example, the European countries have countless customs that sound peculiar or even counterproductive to any foreigner but which local managers support heavily: thirty-five-hour workweeks in France, Mitbestimmung (co-determination) in Germany, late-night work hours in Spain, and so on. These drawbacks can easily be overcome by hiring a competent local general manager.

Kraft Foods Australia

Kraft Foods is one of the world's largest food and beverage companies, with sales in more than 145 countries. Kraft was acquired in 1988 by Philip Morris Companies, which also purchased Miller Brewing in 1985 and Nabisco Holdings in 2000. Philip Morris changed its name to Altria Group in 2003 to reflect its more diversified business ventures.

In 2002, Kraft Foods Australia acquired a manufacturing plant in Broadmeadows, Australia, as a wholly owned subsidiary to manufacture its cookies. The Australian facility, which had been built in 1964, employed 151 people. Kraft then embarked on a strategy to improve the performance of the facility, reduce costs, and maintain quality; however, the cost reductions were not sufficient, and the older plant did not have the capacity to support an expanding market. On March 31, 2006, Kraft Foods Australia closed the cookie manufacturing facility and moved the manufacturing of cookies to a regional facility in Suzhou, China. Later that year, Kraft Foods Australia announced that it would close its distribution center in Port Melbourne and a dairy plant in Strathmerton that manufactured cheese and Vegemite, a dark brown Australian food paste made from yeast extracts, a uniquely Australian product (see Figure on top right).

However, all the product lines would

continue to be sold in Australia, with a third-party-logistics distributing these products.

The employment contracts that Kraft had negotiated with its unions and the laws of Australia required the company to provide substantial support to its laid-off workers in both locations: the laid-off workers had to be paid a severance package that included four weeks' pay for each year worked at the plant (a benefit called an "entitlement"), and given access to outplacement services for a minimum of eight weeks (called a "redundancy package").[26]

Kraft Foods vice president and area director for Australia/New Zealand Chris Bell said, "Kraft is especially mindful of the impact this decision will have on our employees, as we greatly value the support that all our employees give to Kraft Foods Australia. We will ensure that all affected [...] employees are given access to every support during this difficult period, and they are guaranteed to be paid their appropriate entitlements, including a redundancy package. Employees will also have access to comprehensive career transition support services."[27] When it purchased the Broadmeadows plant in 2002 as a wholly owned Australian subsidiary, Kraft had undoubtedly anticipated the additional costs of its legal obligations to its new workforce and had considered the employees when it decided to close the plant. Not all companies who invest abroad consider those factors.

4.5 Parallel Imports

One of the greatest problems faced by a firm involved in several markets is the risk of parallel imports. The problem is particularly acute if the firm has relinquished some control over its goods' prices. That would often be the case if the company is using distributors, for example.

Parallel imports—or gray market goods—are goods that are sold outside a company's regular distribution channels, usually because there is a discrepancy between the price charged in one country and the price charged in another. Gray

parallel imports
Goods purchased in one country by unauthorized intermediaries and sold to unauthorized retailers in another country.

gray market goods
Goods purchased in one country by unauthorized intermediaries and sold to unauthorized retailers in another country.

Figure 4.13: Parallel Imports

market goods are not counterfeit or shoddy goods: they are legitimate items, but are sold outside the channel chosen by the company (see Figure 4.13 on the preceding page). For example, a small kitchen appliance may sell at a different price in Turkey than in Germany, and, for whatever reason, the Turkish version of the product is significantly cheaper. An entrepreneur then buys the appliances at their retail price in Turkey, ships them to Germany, and sells them through a discount store. The price a consumer pays in Germany for the Turkish version of the product ends up being lower than the price of the German version. Since the sale is "outside" of the regular distribution channel set up by the manufacturer in Germany, it is considered a parallel import. The legitimate retailer in Germany is not happy to be undersold and the appliance manufacturer has lost some control over the marketing of its products.

Parallel imports occur in many different product lines, from shampoo to cars to spare parts; however, it is a particularly sensitive issue in luxury goods, such as watches, electronics, and high-end automobiles. While there are ways to combat parallel imports, which can be found in any good textbook in international marketing, the best strategy is to avoid having discrepancies in prices from one country to another, which usually requires the firm to have a coherent entry strategy.

On a final note, there is no legal recourse possible for parallel imports, as the product is a legitimate product, manufactured by an authorized plant. In the United States, the Supreme Court affirmed this point explicitly: once a firm has sold a product, it has no right to continue controlling it. In Justice John Paul Stephens's words: "The whole point [...] is that once the copyright owner places a copyrighted material in the stream of commerce by selling it, it has exhausted its exclusive statutory right to control its distribution."[28] The U.S. Customs and Border Protection Service will not stop gray market goods unless they differ from the goods sold by the traditional distribution channel in the United States. That is the case, for example, for products sold under the same brand name, but with a different chemical composition to satisfy foreign requirements or consumer tastes abroad.[29] Other countries have taken similar stances.

4.6   Counterfeit Goods

counterfeit goods
Goods manufactured to look like original products, but whose manufacturing was not approved by the brand owners.

One other significant issue that a firm encounters when it starts to expand abroad is the increased probability that unscrupulous competitors —and sometimes partners—manufacture and distribute counterfeits of the original product. Counterfeit goods are copies of the original products sold under the same (or a very similar) brand name, are generally of lower quality, and are also generally sold at much lower prices than the original. Most of the time, the purchasers are well aware that they are not purchasing the genuine product, but do not feel that they are doing anything wrong; they intend to save money or are interested in obtaining the status that the brand conveys, without paying for it.

Counterfeiting generally happen when there is a substantial discrepancy between the variable cost of manufacturing the product and the price at which it sells. Counterfeits are therefore abundant in the software and entertainment industries; a DVD of a movie or a CD of a software program can be reproduced for a few pennies but sell for much more. Most of the counterfeit goods that U.S. Customs and Border confiscated in 2014[30] were luxury goods (handbags, watches, clothing), pharmaceutical drugs, and cigarettes, all of which exhibit the same characteristics: low manufacturing costs and high selling prices. The probability increases further if the product is physically small and light enough that it can be sold easily and discreetly on the streets: sidewalk peddlers constitute the most common distribution channel for counterfeit goods.

The existence of counterfeiting activity does not depend on the chosen method of entry. Thus, whether a firm enters a foreign market through licensing, contract manufacturing, or a wholly owned subsidiary, does not matter. Counterfeit manufacturing is generally present in countries where government authorities have other priorities than defending the intellectual property rights of (foreign) firms. China and India are commonly accused of ignoring counterfeiting activities, but they are just the most visible targets. Counterfeiting happens in all countries.[31] Defending a company against counterfeit goods that imitate its products remains daunting. Counterfeiting is difficult to prosecute, and most consumers—as well as local law enforcement officials who are also consumers—see counterfeiting as a crime that benefits them and hurts only the large foreign corporations, with whom they do not empathize.[32]

The tide seems to be turning, though. Since the beginning of the twenty-first century, many countries have cracked down on counterfeiting, for several reasons. Governments have realized that counterfeiting is not a crime that affects just the profits of foreign firms, it also affects the health of their citizens. The most notorious examples happen in China when unscrupulous local businesses sold counterfeit baby formula and adulterated milk. The problem was so widespread that the Chinese government found 15,000 instances of tainted food products, and shut down 5,700 food businesses.[33]

4.7   Other Issues in Methods of Entry

Companies should consider several other factors to make an appropriate decision regarding their method of entry into a foreign market.

4.7.1   Foreign-Trade Zones

Foreign-trade zones (FTZs) are areas of a country that have acquired a special customs status, with the specific purpose of encouraging foreign investments and exports. Effectively, a foreign trade zone—sometimes also called a free-trade zone—is an area of a country that is, for customs purposes, "outside" of the country; goods can be shipped to the FTZ without being subject to duty and quotas. Once in the FTZ, the goods can be transformed, assembled, repackaged, and eventually shipped to customers. If the goods are re-exported, they never

foreign trade zone
An area that is physically within the borders of a country, but that is considered outside of its borders for customs' purposes.

duty
The amount of tax paid to customs authorities in the importing country on imported goods.

pay duty in the host country in which the FTZ is located; if they are sold in the host country, duty is only paid when the goods leave the FTZ.[34]

FTZs exist in one form or another in nearly every country. Some countries use them aggressively to encourage foreign investments by allowing just about any economic activity within the zone, including manufacturing; goods come in the trade zone duty-free; are transformed in the zone into a final product, creating jobs in the host country; and the product is then re-exported abroad or into the host country. In China, the Waigaoqiao Free Trade Zone, near Shanghai, is home to 104 of the world's 500 largest companies, employs 170,000 people, including 8,600 foreign workers, and had added RMB 67 billion (about U.S. $9 billion) to the Chinese economy.[35] Uruguay has aggressively promoted the creation of free-trade zones, and the 1,600 companies operating in its twelve large FTZs account for more than 14 percent of the country's total exports.[36]

FTZs are particularly attractive to a manufacturer if the host country has an inverted tariff structure (*i.e.*, the tariffs charged on parts are higher than the tariffs charged on the final product).[37] FTZs can also be advantageous to hold goods in inventory until sold, or to wait for a numerical quota to open. However, in view of the progress made in the last few years by the WTO to lead countries to lower tariffs and increase trade, FTZs may have a limited future because their advantages are dwindling. Nevertheless, they remain attractive and should be considered as a possible alternative site for a foreign investment, whether a sales subsidiary, a joint venture, or a WOFE.

4.7.2   Maquiladoras

maquiladora
A plant located in Mexico that have the same status as a foreign trade zone located both in the United States and Mexico.

Maquiladoras are companies in Mexico with a customs status similar to that of an FTZ located both in Mexico and in the United States. They can import goods from the United States duty free, transform these goods by assembling them into products, and then re-export them to the United States, where the goods are assessed duty only on the value added in Mexico. Originally, maquiladora status could be obtained in only a geographic band located just south of the United States' border with Mexico, but it was expanded to the rest of the country in the late 1980s. Today, with the completion of the North American Free Trade Agreement (NAFTA), maquiladoras have limited attractiveness to a foreign investor, but this alternative is still available, and many plants located in the Northern part of Mexico have retained that status.

4.7.3   Foreign Sales Corporations

foreign sales corporation
A subsidiary, created for tax-reduction purposes only, that handles an exporter's overseas sales.

Foreign sales corporations (FSCs) were created in the United States as tax breaks for exporters. FSCs were not a method of entry, but rather a way for U.S.-based corporations to lower their income tax. The only conditions were that the corporation had to export products with a 50-percent U.S. content and had to incorporate a subsidiary in one of several pre-approved foreign locations, such as the U.S. Virgin Islands, Barbados, or Jamaica. By channeling its export sales through an FSC, a corporation was eligible to reduce its tax rate on profits earned on export sales of fifteen percentage points, from 45 percent to 30 percent.[38] It was essentially a tax incentive available to exporters, regardless of the method used for export.

The European Union brought a complaint to the World Trade Organization (WTO) that the FSC concept subsidized exports, a practice that is prohibited by the agreement. The WTO ruled against the United States in August 1999. Subsequently, the U.S. Congress created the Extraterritorial Income Exclusion (ETI) Act, which offered roughly the same benefits to U.S. exporters, but under a different legislation.[39] The ETI was also found to be contrary to WTO rules in 2004 under the same argument; export sales were not taxed, and therefore the ETI was considered a form of export subsidy, contrary to WTO rules. In 2005, the U.S. Congress created a new provision to counter that setback, the Domestic Production Activities Deduction (DAPD). Although it is available to all companies operating in the United States,[40] it is designed to provide favorable tax treatments to exporters: 9 percent of net income earned on foreign sales is non-taxable, but the non-taxable amount cannot exceed 50 percent of payroll expenses for export activities.[41] The provisions of the DPAD were written so that they would be immune from WTO scrutiny, and that seems to have been effective.[42]

Another tax incentive available to U.S. exporters is the Interest-Charge Domestic International Sales Corporation [IC-DISC]. It allows an exporter to create a separate subsidiary to which it pays a commission on its foreign sales. The tax rate that the subsidiary pays on these commissions is 15 percent, a much-lower rate than the 35 percent that corporations pay on ordinary income.[43] The provisions of this export incentive were also designed to avoid conflict with WTO rules, and no WTO challenge had been undertaken as of October 2016.[44]

4.7.4 Anti-Bribery Conventions

One of the last aspects of significant concern in selecting a method of entry in a foreign country is the fact that business practices in some countries tend to include corruption and bribery. The Organisation for Economic Co-operation and Development (OECD) has tried to ban such practices by developing its Anti-Bribery Convention (ABC), which 41 countries had ratified as of November 2016. One aspect of the convention is that it asks the developed countries' governments to cease the practice of letting firms deduct bribery as a business expense.

Anti-Bribery Convention
An OECD convention that requires countries to penalize companies engaging in bribery.

Eleven countries (Australia, Bulgaria, Finland, France, Hungary, Iceland, Italy, Luxembourg, Mexico, Norway, and Switzerland) incorporated measures outlined in the ABC in their penal codes, and five (Canada, Germany, Greece, Korea, and the United States) passed specific separate legislation. Two of the signatory countries (Japan and the United Kingdom) wrote statutes penalizing companies and officers of companies involved in the bribery of foreign officials.[45]

A precursor of the OECD's anti-bribery convention, the United States implemented in 1977 a punitive Foreign Corrupt Practices Act (FCPA), which fines heavily companies that are caught using bribery to gain foreign contracts. The FCPA is far-reaching and prohibits "all officers and employees and anyone else acting

Foreign Corrupt Practices Act
A U.S. law that punishes severely U.S. companies engaging in bribery outside of the borders of the United States.

on behalf of the firm and its subsidiaries [from] offer[ing] any payments, direct or indirect, or through a third party, to government officials in return for getting or keeping business."[46] This includes payments made by an agent to a foreign official, or "special incentives" given to a well-connected partner in exchange for having won a contract. Anything that is not contractual is deemed suspect. The U.S. government prosecutes the firms that it thinks have violated the law, and the officers of the firm, whether they knew of the practice or not, and fines can run in the millions of U.S. dollars.[47]

The FCPA is often understood to be aimed at preventing the bribery of high-level foreign officials; while this was originally the case, it was amended in 1998 and now targets attempts at influencing all levels of foreign officials, including such practices as asking for a favorable treatment of a customs entry or a reduced tariff rate.[48]

The FCPA and the ABC are attempts by developed countries' governments to clean up business practices abroad, and prevent firms from being subject to extortion by corrupt foreign government officials. So far, there seems to be minimal evidence that these efforts have been effective, but they have taught foreign officials that it was useless to request bribes from developed countries' companies, and, in that respect, these efforts have worked. There is substantial grumbling, though, in the export community that the FCPA and the ABC have cost developed countries' exporters billions of dollars in lost business to foreign competitors that are unimpeded by such laws and can deduct bribes as a business expense.

From a practical standpoint, for any exporter, the rules are fairly simple: business abroad must be conducted aboveboard and remain within the boundaries set in the original agency or distributorship contracts.

Review and Discussion Questions

1. What are the principal differences between an agent and a distributor?

2. What are the different methods of entry regrouped under the term "indirect export"?

3. Using a product and country of your choice, determine what would be the best method of entry for an exporter interested in that market. Justify your decision using the guidelines provided in the chapter.

4. Why would a company decide to franchise abroad?

5. What advantages does a foreign trade zone represent for an importer/exporter?

6. What are the advantages and disadvantages of using a subsidiary rather than a joint venture, for a firm interested in manufacturing abroad?

Notes

[1] Pomerantz, Kenneth, and Steven Topik, *The world that trade created*, 2013, M.E. Sharpe, Armonk, New York, 2013.

[2] *Foreign Market Entry, Breaking into the Trade Game*, Small Business Administration, 3rd ed.,http://www.tfrec.wsu.edu/pdfs/P2345.pdf, retrieved October 1, 2016.

[3] Root, Franklin R., *Entry Strategies for International Markets*, Revised and Expanded Edition. New York: Lexington Books, 1994.

[4] Lymbersky, Christoph, *Market Entry Strategies*, First International Edition, Management Laboratory Press, Hamburg, Germany, 2008.

[5] Phillips, Michael M., "Carving out an Export Industry, and Hope, in Africa," *The Wall Street Journal*, July 18, 1996, p. A10.

[6] Ghana Trade, http://ghanatrade.gov.gh/Handicraft-Gift-Items/, retrieved November 4, 2016.

[7] Dugger, Celia, "Peace Prize to Pioneer of Loans to Poor No Bank Would Touch," *The New York Times*, October 14, 2006.

[8] Lacey, Marc, "US Trade Law Gives Africa Hope and Hard Jobs," *The New York Times*, November 14, 2003

[9] Bello, Daniel C., and Ritu Lohtia, "Export Channel Design: The Use of Foreign Distributors and Agents," *Journal of the Academy of Marketing Science*, Spring 1995, pp. 83Ü93.

[10] Root, Franklin R., *Entry Strategies for International Markets*, Revised and Expanded Edition. New York: Lexington Books, 1994.

[11] Shirouzu, Norihiko, "In Japan, Breaking Up Can Be Hard to Do," *The Wall Street Journal*, December 31, 1997, p. A7.

[12] Whalen, Jeanne, "Cool in Kyrgyzstan: a Scottish Pet Store and its Red Parrot," *The Wall Street Journal*, May 2, 2000, p. A1, http://www.wsj.com/articles/SB957220318617993860, retrieved November 22, 2016.

[13] Martin, Josh, "Profitable Supply Chain," *The Journal of Commerce*, March 11, 1998, p. 1C.

[14] Bianchi, Stefania, and Sabrina Cohen, "Libya Opens Doors to Foreign Banks," *The Wall Street Journal*, February 16, 2010.

[15] "McDonald's," *Entrepreneur*, https://www.entrepreneur.com/franchises/mcdonalds/282570, retrieved December 5, 2016.

[16] McDonald's Corporation, *Discover McDonald's Around the World*, http://corporate.mcdonalds.com/mcd/country/map.html, retrieved November 25, 2016.

[17] *List of countries with McDonald's restaurants*, wikipedia.org, https://en.wikipedia.org/wiki/List_of_countries_with_McDonald's_restaurants, retrieved November 25, 2016

[18] Gibson, Richard, "Some franchisees say Moves by McDonald's hurt their Operations," *The Wall Street Journal*, April 17, 1996, p. A1

[19] "Management's Discussion and Analysis of Financial Condition and Results of Operations," *McDonald's 2012 Annual Report*, http://www.aboutmcdonalds.com/mcd/investors/annual_reports.html, retrieved
June 10, 2013.

[20] Hennessy, Selah, "McDonald's Olympic Restaurant is Company's Busiest," *Voice of America*, August 7, 2012, http://www.voanews.com/content/temporary_olympic_park_mcdonalds_company_busiest/1475424.-
html, retrieved June 10, 2013.

[21] *McDonald's 2015 Annual Report*, http://corporate.mcdonalds.com/content/dam/AboutMcDonalds-

/Investors 2/2015 Annual Report.pdf, retrieved November 25, 2016.

[22] Engardio, Pete, and Michael Shari, "The Suharto Empire," *Business Week*, August 19, 1996, pp. 46-50.

[23] Garcia-Castro, Roberto, "Governing Joint Ventures In China: Lessons from Success and Failure," *The IFCAI [Institute of Chartered Financial Analysts of India] University Journal of Mergers and Acquisitions*, March 2009, http://www.iupindia.org/309/IJMA_Governing_Joint_Ventures_7.html.

[24] Bradsher, Keith, "After Latin Venture Fails, Volkswagen Succeeds and Ford Scrambles," *The New York Times*, May 16, 1997.

[25] "Global FDI Recovery Derails," *Global Investment Trends Monitor*, January 23, 2013, unctad.org/en/PublicationsLibrary/webdiaeia2013d1_en.pdf, retrieved June 10, 2013.

[26] Ross, Emily, "Sack with Care," *Business Management*, Compak 2006 Supplement, http://www.vcta.asn.au/files/2006%20files/compak06/May/BM206_2.pdf, accessed June 6, 2006.

[27] "Kraft Foods Cuts Australian Jobs, Moves to China," *China SCR: News & Views on Corporate Social Responsibility in China*, January 12, 2006, http://www.chinacsr.com/2006/01/12/kraft-foods-cuts-australian-jobs-moves-to-china.

[28] Greenhouse, Linda, "Court Ruling Helps 'Gray Market' in U.S. Goods," *The New York Times*, March 10, 1998.

[29] Chester, James, "Policing and Protecting U.S. Intellectual Property Rights at the Border," Chester and Associates, March 28, 2008, http://www.tradelawfirm.com/sitebuildercontent/sitebuilderfiles/protect_ip_at_border.pdf.

[30] "Intellectual Property Rights—Fiscal Year 2014 Seizure Statistics," February 25, 2015, U.S. Customs and Border Protection, https://www.cbp.gov/sites/default/files/documents/2014 IPR Stats.pdf, retrieved November 26, 2016.

[31] Balfour, Frederik, "Fakes: The Global Counterfeiting Business is Out of Control, Targeting Everything from Computer Chips to Life-Saving Medicines. It's So Bad That Even China May Need to Crack Down," *Business Week*, February 7, 2005, pp. 54-64.

[32] Fishman, Ted C., "Manufaketure," *The New York Times*, January 9, 2005.

[33] McDonald, Mark, "From Milk to Peas, a Chinese Food-Safety Mess," *The New York Times*, June 21, 2012.

[34] Chester, James, "Foreign Trade Zones; Creating Profits through Savings," Chester and Associates, March 28, 2008, http://www.tradelawfirm.com/sitebuildercontent/sitebuilderfiles/FTZ_ppt.pdf.

[35] "Waigaoqiao: the First Free Trade Zone in China," *China Economic Review*, May 12, 2009, http://www.chinaeconomicreview.com/node/49471, retrieved June 10, 2013.

[36] *Free Zones in Uruguay*, January 2015, Uruguay XXI, Investment and Export Promotion Agency, http://www.uruguayxxi.gub.uy/guide/descargas/Zonas Francas - Uruguay XXI.pdf, retrieved November 27, 2016.

[37] Calabrese, Dan, "Business Guide to Tax Evasion (Relax, It's Perfectly Legal)," *Inbound Logistics*, January 2009, pp. 171-179.

[38] Tirschwell, Peter, "The ABCs of FSCs," *The Journal of Commerce*, November 29, 1997, p. 1C.

[39] "Overview of the Foreign Sales Corporation/Extraterritorial Income (FSC/ETI) Exclusion," The Tax Foundation, January 2, 2002, http://www.taxfoundation.org/news/show/154.html, retrieved June 10, 2013.

[40] Losi, Ryan, "The Domestic Production Deduction: Does it apply to you?", Virginia International Trade, http://www.exportvirginia.org/newsletter/articles/archives/piascik.htm, retrieved May 23, 2009.

[41] Heafield, Karl, and Stanley Rose, "United States: Double-Dipping Deductions with DPAD," August 15, 2016, *Mondaq*, http://www.mondaq.com/unitedstates/x/519022/Corporate+Tax/DoubleDipping-+Deductions+With+DPAD, retrieved November 22, 2016.

[42] *Ibid.*

[43] Zerbe, Dean, "IC-DISC: The Big Tax Break for Exporters," *Forbes*, March 29, 2011, http://www.forbes.com/sites/deanzerbe/2011/03/29/ic-disc-the-big-tax-break-for-exporters/, retrieved June 10, 2013.

[44] Buck, Samuel, "Benefits of Interest Charge Domestic International Sales Corporations," December 1, 2014, *The Tax Adviser*, http://www.thetaxadviser.com/issues/2014/dec/tax-clinic-01.html, retrieved November 22, 2016.

[45] *Annual Report 2013*, OECD Working Group on Bribery, http://www.oecd.org/daf/anti-bribery/oecd-workinggrouponbribery-annualreport.
htm, retrieved June 10, 2013.

[46] "Update of Country Descriptions of Tax Legislation on the Tax Treatment of Bribes," Organisation for Economic Co-operation and Development, October 1, 2007, http://www.oecd.org/dataoecd/42/43/-37116153.pdf, retrieved June 10, 2013.

[47] "FCPA penalties for individuals and entities," World Compliance, http://www.fcpa-worldcompliance.com/resources/fcpa-penalties.html,
retrieved June 10, 2013.

[48] Chester, James, "Guide to the FCPA," Chester and Associates, April 17, 2007, http://www.tradelawfirm.com/sitebuildercontent/sitebuilderfiles/fcpa.pdf.

Chapter 5

International Contracts

When a firm gets involved in international business, it enters into several contracts, either written or implied, with many partners, some of which are located abroad. Examples of such contracts include:

- The contract of sale between the exporter and the importer

- The contract of insurance between the exporter or the importer (depending on the terms of sale, which will be covered in Chapter 6) and an insurance company (covered in Chapter 10)

- The contract of carriage between the exporter or the importer and the shipping line

- The contract between an exporter and its agent or distributor

- The contract between an exporter or an importer and its bank, regarding payment arrangements such as documentary collection or letters of credit (concepts that will be covered in Chapter 7)

These contracts are formed under the precepts of many traditions, local laws, multilateral governmental agreements, and international treaties that are sometimes not ratified or only partially ratified by some countries. Frequently, these contracts are further complicated by a profoundly different understanding of what a contract represents. Nevertheless, international traders and logistics managers have learned to operate within this complex framework.

5.1 *Lex Mercatoria*

Lex Mercatoria
The body of laws and international agreements that govern the relationships and contracts between international parties.

When a contract is established between two parties in the same country, the law governing the execution of this contract is clearly determined by that country's legal system. In the United States, for example, it is the Uniform Commercial Code (UCC), in France, it is the *Code de Commerce Français*, in Germany, it is the *Handelsgesetzbuch*, and in Japan it is the *shōhō*. All domestic legal systems include ample jurisprudence and expertise to determine how contracts should be executed. However, when the contract is between two parties in different countries, no specific laws govern this contract, except what is called *Lex Mercatoria*—trade law—which is composed of a multitude of international agreements and international trade customs, all of which complement domestic laws.

Lex Mercatoria is complex because it includes many different sources of law and jurisprudence. It includes United Nations treaties and other decisions; international agreements, such as the General Agreement on Tariffs and Trade (GATT), which has given rise to the World Trade Organization (WTO) with its own rules and court system; multilateral agreements on specific industry issues, such as the Warsaw Convention on international air transport or the textile Multi-Fiber Agreement; regional agreements, such as the European Union and the North American Free Trade Agreement (NAFTA); bilateral agreements, such as the Open Skies agreement between the United States and the Netherlands (see Chapter 12) and the special status granted to Hong Kong by the People's Republic of China; International Chamber of Commerce rules, such as the Incoterms® rules for terms of trade (see Chapter 6) and the UCP-600 for bank documentary credits (see Chapter 7); and arbitration decisions and jurisprudence, established by the International Chamber of Commerce Arbitration Court or private arbitrators. In addition, many states*—countries—pick and choose which treaties they will ratify and, on occasion, which articles of the treaties they will ratify. They can also choose to become only signatories to a treaty, which means they do not make a full commitment to its terms. In addition, states can decide to abide by the terms of a treaty, but not ratify it. Finally, things get even more interesting when courts decide that some domestic principle cannot be violated by an international convention or custom, even if the country has ratified the agreement.

The United States is an exception in many ways regarding its compliance with *Lex Mercatoria.* The courts of the United States generally do not use jurisprudence established in other countries, or decisions made by international bodies, in their decisions. The courts' position is that laws are the results of a democratic process and that neither foreign courts nor international bodies are elected by U.S. nationals, and therefore their decisions cannot be binding.[1] The counter-argument is that the United States, by following such policies, is isolating itself from the rest of the world. The debate is far from settled.[2]

This chapter does not attempt to cover *Lex Mercatoria* in depth. Only an overview of three of its major elements is presented here. The first part of the Chapter covers the issues regarding the contract of sale between an exporter and an importer, which, for most countries, are covered by the United Nations Convention on Contracts for the International Sale of Goods (CISG), also known as the Vienna Convention. The second part of the chapter covers the issues regarding contracts between exporters and agents and contracts between exporters and distributors, as well as the resolution of eventual disputes through the arbitration system. The third part of the chapter lists the primary clauses of typical contracts between exporters and their international partners.

The specific aspects of contracts as they pertain to the terms of sale—the International Commercial Terms (Incoterms® rules) of the International Chamber of Commerce (ICC)—will be covered in Chapter 6. Contracts relating to banking and payments will be covered in Chapter 7, insurance contracts will be covered in Chapter 10, and contracts of carriage between shippers and carriers will be covered in Chapters 11 and 12.

5.2 International Sales Contracts and the CISG

Whether a sales contract is considered "international" is not always evident. Courts generally look at two criteria to decide whether a contract is international:

Convention on Contracts for the International Sale of Goods
A United Nations' treaty that acts as international sales law.

---

*It is important to note that, in an international context, the meaning of "state" is that of "country." Readers in the United States should be mindful of the distinction. International agreements are signed by the United States of America at the federal level, and individual U.S. states do not have the power to enter into international agreements.

the economic criterion, that is, whether there was a transaction that involved a transfer of merchandise from one country to another, and its mirror image of a transfer of funds; and the judicial criterion, which is based on whether the transaction has links to the laws of different states.[3] For example, a sale of office supplies to a French company's subsidiary located in Germany by a German supplier is not considered international, because it does not involve two countries; however, the same sale to the company's headquarters, located just across the border, is international. Whenever there is a sales contract between two parties in two different countries, the domestic laws no longer apply, and it is governed by the Vienna Convention.[4]

Figure 5.1: The United Nations Complex in Vienna, Austria
Photo ©Radu Bercan/Shutterstock. Used with permission.

Vienna Convention
Another name for the Convention on Contracts for the International Sale of Goods.

The Vienna Convention, or CISG, was born in 1980 of two other conventions, the Uniform Law for the International Sale of Goods (ULIS) and the Uniform Law on the Formation of Contracts for the International Sale of Goods (ULF). Both had been written in The Hague in 1964 but had been ratified by only a few countries because they were somewhat deficient.[5] In contrast, the CISG has been ratified by more than 84 countries,[6] whose export and import activities represent more than 80 percent of all world trade. The major exception to the list of developed countries that have signed the CISG is the United Kingdom, whose "[m]inisters do not see the ratification of the Convention as a legislative priority" and therefore have not taken the time to introduce legislation to ratify it in the last 36 years.[7] As often is the case, though, several countries, including the United States, have not ratified all of the Convention and have left out some provisions, some of which may have conflicted with domestic law.

The CISG has nevertheless become the law of international contracts, as traders will often elect to have their contracts governed by the laws of a contracting state, and therefore the CISG will apply. For example, even though the United States is not a full signatory to the CISG, transactions between United States companies and their counterparts abroad fall under the Vienna Convention if the country of the other party is a signatory to the CISG. In addition, U.S. companies have the right to "opt in" or "opt out" of the CISG by specifying, in the language of the contract, the particular law to apply to the contract. This point must be specific, though: "The choice-of-law provision must expressly exclude application of the CISG because without an express exclusion, CISG will govern."[8] By choosing to have "the laws of the State of Texas" apply to a contract, a company actually elects to have the CISG apply, because the State of Texas operates within the U.S. federal system, which includes all treaties in force, including the CISG.[9]

The CISG is substantially different from the UCC—the Uniform Commercial Code, or the commercial law of the United States—in a few of its aspects, notably the contract formation and remedies for non-conforming goods or late delivery. It also differs from several other countries' domestic laws, as evidenced by the number of countries that have not ratified specific articles of the CISG. Although these exclusions may make good political fodder, they may not be acceptable to courts that handle disputes between traders located in countries that have adopted different versions of the CISG, or have amended it to include some other interpretation.[10]

5.2.1 Contract Formation

The CISG does not consider that a contract has been accepted until both parties agree to all terms. It is customary for a seller to make an offer. The buyer may respond positively, but indicate that it wants a different schedule of delivery or term of payment, or some other aspect of the transaction to be handled differently. Under the UCC of the United States, such a response is construed as an acceptance of the offer. Under the CISG, it is understood as a rejection of the offer, and as a counter-offer by the buyer, unless the suggested changes do not materially affect the contract. The CISG specifies that changes to "price, payment, quality, and quantity of the goods, place, and time of delivery, extent of one party's liability to the other—most likely to be understood as an Incoterms® rule (see Chapter 6)—or the settlement of disputes are considered to alter the terms of the offer materially," and therefore that no acceptance is made in those cases.[11]

Another difference between the UCC and the CISG regarding offer and acceptance of a sales contract is what is referred to by U.S. lawyers as the "Battle of the Forms." For most businesses, an offer or an acceptance is made on a

simple signatory
The first step in the acceptance of a treaty by a state. It signs it to indicate that it agrees with its premises, but it will need to ratify it before it is bound by it.

full signatory
The acceptance of a treaty by a state. It signs it to indicate that it agrees with its premises, without further ratification.

ratification
The process by which a state fully accepts to be bound by an international treaty. It makes it part of its national legislation by having its Congress vote on it.

Uniform Commercial Code
The set of federal laws that govern commercial contracts in the United States.

offer
The first step in the formation of a contract. The contract is initiated when one of the parties makes an offer to the other.

acceptance
The second step in the formation of the contract. After the offer is made, the other party accepts the terms offered.

rejection
An intermediary step in the formation of the contract. After the offer is made, the other party rejects the terms offered and makes a counter-offer.

standard business form, with many small-print statements pre-printed on it, designed to protect the interests of the party writing the offer (or the acceptance). In most instances, these pre-printed clauses do not match. Under the UCC, the courts have determined that these differences do not matter in the formation of a contract, unless they significantly affect the contract terms, and regard these differing terms as additions to the contract terms, to be sorted out by the court in case of conflict. Under the CISG, the requirement of a mirror image may signify a return to what, for Americans, would be the pre-UCC rules, where the contract terms are determined by the terms pre-printed on the form of the party "firing the last shot." Then again, it may signify that there is no contract until all terms match, with little tolerance for differences.[12] There is little evidence that the second interpretation is likely to prevail, especially if both parties thought there was a contract and acted accordingly.

counter-offer
An intermediary step in the formation of the contract. After the offer is made, the other party does not accept the terms offered, and proposes modifications ot the terms of the contract.

5.2.2   Creation of the Contract

The CISG treats the length of time during which the offer is considered outstanding differently than the UCC does. Most offers contain a clause stating that the offer is open until a certain date; under the UCC, however, the offer can be withdrawn at any time, without prejudice, for almost any reason. Under the CISG, the offer cannot be withdrawn by the seller (or the buyer) before its expiration date, and the other party can accept it at any time until that time. The offer is considered irrevocable.

The CISG does not dictate that contracts of sale must be written: any agreement between a seller and a buyer can form a contract. Obviously, the issues of the proof of the existence of a contract, and of the terms of the contract, then become difficult to determine unless there are witnesses to the discussion between seller and buyer. Even when a contract of sale is signed, the written contract terms can be superseded by an oral exchange between the two parties, as long as there is evidence that it was the intent of both parties. In one of the jurisprudence cases contained in the United Nations Commission on International Trade Law (UNCITRAL) database—called CLOUT, for the Case Law on UNCITRAL texts—two witnesses corroborated that the written terms of the contract had been modified orally by the seller and the buyer, and the modifications were used by the court in determining the case.[13] In contrast, the UCC requires that any sales agreement above U.S. $500 be in writing.

5.2.3   Breach of Contract

breach
In the event that one of the parties to a contract does not meet its obligation, that is in *breach* of the contract.

Finally, the CISG treats non-conforming goods and delays in shipments much differently than the UCC. Whereas the UCC applies the "perfect tender" principle (*i.e.*, the goods must exactly conform to the goods contracted and be delivered within the framework specified in the contract), the CISG grants the seller more latitude. For example, the buyer cannot refuse or cancel delivery unless the non-conformity or the delay "substantially deprives the buyer of what it was entitled to expect under the contract and, even then, only if the seller foresaw, or a party in its position would have foreseen, such a result."[14] In other words, the buyer cannot avoid the contract unless the seller performs a fundamental breach of the contract. Therefore, firms operating on a just-in-time basis should specifically notify their suppliers that they are following a just-in-time manufacturing policy, so that suppliers can then "foresee" the problem that a delay in shipment causes.

In counterbalance, the CISG allows the buyer to unilaterally apply a price reduction to the contracted amount for non-conforming goods. Such a price reduction should be proportional to the goods' loss of value (percentage that is non-conforming) or to the loss of market incurred by the buyer in the event of a delay. However, the burden placed on the buyer to notify the seller in a timely manner, and to explain which remedy it will seek has a high threshold. The notification must be made as soon as possible; it must be clear and painstakingly detailed in the description of the problem, and it must be extremely clear and specific in the remedies sought. Several cases in CLOUT (given by McMahon[15]) show that the burden placed on the buyer by the courts seems unduly harsh. In addition, this issue is somewhat moot for a buyer paying on a letter of credit (see Chapter 7), because it is committed to pay the full amount in all cases. Finally, the buyer's notification to the seller that a price reduction will unilaterally be applied must be made within two years; such a long upper limit is also of concern, because the statute of limitations for claims against a carrier may be shorter than two years in some countries, preventing the seller from recovering damages caused by a carrier.[16]

5.3 Agency versus Distributorship Legal Issues

The second type of contract of interest are contracts between an exporter and its representatives in foreign markets—either an agent or a distributor. To briefly repeat content covered in Chapter 4, an agent is a representative located abroad that earns a commission on the sales it makes on behalf of the exporter. An agent cannot negotiate prices, delivery, or other sales terms with the buyer, but only represents the decisions made by the exporter. In contrast, a distributor is also located abroad, but it purchases goods from the exporter, with the intention of reselling them in its country, earning a profit in the process. The distributor sets its own prices and has an inventory of goods to sell. It is also most often responsible for after-sale service.

It is difficult to generalize about agency and distributorship agreements: there is no international agreement on the way each of these relationships is governed. In most cases, the country of residence of the agent or distributor considers that it has jurisdiction over the agreement, and in many cases, regardless of the fact that the agreement may specify that the laws of another country apply to the contract (see Section 5.7.8 on page 165 and Section 5.7.9 on page 166 for specific information regarding the Choice of Law and the Choice of Forum in an international distribution contract). Because each country has its own laws and regulations regarding these distribution agreements and because the jurisprudence of each country may differ on similar statutes, it is difficult to be specific without getting into tedious listings of countries. Therefore, only broader issues will be covered, to determine which aspects of a distribution contract should be examined.

5.3.1   Contract Law versus Labor Law

distribution contract
A contract between an exporter and an overseas intermediary, whether an agent or a distributor.

In the absence of specifics, agreements between an exporter and an agent and agreements between an exporter and a distributor will be called distribution contracts. One of the greatest differences among countries is whether the countries consider such distribution agreements as contracts between equal or unequal partners.

If the contract is regarded as being between two equal parties, courts will consider the terms of the contract when handling a dispute. This approach is referred to as contract law or case law, where the question is resolved by trying to interpret the meaning of the contract between the two parties. Both parties are considered to have equal sophistication in dealing with legal matters, and therefore neither of the parties would have entered a contract without understanding its terms. Most countries, but certainly not all, consider that agreements between an exporter and a distributor are agreements between equals. The contract between the two parties is the framework that courts use in deciding a dispute between the two parties. When the contract is silent about the point in contention, then the courts use jurisprudence based on what other contracts of the same type have established.

contract law
A set of laws that govern relationships established by contracts between two parties.

labor law
A set of laws that govern relationships between employees and employers.

In other cases, though, countries equate an international distribution agreement as something like an employment contract, where the parties are considered unequal in their ability to interpret and understand a legal contract, and therefore the weaker party must be protected. This point of view calls for the application of labor law, or for the application of special statutes that specifically deal with the relationship between an exporter and an agent, or an exporter and a distributor. Such statutes cannot be overruled by the terms of the contract. Therefore, the courts, in ruling in a dispute between the two contract parties, will ignore the terms of the contract and use the laws of the country in which the agent or distributor is located. Most countries that follow such an interpretation tend to protect agents rather than distributors—Belgium being the lone country protecting distributors but not agents[17]—but several protect both. In addition, this point of view does not depend on whether the agent or distributor is an individual or a corporation. Labor law has been used to supersede contracts between an exporter and an incorporated agent.

5.3.2   Home Government Restrictions

Some countries use specific statutes to regulate international distribution agreements because they feel that they need to protect agents or distributors against contracts that may not be fair or equitable. Specifically, countries want to protect agents or distributors against wrongful or abusive termination (this aspect of international distribution contracts is covered in Section 5.4 on page 156).

In addition, those governments can also construct complicated systems to manage agents and distributors operating within their borders. The governments can require the agents and distributors to formalize and legally record their relationships with their principals. This process of registration is not unlike the process of joining a professional association, but it often doubles as a tax. Governments can also require that the agents and distributors be nationals of the country in which they represent the exporter; such is the case in most Middle Eastern countries. Governments can also mandate that the terms of the contracts be inspected by their administration—to monitor the commissions paid to agents, for example, which they sometimes limit with a floor or a ceiling. Other governments allow only exclusive agents or distributors—a single agent or distributor within a specific geographic area, usually the country itself—as do most South American countries. Finally, some governments simply do not allow agents at all—they mandate a distributor—or not allow any third-party representation, coercing exporters to establish a subsidiary, from which they can then collect income tax. Unfortunately, it is difficult to generalize about these different requirements, as they are country specific. They even vary from one region of a country to another, as shown in the laws of the State of Louisiana, which are in contrast with the laws of nearly all other states in the United States, or of the laws of the Alsace-Lorraine region, which are significantly different from those in the remainder of France. In addition, such regulations can change at any time. Specific legal expertise and advice is therefore necessary before writing a distribution contract in any country.

registration
For an agent or a distributor, the process of notifying the importing country's government that it is entering a distribution agreement with an exporter.

5.3.3 Other Issues in Agency and Partnership Agreements

There are two additional issues with which an exporter should be familiar in the context of an international distribution agreement, whether with a foreign agent or with a foreign distributor.

- The first is specific to U.S. exporters: because the agent or the distributor acts as a representative of the U.S. exporter, the Foreign Corrupt Practices Act applies (see Section 4.7.4 on page 141). Therefore, the exporter is liable for unlawful actions taken by the agent or distributor, even if the exporter had no knowledge of or control over the agent's actions.[18] This law places a particular burden on U.S. exporting companies that other countries governed by the OECD's Anti-Bribery Convention and their exporters do not have to carry. Other countries' courts do not recognize agents as a "directing mind" employed by the exporter.[19]

- The second is valid for all exporters: whenever an exporter enters an international distributorship agreement with an agent or a distributor, it must guard against the possible perception that the parties are entering into a partnership agreement, rather than a contract in which one party is committing to using the services of the other. If the exporter and its agent or distributor are portraying themselves as partners to other parties, then they are also indicating that they are jointly assuming each other's liabilities. This representation can present substantial risk for both parties.[20]

5.4   Termination

The most sensitive issue in an international distribution contract is the issue of termination, or the act of ending the relationship between the exporter and the agent or the exporter and the distributor. All contracts contain a termination clause, which includes a pre-termination notice and specifies termination compensation.

- A pre-termination notice specifies how many days the exporter must give to the agent or the distributor before the termination becomes effective. This duration usually is shorter for agents than it is for distributors, but country statutes can extend it beyond the contractual agreement. Some contracts call for no pre-termination notice—the contract is canceled immediately upon notice[21]—and some go for as long as one year.

- Termination compensation, often called a "goodwill compensation," is equivalent to the amount of income the agent or distributor would have earned for a certain period. This compensation can be as low as zero, and as high as two years' worth of income. Again, this provision of the contract may be rendered null by the importing country's statutes, which may mandate a specific compensation.

Pre-termination notice and termination compensation can be determined by the terms of the contract, but the terms are often superseded by the statutes of the country in which the agent or the distributor is located. There are so many disparities and criteria that it is difficult to determine the requirements of a particular country. The European Union has attempted to reduce the differences between its member states' requirements,[22] but has not been successful.

The specific elements of a termination clause depend on the reason behind the termination of the contract, which can be for either just cause or convenience.

5.4.1   Just Cause

termination for "just cause"
The unilateral decision, by one of the parties to a contract, to terminate the contract because the other party has not met the terms of the agreement.

Termination for "just cause" is triggered when either of the parties (exporter, agent, or distributor) is not honoring the contract terms. Generally, the agent or distributor is not doing something that it is contractually obligated to do, such as meeting the sales performance objectives, spending a certain percentage of sales on advertising, or maintaining the type of establishment spelled out in the contract. Alternatively, the representative is doing something that it is contractually not allowed to do: for example, selling competitors' products, applying for patent protection on the improvements it has made to the products, or keeping the list of customers a secret. Section 5.7.1 explains these terms in greater detail. Only in a few cases is just-cause termination due to the exporter not performing its obligations, such as not providing the agent with prompt *pro forma* invoices or not shipping diligently, but it can happen.

In any case, it is relatively easy to terminate a contract for just cause, as there is a reason to terminate it. In most instances, the guilty party is not entitled to much compensation or many days' notice. Nevertheless, national statutes may still supersede the agreement in such cases, and mandate a minimum notice period and a minimum compensation, even though there is breach of the contract.

5.4.2 Convenience

Termination for convenience can occur for any reason other than non-performance. Termination for convenience can be triggered by any of the parties, but generally, the exporter is the party seeking to terminate the contract. One of the most egregious—but unfortunately common—reasons is that the representative is very successful and the exporter realizes that the agent is earning too much in commissions and wants to replace it with a sales subsidiary. Another reason for termination is a change in the exporter's strategy that modifies how the exporter intends to enter foreign markets, or, worse, necessitates a complete retrenchment in the domestic market. In any case, the termination is not linked to a lack of performance by one of the parties on the terms of the contract, but due to some other, non-contract-related, reason.

> **termination for "convenience"**
> The unilateral decision, by one of the parties to a contract, to terminate the contract for reasons unrelated to the performance of the contract by the other party.

A termination for convenience should be handled with great care, as the potential for damages to the spurned party can be substantial; in those cases, a lengthy termination notice, as well as a generous goodwill compensation package, is the only way to ensure no litigation and a smooth(er) termination. If there are issues to resolve, such as inventories of unsold merchandise or outstanding orders, every effort should be made by the exporter to compensate the distributor or the agent. If compensation is not offered, the representatives can easily ask courts to intervene. In most instances, courts look upon terminations for convenience harshly, sometimes assimilating distributors to agents so as to give them the advantages that the statutes of their country give agents. These statutes usually mandate long notice periods and generous compensation packages. Belgian courts granted three months of income to a distributor in compensation for a contract that lasted only four months, and three years of profits in compensation to a distributor who was associated with a manufacturer for 22 years but had been fairly unsuccessful, with yearly sales of only BFr. 1,400,000 or roughly U.S. $28,000 at that time.[23]

> **litigation**
> The final process by which parties to a contract have to settle a dispute, in a court of law.

Unfortunately, in a termination for convenience, going to court may be the best-case scenario, as several injured representatives have sabotaged the efforts of the exporter later on, through various means, from mentioning to customers the callous treatment suffered at the hands of the exporter, to attracting new competitors into the market.

5.5   Arbitration

arbitration
A process by which parties
to a contract choose to
settle a dispute. An
arbitration decision is
binding on both parties.

Arbitration is fast becoming the preferred way of resolving disputes between international partners. In 1960, the International Chamber of Commerce (ICC) received about 50 requests for arbitration; in 1999, it received 529 requests, [24] and in 2014, 791 requests. On these 791 requests, the ICC rendered approximately 500 awards.[25] The ICC developed its own *Rules of Conciliation and Arbitration* in 1988, and revised them in 2011, as *Arbitration and ADR Rules*[26] (ADR stands for Amicable Dispute Resolutions) which are translated in thirteen languages. However, there are many alternative venues for arbitration: the London Court of International Arbitration oversaw 288 disputes in 2015, the International Centre for Dispute Resolution presided over 1,052 arbitrations, the Stockholm Chamber of Commerce managed 77, the China International Economic and Trade Arbitration Commission oversaw 386 international cases,[27] and countless individual law firms that specialize in this function, many of which are in Switzerland.

The advantages of arbitration over court litigation are many:

- Arbitration tends to be perceived as fair. Arbitration panels are not a court

Figure 5.2: The Arbitration Building in Lipetsk, Russia
Photo ©Sergey Lavrentev/Shutterstock. Used with permission.

in either of the parties' countries, and therefore are perceived as being more independent and even-handed. This is, of course, only a perception, because courts in any developed country using a modern commercial code are fair, but this perception is often important when dealing with sensitive litigants.

- Arbitration tends to be more expeditious than litigation. Arbitration panels are numerous and do not have the backlog that traditional courts have, which are generally understaffed and overworked. In some countries, commercial disputes can drag on for years: in India, one of the worst cases, there are more than 31 million backlogged civil cases—by the government's own admission—many of which have gone on for more than ten years! In 2010, the High Court estimated that it would take 320 years to clear the backlog.[28]

- Arbitration tends to be more efficient. Because arbitration panels do not have to follow the same rules of evidence as courts, proceedings go much faster, and testimony can be given more efficiently. Because other procedures are also simplified—there is no pre-trial discovery—an arbitration meeting generally lasts a few days, whereas a lawsuit can take weeks or longer.

- Arbitration panels tend to provide more creative solutions. Arbitrators seek to resolve the dispute to the satisfaction of both parties and can find compromises that are impossible in a formal court, where one party has to win, and the other party loses. There is also the possibility of iterative negotiations between the parties and the arbitration panel, a process that can lead to an acceptable compromise. Courts do not have this freedom.

- Arbitration tends to be more effective. Arbitrators generally have a wealth of experience in international business matters and can quickly understand the pertinent issues, draw on their experience and knowledge of arbitration jurisprudence, and settle the dispute to the satisfaction of both parties more effectively than a local court that has to adjudicate mostly domestic cases, and therefore has limited international-business experience.

- Arbitration is not open to the public. Whereas court decisions are generally published and available to all, arbitration decisions are private, and only the parties involved know what steps were taken to resolve the dispute. This can lead to compromises that some litigants would not accept if they were made public.

- Probably most importantly, arbitration is cheaper. All the previous advantages tend to lower litigation costs. In addition, these lower costs are generally shared by the parties in dispute, whereas court costs are usually borne by the loser, a custom called "European rules"; however, in court disputes adjudicated in the United States, both parties pay their own costs.

litigation
The final process by which parties to a contract have to settle a dispute, in a court of law.

The only way to ensure arbitration in the case of a dispute between the exporter and its representatives abroad is to include a clause directing that "any dispute [...] shall be finally settled in accordance with the *Arbitration and ADR Rules* of the International Chamber of Commerce."

5.6 Mediation

mediation
A process by which parties to a contract choose to find a compromise in a dispute. A mediation recommendation is not binding.

Mediation is a process by which a third party attempts to find a middle ground between the parties that are having a dispute. The mediator often shuttles between the two companies and seeks to find a solution acceptable to both parties. Most mediators have a legal background or know the particulars of an industry; mediators can be found through referrals and within the trade associations of many industries.

Mediation presents several advantages over litigation or arbitration, including:

- Mediation is less formal. The parties in a dispute are often reluctant to enter arbitration because it is a formal process, taking place over a few days, involving meetings in a neutral venue, and restricted to a few individual managers. Litigation is even more formal. Mediation is often conducted over a longer period, each party having the opportunity to meet with the mediator in its own corporate environment, and the mediator meeting with many different people in both organizations, to get a better idea of the issue.

- Mediation is non-binding. It can be the first step in resolving a dispute and can help both parties assess how their positions are perceived by unrelated parties. In other words, it is an indicator to both parties of the strength of their respective positions and of their probabilities of winning an arbitration hearing or a court case.

- Mediation is more practical for smaller disputes and when parties are interested in keeping a business relationship. Unfortunately, arbitration—and certainly litigation—commonly results in severing all commercial relationships between both parties. Mediation allows both parties to resolve a dispute without affecting the remainder of their business.

- Mediation is often best for disputes that have arisen from misunderstandings. Both parties are unable to reach a compromise because they do not understand what the other was trying to accomplish, and the mediator can help them reach that middle ground.

Mediation is often the best approach when there is a genuine interest on the part of both parties to resolve the dispute in a manner that is fair to both parties, and when both parties are interested in resuming normal business relationships as quickly as possible.

Figure 5.3: The Imposing Façade of a Courthouse in Nice, France
Photo ©Victor Kiev/Shutterstock. Used with permission.

5.7 Elements of an Agency or Distributor Contract

There are several points that must be covered in any contract, regardless of the country in which it is used. This section explores many of these mandatory contract elements. Some country-specific requirements can obviously still influence each one.

5.7.1 Contract Language

Because distribution agreements are usually entered into by two parties who do not share a common language, it is often necessary to have these contracts written in two languages. However, as any speaker of a foreign language can attest, it is impossible to accurately and precisely translate contract terminology from one language to another. It is therefore critical to include a clause that specifies that the contract written in Language A is the original contract, the contract written in Language B a translation, and that in case of a dispute or problems of interpretation, the original contract should prevail.

There are exceptions to this practical rule, however. Most international agree-

contract language
The language in which a contract is written. If the contract exists in other languages, those versions are considered translations, and not the original contract.

ments between countries, such as the CISG or the International Chamber of Commerce's Incoterms® rules, are written in several languages, all of which are given the same legal status; they are all "originals," which can sometimes present problems when translations cannot precisely duplicate the meaning of the original agreement. These problems can be avoided in a distribution agreement by having one original agreement and the other clearly labeled as a translation.

5.7.2   Good Faith

good faith
The assumption that both parties entering a contract do not have ulterior, undisclosed, motives.

Another mandatory clause in a distribution agreement states that both parties enter into the agreement in good faith. A contract is entered in good faith when neither party has any ulterior motive about the agreement. It's best to understand good faith as the prerequisite for a contract to be formed: both parties must want to fulfill the terms of the contract, rather than use the contract agreement to dupe the other party into providing some necessary material toward another goal.

The same interpretation of good faith also applies to the terms of the contract; both parties agree that they will adhere to the terms of the contract in good faith (*i.e.*, interpret the terms without trying to distort them to their advantage). Both parties agree to deal fairly with each other and not to attempt to find, in the terms of the contract, loopholes or ways to interpret a clause to their advantage and to the detriment of the other party.

5.7.3   *Force Majeure*

force majeure
An event beyond the control if any of the parties in an agreement that prevents one of the parties from fulfilling its obligations.

All contracts contain some sort of a *force majeure* clause. This is a French expression that translates loosely as "overwhelming power" but which refers to any event that cannot be avoided and for which neither contract party is responsible. Examples of such events include a major storm that sinks the ship carrying products to the distributor, or a fire that prevents a firm from producing the goods on time, civil unrest, or a lengthy strike at a port that delays the delivery of the goods. Contracts always contain a clause that absolves either party from not fulfilling its responsibilities in case of *force majeure*, or a cause of non-performance beyond its control. Generally, there is also some statement that qualifies such exemption of liability to perform, "as long as the affected party resumes the performance of this agreement" after the *force majeure* statement.

Contracts may also contain another legal term, "Acts of God," to address events beyond the control of the parties. However, the concept of *force majeure* is broader. The term "Acts of God" defines only large-scale natural disasters, such as floods or volcanic eruptions, whereas the term *force majeure* defines all events beyond the control of the parties that prevent the fulfillment of the terms of the contract.

5.7.4   Scope of Appointment

The scope-of-appointment clause defines the function that the representative will perform; this clause defines whether the representative is an agent or a distributor. It is generally the first clause in the contract.

The scope-of-appointment clause also indicates the products to which the contract applies, and defines the product lines that the agent or distributor is contracted to sell, identifying which product lines it is allowed to sell and which it is not allowed to sell. There is often language indicating that the representative cannot select the most profitable products and ignore the remainder of the lines; this latter requirement may be expressed in quantitative terms. In addition, a specific list of the products that the representative can sell is often placed in an Appendix and made part of the contract.

The scope-of-appointment clause also refers to the territory of the agreement and to corporate accounts, both of which are defined later in the agreement.

scope of appointment
The scope [products, territory, customers] to the contract applies.

5.7.5 Territory

The territory clause defines the geographical limits within which the agent or distributor is authorized (expected) to sell. It is generally the entire country in which the representative is located, with some possible exceptions. In large countries, there may be a regional appointment, and for regions with limited sales potential, there may be several countries included. The clause also spells out whether the agreement makes the agent or distributor an exclusive representative in that territory, which essentially grants a monopoly to the representative.

territory
The geographical area in which the agent or distributor is restricted/expected to sell.

There are several problems associated with the definition of an exclusive territory, specifically in the European Union (EU). While it is possible to write a contract limiting a representative to a single country's territory, the EU considers that a firm operating in one EU country can also legally sell in any other. It is therefore difficult for the exporter to limit the activities of a representative to a single country—it is contrary to the laws of the EU and has been construed as an antitrust violation[29]—and it is difficult to grant exclusive rights to a territory when neighboring representatives have the right to sell there as well.

exclusive representative
An agent or a distributor that has been granted the right to be the sole representative of the exporter in a given territory.

In many South American countries, the issue is different: unless an international representation agreement specifically spells out that it is non-exclusive, it is always interpreted as an exclusive agreement in that territory.[30]

5.7.6 Corporate Accounts

Some agreements specify which customers remain corporate accounts, or customers to which the representative is not allowed to sell. Generally, corporate accounts are large customers who have negotiated terms that apply to all purchases worldwide. The agreement always includes some provisions under which the list of corporate accounts can be amended.

corporate accounts
The customers to which the agent or distributor is not allowed to sell. These accounts are handled directly by the exporter.

It is important for an exporter to pay close attention to the number of corporate accounts that are included in a representation agreement, because too many of them may discourage the representative. An example of such a counterproductive agreement is one that specifies that all accounts above a certain level of sales automatically become corporate accounts; consequently, a successful agent, after having developed an account and reached that critical level of sales, would see the account removed from its commission basis, and therefore from its income. This is certainly not the way to reward a good representative intent on excelling, and is likely to limit the sales of the exporter, as such a policy encourages the representative to keep sales just below the critical threshold. Thus, accounts originally developed by the agent should be exempt from this policy.

5.7.7   Term of Appointment

term of appointment
The initial duration of the distribution contract, and the duration of its eventual renewal periods.

The term-of-appointment clause determines the duration of the appointment of the representative. The duration must always be a definite period, with the possibility of renewal if certain performance criteria are met.

It is critical to determine the original duration of the contract appropriately. Finding the balance between a sufficiently long appointment period, so that the representative has enough time to develop the market to the point where it is a sustainable venture, and a sufficiently short period, so that an ineffective representative may be removed and replaced without too much of an opportunity cost to the exporter, is a delicate task. Most of the time, the initial appointment period is dictated by market conditions and by the type of product sold. If the representative is expected to do "pioneer sales," in which it must sell a new product with little brand awareness and unique characteristics, a longer period is necessary than for a standard product with a well-known brand and multiple competitors. If the market is characterized by personal contacts and long-term relationships between customers and suppliers, then a longer period is necessary than in a market that is more competitive and fluid.

Once the initial appointment period is complete, the clause also specifies the renewal period and, importantly, the conditions under which the contract will be renewed for that duration. Renewal periods can be similar in duration to the initial appointment period or can be shorter; there are no specific recommendations either way. However, it is important to specify clearly the performance criteria for renewal: level of sales reached, market share obtained, number of customers contacted, amount spent on advertising, number of sales calls made, and so forth. The issue is to make sure that the contract is not automatically renewed.

Should the representative not meet the criteria for renewal at the end of the initial appointment period, then the exporter has two alternatives. It can terminate the contract, which is often a bad solution, unless the representative has done particularly poorly. This is because the exporter is now confronted with the task of finding another representative and providing training to that new representative, possibly delaying the venture by a year or more. Termination also creates ill will: the slighted representative can always retaliate and create problems for the next appointed representative and alienate existing customers by giving them the impression that the exporter is not committed to that market.

The other alternative is to renew the contract. The representative may have failed to achieve the objectives set in the original agreement because of circumstances beyond its control, or because the difficulties of entering the market were underestimated, or because the market potential had been overestimated. In any case, when renewing the contract, it is important to make clear to the representative, in a carefully worded communication, that the terms of the renewal were not met, although the exporter is willing to renew because of the circumstances.

Should such a communication be omitted and the contract be renewed anyhow, it could then be construed by a court as an evergreen contract, that is, a contract with no determined duration, and a contract that can no longer be terminated for non-performance, as there is a precedent of non-performance and simultaneous renewal. Although generally a couple of instances are necessary before such a conclusion is reached, some overprotective courts may not see it that way.

evergreen contract
A contract that, by design or by default, does not have a specified duration.

5.7.8 Choice of Law

Because an international contract has links to the laws of two different countries, different interpretations of specific clauses are quite possible. To avoid interpretation problems, every contract includes a clause that identifies which of the two sets of laws should be used by a court or arbitration panel when a conflict arises. In general, the choice of law is made by the exporter rather than the agent or distributor; however, this does not preclude a possible resolution in the courts of the importing country, which may assume jurisdiction over the contract because of the country's statutes regarding agents or distributors. This is the case when the importing country determines that agency contracts are governed by labor law, for example. In such cases, the contract clause that assigns the choice of law to the exporter's country is ignored: the court will recognize it, but explain why it is not valid.

choice of law
The national laws that govern the terms of the contract.

The choice of law can make a substantial difference in the way a case is resolved. In a well-publicized case, individual American investors in Lloyd's of London insurance syndicates tried to sue the company in U.S. courts to circumvent an exemption from liability from negligence that the company enjoys in the United Kingdom. However, because the contract between the investors and Lloyd's clearly stated that the laws of the United Kingdom would prevail in case of dispute—the choice of law clause—the U.S. Supreme Court ruled that the U.S. courts had no jurisdiction over the dispute,[31] even though such an exemption is contrary to generally accepted principles of law in the United States. The peculiarities of Lloyd's insurance market, as well as its problems with investors, are covered in Section 10.7 on page 370.

The International Chamber of Commerce (ICC) model contracts for agency[32] and for distributorship[33] approach the choice of law innovatively, by giving the contract writer two possibilities, the first being the traditional choice of a specific country's laws, and the second being the "principles of law generally recognized in international trade as applicable to international agency [distribution] contracts,"[34] or those principles that constitute the *Lex Mercatoria*. As more and more arbitration jurisprudence accumulates, this alternative may become the preferred way of wording choice of law clauses, as it shields both parties from unexpected outcomes.

5.7.9　Choice of Forum or Venue

choice of forum
The court in which disputes regarding the contracts will be resolved.

choice of venue
The court in which disputes regarding the contracts will be resolved.

Strongly linked to the choice of law is the choice-of-forum—or choice-of-venue—clause. In it, both parties agree on the location of the court that will rule on a dispute, using the laws selected in the choice-of-law clause. In most instances, the choice of law somewhat dictates the choice of forum, as it makes logical sense to link both, and benefit from a court experienced in the jurisprudence of the laws governing the contract.

One of the preferences of exporters—and of their legal representatives—is to choose courts with which they are familiar, and that generally means a court in the exporting country. While this has obvious advantages of convenience for the exporter, it may present difficulties when it comes time to ask a foreign court to enforce the decision. In general, foreign courts look more favorably upon enforcing the resolution of a dispute in another court if the terms of the contract are clearly international, that is, if the contract uses terminology and concepts that are specifically international—for example, the CISG, the ICC's Incoterms® rules, and/or arbitration under ICC rules.

5.7.10　Arbitration Clause

arbitration
A process by which parties to a contract choose to settle a dispute. An arbitration decision is binding on both parties.

An increasing number of contracts include a clause calling for an arbitration panel to settle disputes, rather than a court. Either the arbitration panel is decided upon at the outset of the contract, or a mention is made of the *Arbitration and ADR Rules* of the International Chamber of Commerce, which outline how the panel should be chosen. The panel is generally made up of three arbitrators, with each of the parties choosing one and the third being chosen by an arbitration organization, such as the ICC.

arbitration panel
A group of arbitrators who are empowered by both parties to resolve a contract dispute. Their decision is binding on both parties.

In many instances, the clause states that the dispute will be "finally settled"[35] by the panel (*i.e.*, that the panel's decision is binding on both parties). If the country in which the arbitration takes place is one of the 130 signatory countries to the Convention on the Recognition and Enforcement of Foreign Arbitral Awards, also known as the New York Convention, then the ruling can be enforced almost anywhere;[36] unfortunately, China, although a signatory, has stood out as the only country where arbitration awards have to be reviewed by a local court, and that requirement makes it difficult to arrange for redress.[37] Foreign companies should be wary about arbitration solutions in that unusual environment.

Despite this obstacle, there are several advantages to settling a dispute through arbitration rather than through the courts, many of which were outlined in Section 5.5.

5.7.11　Mediation Clause

For many contractual disputes, the possibility of mediation or conciliation is encouraged before undertaking arbitration or litigation. A mediator is an individual who encourages and facilitates communications between both parties in a dispute, so that they can reach a compromise satisfactory to both. A mediator does not reach a decision for the parties, but leads the parties toward a compromise.

Mediation is not binding, which means that the decision cannot be enforced and must be agreed upon by both parties. Because mediation is also done in private, there are no public records of mediation, and it is an appropriate alternative to settling disputes when one of the parties is concerned about "saving face."[38] Mediation is sometimes initiated by the arbitration panel or the court for resolutions of disputes where both parties seem open to conciliation. (The advantages of mediation over arbitration and litigation are outlined in Section 5.6)

mediation
A process by which parties to a contract choose to find a compromise in a dispute. A mediation recommendation is not binding.

5.7.12 Profitability or Commission

The profitability or commission clause is worded differently if it defines the amount of commission that the agent will earn or, reciprocally, the price at which the distributor is expected to sell the product, or the markup that it is expected to add to its costs.

For agency agreements, the exporter specifies the commission that the agent will earn for sales in its territory. The commission may vary from product to product, so that the agent is given a financial incentive to sell a specific product, but it is usually around five percent of the selling price of a product, depending on the industry in which the agreement takes place. A savvy exporter sometimes adds the possibility of negotiating the commission with its agent to win a contract for which the price is critical. Agents usually go along with such reduced commissions on the philosophy that a lower commission is better than no commission at all, if the sale is not successful. For sales outside of the territory that the agent may generate accidentally—for example, by attending a trade show and meeting some prospect from a different country—the contract often calls for a lower commission.

Finally, the commission clause also defines when the commission is paid to the agent. The commission is always paid some time after the customer has paid the exporter. Once the exporter is paid, it then pays the commission to the agent. Commissions can be paid as they are earned, or monthly, quarterly, or even semi-annually or annually.

For distributorship agreements, the issue of price can be difficult; if the distributor is free to set its own prices, then there is always the possibility of having substantially different prices for the same product in different countries, thereby creating the possibility of parallel imports (see Section 4.5 on page 137) and risking the aggravation of customers and distributors alike.

However, if an exporter is attempting to limit the probability of parallel imports, for example by trying to control the price at which the distributor sells the product or the markup that the distributor can add to the cost of the product, then there is always the possibility that such a clause will be construed as price fixing and therefore an attempt at reducing competition. Nevertheless, several versions of such clauses exist: some companies bluntly set the same price worldwide and argue that they do not want their distributors to compete on price, but rather on other attributes like service, assortment, and repair facilities. Other exporters make advertising support and other sales help conditional upon the distributor keeping the price in line with the exporter's guidelines. Still other exporters do not contractually state anything, but make explicit threats of possible delays in delivery for those distributors who do not respect guidelines. Obviously, all these attempts can be struck down by courts as collusion, but such agreements exist worldwide. Obtaining advice from an experienced lawyer in drafting such clauses is money well spent.

5.7.13   Intellectual Property

trademark
An intellectual property item that refers to a brand, a commercial name, or a slogan.

patent
An intellectual property item that refers to a process, material, or design.

copyright
An intellectual property item that refers to a musical piece, a piece of art, or a written product.

confidentiality
A promise by both parties to a contract to not disclose what they have learned about each other's business to other parties.

Exporters who benefit from substantial advantages due to intellectual property items should also specify the handling of trademarks, patents, and copyrights particularly carefully in a contract between an exporter and an agent or a distributor.

While the exporter can protect its intellectual property by following the proper registration procedures in the importing country, it is often useful to specify and define the intellectual property issues in the contract, especially in countries where intellectual property protection is lax. By including an intellectual property clause in the contract, the exporter transforms the protection of patents, trademarks, and copyrights into contractual issues, which are more likely to be enforced by a court. There are countless instances, unfortunately, of distributors or agents who violate intellectual property items nevertheless, but a good contract can dissuade them from attempting to do so.

The contract should also include a confidentiality clause to determine how trade secrets and other strategic advantages are handled. The International Chamber of Commerce provides a model agreement for the international protection of confidential information.[39]

Finally, the contract should specify how improvements to existing products made by the agent or the distributor are handled. Although they traditionally become the property of the exporter, the compensation to which the agency or the distributor is entitled should be defined. This is an important aspect of contracts for all parties. Chapter 4 shows that two of the most popular products sold by McDonald's Corporation were first created by franchisees: the Big Mac and the Egg McMuffin.

5.7.14   Miscellaneous Other Clauses

There are many more clauses in a foreign distribution contract, whether with an agent or distributor, many of which are more managerial in nature and become specific to the industry, the strategy of the exporter, and its representatives than can be generalized.

facilities and activities
The specific facilities and activities that each party to a contract is committing to maintaining.

For example, the **facilities-and-activities** clause defines what the exporter and the agent or distributor have agreed upon with respect to the type of establishment that the representative will maintain, the size of the retail establishments it will build, the amount of inventory they will carry, the type of training that employees will receive, and the expectations of managerial policies toward customer complaints, all of which are specific to an industry or a corporate strategy.

McDonald's has much more stringent requirements in this respect than would an exporter of agricultural by-products.

The same is true regarding the **advertising** clause, which spells out the obligations of both parties regarding promotional activities such as advertising, trade show attendance, ownership of ideas for advertising campaigns and sales promotion items, and, very importantly, how the costs of such promotional activities will be shared. For many consumer products, advertising costs are shared by the exporter and the representative in some varying percentages, but for industrial products, the spectrum can go from entirely the responsibility of the exporter to entirely the responsibility of the representative. Cost responsibility may also vary as a function of the country in which the representative operates. A word of caution, though: if there are discrepancies among the cost burden of distributors in different countries, the sale price may be affected and trigger parallel imports, which is something that an exporter should attempt to avoid.

advertising
The promotional activities that each party to a contract is committing to pursue.

The clause regarding **competing lines** spells out how an agent or distributor will be allowed to handle products manufactured by competitors. In most instances, an agent is not allowed to represent firms that are competing directly with the exporter's products, but a distributor can. Both are encouraged to carry products that complement the exporter's product line, with the understanding that complementary products can increase the attractiveness of the agent or the distributor's portfolio of goods. Some exporters, though, prefer that the agent or the distributor sell their products at the exclusion of all others, to ensure that the representative is concentrating its efforts on the exporter's products. Such decisions are made generally as a function of the bargaining strength of the parties: a Japanese *sogo shosha* will carry whatever it pleases, whereas a small dealer involved in distributing products manufactured by a large firm, such as Caterpillar, will have to abide by whatever its principal dictates.

competing lines
Products manufactured by a company other than the principal that compete directly with the principal's products.

Finally, the **ownership of the customers' list** must be resolved for distributors. Because distributors sell to their own accounts, the exporter is usually not privy to the identity of these customers. In some cases, the exporter may find out who the distributor's customers are when the customers are requested to fill out warranty registration forms, but in general, they are unknown to the exporter. Some exporters demand that the distributor report the names of its customers, while others prefer to leave this issue alone. Except for warranty issues, the only reasons an exporter would want to know the names of the distributor's customers are in expectation of the distributor's poor performance or in expectation of the creation of a sales subsidiary in the future, neither of which represent a good basis on which to start a contract. As far as agents are concerned, because the exporter is shipping and billing directly to the customers to whom the agent sold, the exporter is aware of the customers' identities, and therefore the issue is less significant.

customers' list
The list of the customers to which the agent or distributor sells the principal's products.

Review and Discussion Questions

1. What are the general provisions of the United Nations Convention on Contracts for the International Sale of Goods?

2. What issues are created by the concept of labor law in an international distribution agreement?

3. Describe three clauses generally found in an agency or distributorship agreement.

4. What are the differences between the "choice of law" and "choice of forum" clauses? How are they related?

5. What are the two possible forms of termination? How differently will they be handled by a court of law?

6. What are the differences between mediation and arbitration? How do they differ from a proceeding in a court of law?

Notes

[1] Feldman, Noah, "When Judges Make Foreign Policy," *The New York Times*, September 25, 2008.

[2] Associated Press, "Supreme Court Justices Spar over International Law," Law.com, January 18, 2005, http://www.law.com/jsp/article.jsp?id=1105364112559, retrieved June 11, 2013.

[3] Gourion, Pierre-Alain, and Georges Peyrard, *Droit du Commerce International*, 1997, Librairie Générale de Droit et de Jurisprudence, 14, rue Pierre et Marie Curie, 75005 Paris, France.

[4] JBC International, "Think You Understand the Vienna Convention? Then Read This Sad Tale," *The Journal of Commerce*, June 24, 1998, p. 12C.

[5] Lookofsky, Joseph M., *Understanding the CIGS in the USA: A Compact Guide to the 1980 United Nations Convention on Contracts for the International Sale of Goods*, 1995, Klumer Law International, Boston, The Hague, London.

[6] Kritzer, Albert, "CISG: Table of Contracting States," Pace Law School Institute of International Commercial Law, Janaury 8, 2016, http://www.cisg.law.pace.edu/cisg/countries/cntries.html, retrieved November 11, 2016.

[7] Moss, Sally, "Why the United Kingdom has not ratified the CISG," *Journal of Law and Business*, 25, 2005-2006, pp. 483-485.

[8] Murray, Timothy, "CISG: Opt out or not? The CISG in a nutshell," http://www.mhandl.com/content-/cisginanutshell, retrieved November 29,2016.

[9] Chester, James, personal e-mail communication, January 19, 2009.

[10] Ziegler, Jacob, "Canada Prepares to Adopt the International Sales Convention," *Canadian Business Law Journal*, vol. 18, issue 3, Fall 1991.

[11] Winship, Peter, "Formation of International Sales Contracts under the 1980 Vienna Convention," *International Lawyer*, 1983, http://www.cisg.law.pace.edu/cisg/biblio/winship3.html, retrieved November 26, 2016.

[12] Gellman, Gila E., "Forming International Sales Pacts," *Marketing Management*, Winter 1994, pp. 60-62.

[13] Ferrari, Franco, "What Sources of Law for Contracts for the International Sale of Goods; Why One has to look beyond the CISG," *International Review of Law and Economics*, 25, September 2005, pp. 314-341.

[14] Walt, Steven, "The CISG Expansion Bias: A Comment on Franco Ferrari," *International Review of Law and Economics*, 25, September 2005, pp. 342-349.

[15] McMahon, John P., "Applying the CISG: Guide for Business Managers and Counsels," Pace Law School Institute of International Law, http://www.cisg.law.pace.edu/cisg/guides.html, accessed May 23, 2009.

[16] Huber, Peter, and Alastair Mullis, *The CISG: A new Textbook for Students and Practioners*, Munich: Sellier European Law Publisher, 2007.

[17] Heron, Karl G., and David D. Knoll, "Negotiating and Drafting International Distribution, Agency, and Representative Agreements: The United States Exporter's Perspective," *The International Lawyer*, Fall 1987, pp. 939-983.

[18] Deming, Stuart, *The Foreign Corrupt Practices Act and the New International Norms*, Chicago: American Bar Association, 2005.

[19] Carr, Indira, and Opi Outhwaite, "The OECD Anti-Bribery Convention Ten Years On,", *Manchester Journal of International Economic Law*, 5, Issue 1, 2008, pp. 3-35.

[20] Chester, James, personal e-mail communication, January 19, 2009.

[21] Puelinckx, A. H., and H. A. Tielemans, "The Termination of Agency and Distributorship Agree-

ments: A Comparative Survey," *Northwestern Journal of International Law and Business*, Fall 1981, 3:542, pp. 452-495.

[22]Miller, Edward, and Larry Coltman, "International Commercial Agency Agreements and Private International Law," July 8, 1999, m.reedsmith.com/files/Publication/23acd8f4-c3c3.../Comag3.pdf, retrieved June 11, 2013.

[23]*Ibid.*

[24]Ulmer, Nicolas C., "Bullet-proofing Your International Arbitration: Part 2 of 2," *World Trade*, August 2000, p. 68.

[25]"Parties' Preferences in International Arbitration: The Latest Statistics of the Leading Arbitral Institutions," Global Arbitration News, August 5, 2015, https://globalarbitrationnews.com/parties-preferences-in-international-arbitration-the-latest-statistics-of-the-leading-arbitral-institutions-201508-05/#982971-v1-GAN_Article_Arbitration_Institutions.docx, retrieved December 11, 2016.

[26]"ICC Rules of Arbitration," International Chamber of Commerce, http://www.iccwbo.org/Products-and-Services/Arbitration-and-ADR/
Arbitration/ICC-Rules-of-Arbitration/, retrieved June 11, 2013.

[27]*Ibid.*

[28]"Courts will take 320 years to clear backlog cases: Justice Rao," *The Times of India*, March 6, 2010, http://articles.timesofindia.indiatimes.com/2010-03-06/india/28143242_1_high-court-judges-literacy-rate-
backlog, retrieved June 11, 2013.

[29]Heron, Karl G., and David D. Knoll, "Negotiating and Drafting International Distribution, Agency, and Representative Agreements: The United States Exporter's Perspective," *The International Lawyer*, Fall 1987, pp. 939-983.

[30]Dubberly, David E., "When Giving Your Rep the Boot: In Latin America, Labor Laws May Prove Surprisingly Costly, Unless You Plan Ahead," *Export Today*, May 1998, p. 26.

[31]"Lloyd's Revamp Won't Be Challenged," Associated Press News Release, June 23, 1997.

[32]*The ICC Model Commercial Agency Contract*, 2nd ed., 2002, publication No. 644 of the International Chamber of Commerce, ICC Publishing, 156 Fifth Avenue, New York, NY 10010, USA and ICC Publishing SA, 38, Cours Albert 1er, 75008 Paris, France.

[33]*The ICC Model Distributorship Contract*, 2002 ed., publication No. 646 of the International Chamber of Commerce, ICC Publishing, 156 Fifth Avenue, New York, NY 10010, USA and ICC Publishing SA, 38, Cours Albert 1er, 75008 Paris, France.

[34]*The ICC Model Commercial Agency Contract*, 2nd ed., 2002, publication No. 644 of the International Chamber of Commerce, ICC Publishing, 156 Fifth Avenue, New York, NY 10010, USA and ICC Publishing SA, 38, Cours Albert 1er, 75008 Paris, France.

[35]*The ICC Model Distributorship Contract*, 2002 ed., publication No. 646 of the International Chamber of Commerce, ICC Publishing, 156 Fifth Avenue, New York, NY 10010, USA and ICC Publishing SA, 38, Cours Albert 1er, 75008 Paris, France.

[36]Ulmer, Nicolas C., "Bullet-proofing Your International Arbitration: Part 2 of 2," *World Trade*, August 2000, p. 68.

[37]Howell, David, James Rogers and Matthew Townsend, "Chinese Arbitration—Still Distinctive," Harvard Business Law Review, April 2013, pp. 196-202.

[38]Connors, Kathleen, "Arbitration Taking Hold in Asia with Help of International Chamber," *The Journal of Commerce*, April 2, 1997, p. 8A.

[39]*The ICC Model Confidentiality Agreement*, 2006 ed., publication No. 664 of the International Chamber of Commerce, ICC Publishing, 156 Fifth Avenue, New York, NY 10010, USA and ICC Publishing SA, 38, Cours Albert 1er, 75008 Paris, France.

Chapter 6

Terms of Trade or Incoterms® Rules

Whenever an exporter sells goods to a foreign company, whether through an intermediary such as an agent or distributor or directly to an importer, there are many steps involved in getting the goods to the customer:

- The goods must be cleared for export.

- The transport of the goods between the exporter and the importer must be arranged, often using several means of transportation—also called means of conveyance—, including at least three distinct legs in that journey:

  - pre-carriage, or the transportation that takes place in the country of export.

  - main carriage, or the international transportation between the country of export and the country of import.

  - on-carriage, or the transportation that takes place in the country of import.

- The goods must clear customs in the importing country.

The terms of trade used in the contract of sale determine which steps are the responsibility of the exporter and which are the responsibility of the importer. Often, the number of issues involved in an international shipment is substantial, and determining the way these tasks should be divided between the exporter and the importer for each shipment would be a daunting task. In addition, it would be virtually impossible to anticipate everything that could go wrong during transit and determine at the time of the contract which of the parties should be responsible for each incident.[1]

6.1   International Commercial Terms

Fortunately, standardized terms of trade were created in 1936 by the International Chamber of Commerce (ICC): these terms have evolved into eleven International Commercial Terms rules, from which the acronym Incoterms® is derived. These Incoterms® rules were revised in 1953, 1967, 1976, 1980, 1990, 2000, and most recently in 2010.[2]

It significantly benefits both parties to use one of these Incoterms® rules because ample information is available for each, and substantial jurisprudence has accumulated for each through the ICC arbitration system. Incoterms® rules are used in all the documents used in an international transaction. For example, a *pro forma* invoice would read:

FCA · **2300 Industrial Parkway, Milwaukee, WI 53223, USA, Incoterms® 2010.**

pre-carriage
The portion of an international shipment that takes place in the exporting country.

main carriage
The portion of an international shipment that takes place between the exporting country and the importing country.

on-carriage
The portion of an international shipment that takes place in the importing country.

International Chamber of Commerce (ICC)
The largest business organization in the world. Its goal is to champion international business growth and its members are the national chambers of commerce.

Incoterms® Rules
A series of eleven international terms of trade standardized by the International Chamber of Commerce.

Figure 6.1: The International Chamber of Commerce Incoterms® Rules Logo
Photo ©ICC. Used with permission.

to indicate which tasks the exporter is willing to perform and which tasks remain the responsibility of the importer. When faced with an Incoterms® rule,* exporters and importers know precisely what tasks they must complete, which costs they have to bear, and the exact point at which the responsibility for the goods transfers from the exporter to the importer.

6.2   Understanding Incoterms® Rules

The term of trade or Incoterms® rule that the exporter and the importer agree to use in a transaction defines five aspects of an international sale:

- Which tasks the exporter performs

- Which tasks the importer performs

- Which activities are paid by the exporter

- Which activities are paid by the importer

- When the transfer of responsibility for the goods takes place

This point at which the transfer of responsibility takes place is complicated: it is necessary to distinguish between (1) the transfer of responsibility for the goods between the exporter and the importer and (2) the transfer of title between the exporter and the importer. The transfer of responsibility (transfer of risk) is dictated by the Incoterms® rule. The transfer of title (transfer of ownership) usually takes place when the importer has either paid the exporter—and obtained the original bill of lading (see Chapter 9)—, accepted to sign a draft (see Chapter 7), or performed some other event specifically outlined in the contract of sale. The transfer of responsibility coincides with the delivery of the goods, a point that is clearly outlined in each of the Incoterms® rules, and in most cases, delivery occurs chronologically much earlier than the transfer of title.

transfer of responsibility
In an international voyage, the point at which the exporter ceases to be responsible for the goods.

transfer of title
The point in time at which the ownership of the goods changes from the exporter to the importer.

delivery
In an international voyage, the point at which the responsibility for the goods switches from the exporter to the importer.

---

*Incoterms® is a trademark of the International Chamber of Commerce (ICC).

The transfer of responsibility of the exporter never extends beyond the services for which that company has paid. There are several Incoterms® rules, however, where the exporter is obligated to pre-pay a portion of the transportation costs—main carriage and on-carriage—even though the exporter is no longer responsible for the goods. Such is the case for the so-called C-terms, the terms whose three-letter acronyms start with the letter C.

6.3   Incoterms® Rule Strategy

The proper choice of an Incoterms® rule is therefore contingent upon the exporting firm's strategy, but is also somewhat constrained by the following parameters:

- The type of product sold: several industries (commodities in particular) prefer using some specific terms of trade rather than others.

- The method of shipment: goods shipped by ocean or barge are sold under different Incoterms® rules than cargo shipped by air or by ground transportation—rail or road.

- The package size: containerized goods, small packages, and large crates are transported under different Incoterms® rules and use different transportation modes.

- The ability of either the exporter or importer to perform the tasks involved in the shipment.

- The amount of trust placed by either the exporter or the importer toward the other.

Nevertheless, the greatest criterion used to choose the proper Incoterms® rule for a transaction is the willingness of both parties to perform and pay for some of the tasks involved in the shipment. In some cases, an exporter can gain a strategic advantage and facilitate the sale of its products by assisting the importer with the tasks involved in the shipment. In others, an importer can obtain a lower price if it performs all or most of the tasks involved in the shipment. However, most companies do not determine which Incoterms® rule to use on a case-by-case basis, but instead determine which term of trade should be used regularly, given the company's strategy, its product line, its customers' expectations, and its trade volume. Sophisticated exporters offer more than one Incoterms® rule choice to their customers (see Section 6.17 on page 202) to gain a tactical advantage over their competitors.

Another issue to recognize in this decision is that, regardless of the Incoterms® rule chosen, the importer always pays for the transportation and other costs of shipping internationally. The fact that the exporter pre-pays and arranges for certain aspects of the shipment is reflected in the invoice price; therefore, the importer is charged for them. In addition, it is likely, although not always the case, that the exporter's invoice includes a charge that is higher than

International Commercial Terms

Main Carriage by Any Means of Transportation

EXW	Ex Works
FCA	Free Carrier
CPT	Carriage Paid To
CIP	Carriage and Insurance Paid to
DAT	Delivered At Terminal
DAP	Delivered At Place
DDP	Delivered Duty Paid

Main Carriage by Ocean

FAS	Free Alongside Ship
FOB	Free On Board
CFR	Cost and Freight
CIF	Cost, Insurance and Freight

Table 6.1: International Terms of Trade Abbreviations

the actual cost of the service. Many exporters add a premium to these expenses to reflect the cost of time and effort to arrange for those services.[3]

Nevertheless, the choice of Incoterms® rule is often the exporter's decision: it is difficult for an exporter to adapt its Incoterms® rule strategy to accommodate the requirements of an importer, as it may require the exporter to be responsible for tasks that it has decided it would rather not perform. Should the importer feel that the exporter is not providing a service that is adequate, it can always purchase from another source. However, should the importer want to perform more tasks than the exporter prefers, it is possible for the exporter to do less than what it expected, and use a different Incoterms® rule for that transaction, one for which it is responsible for fewer aspects of the shipment.

Finally, the choice of the proper Incoterms® rule is a critical decision for a firm, as the choice is an integral part of the firm's export strategy and linked to the level of customer service it wants to provide.[4]

In this chapter, all eleven Incoterms® rules are reviewed in depth. They are first divided into two groups; those Incoterms® rules that are appropriate for all forms of international transportation (the main carriage), and those that can only be used with ocean shipments. In each group, the Incoterms® rules are then reviewed in an order that reflects increased services provided by the exporter (see Table 6.1).

6.4   Ex-Works (EXW)

The Ex-Works (EXW) Incoterms® rule can be used for any merchandise and for any means of transportation. It should be used with the following syntax:

EXW · 2400 Progress Drive, Poughkeepsie, New York 12601, USA, Incoterms® 2010.

where the address is the location at which the exporter will hold the merchandise available to the importer. This location is in the exporting country.

EXW is the easiest of the Incoterms® rule for the exporter, and the most difficult for the importer. In an EXW transaction, the exporter is only required to "place the goods at the disposal of the buyer" and "render every assistance [...] in obtaining [...] any export license or other official authorization necessary for the export of the goods." [5] In addition, the exporter must package the goods for export, but the exporter does not have to load the goods onto the importer's prearranged vehicle. It should be evident that EXW is not an advantageous Incoterms® rule from the importer's perspective: arranging to pick up goods in a foreign country, providing domestic transportation, and clearing goods for export in a foreign country, are not easy tasks.

Because of these restrictions, the International Chamber of Commerce (ICC) is directing exporters to limit the use of EXW to international shipments that are transported by small-package companies, such as FedEx or DHL.[6] In that case, the goods are clearly placed at the disposal of the buyer, who can instruct the small-package carrier to collect them at the exporter's place of business. The goods are small enough that there is no concern about placing the goods on board the means of conveyance. The small-package company then transports the goods to their destination in the importing country, under a single bill of lading. Under these circumstances, an EXW Incoterms® rule is attractive to importer, since there is little effort extended to arrange for the collection and shipment of the goods.

6.4.1   Delivery under EXW

The EXW Incoterms® rule does not specify anything regarding the delivery of the goods. Delivery occurs at the time at which the importer (or the importer's agent) picks up the goods at the exporter's plant. This delivery must take place at a mutually convenient time. The exporter is required to notify the importer that the goods are available for pickup and the importer is required to notify the exporter of the time at which the goods will be picked up.

There is no specific transportation document corresponding to the delivery of the goods under the EXW Incoterms® rule, although, if a transportation company picks up the goods, the exporter is generally given a copy of the bill of lading or some form of receipt for the goods.

Figure 6.2: Small-Packet Delivery Vehicle in Amsterdam, on its way to pick up an EXW shipment

Photo ©DNiewland/Shutterstock. Used with permission.

6.4.2 Responsibilities of the Exporter and the Importer under EXW

Under EXW, the exporter's responsibilities are limited to the most basic functions: make the goods available to the buyer, package the goods for export shipment, assist in the export clearance procedures, and provide the documents to the importer so that the goods can clear customs in the importing country or be insured. None of these requirements are trivial, though.

The exporter must package the goods so that they are protected during their international voyage. That packaging requirement means that the exporter should identify the means of transportation and ensure that the goods are adequately packaged to prevent damage. If the goods are damaged in transit due to improper packaging, the exporter is responsible and the insurance coverage contracted by the importer will not cover the costs of the damage. This requirement is, however, easy to meet for a small package traveling by air, since the packaging requirements are similar to those for a small package traveling domestically.

The exporter also has to provide all the documents necessary for the importer to clear customs in the importing country; this means that the invoice must be a good international invoice and include product description, Harmonized System numbers, weights, volume measures, unit price, total price, and so on (see Chapter 9 for further details and examples), that the other documents are prepared carefully and accurately (certificate of origin, packing list, and so on), and that the correct number of originals and copies are included. The exporter must provide these documents, but can charge the importer for the cost of providing them. Because the importer is also in charge of exporting the products, the exporter has to provide the documents necessary to clear the goods for export in the exporting country.

At export, the United States handles EXW shipments in a way that is somewhat at odds with the Incoterms® rule. Under EXW rules, the importer clears the goods for export, and therefore is the exporter of record. However, in the United States Electronic Export Information (EEI) declaration (an export document explained in Section 9.3.1), with which the Census Bureau records the exporter's identity, the seller-exporter must be listed as the "U.S. principal party in interest."[7] This terminology was specifically created to allow the U.S. Census to record the exporter of a specific shipment under an EXW sale, rather than record the importer of the goods: actually, the term "exporter" has been stricken from the EEI. Because of this requirement, the United States government has placed the responsibility of providing the correct Export Commodity Classification Number (ECCN) and any information that could affect an export license on the exporter in an EXW transaction.[8]

The importer is responsible for all other aspects of the shipment in an EXW transaction: arranging for main transportation, clearing customs in the importing country, purchasing insurance, and providing on-carriage (transportation) in the importing country.

6.5 Free Carrier (FCA)

The Free-Carrier (FCA) Incoterms® rule can be used for any merchandise and for any means of transportation, but it was created for goods shipped through multimodal transportation (*i.e.*, merchandise that is shipped through multiple means of transportation—without being "handled" between means of transportation because it is containerized—and under a single bill of lading). The FCA Incoterms® rule can be used for shipments of either full-container loads (FCL) or less-than-container loads (LCL). FCA has become one of the most popular Incoterms® rules as the number of multi-modal shipments has increased. The FCA Incoterms® rule should be used with the following syntax:

> **FCA · Bâtiment B, 46 Allée Corbière, F-81000 Castres, France, Incoterms® 2010**

FCL shipment
An international shipment that uses, by weight or volume, the entire capacity of a container.

LCL shipment
An international shipment that is combined with other shipments in a single container.

where the address is the location at which the delivery takes place. Delivery usually takes place in the exporting country or in a neighboring country.

The goods can be given to the carrier at the exporter's premises, or they can be delivered by the exporter to the carrier's place of business. In the first case, it is common to refer to the transaction as an FCA "exporter's premises" and in the second case to an FCA "carrier's premises." The location depends on the agreement between the importer and the exporter, but the importer selects the carrier. In either FCA "exporter's premises" or FCA "carrier's premises," the exporter is responsible for loading the goods on the means of transportation.

Because FCA is a recent Incoterms® rule—it was created in 1990—great care has been taken to define which responsibilities are borne by the exporter, and which are borne by the importer. In the 2010 version of Incoterms® rules, the ICC indicated that it would prefer international shipments of goods other than small packages to be conducted under FCA rather than under EXW when the exporter and the importer agree that the exporter's role in the international shipment should be minimal.

6.5.1 Delivery under FCA

Under FCA, the delivery takes place when one of two conditions is met:

- If it is an FCA "exporter's premises" transaction, the delivery takes place when the goods are loaded, by the exporter and at its expense and risk, onto the carrier's truck.

- If it is an FCA "carrier's premises" transaction, the delivery takes place when the goods are made available to the carrier (*i.e.*, when the goods have arrived at the carrier's dock). The goods are delivered even though they have not been unloaded from the exporter's truck. They are unloaded by the carrier and at the carrier's expense (*i.e.*, at the importer's expense), and at their risk.

The document that corresponds to the transfer of responsibility for an FCA shipment is the receipt given by the carrier to the exporter; it is generally a multimodal bill of lading.

6.5.2 Responsibilities of the Exporter and the Importer under FCA

Under FCA, the exporter packages the merchandise for export, as it does under EXW. However, if the transaction is an FCA exporter's premises, the exporter's responsibilities also include loading the merchandise into a container provided by the carrier, and loading the container onto the truck provided by the carrier, or loading the non-containerized goods onto the means of conveyance provided by the carrier. If the transaction is an FCA carrier's premises, then the exporter is responsible for loading the goods onto its own truck and delivering the merchandise to the carrier's facilities.

In addition, the exporter clears the merchandise for export, and must provide whatever information and documents are needed by the importer to clear customs in the importing country and to obtain insurance. In the United States, the exporter fills out Electronic Export Information (EEI) declaration and is the "U.S. principal party in interest." For shipments originating in countries where export authorities require a pre-shipment inspection (see Chapter 17), the exporter must pay for it.

The exporter also provides all the documents necessary for the importer to clear customs in the importing country; the exporter can charge the importer for the costs of providing them.

The importer is responsible for arranging the main carriage and on-carriage (*i.e.*, finding a carrier between the exporter's town and the final destination) and communicating which carrier has been selected to the exporter. The importer is also responsible for arranging for insurance and for clearing customs in the importing country. If the importing country requires a pre-shipment inspection, the importer has to pay for it.

6.6   Carriage Paid To (CPT)

Under the Carriage-Paid-To (CPT) Incoterms® rule, the exporter and the importer agree that the exporter should pre-pay the main carriage for the goods. This Incoterms® rule is designed to be used for all cargo types and all means of transportation. CPT is most commonly used for goods transported by surface or air transportation, but it can be used for goods transported by ocean; however, CPT is rarely used for cargo that is directly delivered by the exporter to an ocean carrier in a port. In addition, CPT is more likely to be used for cargo that is not containerized, such as roll-on/roll-off cargo or large crates. The CPT Incoterms® rule should be used with the following syntax:

> **CPT · Graacher Straße 20, Köln, Deutschland D-50969, Incoterms® 2010.**

where the address refers to the location in the city of destination in which the importer takes control of the goods. This location is generally in the importing country or a neighboring country.

In a CPT transaction, delivery does not take place in the city of destination (at the address mentioned in the Incoterms® rule) but at the point where the exporter delivers the goods to the carrier in the exporting country. Unless unusual circumstances prevail, shipping charges do not include the unloading of the merchandise in the destination city.

6.6.1   Delivery under CPT

Under the CPT Incoterms® rule, delivery takes place in the exporting country when the exporter provides the goods to the first carrier. This is the case even though the exporter has pre-paid shipping charges to the city of destination (pre-carriage, main carriage and on-carriage) and the contract of carriage is in the exporter's name. Proof of delivery is obtained when the exporter is given a bill of

Figure 6.3: CPT Delivery: Sugar Bags are Loaded in the First Means of Conveyance in Thailand

Photo ©Amarin Jitnathum/Shutterstock. Used with permission.

lading or equivalent document (air waybill, sea waybill, multi-modal bill of lading) by the carrier.

6.6.2 Responsibilities of the Exporter and the Importer under CPT

In a CPT transaction, the exporter is responsible for packaging the goods for export, shipping them to the carrier, and pre-paying the shipping costs to the city of destination. In the United States, the exporter fills out the Electronic Export Information (EEI) declaration and is the "U.S. principal party in interest," or the exporter of record. In countries where export authorities require a pre-shipment inspection, the exporter must pay for it.

The exporter also must provide all the documents necessary for the importer to clear customs in the importing country; the exporter can charge the importer for the cost of providing them.

The importer assumes responsibility for the goods when the exporter delivers them to the first carrier. The importer is responsible for unloading the goods from the carrier's truck in the importing country, clearing customs, and for paying inland transportation (if any) beyond the city of destination. If the importing country requires a pre-shipment inspection, the importer pays for it.

6.7   Carriage and Insurance Paid To (CIP)

The Carriage-and-Insurance-Paid (CIP) Incoterms® rule is a modification of the CPT Incoterms® rule for which the exporter also purchases insurance for the cargo while it is in transit. The CIP Incoterms® rule can be used for all goods and all means of transportation, but is mostly designed for non-containerized cargo that travels by surface or air. It is possible to use CIP for ocean cargo, as long as the cargo is not given to an ocean carrier in a port. The CIP Incoterms® rule should be used with the following syntax:

> **CIP · Ulitsa Poruchik Nedelcho Bonchev, Sofia, Bulgaria,**
> **Incoterms® 2010**

where the address refers to the location in the city of destination where the importer takes control of the goods. This location is in the importing country or a neighboring country.

In a CIP transaction, the delivery does not take place in the city of destination, but in the city where the exporter delivers the goods to the first carrier. In addition to the responsibilities the exporter has under the CPT Incoterms® rule, it must pre-pay for insurance until the city of destination.

Under the CIP Incoterms® rule, the amount insured must be at least 110 percent of the value of the goods, a custom that dates to 1906, when Great Britain instituted the Marine Insurance Act[9] and introduced the maritime equivalent to the CIP Incoterms® rule (see 6.14 on page 196).

The insurance coverage required by the ICC is Coverage C of the Institute Cargo Clauses (see Section 10.5.2 on page 356), and therefore minimum-cover insurance. Expectedly, a modification to the CIP Incoterms® rule has emerged, called an Incoterms® rule variant, that requests that the exporter provide coverage A of the Institute Cargo Clauses, or maximum-cover insurance. The syntax must accommodate the fact that Incoterms® rule variants are not regulated by the ICC and should therefore read:

Incoterm® rule variant
A modification to an Incoterm® rule, not sanctioned by the ICC, that changes one or more of its parameters.

> **CIP · Ulitsa Poruchik Nedelcho Bonchev, Sofia, Bulgaria,**
> **Incoterms® 2010, maximum cover**

Certain countries (see Table 6.2 on page 198) do not allow their importers to purchase insurance abroad, and therefore prevent any import using the CIP Incoterms® rule.

6.7.1   Delivery under CIP

Under CIP, delivery takes place when the exporter provides the goods to the first carrier in the exporting country. This is the case even though the exporter has pre-paid shipping charges to the city of destination (pre-carriage, main carriage and on-carriage) and the contract of carriage is in the exporter's name. Proof of delivery is obtained when the exporter is given a bill of lading or equivalent document (air waybill, sea waybill, multi-modal bill of lading) by the carrier.

6.7.2   Responsibilities of the Exporter and the Importer under CIP

In a CIP transaction, the exporter is responsible for export packing, transportation costs (pre-carriage, main carriage and on-carriage) to the city of destination, and for minimum-insurance costs. In addition, the exporter is responsible for clearing the goods for export. In the United States, the exporter fills out the Electronic Export Information declaration and is the "U.S. principal party in interest" or the exporter of record. In countries where export authorities require a pre-shipment inspection, the exporter must pay for it.

The exporter also must provide all the documents necessary for the importer to clear customs in the importing country; the exporter can charge the importer for the costs of providing them.

The importer's responsibility starts when the exporter delivers the goods to the first carrier. The importer is responsible for unloading the carrier's truck, clearing customs in the importing country, and for transportation costs beyond the city of destination. If the importing country requires a pre-shipment inspection, the importer has to pay for it.

6.8   Delivered At Terminal (DAT)

The Delivered-At-Terminal (DAT) Incoterms® rule was created in 2010. The DAT Incoterms® rule reflects the practice that containerized cargo often transits through a container terminal, whether in the exporting or importing country. DAT is intended to be used for all modes of transportation and all types of cargo, but fits closely with intermodal containerized shipments. A terminal, or more precisely an intermodal terminal, is a location where cargo shifts from one mode of transportation to another; from truck to rail, or from rail to ocean, for example. The DAT Incoterms® rule should be used with the following syntax:

container terminal
A location where containerized cargo changes mode of transportation.

> **DAT · Paranaguá Container Terminal, Avenida Portuária, Paranaguá, Parana 83206-410, Brazil, Incoterms® 2010.**

where the address refers to the terminal in which the importer takes control of the goods. The address can be located in the exporting country, in which case the importer is responsible for the main carriage, or it can be located in the importing country, in which case the exporter is responsible for the main carriage. The DAT Incoterms® rule is quite flexible.

6.8.1 Delivery under DAT

In a DAT transaction, delivery takes place in the terminal, when the goods are unloaded from the means of transportation provided by the exporter. If the terminal is in the port of origin, then the exporter delivers the goods when they are unloaded from the truck that took them to the terminal. If the terminal is in the port of destination, the transfer of responsibility takes place when the goods are unloaded from the ship. Proof of delivery is generally provided by the terminal with a terminal receipt.

Figure 6.4: DAT Delivery: Unloading a Container at Lat Krabang Intermodal Terminal in Bangkok, Thailand
Photo ©Sod Tatong/Shutterstock. Used with permission.

6.8.2 Responsibilities of the Exporter and the Importer under DAT

Under DAT, the exporter is responsible for export packing and transportation costs to the terminal of destination. Depending on the location of the terminal, the transportation costs may include pre-carriage, main carriage and possibly on-carriage. The exporter is also responsible for the cost of unloading the goods at the terminal. In addition, the exporter is responsible for clearing the goods for export and, in the United States, is the "U.S. principal party in interest," or the exporter of record on the Electronic Export Information (EEI) declaration. In countries where export authorities require a pre-shipment inspection, the exporter pays for it.

The exporter also has to provide all the documents necessary for the importer to clear customs in the importing country; the exporter can charge the importer for the costs of providing them.

The importer's responsibility starts when the exporter has delivered the goods in the terminal. The importer is responsible for clearing customs in the importing country, and for transportation costs beyond the terminal. Depending on the terminal's location, the transportation costs may include main carriage, on-carriage, and possibly pre-carriage. If the importing country requires a pre-shipment inspection, the importer pays for it.

6.9   Delivered At Place (DAP)

The Delivered-At-Place (DAP) Incoterms® rule was created in 2010. The DAP Incoterms® rule allows the exporter to provide a high level of service by delivering the goods to the importer's place of business—or some other location chosen by the importer. DAP is intended to be used for all modes of transportation and all types of cargo. The DAP Incoterms® rule should be used with the following syntax:

> **DAP · 97 Brisbane Street, Sydenham 8023, New Zealand, Incoterms®
> 2010.**

The DAP Incoterms® rule was designed to replace a former Incoterms® rule called DDU—Delivered Duty Unpaid—which had been frequently used, but could not be used for domestic transactions, since there is no duty that a seller has to consider in a domestic transaction. The two terms—the former DDU and the new DAP—are essentially similar; for a manager accustomed to DDU, a change to DAP will be smooth and require few adjustments.

6.9.1   Delivery under DAP

In a DAP transaction, delivery takes place when the goods arrive, still loaded on the means of transportation provided by the exporter, at their destination. Since the delivery generally takes place at a location that is the importer's place of business, the proof of delivery is the arrival of the goods, ready to be unloaded. It is customary for the exporter to provide a copy of the bill of lading to the importer.

Incoterms®2010 Rules in Domestic Trade

The 2010 version of Incoterms® rules created a group of commercial terms of trade that could be used for both domestic and international trade, as is clearly stated in the ICC document: Incoterms® rules are the "ICC rules for the use of domestic and international trade terms."

There are several reasons for this change; the first is that, in 2002, the American Law Institute and the National Conference of Commissioners on Uniform State Laws eliminated the definitions of shipping and delivery terms from the United States Uniform Commercial Code (FOB factory, FOB destination).[10] Even though none of the fifty states had incorporated these changes by 2010, it was expected that they would eventually be adopted and the ICC thought that the Incoterms® 2010 rules could fill the void. However, in May 2011, the American Law Institute withdrew that elimination, and reinstated the traditional shipping and delivery terms of the UCC.[11]

The second reason is that Incoterms® rules are revised and reviewed at periodic intervals. That fact allows for the terms to reflect the trade practices and creativity of domestic and international shippers. Consider that the UCC's version of FOB was written in 1941, before the major innovations of the past sixty years: containers, widespread air shipments, and computers. The Incoterms® rules are more in tune with current shippers' practices.

The third reason is that companies and managers are increasingly multi-national, and operate in many domestic markets in addition to their international activities. By following Incoterms® rules, managers can learn only one set of rules, rather than several domestic rules, many of which contradict one another. For example, the UCC's Free On Board is radically different from the *franco à bord* or from the *franco de port* of the French, from the *frei an Bord* of the German, and from the Free On Board of the Incoterms® rules.

It is unknown whether Incoterms® rules will eventually gain usage as domestic terms of trade. However, the modifications made by the International Chamber of Commerce would likely enhance that possibility.

6.9.2 Responsibilities of the Exporter and the Importer under DAP

Under DAP, the exporter is responsible for export packing and transportation costs to the destination mentioned on the Incoterms® rule statement. Generally, the transportation costs include pre-carriage, main carriage and on-carriage. The exporter is not responsible for the cost of unloading the goods at their destination, which are paid by the importer. The exporter is responsible for clearing the goods for export, and, in the United States, the exporter is the "U.S. principal party in interest" or the exporter of record on the Electronic Export Information (EEI) declaration. In countries where export authorities require a pre-shipment inspection, the exporter pays for it.

The exporter also has to provide all the documents necessary for the importer to clear customs in the importing country; the exporter can charge the importer for the costs of providing them.

The importer pays the costs of unloading the goods from the means of conveyance used for the on-carriage, and has to clear customs in the importing country, using the documents provided by the exporter.

6.10 Delivered Duty Paid (DDP)

The Delivered-Duty-Paid (DDP) Incoterms® rule can be used for any merchandise and for any means of transportation. The DDP Incoterms® rule should be used with the following syntax:

> **DDP · Kopparbergsgatan 226, Malmö 214 44, Sverige/Sweden, Incoterms® 2010.**

where the address is the location at which the importer takes control of the goods. This location is generally the importer's place of business, but can be any other location in the importing country or in a neighboring country that the importer selects.

Choosing the DDP Incoterms® rule requires the exporter to provide the ultimate level of customer service. The exporter handles everything for the importer, including shipment to the customer's plant and customs clearance in the importing country. For the importer, a DDP transaction is exactly equivalent to receiving a domestic shipment from a domestic supplier: the only thing left to the importer's care is unloading the merchandise, something that is usually the importer's responsibility under a domestic shipment.

In some cases, it may be advantageous for pragmatic reasons to use a variant of the DDP Incoterms® rule: in many countries, the customs authorities collect not only duty on the imported goods but also a Value Added Tax (VAT) on the value of the goods (see Chapter 17). Because of the peculiarities of VAT accounting, it is often more convenient for the importer to pay the VAT than it is for the exporter. In those circumstances, the DDP VAT unpaid Incoterms® rule variant may be used. The syntax for this variant should be:

> **DDP · Kopparbergsgatan 226, Malmö 214 44, Sverige/Sweden, Incoterms® 2010, VAT unpaid.**

6.10.1 Delivery under DDP

Under the DDP Incoterms® rule, delivery takes place when the exporter places the goods at the disposal of the importer at the delivery address mentioned in the Incoterms® rule. The goods are delivered loaded (*i.e.*, it is the responsibility of the importer to arrange and pay for unloading the goods). However, this is often a very minor point, as the destination of the delivery is often the importer's plant, which can obviously unload a truck.

Although there is no transportation document that corresponds to delivery, a commonly used alternative is for the exporter to provide the bill of lading at delivery.

6.10.2   Responsibilities of the Exporter and the Importer under DDP

The exporter assumes all responsibilities in a DDP shipment: clearing the goods for export, transporting them to the importer's facilities, and clearing customs in the importing country. All costs and responsibilities are for the account of the exporter.

The importer only has the responsibility of receiving the goods at delivery and unloading them.

6.11   Free Alongside Ship (FAS)

Although the Free-Alongside-Ship (FAS) Incoterms® rule can be used for any merchandise, it is specifically designed for ocean transportation, and is not meant for any other means of transportation or for merchandise that is not destined to be handed to an ocean shipping line at the port of departure. The practices followed by international shippers make FAS an Incoterms® rule that should be used sparingly—or not at all—with containerized cargo, which should be best handled under a DAT Incoterms® rule. The FAS Incoterms® rule should be used with the following syntax:

> **FAS · Waalhaven Noordzijde 2089, Rotterdam, 3089KM, The Netherlands, Incoterms® 2010.**

where the address refers to the dock in the port where the delivery takes place. This port is usually located in the exporting country or a neighboring country.

In an FAS transaction, the exporter is responsible for bringing the goods to the port, on a quay "alongside" a ship designated by the importer, at which time the responsibility shifts to the importer.

6.11.1   Delivery under FAS

Under FAS, the delivery officially takes place when the exporter delivers the goods "alongside" a ship designated by the importer. The problem with this Incoterms® rule is that ports no longer keep merchandise "alongside" a ship, or on a quay waiting for a ship. Instead, the delivery takes place in a holding area, then the goods are cartaged (transported within the port area) from the holding area to

Figure 6.5: FAS Delivery: Steel Wire Coils Delivered Alongside the Ship in the Port of Odessa, Ukraine

Photo ©Aleksandr Lesik/Shutterstock. Used with permission.

the ship before the stevedoring (loading onto the ship) takes place. However, there are some merchandise types that are delivered next to the ship, such as large crates or bulk cargoes.

Compounding this difficulty is the fact that there is no transport document corresponding to a delivery to a holding area or to the quay alongside the ship. The ICC recognizes that the exporter may not be able to obtain "a receipt or a transport document from the carrier"[12] since no ocean carrier will issue a bill of lading until the goods have been received in good condition onboard the vessel. However, the ICC adds that the exporter must then "provide some other document to prove that the goods have been delivered" [13] but does not suggest what it may be. A dock receipt from the port authorities may be sufficient; however, this lack of clear physical evidence of delivery can be a substantial deterrent to using the FAS Incoterms® rule. However, the use of Electronic Data Interchange (EDI) by the parties involved can remedy this problem: the exporter can notify the importer that delivery has been made in the port of departure and the terminal operator can also do the same. However, the ICC did not list such notices as acceptable proofs of delivery.

It is for those reasons that the DAT Incoterms® rule was developed; there is a clear point at which the responsibility for the goods shifts from the importer to the exporter.

6.11.2 Responsibilities of the Exporter and the Importer under FAS

Under FAS, the exporter is responsible for packing the goods for export, transporting them to the port, and unloading them onto the quay or holding area in the port. The exporter is responsible for clearing the goods for export, providing whatever documents and assistance the importer may need to clear customs in the importing country and to obtain insurance. In the United States, the exporter fills out the Electronic Export Information declaration and is the "U.S. principal party in interest," or the exporter of record. In countries where export authorities require a pre-shipment inspection, the exporter must pay for it.

The importer is responsible for the shipment starting from the point of delivery. Therefore the importer is responsible for port handling charges, stevedoring (loading the goods in the vessel), and for ocean transportation costs, as well as insurance (if purchased), unloading in the port of arrival, and customs duties in the importing country. If the importing country requires a pre-shipment inspection, the importer has to pay for it.

6.12   Free on Board (FOB)

Although the Free-On-Board (FOB) Incoterms® rule can be used for any merchandise, it is specifically designed for ocean transportation, and is not meant for any other means of transportation or for merchandise that is not destined to be handed to an ocean shipping line at the port of departure. The practices followed by international shippers make FOB an Incoterms® rule that should be used sparingly—or not at all—with containerized cargo, which is best handled under a DAT Incoterms® rule. The FOB Incoterms® rule should be used with the following syntax:

> **FOB · Breakbulk Terminal, 660 Duncan Road, Cape Town, South Africa, Incoterms® 2010.**

where the terminal indicated is the location in the port where the goods are placed onboard the vessel and delivery takes place. This port is generally located in the exporting country or a neighboring country.

Under the FOB term, the exporter is responsible for the goods until they are placed on the ship. The importer is responsible for them after that.

Free On Board, sometimes incorrectly called Freight On Board, is one of the oldest maritime terms of trade. Unfortunately, that means that the division of responsibilities between the exporter and the importer is somewhat dependent on the practices of the port in which the goods are loaded. These differences matter because of the way the loading costs are billed: some ports have the tradition to include loading, stowing, and securing the goods in the hold of the ship as part of the stevedoring costs, while other ports bill these services as part of the ocean cargo costs. The shipping line contracted by the importer obviously should be able to communicate what the port's practice is. However, these differences in practices have triggered the need for a variant to the FOB Incoterms® rule to reflect which of the trade partners is responsible for handling costs on the ship; either "FOB stowed" or "FOB stowed, trimmed, and secured"[14] can be used to denote that the exporter is responsible for those specific costs. Here again, because the ICC does not regulate Incoterms® rule variants, the correct syntax should be:

> **FOB · Breakbulk Terminal, 660 Duncan Road, Cape Town, South Africa, Incoterms® 2010, Stowed, Trimmed and Secured.**

For these reasons, it may be preferable to use the DAT Incoterms® rule which outlines clearly the responsibilities of the exporter and the importer.

6.12.1 Delivery under FOB

Under FOB, the point at which the responsibility for the goods shift from the exporter to the importer is when the goods are "onboard" the vessel. This interpretation of the delivery point is new with Incoterms® 2010 rules, and little jurisprudence has accumulated regarding what constitutes "onboard." It is expected to mean that the goods are delivered when they are in the hold of the ship, but remain to be stowed—placed in the exact location on the deck. The point at which the responsibility for the goods shifts from the exporter to the importer is called the "FOB point."

The document associated with the FOB delivery is quite clear however: the proof of delivery is an ocean bill of lading or a sea waybill. Since the ocean bill of lading certifies that the goods have been received onboard the ship, there is a perfect match between the documents available and the requirements of the Incoterms® rules. Only after receiving the goods will the shipping line issue this document, giving a copy to the exporter.

6.12.2 Responsibilities of the Exporter and the Importer under FOB

In an FOB transaction, the exporter is responsible for packaging the goods for export, shipping them to the port of departure, and paying to have them loaded onto the ship by a stevedore. The exporter is responsible for clearing the goods for export, and must provide whatever documents and assistance the importer may need to clear customs in the importing country and to obtain insurance. In the United States, the exporter fills out the Electronic Export Information declaration and is the "U.S. principal party in interest" or the exporter of record. In countries where export authorities require a pre-shipment inspection, the exporter must pay for it.

stowed
Goods are considered stowed when they are aboard the ship and placed in the position in which they will be transported.

trimmed
A ship is considered trimmed when the cargo aboard the ship is balanced side-to-side and front-to-back.

secured
Once goods are stowed and the vessel trimmed, the goods are tied to the vessel by means of ropes or chains.

stevedore
Historically, an individual, and today a company, that loads and unloads goods from a vessel.

Figure 6.6: FOB Delivery: Steel Coils Loaded and Stowed in the Hold of a Ship, Port of Singapore

Photo ©Wathit Kettap/Shutterstock. Used with permission.

The importer is responsible for arranging and paying for ocean transportation from the port of departure to the goods' destination, clearing customs in the importing country, and eventually arranging and paying for insurance. If the importing country requires a pre-shipment inspection, the importer must pay for it.

6.13   Cost and Freight (CFR)

Although the Cost-and-Freight (CFR) Incoterms® rule can be used for any merchandise, it is specifically designed for ocean transportation, and is not meant for any other means of transportation or for merchandise that is not destined to be handed to an ocean shipping line at the port of departure. The practices followed by international shippers make CFR an Incoterms® rule that should be used sparingly—or not at all—with containerized cargo, which is best handled under a DAT Incoterms® rule. The CFR Incoterms® rule should be used with the following syntax:

CFR · ENL Multi-purpose Terminal, Apapa Wharf, Lagos, Nigeria, Incoterms® 2010.

where the terminal in the port of destination is the location at which the importer takes physical control of the goods. The port of destination is usually located in the importing country or in a neighboring country. The port of destination is not the point of delivery. In a CFR transaction, the delivery (the transfer or responsibility or the transfer of risk) does not take place in the port of destination, but in the port of departure.

The CFR term is also one of the oldest maritime terms of trade, and it was known until the 1990 version of Incoterms® rules as C&F or C+F, abbreviations which are now obsolete. The exporter is responsible for the goods until they are placed onboard the ship in the port of origin in the exporting country, and the importer is responsible for them after that. However, the exporter pre-pays the ocean freight.

Unfortunately, because CFR is such an old term of trade, its meaning depends on the practices of the port in which the goods are unloaded. These practices affect the way the unloading costs are billed: some ports traditionally bill separately for the unloading of the goods as stevedoring costs, and others ask shipping lines to bill for these services as part of the ocean cargo costs. The shipping line contracted by the exporter can communicate what the practice is at a given port of discharge. Nevertheless, to account for these differences in practices, variants to the CFR Incoterms® rule were created to reflect which trade partner is responsible for unloading costs. "CFR landed" explicitly states that the costs of unloading are borne by the exporter, and "CFR undischarged" notes unloading costs are borne by the importer.[15] In these cases, the correct syntax is:

CFR · ENL Multi-purpose Terminal, Apapa Wharf, Lagos, Nigeria, Incoterms® 2010, landed.

6.13.1 Delivery under CFR

In a CFR transaction, delivery does not take place in the port of destination (the port mentioned in the Incoterms® rule) but in the port of departure, where the exporter delivers the goods to the carrier. In a CFR transaction, the point of delivery is the "FOB point." Until the merchandise is onboard the ship, it is the responsibility of the exporter; after that, the responsibility shifts to the importer.

The document associated with the CFR term is the proof of delivery in the port of departure: an ocean bill of lading or a sea waybill. Only after receiving the goods will the shipping line issue this document, giving one of the originals to the exporter.

6.13.2 Responsibilities of the Exporter and the Importer under CFR

Under CFR, the exporter is responsible for packaging the goods, shipping them to the port of departure, loading them onto a ship "of a kind normally used for the transport of goods of the contract description,"[16] and pre-paying for the main carriage. Depending on the practices at the port of destination, this pre-paid contract of carriage may include the costs of unloading the goods. If it does not, then the importer must pay for unloading the ship. The exporter is also responsible to clear the goods for export, assist the importer in providing the documentation necessary to clear customs in the importing country and obtain insurance. In the United States, the exporter fills out the Electronic Export Information declaration and is the "U.S. principal party in interest" or the exporter of record. In countries where export authorities require a pre-shipment inspection, the exporter has to pay for it.

The importer takes responsibility for the goods at the delivery point (*i.e.*, once the goods are aboard the ship in the port of departure), even though the exporter contracts for the ocean shipping of the goods. Depending on the practice at the port of destination, and the possible Incoterms® rule variant used, the importer may also have to pay the unloading costs. It is also responsible for clearing customs in the importing country and for inland on-carriage after that. If the importing country requires a pre-shipment inspection, the importer must pay for it.

6.14 Cost, Insurance, and Freight (CIF)

Although the Cost-Insurance-and-Freight (CIF) Incoterms® rule can be used for any merchandise, it is specifically designed for ocean transportation, and is not meant for any other means of transportation or for merchandise that is not destined to be handed to an ocean shipping line at the port of departure. The CIF Incoterms® rule is also mostly designed for non-containerized cargo; containerized cargo is better handled through a DAT Incoterms® rule. The CIF Incoterms® rule should be used with the following syntax:

> **CIF · Naigai Lines, 176 Higashi-Machi, Chuo-Ku, Kobe 650-0031, Hyogo, Japan, Incoterms® 2010.**

where the point at which the importer takes control of the goods is a specific terminal in the port of destination. In a CIF transaction, the delivery does not take place in the port of destination, but in the port of departure, when the goods are placed onboard the vessel.

The CIF Incoterms® rule is similar to the CFR term, with the exception that the exporter has the additional responsibility to pre-pay for marine cargo insurance until the port of destination. Unfortunately, the mandate of the ICC is for "minimum cover," or Coverage C of the Institute Cargo Clauses (see Section 10.5 on page 354), a practice that results in the creation of yet another Incoterms®

rule variant,[17] CIF maximum cover—mandating Coverage A of the Institute Cargo Clauses—in addition to the predictable CIF undischarged and CIF landed, which are mirrors of their CFR equivalents. The syntax again must accommodate the fact that Incoterms® rule variants are not regulated by the ICC and should read:

CIF · Naigai Lines, 176 Higashi-Machi, Chuo-Ku, Kobe 650-0031, Hyogo, Japan, Incoterms® 2010, maximum cover, landed.

Finally, under the CIF Incoterms® rule, the amount insured must be at least 110 percent of the value of the goods, a custom that dates to 1906 and the British Marine Insurance Act.

One aspect of CIF is also unusual: certain countries (see Table 6.2 on the next page) do not allow their importers to purchase insurance abroad, and therefore prevent any import on a CIF or CIP basis.[18] This restriction is in place to conserve foreign currency—it obligates importers to purchase insurance locally in local currency—and to subsidize the national insurance industry; all the countries practicing this restriction are relatively small traders. Import restrictions generally prevent exporters from offering CIP or CIF if the importer is expected to purchase insurance.

6.14.1 Delivery under CIF

In a CIF transaction, delivery is the "FOB point," the point at which the responsibility shifts from the exporter to the importer. Until the merchandise is onboard the ship, it is the responsibility of the exporter; after that, the responsibility shifts to the importer. The document associated with the CIF term is also quite clear: the proof of delivery is an ocean bill of lading or a sea waybill. Only after receiving the goods will the shipping line issue this document, giving one of the originals to the exporter.

6.14.2 Responsibilities of the Exporter and the Importer under CIF

Under CIF, the exporter has to package the goods for export, and pay for shipping costs and minimum insurance costs to the port of destination. The exporter is also responsible for clearing the goods for export. In the United States, the exporter fills out the Electronic Export Information declaration and is the "U.S. principal party in interest" or the exporter of record. In countries where export authorities require a pre-shipment inspection, the exporter must pay for it.

The importer takes responsibility for the goods once they are onboard the ship in the port of departure, even though the contract of carriage is between the seller and the ocean shipping line. The importer is responsible for clearing customs in the importing country and for inland transportation after that. If the importing country requires a pre-shipment inspection, the importer pays for it.

Countries with Restrictions on Insurance Purchases

Country	Import	Export	Country	Import	Export
Algeria	■		Laos	■	■
Angola	■		Libya	■	
Bangladesh	■		Malaysia	■	
Barbados	■		Mali	■	
Benin	■		Mauritania	■	
Burkina Faso	■		Morocco	■	
Burundi	■	■	Myanmar/Burma	■	■
Cameroon	■		Nicaragua	■	
Central African Republic	■		Niger	■	
Chad	■		Nigeria	■	
Congo (Brazzaville)	■		Oman	■	■
Congo (Kinshasa)	■	■	Pakistan	■	
Cuba	■	■	Papua New Guinea		■
Djibouti	■		Qatar	■	■
Dominican Republic	■		Russia	■	
Ecuador	■		Rwanda	■	■
Ethiopia	■		Senegal	■	■
Gabon	■		Serbia	■	■
Georgia		■	Sierra Leone	■	
Ghana	■		Solomon Islands	■	
Guatemala		■	Sudan	■	
Guinea	■		Syria	■	
Haiti	■		Tanzania	■	
Indonesia	■		Thailand	■	■
Iran	■		Togo	■	
Iraq	■		Tunisia	■	
Ivory Coast	■		Uganda	■	■
Jordan		■	Venezuela	■	■
Kenya	■		Yemen	■	■

Table 6.2: Countries with Restrictions on Insurance Purchases for Incoterms®
Rules Sales
American Institute of Marine Underwriters.

6.15 Summary of the Division of Responsibilities between Exporters and Importers

Table 6.3 summarizes the responsibilities of the exporter and those of the importer for each Incoterms® rule. When the exporter is responsible for an aspect of a shipment, the column is marked with an X. When the importer is responsible, it is marked with an I. When it could be either the exporter or the importer, then the column is marked with an asterisk. A dash signifies that there are no requirements to purchase insurance.

For example, under FCA, if the term "exporter's premises" is used, then the pre-carriage is the responsibility of the importer. If "carrier's premises" is specified, then the pre-carriage is the responsibility of the exporter. Similarly, under DAT, the main carriage can be the responsibility of the exporter if the delivery takes place in a terminal in the importing country, or the responsibility of the importer if the delivery takes place in a terminal located in the exporting country.

Under CFR and CIF, the responsibility for unloading the goods in the port of destination is determined by the customs of that port. If the contract of ocean carriage includes unloading the goods, that expense is the responsibility of the exporter; if it does not, the expense is borne by the importer.

Division of Responsibilities under Incoterms® Rules

Task	All-methods-of-transportation Incoterms® rules							Maritime Incoterms® rules			
	EXW	FCA	CPT	CIP	DAT	DAP	DDP	FAS	FOB	CFR	CIF
Export Packing	X	X	X	X	X	X	X	X	X	X	X
Export Clearance	I	X	X	X	X	X	X	X	X	X	X
Pre-Carriage Loading	I	X	X	X	X	X	X	X	X	X	X
Pre-Carriage	I	*	X	X	X	X	X	X	X	X	X
Main Carriage Loading	I	I	X	X	*	X	X	I	X	X	X
Main Carriage	I	I	X	X	*	X	X	I	I	X	X
Insurance	—	—	—	X	—	—	—	—	—	—	X
Main Carriage Unloading	I	I	X	X	*	X	X	I	I	*	*
On Carriage	I	I	X	X	I	X	X	I	I	I	I
On Carriage Unloading	I	I	I	I	I	I	X	I	I	I	I
Import Clearance	I	I	I	I	I	I	X	I	I	I	I
Import Duty	I	I	I	I	I	I	X	I	I	I	I

Table 6.3: Summary of Incoterms® Responsibilities

X=exporter; I=importer; * =depends on point of delivery; —=undetermined.

6.16   Common Errors in Incoterms® Rules Usage

6.16.1   Confusion with Domestic Terms

Some of the most commonly made errors in international terms of trade is the substitution of domestic terms of trade for international terms of trade: an inexperienced exporter will use "FOB factory" rather than the correct corresponding Free Carrier, exporter's premises, or FCA Incoterms® rule; similarly, rather than the correct Delivered Duty Paid (DDP) Incoterms® rule, the same inexperienced exporter uses "FOB destination."

"FOB factory" (also known as "FOB origin") is a term of trade used in the United States (see vignette on page 188) for domestic sales that limits the responsibility of the seller to loading the merchandise onto a vehicle owned or hired by the buyer. When the merchandise is loaded onto the vehicle, the title of the merchandise transfers to the buyer. There are therefore several differences between "FOB factory" and its closest Incoterms® rule equivalent, which is Free Carrier (FCA) exporter's premises. First, "FOB factory" shows a transfer of title, which none of the Incoterms® rules do, rather than a transfer of responsibility, the only concept to which the Incoterms® rules refer. Second, "FOB factory" does not refer to any form of documentation, which is critical to the international buyer because such documents are needed to clear customs. Third, "FOB factory" applies to any form of transportation, and not only to ocean transportation, as the FOB Incoterms® rule does. Finally, "FOB factory" does not have any specific packaging requirements, whereas FCA clearly requires packaging sufficient to withstand an international voyage.

"FOB destination" (also known as "FOB delivered") is another term used in the United States for domestic sales that extends the responsibility of the seller to the delivery point at the buyer's place of business; the seller pays for the carriage cost to the point of delivery. When the merchandise is unloaded from the vehicle, the title transfers to the buyer. The "FOB destination" term of sale is not equivalent to the DAP Incoterms® rule. First, "FOB destination" also refers to the transfer of title, whereas the DAP Incoterms® rule does not. Second, it makes no reference to customs clearance, which DAP excludes, but DDP requires.

Other terms that are also used incorrectly in international trade are "Freight Pre-Paid" and "Freight Collect," which are also UCC terms and refer to the fact that the seller either includes the cost of shipment in the invoice or excludes it. Neither of these terms work in an international environment for essentially the same reasons that "FOB factory" and "FOB destination" do not.

On occasion, there are some other terms used in international trade that have their roots in domestic trade, although they have become obsolete. For example, some invoices will reflect a *franco* price, which is conceptually equivalent to the "FOB factory" term; however, the *franco* price does not require the loading of the merchandise onto the vehicle provided by the buyer. There are reasons to use this term of trade domestically, but a multitude of reasons not to use it internationally.

6.16.2 Confusion with Older Incoterms® Versions

The International Chamber of Commerce modified the Incoterms® rules in 1980, 1990, and 2000. It eliminated some Incoterms® rules, modified others and created new ones. For many reasons, several exporters have failed to adapt to these changes.

Older ICC versions included several Incoterms® rules that have since disappeared: FOB rail (which eventually changed to FOR, "Free on Rail" in 1980, and eventually was abandoned altogether in 1990), FOB truck (which became FOT, "Free on Truck" in 1980, and which was also abandoned in 1990), and FOB airport (eliminated in 1990). On occasion, though, these older Incoterms® rules are still used on invoices. Although this practice is allowed under ICC rules, the use of such obsolete Incoterms® rules is more due to carelessness than to a deliberate attempt at using an Incoterms® rule that has advantages over the current version. It is therefore preferable to use the Free Carrier (FCA) Incoterms® rule instead of the previous similar Incoterms® rules, as fewer and fewer people are familiar with the specific requirements of the former Incoterms® rules.

Another problem with older Incoterms® rules is the use of C&F or C+F rather than CFR to communicate that an ocean shipment is made under a Cost and Freight Incoterms® rule. Not only has the abbreviation changed, but the transfer of responsibility has changed from the point at which the goods crossed the ship's rail to the point at which they are onboard the vessel. Therefore, such older abbreviations should be avoided: they could confuse the importer and present challenges, should the shipment experience a mishap.

Another obsolete term is "Free Domicile," although there is no evidence that such a term was ever part of the recognized Incoterms® rules. This pricing term is used when the exporter pays all the applicable duties and all the transportation and other charges until the shipment is delivered to the importer's premises. Because this term is not recognized by the ICC Arbitration Panel, it should be replaced by either the Delivered At Place (DAP) or the Delivered Duty Paid (DDP) Incoterms® rule.

6.16.3 Improper Use of Correct Incoterms® Rules

Sometimes shippers use the correct Incoterms® rule, but for the incorrect commodity. Table 6.4 on the next page outlines the proper use of Incoterms® rules for specific shipments. For example, a containerized shipment should not be shipped EXW, could be shipped CIF or CFR, but should be shipped FCA, DAT or DAP.

Another misuse of Incoterms® rules is when a shipper uses FOB for an air shipment, even though FOB is an ocean-shipment term. The correct Incoterms® rule to use for an air shipment via Free Carrier (FCA), to clearly outline the responsibilities of the exporter and of the importer. Table 6.5 on the following page outlines the proper use of Incoterms® rules by mode of transportation.

Appropriate Incoterms® Rule per Type of Shipment

Task	All-methods-of-transportation Incoterms® rules							Maritime Incoterms® rules			
	EXW	FCA	CPT	CIP	DAT	DAP	DDP	FAS	FOB	CFR	CIF
Bulk Cargo	−	+	−	−	+	+	+	+	++	++	++
Breakbulk Cargo	−	++	+	+	++	+	+	++	++	++	++
Roll-on-Roll-off Cargo	−	++	+	+	++	+	+	+	+	+	+
Containerized Cargo	−	++	+	+	++	++	+	−	−	−	−
Small Packet	++	+	+	+	−	+	+	−−	−−	−−	−−

Table 6.4: Summary of Incoterms® Rule Choice by Types of Cargo
−− inappropriate; − discouraged; +appropriate; ++best fit.

Appropriate Incoterms® Rule per Main Carriage

Task	All-methods-of-transportation Incoterms® rules							Maritime Incoterms® rules			
	EXW	FCA	CPT	CIP	DAT	DAP	DDP	FAS	FOB	CFR	CIF
Ocean	−	+	−	−	+	+	+	+	+	+	+
Air	++	+	+	+	−	+	+	−−	−−	−−	−−
Rail	−	++	+	+	++	++	+	−	−	−	−
Road	++	+	+	+	−	+	+	−−	−−	−−	−−
Multi-modal (FCL)	−	++	+	+	++	+	+	++	+	++	++
Multi-modal (LCL)	−	++	+	+	++	+	+	+	+	+	+

Table 6.5: Summary of Incoterms® Rule Choice by Means of Transportation
−− inappropriate; − discouraged; +appropriate; ++best fit.

6.17   Incoterms® Rules as a Marketing Tool

As mentioned earlier, the greatest criterion used in the choice of an Incoterms®
rule is the willingness of the exporter and importer to perform and pay for some
of the tasks involved in an international shipment. In some cases, a tactical
advantage can be gained by an exporter willing to facilitate the sale of its products
by assisting a novice importer in handling a shipment. In other cases, a price

advantage may be obtained by an experienced importer willing to perform all or most of the tasks involved in the shipment.

Usually, an exporter does not determine which Incoterms® rule to use on a case-by-case basis. Instead, the exporter adopts a policy to include in international quotes those services that it feels it can provide efficiently. It is difficult for an exporter to adapt its Incoterms® rule strategy to accommodate the requirements of an importer, as it may require the exporter to be responsible for tasks that it has decided it would rather not perform. However, should the importer want to perform more tasks than what the exporter prefers, it is possible for the exporter to do less than what it expected, and use a different Incoterms® rule on that transaction that allows the importer to do more.

The choice of the proper Incoterms® rule is a critical decision for a firm: it is an integral part of its export strategy and linked to the level of customer service it is aiming to provide. From this perspective, therefore, it makes most sense for an exporter to become as well-versed as possible in international logistics and be prepared to include as many of the transportation functions as possible in its quote.

An exporter intent on increasing its sales should therefore offer to provide the importer with the most customer-friendly Incoterms® rule quotes (either DAP or DDP), if only by using the services of a competent freight forwarder. Should the importer want to shoulder more responsibilities, it is always possible for the exporter to reduce its involvement and quote FCA or even EXW. The best quote is one in which the exporter lists different prices for different Incoterms® rules, leaving the importer choose which is best for its specific case.

For example, an exporter could submit a quote that reads:

FCA · 2500 Industrial Parkway, Cleveland, OH 44114, USA _____ $10,000

FCA · Terminal 5, Cincinnati Airport, Covington, KY 41048, USA ___ $11,000

CIP · CDG Cargo, route des badaux, 95700 Roissy, France _____ $15,500

DAP · 114 rue de Prat, 63100 Clermont-Ferrand, France _____ $16,500

DDP · 114 rue de Prat, 63100 Clermont-Ferrand, France _____ $17,800

and leave the importer decide which of the Incoterms® rules it would like to choose.

Review and Discussion Questions

1. Choose two Incoterms® rules and describe them.

2. What is the Incoterms® rule that is most importer friendly? Least importer friendly? Justify your answer.

3. Which the Incoterms® rules include a requirement of insurance by the exporter? How is that insurance requirement handled?

4. The Delivered Incoterms® rules (DAT, DAP, and DDP) do not include insurance. Why not?

5. Choose a product, as well as an importer and an exporter, and determine what would be the ideal Incoterms® rule for a transaction. Make as many assumptions as necessary to justify your decision.

6. Explain why a developing country would want to prevent its importers from purchasing CIF or CIP and instead require CFR or CPT shipments.

7. A certain *sogo shosha* (a Japanese Trading Company) always requests its suppliers to provide an FCA exporter's premises quote. Knowing what you know about trading companies and Incoterms® rules, why do you think this is the case?

Notes

[1]Debattista, Charles, Editor, *ICC Guide to Incoterms® 2010*, International Chamber of Commerce Publication No. 720E, ICC Publishing S.A., 38 Cours Albert 1er, 75008 Paris, France and ICC Publishing, Inc., 156 Fifth Avenue, Suite 417, New York, NY 10010, USA.

[2]*Incoterms® 2010, ICC Rules for the Use of Domestic and International Trade Terms*, International Chamber of Commerce Publication No. 715E, ICC Publishing S.A., 38 Cours Albert 1er, 75008 Paris, France and ICC Publishing, Inc., 156 Fifth Avenue, Suite 417, New York, NY 10010, USA.

[3]Kaye, Simon, "Using Incoterms to Simplify Global Sourcing," *Inbound Logistics*, January 2012, pp. 193-196.

[4]Freudmann, Aviva, "Traders get a Brand-new Bible," *Journal of Commerce*, September 9, 1999, p. 1.

[5]*Incoterms® 2010, ICC Rules for the Use of Domestic and International Trade Terms*, International Chamber of Commerce Publication No. 715E, ICC Publishing S.A., 38 Cours Albert 1er, 75008 Paris, France and ICC Publishing, Inc., 156 Fifth Avenue, Suite 417, New York, NY 10010, USA.

[6]Reynolds, Frank, *Incoterms® for Americans (Completely rewritten for Incoterms® 2010)*, International Projects, Inc., Toledo, Ohio, USA.

[7]"U.S. Principal Party in Interest Overview," United States Census Bureau, https://www.aesdirect.gov/support/usppi_overview.html, retrieved May 18, 2013.

[8]Biederman, David, "New Rules for Exports," *JoC Week*, July 24-30, 2000, pp.10-12.

[9]Reynolds, Frank, "Seminar in Paris Yields Answers to Widely Asked Questions on Incoterms," *Journal of Commerce*, April 22, 1998, p. 2C.

[10]King and Spalding LLP, "UCC Article 2 (Sales of Goods)—Significant Changes on the Way," www.kslaw.com/Library/pdf/UCCArticle2.pdf, retrieved May 18, 2013.

[11]American Law Institute, "Recommendation of the Permanent Editorial Board for the Uniform Commercial Code to Withdraw the 2003 Amendments to UCC Articles 2 and 2A from the Official Text of the Uniform Commercial Code," http://www.theconglomerate.org/2011/05/-withdrawing-the-2003-amendments-to-ucc-articles-2-and-2a.html, retrieved May 18, 2013.

[12]Ramberg, Jan, *ICC Guide to Incoterms® 2010*, International Chamber of Commerce Publication No. 720E, ICC Publishing S.A., 38 Cours Albert 1er, 75008 Paris, France and ICC Publishing, Inc., 156 Fifth Avenue, Suite 417, New York, NY 10010, USA.

[13]*Ibid.*

[14]Raty, Asko, "Variants on Incoterms (Part 2)," in Debattista, Charles, Editor, *Incoterms in Practice*, International Chamber of Commerce Publication No. 505, ICC Publishing S.A., 38 Cours Albert 1er, 75008 Paris, France and ICC Publishing, Inc., 156 Fifth Avenue, Suite 417, New York, NY 10010, USA, 1995.

[15]Raty, Asko, "Variants on Incoterms (Part 2)," in Debattista, Charles, Editor, *Incoterms in Practice*, International Chamber of Commerce Publication No. 505, ICC Publishing S.A., 38 Cours Albert 1er, 75008 Paris, France and ICC Publishing, Inc., 156 Fifth Avenue, Suite 417, New York, NY 10010, USA, 1995.

[16]Ramberg, Jan, *ICC Guide to Incoterms® 2010*, International Chamber of Commerce Publication No. 720E, ICC Publishing S.A., 38 Cours Albert 1er, 75008 Paris, France and ICC Publishing, Inc., 156 Fifth Avenue, Suite 417, New York, NY 10010, USA.

[17]Mikkola, Kainu, "Variants on Incoterms (Part 1)," in Debattista, Charles, Editor, *Incoterms in Practice*, International Chamber of Commerce Publication No. 505, ICC Publishing S.A., 38 Cours Albert 1er, 75008 Paris, France and ICC Publishing, Inc., 156 Fifth Avenue, Suite 417, New York, NY 10010, USA, 1995.

[18]American Institute of Marine Underwriters, "A list of countries with restrictive measures in

the field of marine insurance (August 2008)," http://www.aimu.org/cargoinsurancerestrict.html, retrieved January 18, 2017

Chapter 7

Terms of Payment

One of the greatest concerns an exporting company has is to make sure that it can collect payment from its foreign customers. Although this is also a legitimate concern domestically, an international transaction is generally perceived to involve a greater non-payment risk than a domestic sale, for many reasons.

There are several ways in which an exporting company can ensure that it is paid and paid on time; a company can tailor its international terms of payment to the characteristics of its customers, the countries in which it does business, and its own tolerance for risk. Although these methods are more complex than the open-account arrangements traditionally found in all domestic sales, they are universally accepted, and there is ample jurisprudence to support them. It is therefore relatively simple to choose an international sales term that secures the interests of the exporter.

What is difficult in selecting an international sales term is managing the delicate balance between protecting the interests of the exporter and offering good marketing practices that engender good customer relations.

7.1   International Payment Characteristics

Exporters tend to handle their foreign receivables conservatively and err on the side of caution for several reasons:

- **Credit information**. There is generally much less information on the creditworthiness of a creditor in a foreign market than there is for a domestic customer. Although a few credit reporting agencies, accounting firms, and factoring houses do keep such information, it is not always readily obtainable or does not exist for a specific customer, especially if the customer is a new firm or is in a developing country. Some improvements have been made recently, though, with the creation of centralized credit information portals,[1] which offer links to access foreign countries' credit agencies. Collecting credit information, though, is usually much more expensive and complicated for a foreign customer than for a domestic one, if only because the identity of a domestic firm is easier to establish. The paucity of information about certain countries is often coupled with an unfamiliarity with the diverse business organizations (different types of partnership and corporations) of a foreign country's legal system and an inability to decipher businesses' names.

- **Lack of personal contact**. International transactions tend to be conducted in a more impersonal fashion (through fax, telex, e-mail) than domestic transactions are, which tend to be conducted at least initially with some sort of personal contact (in person or over the phone). This lack of contact can lead to a climate in which the exporter has no way to evaluate the character of the importer, and where the possibility of a greater risk is often therefore assumed. Even when there is personal contact, it is sometimes between people who are not always well versed in intercultural communication and can substantially misunderstand each other. Such communication gaps can foster the perception of a higher risk and encourages a more cautious approach.

- **Difficult and expensive collections.** Should a foreign customer renege on a payment, the collection of a past-due account can be difficult. Although there is a generally well structured collections system for domestic transactions, there are few firms that offer international collection services. Those that do tend to offer the service at a high price, collecting between 5 and 30 percent of the receivable.[2] In some cases, relying on a foreign collection agency can lead a company to unwittingly employ some pretty unsavory characters, a situation that can eventually taint the image of the exporter, as Citibank discovered to its detriment when it used a "strong-arm" collection company in India.[3]

- **No easy legal recourse.** Unlike in a domestic setting, where there is a commercial code (of laws) and abundant jurisprudence, there is little of either in international trade. In addition, there is no court with jurisdiction over international disputes, and therefore a ruling by a court in the exporter's country cannot be easily enforced in the importer's country.

The creation of the United Nations Convention on Contracts for the International Sale of Goods (CISG) and its implementation in 1980 have helped establish a body of legal principles for the sale of goods between companies located in two different sovereign countries. As of January 2017, 84 countries had ratified this treaty, representing about 80 percent of the world's trade, but some countries, such as the United States, have ratified only part of the treaty,[4] presumably those articles that do not conflict with their own code law (Uniform Commercial Code [UCC] for the United States). The United Kingdom has yet to ratify this convention at all.[5] The enforcement of the convention is left to domestic courts' interpretation, and although there is some jurisprudence in this area, it is still fairly scant (all of the available jurisprudence is made accessible through a database created by the United Nations Commission on International Trade Law [UNCITRAL] called CLOUT, for Case Law On UNCITRAL Texts).

Convention on Contracts for the International Sale of Goods
A United Nations' treaty that acts as international sales law.

Exporters are always concerned that conflicts of law between domestic laws and the CISG and differences in interpretation by the courts make the prospect of a court battle more daunting. Section 5.2 outlined several differences between the CISG and the United States UCC.

It is a common misconception that there is some sort of an international court of justice; although the International Court in The Hague, Netherlands (see Figure 7.1 on page 211), arbitrates disputes between governments and between governments and multinational corporations, it never interferes in disputes between corporations. In addition, its rulings are non-binding, as the International Court does not have the executive authority to enforce them.

- **Higher litigation costs.** The cost of international litigation, arbitration, or mediation is generally much greater than that of domestic litigation. Seeking a ruling against an importer in the importer's country is time consuming, can involve several trips abroad, and necessitates hiring foreign law specialists, a process that involves greater expenses than domestic disputes. In some countries, the backlog of civil and commercial cases in the court system renders impossible the probability of a swift decision. In India, for example, a judgment takes five years on average (see Table 7.2 on page 213), and may not be rendered for ten years, with some cases meandering through the system for much longer periods. Other countries, such as China, Russia, Indonesia, and Ukraine, are not much different.[6, 7]

Suing a foreign customer for non-payment in the courts of the exporter's country may be perceived as a means to speed the process up and eventually lower the exporter's costs; however, such suits are followed only by the prospect of having to file suit in the importing country's courts as well, to enforce the judgment rendered against the importer. Most exporters perceive litigation as an absolute last resort.

- **Mistrust**. Finally, there is the perception that the importing company is aware of all these factors and knows that the exporter is unlikely to aggressively pursue an uncollected foreign receivable. This creates a feeling of distrust on the part of the exporter, who can assume the worst intentions on the part of the importer.

litigation
The final process by which parties to a contract have to settle a dispute, in a court of law.

arbitration
A process by which parties to a contract choose to settle a dispute. An arbitration decision is binding on both parties.

mediation
A process by which parties to a contract choose to find a compromise in a dispute. A mediation recommendation is not binding.

7.2   Alternative Terms of Payment

There are four traditional payment methods in foreign transactions, all involving a different level of risk: cash in advance, open account, documentary collection, and letters of credit. Although there are variations in each of these methods, each one is designed to mitigate at least one aspect of the risks involved in an international transaction, and the methods have not changed much in the past fifty years. However, about twenty years ago, an interesting fifth payment method emerged, called TradeCard, and TradeCard promises to become an effective means of securing payment from a customer abroad without involving as many fees or intermediaries as some of the more secure traditional alternatives. However interesting TradeCard is, though, it has not been particularly successful in gaining market share.

Each of these five payment methods presents advantages and disadvantages and can be generally seen as a trade-off between the risk of non-payment and the risk of losing the business to a more aggressive competitor who is willing to accept more risk and therefore present the customer with a simpler form of payment.

Table 7.1 lists examples of the most common perceptions of the trade-off of risk of non-payment versus loss of business. Table 7.1 is an overly simplified summary of the various payment methods. The ultimate choice of a term of sale

Figure 7.1: The International Court in The Hague, Netherlands
Photo ©Ankor Light/Shutterstock. Used with permission.

Term of Payment	Probability of Losing The Business because of the Choice of Method of Payment	Probability of Loss due to Non-Payment
Cash in Advance	High	Nil
Letter of Credit	Fairly High	Almost Nil
Documentary Collection	Low	Low
Open Account	Nil	Relatively High
TradeCard	Low	Almost Nil

Table 7.1: Methods of Payment and Perceived Risks

should be carefully determined as a function of several objective and subjective factors, and each variant of the preferred method should be carefully considered. Unfortunately, if only for the obvious reason of simplifying the sale process, several exporting firms do not have the inclination—nor do they have the time and personnel—to tailor terms of payment to specific customers or countries, and these firms have adopted a single foreign-sales policy that applies to all orders from importers, regardless of where these customers are located or who they are. Such a lack of flexibility tends to lead to conservative policies. One exporter confessed to the author that it considered only cash-in-advance sales orders; undoubtedly this conservative stance never got the exporter's company in trouble, but it likely yielded much lower export sales than a slightly more aggressive approach. Ideally, the terms of sale of a transaction should be evaluated according to the risks attached to the transaction.

7.3   Risks in International Trade

There are three sources of risk in international trade that must be considered. First is the commercial risk, which is also encountered in domestic transactions and relates to the ability (and the willingness) of the importer to pay the invoice in time. However, there is also the country risk which encompasses all the issues related to a country to which an exporter is shipping that may affect payment, regardless of the importer's creditworthiness. Finally, exporters must also consider their exposure, which is the potential financial impact of non-payment or reduced payment on the exporter's business.

7.3.1   Country Risk

country risk
The probability of not being paid by a creditor, because the importer's country does not have the foreign currency or does not allow the creditor to pay—political embargo.

Country risk is an aggregate of political and economic issues.

On the political side, the government's stability should be considered. For example, the possibility that a government may be changed (with a new election) may influence import policies, which, in turn, can mean that goods cannot clear customs as easily, or that tariffs increase, or that other policies are changed to such an extent that the importer will refuse delivery. In a country in which such a political risk is perceived, the exporter should prefer a more secure term of payment. Similarly, a government that is in a weak position may see its policies challenged by a strong public opposition, a situation that can lead to political unrest, as was the case in the French Caribbean islands of Martinique and Guadeloupe, where there was a massive general strike early in 2009.[8] When such general strikes happen, nearly all economic activity stops, and therefore importers do not pay their creditors until the situation stabilizes. The strike in Guadeloupe lasted more than a month. In 2011, the Arab Spring[9] certainly disturbed quite a few international transactions.

Port personnel or other personnel critical to a shipment's timeliness—such as customs officers—strike often in some countries, and this fact should be considered in the choice of payment term. A strike in U.S. West Coast ports lasted only a day in May 2008,[10] but a similar action in 2013 at the International Terminal in the Port of Hong Kong lasted forty days and disrupted many shipments.[11] Sometimes, social movements are so common that businesses must plan around them. The French government tallies an average of at least 2 million worker-days of strike every year, and many more are lost because of the strikes (when non-striking employees cannot make it to work, for example).[12]

In some cases, the government delays payment of international obligations, including trade obligations, whenever it makes sense politically. However, although a few governments have reneged on their public debt, there is no recent evidence of governments refusing to honor their commercial (trade) debt.

The overall health of the economy should also be considered. If there is high unemployment, policies against "job-stealing" imports may be implemented. If there is high inflation, price controls may be initiated. Moreover, the balance of payments of the importing country may also be relevant: if the importing country is badly in a deficit position, imports of goods that are deemed non-essential may be curtailed. Such is the case when the import cover, or the amount of foreign currency that the country has to cover its imports, becomes low; generally, the import cover is expressed in months (*i.e.*, foreign currency reserves can cover the next n months of imports).[13]

A quick survey of the importing country's social system should also be conducted. Some countries' societies foster a climate where fraud is common, or even prevalent (*e.g.*, Nigeria),[14] a situation that warrants much caution on the part of an exporter. The fairness of the legal system should also be considered. An importer located in a country in which claims are handled professionally should be offered more lenient payment terms than one located in a country where the administrative and justice systems are notoriously biased, inadequate, or agonizingly slow. Table 7.2 outlines the number of days that it takes an importer to clear a product for import (once all documents are received), the number of days it takes to export a product, and the average duration of a commercial lawsuit. The World Bank has this information for all countries of the world.[15]

	Time needed to			
Country	Import a Product (hours)	Export a Product (hours)	Settle a Lawsuit (days)	Obtain a Construction Permit (days)
Brazil	183	67	731	426
France	1	1	395	183
Germany	1	37	499	96
India	344	144	1,420	213
Japan	43	25	360	197
Singapore	38	14	164	48
United States	10	4	420	81
Zimbabwe	309	171	410	238

Table 7.2: Time (in hours or days) Required to Perform Certain Tasks, by Country.
The World Bank.

Finally, it is important to note that expectations of currency exchange rate fluctuations do not affect the choice of the term of payment but will affect the choice of the currency of quote (see Chapter 8) and the strategy used to minimize this risk.

7.3.2   Commercial Risk

commercial risk
The probability of not being paid by a creditor, either because the creditor does not have the funds, or because it refuses to recognize the debt.

It is more difficult to obtain accurate and reliable information about commercial risk. If the potential customer is a distributor who does business with other exporting firms, it is often possible to obtain firsthand information from these other exporters. It is considered good commercial practice in the United States to share information on the creditworthiness of a common customer—and in some cases to monitor this customer's payments—with other suppliers.

Commercial risk can also be evaluated from private sources, including credit report companies, factoring houses, some accounting firms, insurance companies, and banks. However, private sources are usually fee-based services, and tend to be focused on larger established firms in developed countries. Private sources are reliable and unbiased, though they tend to be conservative in their evaluations.

Table 7.3 lists several companies offering foreign credit reports on overseas customers. Each of these firms usually issues a report on a foreign customer for about U.S. $200.[16]

Several International Credit Reporting Services

Name	Coverage	website
COFACE	worldwide	coface.com
Dun & Bradstreet	worldwide	dnb.com
International Company Profile	Britain	icpcredit.com
Arab Business Information	Middle East	cedar-rose.com
Cristal Credit International	Latin America	cristalcredit.com
Graydon International	Britain	graydon.co.uk
Rencom International	France	rencom.fr
Owens Online	worldwide	owens.com
AMS Inform Private Limited	Southeast Asia	amsinform.com
Finance, Credit & International Business Association	worldwide	fcibglobal.com

Table 7.3: Several International Credit Reporting Services

7.3.3   Exposure

exposure
The impact of an unpaid receivable for an exporter and its effect on the exporter's financial well-being.

The risk of non-payment, made up of an aggregate of different issues, some political, and some economic, is the probability of not getting paid or of getting paid late, and it therefore dictates the terms of payment chosen by the exporter.

However, another issue to consider is the consequence of the loss of payment on a company, also called the exposure of a company. At equal probabilities of loss, a small business should be much more careful handling a U.S.$ 50,000 export transaction than a large company may be. The amount is a much greater percentage of the small company's business, and the impact of the loss of this amount can be very significant. The greater the exposure of an exporter, the more secure the terms of payment should be.

7.4   Cash in Advance

7.4.1   Definition

In a cash-in-advance transaction, the exporter requests that the customer provide payment in advance, before the goods are shipped. Payment is usually made with an electronic fund transfer from the customer's bank to the exporter's bank, using the network of the Society for Worldwide Interbank Financial Telecommunication (SWIFT).

cash in advance
A method of payment in which an importer has to pay the exporter before the exporter ships the goods.

Cash-in-advance payments are the ultimate risk-free alternative for the exporter. The importer must pay before the goods are shipped; therefore, there are no collection worries, no foreign-exchange fluctuation exposure, no cash-flow problems, and only nominal fees to pay to banks.

SWIFT-Society for Worldwide Interbank Financial Telecommunications
An interbank electronic network for the secure transfer of funds and documents.

In a cash-in-advance transaction, the risk is transferred to the importer. The importer sends cash to the exporter with the expectation that the exporter will ship the goods that were requested, in the quantity that was ordered, in due time, and with the documents necessary to clear customs in the importing country. In addition, this takes place in an atmosphere where the exporter just demonstrated that it has no trust whatsoever in the importer because it is requesting cash in advance.

7.4.2   Applicability

Cash in advance is a recommended way of conducting international transactions in countries in which fraud is rampant, in which there is a substantial risk of political instability or the possibility of foreign exchange freezes, and in which there is no convertible currency. Transactions conducted in some of the republics of the former Soviet Union are probably best conducted on a cash-in-advance basis.

However, the cash-in-advance method is unsound for business conducted in developed countries, and in countries in which there is a significant level of sophistication in international business. In these countries, the probability that an importer will place a cash-in-advance purchase is infinitesimally small if there are other comparable suppliers available, and insisting on this method of payment is likely to create resentment on the part of the importer rather than initiate an amicable business relationship. Thus, in those situations, using a cash-in-advance method of payment should be avoided at all costs.

7.5   Open Account

7.5.1   Definition

open account
A method of payment in
which the exporter sends an
invoice to the importer
along with the goods and
expects the importer to pay
within a reasonable amount
of time.

In an open-account transaction, the exporter conducts international business in a manner similar to the way it conducts business domestically. The exporter sends an invoice to the importer along with the shipment and trusts the customer to pay within a reasonable amount of time—commensurate with the credit usually granted in the importer's country—, usually 30 to 90 days. The open-account method of payment is essentially the conceptual opposite of cash in advance, as the exporter shows complete trust in the importer and ships the merchandise without any guarantee that it will be paid. The only recourse in case of non-payment is legal action in the importing country, a time-consuming and expensive process that exporters rarely undertake.

7.5.2   Applicability

The open-account term of payment should be reserved for established customers, or customers with whom the exporter expects to have an ongoing relationship. Open accounts could possibly be extended to new orders from large companies and/or companies for which commercial credit data is available, and whose credit rating is excellent. At least, that's theoretically the way that this term of payment should be used.

In practice, however, open-account terms of sale have become almost necessary in some markets if the exporter wants any sales. For example, in the European Union, it has become very difficult to conduct business on any other basis. The trend is expected to continue and expand to other markets. For example, European Union companies offer open-account terms of payment to 80 percent of their customers[17] outside of the EU. The main reason is that, historically, European exporters have often benefited from their government's support, and were often offered free (or substantially discounted) commercial insurance on their foreign receivables. Until 1994, for example, a French exporter could obtain insurance from COFACE (Compagnie Française d'Assurance pour le Commerce Extérieur), a government-run insurance company, at a greatly reduced cost; its risk of non-payment had therefore essentially been assumed by the government. Today, COFACE and other European-based companies constitute the largest providers of international commercial credit insurance and are present in many different countries, a position reached through many consolidations. Once exporters learn that it is easy to offer open-account terms to their foreign customers, they tend to continue selling on those terms.

credit insurance
An insurance policy that the
exporter can purchase to
protect itself against the
risk of non-payment by the
importer.

7.5.3   Commercial Credit Insurance

To compete in markets where open-account terms of payment have become the rule, companies must offer this term of payment in their quotes to new customers. However, the associated risks or financial exposure linked to a given transaction should entice an exporter to acquire credit insurance on those sales. Therefore a commercial policy covering credit risks should be contracted either on a blanket basis (*i.e.*, covering all export transactions, up to a certain overall amount) or on a per-sale basis (*i.e.*, each individual transaction is covered by a separate commercial insurance contract). Section 10.5 on page 354 gives more detailed information on these types of coverage.

7.5.4 Factoring

Factoring is a process used most frequently between two domestic parties in which the creditor uses an intermediary, called a factor or a factoring house, to finance a receivable. There are two types of factoring: in the first, called factoring "without recourse," the creditor sells the receivable to the factor, who is then responsible for collecting from the debtor. If the latter does not pay, the factor assumes that responsibility, and the creditor keeps the proceeds of the sale of the receivable. In the second case, called factoring "with recourse," the factor attempts to collect the funds from the debtor but, if it is unsuccessful, can turn to the creditor for assistance. Ultimately, in a factoring transaction with recourse, the creditor is responsible for collecting the funds.

factoring
A means of financing international receivable accounts, by which a firm asks a factoring company to advance funds on the receivable.

In some international transactions, the importer may want credit terms that are beyond what the exporter is comfortable giving. For example, a 90-day credit is requested when the exporter can afford only a 30-day credit. In these situations, the exporter can use international factoring as a means of extending credit to the importer. When two countries are involved, factoring is much more complicated than in a domestic sale: the exporter contacts a factor in the exporting country that in turn contacts a factoring house in the importing country. Once both factors agree to the transaction, the sale is completed on an open-account basis. Once the invoice is sent, the exporter sells the receivable to the exporting country's factor and collects its face value, from which are deducted the fees and interest charges covering the period of time during which credit is extended.[18]

In an international transaction, factoring is generally done without recourse, and the factoring house is responsible for collecting the receivable and cannot turn to the exporter if it is unable to collect. This is the main reason for which factoring houses often involve a second factoring company located in the importing country; its responsibility is to check the creditworthiness of the importer and, in some cases, to act as a collection agent for the factoring company in the exporting country.[19]

If the exporter is unable to provide the importer with the type of credit terms that the importer requests, the importer can also find financing for its purchase by asking a financial institution to lend it funds based upon this incoming inventory. In the United States, for example, the United Parcel Service offers "capital cargo finance," which allows an importer to borrow money against an incoming in-transit shipment.[20]

7.6   Letter of Credit

7.6.1   Definition

letter of credit
A method of payment in which a bank promises to pay the beneficiary (the exporter) on behalf of the applicant (the importer), as long as the exporter has provided the documents requested in the letter of credit.

A letter of credit is a document in which the importer's bank promises to pay the exporter if the importer does not pay. Letters of credit substitute the creditworthiness of the bank for the creditworthiness of the importer. However, letters of credit are substantially more complex than this. The promise of payment is not made upon the exporter meeting certain conditions (or the importer not meeting certain conditions), but instead it is made on the documents of the transaction. This is why a letter of credit is often called a documentary letter of credit and why the process is called documentary credit.

It is fundamental to understand that the transaction documents are the critical elements to a letter of credit. The bank is under no obligation to pay if the documents do not conform to the letter of credit's requirements, even though delivery has been made and the importer has obtained control of the merchandise. Similarly, the bank is obligated to pay if the documents are in order, even though the merchandise may be shoddy or not fit for sale.

The letter of credit is a contractual agreement between the issuing bank and the beneficiary—the exporter—that is undertaken on behalf of the importer. This contractual agreement is independent of the underlying business relationship between the exporter and the importer; only the documents relating to a particular transaction between the exporter and the importer matter.[21] Thus, extreme care must be taken in handling the documents related to a letter of credit; otherwise, errors trigger a very time-consuming and expensive process of amendments and corrections.

An international transaction conducted on a letter-of-credit basis is almost as good as one made on a cash-in-advance basis in that the exporter will be paid. However, a letter of credit involves going through a lot more steps and paying a lot more banking fees. Figures 7.2 on the facing page through 7.4 on page 222 explain the process followed by a letter of credit transaction from issuance to payment.

7.6.2   Process

Issuance

Figure 7.2 describes the issuance of a letter of credit, or the steps that take place before the exporter ships the merchandise to the importer.

- The first step in the process is the negotiation, which takes place between the exporter and the importer, in which it is agreed that the term of payment will be by letter of credit. The exporter then sends a *pro forma* invoice to the importer, which estimates the terms of the transaction as closely as possible (see Section 9.2.2 on page 285 for further details on the elements of a *pro forma* invoice). The exporter also provides a series of instructions to the importer, detailing the terms of the transaction.

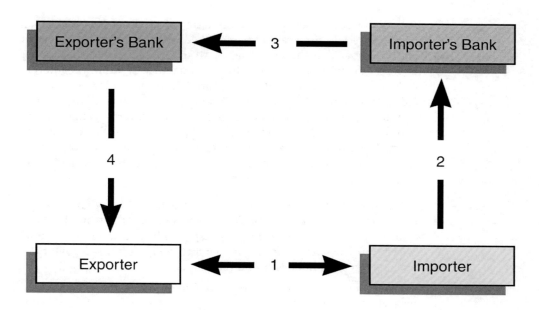

Figure 7.2: The Issuance of a Letter of Credit

- The second step takes place when the importer (the applicant) requests its bank (the issuing bank) to open a letter of credit on the importer's behalf, naming the exporter as the beneficiary. The importer follows the exporter's instructions regarding the terms of the sale and makes sure to include in the application all the documents that it will need to clear customs in the importing country. The importer may also send a copy of the application to the exporter, to ensure that the terms listed on the application are acceptable to the exporter.

  Because the issuing bank is promising to pay if the importer does not pay, it may request that the importer freeze a certain percentage (from 0 to 100 percent) of the amount of the letter of credit in an account or on a line of credit. Freezing these funds ensures that the importer will pay the bank, since the bank has control of the funds before the letter of credit is issued. However, this constraint on cash flow is one reason importers prefer other terms of payment to a letter of credit. Another reason is the fact that the issuing bank requests a fee that varies between 0.5 and 3 percent of the amount of the letter of credit, although most request about 1.5 percent.

- In the third step, the issuing bank sends the letter of credit (generally electronically, using the SWIFT network; or by fax; or, rarely, by mail) to the exporter's bank, which then advises the letter of credit. In this simplified example, the exporter's bank is also the advising bank. The advising bank checks several things: first, that the letter of credit is drawn on a legitimate bank and that its content meets the exporter's requirements. The advis-

issuing bank
The bank that opens the letter of credit on behalf of the importer and pays the exporter if the exporter provides the documents requested in the letter of credit.

beneficiary
The party that will be paid by the letter of credit, the exporter.

applicant
The firm whose payment is supported by the letter of credit, the importer.

advising bank
A bank that reviews the letter of credit on behalf of the beneficiary.

ing bank also wants to ensure that the letter of credit is irrevocable: an irrevocable letter of credit cannot be modified without the express consent of both the issuer and the beneficiary. All letters of credit issued under the Universal Customs and Practice for Documentary Credit of the International Chamber of Commerce (UCP 600) are irrevocable unless specifically marked as "revocable." There are very few instances in which it would make sense for an exporter and an importer to agree to have a revocable letter of credit, or one that can be modified by either party without the approval of the other. The advising bank then also confirms that the letter of credit's information matches the *pro forma* invoice exactly, and that the expiration date is appropriate for the transaction.

- In the fourth step, the advising bank notifies the beneficiary that the letter of credit is acceptable from the bank's perspective. By reviewing the letter of credit, the bank is not engaging its responsibility; it is only acting as an adviser to the exporter and has no liability (will not have to pay) if the issuing bank does not honor its commitment.

The advising bank then forwards the letter of credit to the exporter (the beneficiary), who determines that the terms of the letter of credit are consistent with what was agreed upon between the exporter and the importer. Once the exporter has determined that the letter of credit is acceptable, the exporter can start the shipping process.

Shipment

Figure 7.3 describes the steps that take place once the exporter ships the merchandise to the importer and transmits the sale's documents to the advising bank.

- The fifth step in the letter-of-credit process is composed of two parts.

   1. First the exporter ships the merchandise abroad. Usually, the exporter ships directly to the importer, but in some cases, the shipment may go to another party, such as a wholesaler working with the importer. In all cases, the party to which the exporter ships the goods is called the consignee. In all cases, the exporter ships the goods according to the terms outlined in the letter of credit.

   In the process of shipping the goods, the exporter generates a lot of paperwork, such as an invoice, a certificate of origin, an export license, a packing list, and so on. The exporter also collects a lot of paperwork, such as a bill of lading or an air waybill from the shipping company and miscellaneous certificates (certificate of insurance, certificate of inspection, and so on) from different suppliers (for more information on all of these terms, see Chapter 9). It is critical to ensure that the paperwork matches precisely the requirements of the letter of credit, as the issuing bank's promise to pay is contingent upon presenting the

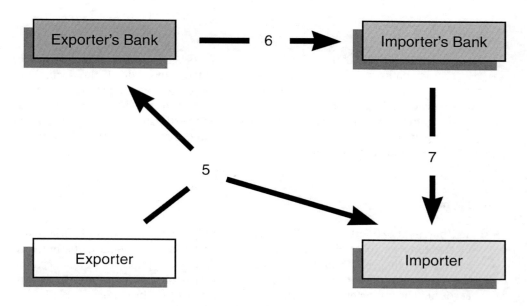

Figure 7.3: Shipment under a Letter of Credit

proper documents. Any error or omission in the documents triggers a discrepancy and delays payment (see Section 7.6.3 on page 223).

2. After the documents are collected, the exporter sends them to its bank (the advising bank), which checks them against the terms of the letter of credit. This is the process that the exporter must follow to provide the importer with the documents that it needs to clear customs in the importing country. No documents travel with the goods; they are sent to the exporter's bank, and eventually are delivered to the importer through the banking system.

- The sixth step happens when the advising bank receives the documents from the exporter. The advising bank sends the documents to the issuing bank if they conform to the requirements of the letter of credit. However, if they do not conform, then the advising bank holds the documents until the issue is resolved. At the point when everything matches the terms of the letter of credit, the advising bank sends the documents to the importer's bank (the issuing bank).

In some cases, depending on the working relationship between the issuing bank and the advising bank, the advising bank may issue a credit (payment) to the exporter at that point. However, this payment is not final and depends on the issuing bank honoring the letter of credit. The simplest example illustrated in Figure 7.3 does not presume such a relationship and assumes that the advising bank will wait until it is paid by the issuing bank before it credits the exporter's bank account.

- The issuing bank then checks the documents again, and determines whether they conform to the requirements of the letter of credit. If the documents conform, the issuing bank notifies the importer that the documents are in order and it exchanges them (paying attention to the original of the bill of lading or the air waybill, which acts as the certificate of title to the goods) against payment by the importer. The importer can then clear customs in the importing country.

Payment

The payment of a letter of credit is a fairly simple process: payment is first made by the importer to its bank, in exchange for the transaction documents. In many cases, since the issuing bank has frozen a portion of the importer's bank account before issuing the letter of credit, the payment is simply processed from this account. The importers' bank then wires the payment to the exporter's bank, and finally the exporter's account is credited (see Figure 7.4).

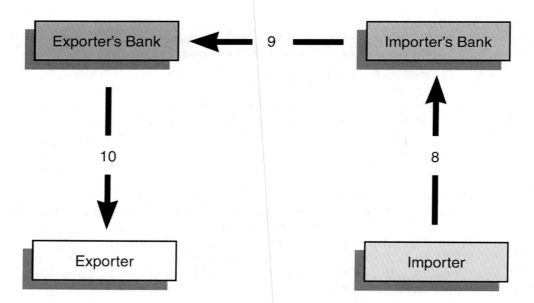

Figure 7.4: Payment under a Letter of Credit

The entire process of a letter of credit is shown in Figure 7.5 on the next page. The reason the process is labeled "simplified" is because several additional parties can get involved in the process, as will be seen in the following section.

7.6.3 Additional Information

Advising Bank

It is not unusual for an exporter's bank to determine that it does not have the expertise to advise a particular letter of credit. This is the case when the letter of credit comes from a country with which the exporter's bank rarely conducts business, or when the letter of credit is issued by a bank with which the exporter's bank is unfamiliar or has no prior business relationship.

In those cases, the exporter's bank declines advising the letter of credit and asks another bank to become the advising bank for that transaction. For that responsibility, the exporter's bank generally seeks the expertise of a large bank located in one of the world's international financial centers (New York, London, or Hong Kong). In such cases, Figure 7.5 would then include an additional bank, the advising bank, separate from the exporter's and the importer's banks, and through which the letter of credit would transit, on its way from the importer's bank to the exporter's bank. The documents would also then transit from the exporter's bank to the advising bank, and then to the importer's bank.

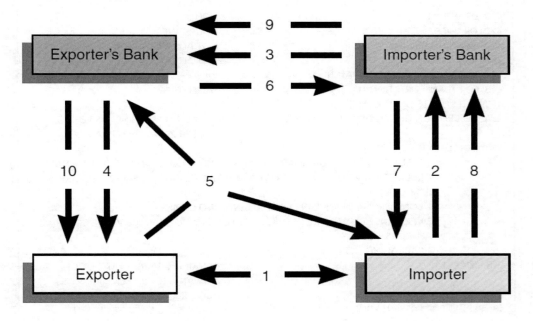

Figure 7.5: Complete, but Simplified Letter of Credit Process

Confirming Bank

In some cases, the exporting company may not be comfortable doing business with the issuing bank, which, after all, is an unknown foreign entity. It may not

```
RECEIVED FROM:    BTTT76XXX UNIVERSAL BANK, TAIWAN
TO:               TDOMCATTTOR TORONTO DOMINION BANK, TORONTO, CANADA


ISSUE OF A DOCUMENTARY CREDIT


40A: FORM OF DOCUMENTARY CREDIT            : IRREVOCABLE
20A: DOCUMENTARY CREDIT NUMBER             : 001/5845
31C: DATE OF ISSUE                         : 15/01/15
31D: DATE AND PLACE OF EXPIRY              : 15/02/20
                                             CANADA
50:  APPLICANT                             : A-TO-Z-IMPORT LIMITED
                                             77, EWE STREET
                                             TAIPEI, TAIWAN
59:  BENEFICIARY                           : EXPORT TRADING INC
                                             21 MAIN ST
                                             TORONTO, CANADA
32B: CURRENCY CODE, AMOUNT                 : USD 50000.00
41D: AVAILABLE WITH...BY...                : YOURSELVES
                                             PAYMENT
42C: DRAFTS AT...                          : SIGHT
42D: DRAWEE                                : YOURSELVES
43P: PARTIAL SHIPMENTS                     : NOT ALLOWED
43T: TRANSHIPMENT                          : NOT ALLOWED
44A: LOADING ON BOARD/DISPATCH...          : VANCOUVER, CANADA
44B: FOR TRANSPORTATION TO...              : TAIPEI, TAIWAN
44C: LATEST DATE OF SHIPMENT               : 15/02/10
45A: DESCRIPTION OF GOODS AND/OR SERVICES  :2 MOLDING MACHINES AS PER P.O
                                             NUMBER 26578 CIF TAIWAN

46A: DOCUMENTS REQUIRED
        1/FULL SET OF CLEAN ON BOARD MARINE BILLS OF LADING MADE OUT TO THE
        ORDER OF UNIVERSAL BANK, TAIWAN MARKED FREIGHT PREPAI AND NOTIFY
        APPLICANT
        2/COMMERCIAL INVOICE IN ORIGINAL AND TWO COPIES
        3/INSURANCE CERTIFICATE IN DUPLICATE FOR 110% OF INVOICE VALUE COVERING
        ALL RISKS
        4 PACKAGING LIST
71B: CHARGES                               : BANKING CHARGES OUTSIDE OF
                                             TAIWAN ARE FOR BENEFICIARY'S
                                             ACCOUNT
48:  PERIOD FOR PRESENTATION               : DOCUMENTS MUST BE PRESENTED
                                             NO LATER THAN 10 DAYS AFTER
                                             DATE OF SHIPPING DOCUMENTS
                                             FOR NEGOTIATION BUT WITHIN
                                             THE CREDIT VALIDITY
49:  CONFIRMATION INSTRUCTIONS             : WITH
53A: REIMBURSEMENT BANK                    : TDOMCATTTOR
72:  SENDER TO RECEIVER INFORMATION        : THIS IS THE OPERATIVE INSTRUMENT
                        * END OF MESSAGE*
```

Figure 7.6: A Letter of Credit Issued under UCP 600

know the bank's creditworthiness, it may feel that the risk of relying on a foreign bank is too high, or it may simply be risk averse or new to the export business. In any case, the exporter can ask the advising bank to confirm the letter of credit; it then becomes a confirmed letter of credit.

A confirmed letter of credit signifies that, in the event the issuing bank does not honor its letter of credit, then the confirming bank will pay the exporter, as long as the documents conform to the terms of the letter of credit. Confirming a letter of credit is a way to substitute the creditworthiness of the confirming (usually domestic) bank for that of the issuing bank. Because the confirming bank is often also the advising bank, the practice is that the confirming bank issues a credit to the exporter upon presentation of the documents at the time of shipment. Thus confirming a letter of credit also speeds up the process of collection by a week or so.

In most cases, confirming a letter of credit is not a wise choice, as banks are creditworthy. In addition, confirming a letter of credit is expensive, costing 0.5 to 1.5 percent of the amount of the letter of credit, a substantial cost considering that foreign banks rarely, if ever, fail. Some U.S. companies have a policy of always confirming letters of credit, generally because they prefer dealing with U.S. banks should there be difficulties in collection; nevertheless, this leads companies to confirm letters of credit drawn on extraordinarily solid banks, such as Crédit Suisse, using less-than-stellar U.S. banks as confirming banks. In addition, most bank failures, when they occur, tend to be rescued by their respective governments and the banks' obligations are honored. The practice of confirming a letter of credit can only be justified based on the grounds that it provides an earlier payment.

Correspondent Bank

In some cases, yet another bank can get involved in the letter-of-credit process. Most banks enter agreements with other banks in which they act as correspondent banks for each other. The purpose of these agreements is for each bank to have representation in a foreign market. The consequence of these agreements is that the banks favor their correspondent banks in financial transactions, and generally direct some of the business they conduct in the correspondent bank's country to that bank. Correspondent banks also keep funds in one another's accounts.

For the sake of example, let's pretend that Bank A in Germany has an agreement with Bank Z in Thailand in which they are each other's correspondent bank. An exporter in Germany, doing business with German Bank B, requests a letter of credit from its Thai customer, which has an account with Bank Z. It is likely for Bank A to be part of the transaction and act as the "courier" between Bank Z and Bank B, or even for Bank Z to request that Bank A become the advising bank. In most cases, it is advantageous for the German exporter to have Bank A involved, as Bank A may release the funds on behalf of the issuing bank, Bank Z (under the International Chamber of Commerce's URR 725 regulations). Therefore, payment would then be collected earlier.

confirmed letter of credit
When a letter of credit is confirmed, should the issuing bank not pay, the confirming bank does.

confirming bank
The bank that confirms a letter of credit. Should the issuing bank not pay, the confirming bank does.

correspondent bank
A foreign bank with which a domestic bank has a preferred business relationship.

UCP 600

UCP 600[22] is the Universal Customs and Practice for Documentary Credit, 2007 revision, Publication 600 of the International Chamber of Commerce (ICC). UCP 600 is a publication that details the responsibilities of the banks involved in letters of credit, as well as the responsibilities of the applicant and the beneficiary. The publication also attempts to address most areas in which there could be misunderstandings between the issuing bank, the advising bank, the applicant, and the beneficiary. Because of the jurisprudence that has accumulated with the almost universal usage of UCP 600 (and its predecessor, UCP 500), it is preferable to always follow its guidelines and to request that the letter of credit be issued "subject to" UCP 600.[23]

Whenever a letter of credit is transmitted through the SWIFT network—the Society for Worldwide Interbank Financial Telecommunications—it is by convention issued under UCP 600 guidelines unless otherwise noted. Because the immense majority of banks belong to the SWIFT network, almost all letters of credit are therefore issued under UCP 600.

Irrevocable Letter of Credit

irrevocable letter of credit
A letter of credit that cannot be altered without the consent of the issuing bank and the beneficiary.

An irrevocable letter of credit cannot be canceled by the issuing bank for any reason, unless the beneficiary agrees to it. A revocable letter of credit can be changed by the importer (or the issuing bank) without prior approval of the beneficiary. It rarely makes sense for a beneficiary to accept a revocable letter of credit. Almost all letters of credit are irrevocable.

Since letters of credit are almost all transmitted through the SWIFT network, they are following UCP 600 guidelines, and are therefore irrevocable. However, this is still a point of confusion: under the previous guidelines (UCP 500), all letters of credit were irrevocable as well. However, before 1993, under the UCP 400 rules, the opposite was true, and all letters of credit were revocable, unless specifically marked as irrevocable. There is still some confusion regarding this important distinction, even though it is more than 20 years old: exporters are still told to make sure that letters of credit are irrevocable. If they are issued under UCP 600, they are irrevocable.

URR 725

The International Chamber of Commerce (ICC) has also published a document entitled Uniform Rules for Bank-to-Bank Reimbursements under Documentary Credits, which is called URR 725 and was implemented in October 2008.[24]

URR 725 rules outline the responsibilities of the banks involved in an international transaction conducted under UCP 600 and in which payment to the exporter is made directly by the advising bank (or by the correspondent bank of the issuing bank). The paying bank is then reimbursed by the issuing bank. This practice is becoming more common to help expedite the process of a letter of credit. The ICC felt that uniform rules were necessary in this matter and created the URR 725 rules to direct banks as to the proper way of implementing the UCP 600 rules. Although these rules apply to banks rather than exporters, it may be advisable to refer to them before requesting payment from the advising or the correspondent bank of the issuing bank.

Discrepancies and Amendments

Unfortunately, and for several reasons, there are often discrepancies between the requirements outlined in the letter of credit and the documents presented by the exporter. Since no payment is made to the exporter (and no document will be released to the importer) if they do not match, the exporter and the importer must resolve any discrepancy that arises so that the transaction can be completed.

discrepancy
A difference between the documents required by the letter of credit and the documents provided or obtained by the exporter.

Such discrepancies can be on shipping dates, changes in the number of packages, changes in part numbers, suppliers' costs (insurance, shipping charges), and a host of different reasons (see Table 7.4)[25]. It is estimated that around 50 percent of all letters of credit have some sort of discrepancy. Given these potential problems, it is crucial for the exporter to pay close attention to the terms of the letter of credit and to attempt to adhere to them as closely as possible.

Source of Discrepancy	Percentage of all Discrepancies
Inconsistent data	25.1%
Absence of documents	8.4%
Late presentation	7.9%
Carrier not named	8.8%
Incorrect goods description	4.1%
Incorrect data	7.1%
Incorrect BOL Endorsement	3.8%
Incorrect Insurance Cover	1.8%
Other discrepancies	33.0%

Table 7.4: Leading Sources of Discrepancies in Documentary Credit
Sitpro.

Great care should be given to the preparation of the *pro forma* invoice, as the issuing bank relies on this document to issue the letter of credit. In those few cases in which the letter of credit does not reflect exactly the *pro forma* invoice (misspellings, for example), it is wise to issue an invoice that matches the letter of credit. While this is difficult to do with an automated invoice processing system, it may save a considerable amount of future aggravation. Many bankers have "horror stories" of issuing banks refusing payment on a letter of credit because there was a typo on it. Many letters of credit are typed by clerks with no knowledge whatsoever of the exporter's language, and therefore it is more difficult to avoid typos and other data-entry errors.

amendment
A change to a letter of credit to which all parties have agreed, from the applicant to the beneficiary.

In those cases where there is a discrepancy between the letter of credit's requirements and the documents presented by the exporter, the exporter and the importer must request their respective banks to negotiate an amendment to the letter of credit. The amendment process is initiated by the advising bank, which requests an amendment to the letter of credit from the issuing bank. Since the amendment is a change to an irrevocable letter of credit, it must be authorized by both parties; the beneficiary and the importer (through the issuing bank) must agree to it. There is usually a fee attached to an amendment, and in some cases an amendment can be difficult to obtain because the importing country's government gets involved (the import license may have to be changed) or because the change is not to the advantage of the importer (a delay in shipping date, for example). In the overwhelming majority of cases, though, the problem can be solved to the satisfaction of both parties; one personal banking acquaintance could recall only one deal "gone bad"—unpaid—in 20 years of letter-of-credit management.

Yet More Complications

Things can get much more complicated in a letter-of-credit transaction as yet more parties get involved. For example, if the exporter's bank feels that it is unqualified to advise the letter of credit, it may request that another, larger or more experienced bank become the advising bank. In those cases, there are at least three banks involved; the importer's bank, the exporter's bank, and the advising bank.

However, letters of credit can involve as many as six banks: the exporter's bank, the importer's bank, an advising bank (to help the exporter's bank), a confirming bank (to reassure the exporter), and the correspondent banks of the latter two (to "simplify" the exchange of documents). When so many banks are involved, the amendment process can quickly become quite confusing (and possibly more expensive), and it may be difficult to ascertain where the documents are at any point in time.

Drafts

draft
A promissory note in which the importer formally recognizes its debt to the exporter.

It is possible to add a draft to a letter of credit. The draft is an instrument that legally binds the importer to paying within a certain period. This allows the exporter to grant commercial credit to the importer whenever it is deemed necessary. If no draft is attached to a letter of credit, the assumption is that the importer is not granted any credit (*i.e.*, that the letter of credit is payable "at sight;" in other words, immediately). The different types of drafts available in an international transaction are explained in Section 7.8.3.

7.6.4 Applicability

A letter of credit used to be the payment term of choice in international transactions, especially in those cases where the exporter had no pre-existing business relationship with the importer, or when the importer was in a country that was considered risky. It still is an excellent method for the exporter to use to make sure it will be paid, and is recommended in situations in which the exporter is risk averse, new to the business of exporting, has substantial exposure in the transaction, or has some uneasiness regarding the creditworthiness of the importer.

However, it is often a disadvantage to request a letter of credit because of the costs (and the cumbersome process) associated with it. It is also unwise to demand payment on such restrictive terms when other competitors can offer open-account terms. Therefore, it may be a more sensible alternative, especially in western Europe, to offer terms that are more favorable to the importer and to use commercial insurance to cover the commercial risk.

7.7   Additional Types of Letters of Credit

In addition to ordinary letters of credit that cover a single transaction, a few additional types have been designed to handle specific cases.

7.7.1   Stand-By Letters of Credit

A stand-by letter of credit is similar to an ordinary letter of credit, with a few exceptions. First, a stand-by letter of credit has a much longer validity period, sometimes longer than a year. Second, a stand-by letter of credit usually applies to more than one shipment from the exporter to the importer. Under such a system, the exporter makes shipments on an open-account basis and will "call" on the letter of credit only if the importer is not meeting its obligations;[26] for example, if the exporter is not paying on time. These qualities make stand-by letters of credit a tool of choice for handling business with a distributor, for example, or making a series of shipments to a customer.

stand-by letter of credit
A letter of credit that is valid for multiple shipments and allows for bills of lading issued on multiple dates.

The stand-by letter of credit is an instrument that was created by U.S. banks as a substitute for bank guarantees, because U.S. banks are prohibited from offering them. Therefore, stand-by letters of credit are often also used to secure the obligations of the seller/exporter (as in a performance bond) (see Section 7.12 on page 238). The sums secured by stand-by letters of credit are vastly superior to the amount secured by traditional letters of credit, as they involve longer, larger-scale contracts.

The rules for stand-by letters of credit are regulated by the International Stand-By Practices ISP98, a series of eighty-nine rules governing the language, documentation, and practices of this type of letter of credit.[27]

7.7.2   Transferable Letters of Credit

A distributor may be interested in exporting products that it must first purchase from a manufacturer. In that case, the exporter may have to demonstrate to the manufacturer that it can pay. The distributor can do that with a transferable letter of credit, with which the beneficiary of a letter of credit (the exporter) asks

transferable letter of credit
A letter of credit that the beneficiary can use as a means to insure its creditors that they will be paid.

the issuing bank to allow the letter of credit to be used to secure the payment of the beneficiary toward others. Generally, banks will not allow a transferable letter of credit to be made transferable to more than one intermediary, that is, the supplier of the goods to the exporter. A transferable letter of credit must be issued as transferable, and the issuing bank is the only party that can allow this transferability.

Because of the number of export trading companies in some parts of Asia, transferable letters of credit are used extensively in China, Taiwan, and Singapore.[28]

7.7.3 Back-to-Back Letters of Credit

back-to-back letter of credit
A letter of credit issued using another letter of credit as a payment guarantee.

When the exporter purchases the goods from a manufacturer and needs to reassure the manufacturer that it will be paid, it is possible to use a back-to-back letter of credit rather than a transferable letter of credit, although the concept is similar.

In a back-to-back letter-of-credit transaction, the exporter obtains a letter of credit from its bank, with which the payment to the manufacturer is secured. This letter of credit is a secondary letter of credit that uses the letter of credit that was issued in the importing country on behalf of the importer—and is therefore called the primary letter of credit—as collateral. The secondary letter of credit is not as secure as a transferable letter of credit, because there is the possibility that the primary letter of credit will not be paid because of some non-performance by the exporter, over which the manufacturer has no control. Nevertheless, back-to-back transactions are relatively common when intermediaries do not have the financial capability to handle large sales.

7.7.4 Red-Clause Letters of Credit

red-clause letter of credit
A letter of credit that allows the beneficiary to obtain funds from the applicant before the goods are shipped.

Sometimes, the exporter may not have enough working capital to finance the manufacturing of the goods that it is selling to the importer. In that case, it is possible to ask the importer to issue a red-clause letter of credit, with which the importer provides the exporter with a cash down-payment, prior to shipment, to finance the production of the goods. The importer—or possibly the issuing bank—lends some or all the funds necessary for the manufacturing of the goods.

7.8   Documentary Collection

7.8.1   Definition

Documentary collection is a process by which an exporter asks a bank located in the importer's country to safeguard the exporter's interests. The exporter asks the bank not to release the documents—specifically the bill of lading, which is the certificate of title to the goods (see Chapter 9)—until the importer satisfies certain requirements, most often paying the exporter or signing a financial document (called a draft or a bill of exchange) promising that it will pay the exporter within a given amount of time. Should the importer decide not to take delivery of the goods, this allows the exporter to have them shipped back to the exporting country and to lose only the costs of shipment rather than the total value of the goods. Another possibility is to find another customer for the goods.

documentary collection
A method of payment in which an exporter enlists the help of a bank in the importer's country to collect payment from the importer.

7.8.2 Process

Although the process can be done with the exporter sending the documents directly to the bank in the importer's country, the process generally starts (see Figure 7.7) with the exporter sending the documents to its own bank, which acts as a conduit for sending the documents to the importer's bank. The exporter's bank is called the remitting bank, and it acts only as an intermediary; it has no responsibility in the process but the safe transmittal of the documents. The reason a remitting bank is used is to help the foreign bank ascertain the legitimacy of the exporter; the bank is not dealing with an unknown exporter, it is dealing with a bank with which it has dealt in the past, or one that can be easily vetted.

remitting bank
In a documentary collection, the remitting bank collects the documents from the exporter and sends them to the presenting bank. It has no other involvement.

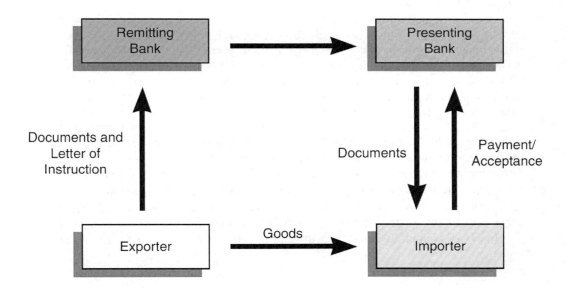

Figure 7.7: The Documentary Collection Process

The remitting bank then forwards the documents, as well as an instruction letter from the exporter, to the presenting bank. The presenting bank can be the importer's bank or another bank in the importing country, but it is most often the correspondent bank of the remitting bank in the importer's country. The presenting bank then follows the instruction letter and alerts the importer that the

presenting bank
In a documentary collection, the presenting bank interacts with the importer and withholds the documents until payment is received or a draft signed.

documents have arrived. It notifies the importer that it will have to either pay for the goods or sign a draft to obtain the documents. Since the importer needs the documents in order to clear customs in the importing country, it complies with the requirements of the presenting bank. If the importer decides not to collect the documents, the bank retains them and follows the exporter's instruction letter to determine its next steps.

Once the presenting bank obtains payment from the importer, it forwards the funds to the remitting bank, which then notifies the exporter that the funds have arrived.

7.8.3   Drafts

The exporter has several alternatives in deciding what it wants the presenting bank to request in exchange for delivering the documents to the importer. It can request immediate payment or it can grant the importer some time to make the payment, and uses a draft to do so. A draft is a promissory note, signed by the importer in the presence of a representative of the presenting bank, in which the importer commits to pay the exporter on a given date.

bill of exchange
Another term for a draft. A promissory note with which the importer formally recognizes it debt to the exporter.

A draft (or a bill of exchange) is a legal document in the importing country in which the importer officially recognizes a commercial debt toward the exporter. This makes it easier to collect payment if the importer decides not to honor its commitment, as the default is now a domestic issue rather than an international one—a dispute over which a domestic court in the importing country would have no problem ruling. Specifically, in the instructions to the presenting bank, it is possible to request a protest in case of non-payment on a draft, which is a legal process that can have serious consequences for an importer; it may be difficult (if not impossible) for the importer to obtain credit after it has been recorded that it does not honor its debt. In some countries, such defaults are even published prominently in the local business press, tarnishing the reputation of a business.

Although drafts are introduced in the section dealing with documentary collections, it is not unusual for a draft to accompany a letter of credit as well. When they accompany a letter of credit, they fulfill the same role; the documents held by the issuing bank are not given to the importer until the importer signs the draft.

Sight Draft

sight draft
A draft in which the importer promises to pay the exporter immediately, "at sight."

The exporter can request that the presenting bank release the documents only upon payment of the invoice by the importer. Such a transaction is called "documents against payment" (D/P) or a sight draft transaction, meaning that the draft (a promissory note) is payable "at sight" (*i.e.,* immediately). In this case, the exporter retains title to the goods, embodied in the bill of lading or air waybill, until payment is made and the bill of lading or air waybill is given to the importer.

Time Draft

In some cases, the exporter may want to grant credit to the importer but still want to ensure it will be paid. In that case, the exporter can request that the bank exchange the documents against a time draft: the importer has to sign (endorse) a document promising it will pay within a certain time after the draft is endorsed. Credit is generally extended for durations that are multiples of thirty days: 30, 60, 90, and 180 days are the most common credit terms. The presenting bank should be instructed to remit the documents when the draft is signed ("documents against acceptance" [D/A]), or to remit them against payment (D/P), in which case the importer will not take title to the goods until after payment is made, a requirement that mostly defeats the purpose of granting credit. Because of problems associated with the custody of the goods between their arrival in the importing country and the time they become the property of the importer, the ICC advises that "collections should not contain bills of exchange [drafts] payable at a future date with instructions that commercial documents are to be delivered against payment."[29]

time draft
A draft in which the importer promises to pay the exporter 30, 60 or 90 days after the importer has signed the draft.

Date Draft

A date draft is another way of granting credit to the importer. The difference is that credit is extended to the importer for 30, 60, or 90 days from the shipment date rather than from the date of the endorsement of the draft. The shipment date is determined by the main contract of carriage, generally the date at which the ocean bill of lading or the air waybill is issued.[30] The advantage of the date draft over the time draft is that the exporter has control over the date at which shipment is initiated (and therefore over the date at which the payment is due), whereas it has no control over the date at which the importer will endorse the draft.

A date-draft transaction therefore alleviates one problem of documentary collection in general: the date at which the importer will endorse the draft. Under the Uniform Rules for Collection of the ICC,[31] the bank must notify the importer as soon as it receives the documents. However, the importer has no incentive to come to the bank to collect them—if the draft is a sight or time draft—because delaying endorsement delays payment as well.

date draft
A draft in which the importer promises to pay the exporter 30, 60 or 90 days after the shipment date of the goods, regardless of the date on which importer has signed the draft.

7.8.4 Instruction Letter

In addition to the documents (*e.g.* invoice, bill of lading, certificates, licenses) and the draft, each documentary collection includes an instruction letter in which the exporter, through the intermediary of the remitting bank, specifies what the presenting bank is expected to accomplish.

The instruction letter is a document in which the remitting bank instructs the presenting bank on the procedures it should follow in its dealings with the importer. For example, the instruction letter specifies whether the documents should be exchanged against payment (D/P), or against an acceptance of the draft

instruction letter
In a documentary collection, a document prepared by the exporter that instructs the presenting bank on the steps to take before releasing the documents to the importer.

(D/A). The instruction letter also indicates what the procedure should be if the importer refuses to sign the draft, if the importer refuses to pay the fees (if any), or if the importer does not honor its signature. The presenting bank could be asked to file a protest, for example.

This instruction letter is the only document that the presenting bank follows in a documentary collection. The bank does not need to find its instructions among the other documents that accompany the documentary collection. The ICC is quite clear about this issue in its Uniform Rules for Collections (URC 522). Despite this *caveat*, it is nevertheless preferable to mention in the instruction letter that the collection is subject to URC 522, for it outlines rules for the timeliness of presentations and information reports.

7.8.5   Acceptance

Trade Acceptance

trade acceptance
In a documentary collection, trade acceptance takes place when the importer signs the draft.

The responsibilities of the presenting bank generally stop at notifying the importer that the documents have arrived, and at requesting that the importer endorse the draft (under D/A terms) or at requesting payment (under D/P terms) before releasing the documents. In those cases, this process is called trade acceptance—sometimes "trader's acceptance"—as the importer has control over the decision to accept or reject the draft and over the timing of the endorsement.

This can be somewhat inconvenient for the exporter, as the importer may delay acceptance of the draft for an inordinate amount of time—a problem that can be solved with a date draft—or even refuse to sign the draft. In such a case, the exporter still has title, but that title is for merchandise that is warehoused in a foreign country. The costs associated with warehousing goods in an unknown location, as well as the risks of pilferage and the exporter's difficulties in arranging for such storage, can lead unscrupulous importers to take advantage of the situation by extorting better terms from the exporter (*e.g.* a discounted price, given the costs of repatriating the goods) before signing the draft. This is a strategy that works only once, but an unscrupulous importer could attempt to use it.

Banker's Acceptance and Aval

banker's acceptance
In a documentary collection, banker's acceptance takes place when the bank signs the draft on behalf of the importer.

aval
In a documentary collection, the promise by the presenting bank that the importer will honor the draft and that, should the importer default, the bank will make the payment.

The problems presented by a trade acceptance can be solved by requesting a banker's acceptance. In this case, it is the presenting bank that endorses the draft on behalf of the importer. The bank usually endorses the draft immediately upon receipt of the documents, and the endorsement of the bank engages the responsibility of the importer: it signs on behalf of the importer. The presenting bank is unlikely to offer a banker's acceptance unless it feels it can aval the draft.

An aval is a promise by the presenting bank that the importer will honor the draft and that, should the importer default, the bank will make the payment. The bank therefore acts as a co-signer of the draft.

Although an aval is theoretically independent and different from a banker's acceptance, in practice the latter is often used as a substitute for aval. Therefore the remitting bank often offers credit to an exporter based upon a banker's acceptance, as it understands that the credit risk is now based upon the credit-worthiness of the presenting bank, which is a situation almost as good as that of a letter of credit, but at a lower cost.

7.8.6 URC 522

The International Chamber of Commerce publishes guidelines for documentary collections in its Uniform Rules for Collections (URC 522).[32] The main benefit of these rules is that they outline the responsibilities of the remitting bank and the responsibilities of the presenting bank, as well as the limits of their responsibilities. For example, the presenting bank must ensure that it promptly notifies the importer to come sign the draft (D/A) and is responsible for ensuring that the draft is signed properly (according to local laws), but the presenting bank has no obligation to determine that the person has the authority to sign. These obligations (and limitations) are well described and explained in the Commentary on URC 522.[33]

The URC 522 mandates the inclusion of an instruction letter to the presenting bank, which clarifies what the presenting bank has to do with the documents. Because URC 522 is becoming the international standard for documentary collection—although it has not reached the universal nature of UCP 600 for letters of credit—it is advisable to always state in the instruction letter that the collection is subject to the Uniform Rules for Collections (URC 522) of the International Chamber of Commerce.

7.8.7 Applicability

Documentary collections are a good way to conduct international sales because they are less cumbersome (and less expensive) than letters of credit and provide a good amount of safety for exporters. The title remains in the hands of the exporter until the importer accepts the draft (D/A) or makes payment (D/P). The exporter's risk is further reduced if a banker's acceptance is requested.

However, documentary collections represent more risk for the exporter than a letter of credit because payment depends on the primary transaction (the contract of sale); the importer can refuse to sign the draft (invoking poor-quality merchandise, for example) or delay signing the draft (until it has resold the merchandise), in which case the exporter retains title but does not get paid. A letter of credit, however, does not depend on the primary transaction, but only on the documents; it ensures payment as long as the documents are in the proper form.

A documentary collection can be used for customers with which there is a fair amount of trust, but for which an open-account transaction is out of the question for other reasons. A banker's acceptance can be used for customers who refuse to conduct business on a letter-of-credit basis and about whose creditworthiness the exporter is uncertain.

7.9   Forfaiting

forfaiting
A means of financing an international sale in which an exporter collects a series of drafts from the importer, and then sells them.

When the importer wants credit terms that are beyond what the exporter is comfortable giving—for example, a five-year payment plan is requested on a piece of machinery when the exporter can extend only a 180-day credit—there is the possibility of using international forfaiting to extend this credit. In an international transaction, forfaiting is generally achieved using a series of drafts from the importer, which have been given an aval by the importer's bank. Forfaiting is used for longer credit terms than factoring, which tends to be used for credit terms of up to 180 days. In contrast, forfaiting can be used for terms as long as seven years.

The exporter, once it has an agreement from the forfaiting firm, obtains this series of drafts, all with different due dates from the importer. The exporter then sells this series of drafts to the forfaiting firm at a discount. The forfaiting firm purchases the drafts without recourse, which means it cannot hold the exporter responsible for non-payment by the importer. Forfaiting usually satisfies the credit requirements of the importer at no risk—and at a fairly moderate cost—to the exporter.

7.10   Purchasing Cards

purchasing cards
Credit cards used by companies to make small purchases, and that can be used in international transactions.

Several banks offer a system of credit cards for their corporate accounts, called purchasing cards. Purchasing cards originate from the observation that companies purchase myriad small items, from office supplies to small maintenance parts. In the past, the traditional process to purchase these parts was through a centralized purchasing department that issued a purchase order, processed a significant amount of paperwork, and then paid an invoice. More recently, companies have been using purchasing cards, also called procurement cards or simply P-cards. P-cards allow each department to make certain purchases directly from a vendor, a much more expedient process. The P-cards are similar in concept to consumer credit cards; the cards have a certain credit limit, are billed directly to the department (or at least can provide an itemized billing statement showing which department is responsible for a specific purchase), and most importantly, allow transactions to be conducted rapidly. in addition, P-card usage can be restricted to specific vendors, allowing the purchasing department to restrict purchases to pre-approved suppliers. Moreover, the supplier is paid immediately—minus a certain transaction percentage, about 2 to 3 percent—and the customer is billed at the end of the month.[34]

Most P-cards are used for domestic purchases, but there are several advantages to using them for international purchases. The first is that the exporter is paid almost immediately after the goods have been shipped. The second is that the exchange rate on the transaction is the best a company can get: because banks process thousands of foreign transactions worth millions of dollars on the same date, the exchange rate is the one that large transactions can earn. Finally, the importer has recourse if the merchandise is defective, much like a consumer using a Visa or American Express card. It is expected that this type of P-card transaction will increasingly take place in international business, particularly for small items (maintenance parts) and will facilitate the handling of rush orders, which will increase the level of customer service a company can offer from its home country.

P-cards seem to present only advantages, and the number of banks offering such a service is increasing rapidly. However, one issue that has negatively affected the use of P-cards is the way that banks have modified their foreign exchange procedures. In 2005, many banks offering P-cards changed their policies on currency exchange and added a fee on foreign currency transactions that varies from 1 to 3 percent of the value of the transaction. This additional cost negates the advantageous exchange rates that procurement cards can offer. Another slight disadvantage is that the exchange rate in effect on the processing date may differ from the rate on the date used for the transaction, resulting in a slightly different currency exchange rate than was initially anticipated. As of February 2017, multiple banks had abandoned the foreign-exchange fee, making the option of a P-card quite palatable.

7.11 TradeCard

Created by the World Trade Centers Association in 1994, TradeCard is a proprietary electronic system that is gaining greater acceptance in the trade community and is an alternative that combines the advantages of letters of credit and procurement cards:

TradeCard
A proprietary process that combines payment and documents and facilitates international transactions.

- No payment is made until all the documents are in order and there are no discrepancies.

- The buyer is obligated to pay if the documents are in order.

- The system is expedient (payment is received quickly).

TradeCard also has two advantages over both of letters of credit and procurement cards in that it is extremely inexpensive—charging only $150 for a transaction up to U.S.$ 100,000, in contrast to 1 to 3 percent for letters of credit and 2 to 3 percent for procurement cards—and combines document handling and payments.

TradeCard encompasses several electronic tools. First, it has a secure system for transmitting documents, from the *pro forma* invoice to the bill of lading, packing list, and other transportation documents. TradeCard also has a system that checks the customer's creditworthiness and, should the importer be deemed creditworthy, guarantees payment to the exporter if the documents conform. This service is offered through a partnership with COFACE. Finally, TradeCard automatically settles invoices once the documents are in order and without discrepancies.

Unfortunately, TradeCard had not achieved a critical mass of customers (enough customers to make it a standard form of payment), and therefore, as of 2017, despite its gains, it remains an unusual form of payment in international trade, far behind letters of credit, documentary collections, and open accounts. When an exporter suggests payment using TradeCard, it is unlikely that the importer already has an account with TradeCard, and therefore it is unlikely that the transaction will be completed under this term of sale. The reciprocal is also true: a savvy importer may have a TradeCard account, but the exporter may not. If the two begin to do business frequently, the TradeCard customer may eventually convince the other of the advantages of such a system.

In addition, importers and exporters often ask their bankers for advice in such matters, and bankers are generally quite conservative in their recommendations. It also should be noted that banks collect substantial fees from letters of credit, and none on TradeCard transactions. Thus it becomes clear why this method of payment has not gained as much momentum as was originally anticipated. Nevertheless, TradeCard presents such advantages over the other forms of international payment that it is expected to become a dominant method of payment in the 2020s.

In early 2013, TradeCard merged with GT Nexus, a cloud-based business network that provides supply-chain solutions to multinational companies, and this development may help TradeCard develop a greater market share. GT Nexus subsequently made TradeCard part of its Supply Chain Finance products, but GT Nexus does not publish the number of transactions that are completed under this program.

7.12   Bank Guarantees

7.12.1   Definition

bank guarantee
A contract from a bank in which the bank guarantees that the exporter will perform as required by the importer.

guarantor
The bank that provides the bank guarantee.

A bank guarantee is another instrument used in international trade, but in different situations. A bank guarantee is usually requested to secure the performance of the seller (exporter), rather than to ensure payment from the buyer (importer). Bank guarantees happen in cases in which the exporter is a company contracting to build a plant, establish a drilling platform, or install a sewer system; for example, companies like Bechtel and Bouygues are often asked to provide bank guarantees.

A bank guarantee applies to all long-term contracts in which the importer wants to ensure that the work will be completed. Frequently, the bank guarantee is offered by a group of banks rather than a single bank, because of the amounts involved. Finally, a bank guarantee is usually for an amount that is only a fraction of the total amount of the contract. By law, U.S. banks are not allowed to offer bank guarantees, so those are always provided by banks based outside of the United States.

Like a letter of credit, a bank guarantee is an independent contract between the bank giving the guarantee (guarantor) and the beneficiary.

7.12.2   Guarantee Payable on First Demand

A bank guarantee payable on first demand—at first request—is one in which the beneficiary does not have to provide any evidence that the terms of the underlying contract between the contractor and the beneficiary have not been met; the issuing bank must pay at the first request of the beneficiary, solely upon the presentation of a request for payment, sometimes accompanied by a statement from the beneficiary stating that the contractor is not meeting its obligations. No other proof is necessary. This type of bank guarantee is the most common one.

7.12.3   Guarantees Based upon Documents—Cautions

In some cases, a guarantee can be made conditional upon presentation of certain documents rather than on first demand. The beneficiary must present documents that demonstrate that the contractor is not meeting its obligations; such a document may be a court ruling, or some other evidence as agreed upon in the terms of the guarantee.

The ICC has issued a series of conventions regarding documentary bank guarantees in Publication No. 325, Uniform Rules for Contract Guarantees. These rules are not widely used,[35] primarily because documentary guarantees are rarely used.

7.12.4   Stand-By Letters of Credit

Because U.S. law prohibits bank guarantees, American banks offer an alternative to bank guarantees with stand-by letters of credit. The only difference between a stand-by letter of credit and a bank guarantee is that the stand-by letter of credit is always documentary (*i.e.*, the beneficiary must present a document before collecting from the bank). A simple statement that the contractor is not performing is usually considered sufficient.[36]

7.12.5   Types of Bank Guarantees

Several types of bank guarantees—or stand-by letters of credit—are available:

- The tender guarantee or bid guarantee is requested by a beneficiary to ensure that the contractor is bidding in good faith and will enter the contract if awarded.

- The performance guarantee is the most commonly used type of guarantee and is used to ensure that the contractor finishes the project.

- The maintenance guarantee is used to ensure that the contractor performs the services necessitated by the contract after the completion of the project (*i.e.*, maintenance and after-sale service).

- The advance-payment guarantee or repayment guarantee is used to ensure that payments made by the beneficiary in advance of the work (to enable the contractor to purchase supplies or machinery) are reimbursed if the contractor fails to start the project.

- The payment guarantee is used in a different context. It covers the obligations of the buyer (often a distributor) toward the exporter, and is essentially a stand-by letter of credit.

7.13   Terms of Payment as a Marketing Tool

An exporter has several alternatives from which to choose when negotiating terms of payment with the importer. Although the choice of payment term depends on the level of experience of both the exporter and the importer as well as on the exporter's confidence that the importer has in the ability to make the payment, certain payment terms are definitely preferable and will increase an exporter's probability of closing the sale.

In most situations, an importer obtains several possible quotes from several exporters located in different countries. For example, a Brazilian newspaper looking to replace a printing press will seek bids from many suppliers that could be located in the United States, Germany, Japan, Switzerland, Taiwan, and Canada. Although the alternative bids are likely to be evaluated on a large combination of criteria (price, specific capabilities, after-sale service, delivery terms, credit terms, financing, and so on), one of the criteria will be the ease with which the purchase transaction will take place. From the importer's perspective, the easiest alternative—and the one that does not demand that cash flow be affected—is to purchase on an open-account basis. It is likely that at least one of the potential suppliers will offer such terms, and that others will ask for a letter of credit. Therefore, the supplier offering an open-account transaction has a competitive advantage over the others and, if it has purchased credit insurance, has not affected its probability of getting paid.

There are some regions of the world in which letters of credit are still playing a significant role (see Table 7.5 on the facing page).[37] However, in nearly all cases, more than half of international transactions, and more than 90 percent of the transactions in which the importer is located in the fifteen original European Union countries or North America, are conducted using some other means of payment.

Percentage of Transactions Conducted on Letters of Credit
(based on the location of the importer)

European Union [15]	9%
Rest of Europe	20%
North America	11%
Latin America	27%
Middle East	52%
Asia-Pacific	43%
Africa	49%
Asia	46%
Australia-New Zealand	17%

Table 7.5: Percentage of Transactions Conducted on a Letter-of-Credit Basis
Sitpro.

Although no specific information is known, it is likely that the rank order of the other methods of payment are:

1. Open account (with or without credit insurance)

2. Documentary collection

3. Procurement cards (for smaller purchases)

4. TradeCard (for larger purchases)

5. Cash in advance

An exporter intent on increasing its sales should show that it is confident in the ability of the importer to pay for the goods by using an open account. After all, this is the way its domestic sales are conducted—and generally the way many other competing exporters are selling. If the exporter is unsure about the ability of the importer to pay, it should consider purchasing a credit-insurance policy.

Review and Discussion Questions

1. Why is it more difficult and riskier to collect receivables from a foreign purchaser?

2. What are the differences between the political and commercial risks of non-payment?

3. Describe the concept of cash in advance.

4. Describe the process of documentary collection.

5. Describe the mechanism of a letter of credit, from the exchange of the pro forma invoice to final payment.

6. What is credit insurance? Why is it associated with open-account transactions?

7. Several people claim that letters of credit will soon be replaced by the concept of TradeCard. What is this product, and why do some people think it has such a bright future?

8. Describe the concept of bank guarantees. What are the different types of bank guarantees?

Notes

[1] Worldwide Credit Reports, http://fcibglobal.com/credit-country-reports/worldwide-credit-reports.-html, retrieved January 24, 2017.

[2] Green, Paul, "The Hidden Costs of Managing your Accounts Receivable," *Advantage Business Magazine*, October 28, 2014, http://advantagebizmag.com/blog/2014/10/28/hidden-cost-managing-accounts-receivable/, retrieved January 28, 2017.

[3] Stecklow, Steve and Jonathan Karp, "Citibank in India Used Collectors Accused of Strong-Arm Tactics," *The Wall Street Journal*, May 5, 1999, p. A1.

[4] Kritzer, Albert, "CISG: Table of Contracting States," Pace Law School Institute of International Commercial Law, http://www.cisg.law.pace.edu/cisg/countries/cntries.html, retrieved January 28, 2017.

[5] Moss, Sally, "Why the United Kingdom has not ratified the CISG," *Journal of Law and Business*, 25, 2005-2006, pp. 483-485.

[6] Freedman, Michael, "Judgment Day: U.S. Companies Complain They Can't Get a Fair Shake from America's Plaintiff-Friendly Juries. Try Resolving a Dispute in Russia, Indonesia, or Ukraine," *Forbes*, June 7, 2004, pp. 97-98.

[7] Dolven, Ben, "Foreign Investors Find that China's Legal System Resolves Few Disputes," *The Wall Street Journal*, April 7, 2003, p. A14.

[8] Chrisafis, Angelique, "France faces revolt over poverty in its Caribbean Islands," *The Guardian*, February 12, 2009, http://www.guardian.co.uk/world/2009/feb/12/france-revolts-guadeloupe-martinique, retrieved February 12, 2009.

[9] Goldberg, Jeffrey, "The Modern King in the Arab Spring," *The Atlantic*, April 2013, pp. 17-24.

[10] Yardley, William, "Union's War Protest Shuts down West Coast ports," *The New York Times*, May 2, 2008, http://www.nytimes.com/2008/05/02/us/02port.html.

[11] Foxman, Simone, "Hong Kong port strike ends with 9.8% raise for dockworkers—plus potty breaks," *Quartz*, May 6, 2013, http://qz.com/81552/40-day-hong-kong-port-strike-finally-ends-with-a-deal-in-writing/, retrieved May 23, 2013.

[12] Ministère du Budget, des Comptes Publics et de la Fonction Publique, Rapport Annuel sur l'Etat de la Fonction Publique: Faits et Chiffres 2007-2008, Volume 1, p. 591, http://lesrapports.ladocumentationfrancaise.fr/BRP/084000616/0000.pdf, accessed May 24, 2009.

[13] "Total Reserves in Months of Import," The World Bank, http://data.worldbank.org/indicator/FI.-RES.TOTL.MO, retrieved January 28, 2017.

[14] Shoenmakers, Y. M. M., E. De Vries Robbé, and Anton Van Vijk, *Mountains of Gold: An Exploratory Research on Nigerian 419 Fraud: Backgrounds*. Amsterdam: SWP Publishers, 2009.

[15] "Doing Business: Trading Across Borders," International Finance Corporation, The World Bank, http://www.doingbusiness.org/data/exploretopics/trading-across-borders, retrieved January 28, 2017.

[16] "International Credit Reports," Kansas Department of Commerce—Trade Development, http://-kdoch.state.ks.us/KDOCHdocs/TD/CofaceInternationalCreditReportsFlier.pdf, retrieved May 24, 2009.

[17] Banham, Russ, "Credit Clout: Export Credit Insurance Offers Low-Cost Insurance that Protects Shippers from Non-Payment," *International Business*, March 1997, pp. 8-44.

[18] Pereira, Ray, "International Factoring: The Viable Financing Alternative," *World Trade*, December 1999, pp. 68-69.

[19] International Factoring Association, http://www.factoring.org/, retrieved January 28, 2017.

[20] "UPS Capital Cargo Finance," United Parcel Service, http://www.upscapital.com/solutions/cargo-_finance.html, accessed October 13, 2008.

[21] Wood, Jeffrey, "Drafting Letters of Credit; Basic Issues under Article 5 of the Uniform Commercial

Code, UCP 600 and ISP 98," *Banking Law Journal*, February 2008, pp. 103-149.

[22] *Uniform Customs and Practices for Documentary Credits*, UCP 600, 2007 Revision, Publication No. 600 of the International Chamber of Commerce, ICC Publishing S.A., 38 Cours Albert 1er, 75008 Paris, France and ICC Publishing, 156 Fifth Avenue, New York, NY 10010.

[23] *User's Handbook for Documentary Credits under UCP 600*, Publication No. 694 of the International Chamber of Commerce, ICC Publishing S.A., 38 Cours Albert 1er, 75008 Paris, France and ICC Publishing, 156 Fifth Avenue, New York, NY 10010.

[24] *Uniform Rules for Bank-to-Bank Reimbursements under Documentary Credits*, URR 725, 2008, publication No. 725 of the International Chamber of Commerce, ICC Publishing S.A., 38 Cours Albert 1er, 75008 Paris, France and ICC Publishing, 156 Fifth Avenue, New York, NY 10010.

[25] Adapted from "Report on the Use of Export Letters of Credit 2001/2002," dated April 11, 2003, Sitpro, Simplifying International Trade, http://sitpro.org.uk/reports/lettcredr, accessed May 25, 2009.

[26] Tyler, Joseph, "Financing Exports," in *Export Practice: Customs and International Trade Law*, Terence P. Stewart, ed., New York: Practicing Law Institute, 1994.

[27] *International Standby Practices*, ISP98, Institute of International Banking Law and Practice, Inc., Publication No. 590 of the International Chamber of Commerce, ICC Publishing S.A., 38 Cours Albert 1er, 75008 Paris, France and ICC Publishing, 156 Fifth Avenue, New York, NY 10010.

[28] Borcky, Ron, "Understanding and Using Letters of Credit: Part II," Credit Research Foundation, http://www.crfonline.org/orc/cro/cro-9-2.html, retrieved June 17, 2013.

[29] *Uniform Rules for Collection*, URC 522, 1995, publication No. 522 of the International Chamber of Commerce, ICC Publishing S.A., 38 Cours Albert 1er, 75008 Paris, France and ICC Publishing, 156 Fifth Avenue, New York, NY 10010.

[30] Reynolds, Frank, "Use Caution with Semi-Secured Terms," *The Journal of Commerce*, October 20, 1999, p. 10.

[31] *Uniform Rules for Collection*, URC 522, 1995, publication No. 522 of the International Chamber of Commerce, ICC Publishing S.A., 38 Cours Albert 1er, 75008 Paris, France and ICC Publishing, 156 Fifth Avenue, New York, NY 10010.

[32] *Ibid.*

[33] *Commentary on the ICC Uniform Rules for Collections*, 1995, Publication No. 550 of the International Chamber of Commerce, ICC Publishing S.A., 38 Cours Albert 1er, 75008 Paris, France and ICC Publishing, 156 Fifth Avenue, New York, NY 10010.

[34] "Purchasing Card Introduction: What, Why, How, Who," Professional Association for the Commercial Card and Payment Industry, http://www.napcp.org/?page=PCardIntro, retrieved June 17, 2013.

[35] Bertrams, R. I. V. F., *Bank Guarantees in International Trade*, Kluwer Law and Taxation Publishers, Deventer, The Netherlands, 1990.

[36] *Ibid.*

[37] "Ninth Survey of International Services Provided to Exporters," commissioned by the Institute of Exporters, and reproduced in the *Report on the Use of Export Letters of Credit 2001/2002*, April 11, 2003, Sitpro, Simplifying International Trade, http://sitpro.org.uk/reports/lettcredr, accessed June 1, 2006.

Chapter 8

Managing Transaction Risks

The previous chapters have shown that, for each international sale, the exporter and the importer must agree on two points:

term of trade
An element of the contract of sale that specifies the responsibilities of the exporter and those of the importer in the shipment of the goods.

term of sale
An element of the contract of sale that specifies the method of payment used in an international transaction.

- The terms of trade under which the sale is conducted (*i.e.*, the costs the exporter should pay, the costs the importer should pay, and the point at which the responsibility for the cargo shifts from one to the other). These responsibilities are determined by the chosen Incoterms® rule.

- The terms of sale under which the transaction is performed (*i.e.*, at what point in the transaction the exporter wants to be paid, and its level of confidence in the importer's ability to pay). The exporter and the importer can choose from several alternative terms of sale, from cash in advance to an open-account transaction to TradeCard.

currency
The monetary unit used to settle economic transactions in a given country.

However, there is one more issue for the exporter and the importer to consider: the currency that will be used in the transaction. While the exporter and the importer have several options, they must agree on a currency, based on the advantages and disadvantages of each possible alternative.

exchange rate risk
The risk presented by the fluctuations in exchange rates between the time at which the sale is made and the time at which it is paid.

Once the transaction's currency is determined, at least one of the parties is left with a potential currency-fluctuation risk, since there is always a time lag between the time at which the transaction amount is set and the time at which payment is made. The party at risk must then determine how it will manage that risk.

8.1   Currency Used in the Sales Contract

The exporter and the importer have three alternatives when determining the currency that will be used in an international transaction. The sale can be conducted using the exporter's currency, the importer's currency, or a third country's currency. When considering these options, the exporter and the importer should weigh two factors:

- **The risk of currency fluctuation**. Currency-fluctuation risk is a speculative risk, that is, a risk for which there is the possibility of a gain or a loss, depending on which way the exchange rate fluctuates, and whether the exporter or the importer is holding the currency risk. If the transaction is conducted in the exporter's currency, then the importer carries the exchange rate risk. If the transaction is conducted in the importer's currency, then the exporter assumes the exchange rate risk. The two vignettes on pages 248 and 249 illustrate this point.

hard currency
A currency that can be easily converted into another currency.

- **The convertibility of the currency**. Currency-convertibility risk is a pure risk—there can only be a loss— that reflects the degree to which a currency can be converted into other currencies. Major countries' currencies are fully convertible—they are called hard currencies—and these currencies can be freely exchanged, at a moment's notice. These currencies are also called convertible currencies.

Figure 8.1: Foreign Exchange Quotes of Convertible Currencies
Photo ©3D_Creation/Shutterstock. Used with permission.

The ability to convert a currency into hard currency is generally measured in "months of foreign exchange cover" or an approximation of the size of the hard currency stock a country has, expressed in months of import activities that this stock can cover. The World Bank publishes these data and most countries have two to four months' cover.[1]

convertible currency
A currency that can be converted into an other currency.

However, some developing countries' currencies are not readily convertible into hard currencies, because the country has few exports and its government controls which imports get paid first. Those countries have little foreign currency cover. In most cases, the lack of currency convertibility just delays the date at which the currency can be exchanged for hard currency. All currencies that are difficult to convert into hard currencies are called soft currencies. In some rare cases, the currency is not convertible at all (*i.e.*, the currency cannot be exchanged for any other currency, at any time), or more commonly, the currency has a different exchange rate for purchases and for sales. Finally, some currencies can be purchased, but not sold. Such currencies are collectively called inconvertible currencies.

soft currency
A currency that cannot always be converted into an other currency.

inconvertible currency
A currency that cannot be converted into an other currency.

Figure 8.1 illustrates the way the exchange rates between two convertible currencies can be displayed.*

---

*All currencies are abbreviated with three letters: the first two letters being the abbreviation of the country's name, and the third being, generally, the first initial of the currency's name

8.1.1   Exporter's Currency

In this first alternative, the exporter and the importer agree that the transaction's currency will be the currency of the exporter's country. For example, if the exporter is located in Germany and the importer is located in Colombia, then the transaction takes place in euros (EUR), the currency of (most of) the European Union.

In this case, the exchange rate risk is nil for the exporter; all currency risks are borne by the importer, and it must determine how it will handle its transaction risks. In addition, the importer has to resolve any possible convertibility problems. Here, because the Colombian peso (COP) is fully convertible, this is not an issue.

When the Exporter Carries the Exchange Rate Risk

The choice of a currency is a fundamental aspect of an international sale: the choice of currency can substantially affect the profitability of a sale for the exporter. Take for example a sale for U.S.$ 1,000,000 on which an exporter is expecting to generate a 10 percent profit margin; its expected profits are therefore U.S.$ 100,000.

Suppose the exporter and the importer agree to conduct this transaction in the importer's currency, the European euro. The exporter then assumes the exchange rate risk. If the exchange rate at the time of the sale is U.S.$ 1.2761/€ 1; the exporter bills the importer for € 783,637.65.

If the value of the euro declines by 2 percent before the payment is made about a month later, then the exchange rate at that time of payment be U.S.$ 1.2506/€ 1. When the customer pays the invoice for € 783,637.65, the U.S. exporter converts that amount of money into U.S. dollars, and collects U.S.$ 980,017.24 if there are no banking fees collected, which we will assume for the sake of this example. The importer pays exactly what had been agreed, and carries no currency fluctuation risk whatsoever.

The U.S.$ 100,000 profit that the exporter was anticipating has been reduced to U.S.$ 80,017.24 [$ 980,017.24 − $ 900,000], which is about 20 percent less than anticipated.

The reverse can also happen: the exporter's profitability can be drastically affected by an increase in the value of the currency that it uses to pay for merchandise. For example, if the exchange rate had moved in the other direction, and the euro had increased in value by 2 percent, the new exchange rate would have been U.S.$ 1.3016/€ 1, which means that the U.S. exporter, after collecting the payment of € 783,637.65, would have been able to convert the currency into U.S.$ 1,019,982.77, for a profit of U.S.$ 119,982.77, an increase of roughly 20 percent.

8.1.2 Importer's Currency

In this alternative, the exporter and the importer determine that the transaction's currency will be that of the importer's country. For example, if the exporter is located in Jordan and the importer is located in the United States, then the transaction takes place in U.S. dollars (USD), the currency of the United States.

In this case, the exchange rate risk is nil for the importer; all currency risks are borne by the exporter, and it must determine how it will handle its transaction risks. The exporter is also ultimately responsible for converting the currency, so any convertibility problem will have to be resolved by the exporter. Here, there is no issue as the Jordanian dinar (JOD) is fully convertible.

When the Importer Carries the Exchange Rate Risk

If the exporter and the importer agree to conduct the transaction in the exporter's currency (U.S. dollars) rather than in the importer's currency (euros), then the importer assumes the exchange rate risk. For the sake of simplification, take the same sale: the exporter sells the goods for U.S.$ 1,000,000 and its expected profits are U.S.$ 100,000. Suppose also that the exchange rate at the time of the sale is still U.S.$ 1.2761/€ 1: the exporter bills the importer for U.S.$ 1,000,000, and the importer equates this amount to a payment of € 783,637.65. If the value of the euro declines 2 percent before the payment is made, about a month later, the exchange rate at the time of payment will be U.S.$ 1.2506/€ 1. When the customer pays the invoice for U.S.$ 1,000,000, the U.S. exporter collects exactly what it anticipated, but the importer needs to supply its bank with € 799,616.18, assuming no banking fees.

The importer anticipated paying € 783,637.65 for these goods, but it actually has to pay € 799,616.18, which is about 2 percent more. If the importer was anticipating selling the goods at a price of € 950,000, a markup of approximately 21 percent, its profits are reduced from € 166,262.35 to € 150,383.82, a reduction of nearly 9.6 percent. The reverse can also happen: the importer's cost can be lower if the value of its country's currency increases. For example, if the euro had increased 2 percent, the exchange rate would have been U.S.$ 1.3016/€ 1, which means that for the importer, to pay the U.S.$ 1,000,000 that it owes the exporter, needed to convert only € 768,285.19, or 2 percent less. That would have increased its profits from € 166,262.35 to € 181,714.81, or approximately 9.3 percent.

Since the creation of the euro, there have been at least 129 instances in which the exchange rate between the U.S. dollar and the euro changed by more than 2 percent over a month's time, when that determination is calculated on a week-by-week basis.

8.1.3 Third Country's Currency

Finally, the exporter and the importer can agree that the transaction's currency will be a third country's currency. For example, if the exporter is located in Thailand and the importer is located in India, they may decide to use the U.S. dollar as the transaction currency.

Using a third country's currency presents several advantages for both the exporter and the importer: for example, both bear the risks of currency fluctuation for their respective country's currency against the currency of the transaction. In this example, the exporter is responsible for the fluctuations of the baht (THB) against the dollar, and the importer is responsible for the fluctuations of the rupee (INR) against the dollar.

Special Drawing Rights
An artificial currency whose value is determined by the the value of a basket of currencies.

In some cases, the exporter and the importer choose an artificial currency (a non-circulating currency) for a transaction, such as the Special Drawing Rights (SDR) of the International Monetary Fund, which are sometimes used for international contracts; such is the case of the Liability Conventions of the ocean shipping industry (see Section 11.5 on page 411).

All three of the alternatives for choosing a transaction currency present challenges and call for some management of the risks presented by exchange rates.

USD	33.66	35.33	36.14
EUR	37.48	39.44	40.74
GBP	49.26	51.21	52.93
JPY	0.2989	0.3183	0.3374
CNY	4.87	0.00	5.75

Figure 8.2: The Most Frequently Used Third-Country Currencies
Photo ©Bankoo/Shutterstock. Used with permission.

8.1.4 The Special Status of the Euro

The euro was first created as an artificial currency; in its early years, when it was known as the European Currency Unit (ECU), the currency's value was determined by the value of a basket containing the various currencies of the European Union.

When the euro was officially unveiled in 1999, its value relative to of each of the eleven (later twelve, with the inclusion of Greece) currencies of the participating EU countries was set at a fixed rate. Only in January 2002 did the euro become a circulating currency, losing its status as an artificial currency. When seven other countries joined the euro, their legacy currency's value was also translated using a fixed currency exchange rate with the euro.

Value of the Euro and Date of Conversion

Country	Currency	Value	Date
Austria (schilling)	ATS	13.7603	December 31, 1998
Belgium (franc)	BEF	40.3399	December 31, 1998
Finland (markka)	FIM	5.94573	December 31, 1998
France (franc)	FRF	6.55957	December 31, 1998
Germany (mark)	DEM	1.95583	December 31, 1998
Ireland (punt)	IEP	0.787564	December 31, 1998
Italy (lira)	ITL	1,936.27	December 31, 1998
Luxembourg (franc)	LUF	40.3399	December 31, 1998
The Netherlands (guilder)	NLG	2.20371	December 31, 1998
Portugal (escudo)	PTE	200.482	December 31, 1998
Spain (peseta)	ESP	166.386	December 31, 1998
Greece (drachma)	GRD	340.750	June 19, 2000
Slovenia (tolar)	SIT	239.640	July 11, 2006
Cyprus (pound)	CYP	0.585274	July 10, 2007
Malta (lira)	MTL	0.429300	July 10, 2007
Slovakia (koruna)	SKK	30.126	July 8, 2008
Estonia (kroon)	EEK	15.6466	June 13, 2010
Latvia (lats)	LVL	0.702804	July 9, 2013
Lithuania (litas)	LTL	3.4528	July 23, 2014

Table 8.1: Value of the Euro in Legacy National Currencies at Adoption
European Central Bank.

The euro is a unique case of a truly international currency; not only has it become the official domestic currency of 19 of the 28 European Union countries, but the euro is also used for all intra-European trade in the Eurozone and is therefore used extensively to settle international debts. The stated goal of the European Union is to eventually transform the euro from a challenger to the U.S. dollar to the preferred third-country currency.

euro
The common currency of 19 of the 28 countries in the European Union.

Eurozone
The nineteen countries of Europe in which the euro is the currency.

Table 8.1 lists the rate at which the legacy currencies of the European Union countries were converted to the euro and Table 8.2 lists the status of the conversion for the thirteen countries of the European Union that have not yet adopted the euro.[2]

European Countries That Have Not Yet Adopted the Euro		
Bulgaria (lev)	BGN	Bulgaria plans to adopt the euro in 2018. The lev is not part of the ERM-II system, but its value is pegged to the euro.
Croatia (kuna)	HRK	Croatia may not adopt the euro until 2020. The kuna does not participate in the ERM-II system.
Czech Republic (koruna)	CZK	The Czech Republic will probably not adopt the euro until 2020. The koruna does not participate in the ERM-II system.
Denmark (krone)	DKK	Denmark rejected the euro by referendum on September 28, 2000. The krone is part of the ERM-II system (semi-pegged to the euro).
Hungary (forint)	HUF	Hungary may not adopt the euro until 2020. The forint does not participate in the ERM-II system.
Poland (złoty)	PLN	Poland has no plan to introduce the euro. The złoty does not participate in the ERM-II system.
Romania (leu)	RON	Romania has plans to adopt the euro in 2019. The leu does not participate in the ERM-II system.
Sweden (krona)	SEK	Sweden rejected the euro by referendum on September 13, 2003. The krona is not part of the ERM-II system.
United Kingdom (pound)	GBP	The United Kingdom is officially not in favor of adopting the euro. It is planning to leave the European Union.

Table 8.2: European Countries and Plans for Adoption of the Euro
European Community.

8.2   The System of Currency Exchange Rates

To manage exchange rate risks (the risks presented by currency exchange rate fluctuations), it is necessary to have a good understanding of the functioning of the system of exchange rates. Unfortunately, this section can only be a cursory review of the current knowledge in this area; a reader interested in obtaining a greater understanding of international corporate finance should refer one of any number of excellent textbooks in this field.[3,4,5]

8.2.1   Types of Exchange Rate Quotes

The exchange rate of two currencies is the value of one currency expressed in units of the second. For example, on February 14, 2017 the exchange rate for the euro against the U.S. dollar was $1.0579/€ 1 (*i.e.*, one euro was worth U.S. $1.0579).[6] According to the *Wall Street Journal*, the exchange rate is the

Spot Exchange Rates for Selected Currencies

Country	Currency	Direct Quote (in U.S.$)	Indirect Quote (per U.S.$)
Argentina	Peso [ARS]	0.0646	15.4768
Australia	Dollar [AUD]	0.7663	1.305
Brazil	Real [BRL]	0.3241	3.085
Canada	Dollar [CAD]	0.765	1.3073
Chile	Peso [CLP]	0.001561	640.50
China	Yuan [CNY]	0.1456	6.8668
Czech Republic	Koruna [CZK]	0.03915	25.544
Denmark	Krone [DKK]	0.1422	7.0323
Egypt	Pound [EGP]	0.0606	16.5065
Hong Kong	Dollar [HKD]	0.1289	7.7597
Hungary	Forint [HUF]	0.003434	291.17
India	Rupee [INR]	0.01496	66.8449
Indonesia	Rupiah [IDR]	0.000075	13,326
Israel	Shekel [ILP]	0.2668	3.7478
Japan	Yen [JPY]	0.00875	114.26
Kuwait	Dinar [KWD]	3.2751	0.3053
Malaysia	Ringgit [MYR]	0.2247	4.4504
Mexico	Peso [MXN]	0.0494	20.2587
New Zealand	Dollar [NZD]	0.7169	1.3949
Norway	Krone [NOK]	0.1191	8.3995
Pakistan	Rupee [PKR]	0.00954	104.83
Peru	New Sol [PEN]	0.3066	3.2619
Philippines	Peso [PHP]	0.02	49.952
Poland	Zloty [PLN]	0.2459	4.0664
Russia	Rouble [RUB]	0.01753	57.058
Saudi Arabia	Riyal [SAR]	0.2667	3.7504
Singapore	Dollar [SGD]	0.7038	1.4208
South Africa	Rand [ZAR]	0.0763	13.1064
South Korea	Won [KRW]	0.000878	1138.9
Sweden	Krona [SEK]	0.1119	8.9342
Switzerland	Franc [CHF]	0.9936	1.0064
Taiwan	Dollar [TWD]	0.03254	30.74
Thailand	Bhat [THB]	0.02856	35.02
Turkey	Lira [TRY]	0.274	3.6503
United Kingdom	Pound [GBP]	1.2467	0.8021
	SDR	1.51423	0.660402
European Union	Euro [EUR]	1.0579	0.9453

Table 8.3: Spot Exchange Rates of Selected Currencies, February 14, 2017
The Wall Street Journal.

midpoint between the bid and offer rates for exchanges of a value greater than $1,000,000 between banks. The *Financial Times* published the midpoint, as well as the bid-offer spread.[7] The actual exchange rate offered to a company seeking to purchase euros is different: the company would have to pay more, say $1.08, for every euro purchased. Reciprocally, the exchange rate offered to a company seeking to sell euros is lower: the company would collect less, say $1.03, for every euro sold.

Traders in foreign exchange quote a currency in two ways:

direct quote
The value of a foreign currency expressed in units of the domestic currency.

- The first way to value a currency is the direct quote, in which the value of the foreign currency is expressed in units of the domestic currency. For example, the direct quote for the euro in U.S. dollar terms was $1.0579/€ 1, as of February 14, 2017. This is the preferred way of quoting the euro, the British pound, the Australian dollar, and the New Zealand dollar.

indirect quote
The value of the domestic currency expressed in units of a foreign currency.

- The second way to value a currency is the indirect quote, in which the value of the domestic currency is expressed in units of the foreign currency. For example, the indirect quote for the Japanese yen against the U.S. dollar was ¥114.26/U.S.$ 1 as of February 14, 2017. Most currencies are traditionally expressed as indirect quotes: the Canadian dollar, the Swiss franc, and the Japanese yen, for example.

It should be self-evident that there is an inverse relationship between the two ways of quoting a currency exchange rate between two currencies:

$$\text{Direct quote} = \frac{1}{\text{Indirect Quote}}$$

Spot Exchange Rate

spot exchange rate
The exchange rate of a foreign currency for immediate delivery (within 48 hours).

The first type of exchange rate is the spot exchange rate, or the exchange rate for a foreign currency for immediate delivery. This "immediate delivery" is subject to interpretations that vary from country to country and, within one country, from one currency to another; however, the spot exchange rate is (roughly) the price of a foreign currency to be delivered within forty-eight hours.

The spot exchange rate is the exchange rate with which most international travelers are familiar: it is the one used by foreign exchange kiosks and banks worldwide (see Table 8.3 on the previous page)[8]. Comprehensive spot currency exchange rates are published daily in *The Wall Street Journal* and many dailies. The *Financial Times* is the most comprehensive of all periodicals in that respect, quoting daily the spot currency exchange rates for more than 150 currencies against the U.S. dollar, the British pound, the European euro, and the Japanese yen.[9] These quotes are available online for free.

Forward Exchange Rates

The second type of exchange rate is the forward exchange rate, or the exchange rate for a foreign currency to be delivered some number of days in the future.

Financial newspapers such as *The Wall Street Journal* publish forward exchange rate quotes for 30 days, 90 days, 180 days, or one year in the future. A party entering into a forward currency contract is committing to purchasing one currency with another at a certain price on a certain date. The exchange rate quotes given[10] are the mid-points for transactions of U.S. $1,000,000 or more that take place between banks; the actual exchange rate obtainable by a company involved in international trade is less favorable.

forward exchange rate
The exchange rate of a foreign currency for delivery in 30, 60 or 180 days from the day of the quote.

Forward Exchange Rates for Selected Currencies

Country	Currency		Direct Quote (in U.S.$)	Indirect Quote (per U.S.$)
Canada	Dollar [CAD]	Spot	0.7607	1.3146
		Forward 30 days	0.7608	1.3144
		Forward 90 days	0.7613	1.3135
		Forward 180 days	0.7622	1.3120
Japan	Yen [JPY]	Spot	0.008793	113.73
		Forward 30 days	0.008800	113.64
		Forward 90 days	0.008826	113.30
		Forward 180 days	0.008867	112.78
Switzerland	Franc [CHF]	Spot	0.9905	1.0096
		Forward 30 days	0.9919	1.0082
		Forward 90 days	0.9957	1.0043
		Forward 180 days	1.0020	0.9980
United Kingdom	Pound [GBP]	Spot	1.2477	0.8015
		Forward 30 days	1.2483	0.8011
		Forward 90 days	1.2503	0.7998
		Forward 180 days	1.2535	0.7978
Europe	Euro [EUR]	Spot	1.0541	0.9487
		Forward 30 days	1.0552	0.9477
		Forward 90 days	1.0584	0.9448
		Forward 180 days	1.0636	0.9402

Table 8.4: Forward Exchange Rates of Selected Currencies on February 15, 2017
www.investing.com.

A forward rate can be quoted in two ways. The first way is to quote the outright rate, which is the rate at which a commercial customer purchases or sells a foreign currency forward. The outright rate is the exchange rate quote shown in Table 8.4. However, in the interbank market, there is another way of quoting forward exchange rates, called the swap rate. Such a forward rate is expressed in points that must be subtracted or added to the spot rate to arrive at the forward exchange rate. A point is the unit of the last digit quoted: for example, if the spot exchange rate for the Japanese yen was $0.008793/¥ on a given date, and the forward swap rate for 90 days was expressed at a 33 points premium on the same day, then the 90-day forward exchange rate would be $0.008793 + 0.000033, for a forward exchange rate quote of $0.008826/¥ for a delivery 90 days from that date, as shown in Table 8.4 on the previous page.

A foreign-currency swap refers to the practice of a simultaneous purchase of one currency on the spot market and the sale of the same currency, in the same amount, on the forward market. A foreign-currency swap can also refer to purchasing and selling the same currency forward, but with two different maturity dates. That is, a swap transaction is either a spot transaction and a forward transaction, or two forward transactions.[11] The swap market is much larger than either the spot market or the forward market. The swap rate is used by banks and companies that have funds readily available in one currency and temporary needs in another currency; they exchange the currencies on the spot market, and know at what exchange rate they will be able to change them back, at some predetermined time in the future.

Currency Futures

currency future
The value of a fixed quantity of a foreign currency, to be delivered at a fixed date in the future.

Finally, some currencies are also traded in the currency futures' market as commodities: in the United States, futures for six currencies are traded on the Chicago Mercantile Exchange.

A futures' contract is an agreement between two parties: the seller (called the "short") who promises to deliver the currency on a certain date, and the buyer (called the "long") who agrees to buy the currency at a price that is agreed upon ahead of time.

Futures' contracts were first created for commodities other than currencies (such as corn or wheat) and fulfill different purposes for the parties that use them. Generally, the futures' contract takes place between a party that wants to limit its risk and a party that is speculating. For example, a farmer anticipates that he will be able to harvest a certain amount of corn; to limit his uncertainty regarding the price at which he can sell this commodity, he enters into a futures contract, which obligates him to deliver a specified amount of corn on a certain date, at a set price. The other party to the contract is a speculator who is not interested in the corn at all, but is intent on reselling it immediately upon delivery to another party and speculates that the corn, on that date, will fetch a higher price than what he promised to pay the farmer.

Similarly, a company that uses wheat for a particular purpose may enter into a futures' contract to make sure it can purchase a certain amount of that commodity on that date at a set price. The other party to the futures' contract is a speculator who thinks that he can obtain the wheat on that date for less than what he can sell it to the company.

In the first case, the farmer is intent on minimizing his risk (for example, a bumper crop lowers the value of his corn), and in the second case, the company is looking to minimize its uncertainty regarding the price of one of its raw materials. In both cases, the speculator is taking the risk; if the corn supply is lower than what the market anticipated, the speculator can take delivery from the farmer at a price lower than the spot price and make money. In the second case, the speculator makes money if the supply of wheat is larger than the market anticipated. If the speculator is incorrect, he loses money, but he nevertheless must make good on his promise to purchase the corn or sell the wheat at the price that he had promised to pay or sell the commodity.

There are two major differences between a forward contract and a futures' contract as they apply to currency exchange rates:

1. The amount of the foreign currency for which a company can purchase futures is fixed; in the United States, currency futures are only available in increments of 100,000 Australian dollars, 62,500 British pounds, 100,000 Canadian dollars, 125,000 euros, 12.5 million Japanese yen, and 500,000 Mexican pesos. This is in contrast with the forward market, in which any amount can be purchased or sold.

2. The date at which the future must be settled (purchased or sold) is fixed: in the United States, the settlement date is always the third Wednesday of the months of March, June, September or December. This is in contrast with the forward market, in which any date can be chosen in advance.

Because of this lack of flexibility, companies involved in international trade do not use futures' contracts for currencies as frequently as they use forward contracts.

Currency Options

In addition to the futures market, there is also a currency options' market, which takes place, in the United States, at the Philadelphia Stock Exchange's United Currency Options Market.

currency option
The right—but not the obligation—to purchase (or sell) a currency at a certain price some time in the future.

An option contract differs substantially from a futures' contract. In a futures' contract, both parties are obligated to deliver (or buy) the currency on the date at which the futures' contract is settled. In contrast, in the options' market, the buyer of the option is purchasing the right (the option) to buy or sell a particular currency at a predetermined price. However, the buyer of the option is not required to exercise that option; the option buyer can decline instead to purchase or sell at that price. If the option buyer elects to exercise the option, however, the seller of the option is obligated to comply.

There are two types of options: call options and put options. A call option is the right, but not the obligation, to buy a predetermined amount of foreign currency at a predetermined price (called the strike price) on a predetermined date. A put option is the right, but not the obligation, to sell the same. If the option buyer decides not to exercise the option, it only loses the amount that it paid for that option. The seller of the option keeps the amount that it charged for the option, regardless of what the buyer decides to do.

call option
A currency option with which a firm buys the right to buy a currency at a given price some time in the future.

put option
A currency option with which a firm buys the right to sell a currency at a given price some time in the future.

strike price
The price at which a currency option is exercised.

To add to the complexity, there are two styles of options: the U.S.-style option gives a company the right to exercise its option at any time until the expiration date, while a European-style option only allows the option buyer to exercise that option on the expiration date. Options are priced by the market, the aggregate of companies wanting to purchase options and speculators and other companies selling options. Several mathematical models can be used to determine the pricing of options, but their complexity is beyond the scope of this textbook.

How Does the Options Market Work?

Call Options:

A United States firm purchases a call option—the right to buy—British pounds on November 1, at a predetermined exchange rate of £ 1.00/U.S. $1.88; this price is called the strike price. The firm has to pay U.S. $4,000 for the option.

On November 1, the firm can exercise its call option and tell the seller of the option that it wants delivery of the currency, and the seller of the option must comply. The buyer of the option only exercises the option if the spot exchange rate of that currency on November 1 is higher that the agreed-upon strike price, say £ 1.00/U.S. $1.90, because buying British pounds on the spot market on that date is more expensive than exercising the option.

If the spot exchange rate is lower, say £ 1.00/U.S. $1.84, the buyer of the option does not exercise its option, and purchases the currency on the spot market instead; the firm willingly foregoes what it paid for the option, or U.S. $4,000.

Put Options:

A German firm purchases a put option—the right to sell—European euros on December 1, at a predetermined exchange rate of € 1.00/U.S. $1.26; that price is called the strike price. The firm must pay € 3,000 for that option.

On December 1, the firm can exercise its put option and tell the seller of the option that it wants the money for the currency, and the seller of the option must comply (buy the currency from the German firm). The buyer of the option exercises the option if the spot exchange rate of that currency on December 1 is lower that the agreed-upon strike price, say € 1.00/U.S. $1.24, because selling the euros on the spot market is more attractive than exercising the option.

If the spot exchange rate is higher, say € 1.00/U.S. $1.30, the buyer of the option does not exercise its option and sells the currency on the spot market instead; the company willingly foregoes what it had paid for the option, or € 3,000.

8.2.2   Types of Currencies

In determining the exchange rate risks carried by a specific transaction, it is helpful to determine the type of currency with which the exporter (or importer) is dealing. There are three types of currencies.

Floating Currencies

Floating currencies are foreign currencies whose value changes (or can change) continuously against other currencies. For example, the U.S. dollar continuously changes in value as it is traded between companies that have dollars and companies that want dollars; only the market determines its value. Figure 8.3 illustrates the exchange rate between the U.S. dollar and the European euro since the euro was placed in circulation in January 2001.[12] The countries representing the greatest percentage of world trade all have floating currencies.

floating currency
A currency whose value is determined by market forces. A floating currency's value changes frequently.

The fact that a currency is floating does not always represent unpredictability for a company involved in international trade; most currencies are relatively stable in their values in the short term. However, those currencies that are considered volatile (*i.e.*, currencies that can experience a great deal of variation in their exchange rates from one day to the next) can present a significant risk. Even though the euro has fluctuated substantially against the U.S. dollar—almost 100 percent, from a low of € 1.00/U.S.$ 0.8270 on October 25, 2000, to a high of € 1.00/U.S.$ 1.601 on April 22, 2008—in the seventeen years since its inception, neither the euro nor the U.S. dollar are considered volatile currencies.

To squelch some of this volatility, floating currencies are sometimes supported by their country's government, which intervenes in the foreign exchange markets to sustain the value of a currency. Such policies can be quite onerous for countries: to support the value of a currency, the government must purchase it on the open market, and that is only achieved by selling foreign exchange, or

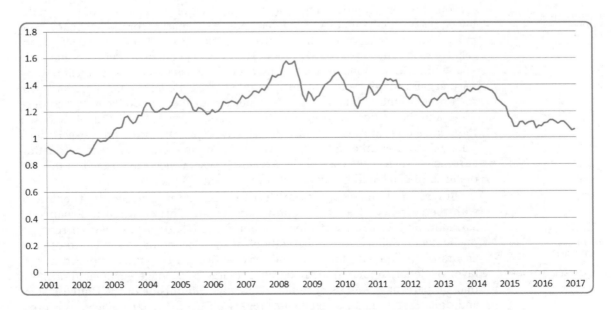

Figure 8.3: The Euro-U.S. Dollar Exchange Rate, January 2001-January 2017
Federal Reserve System.

the proceeds of export sales. George Soros made a fortune (more than U.S. $1 billion) by betting against the British pound in September 1992, at a time when the British government was intent on shoring up the pound's value.[13]

Over the long run, a country can adopt policies that reduce the value of its currency against others. Such policies have the result of lowering the relative price of exports from that country, increase total exports, and decrease imports by making them more expensive. As Figure 8.3 on the previous page shows, the value of the dollar went down from approximately 2001 to 2008: as the price of a euro goes up, the purchasing power of the dollar goes down. Some finance ministers (Brazil and India particularly) accused the United States of having engaged in a "currency war" by decreasing the value of its currency, a charge that was dismissed by Ben Bernanke, former Chair of the Board of Governors of the United States Federal Reserve, as late as January 2016:[14] "Although the Fed's monetary policies of recent years likely put downward pressure on the dollar, [...there is] little support for the claims that the Fed has engaged in currency wars."

Most the developed countries have stable floating currencies, that is, currencies for which it is reasonable to expect a predictable exchange rate in the short term. It's only under those conditions that an international firm will accept payment—or agree to pay—in that country's currency.

Pegged Currencies

pegged currency
A currency whose value is determined by a fixed exchange rate with a more widely traded currency, such as the dollar or the euro.

Several countries have been plagued with volatile currencies. There are several reasons for this situation, most notably the lack of a sustained level of trade, giving rise to substantially varying demands in the market for that currency from one month to the next. Pegging a currency makes it worth a fixed exchange rate relative to another, stronger currency. The exchange rate is therefore predictable at any time. In most instances, the currency chosen is that of the greatest trading partner, and therefore it is often the United States dollar or the European euro; for example, the Lithuanian litas was pegged to the U.S. dollar until February 2002, and then it became pegged to the European euro, before Lithuania adopted the euro as its currency on July 23, 2014. Some currencies are pegged for a time, often to weather a turbulent economic period, and then become floating currencies; such is the case of the Argentine peso, which was pegged to the U.S. dollar until 2002, and has been a floating currency since.

dollarization
The decision by a country to replace its domestic currency with the dollar.

In rare cases, the country can elect to eliminate its currency and replace it with the currency of another country altogether. This occurred in Panama, El Salvador, and Ecuador, which have adopted the U.S. dollar as their currency, a phenomenon dubbed the "dollarization" of these economies. The Board of Governors of the United States Federal Reserve System is neither opposed nor in favor of dollarization,[15] mostly because a large percentage—estimated at more than 50 percent[16]—of U.S. currency is already held outside of the United States, and dollarization has no significant impact on U.S. monetary policy. However, for the countries adopting the U.S. dollar as their currency, their government's ability to influence their economies through monetary policy is eliminated.[17]

Floating Currency Blocs—European Monetary System

Finally, some countries trade so much with each other that they decide to create a currency bloc. Such was the case of the European Monetary System (EMS), which eventually gave rise to the common currency of the European Union, the euro.

currency bloc
A group of currencies whose values fluctuate in a parallel fashion with other currencies and whose values vary within a small percentage among themselves.

The EMS was designed so that the value of the currencies of the member countries had to stay within a few percentage points of each other's value, a policy that was called the Exchange Rate Mechanism (ERM). In the beginning of this experiment, the maximum variation allowed was 5 percent, and toward the end of the system, it was as low as 1 percent. Such variations were continuously controlled by the governments of the European countries, which intervened in the foreign exchange markets by buying and selling their own currencies. Such a system allowed the EMS currencies to float as a bloc against other non-EMS currencies, while maintaining a stable foreign exchange environment within the European Union, a situation that greatly promoted trade among the Union members.

Eventually a currency bloc can evolve into a fixed exchange rate between all the internal currencies. In Europe, the fixed exchange rates were established in terms of an artificial currency, the European Currency Unit (ECU), which was created in January 1999, and whose value was determined by the value of a basket of the internal currencies. The European Currency Unit was named the euro soon thereafter. Finally, on January 1, 2002, all internal currencies were eliminated and the European euro became the only circulating currency for twelve of the European countries (see Table 8.1 on page 251). When the European Union was expanded on June 1, 2004, the original ERM was resurrected as ERM-II and many of the new countries' currencies will eventually be replaced by the euro (see Table 8.2 on page 252) after they meet certain requirements for admission, and have been part of the ERM-II system for at least two years.

artificial currency
A currency that does not circulate. After the euro was changed into a circulating currency in 2002, the only artificial currency in the world is the Special Drawing Rights of the International Monetary Fund.

There were other currency blocs and common currencies in the planning stages in the early 2010s. The Gulf Cooperation Council, encompassing Bahrain, Kuwait, Oman, Qatar, Saudi Arabia, and the United Arab Emirates, proposed the creation of a common currency, tentatively called the *Khaleeji*, but Oman withdrew from the project in 2006 and the U.A.E. in 2009,[18] and by 2016, the project appeared to be doomed. In addition, since the GCC countries' currencies are all pegged to the U.S. dollar (except for Kuwait), this new currency was more symbolic than substantial.

8.3 Theories of Exchange Rate Determinations

For a company to determine its risks in an international currency transaction, it is imperative to understand how exchange rates are determined. Once a company's management understands the theories behind exchange rate fluctuations, it can then forecast them, and determine its best strategy for a specific transaction.

There are five different, but complementary, theories that help explain the variations between two countries' exchange rates.

Price of the Big Mac in Selected Countries

Country	Price in the Local Currency	Price in U.S.$	Percentage of U.S. price
United States	USD 5.06	5.06	100%
Argentina	ARS 55.00	3.47	69%
Australia	AUD 5.80	4.28	85%
Brazil	BRL 16.50	5.12	101%
Britain	GBP 3.09	3.73	74%
Canada	CAD 5.98	4.51	89%
Chile	CLP 2,450	3.64	72%
China	CNY 19.60	2.83	56%
Czech Republic	CZK 75.00	2.91	57%
Denmark	DKK 30.00	4.22	84%
Egypt	EGP 27.49	1.46	29%
Euro area	EUR 3.88	4.06	80%
Hong Kong	HKD 19.20	2.48	49%
Hungary	HUF 900	3.05	60%
India	INR 170	2.49	49%
Indonesia	IDR 31,000	2.33	46%
Israel	ILS 16.90	4.38	87%
Japan	JPY 380	3.26	64%
Malaysia	MYR 8.00	1.79	35%
Mexico	MXN 49.00	2.23	44%
Norway	NOK 49.00	5.67	112%
Pakistan	PKR 375	3.58	71%
Philippines	PHP 133	2.68	53%
Poland	PLN 9.60	2.30	45%
Russia	RUB 130	2.15	43%
Singapore	SGD 5.60	3.89	77%
South Africa	ZAR 26.32	1.89	37%
South Korea	KRW 4,400	3.68	73%
Sri Lanka	LKR 350	2.33	46%
Sweden	SEK 48.0	5.26	104%
Switzerland	CHF 6.50	6.35	125%
Taiwan	TWD 69.00	2.16	43%
Thailand	THB 119	3.35	66%
Turkey	TRY 10.75	2.75	54%
Ukraine	UAH 42.00	1.54	31%
Venezuela	VEF 3,550	5.25	104%

Table 8.5: The Price of Mc Donald's Big Mac in Selected Countries in January 2017
The Economist.

8.3.1 Purchasing Power Parity

In its absolute form, the Purchasing Power Parity theory holds that exchange rates reflect the price differences of each and every product between countries. The idea is that exchange rates fluctuate to equalize the price differences of similar products between countries, so that a set amount of currency purchases the same goods in any country of the world.

purchasing power parity An economic theory that holds that exchange rates should reflect the price differences paid by consumers.

However, purchasing power parity is impossible to achieve (and measure), given the disparity of goods and services that are purchased worldwide. Even for a perfectly uniform good, there are wide price discrepancies from one country to the next.

This inconsistency is well illustrated with the Big Mac Index, published by *The Economist* (see Table 8.5 on the facing page),[19] which shows the price of a McDonald's Big Mac sandwich can vary from 29 percent (in Egypt) to 125 percent (in Switzerland) of the U.S. price. In effect, the price of a Big Mac is 4.3 times as much in Switzerland as it is in Egypt.

Practically speaking, purchasing power parity is determined by calculating how much domestic currency an average person must spend to purchase a basket of goods. The World Bank uses this model of purchasing power parity to determine the GDP per capita (PPP adjusted) of all the world's nations.

In its relative form, as used in international finance to determine changes in exchange rates, Purchasing Power Parity is calculated using inflation rates, which is only a slightly different methodology, because in each country, inflation rates are determined by taking the prices of a basket of goods. Therefore, the only differences between the Purchasing Power Parity determined by the World Bank and Purchasing Power Parity determined through inflation rates is that the World Bank attempts to use an identical basket of goods in each country, whereas the inflation rate is calculated using different baskets of goods in different countries. In addition, the basket of goods used for inflation determination tends to include more items.

The Purchasing Power Parity Theory holds that exchange rates reflect the differences in inflation rates between countries. In other words, if the inflation rate is higher in one country, then its currency should decrease in value relative to other currencies.

This relationship can be illustrated mathematically as:[20]

$$\frac{\text{Spot value of currency F at time } t \text{ in Country D}}{\text{Spot value of currency F at time } 0 \text{ in Country D}} =$$

$$\frac{(1 + \text{inflation rate in Country D})^t}{(1 + \text{inflation rate in Country F})^t}$$

and symbolically as:

$$\frac{S(e_t)}{S(e_0)} = \frac{(1 + \text{inf}_D)^t}{(1 + \text{inf}_F)^t}$$

8.3.2   Fisher Effect

The Fisher Effect is the observation that a country's nominal interest rate (what a borrower pays for a loan) comprises both the inflation rate in that country and the real interest rate that borrowers pay.

The real interest rate is the rate that borrowers pay to borrow money anywhere in the world and the real interest rate is expected to be uniform throughout the world. This expectation is only partially realistic; while large corporations have access to many financial markets, most businesses and individuals are restricted to one. However, the Fisher Effect theory asserts that people expect to pay the same real interest rate in every country, at all points in time.

In consequence, individuals in countries with high inflation rates should expect to pay high nominal interest rates, and individuals in countries with low inflation rates should expect low nominal interest rates.

The mathematical representation of this phenomenon is:

$$(1 + \text{real interest rate}) \times (1 + \text{inflation rate}) = 1 + \text{nominal interest rate}$$

and symbolically as:

$$(1 + \text{rir}) \times (1 + \text{inf}) = 1 + \text{nir} \iff \text{nir} = \text{rir} + \text{inf} + (\text{nir} + \text{inf}) \approx \text{rir} + \text{inf}$$

8.3.3   International Fisher Effect

The International Fisher Effect is the observation that spot exchange rates reflect the differences between nominal interest rates in different countries. The International Fisher Effect theory posits that, if nominal interest rates are higher in country F than in country D, then country F's currency should decrease in value relative to country D's currency.

Conceptually, the expected spot rate reflects the fact that an investor gets the same yield on an investment, whether it is made in country D or country F.

Mathematically, this can be described as:

$$\frac{\text{Spot value of currency F at time } (t + 1) \text{ in Country D}}{\text{Spot value of currency F at time } (t) \text{ in Country D}} =$$

$$\frac{1 + \text{nominal interest rate in Country D}}{1 + \text{nominal interest rate in Country F}} =$$

and symbolically as:

$$\frac{S_{e_{t+1}}}{S_{e_t}} = \frac{1 + \text{nir}_D}{1 + \text{nir}_F}$$

8.3.4 Interest Rate Parity

The Interest Rate Parity Theory links the forward exchange rate of a foreign currency to its spot rate, using the differences in nominal interest rates between the foreign country and the domestic country. The principle is that the forward exchange rate should be expressed as a discount if the foreign country is experiencing higher nominal interest rates than the domestic country, and should reflect a premium if the foreign nominal interest rates are lower.

In other words, at time t, the forward exchange rate $F_{t+1}(e_t)$ for delivering currency F n days from t (that is, at time $t + 1$) reflects the difference between the nominal interest rate in country D and the nominal interest rate in country F, adjusted for the length of n days. This relationship always holds in the real world unless prevented by government action.

This relationship translates mathematically as:

$$\frac{F_n(e_t) - S(e_t)}{S(e_t)} \times \frac{360}{n} = \text{nir}_D - \text{nir}_F$$

interest rate parity
An economic theory that holds that the forward exchange rate between two currencies should reflect the differences in nominal interest rates between these two countries.

8.3.5 Forward Rate as Unbiased Predictor of Spot Rate

The Forward Rate as an Unbiased Predictor of the Spot Rate theory holds that forward exchange rates—and related futures exchange rates (see Figure 8.4)—for currencies are good predictors of the future spot exchange rates of that currency.

Figure 8.4: Currency Futures Trading Pit in São Paulo, Brazil
Photo ©Alf Ribeiro/Shutterstock. Used with permission.

In other words, if the forward rate for a currency shows a discount of 2 percent for a maturity date of n days, then the spot rate in n days should be 2 percent lower than it is today.

Conceptually, the relationship is that the forward exchange rate of currency F at time t in Country D for delivery at time $t + 1$ is the expected (average) spot value of currency F at time $t + 1$ in country D.

The Interest Rate Parity theory can be expressed mathematically as:

$$F_{t+1}(e_t = S(e_{t+1})$$

8.3.6   Entire Predictive Model

The five relationships can be combined to understand how each can be used to forecast expected spot exchange rates, as shown in Figure 8.5.[21]

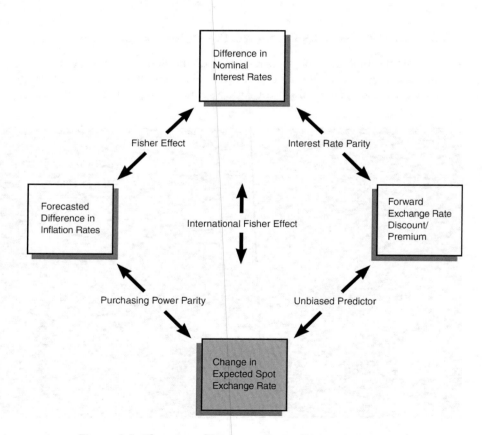

Figure 8.5: Theories of Exchange Rates Determination

8.4 Exchange Rate Forecasting

It should now be evident that forecasting exchange rates is difficult. In addition to the five theories mentioned in the preceding section, there are always political changes, unpredictable economic variations, and the occasional natural catastrophe that influence a currency's exchange rate. Figure 8.6 illustrates the exchange rate of the Japanese yen with the U.S. dollar over the past forty-two years;[22] the exchange rate has been unpredictable, although reasonably stable in the short run. In addition to the U.S. Federal Reserve System,[23] historical exchange rates can easily be obtained, for any currency, from the Bank of Canada[24] and from the Pacific Exchange Rate Service at the University of British Columbia.[25]

Figure 8.6: The Yen-U.S. Dollar Exchange Rate, January 1971-February 2017
Federal Reserve System.

Three general methods can be utilized for forecasting exchange rates, and, again, the reader should refer to textbooks dealing with forecasting to understand these techniques better. Only a cursory review is made here.

8.4.1 Technical Forecasting

So-called technical forecasting methods are all based upon time-series analysis, from simple moving averages (something that can be done easily on a spreadsheet) to sophisticated ARIMA (Auto-Regressive Integrated Moving Average) methods and neural-network models that require dedicated software packages and powerful computers. Several possible sources of technical forecasting exist.[26,27,28,29]

Technical forecasting is based on the premise that future movements in a currency's value are mathematically linked to its past movements, and use techniques that extract patterns from the historical data. These patterns are then applied to recent data to forecast the currency's future exchange rate.

Such technical forecasts are valuable in determining the possible variations of a currency's exchange rate in the short term. In the long run, technical forecasts tend to accumulate errors quickly, as they ignore the economic fundamentals of exchange rate determination.

8.4.2 Fundamental Forecasting

Fundamental forecasting attempts to integrate all the theories presented in Section 8.3 into a mathematical, causal model that uses the exchange rate of a specific currency as the dependent variable and the expected inflation rates, nominal interest rates, forward interest rates, and real interest rates as the independent variables.

Fundamental forecasting uses a large multiple linear regression model and ANOVA—Analysis of Variance—techniques, and can be done with any good spreadsheet program, such as Microsoft® *Excel*. However, there are several pitfalls with causal models, and a good survey of such models should be undertaken before they are used. Several sources can be consulted to learn about these linear models.[30,31,32]

The problem with causal models in general, and especially in the case of foreign exchange forecasting, is the difficulty in accounting for all the possible influences on a given currency's exchange rate (independent variables)—it is impossible to isolate the exchange rate's movements to a single pair of currencies—and, at the same time, limit the inevitable collinearity of the independent variables. Novices tend to increase the number of independent variables, as it increases the coefficient of determination (R^2), but often overlook the problem of collinearity that this strategy brings along.

8.4.3 Market-Based Forecasting

Market-based forecasting is based on the premise that "the market knows best" and that, therefore, the forward exchange rate of a currency is the best unbiased predictor of the future spot rate of that currency.

Because it is likely that speculators conduct their own analytical and mathematical forecasts for a currency, it is logical to conclude that the forward exchange rate includes the entire wisdom of the market, and that, therefore, it is the best predictor of the future value of a currency. This observation is called the Efficient Market Hypothesis.

However, this assumption may be incorrect, as forward rates often reflect the futures' contract rates, which are set by speculators who may include people motivated by different motives than the actual purchase and delivery of a currency. Such was the case with George Soros in 1992 when he decided to bet against the

British pound, driving the government of the United Kingdom to spend a large amount of foreign currency to sustain its value, and eventually forcing the pound out of the Exchange Rate Mechanism (ERM) of the European Union.[33]

Moreover, the forward rates do not account for possible government interventions, which can wreak havoc on the actual spot rates of currencies. For example, in the spring of 2002, the Japanese government consistently kept the value of the yen down to boost the Japanese economy through undervalued exports. The forward rates also do not reflect the possibility of an unexpected change or a currency crisis; such was the case when the Argentinian peso, which was pegged to the U.S. dollar at the rate of U.S.$ 1.00 per peso, suddenly was allowed to float on January 6, 2002, and reached U.S.$ 0.25 per peso on March 25, 2002. The currency stabilized relatively quickly at around U.S.$ 0.35 in 2002, but slowly declined thereafter; it stood at U.S.$ 0.065 in February 2017,[34] at the official rate, but the unauthorized "black market" rate was considerably lower. The Chinese currency, the yuan (also known as the renminbi [RMB]), was also artificially kept at a pegged rate against the U.S. dollar at the rate of ¥8.28/U.S.$ 1 from 1994 until July 2005, when it was changed to "better reflect market conditions" and appreciated to ¥8.11/U.S.$ 1 almost immediately. The yuan has progressively appreciated since, and stood at ¥6.88/U.S.$ 1 in February 2017.[35] Nevertheless, there is a consensus that the yuan is still undervalued, helping Chinese exports while making imports to China more expensive.

8.5 Managing Transaction Exposure

When a company is engaged in an international transaction and agrees to use a foreign currency to conduct this transaction, the company is then exposed to a certain amount of risk, due to possible fluctuations in currency exchange rates. Such risk is called transaction exposure and can be handled in one of two ways: the risk can be retained by the firm, or it can be hedged, or reduced, by using one of three possible techniques, which will be presented in this section.

transaction exposure
The impact of a change in a currency exchange rate for a company involved in international trade and its effect on the company's financial well-being.

Under these general guidelines, firms can pursue one of two strategies:

1. Determine what the decision should be on an invoice-by-invoice basis, depending on the currency involved, the amount of the invoice, and the forecast of the currency's exchange rate.

2. Set a policy that the firm follows for all foreign currency receivables and payables.

In either case, the choice of strategy depends on the forecast that the company makes of the exchange rate; the choice also depends on the size of the firm—and of its ability to weather a currency risk—on the size of the invoice relative to the total sales of the firm—what is called the exposure—and on the company's degree of sophistication in international finance. In general terms, it is almost always better for a firm to hedge its foreign exchange risks, with only a few exceptions; however, certain firms nevertheless choose to retain their exchange rate risks.

8.5.1   Risk Retention

risk retention
A risk management strategy in which a company decides to retain a risk and not insure or hedge against it.

The strategy of risk retention is fairly simple: the company decides that it is best to retain the risk of currency fluctuation. There are three types of companies that systematically retain their currency risks:

- Very large traders—importers and exporters, often in the same currency—that simultaneously carry risks on the "up-side," where they can earn additional income because of a favorable exchange rate change, and on the "down-side," where they can lose money for the same reason. Overall, for these firms, transaction exchange rate risks are a zero-sum game, and it is not necessary to hedge, as the many positions such firms hold offset each other. Nevertheless, large traders tend to be sophisticated in international finance, and they actually hedge their positions, and even speculate in the currency markets.

- Exporters or importers that have little exposure (*i.e.*, which are shipping or buying goods of relatively small value, in fairly small shipments, and therefore for which a currency loss would not have substantial financial consequences). Often, for these firms, the costs of hedging, or of determining whether they should hedge, exceed the benefits that they would accrue.

- Firms that do not evaluate international currency transaction risks clearly. These firms are not following a specific policy; they have no policy, or have a management that is not well versed in the intricacies of international trade. Such firms are also often the ones that cannot afford not to hedge, as they tend to be smaller, have greater exposure, and are more susceptible to a partial loss due to exchange rate fluctuations.

8.5.2   Forward-Market Hedges

forward-market hedge
A technique to reduce exchange rate fluctuation risk that uses forward market exchange rates.

The first of the strategies that a company can follow to protect itself from currency fluctuations is a forward-market hedge. This strategy involves selling forward a future receivable in a foreign currency, or purchasing forward the currency necessary to cover a foreign payable. This strategy varies in its implementation for each situation.

Two examples will make this strategy much clearer:

An Exporter Selling in the Importer's Currency

A U.S.-based company sells a product to an Italian firm on March 2, 2017; the invoice is payable in euros on June 2, 2017 (ninety-day credit). The amount that the firm wants to collect is U.S.\$ 200,000.

The company can use the spot exchange rate on March 2, 2017, which was U.S.\$ 1.2988/€ 1,[†] and bill the customer for € 155,279.50. However, as of March 1, 2017, the ninety-day forward exchange rate for the euro is U.S.\$ 1.2830/€ 1,

---

[†]The exchange rates used in these examples are fictitious and not based on actual exchange rates.

indicating that the market expects a decrease in the value of the euro against the U.S. dollar. The firm therefore invoices its customer for U.S.$ 200,000/1.2830 = € 155,884.65.

In this case, a forward-market hedge consists of the U.S. firm entering a forward contract with a bank, in which it promises to sell € 155,884.65 to the bank on June 2, 2017, at the predetermined (forward) exchange rate of U.S.$ 1.2830/€ 1.

On June 2, 2017, the U.S. company presents € 155,884.65 to the bank and exchanges these funds for the U.S.$ 200,000 it wanted to collect. The U.S. firm is unconcerned about the spot exchange rate of the euro on June 2, 2017.

An Importer Buying in the Exporter's Currency

A German firm purchases a product from a British firm for £ 250,000.00. The machine is delivered on April 4, 2017, and payment is expected (in pounds) on July 6, 2017.

On April 4, 2017, this amount was equivalent to € 294,475.00 because the spot exchange rate between the UK pound and the euro was € 1.1779/£ 1.

However, on April 4, 2017, the pound is expected to rise in value and the 90-day forward exchange rate with the euro is € 1.1920/£ 1. The German firm wants to ensure it knows how much it will spend on the machine, and uses a forward-market hedge by entering into a contract with a bank from which it promises to purchase £ 250,000 on July 4, 2017, at a predetermined (forward) exchange rate of € 1.1920/£ 1. On July 4, 2017, the German firm pays € 298,000.00 to the bank and obtains in exchange the £ 250,000 that it needs to pay its British supplier.

The German firm can determine on April 4, 2017 exactly how much it had to pay for the machine and is unconcerned about the spot exchange rate of the British pound on July 4, 2017.

In either of these cases, the firm has eliminated its exchange rate risk using a forward-market hedge; the firm knew, with total certainty, at the time it entered the forward contract with the bank how much it would collect (U.S. firm) or how much it would pay (German firm). For both of the firms, the forward-market hedge removed the exchange rate risk.

8.5.3 Money-Market Hedges

A money-market hedge uses the banking system of the country of the currency in which the receivable or the payable is going to be paid. The firm that is hedging its exposure either borrows from a bank in the foreign country or deposits money in a bank in the foreign country.

money-market hedge
A technique to reduce exchange rate fluctuation risk that uses the banking institutions of the foreign currency's country.

This can again be explained best with two illustrations:

An Exporter Selling in the Importer's Currency

A firm located in Switzerland sells a piece of machinery to a firm located in Japan, for the equivalent of CHF 150,000.00; to be competitive with Japanese competitors, though, it decided to bill the customer in Japanese yen.

The transaction takes place on January 16, 2017, with a payment date of March 16, 2017. The transaction amount is expressed in Japanese yen, for a total of JPY 14,277,240.00 because the exchange rate on January 16, 2017 is JPY 95.1816/CHF 1.

To protect itself from currency fluctuations, the Swiss firm uses a money-market hedge, by borrowing from a Japanese bank the present value (as of January 16, 2017) of JPY 14,277,240.00 on March 15, 2017. Supposing that the commercial lending rate in Japan on January 16, 2017, is 3 percent *per annum*, or about 0.5 percent for two months. The amount the Swiss firm borrows is then JPY $(1 - 0.005) \times 14,277,240.00 = 14,205,853.80$; the Swiss firm pays the bank back on March 15, 2017, using the payment of JPY 14,277,240.00 made by its customer.

On January 16, 2017, the Swiss firm exchanges the proceeds from the loan (JPY 14,205,853.80) for CHF 149,250.00 (the exchange rate on January 16, 2017 is JPY 95.1816/CHF 1), and gets an amount roughly equal to the payment of CHF 150,000.00 it had expected, although decreased by the cost of getting the money two months earlier. The Swiss firm is unconcerned about the spot exchange rate of the yen on March 15, 2017.

An Importer Buying in the Exporter's Currency

On May 2, 2017, a firm located in Denmark purchases raw materials from a firm located in Australia, which asks to be paid in Australian dollars. The amount of the invoice is AUD 20,000,000, payable six months later, on November 1, 2017.

The Danish firm can eliminate its exposure to exchange rate fluctuations between the Danish krone and the Australian dollar by using a money-market hedge. The Danish firm invests a sum in an Australian bank that will mature to AUD 20,000,000 on November 1, 2017. Assuming an annual interest rate of 4 percent paid on deposits in Australia, the Danish firm must invest AUD $20,000,000/(1 + 0.02) = 19,607,845$ to have enough to cover its obligation on November 1, 2017.

On May 2, 2017, the Danish firm converts DKK 114,531,804.91 into Australian dollars (the exchange rate is AUD 0.1712/DKK 1 on May 2, 2013), and deposits that amount into a bank account in Australia. The Danish firm is unconcerned about the spot exchange rate of the Australian dollar on November 1, 2017.

The money-market hedging strategy is effective because it allows the firm to use the exchange rate on the date of the transaction rather than speculate on the value of the exchange rate on the date of payment. In that respect, a money-market hedge eliminates the risks of currency fluctuations; the only cost to the Swiss firm is the interest it pays to the Japanese bank, in addition to the fees that are charged for the foreign exchange transactions. However, the amount of interest the Swiss firm pays should be the same as what it would have paid by borrowing the same amount in Switzerland, at least if the Interest Rate Parity Theory holds. Similarly, the only cost to the Danish firm—in addition to the fees—is the opportunity cost of the investment, from which the interest earned in Australia must be deducted. Both of these should offset each other approximately as well.

8.5.4 Options-Market Hedges

It is also possible to hedge a foreign currency fluctuation risk with options. An options-market hedge is a more sophisticated alternative, because it amounts to remaining unhedged—retaining the risk—if the exchange rate turns favorable and to purchasing an option, which acts as an insurance policy, to protect against unfavorable exchange-rate fluctuations. If the exchange rate turns unfavorable, the firm can exercise its option—its insurance policy—and is covered. If the exchange rate turns favorable, the firm can still benefit from this situation by not exercising its option, even though it loses the cost of the option.

options-market hedge
A technique to reduce exchange rate fluctuation risk that uses options for a particular currency.

Option-market hedges involve purchasing put or call options, or the option to sell or purchase certain currencies at a certain exchange rate on (European-style options) or before (U.S.-style options) a certain date. This agreed-upon exchange rate is called the strike price. Here again, two examples will illustrate the concepts better than an abstract description:

An Exporter Selling in the Importer's Currency

A company located in the United States sells a large piece of equipment to a firm located in the United Kingdom, and agrees to be paid in pounds. The invoice, for £ 1,000,000, is issued on December 10, 2017, but is not payable until March 10, 2018.

The U.S.-based exporting firm can minimize its currency fluctuation risk by using an option hedge; on December 10, 2017, it purchases a put option—the right to sell £ 1,000,000 on March 10, 2018—at an agreed-upon exchange rate of U.S.$ 1.3615/£ 1. If the spot exchange rate on March 10, 2018, is lower than U.S.$ 1.4615/£ 1, then the American firm exercises its option and sells the currency at that price. If the spot rate is higher than U.S.$ 1.3615/£ 1, the firm will let its option lapse and will sell the currency it received at the spot market rate.

Because the exchange rate on March 10, 2018 is U.S.$ 1.4908/£ 1, the firm sells its pounds without using its option.

The U.S. firm still incurs the cost of the option, which is approximately 1.25 percent of the contract amount, or about U.S.$ 18,268.75; however, this cost is offset by the fact that it sells its British pounds for U.S. $29,300 more than it had anticipated. The net profits on this financial transaction are U.S.$ 11,031.25.

An Importer Buying in the Exporter's Currency

A company located in Spain purchases a plant located in Canada. The contract is signed on June 28, 2017, and the firm agrees to make three installment payments of Can$ 1,000,000 each on December 28, 2017, March 28, 2018, and June 28, 2018 (six months, nine months and twelve months after purchase).

To minimize its currency risks, the Spanish firm uses an options hedge by purchasing the right to buy Can$ 1,000,000—call options—at exchange rates of Can$ 1.3348/€ 1 for December 28, 2017, Can$ 1.2871/€ 1 for March 28, 2018, and Can$ 1.2743/€ 1 for June 28, 2018.

Because the spot exchange rate is Can$ 1.3177/€ 1 on December 28, 2017, the Spanish firm does not exercise its option, purchases the Canadian dollars on the spot market, and sends them to the Canadian supplier.

On March 28, 2018, the spot market is Can$ 1.3020/€ 1, and therefore the Spanish firm exercises its option and purchases the dollars at Can$ 1.2871/€ 1 (the strike price of its option), because it is a more favorable exchange rate than the spot market.

For the future June 28, 2018 payment, the firm still has the possibility of saving money if the spot rate is more favorable than its option rate; if not, it exercises its option.

The cost of these successive options for the Spanish firm was approximately 0.75 percent, 1.25 percent, and 1.5 percent of the contract amounts for November, February, and August, respectively, for a total of approximately € 27,000.00. However, the costs were reduced by the fact that the firm saved € 9,722.17 in December.

The main problem with option hedging is that options are expensive, which is somewhat understandable as they are only covering the "down-side." The second issue is that options are commonly traded for only a limited number of currencies, and that the amounts are not as flexible as in forward markets. Nevertheless, some banks will write options that are tailored to their customers' needs. For the sophisticated firm involved in international trade, the options-market-hedge strategy has great potential.

For further information on this hedging strategy, the other hedging strategies described in this section, as well as additional strategies, the reader should refer to a number of textbooks in international finance[36] or to textbooks on options and futures.[37]

8.6   International Banking Institutions

There are several institutions involved in international banking; however, only a few of these institutions have a function that is linked to international payments. A brief synopsis of each of these institutions is given in this section. A reader interested in gaining more information on these institutions should consult a textbook in International Economics or International Banking.[38,39]

8.6.1   Central National Banks

central bank
The entity that controls the money supply of a nation and functions as a clearinghouse for inter-bank exchanges.

In every country in the world, there is a Central Bank, or some institution that acts as a Central Bank: Great Britain has its Bank of England, the European Union has its European Central Bank (ECB), and the United States has the Federal Reserve System that, although not technically a Central Bank, fulfills the role of one. Each country in the European Union has also retained its Central Bank, because only the control of the monetary supply is in the hands of the ECB; France has its Banque de France and Germany has its cherished BundesBank.

Central banks provide several services to the domestic banks of their respective countries. The first role of a central bank is the creation and control of the monetary supply, through market operations and the control of currency. This role can be one of maintenance or a more active role, such as executing monetary policy operations. The second role of a central bank is its function as a check clearinghouse where checks written on different domestic banks' accounts are settled. In some countries, central banks also manage the exchange rate of the national currency and the national foreign exchange reserves.

8.6.2   International Monetary Fund

The International Monetary Fund (IMF) was created in 1944 at the Bretton-Woods Conference; the IMF was designed to oversee the fixed exchange rate system that the Conference had started. When exchange rates started to float in 1971—the end of the gold standard—the IMF changed its focus to helping countries manage their balance of payments. In particular, the IMF lends money to countries that experience difficulties with their balance of payments. IMF loans are usually accompanied by many conditions to which the country must agree; inflation control and money supply growth are often on the list. The funds necessary for those loans are collected from the countries that become members of the IMF; they are assessed a quota that is determined by the country's economic size.

International Monetary Fund
The international organization created in 1945 to oversee exchange rates and develop an international system of payments.

The IMF is also the curator of an artificial currency called the Special Drawing Rights (SDR), which was designed to supplement the U.S. dollar in its role as the international currency. The SDR's value is determined by a basket of five currencies: the U.S. dollar for 41.73 percent, the European euro for 30.93 percent, the Chinese renminbi (yuan) for 10.92 percent, the British pound for 8.33 percent, and Japanese yen for 8.09 percent.[40]   Although the SDR is not often used by businesses, it is often used by governments to settle their debts with each other. It is also used in the settlement of disputes under the liability conventions of ocean cargo shipping (see Section 11.5 on page 411).

8.6.3   Bank for International Settlements

The Bank for International Settlements was created after World War I to manage Germany's war reparation payments. Since then BIS has evolved into a major international institution, providing support to Central Banks—which constitute its membership—and recently providing guidance to the new Central Banks of the former Eastern Bloc Countries. Although membership was originally limited to European Central Banks, the United States' Federal Reserve System joined in 1994.

Bank for International Settlements
The bank that advises central banks and provides a clearinghouse for exchanges between central banks.

8.6.4   World Bank

The International Bank for Reconstruction and Development—known as the World Bank—was created in 1945 after the Bretton-Woods Conference. Its purpose was to help countries rebuild their infrastructure after World War II, and the World Bank has slowly evolved to become the bank in charge of financing large infrastructure projects. A government that is borrowing World Bank funds must be a member of the IMF, and the loan is usually repaid as a long-term loan.

8.6.5   Ex-Im Bank

The Export-Import Bank (Ex-Im Bank) is a federal agency of the United States' government. The Ex-Im Bank's purpose is to provide assistance to U.S. exporters in the form of loans (only available to large exporters), loan guarantees (available to banks who finance exporters), or political-risk insurance policies available through the Foreign Credit Insurance Association (FCIA). See Section 10.8 on page 372 for further details. The Ex-Im Bank's existence was challenged by the United States Congress in 2015, and it was only re-authorized until 2019 through a piece of unrelated legislation. The Ex-Im Bank's future is uncertain.

8.6.6   Society for Worldwide Interbank Financial Telecommunication (SWIFT)

The Society for Worldwide Interbank Financial Telecommunication (SWIFT) is a corporation supporting an Electronic Data Interchange network that was created by banks to obtain a secure and reliable means of transferring financial information internationally. In particular, it allows the communication of letters of credit and miscellaneous international fund transfers. Because of the high level of security that the network enjoys, documents transferred through the network have the same value as original paper documents.

8.7   Currency of Payment as a Marketing Tool

In an international transaction, the choice of the currency exposes the exporter (or the importer) to the risk of currency exchange rate fluctuation. Rather than consider this risk to be a drawback in an international sale, a good exporter should consider the risk as an opportunity.

There are four main tactics that the exporter can pursue to eliminate this foreign exchange risk:

- Quote in the exporter's currency. Although this is the easiest of the alternatives for the exporter, it shifts the risk onto the importer, who is likely to consider this risk to be a burden. In addition, if the exporter's quote is being evaluated against other quotes, including some domestic proposals, a quote that is presented in a foreign currency is going to be less attractive to the importer.

- Quote in the importer's currency and minimize the risk of exchange rate fluctuation with a forward-market hedge. In this alternative, the importer has no currency fluctuation risk and the exporter knows exactly what its foreign exchange cost is going to be at the time of the transaction. The only drawback is that the exporter may not have easy access to the forward market of some currencies that are not commonly traded in the forward markets (a currency other than the European euro, the Japanese yen, the British pound, or the Australian dollar for a U.S.-based exporter). Nevertheless, these other currencies are traded in the forward market in London and, with some help from a savvy international banker, an exporter can hedge just about any receivable in any currency.

- Quote in the importer's currency and minimize the exchange rate risk with a money-market hedge. In this alternative, the importer has no currency fluctuation risk; the exporter also knows exactly what its foreign exchange cost will be, although this alternative requires knowing what the interest rates are in the importing country. However, the exporter must be experienced—and have an international presence—to borrow from a bank in a foreign market; only a few companies have this option available, although a savvy international banker can provide substantial help.

- Quote in the importer's currency and minimize the exchange rate risk with an options-market hedge. In this alternative, the importer has no currency fluctuation risk and the exporter benefits in two ways. If the exchange-rate fluctuation is favorable, the exporter benefits from it. If the exchange-rate fluctuation is unfavorable, the exporter has minimized its risk. The main issue with options-market hedges is the same as with the forward-market hedges: not all currencies are readily available in the home country of the exporter, and the help of a savvy international banker may be required to purchase options on the London market, for example.

Because of the intense competition that an exporter faces in international markets, it is likely that a significant percentage of its competitors will quote in the importer's currency. Because it is easier for the importer to handle a purchase in its own currency, an exporter that does not quote in that currency is at a strategic disadvantage.

An exporter intent on increasing its sales abroad should therefore consider offering quotes in the importer's currency and discuss with its banker which of the three hedging tactics is most appropriate.

Review and Discussion Questions

1. What are three of the possible choices that an exporter can make (in terms of currency) for a specific transaction?

2. Explain the three different types of exchange rates. Find the three exchange rates for a currency of your choice and explain the values you find.

3. Explain the three different types of currencies. Give an example of each.

4. Choose two theories of exchange rate determination and explain them.

5. What does it mean for a firm to retain its currency-fluctuation risk in a transaction?

6. There are three types of hedges that a firm can use to protect itself against transaction exposure. Choose one type of hedge and explain it.

Notes

[1] "Total Reserves in Months of Import," The World Bank, http://data.worldbank.org/indicator/FI.-RES.TOTL.MO, retrieved June 11, 2013.

[2] Multiple sources, but Wikipedia has generally a series of continuously updated webpages covering the status of all of these countries and their progress toward their accession to the euro.

[3] Eiteman, David K., Arthur I. Stonehill, and Michael H. Moffett, *Multinational Business Finance*, 2015, Fourteenth Edition, Pearson-Addison-Wesley Publishing Company, Reading, Massachusetts.

[4] Madura, Jeff, International Financial Management, 2014, Twelfth Edition, South-Western Publishing, Cincinnati, Ohio.

[5] Shapiro, Alan C., *Multinational Financial Management*, 2013, Tenth Edition, John Wiley & Sons, Hoboken, New Jersey.

[6] "Exchange Rates: New York Closing Snapshot," *The Wall Street Journal*, http://www.wsj.com/mdc-/public/page/2_3021-forex-20170215.html?mod=mdc_pastcalendar, retrieved February 17, 2017.

[7] "Currencies," *Financial Times*, http://markets.ft.com/research/Markets/Currencies, June 12, 2013.

[8] "Currencies," *The Wall Street Journal*, June 11, 2013, p. C6.

[9] "Currencies," *Financial Times*, http://markets.ft.com/research/Markets/Currencies, June 10, 2013.

[10] "Currencies," https://www.investing.com/currencies/, retrieved February 21, 2017.

[11] "Foreign Exchange Swap Transactions," *The Learning Center*, Allied Irish Bank, http://www.fxcenterusa.com/us/learning/FX%20Swaps.pdf, retrieved May 30, 2009.

[12] "Foreign Exchange Rates. H.10," Board of Governors of the Federal Reserve System, http://www.-federalreserve.gov/releases/h10/hist/, retrieved February 21, 2017.

[13] Mallaby, Sebastian, *More Money than God*, Penguin Press HC, New York, New York, 2010.

[14] Bernanke, Ben S., *What did you do in the currency war, Daddy?*, January 5, 2016, Brookings Institute, https://www.brookings.edu/blog/ben-bernanke/2016/01/05/what-did-you-do-in-the-currency--war-daddy/, retrieved February 21, 2017.

[15] Cohen, Benjamin, "U.S. Policy on Dollarisation: A Political Analysis," http://www.polsci.ucsb.edu/-faculty/cohen/recent/dollarization.html, retrieved February 21, 2017.

[16] Porter, Richard D. and Ruth A. Judson, "The Location of U.S. Currency: How Much Is Abroad?," *Federal Reserve Bulletin*, October 1996, p. 883-903.

[17] Wang, Sam, "Examining the Effects of Dollarization on Ecuador," *Council on Hemispheric Affairs*, July 26, 2016, http://www.coha.org/examining-the-effects-of-dollarization-on-ecuador/, retrieved February 23, 2017.

[18] Reuters, "U.A.E. Quits Gulf Monetary Union," *The Wall Street Journal*, May 21, 2009, p. C2.

[19] "The Economist Big Mac Index," *The Economist*, January 12, 2017, http://www.economist.com/content/big-mac-index, retrieved February 23, 2017.

[20] Shapiro, Alan C., *Multinational Financial Management*, 2009, Ninth Edition, John Wiley & Sons, Hoboken, New Jersey.

[21] Peck, Earl, "Prices, Interest Rates, and Exchange Rates in Equilibrium," unpublished research paper, Baldwin-Wallace College, Berea, Ohio.

[22] Board of Governors of the Federal Reserve System, http://research.stlouisfed.org/fred2/series/EX-JPUS/downloaddata, retrieved February 23, 2017.

[23] "Economic Research and Data," Board of Governors of the Federal Reserve System, http://www.federalreserve.gov/econresdata/default.htm, retrieved February 23, 2017.

[24] "10-Year Currency Converter,Ť Bank of Canada, http://www.bankofcanada.ca/rates/exchange/10-

year-converter/, retrieved February 23, 2017.

[25] Antweiler, Werner, "Pacific Exchange Rate Service," http://fx.sauder.ubc.ca/data.html, retrieved February 23, 2017.

[26] Bowerman, Bruce L., Richard L. O'Connell, and Anne Koehler, *Forecasting, Time Series, and Regression*, 2005, Fourth Edition, Southwestern Publishing, Cincinnati, Ohio.

[27] Box, George E., Gwilym M. Jenkins, Gregory C. Reinsel, and Greta M. Ljung, *Time Series Analysis: Forecasting and Control*, 2016, Fifth Edition, John Wiley, Hoboken, New Jersey.

[28] Makridakis, Spyros, Steven C. Wheelwright, and Rob Hyndman, *Forecasting: Methods and Applications*, 1998, Third Edition, John Wiley and Sons, Inc., New York, New York.

[29] McNelis, Paul, *Neural Networks in Finance: Gaining Predictive Edge in the Market*, 2005, Academic Press Advanced Series in Finance, Elsevier, New York, New York.

[30] Fox, John, *Applied Regression Analysis and Generalized Linear Models*, 2016, Third Edition, Sage Publications, Thousand Oaks, California.

[31] Seber, George A.F., and Alan J. Lee, *Linear Regression Analysis*, 2015, Second Edition, John Wiley, Hoboken, New Jersey.

[32] Weisberg, Sanford, *Applied Linear Regression*, 2013, Fourth Edition, John Wiley, Hoboken, New Jersey.

[33] Weiss, Gary, "George Soros, All Warm and Cuddly," *Business Week*, March 4, 2002, p. 68, reporting on Michael T. Kaufmann's *Soros: The Life and Times of a Messianic Billionaire*, 2002, Alfred A. Knopf, New York.

[34] "Commodities and Currencies," *The Wall Street Journal*, February 23, p. B6.

[35] *Ibid.*

[36] Eiteman, David K., Arthur I. Stonehill, and Michael H. Moffett, *Multinational Business Finance*, 2016, Fourteenth Edition, Pearson-Addison-Wesley Publishing Company, Reading, Massachusetts.

[37] Hull, John C., *Options, Futures, and Other Derivatives*, 2014, Ninth Edition, Prentice-Hall, Englewood, New Jersey.

[38] Krugman, Paul, Maurice Obstfeld, and Marc Melitz, *International Economics: Theory and Policy*, 2014, Tenth Edition, Prentice-Hall, Englewood, New Jersey.

[39] Smith, Roy, and Ingo Walter, *Global Banking*, 2012, Third Edition, Oxford University Press, New York, New York.

[40] "Special Drawing Right," April 21, 2017, http://www.imf.org/en/About/Factsheets/Sheets/2016/-08/01/14/51/Special-Drawing-Right-SDR, retrieved May 15, 2017.

Chapter 9

International Commercial Documents

A large number of documents are involved in international transactions, many more than in a purely domestic sale. Some of these documents are required by the exporting country, some by the importing country, some by the banks involved (especially if the shipment is made under a letter of credit), some by the carrier (transportation company), and some by the importer.

Under each of the Incoterms® rules outlined in Chapter 6, the exporter is responsible for generating and collecting all—or almost all—the documents linked to an international transaction. Any error or omission in these documents can create difficulties for both the exporter and the importer, as the goods will be detained by customs in the importing country, the bank will request amendments to process payment, or the carrier will load the goods improperly.

It is therefore imperative for international logistics managers to exert special care and follow best practices in generating the documents linked to every international transaction.

9.1   Documentation Requirements

Most international trade transactions require numerous documents, each of which must be filled out in a specific fashion, depending on the goods' country of destination, the type of goods, the method of transportation, the method of payment, the bank(s) involved, and so on. Each of these documents must also contain detailed information and specific statements, and must often be filed in a certain time frame with a specific administration. Such are the difficulties of generating these documents that a multitude of software packages exist to help the international logistics manager complete the task. Most of these software packages promise that they can help an exporter complete an entire set in "as little as two hours."

In addition, it is common to require more than one original for some of these documents, as well as a multitude of copies—one for nearly every intermediary involved in the shipment. For some transactions, the number of originals and copies can be staggering: a particularly egregious case was a letter of credit from Ethiopia for U.S.\$ 1,067 that called for "15 original invoices, five of them certified by a chamber of commerce."[1] In many cases, the thickness of the export documentation necessary for an international transaction reaches more than 1.5 centimeters (0.5 inch), even for a simple export.

Finally, most countries require these documents to be issued on paper. Although there has been a recent increase in the number of countries that accept electronic submissions of paperwork, most still prefer paper. Many countries require everything on paper; for others, only paper documents have legal status. This is the case in countries that have a legal system based on the old Napoleonic Code and have not updated their laws. Italy, for example, formally started to give an equivalent legal status to electronic documents only in February 2002.[2]

9.2 Invoices

One of the documents common to both international and domestic transactions is the bill (or invoice) that the exporter sends to the importer. However, the content of an international invoice is more complex and should be prepared differently for a foreign customer than for a domestic one.

9.2.1 Commercial Invoice

The invoice that accompanies an international shipment is called the commercial invoice. Depending on the terms of payment (see Chapter 7), the commercial invoice may be sent directly to the importer with the merchandise, or indirectly, through banking channels.

commercial invoice
The document sent by the seller to the buyer that lists the goods purchased and the amount due.

A commercial invoice should present precisely what the importer is being billed for. This seems obvious, but it is a much greater challenge to fulfill this requirement for an international transaction than it is for a domestic transaction. Several areas of the invoice must be carefully written to avoid problems later (see Figure 9.1 on the next page):

- A precise description of the product should be given. In domestic marketing, it is common to just print a part number, the number of units, a per-piece price, and a total. This is insufficient in international trade, as the invoice is one of the documents that is used by the importer (or the exporter, depending on the terms of trade or Incoterms® rule used) to clear customs in the importing country. Because the tariff paid is a function of the classification (type) of the product imported (see Section 17.1.1 on page 574), a clear and accurate description of the product should be written on the invoice, including the Harmonized System Number. In addition, because tariff rates are determined using a multiplicity of criteria, such as the number of units in the shipment, their dimensions, weight, and total value, this information should also be included.

  However, it is not possible to assume that tariffs will be calculated on the same basis everywhere; Switzerland, for example, uses weight to calculate duty for almost all products, including computers.

- The terms of trade (or Incoterms® rule used) should be made quite clear and should indicate that the seller intends to follow the guidelines proposed by the International Chamber of Commerce (ICC). The terms of trade are crucial to clarify whether the exporter or the importer is responsible for paying for several ancillary services and fees: shipping, stevedoring, insurance, dock fees, terminal fees, duty, and so on. A misunderstanding in this area can cause countless problems and cost a substantial amount of money. The use of non-traditional terms of trade or the use of domestic terms of trade in an international transaction, which no one understands, should be avoided at all costs.

EBERT PIPE ORGANS, INC.

INVOICE: 072317-001   **Date:** July 23, 2017

Sold By: **Shipped By:**
Ebert Pipe Organs, Inc.   Ebert Inc. Warehouse
1234 Carnegie Avenue   7200 Industrial Parkway
Cleveland, OH 44111   Cleveland, OH 44111
USA   USA

Sold To: **Shipped To:**
Australian Importers   St. John's Methodist Church
4/2 Wilson Avenue   76 Ewing Road
Brunswick, Victoria 3089   Brunswick, Victoria 3095
Australia   Australia

Crates: 3   **Weight:** 57.55 kg net each   **Volume:** 1.2 x 0.6 x 0.4 m each
                          65.00 kg gross each   0.288 m³ each
                         195.00 kg total   0.864 m³ total

Purchase Order: 062083

Quantity	Description	Unit Price	Total
3	Catalog Item # 095673. Pipe organ blower. HS 8414.59.1000	USD 975.00	USD 2,925.00
	Insurance paid to Brunswick, Australia	USD 128.70	
	Airfreight Costs to Brunswick, Australia	USD 585.00	
	US Domestic Transportation Costs	USD 87.00	
	Total:		USD 3,725.70

Shipped via: Trans-Air   CIP 76 Ewing Road Brunswick,
                                         Australia, Incoterms 2010
Country of Origin: USA

Terms: 1.5% 10 days / net 30 days

Figure 9.1: A Sample Commercial Invoice, with All Details Included
Photo ©Pierre David. Used with permission.

- A detailed list of the items that the exporter has prepaid for the importer should be noted; for example, the amount the exporter paid for international insurance should be indicated in the case of a CIF or CIP shipment, as some importing countries—such as the United States—exclude this amount when calculating duty. Stevedoring charges in the port of departure should be itemized for the same reason. There are probably countries for which it makes sense to list the amounts prepaid for domestic transportation (pre-carriage) in the exporting country as well.

- The terms of payment (see Chapter 7) should also be listed; the terms of payment are the conditions under which the invoice should be paid. The invoice may be accompanied by a letter of credit or a bank draft. It could also indicate that the merchandise has already been paid for (as in a cash-in-advance, a purchasing card, or TradeCard purchase) or show a due date (as in a sale conducted on an open-account basis).

- The currency in which the payment is to be made should be clear. The issues regarding the choice of the currency and ways to manage the risk of currency fluctuations are presented in Chapter 8.

- The shipping information should also be listed; the shipping information should include the ports of departure and destination, the name of the shipping company(ies), the dates of the shipment, the number of boxes or containers, their weight (gross and net), and their size.

- Finally, identifying information for the parties involved should also be provided: the name of the seller-exporter, the name of the buyer-importer, the persons to be contacted, addresses, and so forth. Local telephone access codes should be eliminated, to avoid confusing the foreign customer.*

9.2.2 *Pro forma* Invoice

A *pro forma* invoice is a common international document; despite its name, it is not an invoice at all, but a quote.

An international transaction includes so many variables that it is sometimes difficult for an importer to have a good grasp of what its final costs will be; for example, the cost of the goods is increased by the costs of shipping, insurance, and so forth. To determine these costs, the importer may request a *pro forma* invoice, literally an invoice "as a matter of form" (*i.e.*, an invoice in advance or an accurate and precise preview of what the actual invoice would be like if the transaction were to take place). The importer can then compare this invoice to the other quotes it receives.

When the exporter requests payment on a letter-of-credit basis, the information contained on the *pro forma* invoice is used by the issuing bank to open the

pro forma **invoice**
A quote provided by the exporter to the importer for the purpose of obtaining a letter of credit or an import license.

---

*In the United States, it is necessary to dial the digit "1" before making a phone call to another state. In Great Britain and in France, it is necessary to dial the digit "0" before making a domestic call. These access digits should be omitted from the letterhead.

letter of credit. Because the letter of credit dictates that the documents submitted for payment must match exactly those outlined in the letter of credit, the information included in the *pro forma* invoice will also be present in the letter of credit. Therefore, the actual transaction documents will be reviewed against the information contained in the *pro forma* invoice. Extreme care should therefore be given in writing a *pro forma* invoice: the final commercial invoice should not vary from it. If it does, this situation will likely trigger a discrepancy between the letter of credit and the actual documents, and amendments will have to be made and paid for. It is therefore imperative for the exporter to have a very accurate *pro forma* invoice, including exactly the same type of information as the final commercial invoice would have, in the same amount, with exact quotes from the other suppliers involved (shipping, insurance, and the like).

The *pro forma* invoice should also include an expiration date, or the date after which the quote is no longer valid. The expiration date in an international transaction is treated differently than in a domestic transaction. Whereas under the Uniform Commercial Code of the United States (UCC) and under the domestic laws of many other countries, the offer can be withdrawn at any time, without prejudice, for almost whatever reason, this is not the case in an international transaction conducted under the United Nations Convention on the International Sale of Goods (CISG). Under the CISG, the offer cannot be withdrawn by the seller (or the buyer) before its expiration date, and the other party can accept it at any time until then; it is an irrevocable offer. Most countries have adopted this convention for international sales contracts (see Section 5.2 for further details).

Casual handling of a *pro forma* invoice may cause countless problems later. As *A Basic Guide to Exporting* wisely points out, "problems [...] are more easily avoided than rectified after they occur."[3]

9.2.3   Consular Invoice

consular invoice
An invoice printed on stationery provided by the importing country's Consulate.

For exports to some countries—specifically a decreasing number of Latin American countries—a consular invoice may be necessary. A consular invoice is a regular commercial invoice printed on stationery (paper) provided by the importing country's consulate, and made "official" (stamped, embossed, given a visa, or whatever other procedure is used to legalize it) by the consulate before the invoice can be sent to the importer. The process of obtaining a consular invoice is often time-consuming, as it involves at least one exchange (by mail or in person) with the consulate. Because consulates for most countries are rarely located in a city convenient to the exporter, there are several messenger-service companies that provide couriers who will pick up the invoice, wait in line at the consulate, have it legalized, and return it to the exporting company.

Consular invoices are favored by countries that want to accurately forecast their needs for foreign currency. From these consular invoices, the country can determine its expected foreign currency outflows and therefore accurately manage its needs for foreign currency. However, this process also has the added benefit of generating additional revenue, as the stationery sold by the consulate and the officialization procedure are usually expensive. These fees are also obviously generated in hard currency, which is another benefit.

Fortunately, the requirement for consular invoices is slowly disappearing, as it is often viewed as a non-tariff trade barrier by exporters. As of June 2017, consular invoices were still required in half a dozen countries, mostly in Latin America.

9.2.4 Specialized Commercial Invoices

Some countries require that all commercial invoices be printed on a standard form, which is easily available at a low cost from specialized printers of international stationery, such as Unz & Co. These countries include Canada, Mexico, New Zealand, Brazil, and Israel.[4] In general, the requirement for a specialized invoice is not considered a trade barrier, and it is understood that the form's purpose is to simplify the work of customs employees.

9.3 Export Documents

A country's government may require several documents before a product can be exported. These requirements are motivated by the desire to keep accurate data on what is exported from that country. Such is the case for the Electronic Export Information (EEI) in the United States or the Single Administrative Document for the European Union. In some cases, though, the government also wants to control the outflow of certain types of merchandise, or does not want to trade with certain countries for political reasons (embargoes). In those cases, the country requires the exporter to obtain an export license.

9.3.1 Electronic Export Information

The Electronic Export Information (EEI) is a data-collection process required by the U.S. government for all exports valued over U.S.$ 2,500 per item category, as determined by the Harmonized System Number ($500 for parcels sent through the postal system), and for all shipments that require an Individual Validated Export License. The EEI is not required for exports to Canada, but it is required for shipments to Puerto Rico or the U.S. Virgin Islands, even though those shipments are not exports.[5] The EEI is collected electronically by the U.S. Customs and Border Protection or the Census Bureau as part of the Automated Export System. The EEI replaced a paper form called the Shipper's Export Declaration (SED), which had to be physically filed with CBP at the time of shipment.

The EEI allows the U.S. Census Bureau to tabulate what products are exported from the United States and to determine where these products are sold. The data are available for all commodities and for all countries in the National Trade Data Bank, available on the website of the International Trade Commission[6] with a subscription.

electronic export information
A set of data collected by U.S. Customs detailing the type and value of goods exported, as well as their destination.

The EEI's definition of "exporter" is particular to that process. Because merchandise-classification errors can sometimes be attributable to a lack of understanding of the products being shipped, the exporter of record—called the "U.S. principal party in interest," or USPPI—is now always the manufacturer of the goods, even on an EXW shipment, where the goods are actually under the responsibility of the importer when they leave the United States. With this move, the Census Bureau has effectively forced the seller to provide accurate and timely information to the importer, who is still responsible for filing an EEI. This definition has increased the reliability of the export statistics of the United States.

9.3.2   Single Administrative Document

The Single Administrative Document is a data-collection document required by the European Union for all exports.[7] The document can be filed in paper form or electronically, and must be filed in the country in which the goods are packed, and submitted to the office of the country from which the goods are shipped, if different. The "owner of the goods" or its representative is responsible for filing the form.

9.3.3   Export Licenses

export license
The express authorization, granted by the exporting country's government to the exporter, to export a particular product.

An export license is an express authorization by a given country's government to export a specific product before it is shipped. There are many reasons for a government to require an export license, but these reasons are usually triggered by one of the following four viewpoints:

- The government is attempting to control the export of national treasures or antiques. This is the case in India, which prohibits the export of any object older than 100 years old; with Britain and with France, which both control the export of antiques and works of art; with Russia, which prohibits the export of cultural artifacts;[8] and with Turkey, which was recently involved in a high-stakes fight over a trove of antique coins that were discovered in 1984 and eventually smuggled into the United States.[9] Several countries have been successful in repatriating such artifacts: Italy convinced the Metropolitan Museum of Art in New York City to return some 15 objects,[10] Greece repatriated several objects from the Getty Museum in Los Angeles, and the Boston Museum of Fine Arts returned the coins to Turkey.[11,12]

- The country's government is controlling the export of some raw materials, generally to conserve natural resources and promote domestic industry. In 2011, China restricted the export of rare earths—chemical elements critical to the manufacturing of some electronic components—of which it controls 90 percent of the world's production.[13] Vanuatu—an island country in the middle of the South Pacific—controls the export of phosphates, the only source of export for the country, and the primary industry on the island. The country of Malaysia controls the export of some types of wood. Figure 9.2 on page 290 is an export license granted by the Malaysian Timber

Industry Board to export wooden rods to the United Kingdom. The Organisation for Economic Co-Operation and Development (OECD) tallies a comprehensive list of raw materials that cannot be legally exported without an export license.[14]

- The country can also implement export controls for political reasons. Following an internal struggle between the president-elect and the outgoing president of the Ivory Coast, the country banned the export of cocoa in January 2011.[15] Belarus stopped the export of butter, cheese and macaroni in 2011 in an attempt to maintain lower consumer prices in the country.[16]

- The government is trying to exert control over foreign trade for political or military reasons: this is mostly the way the United States government manages its export licensing program; the process it follows is described further in the next section. Some other countries also pursue similar objectives: China seized and prohibited from export a book published by an American firm but printed in China, as it depicted opinions with which the Chinese government was at odds.[17] The European Union prohibits the export of personal data gathered on customers or consumers.[18]

Many countries have export restrictions: the OECD found more than 50 countries with some form of export restrictions or controls.[19]

9.3.4 U.S. Export Controls

The U.S. government's policy regarding export controls is anchored in several milestones: the existence of a (once secret) agreement between Western countries to deny access to certain military technologies (nicknamed CoCom), that ceased to exist in 1994;[20] the Export Administration Act, which controlled the type of goods that could be exported to certain "unfriendly" countries, that lapsed in 1992; the Fenwick Anti-Terrorist Amendment of the Export Administration Act, written to prevent exports to nations supportive of international terrorism; and the Comprehensive Anti-Apartheid Act, which created a number of regulations for exports to South Africa. These documents brought into existence the current Commerce Control List, which details which commodities and products can and cannot be shipped to certain countries. The list is updated regularly and published in the U.S. Export Administration Regulations (EAR).[21] In 1996, the EAR was completely revised to reflect a major shift from a policy of "everything that is not explicitly authorized needs an export license" to a policy of "everything is authorized unless specifically prohibited." Finally, in April 2002, the Bureau of Export Administration, which administers the EAR, changed its name to the Bureau of Industry and Security.

For some products, therefore, the U.S. government wants to ascertain that the goods are purchased for a legitimate commercial purpose (and not a military or a criminal one) and that there is no risk of diversion (sale to another unfriendly company or country). This is particularly true of products that have a dual use (*i.e.*, products that can be used for several purposes, one of which is commercial

LEMBAGA PERINDUSTRIAN KAYU MALAYSIA
(Malaysian Timber Industry Board)

MTIB

No. Permohonan :
Application No.

LESEN EKSPORT
EXPORT LICENSE

No. Pendaftaran MTIB/*Registration No* : **W05353**

1. Konsainor /Pengeksport (Nama dan Alamat) *Consignor / Exporter (Name and Address)*	6. Pelabuhan Pemunggahan/ *Port of Discharge* SOUTHAMPTON-EASTLEIGH APT.	7. Tarikh Eksport/*Date of Export* 22/01/2016

CKF RODS SDN BHD
NO.37-2, JALAN USJ 21/10
UEP SUBANG JAYA
47630 SUBANG JAYA SELANGOR

8. Negara Asal / *Country of Origin* MALAYSIA MY	9. Negara Destinasi Terakhir / *Country of Final Destination* UNITED KINGDOM GB

10. Kod Matawang / *Currency Code* USD	11. Amaun yang telah / akan diterima *Amount received / to be received* £ 104.87

2. Konsaini / Pengimport (Nama dan Alamat)
Consignee / Importer (Name and Address)

12. Bayaran bagi barang telah / akan diterima dari :/*Payment for goods received /to be recieved from:* UNITED KINGDOM	13. Insuran / *Insurance*	14. Tambang / *Freight*
	15. Nilai FOB / *FOB Value* MYR	

16. Berat Kasar / *Gross Wt.* (Kg)	17. Ukuran / *Measurement* (m3)

3. Cara Pengangkutan / *Mode of Transport*
1. Laut / *Sea* 2. Keretapi / *Rail*
3. Jalan Raya / *Road* 4. Udara / *Air*
5. Lain-lain (Nyatakan) / *Others (Specify)*................ — 1

Saya mengesahkan ikrar / maklumat ini benar dan lengkap
I hereby certify that this declaration/ information is true and complete

18. Nama / *Name* :   Mun Sam

19. No. Kad Pengenalan / Pasport / *I.C / Passport No* : 670801-10-

20. Jawatan Pemohon / *Designation of Application* : Director

21. Tarikh / *Date* : 18/01/2016

CETAKAN KOMPUTER DAN TIDAK MEMERLUKAN TANDATANGAN
This is computer generated licence, no signature is required

4. No./Nama Kapal/Penerbangan/Kenderaan *No./Name of Vessel/Flight /Conveyance* NORTHERN PRECISION V.15009E/HYUNDAI VICTORY V.008W02	5. Pelabuhan / Tempat Eksport *Port / Place of Export* PORT KELANG (SWETTENHAM)	MYPKG

22. Tanda dan No. Kontena *Container Marks and Nos.*	23. Bil. *No.*	24. No. dan Jenis Bungkusan *No. and Type of Package*	25. Keterangan Barang(Dokumen berkenaan hendaklah dikemukakan) *Description of Goods(Relevant document must be submitted)*	26. Kuantiti Mengikut Unit Tarif Kastam *Qty. Based on Customs Tariff Unit*	27. Tarif Kastam Malaysia *Malaysian Customs Tariff*	
					27. (a)No. Kod *Code No.*	27.(b)Unit *Unit*
		6 PALLET (GENERAL) OTHER ARTICLES OF WOOD - OTHER ARTICLES OF WOOD, NES - LAIN-LAIN				
			1. - (6 PALLET (GENERAL)) T(inch)=0-0; L(inch)=0-0; P((feet)=0-0 T(mm)=28-35; L(mm)=28-35; P(M)=1.5-3		442190990	KGM
			2. - (3 CARTON) T(inch)=0-0; L(inch)=0-0; P((feet)=0-0 T(mm)=10-10; L(mm)=66-66; P(M)=.066-.066			

UNTUK KEGUNAAN PEJABAT / *FOR OFFICIAL USE*

28. Tarikh Kelulusan *Date Of Approval*	29. Tarikh Lesen Sah Sehingga *Expiry Date Of License*	30. Kadar Levi *Levy Rates*	31. Kadar Ses *Cess Rates*	32. Jumlah Bayaran *Total Charges*
19/01/2016	19/03/2016	0.00	0.00	0.00

33. Lesen Eksport No. / *Export License No.* MTI061201001452016	34. No. Resit / *Receipt No.*

Dikeluarkan Kepada : CKF RODS SDN BHD
Untuk Mengeksport: OTHER ARTICLES OF WOOD
Kod Tarif: 442190990
Eksport Ke: UNITED KINGDOM
Diluluskan Sebanyak: 12.17 M3

AKTA KASTAM 1967 [AKTA 235]
SUBSEKSYEN 31(1)
PERINTAH KASTAM (LARANGAN MENGENAI EKSPORT) 2012

SAUPI MAT NAWI

b/p Ketua Pengarah MTIB / *for Director General of MTIB*
PERINTAH SES KAYU 2000
LEMBAGA PERINDUSTRIAN KAYU MALAYSIA

CETAKAN KOMPUTER DAN TIDAK MEMERLUKAN TANDATANGAN
This is computer generated licence, no signature is required

Page 1 of 1   Dicetak oleh/ *Printed by* :   19/01/2016 04:29:06

Figure 9.2: An Export License from the Timber Board, in Malaysia
Photo ©Malaysian Timber Industry Board. Used with permission.

and the other military). For example, the Polaroid Corporation was affected by a dual-use issue: its employees needed to use night-vision goggles to assemble some instant cameras. When sales of the product surged in Japan, the company tried to expand its manufacturing facility in Mexico and attempted to ship more night-vision goggles there, but was rebuffed by the Bureau of Export Administration (BXA)—the predecessor of the BIS—because these instruments have a dual use.[22]

The U.S. export control policies focus on three elements: the product considered for export, the entity abroad buying the product or an intermediary (abroad or in the United States) involved in the sale of the product, and finally, the ultimate country of destination for the product.

Internet Encryption

The internet is a growing area of interest for companies that want to conduct business using this international network. However, conducting business transactions through a computer network necessitates keeping certain data, such as credit card information, confidential and secure.

It is possible to keep data secure with encryption software, a type of computer program that scrambles data so that it cannot be read intelligibly by anyone but the intended recipient equipped with the same software. However, the United States government has long regarded encryption technology as sensitive—it can be used for military purposes—and therefore has kept encryption software on its Commerce Control List.[23]

For years, the U.S. government steadfastly refused to allow companies to use encryption software on the internet, as it considered the software's use to be an export because the web is essentially borderless. Only banks, subsidiaries of U.S. firms, health and medical facilities, and certain online merchants could have access to U.S. encryption technology abroad.

The Bureau of Industry and Security (BIS) has only recently allowed low-level encryption to be sold freely outside of the United States; the terminology used by BIS is "mass-market encryption," or encryption items available to the public that cannot be easily modified beyond their original intent. However, software products containing relatively low-level encryption are still listed in the Commerce Control List, and every potential export must be reviewed by the BIS.[24]

The Product Exported

To determine which products fall under the possible control of the EAR, the BIS publishes a Commerce Control List (CCL) on which it lists all products for which the BIS has deemed that exports should be of concern to the United States. Each product on the CCL is given an Export Control Classification Number (ECCN)—which is different from the Harmonized System Number used by customs—and determines whether exporting the product will necessitate an export license.

All the products that do not fall on the CCL list are given the classification "EAR99" by the BIS. However, a few of the EAR99 products can still require an export license if they fall under the jurisdiction of another government entity that controls export. For example, the Drug Enforcement Administration controls the export of pharmaceuticals under the authority of the Controlled Substances Act and can require an export license for some products.

The BIS gives the reason each product is included on the CCL. Items are listed for reasons of national security, anti-terrorism, crime control, chemical and biological weapons control, nuclear non-proliferation, regional stability, encryption, short supply, United Nations embargo, or "significant item."

Depending on the reason for their listing, ECCN commodities do not require a license for some countries, but do for others. The BIS maintains a Product/Country License Determination Matrix to help the exporter determine its obligations.[25]

The Purchaser of the Product

When the ECCN classification does not require an export license, or when the product is classified as EAR99, the exporter must still determine whether the importer or an intermediary involved in the sale is on one of several lists:

- **The Entity List.** This list identifies people, companies, and organizations engaged in weapon proliferation, drug smuggling, or terrorism, and to which the U.S. government wants to control exports. Sales to persons or organizations on the Entity List require an export license. The Entity List is maintained by the BIS.

- **The Unverified List.** This list identifies individuals, companies, and organizations that are suspected of engaging in activities that the BIS considers illegal. Before making a sale to a person on the Unverified List, the exporter must check with the BIS about possible issues. The Unverified List is also maintained by the BIS. In addition, the exporter must report a suspect transaction when the transaction has elements that the BIS considers "red flags," such as when a cash sale is made for a product that is generally purchased on credit, or when a product is sold to a company that does not appear to be in the exporter's main line of business.

- **The Specially Designated Nationals List.** The Specially Designated Nationals List contains the names of persons located abroad with whom exporters are expressly warned not to do business. These persons have been deemed to represent countries to which the United States does not want to export, or they represent companies or organizations engaged in terrorism or trafficking. Some of these companies are located in the United States. The Specially Designated Nationals List also identifies U.S. persons, companies, or organizations "whose export privileges have been revoked." The list is maintained by the Department of the Treasury.

- **The Debarred List.** An exporter is expressly prohibited to sell to a person on the Debarred List, and a company that is contacted (even for a domestic sale) by one of these companies must notify the BIS. The Debarred List is maintained by the United States Department of State.

The Country of Import

The Commerce Control List determines whether a product, for which an ECCN exists, can be sold to a specific country. There are substantial differences in an exporter's ability to export to countries that the United States considers friendly and to countries that it considers unfriendly.

In addition, though, the United States has embargoes on sales of certain products to several countries. Exporters cannot sell any of these products and will never be able to obtain an export license. Finally, the United States has a total embargo on five countries; no products whatsoever can be exported to Cuba, Iran, North Korea, and Syria. The United States has limited embargoes on several other countries, including Belarus, Burundi, Central African Republic, the Democratic Republic of the Congo, Iraq, the Ivory Coast, Lebanon, Libya, Somalia, Venezuela, Yemen, and Zimbabwe.[26]

When a license is necessary, the U.S. government requires an exporter to obtain an Individual Validated Export License, or an express authorization to ship that product to a particular country, and to write the following Destination Control Statement on the commercial invoice and the Electronic Export Information declaration: "This merchandise licensed by U.S. for ultimate destination [country]. Diversion contrary to U.S. Law prohibited." An Individual Validated Export License is generally granted with very specific terms and conditions to which the exporter is required to adhere.

Individual Validated Export License
The express authorization, given by the U.S government, to export a particular commodity.

Deemed Export

The U.S. Bureau of Industry and Security controls the export of products that could be used against the United States. However, the BIS also considers that products sold to foreign nationals in the United States are "deemed exports," and therefore fall under its jurisdiction. For example, companies should carefully monitor the access of their foreign employees to technology (computers that have access to certain databases, or hold certain programs), and apply for an export license to allow them access. All foreign employees are subject to this rule, except those who are permanent residents of the United States.[27]

deemed export
A product sold in the United States to a non-U.S. citizen.

Fines

The fines levied by the BIS can be staggering and are meant to strongly enforce compliance. Here are a few cases from a BIS booklet called *Don't Let This Happen to You! Actual Investigations of Export Controls and Anti-Boycott Regulations*:[28]

- Schlumberger Oilfield Holdings, a wholly-owned subsidiary of Schlumberger, a Curaçao-based company with headquarters in Sugarland, Texas, agreed to pay over $232 million for trading with Iran and Sudan.

- Hetran, located in Pennsylvania, manufactured a large horizontal lathe, which it sold for $800,000 to a company in the United Arab Emirates. Since Hetran's president knew that the shipment was ultimately being sent to an Iranian company named Falcon Instrumentation and Machinery, he pleaded guilty and was sentenced to a fine of $837,500.

- Gary Tsai pleaded guilty to illegally export high-precision milling machines to his father, Alex Tsai, in Taiwan. These milling machines needed a Validated Export License that was not obtained. Alex Tsai was sentenced to two years in prison.

- Weatherford International conducted business in Cuba, Iran, Sudan and Syria through Weatherford's subsidiary in the United Kingdom. Combined, Weatherford generated approximately $110 million in revenue from sales to these countries. The company was fined $100 million.

- EgyptAir Airlines Company, the flag carrier airline of Egypt, leased two Boeing 737 aircraft to Sudan. EgyptAir agreed to pay a fine of $140,000 for having re-exported the aircraft without a Validated Export License.

A product not on the Commodity Control List or whose Export Control Classification Number does not call for an export license is classified as EAR99, a classification that needs to be included on the Electronic Export Information (EEI) declaration. If a Validated Export License was issued, it is compulsory to include it on the EEI, and include the following statement: "This merchandise licensed by U.S. for ultimate destination [country]. Diversion contrary to U.S. Law prohibited."

9.3.5   End-Use Certificates

end-use certificate
A certificate, required by the exporting country, that attests that the goods are purchased for a legitimate purpose.

In some cases, and particularly for shipments of military equipment, an importer is required to provide the exporter with an End-Use Certificate, or a document that certifies that the product is going to be used for a legitimate purpose, such as military training, and that the product will not be diverted to another, less acceptable task, such as police ammunition against a civil unrest. Most of these certificates are provided by the governments of the importing country.

9.3.6 Export Taxes

Several countries require exporters to pay an export tax on certain commodities.[29] While this appears to be quite counterproductive—discouraging exports prevents a country from earning foreign currency with which it could import other products, and is likely to affect negatively its balance of trade—export taxes can make sense in the case when the goods are minerals in short supply, or when the product has been heavily subsidized by the government. This was the case for the European Union when it decided to tax the export of wheat in 1996.[30] However, although export taxes may seem attractive to some governments to raise funds quickly, they can be politically difficult to implement: in 2008, after the Kirchner government in Argentina implemented an export tax increase on agricultural products from a fixed 35 percent to a floating rate as high as 44 percent, farmers rebelled and the measure was defeated in the Argentinian Parliament.[31]

export tax
A tax collected on the value of the goods exported.

9.3.7 Export Quotas

In the same spirit, several countries have export quotas, which physically limit the amount of a certain category of goods that can be exported from the country. This strategy can be used to control scarce resources, such as in Vietnam, which had an export quota of 5 million metric tonnes of rice for several years, which it increased to 5.2 million metric tonnes in 2009 because of a large crop, and eventually completely abandoned.[32] An export quota can also be used to attempt to control the prices of a commodity on which the country has a monopoly. Such was the case with Russia, which imposed strict export quotas on platinum, palladium, rhodium, and ruthenium, commodities for which it is one of the very few world suppliers. After its application to join the World Trade Organization (WTO) was denied in part because of these export quotas, Russia lifted them in 2008.[33] Russia acceded to WTO membership in August 2012.[34]

export quota
A limit on the quantity of a particular commodity that can be legally exported.

9.4 Import Documents

A significant number of documents are required by countries in which goods are imported. There are several reasons for these requirements. These documents:

- ensure that no goods of shoddy quality are imported,

- help determine the appropriate tariff classification,

- help determine the correct value of the imported goods,

- protect importers from fraudulent exporters, and

- limit (or eliminate) imports of products that the government finds inappropriate for whatever reason.

NO.:FWO/MON/GDOD

REPUBLIC OF GHANA
MINISTRY OF MINES
ACCRA GHANA

Date: 08/06/2016

Certificate Of Origin

This Certificate is in accordance with Paragraph 61, Section 134 Sub-Section 9 of Certificate of Origin Act of 1962 defining the legal authorization related to Possession, assignment, traffic, exportation and manufacturing of precious mineral materials, amended by the decree number: 66-256 of 1971.

I, the Senior Manager in-charge of the department of Mines, undersigned, certify that the fact hereunder stated

BENEFICIARY	DESCRIPTION	WEIGHT
RE-NO: NKA52/30 PATRICK M. SABANYONI, 58 ASHWOOD MANOR, PAULSHOR, SANDTON JOHANNESBURG, SOUTH AFRICA	10 KILOGRAM OF GOLD	24 Karat
Remarks: Rough Diamond/Gold of none bankable condition		

Belonging to ■■ **MS. JUDE DANIELS of REPUBLIC OF GHANA**

This Certificate of Approval is hereby established to deserve merit.

ORIGINAL

MINISTRY OF MINES
MINISTER

Figure 9.3: A Certificate of Origin from Ghana

Photo ©Ministry of Mines, Republic of Ghana. Used with permission.

However, there is also the possibility that the country is trying—not so subtly—to hinder imports and therefore adopt a protectionist stance. In Russia, for example, it takes an average of 36 days to clear customs, and shipments require 11 documents before clearance is given. The Doing Business database of the World Bank gives this information for all countries of the world, and Russia is far from being the worst offender; it takes 17 documents to enter the Central African Republic and 101 days to clear customs in Chad. In contrast, it takes 2 documents for France and 4 days in Singapore.[35]

9.4.1 Certificate of Origin

The most common required document is a Certificate of Origin (COO), which the exporter must have signed by its Chamber of Commerce (see Figure 9.3 on the facing page). In most instances, the Chamber of Commerce delegates that responsibility to the exporter and allows the exporter to sign the certificate of origin on its behalf. Some importing countries do not allow that substitution.

certificate of origin
A certificate, signed by the exporter's chamber of commerce, that attests that the goods originated in the country in which the exporter is located.

The certificate of origin states that the goods originated in a particular country; it does not attest to the location where the product was manufactured, but only that the goods were shipped from a specific locale. This situation sometimes leads to abuses (fraud), in which merchandise is shipped from a different country than the one in which it was manufactured, often to avoid numerical quotas or higher tariffs. To prevent these practices, the Certificate of Manufacture was instituted.

The certificate of origin is used by importing countries to determine the tariff applied to the goods, as most countries apply a multi-column tariff system—different groups of countries pay different tariffs (see Chapter 17)—and to compile trade statistics. As in the case of commercial invoices, some countries require a specialized Certificate of Origin; for example, there is a specific certificate of origin for the North American Free Trade Area.

In most countries, more than one original copy of the certificate of origin must be provided; in the countries that were formerly part of the Soviet Union, three copies are required, but, in addition, all of these copies must be notarized—embossed—and signed.[36]

9.4.2 Certificate of Manufacture

A Certificate of Manufacture is like a certificate of origin, except that it attests to the location of manufacture of the exporting products; the certificate of manufacture must also be signed by the Chamber of Commerce of the exporter. In general terms, a certificate of manufacture attests that the products exported meet the minimum-content requirements of a trade agreement between two countries, which can be a 100-percent requirement. Figure 9.4 on the next page shows a certificate of origin used by a Chinese exporter who was asked to provide evidence that the goods that it intends to export meet the requirements of the China-Costa Rica Free Trade Agreement. This certificate of origin is actually a certificate of manufacture.

certificate of manufacture
A certificate, signed by the exporter's chamber of commerce, that attests that the goods were manufactured in the country in which the exporter is located.

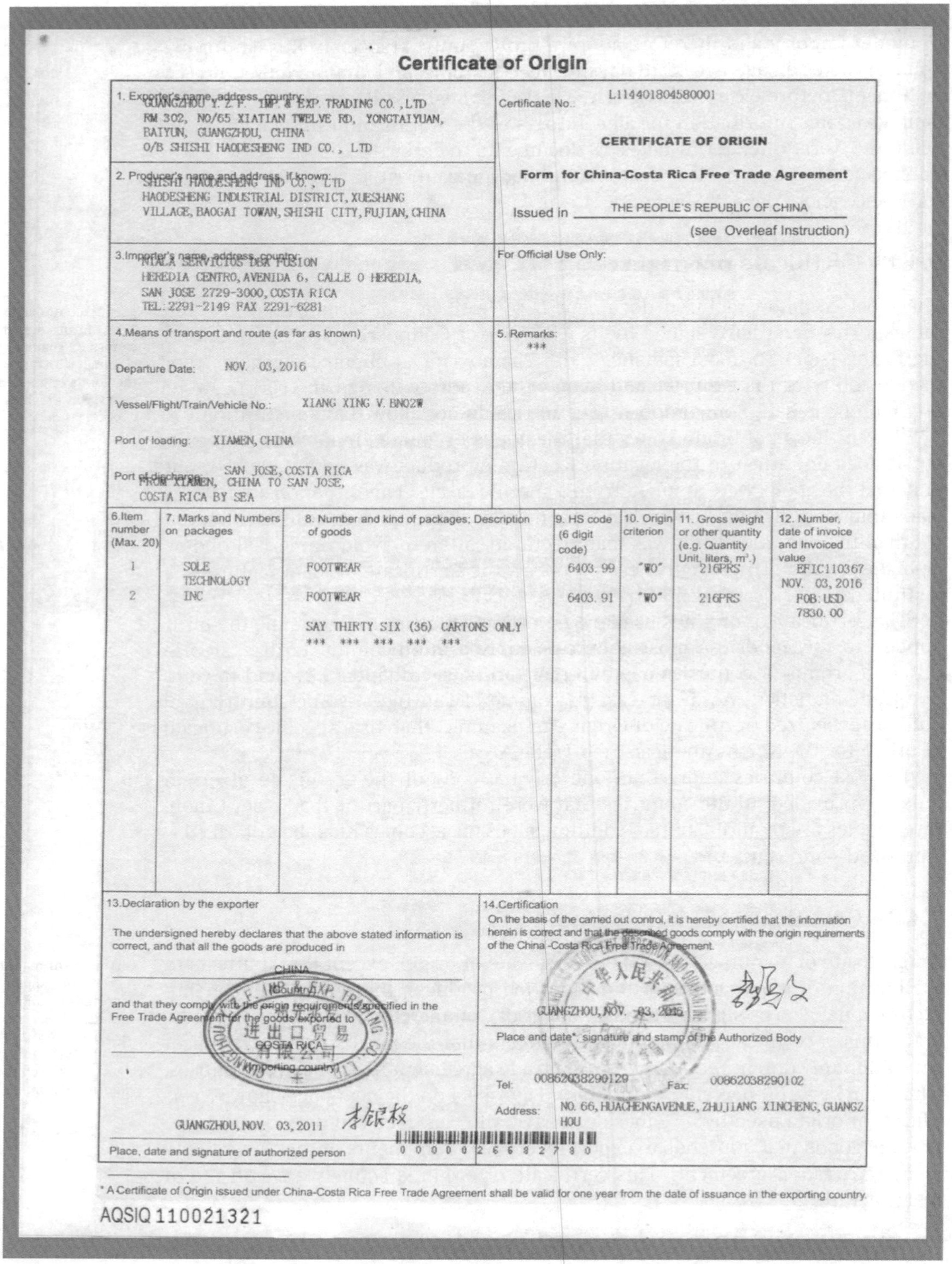

Certificate of Origin

1. Exporter's name, address, country GUANGZHOU Y.Z.F. IMP. & EXP. TRADING CO.,LTD RM 302, NO/65 XIATIAN TWELVE RD, YONGTAIYUAN, BAIYUN, GUANGZHOU, CHINA O/B SHISHI HAODESHENG IND CO., LTD	Certificate No.: L114401804580001
	CERTIFICATE OF ORIGIN
2. Producer's name and address, if known SHISHI HAODESHENG IND CO., LTD HAODESHENG INDUSTRIAL DISTRICT, XUESHANG VILLAGE, BAOGAI TOWAN, SHISHI CITY, FUJIAN, CHINA	**Form for China-Costa Rica Free Trade Agreement** Issued in _____ THE PEOPLE'S REPUBLIC OF CHINA _____ (see Overleaf Instruction)
3. Importer's name, address, country NUALA SERVICIOS DEL FUSION HEREDIA CENTRO, AVENIDA 6, CALLE 0 HEREDIA, SAN JOSE 2729-3000, COSTA RICA TEL.: 2291-2149 FAX 2291-6281	For Official Use Only:
4. Means of transport and route (as far as known) Departure Date: NOV. 03, 2016 Vessel/Flight/Train/Vehicle No.: XIANG XING V. BN02W Port of loading: XIAMEN, CHINA Port of discharge: SAN JOSE, COSTA RICA FROM XIAMEN, CHINA TO SAN JOSE, COSTA RICA BY SEA	5. Remarks: ***

6. Item number (Max. 20)	7. Marks and Numbers on packages	8. Number and kind of packages; Description of goods	9. HS code (6 digit code)	10. Origin criterion	11. Gross weight or other quantity (e.g. Quantity Unit, liters, m³.)	12. Number, date of invoice and Invoiced value
1	SOLE TECHNOLOGY INC	FOOTWEAR	6403.99	"WO"	216PRS	EFIC110367 NOV. 03, 2016
2		FOOTWEAR	6403.91	"WO"	216PRS	FOB: USD 7830.00
		SAY THIRTY SIX (36) CARTONS ONLY *** *** *** *** ***				

13. Declaration by the exporter	14. Certification
The undersigned hereby declares that the above stated information is correct, and that all the goods are produced in _____ CHINA _____ (Country) and that they comply with the origin requirements specified in the Free Trade Agreement for the goods exported to _____ COSTA RICA _____ (Importing country) GUANGZHOU, NOV. 03, 2011 Place, date and signature of authorized person	On the basis of the carried out control, it is hereby certified that the information herein is correct and that the described goods comply with the origin requirements of the China-Costa Rica Free Trade Agreement. GUANGZHOU, NOV. 03, 2015 Place and date*; signature and stamp of the Authorized Body Tel: 00862038290129 Fax: 00862038290102 Address: NO. 66, HUACHENG AVENUE, ZHUJIANG XINCHENG, GUANGZHOU

* A Certificate of Origin issued under China-Costa Rica Free Trade Agreement shall be valid for one year from the date of issuance in the exporting country.

AQSIQ 110021321

Figure 9.4: A Certificate of Manufacture—Certificate of Origin for the China-Costa Rica Free Trade Agreement

Photo ©cargofromchina.com. Used with permission.

9.4.3 Certificate of Inspection

In some cases, an importer requests a Certificate of Inspection, which is a document signed by an independent company—a third party—which attests to the authenticity and accuracy of the shipment. The independent company determines that the product being shipped is actually the product shown on the invoice, that the quantity shipped is actually the one for which the importer is invoiced, that the product is in the same condition as the importer expects (new rather than used, for example), and so forth. This inspection takes place in the port of departure of the goods, before the goods are placed in the main carriage, *i.e.* the ship, aircraft, or truck on which they will travel internationally.

A certificate of inspection is useful to the importer in several situations; for example, in a purchase conducted on the basis of documentary collection, or with a letter of credit, the documents are the only items that the bank inspects before making payment on behalf of the importer, or before committing the importer to pay (see Chapter 7). There is no way to refuse payment if there is a problem with the merchandise, and generally no way to inspect the merchandise without first taking delivery. A certificate of inspection provides evidence that there were no problems with the goods when they left the exporting country.

Some countries require pre-shipment inspections (PSIs) and the submission of a certificate of inspection for all or some of their imports (see Table 9.1)[37], and these countries generally have this requirement for reasons similar to the motivations of the importers. The countries want to protect their importers from unscrupulous exporters, but they also find it a convenient way to ensure the correct classification and valuation of the goods upon entry. Once classification and valuation are established by an independent inspection company in the exporting country, it prevents the potential corruption of local customs officials and generally speeds up the process of customs clearance and the duty collection.[38]

There are several companies that provide PSI services; the largest—with an estimated 60 to 70 percent of the world's business—are the Société Générale de Surveillance (SGS) of Switzerland, Bureau Veritas of Belgium (now headquartered in France), Cotecna of Switzerland, and Intertek of Great Britain. In some cases, an inspection company can enter an exclusivity agreement with a country, so that all shipments made to that country must have a Certificate of Inspection signed by that company. Such is the case of SGS with Indonesia, for example.

Exporters often consider PSIs to be a major annoyance, because inspection companies delve into information that exporters feel should not be divulged to a third party. In addition, because the inspection companies must ensure that the shipment is valued correctly, they can—and sometimes do—recommend a change in the value of the merchandise on the invoice. This generally infuriates sellers (justifiably) especially when they feel that the inspection company inflates the value of the goods to increase tariff revenues in the importing country.

Figure 9.5 on the following page shows a fictitious certificate of inspection for two rolls of stainless steel from China. It provides the importer with specific information about the characteristics of the goods prior to shipment.

certificate of inspection
A certificate, provided by an independent company, that attests that the goods conform to the description contained in the exporter's invoice.

pre-shipment inspection
The inspection, conducted by an independent company, that allows the determination that the goods conform to the description contained in the exporter's invoice.

HFQ Inspection Company
Nanlu Highway, 235
Shanghai, 200134
People's Republic of China
+86 21 61410151

CERTIFICATE NO.: **14202647-A**

INSPECTION REPORT

Order No.:	14202647-A
Client:	SHANGHAI WORLD EXP CO., LTD
Declared Commodity:	HOT ROLLED STAINLESS STEEL SHEET IN COIL, 430 NO. 1 FINISH, PRIME QUALITY, MILL EDGE, WITH PAPER INTERLEAVED.
Weight:	Gross Weight 22.18MT as per weighing-bridge
LC No.:	OIK10121LS1353819
Quantity:	2 coils
Place of Inspection:	Shanghai Warehouse and Linglong Warehouse, YangShan Port
Date of Inspection:	November 14, 2016
Scope of Inspection:	Weighing supervision and supervision of loading

In accordance with instructions received from SHANGHAI WORLD EXP CO., LTD, we, HFQ Co., Ltd., attended the above-mentioned location for purpose of following inspection and report as following:

Weather:
Weather condition at time of survey: Fine
Storage and identification of the goods:
Cargo presented for inspection was found stored in a truck in Shanghai Warehouse in YangShan Port.
By visual checking during inspection and from documents provided by client, it was confirmed that the cargo was hot rolled stainless steel sheet and coil. Detail size as following:
      2 coils
      8*1500*C
      8*1500*C
Packing:
2 coils were packed consisting of the following: half piece plastic cylinder, secured by 1 or 5 steel straps (width 30mm, thickness 1 mm) around the circumference.

Xudong "John" Da

HFQ Record 458102-14202647

Figure 9.5: A *fac simile* Certificate of Inspection Conducted by HFQ

Countries Requiring PSIs

Angola	Indonesia
Bangladesh	Iran
Benin	Kenya
Burkina Faso	Kuwait
Burundi	Liberia
Cambodia	Madagascar
Cameroon	Malawi
Central African Republic	Mali
Comoros	Mauritania
Republic of Congo (Brazzaville)	Mexico
Democratic Republic of Congo (Kinshasa)	Mozambique
Cote d'Ivoire	Niger
Ecuador	Senegal
Ethiopia	Sierra Leone
Guinea	Togo
India	Uzbekistan

Table 9.1: Countries Requiring Pre-Shipment Inspections

Inspection companies provide a valuable service to the importer; had Daewoo used their services, it would have discovered that its Chinese supplier shipped 15 containers of cement blocks rather than the expected plastic videocassette holders. Because the shipment was made on a letter of credit and because the documents were in perfect order, Daewoo had to pay for the shipment.[39]

9.4.4   Certificate of Analysis

A Certificate of Analysis attests to the composition of certain products; for example, a certificate of analysis is used to determine the purity of certain chemicals (for example, the exact percentage of alcohol in a pure-alcohol shipment, which always has some amount of water) or the exact composition of certain mixtures (cement, steel alloys, plastic polymers) or the purity and composition of an agricultural or pharmaceutical product, as seen in Figure 9.6 on the next page.

A certificate of analysis is usually provided by an independent laboratory or another independent inspection company, such as the Société Générale de Surveillance or Bureau Veritas, or by a governmental agency, such as the exporting country's Department of Agriculture or Bureau of Standards. In some cases, the exporter's laboratory is accredited by the exporting country's authorities and can provide its own certificate of analysis.

certificate of analysis
A certificate, provided by an independent company, that attests that the goods conform to the physical description contained in the exporter's invoice.

Vinacontrol HoChiMinh City
80 Ba Huyen Thanh Quan Str., Dist 3.,
Ho Chi Minh City
Tel : (84.8) 38.438624 - 39.316323 - 39.316704
Fax : (84.8) 39.316961 - 38.437861
E : vinahochiminh@vinacontrol.com.vn
www.vinacontrol.com.vn

ANALYSIS CERTIFICATE

NO.   : 14G04ND03351-01
DATE : APR. 29, 2017

Applicant for analysis	:	CASHEW NUT SHELL LIQUID CO.,LTD
Name of sample	:	CASHEW NUT SHELL LIQUID (CNSL)
Number of sample	:	01 SAMPLE
Date of sample receiving	:	APR. 27, 2017

RESULTS OF ANALYSIS

At request of CASHEW NUT SHELL LIQUID CO.,LTD, the supplied sample was analysed in the laboratory of Vinacontrol Hochiminh city. The results are as follows:

Specification	Unit	Method of analysis	Result
Viscosity at 25^0 C	cp	ASTM D-445	152.8
Gravity at 25^0 C	Kg/l	ASTM D-1298	0.9567
Foreign matter	%	ASTM D-473	0.92
Ash content	%	ASTM D-482	0.87
Water content	%	ASTM D-95	0.35

SURVEYOR   DEPUTY MANAGER

THAY MẶT CÔNG TY
Vinacontrol
G4

Ho Thi Hong Nhung
MS VNC1047

Nguyen Quoc Hung
MS VNC1045

TEM CHỐNG GIẢ
Vinacontrol
WWW.TEMCHONGGIA.COM

Improve quality, toward success

Figure 9.6: A Certificate of Analysis from Vietnam
Photo ©VinaControl. Used with permission.

9.4.5 Phyto-Sanitary Certificate

In transactions involving agricultural products and foodstuffs, the importing country often requires a Phyto-Sanitary Certificate. Such a certificate is used to ensure that the product being shipped is free of (certain) diseases, that it is fit for human (or animal) consumption, that it is free of pests, and so forth.

The phyto-sanitary certificate is often written by the governmental agency in charge of agricultural and food services in the exporting country (such as the U.S. Department of Agriculture [USDA] or the U.S. Food and Drug Administration [FDA]), but it also can be obtained from a commercial third party. Figure 9.7 on the following page shows a Phyto-Sanitary Certificate from Indonesia, certifying that coconuts shipped to China are free from pests.

phyto-sanitary certificate
A certificate, provided by the agricultural authorities of the exporting country, that attests that the agricultural products exported are free of disease and pests.

9.4.6 Certificate of Certification

Several countries have industrial standards that clearly define the technical characteristics that a part or product must possess before being sold in that country. For example, Germany has the *Deutsche Industrie Normen* (DIN), Japan has the Japanese Industrial Standards (JIS), and France has the *Normes Françaises* (NF). The United States has several standard setting organizations as well, including the American National Standard Institute (ANSI), the American Petroleum Institute (API), the Society of Automotive Engineers (SAE), the American Gas Association (AGA), all of which have developed performance standards for the products their member companies use.

An importer may require a Certificate of Certification to ascertain that the product meets the requirements of the standard and that the product can "pass" whatever certification procedures are required by the standard. In some countries, this certificate is called a Certificate of Conformity. Figure 9.8 on page 305 shows a certificate of certification issued by the German national railroad company on behalf of a Spanish supplier that manufactures structural-steel parts for railroad cars. The supplier's parts are certified to meet the European norms for these products.

Although there are no well-defined procedures for a certificate of certification, the certificate is often written by an independent company or a trade association's representative. However, there are some cases in which the exporter writes and signs the certificate and has it countersigned by its Chamber of Commerce, much like a certificate of origin is obtained.

certificate of certification
A certificate, issued by an independent company, that attests that the goods conform to the industrial standards of the importing country.

certificate of conformity
Another name for a certificate of certification.

9.4.7 Certificate of Free Sale

A Certificate of Free Sale attests that the product sold by the exporter can be legally sold in the country of export. Such a certificate is usually written and signed by the exporter, and is countersigned by the local Chamber of Commerce or the regulatory agency that is responsible for this type of product. In the United States, that can be the United States Department of Agriculture or the Food and Drug Administration. Figure 9.9 on page 306 shows a Certificate of Free Sale

certificate of free sale
A certificate, issued by the exporter, that attests that the goods can be legally sold in the exporting country.

kt 10

REPUBLIC OF INDONESIA
MINISTRY OF AGRICULTURE
AGENCY FOR AGRICULTURAL QUARANTINE

KT-10   No. 0139804

PHYTOSANITARY CERTIFICATE
No. : 2015.2.04.01.K10.E.005290

TO : PLANT PROTECTION/QUARANTINE ORGANIZATION
     OF. CHINA

I.   DESCRIPTION OF CONSIGNMENT

Name and address of exporter : CV. ALOHA COCONUT FIBER
JL. PERMATA PERING 9 X DESA PERING, KEC. BLAHBATUH, KAB. GIANYAR - BALI - INDONESIA

Declared name and address of consignee : SHANGHAI LULONG INDUSTRIAL CO., LTD
XINDU ROAD 2688, BLDG 30-1102, MINHANG DISTRICT, SHANGHAI 201108, CHINA

Number and description of packages :
900 BAGS = GW : 28,480.00 KGS   NW : 28,430.00 KGS

Distinguishing marks : ....
N/M

Place of origin : SURABAYA, INDONESIA
Declared means of conveyance : NAJADE V. 1110
Declared point of entry : HAIKOU, CHINA
Name of produce and quantity declared :
900 BAGS OF FRESH COCONUTS SEMI HUSKED

Botanical name of plants : *Cocos nucifera*

This is to certify that the plants or plant products or other regulated articles described herein have been
inspected and/or tested according to appropriate official procedures and are considered to be free from
the quarantine pests specified by the importing contracting party and to conform with the current
phytosanitary requirements of the importing contracting party, including those for regulated non-
quarantine pests.
They are deemed to be practically free from other pests.

II. ADDITIONAL DECLARATION

XXX NONE XXX

III. DISINFESTATION AND /OR DISINFECTION TREATMENT

Date. XXX   Treatment. XXX
Chemical. XXX   Duration and temperature. XXX
Concentration. XXX
Additional information. XXX

(Stamp of Organization)   Place of issue : Surabaya
                                       Name of authorized officer : DAMARIS LANDE
                                       Date : May.06, 2015

                                                     (Signature)

*No financial liability with respect to this certificate shall attach to Plant Quarantine Service of Indonesia or
to any of its officers or representatives.*

Figure 9.7: A Phyto-Sanitary Certificate from Indonesia for a Chinese customer
Photo ©Ministry of Agriculture, Republic of Indonesia. Used with permission.

Zertifikat-Registrier-Nr.: 3832014

Herstellerbezogene Produktqualifikation
zur Fertigung von Produkten für Schienenfahrzeuge

Der Hersteller

FORGING PRODUCTS Trading S.L.
B. Arregui s/n
48340 Amorebieta (Vizcaya)
Spanien

ist für die Fertigungsschritte

Warmformgebung und Wärmebehandlung

zur Herstellung von

Naben für Bremsscheiben gemäß EBN 918 278 sowie
Schmiedeprodukten aus Stahl im sicherheitsrelevanten Bereich
gemäß EN 10025 und EN 10083,
z.B.: Radsatzlenker, Radsatzführungen, Konsolen, Motorhalter,
Schlingerdämpferkonsolen, Bremshebel und Hebel für Drehstabfedern

qualifiziert.

Verwendetes Herstellerzeichen

 oder **FP**

Grundlagen der Qualifikation:
- Antrag zur Herstellerbezogenen Produktqualifikation vom 19.11.2013
- Bewertung der Fertigungs- und Prüfeinrichtungen vom 19. – 22.05.2014
- Prüfbericht der Forging Products Trading S.L., Nr. 80508445 vom 11.04.2014
- Abschlussbericht 070/01031/14 vom 29.07.2014

Einschränkungen:
- nur gültig in Zusammenhang mit Schreiben TEF4.Sy vom 29.07.2014

Geltungsdauer der Qualifikation: **Juli 2017**

Deutsche Bahn AG
Vorstandsressort Technik und Umwelt
Qualitätssicherung Schienenfahrzeuge
und Ersatzteile TEF 4

Berlin, 29.07.2014

i.V. _____   i.A. _____
       Bismark   Staudy

Figure 9.8: A Certificate of Certification from the German National Railroad Company on Behalf of a Spanish Supplier

Photo ©Deutsche Bahn. Used with permission.

ΕΛΛΗΝΙΚΗ ΔΗΜΟΚΡΑΤΙΑ
ΥΠΟΥΡΓΕΙΟ ΥΓΕΙΑΣ ΚΑΙ ΚΟΙΝΩΝΙΚΗΣ
ΑΛΛΗΛΕΓΓΥΗΣ

ΕΘΝΙΚΟΣ ΟΡΓΑΝΙΣΜΟΣ ΦΑΡΜΑΚΩΝ
www.eof.gr
Μεσογείων 284 , 155 62 , Χολαργός , ΕΛΛΑΔΑ

ΔΙΕΥΘΥΝΣΗ ΑΞΙΟΛΟΓΗΣΗΣ ΠΡΟΪΟΝΤΩΝ
Τμήμα: Αξιολόγησης Υγειονομικού Υλικού
Πληροφορίες: Μ. Περπιράκη, perpiraki@eof.gr
Τηλ: +30213 2040407

Αρ. Πρωτ.: 83085/23-11-2012

Προς: **ΗΛΕΚΤΡΟΔΥΝΑΜΙΚΕΣ ΚΑΤΑΣΚΕΥΕΣ
      ΜΟΝ.ΕΠΕ (PULSE DYNAMICS),
      ΜΑΡΚΟΠΟΥΛΙΩΤΗ 26,
      Τ.Κ. 11744 ΑΘΗΝΑ**

HELLENIC REPUBLIC
MINISTRY OF HEALTH AND SOCIAL
SOLIDARITY
NATIONAL ORGANIZATION FOR MEDICINES
www.eof.gr
Messogion Ave. 284 , Holargos , 155 62 , HELLAS

EVALUATION DIVISION

Medical Devices Section
Information: Μ. Περπιράκη, perpiraki@eof.gr
Tel.: +30213 2040407

Our Ref.: 83085/23-11-2012 (Issue Date)

To: **ELECTRODYMAMICS MANUFACTURING L.t.d.
    (PULSE DYNAMICS),
    26 MARKOPOULIOTI STREET,
    11744 ATHENS, ATTICA, HELLAS**

**ΠΙΣΤΟΠΟΙΗΤΙΚΟ ΕΛΕΥΘΕΡΗΣ
ΚΥΚΛΟΦΟΡΙΑΣ**

Βεβαιώνουμε ότι, σύμφωνα με τα στοιχεία μας
και σύμφωνα με τα στοιχεία που προσκομίσθηκαν
από την εταιρεία ΗΛΕΚΤΡΟΔΥΝΑΜΙΚΕΣ
ΚΑΤΑΣΚΕΥΕΣ ΜΟΝ.ΕΠΕ (PULSE DYNAMICS),
ΜΑΡΚΟΠΟΥΛΙΩΤΗ 26, Τ.Κ. 11744 ΑΘΗΝΑ
το προϊόν
**Ηλεκτρομαγνητικές θεραπευτικές
γεννήτριες ωστικού τύπου - Σειρά Papimi
UMDNS 12-415**

που αναγράφεται στο Πιστοποιητικό CE
Νο 44232066844/16-10-2012 που έχει
χορηγηθεί από τον Κοινοποιημένο Οργανισμό
TUV NORD CERT No 0044 και ισχύει μέχρι 15-
10-2015, σύμφωνα με την Οδηγία 93/42/ΕΟΚ,
μπορεί να κυκλοφορεί ελεύθερα στην Ελληνική
και την αγορά της Ευρωπαϊκής Ένωσης.
Το παρόν χορηγείται για εξαγωγικούς σκοπούς.

FREE SALES CERTIFICATE

It is hereby certified that, according to our data
and the data provided by the company
ELECTRODYMAMICS MANUFACTURING L.t.d.
(PULSE DYNAMICS), 26 MARKOPOULIOTI
STREET, 11744 ATHENS, ATTICA, HELLAS
the product
**Electromagnetic therapeutic impulse
generators - Papimi Serie UMDNS 12-415**

which is included in the EC Certificate No
44232066844/16-10-2012 issued by the Notified
Body TUV NORD CERT No 0044 (valid until 15-10-
2015), according to the 93/42/EEC Directive, is sold
freely in the Greek and the European Union market.

This certificate is issued for exports.

Η ΠΡΟΪΣΤΑΜΕΝΗ ΤΗΣ ΔΙΕΥΘΥΝΣΗΣ
ΑΞΙΟΛΟΓΗΣΗΣ ΠΡΟΪΟΝΤΩΝ
Evaluation Division Director

Ε. Μ. ΚΡΗΤΙΚΟΥ
Ε. Μ. KRITIKOU

Figure 9.9: A Certificate of Free Sale from Greece
Photo ©Ministry of Health, Hellenic Republic. Used with permission.

delivered by the Ministry of Health of Greece for a medical-equipment manufacturer.

A government or importer concerned that the exporter might attempt to send defective or second-rate products that it could not sell in its home country should require a Certificate of Free Sale to protect itself from this possibility. Neither the importing government nor the importer wants to be perceived as a possible dumping ground for products that could not legally be sold in the exporting country. This is a common fear if the importing-country's manufacturing or consumer-protection requirements are in some way less stringent than the ones of the exporting country.

A certificate of free sale has become common for pharmaceutical imports. Because of stringent regulations, medical supplies have a relatively short shelf life in most developed countries, and some pharmaceutical firms sell or donate expired or soon-to-expire drugs to relief agencies to generate tax write-offs and generate goodwill.[40] While some may perceive this behavior as unethical, the companies argue that most drugs are equally useful beyond arbitrarily determined expiration dates. Nevertheless, the governments of countries where these products are sold are requiring certificates of free sale with increasing frequency to avoid being sent products past their expiration dates.

In commercial transactions, a possible example of the use of a certificate of free sale would have been when Coca-Cola introduced its Dasani purified water in the United Kingdom. By adding calcium to its purified water, the company also inadvertently added bromates at a level that exceeded the standards of the United Kingdom, but not those of the remainder of the European Union and of the United States.[41,42] A concerned importer may have wanted to get a certificate of free sale to make sure that it was not sold sub-standard products.

9.4.8 Import License

Some countries, notably developing countries, require the importer to obtain an import license, or an express authorization to import a given product or commodity. Often, this requirement is instituted to prevent the import of items considered luxurious or nonessential, especially in countries in which there is a short supply of foreign currency, which the government would rather spend on imports that enhance the country's economic position.

import license
The express authorization, granted by the importing country's government to the importer, to import a certain product.

The process by which an importer obtains an import license varies from country to country, but it is often the responsibility of the importer to request a license. The importer will probably need a *pro forma* invoice before requesting an import license.

9.4.9 Consular Invoice

In some cases, an importing country can require the exporter to provide a consular invoice. A consular invoice is a regular commercial invoice that is printed on stationery provided by the country of import and officialized by its consulate in the exporter's country. For more details, see Section 9.2.3 on page 286.

MARINE CARGO INSURANCE CERTIFICATE

CLIENT NO	AGENCY NO	POLICY NO	ENDORS NO	OPEN COVER NO	FLOTAN POLICY NO	PROPOSAL DATE	LOADING DATE
867010	500025	200200008041789	0	200200006641522		19/02/2017	19/02/2017

POLICY HOLDER NAME	:	**ELECTRONIC CARD EXPORTER COMPANY SA**
ADDRESS	:	Polígono San Sebastián, Nave 40 Arganda del Rey - 24500 Madrid Spain
ASSURED'SNAME	:	**TAIWAN WASTEWATER ENGINEERING CO.**
ADDRESS	:	No. 40, Shuang Lien Street Taipei City, 100 Taiwan
MORTGAGE	:	

DETAILS OF SUBJECT MASTER INSURED AND THE VESSEL

KIND OF GOODS	: **ELECTRONOC CARDS**		VESSEL	: MSC NEWYORK, 151 Q 12
QUANTITY	: **10000 PIECES**			:
WEIGHT (NET)	: **12000KGS**			:
WEIGHT (GROSS**	: **15000KGS**			
PACKING	: **1000 CARTONS**			
PORT OF LOADING	: **VALENCIA SEAPORT; SPAIN**			
PORT OF DISCHARGE	: **PORT OF TAIPEI, TAIWAN**			

SUM INSURED

SUM INSURED IN EUR	ADD. S/I IN EUR(%0)	TOTAL SUM INSURED IN EUR
29,080.00	0.00	29,080.00

INSURANCE CONDITIONS AND PREMIUM

CONDITIONS	SUM INSURED VALUE	RATE %	NET PREMIUM EUR
ICC (A)	29,080.00	0.06	17.45

TOTAL NET PREMIUM :	17.45	EUR
TRANSACTION TAX :	0.00	EUR
GROSS PREMIUM :	17.45	EUR

DETAILS OF THE CONDITIONS

Marine Cargo General Conditions.

Warranted as per attached Institute Cargo Clauses (A)
Electronic Date Recognition Clause, Institute Radioactive Contamination, Chemical, Biological, Bio-chemical and Electromagnetic Weapons Exclusion Clause 10/11/2003 and Institute Cyber Attack Exclusion Clause 10/11/2003, Cyber Risk Exclusion Clause

EUR

In case of loss occurance, the indemnity amount to be paid, will be calculated in € , by applying the rate of exhange stated hereinabove. The settlement will be made either in € or in Foreign currency equivalent of the € amount on the date of payment. In consideration on the payment to us by or on behalf of the premium specified in this policy and subject to the general conditions, clauses or special conditions attached to the forming part of the policy. We hereby agree to insure against loss or damage incurred at the cargo specified under this policy. In the event of loss or damage which may result in claim under this insurance immediate notice must be given to company in order that surveyor is appointed who will examine the goods and issue a survey report. No servey report shall be valid unless signed by the appointed surveyor.

TERMINATION OF TRANSIT CLAUSE (TERRORISM), INSTITUTE STRIKES CLAUSES
CLAIMS ARE PAYABLE IN TAIWAN IN THE SAME CURRENCY

ISSUED AT :
DATE OF ISSUANCE :   19/02/2017

SPAIN WELL KNOWN INSURANCE COMPANY

Figure 9.10: A Certificate of Insurance from Spain
Photo ©Özgür Eker, advanceontrade.com. Used with permission.

9.4.10 Certificate of Insurance

Depending on a shipment's term of trade—and particularly on whether contracting insurance for the shipment is the responsibility of the exporter or of the importer, a responsibility determined by the Incoterms® rule chosen—the importer or the importing country can require a Certificate of Insurance with the shipment. This certificate of insurance is easily obtainable from the insurance company that insures the cargo. The insurance policy can be contracted for a single shipment or can be an umbrella policy, covering all of an exporter's shipments. Figure 9.10 on the facing page shows an example of a single shipment's certificate of insurance for a shipment covered with the maximum insurance coverage available, Coverage A of the Institute Cargo Clauses. For further details on the content of insurance policies in international shipments, see Chapter 10.

certificate of insurance
A certificate, issued by the exporter's insurance company, that attests that a particular shipment is insured.

9.5 Transportation Documents

9.5.1 Ocean Bill of Lading

An ocean bill of lading is a fundamental international shipping document used in ocean transportation. Its (almost) equivalent for air shipments is called the air waybill (see Section 9.5.4). A bill of lading (see Figure 9.11 on the next page) is the contract of carriage used for shipping containers, automobiles, crates, and any form of cargo that does not requisition the capacity of the entire ship; when a shipment requires the use of the entire capacity of a ship—generally a bulk shipment of oil or other commodities—another document, called a charter party, is used (see Section 9.5.5).

ocean bill of lading
The contract of carriage between an ocean carrier and the shipper.

The ocean bill of lading when issued by an ocean carrier (a steamship company) is also frequently called a master bill of lading. When the bill of lading is issued by a Non-Vessel-Operating Common Carrier (NVOCC), it is often called a house bill of lading. A house bill of lading indicates the name of the ocean carrier and the master bill of lading.

carrier
The company that transports the goods on its vessel, truck, or train.

The bill of lading is extremely important because it fulfills three roles in an international transaction:

non-vessel-operating common carrier
A shipment consolidator or freight forwarder that does not own means of transportation, but issues its own bills of lading, and therefore acts as a carrier.

- The bill of lading is a contract. The shipping company agrees with the shipper—either the exporter or the importer, depending on the terms of trade (or Incoterms® rule) of the shipment, see Chapter 6—to transport the merchandise from one port to another for a given amount of money; it is a contract of carriage.

shipper
The party in an international transaction—exporter or importer—that is responsible for arranging the main carriage.

- The bill of lading is a receipt for the goods. When the shipping company signs the bill of lading, it is acknowledging that it has received the goods in good condition and that everything seems in proper order. The document acts as a receipt for the goods; the shipping company accepts responsibility for the goods until their port of destination.

FORMAN SHIPPING U.S.A INC.   **BILL OF LADING**

SHIPPER/EXPORTER (2) (Complete Name and Address)	DOCUMENT NO. (5)	BOOKING. NO. a)
PT. ERA MANDIRI CEMERLANG JL. MUARA BARU RAYA NO. 30 UNIT C1 JAKARTA UTARA 14440 INDONESIA		

CONSIGNEE (3) (Complete Name and Address)	FORWARDING AGENT - REFERENCES (7)
	PT.KARYA ABADI MAESTRO RAHARDJO BUILDING 6TH FLOOR SUITE #606# ROA MALAKA UTARA KAV 5 - 6 JAKARTA 11220 INDONESIA
UNITED STATES OF AMERICA	POINT AND COUNTRY OF ORIGIN (8)

NOTIFY PARTY (4) (Complete Name and Address)	DOMESTIC ROUTING/EXPORT INSTRUCTIONS
	FORMAN SHIPPING USA INC. 21148 S, FIGUEROA ST, 2ND CARSON, CA 90745 TEL : 310-787-0116 FAX: 310-787-7859,310-361-7825 PIC: MR PIUS KIM
UNITED STATES OF AMERICA	

PLACE OF RECEIPT (10)
TG.PRIOK,JAKARTA, INDONESIA

OCEAN VESSEL (11)	PORT OF LOADING (12)	ONWARD INLAND ROUTING (15) FINAL DESTINATION (BY MERCHANT)
DAJI V.7031W	TG.PRIOK,JAKARTA, INDONESIA	
PORT OF DISCHARGE (13)	PLACE OF DELIVERY (14)	
MIAMI, FL	MIAMI, USA	

PARTICULARS FURNISHED BY SHIPPER

MARKS AND NUMBERS	NO. OF PKGS OR OTHER PKGS	DESCRIPTION OF GOODS	GROSS WEIGHT	MEASUREMENT
CCLU8547383/FG070948	(17)	**SHIPPER'S LOAD, COUNT & SEALED** **1 X 40' REEFER HIGH CUBE SAID TO CONTAIN :** 1,713 MASTER CARTONS OF FROZEN YELLOWFIN TUNA FILLET 675 MC CENTER CUT TUNA LOIN 5/12 LBS 438 MC TUNA STEAK 8 OZ 600 MC TUNA STEAK 4-14 OZ NW = 40,080.00 LBS / 18,218.00 KGS GW = 42,987.00 LBS / 19,540.00 KGS FDA REG NO : 18241565024 PO NUMBER : 1714 TEMPERATURE -20 DEGREES CELCIUS FREIGHT PREPAID	(19) GW = 19,540.00 KGS NW = 18,218.00 KGS	(20) SHIPPED ON BOARD AT TANJUNG PRIOK JAKARTA, INDONESIA ON AUGUST 06, 2016 BY DAJI V.7031W INTENDED TO CONNECT CMA CGM FIDELIO V.FA090E
CY/CY "FREIGHT PREPAID"				

FREIGHT and CHARGES PAYABLE BY	(Complete Name and Address)	AT

INCONNECTION WITH FREIGHT SEE CLAUSES 14 AND 16 ON REVERSE SIDE OF THIS BILL OF LADING	PREPAID	COLLECT	IN ACCEPTING THIS BILL OF LADING, the Shipper, Consignee, Holder hereof, and Owner of the goods, agree to be bound by all of its stipulations, exceptions and conditions, whether written, printed or stamped on the front or back hereof, as well as the provisions of the above Cartier's published Tariff Rules and Regulations, as fully as if they signed such Shipper, Consignee, Holder or Owner, and it is further agreed that Containers are stowed in clause 6.
			In WITNESS WHEREOF ... vessel has affirmed this Bill of Lading and autorized signature. By: FORMAN SHIPPING U.S.A. INC. PT. KARYA ABADI MAESTRO
	PREPAID		Number of originals issued **3 (THREE)** (if more than one originals issued, the others stand void when ONE is accomplished.)
			BILL OF LADING NO. DATED
TOTAL			MAESTRO-JKT-0707177 JAKARTA AUGUST 06, 2016

TERMS OF BILL OF LADING CONTINUED ON REVERSE SIDE

ORIGINAL

Figure 9.11: An Ocean Bill of Lading for a Container of Frozen Tuna from Indonesia to the United States

However, in some cases, the shipping company finds that something is wrong with the merchandise it is picking up (*e.g.*, the drums in which the merchandise is contained are rusty, there are some damaged crates, the merchandise was loaded when it was raining, the merchandise was packaged in crates that are too weak to sustain an ocean voyage) and it does not want to assume responsibility for that condition. In those cases, the shipping company will make a note about the issue or write an exception on the bill of lading of what it has observed. The bill of lading then becomes a soiled bill of lading or a foul bill of lading.

soiled bill of lading
A bill of lading that reflects the fact that the carrier did not receive the goods in good condition.

foul bill of lading
A bill of lading that reflects the fact that the carrier did not receive the goods in good condition.

In the opposite situation (*i.e.*, when the shipping company finds everything in proper order at the time of loading and does not record any reservations at the receipt of the goods), the bill of lading is considered clean.

clean bill of lading
A bill of lading that reflects the fact that the carrier received the goods in good condition.

In general, letters of credit and documentary collection transactions require a clean bill of lading; a soiled bill of lading would require an amendment to the letter of credit. Carriers may not accept goods for transportation if loading them results in a soiled bill of lading.

- The bill of lading is a certificate of title. The document that the shipping company needs to authorize the release of the goods in the port of destination is also the bill of lading. The company that is in possession of the original the bill of lading is considered to be the one to which the goods belong; the bill of lading is a certificate of title.

There are two types of bills of lading in this respect: the straight bill of lading is one on which the name of the consignee (the person or company that will pick up the goods at the port of destination) is specified. On the other hand, a to-order bill of lading is one in which the name of the consignee is left blank or the term "to order" is written. This means that the bill of lading is negotiable; in other words, it allows the sale of the cargo while it is at sea. This is a common occurrence in certain industries, notably in the oil business, in which it is not unusual to see a specific cargo change hands several times during a given voyage. In some cases, the cargo is sold to a company that wants it delivered to a different port, and the shipping company is asked to arrange for that alternative.

straight bill of lading
A bill of lading on which the name of the consignee has been entered.

consignee
The party to whom the goods should be surrendered at destination.

to-order bill of lading
A bill of lading on which the name of the consignee is marked "to order." A negotiable bill of lading.

negotiable bill of lading
A bill of lading on which the name of the consignee has been left blank.

9.5.2 Uniform Bill of Lading

The uniform bill of lading fulfills the same functions as an ocean bill of lading but is used either for inland transportation between the exporter's place of business and the port of departure, or for land transportation (rail or road) between the exporter and a foreign customer. In the majority of cases, the uniform bill of lading is a straight bill of lading. The uniform bill of lading also acts as a receipt for the goods and as a contract between the shipper and the carrier.

uniform bill of lading
A bill of lading used for transportation by truck or train, domestically or internationally.

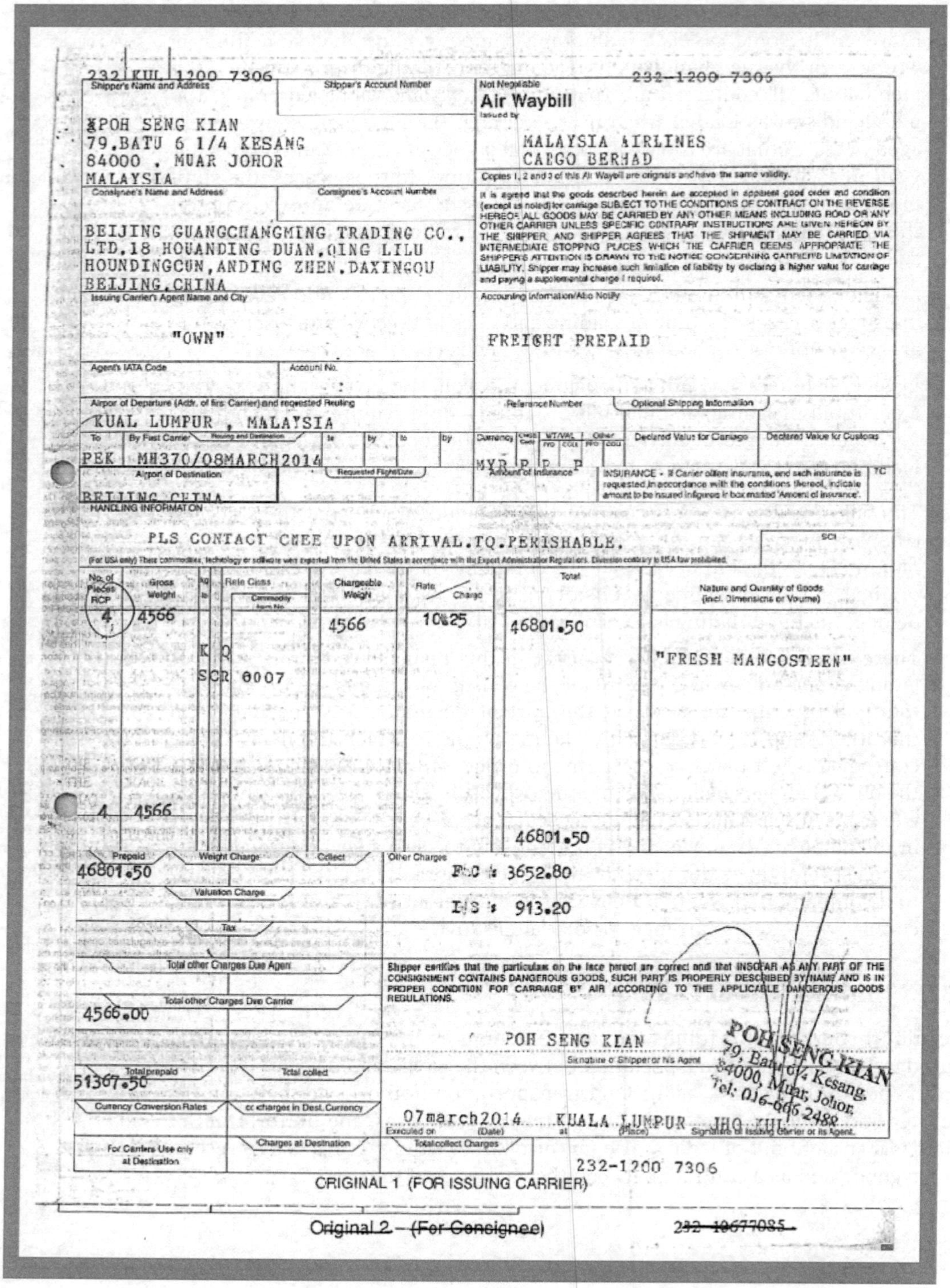
232 KUL 1200 7306 232-1200 7306

Shipper's Name and Address | Shipper's Account Number | Not Negotiable

Air Waybill

Issued by MALAYSIA AIRLINES CARGO BERHAD

POH SENG KIAN
79,BATU 6 1/4 KESANG
84000 . MUAR JOHOR
MALAYSIA

Copies 1, 2 and 3 of this Air Waybill are originals and have the same validity.

Consignee's Name and Address | Consignee's Account Number

BEIJING GUANGCHANGMING TRADING CO., LTD,18 HOUANDING DUAN,QING LILU HOUNDINGCUN,ANDING ZHEN,DAXINGOU BEIJING,CHINA

It is agreed that the goods described herein are accepted in apparent good order and condition (except as noted) for carriage SUBJECT TO THE CONDITIONS OF CONTRACT ON THE REVERSE HEREOF. ALL GOODS MAY BE CARRIED BY ANY OTHER MEANS INCLUDING ROAD OR ANY OTHER CARRIER UNLESS SPECIFIC CONTRARY INSTRUCTIONS ARE GIVEN HEREON BY THE SHIPPER, AND SHIPPER AGREES THAT THE SHIPMENT MAY BE CARRIED VIA INTERMEDIATE STOPPING PLACES WHICH THE CARRIER DEEMS APPROPRIATE. THE SHIPPER'S ATTENTION IS DRAWN TO THE NOTICE CONCERNING CARRIER'S LIMITATION OF LIABILITY. Shipper may increase such limitation of liability by declaring a higher value for carriage and paying a supplemental charge if required.

Issuing Carrier's Agent Name and City: "OWN"

Accounting Information/Also Notify: FREIGHT PREPAID

Agent's IATA Code | Account No.

Airport of Departure (Addr. of first Carrier) and requested Routing: KUAL LUMPUR , MALAYSIA

Reference Number | Optional Shipping Information

To: PEK | By First Carrier: MH370/08MARCH2014 | Currency: MYR | WT/VAL: P | Other: P | Declared Value for Carriage | Declared Value for Customs

Airport of Destination: BEIJING CHINA | Requested Flight/Date | Amount of Insurance

INSURANCE - If Carrier offers insurance, and such insurance is requested in accordance with the conditions thereof, indicate amount to be insured in figures in box marked 'Amount of insurance'.

Handling Information: PLS CONTACT CNEE UPON ARRIVAL.TQ.PERISHABLE.

(For USA only) These commodities, technology or software were exported from the United States in accordance with the Export Administration Regulations. Diversion contrary to USA law prohibited.

No. of Pieces RCP	Gross Weight	kg lb	Rate Class / Commodity Item No.	Chargeable Weight	Rate / Charge	Total	Nature and Quantity of Goods (incl. Dimensions or Volume)
4	4566	K	Q SCR 0007	4566	10.25	46801.50	"FRESH MANGOSTEEN"
4	4566					46801.50	

Prepaid / Weight Charge / Collect: 46801.50

Other Charges: FSC : 3652.80 / ISS : 913.20

Valuation Charge

Tax

Total other Charges Due Agent

Total other Charges Due Carrier: 4566.00

Shipper certifies that the particulars on the face hereof are correct and that INSOFAR AS ANY PART OF THE CONSIGNMENT CONTAINS DANGEROUS GOODS, SUCH PART IS PROPERLY DESCRIBED BY NAME AND IS IN PROPER CONDITION FOR CARRIAGE BY AIR ACCORDING TO THE APPLICABLE DANGEROUS GOODS REGULATIONS.

POH SENG KIAN
Signature of Shipper or his Agent

POH SENG KIAN 79, Batu 6 1/4 Kesang, 84000, Muar, Johor. Tel: 016-666 2488

Total prepaid: 51367.50 | Total collect

Currency Conversion Rates | cc charges in Dest. Currency

07march2014 KUALA LUMPUR JHO KUL
Executed on (Date) at (Place) Signature of Issuing Carrier or its Agent

For Carriers Use only at Destination | Charges at Destination | Total collect Charges

232-1200 7306

ORIGINAL 1 (FOR ISSUING CARRIER)

~~Original 2 – (For Consignee)~~ ~~232-10677085~~

Figure 9.12: An Air Waybill for a Shipment of Mangosteens from Malaysia to China

Photo ©Malaysia Airlines. Used with permission.

9.5.3 Intermodal Bill of Lading

The intermodal bill of lading reflects the substantial increase in the number of international shipments in which the exporter delivers the goods to a carrier that arranges for the transportation and delivery of the shipment until its final destination; it is also called a multimodal bill of lading in Europe or a combined-transport bill of lading in Asia, depending on the location of the carriers. Because the shipment is likely to take more than one mode of transportation, it is called an intermodal or multimodal shipment.

Intermodal bills of lading cover several legs of an international shipment. They are straight bills of lading in most cases. Intermodal bills of lading are also receipts for the goods and evidence of a contract of carriage between the shipper and the carrier.

intermodal bill of lading
A bill of lading used for transportation that uses more than one mode of transportation, domestically or internationally.

9.5.4 Air Waybill

An air waybill fulfills the same function as an ocean bill of lading, but applies only to airfreight. An air waybill is always a straight air waybill and is therefore non-negotiable (see Figure 9.12 on the facing page). This can be easily understood because, in most cases, the documents and the merchandise arrive approximately at the same time in the country of destination, and there is literally no time to sell the cargo while it is in transit. As with other bills of lading, it is also a receipt for the goods and a contract between the shipper and the air carrier.

air waybill
A bill of lading used for transportation by air, domestically or internationally.

9.5.5 Charter Parties

Whenever an exporter is shipping bulk commodities (oil, ores, grains, polymers, sand, cement, sugar, and so on), it does so in such large quantities that an entire ship is often necessary to accommodate the goods. In those cases, the contract between the carrier and the shipper is called a charter party rather than an ocean bill of lading.

Charter parties are complex, as they can be negotiated for a single shipment (a voyage charter party), or for a period of time (a time charter party); charter parties that cover more than one voyage but do not demand the exclusive use of the ship for a specific period (for example, one shipment every other month) are called contracts of affreightment. Moreover, some shippers negotiate charter parties that only include the use of the ship, exclusive of the boat's crew, as the shipper provides the captain and the crew (a bareboat charter party). Finally, because there are differing requirements for various commodities, most charter parties are industry specific (oil, grain, gas, and so forth).

The owner of a freight aircraft can lease its equipment under four types of leases, whether for a single voyage or for a duration of time: (1) A wet-lease agreement under which the owner of the aircraft provides the airplane, a flight crew, maintenance services, insurance, and fuel. (2) An ACMI lease that includes aircraft, crew, maintenance and insurance, but not fuel. (3) A dry lease, under which the owner provides only the aircraft. (4) A damp lease under which the

charter party
A type of contract of carriage, in which the shipper uses all or most of the carrying capacity of the ship to transport commodities.

wet lease
A type of leasing contract in which an airplane is leased, along with a crew, maintenance services, insurance, and fuel.

ACMI lease
A type of leasing contract in which an airplane is leased, along with a crew, maintenance services, and insurance.

dry lease
A type of leasing contract in which only the airplane is leased.

damp lease
A type of leasing contract in which an airplane is leased, with maintenance and insurance, but no crew.

owner provides fewer services than in a wet lease, but more than in a dry lease. For example, a damp lease could include the aircraft, maintenance, and insurance, but not the crew, which would need to be hired by the lessee. In all cases, the lessee must cover the additional costs of operating the aircraft, from simply paying landing fees in a wet lease, to obtaining a crew, securing insurance and providing maintenance in a dry lease.

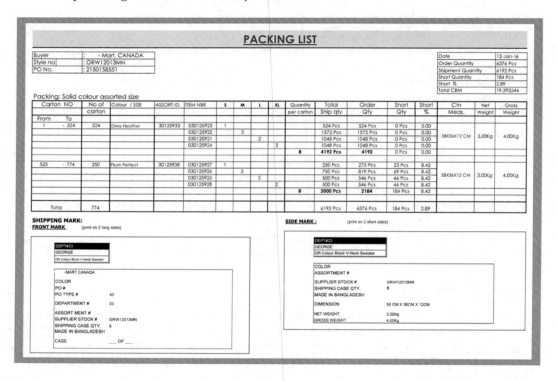

Figure 9.13: A Packing List for a Shipment of Clothing from Bangladesh to Canada
Photo ©Pierre David. Used with permission.

9.5.6 Packing List

packing list
A detailed list of the contents of a shipment.

A packing list always accompanies an international shipment. The packing list is a detailed document provided by the exporter that details how many containers are in the shipment and which merchandise is packaged in each container or packaging unit (see Figure 9.13 for an example). Because of the recent emphasis placed on security by the International Maritime Organization and world governments, packing lists have become more precise; while at one time it was acceptable to mention "freight all kinds," often abbreviated FAK, it is now necessary to list all items in a shipment, in as detailed a manner as possible. Whenever authorities determine that a shipment presents risks and should be inspected, a detailed packing list can prevent a lengthy inspection and avoid further delays.

9.5.7 Shipper's Letter of Instruction

A Shipper's Letter of Instruction is delivered to the shipping company when the shipper—again, either the exporter or the importer, depending on the terms of trade, or Incoterms® rule chosen for the transaction—wants specific steps taken during the transport of the merchandise. For example, the shipper may request that the cargo be stowed below deck (if the cargo is susceptible to become wet) or stowed at the "water line" (*i.e.*, the location in the ship that experiences the least movement), or even above deck (if the cargo is dangerous). When the cargo is livestock, the Shipper's Letter of Instruction explains what to do in most situations.

shipper's letter of instruction
A document in which the shipper spells out how it wants the carrier to handle the goods while they are in transit.

Shipping Live Animals

The business of shipping live animals is quite substantial: each year, many racehorses fly from one track to another,[43] and many exotic animals fly from one zoo to another. In 2011, the Chicago Shedd Aquarium shipped seven whales and two dolphins from Chicago to Connecticut and back during the renovation of its oceanarium.[44]

When shipping live animals internationally, the Shipper's Letter of Instruction is critical, as every shipment is different because every animal has its own requirements regarding temperature, humidity, and its tolerance for shipment delays.

As he related it in a lengthy article,[45] Barry Lopez spent days accompanying airfreight cargo pilots on 40 flights, totaling 110,000 nautical miles, to report on this part of international lore. In some legs of his journey, the cargo included Vietnamese potbelly pigs, a killer whale, racehorses, and ostriches. In these situations, the shipper can ask for specific considerations. Lopez reports that on his flight from Chicago to Tokyo, during which he traveled with sixteen horses, "[t]he pilot made a shallow climb out of Chicago to lessen the strain on the horses' back legs." (It has since become common practice to ship horses facing the rear of the plane to lessen the strain on their necks and front legs.) When the plane hit some turbulence, the pilot changed altitude and a handler went in the cargo hold to soothe the animals.

Actually, the business of shipping live animals by air is so difficult to manage that the International Air Transport Association created a set of Live Animal Regulations.[46] Live animals are also shipped by ocean. Australia, New Zealand, and Argentina ship a large number of sheep to the Middle East, and live cattle travels from Australia to Southeast Asia. These shipments of animals require much care while they travel thousands

Figure 9.14: Horses Shipped by Air Require a Detailed Letter of Instruction
Photo ©Bill Strauss. Used with permission.

of miles to their destination. The World Organisation for Animal Health (OIE) has developed guidelines for the transport of animals by sea,[47] but here again, the shipper communicates its requirements for the handling of the live cargo with precise instructions in its Letter of Instruction.

9.5.8   Shipments of Dangerous Goods

International shipments of dangerous goods are regulated by either the International Maritime Organization's International Maritime Dangerous Goods Code,[48] by the International Air Transport Association's Dangerous Goods Regulations,[49] by the International Civil Aviation Organization's Technical Instructions for the Safe Transport of Dangerous Goods by Air,[50] or by local shipment codes, such as the United States Code of Federal Regulations, Title 49 (abbreviated 49CFR).[51]

There are such an extensive number of regulations that can affect a shipment of hazardous goods that it is always best to entrust a specialized shipper to handle the paperwork associated with such a shipment. This statement is also true for packing and labeling the hazardous goods as there are often specific forms to be filled out; in the case of an air shipment, a Shipper's Declaration for Dangerous Goods must be provided, and a specific mention must be made on the air waybill that the shipment contains dangerous goods. In some cases, the air waybill must also specify that the cargo cannot be shipped on a passenger airplane, but only on a cargo airplane. Similar restrictions must also be observed for ocean, road, and railroad cargoes.

9.5.9 Manifest

The manifest is a shipping document that is quite unlike the documents seen so far in this chapter. The manifest is created by the carrier, or shipping company—the operator of the ship or the aircraft—that lists the exact makeup of the cargo, its ownership, its port of origin and its port of destination, whether there are specific handling instructions, and so forth. Although officially an internal document of the shipping company, the manifest is often used by public authorities to verify that rules and regulations are respected. The following example may clarify this point.

manifest
A document, internal to the shipping company (carrier), that lists all cargoes onboard the transportation vehicle.

Several Middle Eastern countries—Jordan, Saudi Arabia, the United Arab Emirates, Syria, Kuwait, Iraq, Iran, and Libya—engaged in what was referred to as the Arab embargo of Israel; no ship that delivered goods to these Arab nations could have stopped (or be planning to stop) in any Israeli port or have cargo coming from or going to Israel. The manifest is used by authorities in those countries to determine whether the ship or its cargo has had any "unlawful" contact with Israel.[52] American firms dealing in that region were prohibited from honoring this embargo, a situation that made for complicated arrangements, which both Israel and its neighbors conveniently chose to ignore—business is business, after all. In its heyday, the boycott was somewhat bothersome, but was widely derided as ineffective; in 2017, the boycott has essentially disappeared, with Jordan having signed a peace treaty with Israel, and the Gulf Cooperation Council countries no longer honoring the embargo and having called for an end to it. Syria, Lebanon, and Iran are the only countries that are still enforcing it, but with decreased vigor.

9.6 Electronic Data Interchange

9.6.1 Proprietary Commercial Electronic Data Interchange

An alternative way to send documents overseas is through Electronic Data Interchange (EDI) rather than by airmail. The best way to define EDI is to determine what it is not: first, EDI is not a fax, which transmits only a reproduction of a paper document. A fax is essentially a copy machine where the original is in one location and the copy is in another location. Second, EDI is not e-mail (electronic mail). E-mail is only the electronic transmission of text, as in a letter or a memo, for which there is no need to have a specified format ahead of time.

electronic data interchange (EDI)
A method to send documents from one company to another, using electronic means.

EDI is an electronic exchange of documents, from computer to computer, following a format to which both the sending and the receiving parties have agreed.

There are two areas in which the agreement to a common format is crucial:

- First, the sender and the recipient must agree to a technical EDI understanding; for example, the choice of a computer protocol, the determination of a standard outline—which electronic field corresponds to which information on the document (sender, consignee, product description, purchase order number, invoice number, and so forth)—and the possible use of a third-party intermediary to translate one electronic format into another or archive the transmissions between the parties. Such translating service providers are called Value-Added Networks (VANs). They also archive whatever transmission takes place between the two parties.

  Currently, there are only a few international agreements on EDI formats; they tend to be company, industry, or country specific. The most likely to prevail internationally is the standard developed by the United Nations Working Party on the Facilitation of International Trade Procedures of the Committee on Trade of the Economic Commission for Europe (nicknamed WP4, for short), called the United Nations Electronic Data Interchange for Administration, Commerce, and Transport (UN-EDIFACT), which has been accepted by a significant number of countries, including the United States. Some U.S. firms have adopted EDIFACT for all of their EDI communications with suppliers; however, the prevailing EDI standard in the United States for domestic transactions is the ANSI X12 format.

- The second issue is the existence of a legal agreement between the parties; not only should the definition of responsibilities (acknowledgment of an EDI transmission, procedure to follow when there is a defective transmission, confidentiality of the data) be specified, but legal issues must be addressed, such as the timing of the contract formation, liability for communication errors, and the evidentiary value of messages—whether and how they can be introduced in a court proceeding.

To date, there have been several efforts to create a universal EDI agreement; the International Chamber of Commerce has Uniform Rules of Conduct for Interchange of Trade Data by Teletransmission (UNCID), and several EDI associations have created their own versions. Nevertheless, there is no agreement that has international acceptance, and courts still tend to rely on laws designed for written documents whenever there are problems.

9.6.2   Network Electronic Data Interchange

Another well-developed EDI system is the one that was developed by the Society for Worldwide Interbank Financial Telecommunication (SWIFT) to facilitate the exchange of banking documents such as letters of credit. Since banks are essentially all members of the SWIFT system, they can exchange secure messages with each other. Because of significant safeguards in the network, banks can rely on the data transmitted over the network, and a letter of credit transmitted by SWIFT is considered genuine (as good as a paper original). In addition, the SWIFT network adds new services regularly, such as Interbank File Transfers (in free form such as database files, graphs, spreadsheets) over a secure network, a requirement that is of paramount importance to the banks. The security and reliability of the SWIFT network is ascertained by the protocols that the computers in the network must follow. Each login is recorded and must be cleared, messages must first be stored before they are sent, there must be positive confirmation of each message by the recipient, there are redundant links, there is a double backup of each file, and so forth.

Because of the reliability of its system—and its experience in that area—SWIFT created the Bolero network. Bolero is similar to the SWIFT banking network, but it allows the transmission of all sorts of documents (specifically logistics documents) such as invoices, bills of lading, certificates, and so on; however, Bolero does not support payment through the network.

Bolero is shared by several hundreds of customers worldwide, which makes it very different from proprietary EDI systems because communications between member parties are authenticated and there is a common standard. Therefore, the issues of proprietary EDI are overcome. It is a much more efficient way of exchanging information.

Bolero is currently competing with TradeCard on many points; Bolero has the distinct advantage that it is supported by a company with which bankers have dealt for a long time and trust. TradeCard has the advantage of offering payment options through its network; time will tell whether both of these systems will remain or whether one will start dominating the business.

While it may appear that paper documents are in jeopardy with the advent of EDI, this is not the case. Many countries' judiciaries have a strong preference for paper, and the vast majority of international shipments are still conducted using paper documents.

9.7 Document Preparation as a Marketing Tool

It should be relatively clear by now that accurate and timely documents are an essential part of international logistics and of the smooth transfer of goods from an exporter to an importer:

- The *pro forma* invoice must be a perfect preview of the actual invoice. Otherwise, payment through the letter of credit can be affected (*i.e.*, the actual invoice does not match the requirements of the letter of credit and both parties must pay for amendments) or customs clearance can be delayed because the actual invoice does not match the import license.

- The commercial invoice must be clear, detailed, and precise. It must include all the information that is necessary for the importer to clear customs and minimize the duty that it must pay (*i.e.*, description, Harmonized System number, weight, size, number of packages, domestic transportation costs, insurance costs, terminal charges, stevedoring charges, international transportation costs, and so on). It also minimizes the probability of an inspection.

- Certificates of many kinds must be provided. These certificates have to be properly prepared, signed, and occasionally stamped and notarized to facilitate the goods' customs clearance in the importing country.

- The correct number of originals and copies of a multitude of documents must be prepared (invoices, certificates, and so on) or collected (bill of lading). A discrepancy in the number of originals can delay customs clearance until another original is express mailed to the importer.

- The packing list must be prepared carefully and precisely. An incomplete or imprecise packing list increases the probability of a customs inspection.

- The export paperwork must be prepared and filed correctly and in a timely manner. Several countries, including the United States, will not allow goods to be loaded if there are issues with the export paperwork (SED).

Any failure to provide these documents, or to provide complete and accurate documents in a timely manner, is likely to delay a shipment, generate additional costs by requiring last-minute mailings of critical documents, or create "headaches" for one or more of the parties involved in the transaction. Unfortunately, problems with documents are common, although they are avoidable in most instances.

Because the responsibility of proper document preparation falls mostly on the exporter, regardless of the Incoterms® rule used in a transaction, an exporter can turn its ability to do a good and thorough job preparing international shipment documents into a marketing advantage. An exporter intent on increasing its sales should therefore be thorough and meticulous in the way it prepares the documents needed the importer. This careful preparation should be reflected in the first contact, the *pro forma* invoice, and be communicated to the importer by emphasizing the experience of the company at providing accurate and thorough documents for international shipments.

Review and Discussion Questions

1. There are three types of invoices mentioned in this chapter. Explain each one and identify which is truly an invoice and which is not.

2. What documents are necessary for exporting from the United States?

3. There are many different types of certificates that can be requested by the importing country or the importer. Describe three of these certificates.

4. A pre-shipment inspection certificate can be requested by the importing country or by the importer. Why would a country request one? Why would an importer request one?

5. The ocean bill of lading has three general functions. Explain each function in detail and identify the alternative "types" of ocean bills of lading.

6. What are the advantages of conducting international trade using electronic document transmissions, such as EDI, Bolero, and TradeCard?

Notes

[1] Mehta, Ravi R. Singh, "Freak and Faulty L/C's from Third World and Eastern Europe," *The Exporter*, September 1997, pp. 15-17.

[2] Scannicchio, Tommaso, "Important Decision of the Italian Supreme Court of Cassazione in the Matter of Electronic Documents," *Electronic Law Journals*, JILT 2002, http://www2.warwick.ac.uk/fac/-soc/law/elj/jilt/2002_2/scannicchio/#a3, retrieved May 27, 2009.

[3] *A Basic Guide to Exporting*, Export.gov, http://export.gov/basicguide/eg_main_017244.asp, retrieved June 17, 2013.

[4] *Ibid.*

[5] Customs and Border Protection, "When to apply for an Electronic Export Information (EEI)," https://help.cbp.gov/app/answers/detail/a_id/292//when-to-apply-for-an-electronic-export-information-(eei), retrieved March 5, 2017.

[6] "Interactive Tariff and Trade DataWeb," United States International Trade Commission, http://dataweb.usitc.gov/, retrieved March 5, 2017.

[7] European Commission, Taxation and Customs Union, "Export Procedures," http://ec.europa.eu/-taxation_customs/business/customs-procedures/what-is-exportation/export-procedure_en, retrieved March 6, 2017.

[8] Schwirtz, Michael, "Tourist in Russia Stumbles into Legal Predicament," *The New York Times*, August 27, 2007.

[9] Meier, Barry, "The Costly, Bitter Case of the Coins of Elmali," *The New York Times*, September 24, 1998.

[10] Eakin, Hugh, and Elizabetta Povoledo, "Ceding Art to Italy, Met Avoids Showdown," *The New York Times*, February 21, 2006.

[11] Eakin, Hugh, "Getty Museum Will Return 2 Antiquities to Greece," *The New York Times*, July 10, 2006.

[12] "Elmalı Treasure Finally on Display at Home," *Hurriyet Daily News*, October 2, 2009, http://www.-hurriyetdailynews.com/default.aspx?pageid=438&n=elmali-sikkeleri-ait-oldugu-topraklarda-2009-10-27, retrieved June 17, 2013.

[13] Bradsher, Keith, "Specialists in Rare Earths Say a Trade Case Against China May Be Too Late," *The New York Times*, March 13, 2012.

[14] Organisation for Economic Co-Operation and Development, "Export Restrictions on Industrial Raw Materials," http://qdd.oecd.org/subject.aspx?Subject=ExportRestrictions_IndustrialRawMaterials, retrieved March 6, 2017.

[15] Blas, Javier, "Cocoa Soars as Traders back Ivory Coast Ban," *Financial Times*, January 25, 2011, p. 23.

[16] Kramer, Andrew, "Restrictions on Exports Ignite Protests in Belarus," *The New York Times*, June 13, 2011.

[17] Kirkpatrick, David, "China Seizure Halts Delivery of U.S. Book," *The New York Times*, August 28, 2000.

[18] Clayton, Gary E., "Eurocrats Try to Stop Data at Border," *The Wall Street Journal*, November 2, 1998, p. A34.

[19] Kim, Jeonghoi, "Recent Trends in Export Restrictions," *OECD Trade Policy Papers*, No. 101, OECD Publishing, 2010. http://dx.doi.org/10.1787/5kmbjx63sl27-en.

[20] Litman, Gary V., and John M. Breen "Overview of Federal Export Restriction Programs," in *Export Practice: Customs and International Trade Law*, Terence P. Stewart, ed. New York: Practicing Law Institute.

[21] U.S. Export Administration Regulations Database, Bureau of Export Administration, https://www.bis.doc.gov/index.php/regulations/export-administration-regulations-ear, retrieved March 6, 2017.

[22] Klein, Alec, "The Techies Grumbled, but Polaroid's Pocket Turned into a Huge Hit," *The Wall Street Journal*, May 2, 2000, p. A1.

[23] Gallacher, David, "Encryption Export Restrictions Loosened under New Rules that Reduce Pre-Review and Reporting Requirements," Government Contracts Blog—Sheppard-Mullin, November 17, 2008, http://www.governmentcontractslawblog.com/2008/11/articles/export-controls/encryption-export-restrictions-loosened-under-new-rules-that-reduce-prereview-and-reporting-requirements, retrieved June 18, 2013.

[24] U.S. Export Administration Regulations Database, Bureau of Export Administration, https://www.bis.doc.gov/index.php/regulations/export-administration-regulations-ear, retrieved March 6, 2017.

[25] *Introduction to Commerce Department Export Controls*, March 2007, Bureau of Industry and Security, http://www.bis.doc.gov/licensing/bis_exports2.pdf, retrieved May 28, 2009.

[26] "Sanctions Programs and Country Information," U.S. Department of the Treasury, Office of Foreign Asset Control, https://www.treasury.gov/resource-center/sanctions/Programs/Pages/Programs.aspx, retrieved March 6, 2017.

[27] IPC, Association Connecting Electronic Industries, "Deemed Exports 101: Exporting without Crossing Borders," http://www.ipc.org/ContentPage.aspx?pageid=Deemed-Exports-Exporting-Without-Crossing-Borders, retrieved March 6, 2017.

[28] *Don't Let This Happen to You! Actual Investigations of Export Controls and Anti-Boycott Regulations*, September 2016 Edition, Bureau of Industry and Security, United States Department of Commerce, https://www.bis.doc.gov/index.php/forms-documents/enforcement/1005-don-t-let-this-happen-to-you-1/file, retrieved March 6, 2017.

[29] Kim, Jeonghoi, "Recent Trends in Export Restrictions," *OECD Trade Policy Papers*, No. 101, OECD Publishing, 2010. http://dx.doi.org/10.1787/5kmbjx63sl27-en.

[30] Wilson, William, D. Demcey Johnson, and Bruce L. Dahl, "Transparency and Export Subsidies in International Wheat Competition," *Agricultural Economic Reports*, No. 415, May 1999, http://ageconsearch.umn.edu/bitstream/23208/1/aer415.pdf.

[31] Barrionuevo, Alexei, "Argentina Blocks Farm Export Tax," *The New York Times*, July 18, 2008.

[32] Nguyen, Tri Khiem, "Vietnam Rice Trade, Policy and Future Outlook," Agri Benchmark Project, www.agribenchmark.org/fileadmin/...rice/rice_trade_VN_130319.pdf, retrieved June 18, 2013.

[33] "Quota Removal Secures Russia Platinum Exports," Reuters, January 17, 2007, http://uk.reuters.com/article/businessIndustry/idUKL1532931620070117, retrieved June 18, 2013.

[34] Rose, Scott, "WTO Admits Russia as 156th Member to Cap 18-Year Talks: Economy," Bloomberg News, August 22, 2012, http://www.bloomberg.com/news/2012-08-22/wto-admits-russia-as-156th-member-after-two-decades-of-talks-1-.html, retrieved June 18, 2013.

[35] "Doing Business: Trading Across Borders," International Finance Corporation, The World Bank, http://www.doingbusiness.org/data/exploretopics/trading-across-borders, retrieved June 16, 2013.

[36] Rao, N. Vasuki, "Indian Customs System Stuck in Miles of Thick, Red Tape," *The Journal of Commerce*, January 7, 1998, p. 4A.

[37] "When Is Pre-Shipment Inspection Required?", http://2016.export.gov/logistics/eg_main_018120.asp, retrieved March 6, 2017.

[38] Wilmott, Peter, "Pre-Shipment Inspection—A Force for Good?", *American Shipper*, November 2006, pp. 24-27.

[39] Mottley, Robert, "Shippers' Case Law: Consignee, NVOs Clash Over Sealed Shipments," *American Shipper*, April 2000, p. 69.

[40] Russell, Timothy, *The Humanitarian Relief Supply Chain: Analysis of the 2004 South-East Asia Earthquake and Tsunami*, Master's of Engineering in Logistics thesis, Massachusetts Institute of Tech-

nology, June 2005, http://ctl.mit.edu, August 1, 2006.

[41] Jones, Chris, "Coke Admits Defeat in Dasani Rollout," *Food and Drink Europe*, March 26, 2003, http://www.foodanddrinkeurope.com/Products-Marketing/Coke-admits-defeat-in-Dasani-rollout, retrieved May 23, 2009.

[42] "Dasani UK Delay Cans Europe Sales," *BBC News*, March 24, 2004, http://news.bbc.co.uk/1/hi/business/3566233.stm, retrieved May 23, 2009.

[43] Sowinski, Lara, "A Flying Barn," *World Trade 100*, January 2011, p. 50.

[44] "Precious cargo; Transporting Animals by Air," *Air Cargo World*, May 2011, pp. 27-28.

[45] Lopez, Barry, "On the Wings of Commerce," *Harper's*, October 1995, pp. 39-54.

[46] *2012 Live Animal Regulations Manual*, Live Animals and Perishables Board, http://www.iata.org/publications/Pages/live-animals.aspx, retrieved June 19, 2013.

[47] Section 7, *Terrestrial Animal Health Code*, Organisation for Animal Health (OIE), http://www.oie.int/fileadmin/Home/eng/Health_standards/tahc/2010/en_titre_1.7.htm, retrieved June 19, 2013.

[48] *2014 International Maritime Dangerous Goods Code*, International Maritime Organization, 4 Albert Embankment, London SE1 7SR, United Kingdom, http://www.imo.org/publications/imdgcode/Pages/Default.aspx, retrieved March 8, 2017.

[49] *Dangerous Goods Regulations*, 2017, 58th Edition, International Air Transport Association, 33 Route de l'Aéroport, Case Postale 672, CH-1215 Genève 15 Aéroport, Switzerland and 800 Place Victoria, Montréal, Québec, Canada H4Z 1M1, http://www.iata.org/publications/store/Pages/dgr-print-manuals.aspx, retrieved March 8, 2017.

[50] *2015-16 Technical Instructions For The Safe Transport of Dangerous Goods by Air* (Doc 9284), International Civil Aviation Organization, 999 University Street, Montréal, Québec H3C 5H7, Canada, http://www.icao.int/safety/DangerousGoods/Pages/technical-instructions.aspx, retrieved March 8, 2017.

[51] *Electronic Code of Federal Regulations—Chapter 49*, U.S. Government Printing Office, http://www.ecfr.gov/cgi-bin/text-idx?tpl=/ecfrbrowse/Title49/49tab_02.tpl, retrieved March 8, 2017.

[52] Lelyveld, Michael S., "Peace Dividend: Easing in Arab Boycott of Israel," *The Journal of Commerce*, February 17, 1997.

Chapter 10

International Insurance

One of the most complex issues in international logistics is international insurance. Not only is the topic difficult to understand, but international insurance also involves a plethora of vocabulary exclusively used in the marine cargo insurance field, such as jettison, barratry, and *Inchmaree*. In addition, in an international insurance contract, the term "average" denotes something other than the arithmetic mean. The difficulty is compounded by the fact that there are centuries-old traditions and concepts, some of which have essentially not changed for that long, and that can be interpreted either the British way or the American way.

Nevertheless, international insurance is of utmost importance: shipping goods abroad is fraught with perils. A company must knowingly accept these risks or transfer them onto an insurance company. This chapter will first present some of the terms used in international insurance, then explain the risks associated with shipping goods internationally by ocean and by air and introduce possible strategies for dealing with those risks, and finally conclude with more details on the elements of a marine cargo insurance policy, which is the name used for this type of policy, whether the goods travel by ocean or by air.

Eventually, another form of insurance will be presented: commercial credit insurance, which is an alternatives available to cover one of the other great risks of international trade: the possibility that the importer will default on an open-account transaction. For details on open-account transactions and other terms of payment, see Chapter 7.

10.1   Complexity of International Insurance

One of the greatest concerns in international insurance is to ensure that the coverage selected for a shipment is the coverage that the shipper, whether the exporter or the importer, prefers. All too often, a firm finds it is improperly insured only after a loss. This is mostly due to the particularities of the type of policies sold to cover cargo while it is transported internationally.

10.1.1   Particularities of International Insurance

Many differences exist between domestic insurance policies and international cargo policies. This is due to several factors:

- The number of international-insurance-coverage options is substantial. Not only is there a minimum of six different standard insurance policies, but there are also countless variations in the specific clauses that can be included or excluded. Section 10.5 explains these different policies in detail.

- Many of the risks of shipping internationally are misunderstood. Historically, international shippers were located in ports or near ports and had a good understanding of the risks of the sea. Today's international shippers are located mostly inland, and have difficulty comprehending the damage that a bad storm can inflict on cargo. Section 10.2 presents some of the many risks an international shipment faces.

- The Incoterms® rules are somewhat misleading regarding insurance coverage. Although both CIF (Cost, Insurance, and Freight) and CIP (Carriage and Insurance Paid) both mention insurance, they refer to the most basic coverage available, which is inadequate for many goods (see Section 10.5).

- The carriers offer very limited coverage. Under the various international liability conventions, carriers offer very basic coverage, with low limits, and are exempt from liability in many cases, as discussed in Section 11.5 on page 411.

The international logistics manager should therefore become familiar with all the peculiarities and the vocabulary of international insurance to make the best decisions.

10.1.2   Insurance Vocabulary

Insurance uses a precise terminology linked to risks, and it makes sense to understand this terminology before using it to develop a risk management strategy.

- **Average.** A loss incurred on an ocean voyage by a cargo owner. It can be further qualified as a general average or a particular average.

  average
  A loss incurred by a cargo owner on an ocean voyage.

  ○ **General average.** A loss incurred on an ocean voyage that is "general," in the sense that the loss involves all the cargo owners on board. A general average can occur when there is a fire onboard a ship, when a vessel is grounded, or when a ship capsizes. Insurance companies also consider it a general average when the ship's captain takes an action to save the ship, the crew, and the remainder of the cargo; for example, the captain may decide to throw some cargo overboard to save the ship or to ground the ship to prevent it from sinking. The owners of the cargo that was saved by this action are indebted to the owners of the cargo that was sacrificed and to the owners of the damaged ship. The marine insurance industry recognizes that responsibility, and the owners of the cargo that was saved must indemnify the owners of the cargo that was lost and/or the owners of the ship that was damaged. This complex concept is explained in Section 10.5.

  ○ **Particular average.** A partial loss incurred by a cargo owner on an ocean voyage; the cargo may have become wet from seawater or may have been damaged by rough seas. Unlike a general average, the costs of a particular average fall exclusively on the owner of the cargo or its insurance company.

- **Barratry.** An act of disobedience or willful misconduct by the captain or crew of a ship that causes damage to the ship or the cargo.

  barratry
  Willful misconduct on the part of the captain of a ship or the crew.

- **Peril**. An event that brings about a loss. For example, a fire, a collision, and a flood are perils.

peril
An event that causes a loss.

hazard
A situation that increases the probability of a loss.

- **Hazard**. A situation that increases the probability of a peril and therefore of a loss. For example, a hazard is a storm, which increases the probability of the peril of water damage, or a poorly-trained crew, which increases the probability of improper stowing.

- **Jettison**. The act of throwing overboard part of the cargo of a ship (or the fuel of an airplane) to lighten the ship. The purpose of such an action is to save the ship, the remainder of the cargo, and the crew.

- **Risk**. The chance or the probability of a loss. There are different ways to categorize risks:

speculative risk
A risk that can generate a loss or a gain.

  ○ **Speculative risk**. The chance or probability of a loss as well as the chance or probability of a gain (*e.g.*, the risk sustained in a foreign exchange transaction, as described in Chapter 8).

pure risk
A risk that can only generate a loss.

  ○ **Pure risk**. The chance or the probability of a loss only. Pure risks can be insured against (*i.e.*, transferred to an insurance company).

objective risk
A risk whose probability can be calculated.

  ○ **Objective risk**. The chance of a loss that can be accurately calculated, because ample empirical data are available (probability of a fire causing a total loss on a residence) or because a good mathematical model has been developed.

subjective risk
A risk whose probability cannot be relied upon.

  ○ **Subjective risk**. The perceived risk of a loss by an individual or company. Whether this perception is correct can only be settled by calculating the objective risk. Many psychological studies demonstrate that individual managers regularly underestimate the probability of a peril that has a high actual probability, and overestimate the probability of a peril that has low actual probability.[1]

10.2   Perils Faced by International Shipments

When goods are in transit internationally, they face many perils and hazards, simply because they are handled by multiple carriers involved in the pre-carriage (the portion of the trip in the exporting country), the main carriage (the international portion of the voyage), and the on-carriage (the portion in the importing country). As the number of segments in a trip increases, the number of hazards also increases, and international shipments face many more hazards than domestic shipments do. The goods are also exposed to a greater number of risks because they are transferred from one mode of transportation to another, and are therefore handled many more times than domestic shipments are.

The perils of transporting cargo internationally have implications for insurance coverage. However, they also influence the way a company packages its products for export and the way it packs them in containers. Chapter 14 specifically addresses the packing choices available to a shipper.

There are specific perils faced by shipments transported by ocean carriers and by air carriers, which will be illustrated later in this chapter, but all shipments face the risk of theft.

Theft

Cargo theft is a concern for companies shipping internationally. The risks are much greater during pre-carriage and on-carriage than during main carriage, and it has become a major concern of exporters and importers, specifically for cargo that is easy to resell, such as athletic shoes, cellular telephones, consumer electronics, and pharmaceuticals. The total value of cargo thefts is difficult to pinpoint, for two reasons: the police often tally cargo theft data together with other types of thefts, and some companies are reluctant to report cargo theft out of concern for their reputations and fear of increased insurance premiums. The U.S. Federal Bureau of Investigation now collects cargo theft data as a separate category, but only since 2014. The data for 2015 was collected from only 31 of the 50 U.S. states, and the total value of cargo theft was seriously underreported (at U.S.\$ 32 million), but there is an effort underway to determine accurately the extent of the problem.[2] The FBI estimates that cargo theft represents about U.S.\$ 15 billion per year in the United States,[3] and multiple sources estimate cargo theft to represent more than U.S.\$ 30 billion worldwide.[4] Cargo theft can be classified in three ways:

- Pilferage happens when individuals opportunistically steal cargo; such crimes are not planned and usually happen at random. They are more frequent for cargo that can be identified by its markings or packaging, because such cargo makes a more tempting target. Containerization has reduced pilferage because it makes the cargo much more difficult to identify and more difficult to steal in small quantities.

pilferage
An opportunity theft of part of a cargo shipment.

- Organized theft refers to planned operations that are directed at the entire shipment. Organized theft usually targets high-value cargo and often includes a group of individuals, some of whom may be "insiders" in the supply chain and who provide information about the content of the container. A perfect example of organized theft was the theft of U.S.\$ 350,000,000 in diamonds from a parked airplane at the Brussels airport in 2013. The thieves were done in "barely five minutes,"[5] and reportedly were very "professional" in their approach.

organized theft
Theft of a cargo shipment by a group of organized criminals.

- System's theft uses the supply chain's information system to change paperwork, substitute paperwork, or delete files so that cargo can be removed without immediate detection. This type of theft requires either inside accomplices or the ability to gain access to a company's computer system. An example of a system's theft occurred in Malaysia in June 2011, when insiders at the trucking company responsible for pre-carriage stole the entire contents of a container bound for Japan. The container contained 700,000 condoms with a retail value of more than U.S.\$ 1,000,000.[6]

system's theft
Theft perpetrated by someone with access to the shipper's or carrier's computers.

Depending on a company's operating profitability, it can take from $10 to $15 in increased revenue to make up every dollar lost through theft. Corporations should be guided by a strong preventive-security and loss-prevention program. An effective security and loss prevention program is therefore money well spent for most companies whose cargo can be tempting to thieves. Chapter 16 addresses how companies can minimize their security risks, from better packaging and markings to careful screening of employees.

10.2.1   Perils Faced in Ocean Transportation

An ocean shipment is subject to several risks, most of which are only vaguely familiar to a land-based exporter accustomed to shipping by truck or rail to its domestic customers.

However, these risks are frequent, with losses in the billions of U.S. dollars every year. The trade association International Union of Marine Insurance[7] reported 53 ships lost at sea in 2015—not counting passenger vessels and fishing boats—a substantial decrease over the 90 casualties of 2007 and the 122 cargo vessels lost in 2000.[8] There is still roughly one cargo ship lost every week somewhere in the world.

Cargo Movements

cargo movement
The fact that cargo transported internationally will be subjected to several changes of mode of transportation, and to vibrations, jolts, drops, and side-to-side movements during an ocean voyage.

An international shipment sent by ocean carriage is subjected to numerous cargo movements, many more than during a door-to-door domestic shipment. Containerized cargo is placed in the container at the exporter's facility and loaded onto a truck. Generally, stuffing the container with the goods is done carefully, as the exporter's employees are aware of the contents and their value. However, once the goods have left the exporter's shipping dock, they are in the care of carriers who have little knowledge of the shipment's contents. The goods are unloaded in a port, placed in a holding area, tilted when handled by a forklift, possibly pushed and dragged, then subjected to rapid accelerations and decelerations when loaded onto the ship, handled again several times in the same manner in the port of arrival, then loaded onto a truck for final delivery. A typical container is handled four to six times in each of the ports of departure and destination. In some cases, the goods transit through another port before being sent to their final destination. In some cases, such handling damages the container and the cargo.

However, the cargo is subjected to the greatest number of shocks and movements on the ship. A ship can move in six directions, often in an irregular fashion, and repetitively, even during a voyage with good weather. If the weather is stormy, the cargo is shaken in often inconceivable ways: "Boxes [containers] stowed on the outside, on either side of the bow, endure sixty-foot elevator drops. Plus, they are tossed in an arc, up and over, as the ship tilts to starboard. Up and down, over and back, side to side," relates Tom Baldwin, a respected journalist, when he traveled aboard a containership in a near gale.[9]

Ship motions can reach 30 degrees from side to side (roll) and 10 degrees front to back (pitch). These regular movements are accompanied by drops that can reach 10 meters (30 feet), as well as brief movements forward or sideways that end in a violent shock when the ship hits another wave. When a sea voyage lasts two to three weeks, and the motions are repeated every 30 seconds or so, the cargo is subjected to more than 100,000 movements, and it must well packaged to endure this long roller-coaster ride. Figure 10.1 shows what can happen to cargo that is not well secured in its container.

Figure 10.1: A Container Damaged by a Poorly Secured Load.
Photo ©Will Van Dorp. Used with permission.

Water Damage

Bad weather also affects the cargo in another way. As the ship tosses and shakes in a stormy sea, waves wash overboard and can infiltrate the cargo containers or the breakbulk cargo on board (see Figure 10.2 on the following page).

Pacific Ocean storms produce 20-meter (70-foot) swells several times a year, which submerge the decks of many containerships. Avoiding these storms is not always possible, due to the sudden onset of severe weather, or simply because of tight shipping schedules. So-called "rogue" waves, which can reach 35 meters (110 feet) have now been scientifically measured and documented.[10] The result is that there is a strong possibility of water damage to cargo on those ships unless it is very well packed and protected. In some instances, the pounding of the waves

deck
A permanent cover over the ship's hull.

Figure 10.2: A Lumber-carrying Cargo Ship in Rough Seas
Photo ©Kevin Martin. Used with permission.

deforms the container walls and crushes the cargo inside (see Figure 10.3 on the next page).

While it is traditional for a shipper of higher-value merchandise to request that the cargo be stored "under deck" (*i.e.*, inside the ship) rather than "on deck" (outside, exposed to the elements), the way a container or cargo is actually stowed is mostly out of the shipper's control. In addition, on modern hatchless containerships equipped with stack bars, the concept of deck has disappeared, making the distinction moot and increasing the possibility that cargo will be exposed to large quantities of sea- and rainwater.

Another possibility is that a storm will cause cargo to shift on board and to damage the ship to the point where water seeps in the hull: "At some point in the storm, a bulldozer fell off its carriage [a flat container, called a flat-rack], and punched a hole in a fuel tank ... [and] split a seam in the hull. Some 15 feet [4.5 meters] of water and fuel oil subsequently flooded a container-laden hold."[11]

Yet another peril is water damage from the rain, as well as water damage due to a container sitting in a low area in a port that floods during a rainstorm. During Hurricane Katrina in August 2005, several ports reported substantial flooding: all the ports in the states of Mississippi and Louisiana were extensively flooded, particularly in the container staging areas. When southern Brazil experienced unusually heavy rains in December 2008, several ports were flooded and their facilities damaged. Cargo stored on the docks was also under water.

Finally, cargo can be damaged by "container sweat." Most containers are tightly closed, with little to no air circulation. If some of the cargo inside the

container sweat
The humidity that condenses on the inside walls of a container and on its cargo.

Figure 10.3: Containers Damaged by Wave Action during a Storm
Photo ©Danny Cornelissen. Used with permission.

container has a high moisture content (agricultural or forestry products, for example), or if the cargo was loaded in a hot and humid area, then the humidity can condense on the inside walls of the container and damage the remainder of the cargo. A similar problem can happen for breakbulk merchandise placed in a tight cargo hold, as the ship "sweats" as well. These humidity problems can be solved by proper packaging and the use of desiccants. Figure 10.4 on the following page shows the variations in temperature and humidity for a container shipped from Houjie, near Guangzhou (Canton) in the province of Guangdong in the south of China, to Glenwillow, a suburb of Cleveland, Ohio, in the Midwestern United States. For a shipment that traveled in March, the temperatures ranged from a high of 122 degrees Fahrenheit (50 degrees Celsius) to a low of 30 degrees Fahrenheit (−1 degree Celsius), and humidity levels ranged from a high of 91 percent to a low of 13 percent.

Overboard Losses

Another common problem is cargo that is lost overboard in a storm. It is not uncommon for ships to lose containers overboard—actually, worldwide, it is almost

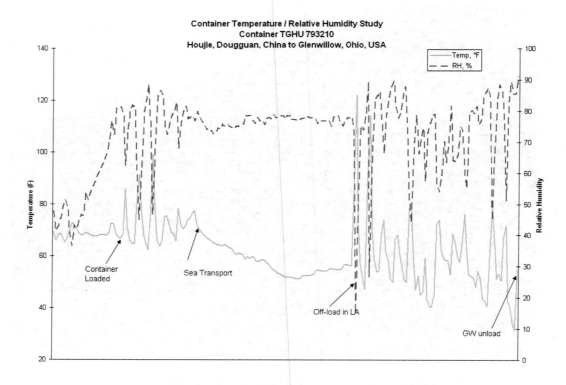

Figure 10.4: Temperature and Humidity Variations in a Container
Diagram courtesy of Royal Appliance Manufacturing Co. Used with permission.

deck stow collapse
A stack of containers placed on deck that collapses in heavy seas.

a daily occurrence. The containers placed on top of the ship's deck are lashed down with bars holding them to the deck and to each other (see Figure 11.9 on page 393). However, the cargo inside a container can shift, causing the container's balance to change. The container can also be improperly tied down, or the cleats holding the container can be damaged, and therefore the lash bars break or become loose, allowing some containers to fall overboard. The remainder of the container stack usually collapses as well, a situation that is called a deck stow collapse and leads to crushed and damaged cargo (see Figure 10.5).

Sometimes, the containers that fall overboard float for weeks, and become hazards to other ships; such "flotsam" (cargo that accidentally falls overboard) and "jetsam" (cargo that was deliberately jettisoned) can still be the carrier's responsibility if they cause damage. If the containers present a risk of environmental damage because they contain hazardous cargo, the carrier is often obligated to retrieve them, especially in U.S. or European waters. Most lost containers eventually sink or wash up on shore, or are retrieved by the Coast Guard (see Figure 10.6).

Figure 10.5: Multiple Container-Stow Collapses on a Containership
Photo ©Marine Nationale Française. Used with permission.

Container Losses

Although container spills are a major loss for any company, two container spills in the trade lanes of the North Pacific have had a silver lining. The spills generated positive results for science by allowing geo-scientists to develop better models of currents in the North Pacific.

Geo-scientists traditionally trace currents by releasing drift bottles at certain points in the ocean and noting where these bottles land on beaches.

Generally, these releases are small: for example, Project North Pacific released 34,000 bottles between 1956 and 1959 in increments of 500 to 1,000 bottles.

A container spill in May 1990 included 80,000 Nike shoes, many of which were eventually recovered by beachcombers on the Northwest coast of the United States and West coast of Canada. Scientists asked beachcombers—who were holding swap meets to find matching pairs—to report where they had found these shoes. From these data, and using models of the North Pacific, scientists improved their knowledge of ocean currents in that region of the world.

However, the most notorious of all spills used for scientific purposes was the loss of 12 containers, one of which was owned by a company shipping plastic bathtub animals, or "rubber duckies." Some 29,000 toys spilled into the ocean in January 1992, and some ten months later, they landed on the beaches of Alaska. Scientists developed a model to simulate the currents that brought these toys back to shore.[12,13] There also were quite a few grins about the methodology, including an article in the *Journal of Irreproducible Results*, but it has now become accepted and is part of what is now called "flotsam science." Newer research efforts in glacier movements are now using rubber duckies, because scientists have learned that the ducks' resilience allows them to be dumped in glacier crevasses. Scientists wait until they resurface a few miles farther down.[14]

Figure 10.6: Recovering a Container Lost at Sea
Photo ©Marine Nationale Française. Used with permission.

Jettison

Not all containers are lost overboard by accident. The captain of a ship—who thinks that this action will save the ship and the remainder of the cargo—is allowed to toss containers or cargo overboard to lighten the ship, to remove a container that may have become dangerous because it became loose, or to throw overboard some cargo to free a stranded ship. Such acts are called "jettison" (or jettisoning) and they are a common occurrence. When jettison occurs, an old maritime tradition, called "general average," dictates how the owners of the jettisoned cargo are compensated (see Section 10.5). All parties on board, the cargo owners whose cargo was saved by this action, pay for this loss.

jettison
The act of throwing cargo overboard to save the ship and the remainder of the cargo.

Fire

Fire is also a significant peril of shipping by ocean cargo containers. Because all dangerous cargo can legally travel internationally only by ocean—and not by air—such cargo is often present on board. Fireworks, explosives, compressed gases, ammunition, and chemicals of all sorts are crowded on deck. If these items happen to be poorly stowed, or are damaged in a storm, they can leak and mix with one another, resulting in fires or explosions. According to John Waite, chief surveyor of the Salvage Association, the most pressing issue for container vessels is fire, because "there is no effective measure by which crews can fight a deck fire on a modern containership."[15] Moreover, he notes that almost all cargo carried above deck is flammable and that chemical products account for 10 to 25 percent of this cargo.

The containership Hyundai *Fortune* was the victim of an explosion on March 21, 2006, which triggered a fire that was not extinguished until three weeks later. The ship lost 40 percent of its cargo in this fire, or approximately 800 containers.[16] The shipping line declared a general average, which is to say that this incident's costs were borne by the owners of all the cargo on board.

In July 2012, the containership MSC *Flaminia* (built in 2001) suffered a major explosion under deck and a massive fire in stacks of containers that were stowed below deck while en route from Charleston to Antwerp, in the North Atlantic (see Figure 10.7 on the following page). The fire was apparently exacerbated by a "discrepancy" in the declaration of certain containers' contents: they had been stowed below deck rather than above deck, even though dangerous cargo must be placed above deck. The fire took five weeks to extinguish.[17] Containers were blown over the side. The crew abandoned ship and was rescued by another ship summoned by the British Coast Guard. It is estimated that 500 containers were lost. On August 20, 2012, the ship was safely towed into Wilhelmshaven, Germany, where the remaining 2,876 containers were discharged. General average was declared for the vessel and cargo losses. The vessel was eventually repaired in Mangalia, Romania.

Figure 10.7: Aftermath of a Fire Aboard the MSC *Flaminia*
Photo ©Maritime Sicherheitszentrum, Deutschland. Used with permission.

Sinking and Capsizing

sinking
In a sinking, a ship is damaged, no longer floats, and goes to the bottom of the sea.

Yet another consequence of bad weather is the possibility of sinking. While not common for modern containerships, the possibility of sinking is always present. Most of the ships lost every year are older bulk ships flying flags of third-world countries (*i.e.*, not always well maintained). However, even the most modern ships can fall prey to a rogue wave and be lost, or seriously damaged at sea, or lose their power and drift toward shore. The International Union of Marine Insurance reports the number of ships lost at sea: in 2015, most of the 53 ships lost at sea were general-cargo ships. However, three of these casualties were tankers, four were breakbulk cargo ships, and six were containerships.[18]

In January 2015, the Roll-On-Roll-Off carrier Hoegh *Osaka*, built in 2000, took on a load of buses and automobiles from the Port of Southampton, Great Britain, to Hamburg, Germany. Due to several cumulative human errors, the ship started to list after a turn—before being in open waters—and the port pilot made the decision to beach the vessel so that it would not be lost. At its worst, the ship listed 52 degrees (see Figure 10.8).[19]

Figure 10.8: The Capsizing of the Hoegh *Osaka* Due to a Series of Human Errors
Photo ©Chris Hunsicker. Used with permission.

Stranding

Another peril facing cargo ships is the possibility of stranding, which also happens fairly frequently. Mechanical breakdown, stormy weather, and sometimes
incompetent crews are responsible for a significant number of grounded ships
every year. The improvements made in navigational technologies, such as the
Global Positioning System, have improved the precision with which ships operate. However, they cannot rely on precise maps. Only about 35 percent of the
world's oceans have been accurately mapped, and many charts rely on data that
were collected—somewhat inaccurately—some 50 to 100 years ago. In addition,
currents, coastal rivers, and strong storms modify the relief of coastal areas frequently; this is why many ports employ pilots to guide ships in their approach to
port.

stranding
In a stranding, a ship runs
into high ground and can no
longer move.

For example, a combination of bad luck and a partially inaccurate map caused
the stranding of the *Queen Elizabeth 2* ocean liner in August 1992 in Martha's
Vineyard Sound, off the coast of Massachusetts. She damaged part of her hull,
passengers had to be evacuated, and Cunard Lines had to put the ship in dry dock
for repairs.[20] This incident shows that strandings can still occur in well-traveled
shipping lanes and with exceptional crews. The four-year-old cruise ship Royal

Caribbean *Monarch of the Seas*, equipped with the most modern technologies, struck a reef in Saint-Maarten in December 1998 and had to be beached to avoid sinking.[21] The *Costa Concordia* ran aground near the island of Giglio, in Italy, on January 13, 2013, because its captain deviated slightly from his assigned route. There were 32 deaths.[22]

On January 18, 2008, the MSC *Napoli*, a Panamax containership, ran into rough weather in the English Channel and the ship started to take on water. The ship was then towed toward a British port, but on the way, it started to list substantially and was eventually grounded purposefully to prevent it from sinking. Overnight, the ship lost over a hundred containers that fell overboard, all of which eventually washed onto the beach, where local residents scavenged motorcycles, car parts, and cosmetics.[23]

Figure 10.9: The Last Moments of the *Luno* in Anglet, France
Photo ©Marine Nationale Française. Used with permission.

On February 4, 2014, the small general-merchandise vessel *Luno* was empty and on its way to the Port of Bayonne, in Southern France. The port pilot had just arrived on board when the ship suffered an electrical malfunction and lost all power and communication. Because the wind was violent, the ship was quickly pushed toward the shore, and became tangled against a breakwall in the town of Anglet. While the crew was being rescued by the French Coast Guard, the ship broke in half. While the aft remained on the rocks of the breakwall, the fore landed on the beach (see Figure 10.9).[24]

Direct damage to cargo is not likely when a ship is stranded. Nevertheless, because stranded vessels can take days or weeks to be freed, the cargo on board can be damaged while it waits; this is obviously the case for refrigerated or produce cargo. In addition, when the ship is freed, cargo is often lightered onto another ship—transferred while at sea—with all the perils associated with a transfer of cargo in less than ideal conditions. If the ship's hull is damaged, there can also be significant water infiltration, and the cargo can be flooded. In other cases, part of the cargo is simply jettisoned to lighten the ship. This is more often the case with bulk cargo of low value rather than with cargo of higher value or containerized cargo.

General Average

The concept of general average is used exclusively in marine insurance. It predates the concept of insurance and was the idea that, when there is an average—a term derived from the French word *avarie*, which means "damage to a ship or its cargo"—or a major loss on a ship, all cargo owners and the ship owner share in the loss. In other words, a general average is a general loss, or a loss affecting all the parties involved in an ocean voyage. General average is based on the principle that the ship's owner as well the cargo owners share the goal of a successful voyage, and that therefore all share in the risks and costs of the venture.

general average
A loss incurred by multiple cargo owners on an ocean voyage. A general loss.

General average is applied in a peculiar fashion: when a portion of the cargo is lost in bad weather, or when there is a major fire on board (see the case of the MSC *Flaminia* presented earlier), or when a portion of the cargo is jettisoned to save the ship, all the cargo owners and the ship owner (or their insurers) pay for the lost cargo if a general average is declared by the ship owner.

It's probably best to explain how this works with an example:

- Assume a bulk cargo ship, valued at $6,000,000, loses power to its rudder and becomes stranded in shallow waters. The ship is carrying iron ore in its fore holds (front of the ship) valued at $1,000,000, and coal in its aft holds, valued at $500,000. To free the ship, the captain calls on a tug and decides that a portion of the iron ore must be jettisoned to allow the bow of the ship to get free. The ship is then towed to a port where several repairs are made to make the ship seaworthy again. After this adventure, the owner of the ship declares a general average, and an adjuster is called to settle the claims.

- First, the adjuster calculates the market value of the jettisoned cargo; in this case, the ore that was jettisoned would have been sold for $100,000. Second, the cost of the salvage operation, including the damage done to the ship while freeing it, is added up: the tug charged $75,000, and damage to the hull, engine, and propeller shaft cost $200,000. Finally, the ratio of the losses to the combined value of the cargo and the ship is calculated:

$$\frac{(100,000 + 75,000 + 200,000)}{(6,000,000 + 1,000,000 + 500,000)} = \frac{375,000}{7,500,000} = 0.05 = 5 \text{ percent}$$

The adjuster then uses this ratio to calculate the liabilities of the cargo owners and of the ship owner:

- The company shipping the iron ore cargo has a liability of $1,000,000 × 5 percent = $50,000. However, because it had a loss of $100,000 for the jettisoned cargo, it collects the difference of $100,000 − $50,000 = $50,000 from the adjuster. Realistically, if the cargo owner is insured, it collects $50,000 from its insurer, and eventually, the insurer will collect $50,000 from the adjuster.

- The company shipping the coal has a liability of $500,000 × 5 percent = $25,000, which it (or its insurance company) pays to the adjuster.

- The company owning the ship has a liability of $6,000,000 × 5 percent = $300,000. Once its direct costs are deducted, though, it ends up paying $300,000 − $275,000 = $25,000 to the adjuster. Most likely, it has a hull-insurance policy, which covers the direct costs of freeing the ship and the repairs, as well as the liability for the general average.

For at least a portion of the cargo owners on board, general average means that the owners of the goods that arrived safely have a liability toward the owners of the goods that did not arrive. Companies with sufficient insurance coverage have only their goods to worry about; companies with no insurance must place a cash deposit with the adjuster of roughly one third of the value of the goods on the ship.[25] Because of its complexity—imagine a ship such as the MSC *Flaminia* with 4,000 containers aboard, most likely owned by a similar number of different owners—the settlement of a general average loss can take years to complete. Every year, there are at least ten situations in which a shipping company declares a general average involving cargo from U.S. shippers.

Piracy

piracy
A violent overtaking of a ship and its crew.

Piracy is the last of the major risks associated with shipping by ocean. Although the mention of this term always raises a chuckle in any audience, it is a serious risk in several parts of the world. Consider that the International Chamber of Commerce (ICC) reported a total of 469 attacks in 2000, the worst year since accurate records have been kept. Figure 10.10 on the next page shows the number of attacks and armed robberies against ships from 1994 to 2016. The problem is so significant that the ICC created the Piracy Reporting Centre in Kuala Lumpur, Malaysia, in October 1992, which issues a monthly piracy report,[26] and advises shipping lines on the best practices to reduce acts of piracy. After a substantial increase in the number of attacks in the Gulf of Aden and Somalia, the center led carriers to adopt strategies that decreased the number of attacks from 439 in 2010 to 297 in 2012, to fewer than 5 in 2016.[27]

The areas of the world in which piracy is still active are the Indonesian archipelago, Nigeria, Togo, and India. Most ships that are attacked are bulk ships, and chemical, oil or product tanker ships carrying commodities that can be easily

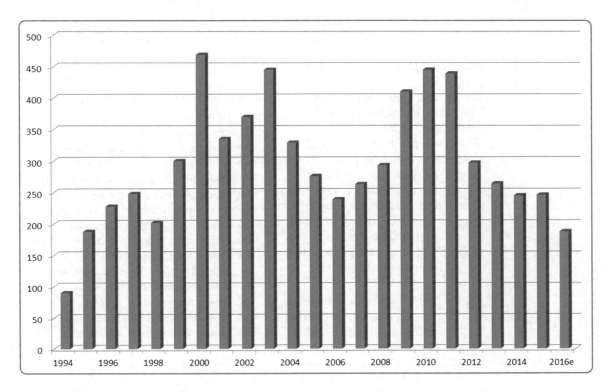

Figure 10.10: Number of Piracy and Armed Robbery Against Ships
ICC International Maritime Bureau.

sold in loosely policed countries; these two categories combined represented more than half of all ships attacked. However, general merchandise ships and containerships represented about 18 percent of piracy victims and are generally held for ransom rather than captured to sell the cargo or the ship.

Many piracy incidents involve thugs attacking a ship and stealing the crew's possessions. However, on several occasions, the ship's crew is transferred to a small boat and left adrift, while the pirates take the ship and its cargo. Still at sea, the ship is renamed, all evidence of its former identity is destroyed, a complete makeover is executed—including a new paint job—and a new set of paperwork is created. Although it may sound impossible to pull this off, the reality is that stealing a ship is a strong possibility, especially for bulk cargo shipped on relatively small ships; there are roughly 40,000 such ships, none of which is particularly distinct from another, which change legal ownership frequently. In addition, in those parts of the world where most piracy attacks occur, the police are either too busy with other pressing matters or cannot be bothered. Despite those odds, the Piracy Reporting Centre has helped recover many of the hijacked ships.

Piracy in the Gulf of Aden

For centuries, pirates have been exploiting the lawlessness of the sea,[28,29] and since they "operate" outside the reach of courts and governments, there is little that governments can do to deter or prevent piracy. While for most people, the word "pirate" conjures up comical images of a man with an eye patch and a parrot on his shoulder, for those sailing ships in certain parts of the world, the actual image is very different.

The Gulf of Aden saw an alarmingly high increase in pirate attacks from the 1990s to the early 2010s. This body of water between North Africa and the Arabian Peninsula is one of the world's busiest shipping lanes, and the attacks were causing major problems for international commerce. The waterway is "an important thoroughfare for goods heading to Europe and the U.S. from Asia," and carries about "4 percent of [the] daily global demand" for crude oil.[30]

Most of the pirates roaming the Gulf came from Somalia, a country which was without an effective government. "Working in small, fast boats, the pirates typically sped up alongside target ships, fired on them with small arms, and then boarded them with simple ladders and grappling hooks."[31] The ships' crew and cargo were usually held for ransom and later released.

Three attacks attracted much attention in 2008-2009, among the more than 50 that took place in that period, and these events triggered a strong response from ship owners, which

eventually all but eliminated the problem.

The *Faina* was taken hostage on September 25, 2008. The Ukrainian ship, bound for Kenya, was carrying "33 T-72 Soviet-era tanks, 150 grenade launchers, 6 anti-aircraft guns and heaps of ammunition,"[32] a fact that was likely unknown to the pirates, but which brought much attention to the incident. The pirates initially demanded a U.S.$ 35-million ransom. For four months, the ship was tracked by American warships determined to prevent the arms from being unloaded. The ship was finally released after the owners paid a ransom of U.S.$ 3.2 million to the pirates.

The hijacking of the *Sirius Star* on November 15, 2008, showed the increasing boldness and resources of the pirates. The Liberian ship was attacked in an area far outside of the pirates' assumed normal operating zone—it was 400 miles off the coast—and the ship was much larger than any of the ships attacked until then. The *Sirius Star* was carrying a cargo of 2.2 million barrels of crude oil, valued at over U.S.$ 100 million.[33] The pirates sailed the ship to the Somali port of Harardhere and demanded a ransom of U.S.$ 25 million. After nearly two months of negotiation, the ship and its crew were released for U.S.$ 3 million.

Finally, the *Maersk Alabama*, with a cargo of 17,000 metric tonnes of U.N. relief supplies and a crew of 21 Americans, was hijacked on April 8, 2009. The captain was held hostage and the pirates demanded a ransom. Because it was a U.S.-flagged ship, the U.S. Navy intervened (to protect a U.S. asset and U.S. lives), surrounding the vessel and the pirates' boat, and the Somali pirates were eventually killed.[34] The movie *Captain Phillips* was inspired by this story.

With the threat of increased violence, ship owners began to seriously combat pirates by diverting some ships away from the Gulf of Aden, and by operating ships at higher speed if they were in that region.[35] Other ship owners hired armed guards to ride on ships (see Figure 10.11), and navies from around the world helped patrol shipping channels.

These efforts have almost eliminated the piracy problem in the Gulf of Aden, with fewer than five incidents in 2016.

Figure 10.11: Armed Guards Aboard a Tanker Ship
Photo ©G. Valeryi/Shutterstock. Used with permission.

Other Risks

Numerous other risks exist in shipping by sea:

- The risk of collision at sea is not substantial, but is still present. Collisions usually happen in crowded shipping lanes, such as the English Channel or the Strait of Gibraltar. Thanks to radar equipment, the risk of collision has been minimized, but it still happens. In August 1999, the *Ever Decent*, a modern containership, collided in the English Channel with the *Norwegian Dream*, a newly built cruise ship.[36] In February 2003, just east of the Port of Singapore, the liquefied-petroleum-gas carrier *Gas Roman* collided with the *Springbok*, a small cargo ship. The collision was of such force that the vessels were not separated until they had drifted to more sheltered waters, to prevent both of them from sinking[37]. In May 2014, the general-cargo ship *Le Sheng* collided with the dry bulker *Cape Med* in the Strait of Gibraltar, just off Algeciras, Spain.[38] Figure 10.12 shows the damage to the *Le Sheng*.

Figure 10.12: Results of a Collision between the *Le Sheng* and the *Cape Med* off Gibraltar

Photo ©Juan G. Mata. Used with permission.

- There is also the risk of collision with non-vessels; floating or sunken containers or debris are present in shipping lanes as well (see Figure 10.6 on page 336), and represent some degree of risk for ships, but little for cargo. Oddly enough, there is still the possibility of collision with icebergs, including huge ones from Antarctica. Icebergs drift continuously in the Antarctic Ocean, and these massive blocks of ice can reach 27 by 36 nautical miles (50 kilometers by 67 kilometers). The position and progress of all very large Antarctic icebergs is monitored by the National Ice Center.[39]

- Other collisions can happen as well. In May 1980, a freighter hit the Skyway Bridge in Tampa, Florida, and caused the collapse of a 420-meter (1,400-foot) span of the bridge,[40] damaging part of the ship and its cargo. In May 2013, in the Port of Genoa, Italy, the *Jolly Nero* crashed into the control tower of the port, killing seven people.[41]

- The risk of having cargo contaminated or affected by other cargo is also present. It is possible for cargo to be contaminated by residues of the cargo that was previously in the same container or in the same ship, particularly foodstuffs contaminated by chemical products. A shipper importing rice found that it was unsellable due to the smell it acquired in the cargo hold of the ship.[42] Another found that its cargo of 2,500 metric tonnes of vinyl pellets was contaminated by a few pounds of styrene left in the hold. Refining costs amounted to $188,000.[43]

- In some cases, other cargo on board can be a hindrance to a shipper. For example, a ship was carrying a load of wheat to the Dominican Republic and stopped in Dakar, Senegal, to pick up an additional load of groundnuts. The nuts eventually proved to be infested with khapra beetles. After the beetles were discovered in the port of destination, the ship was fumigated, twice, which nonetheless failed to rid the cargo of the pests. The ship was then ordered to dump all its cargo—including the wheat—into the sea.[44] The owners of the wheat cargo had done nothing improper; they just happened to have loaded it onto the wrong ship.

- For some ships sailing out of impoverished countries, stowaways are a problem. Young men sneak into the cargo holds or into containers, and hide until they are discovered at sea. In most cases, the stowaways become a larger problem at the port of destination, where police and immigration officials fine the ship and question the crew. In 2015 there were an approximately 2,000 stowaways found aboard cargo ships—and airplane cargo holds—worldwide.[45] Many more were not discovered: U.S. Immigration and Customs Enforcement estimates that about 3,000 stowaways enter the United States every year. In most countries, the responsibility to repatriate discovered stowaways falls on the carrier that brought them into the country. The expense of repatriating stowaways, who frequently are in small groups of two or three and have no identifying papers, runs into thousands of dollars. In a few instances, the fear of these delays, expenses, and fines leads the crews to engage in criminal behavior, such as killing the stowaways or setting them adrift at sea on makeshift rafts.[46]

  stowaway
  A person who hides onboard a ship and travels to the ship's destination.

  The consequences for the cargo beyond the delay are many; most of the time, the cargo is damaged by the stowaways while they are living with the merchandise from a few days to a few weeks. Some of the vehicles going from Mexico to the United States by rail are damaged by stowaways who sleep, eat, and defecate in the cars. Sometimes, the stowaways hide in cargo holds that are closed and where the cargo is often laden with toxic chemicals or fumigated with insecticides. The stowaways die and the cargo is then considered unfit for consumption and destroyed in the country of destination. There are unfortunately no practical ways to prevent this type of occurrence.

- In some cases, and for whatever reason, a government may arrest a ship (*i.e.*, keep it in port rather than let it sail away). Such was the case for five Yugoslav ships that were held in U.S. ports for more than five years, when the U.S. government seized all Yugoslav assets during the Bosnian civil war.[47] The cargo destined for the United States had been unloaded, but the cargo loaded for the return trip was on board for the entire duration of the ordeal.

- In other cases, the ship owners declare bankruptcy while the ship is away, or they abandon the ship and its crew for economic reasons. In June 2016, an Indian company abandoned two of its ships, with crews, in British ports. It was not until January 2017 that the crews of the *Malaviya Seven* and *Malaviya Twenty* were repatriated by the International Transport Workers' Federation,[48] an international union of transportation workers. These occurrences are not infrequent. Cargo aboard these ships is also abandoned.

- In ports where equipment is inadequate or in short supply, some cargo may be unloaded from the ship by taking apart the crates and the merchandise, and reconstructing the goods and the crates on the quay. This can be quite damaging to the cargo. In Chapter 14, this issue, as it relates to packaging and packing the goods, is discussed. The website *World Port Source* publishes a guide to the equipment in place in all the ports worldwide, so that a firm may plan the size of its shipment accordingly.[49]

- Some ports have a history of social unrest, and are shut down for several days by strikes or other civil disturbances. Strikes by French truckers, railroad employees, and airline employees frequently perturb cargo traffic in Europe. Time-sensitive cargo is delayed, and transportation costs increase. Such strikes occur frequently in France and other southern European countries.[50] Strikes in the ports of Japan occur almost annually to force negotiations for higher wages for dockworkers. These actions affect cargo movements in many ways; even if cargo going from Cairo to Bombay is not caught in an Italian strike, it can be delayed because the containership on which it was supposed to sail is delayed.

The possible perils that cargo can encounter at sea and on its way to and from a seaport are many; this list illustrates that many of the risks associated with a sea voyage may be easily underestimated by an exporter or an importer arranging for ocean cargo services. The importer or the exporter, whichever is responsible for the cargo, must be alert in its management of these risks.

10.2.2 Perils Associated with Air Shipments

Compared to the perils of an ocean shipment, the perils of an air shipment are minimal, a situation due mostly to the fact that air transport is, by nature, less perilous than ocean transportation. In addition, the airline industry is still dominated by companies located in, and therefore regulated by, developed countries' governments, which tend to have stringent rules regarding safety, pilot training, and maintenance. Despite the large number of aircraft in operation—in 2016, there were approximately 17,000 commercial airplanes in the world, including 1,770 freighters[51]—and the correspondingly high number of voyages, the number of accidents per year is very small, reflecting the industry's emphasis on safety.

The risks of fire and explosion are greatly diminished, mostly because regulations by the International Civil Aviation Organization and the International Air Transport Association prohibit shipments of dangerous goods by air. The risk of total loss of cargo due to aircraft crashes is essentially nil, as is the risk of loss while the aircraft is aloft. The three biggest concerns for air shipments are:

- **Cargo movement**: while in the aircraft, the cargo is subjected to rough weather and sudden and quick accelerations and decelerations. Because freighter airplanes do not have to worry about passenger comfort, their pilots do not fly around turbulences the way passenger airline pilots do, and the cargo on board can be subjected to sudden and violent bumps. Likewise, the aircraft brakes faster on landing, banks at a wider angle on approach, and is altogether less gentle than if passengers were on board. However, a good percentage of cargo moves in passenger airplanes, which do not experience such conditions; that percentage is expected to continuously decrease, though, as U.S. legislation demands that 100 percent of all cargo be screened before it can travel on a passenger aircraft, a cost-prohibitive and cumbersome measure.

  For air cargo, the greatest hazards remain in the shipping and handling that precede the flight, whether in the truck on the way to the airport, in the warehouse, on the tarmac, or during their counterpart activities in the transit airport and the airport of arrival (forklift truck damage, for example).

- **Theft and pilferage**: while airports control theft while the goods are on the airport premises, this is not often the case in the vicinity of the airports, where problems abound in warehouses, truck terminals, and other satellite locations. Because most cargo sent by air has a high value, it is interesting to thieves, and because the cargo tends to be packaged in cardboard boxes and not palletized, it is more easily pilfered and stolen (sometimes the brands are displayed on the packaging, inciting pilferage). The key to controlling losses in these instances is to ensure that the cargo documents are handled by as few people as possible and that the boxes are not marked to indicate their content.

- **Exposure to inclement weather**: although it seems counterintuitive, goods in transit from a warm place to another warm place may be subjected to very cold weather. For example, the fourth largest freight airport in the world is Anchorage, Alaska (after Hong Kong, Memphis, and Shanghai), where the average high temperature is below freezing from mid-October to early April. Reciprocally, cargo moving from a cold climate to another cold climate may stop at a tropical airport. Such was the case for salmon fry—very young fish—shipped from Alaska to southern Chile, which routinely stopped in Miami, Florida. After it experienced a high mortality, the airfreight company equipped its cargo aircraft with additional fuel tanks so that it could fly directly to its destination. Cargo is commonly left on the tarmac for a couple of hours between flights, and the shipper should anticipate that the cargo will be exposed to atmospheric conditions that are different from the ones in the airports of departure and destination.

There are several other risks associated with air shipment: particularly the cold and the changes in air pressure that can be found in some freighters. Cargo freighters tends to be kept at lower temperatures and lower air pressure during flight than what is practiced in passenger airplanes, to save costs. For most cargo, these slight differences may not be significant, but for some cargo, these differences can be a problem. Because, by definition, sensitive cargo moves by air, care should be taken to ensure that perishable cargo is not kept at temperatures that it cannot handle, or that live cargo and sensitive mechanical instruments are not subjected to air pressures that are too low. However, because such a large percentage of air cargo demands controlled temperatures and pressures, the remainder of the cargo on board benefits from these requirements. Again, the greatest risk is usually not while the freighter is in flight, but while the cargo is on the tarmac, waiting to be loaded, or already loaded and waiting to take off; during these times, tha cargo can be exposed to extreme temperatures as well as rain and snow.

10.3   Insurable Interest

insurable interest
A party who would experience a financial loss in the case of a peril is said to have an insurable interest.

There are several parties interested in the safe arrival of an international cargo shipment. The first, obviously, is the owner of the goods. Whether the owner is the exporter or the importer depends on many factors, principally the transaction's terms of payment (see Chapter 7). However, there are many cases in which non-owners want to ensure that the goods arrive at their destination safely. The terms of trade, or Incoterms® rules used in the transaction between the exporter and the importer (see Chapter 6) indicate the cases in which the exporter is responsible for the goods until that responsibility transfers to the importer. However, even if the importer is not responsible for the goods while they are in transit, it still has an interest in making sure that the goods arrive safely to their destination.

These situations illustrate the concept of insurable interest:

> An insurance contract is legally binding only if the insured has an interest in the subject matter of the insurance and this interest is in fact insurable. In most instances, an insurable interest exists only if the insured [were to] suffer a financial loss in the event of damage to, or destruction of, the subject matter of the insurance.[52]

The use of Incoterms® rules helps the exporter and the importer determine where their respective responsibilities start and end. It should therefore follow that the insurable interest of the exporter ends when possession shifts to the importer, at which time the importer has an insurable interest; unfortunately, while this is correct, it is not that simple. The issue is muddied by several factors. Several examples can be used to illustrate them:

- **Foreign exchange exposure.** An exporter in a developing country sells to an importer in a developed country on a CIF basis. Responsibility transfers once the merchandise is onboard the ship, but the exporter must provide minimum cover insurance (*i.e.*, Coverage C of the Institute Marine Cargo Clauses, which will be explained in Section 10.5 on page 354). If the importer agrees to such minimum coverage, there is still the problem that, should there be a loss, the importer would have to file a claim with the insurer in the developing country, or, at least, an insurer not chosen by the importer. It is possible that the claim processing will take a few months, leaving the importer with the risk of foreign exchange devaluation. Because the terms are CIF, the exporter delivers the goods as agreed—when the goods arrive onboard the ship in the exporting country's port—and therefore the invoice must be paid by the importer, causing a cash-flow problem as well. In this case, the importer has an insurable interest and can obtain coverage in its country to minimize its foreign exchange risk exposure; it would be covered against a loss that happens in transportation and could pay the exporter the amount owed. A similar situation can arise in a CIP shipment.

- **Trust.** An exporter may sell FCA to an importer in a country that mandates that the importer buy insurance in the importing country. The exporter usually ships without evidence of coverage, and correctly so, because the responsibility shifts to the importer as soon as the goods are in the carrier's care. However, should they be damaged in transit, the importer may refuse payment, even though the accident happened under its responsibility. The exporter has therefore an insurable interest in the completion of the trip. Note that the problem is avoided if the exporter sells on a letter-of-credit basis, as the documents for the shipment, including the intermodal bill of lading, would be in order, and the issuing bank would have to pay (see Section 7.6 on page 218).

- **Insufficient coverage.** An exporter agrees to sell to an importer on a CIF basis. The importer requests that the terms be modified to "CIF maximum cover" (*i.e.*, Coverage A of the Institute Marine Cargo Clauses—see

Section 10.5 on page 354) but, because it is an open-account shipment, it does not obtain evidence of this coverage. The goods are slightly damaged in transit by condensation, and the importer seeks to collect compensation under the terms of the insurance policy provided by the exporter. However, the claim is turned down because the exporter did not contract for Coverage A, but for Coverage B or C, which do not allow claims for such damage. Clearly, the importer has an insurable interest in this cargo and can obtain coverage in its country to protect itself from such losses.

While the owner of the goods has a clear insurable interest in the merchandise while it is in transit, non-owners, such as the buyers in the first and third examples above, have an insurable interest that is less direct: this interest is usually qualified as a contingent insurable interest.[53]

10.4   Risk Management

There are three ways in which a company can manage its risks, whether they are international cargo insurance or any other type of risk: the company can retain the risk, transfer the risk, or take a mixed approach, retaining some risks and transferring others.[54] This section will concentrate on the management of international-logistics risks, mainly the risks associated with transporting goods from one country to another.

10.4.1   Risk Retention

risk retention
A risk management strategy in which a company decides to retain a risk and not insure against it.

The strategy of risk retention is fairly clear: the company decides that it is more economical to not purchase insurance to cover the transportation risks. In general, there are four reasons for a company to retain its international-logistics risks:

- **Very large international traders—importers or exporters**—These traders already act somewhat as an insurance company: they have a lot of merchandise in transit, and therefore would have to pay large insurance premiums, but would only occasionally collect on a loss. Therefore, the many savings incurred by not paying premiums end up covering the few losses they do experience. Such firms self-insure, which is the euphemism for not contracting with an insurance company and for paying all risks with current cash flow.

exposure
The impact of a loss for an exporter. Its effect on the exporter's financial well-being.

- **Exporters or importers that have little exposure**—These exporters and importers are shipping or buying goods of fairly small value, in fairly small shipments, and therefore a loss would not have substantial financial or cash-flow consequences for those companies.

- **Exporters or importers that have little relative exposure**—Their international transactions represent a small percentage of their business. The individual international transaction amount may be large, but relative to the size of their domestic sales, it is not significant.

- **Firms that did not evaluate the international transaction risks clearly—** These firms are not insuring because they do not insure their domestic transactions or think that the risks of shipping internationally are not very high. Generally, the firms that choose to retain risks due to ignorance are also the ones that are more likely to incur losses because of improper packing or improper security measures—and for the same reasons. Relying upon the liability coverage provided by the shipping line is also imprudent; the current liability for shipping lines under U.S. law—the Carriage of Goods by Sea Act (COGSA)—provides a maximum coverage of U.S.$ 500 per package, which has been interpreted by some courts as a container, and the shipping lines have 17 specified defenses they can invoke, essentially shielding them from liability except in the most egregious cases. The specifics of this coverage and other alternative liability coverage by the carrier will be covered in Section 11.5.

10.4.2 Risk Transfer

The strategy of risk transfer is also fairly clear: the firm transfers all of its risks to an insurance company. In exchange for paying a premium for an insurance policy, the firm is certain to be covered against losses experienced during international shipments. This strategy is followed for three reasons:

risk transfer
A risk management strategy in which the company decides to insure against its risks.

- **Firms with a lot of exposure—**The value of the goods these firms ship or import is high, and the loss of some or all these shipments would be a substantial financial blow to their operations. In those cases where goods are expensive, though, the insurance companies often request, in cooperation with the firms, to restrict the total amount at risk on any single shipment. Usually this is achieved by having the shipment split over several carriers.

- **Firms with a relatively high exposure—**Even though the shipment amount may be small, it is relatively high in relation to the total sales volume of these firms. A perfect example of such a situation is found in personal effects shipments, which generally are worth small sums, but are quite valuable to their owners.

- **Firms with little experience—**Companies that lack experience in international trade insure because they are uncomfortable with the risks involved or because they are unable to properly assess their exposure.

10.4.3 Mixed Approach

The mixed approach is one where the firm retains some of the risks and transfers the rest. This strategy can be achieved in three different ways:

- The decision is made based upon the maximum amount of exposure that a firm is willing to risk, and is implemented using a deductible. The deductible is the maximum amount for which a firm is responsible. The insurance company is responsible for the portion of a loss that is greater than the deductible and the firm is responsible for the amount of the deductible as well as all losses that have a value lower than the deductible. The deductible can be a cumulative deductible, where the firm pays for losses until the cumulative deductible amount is reached over a period of a year, and the insurance company pays for the losses incurred beyond the amount of the deductible.

- The decision is made based upon the maximum amount of exposure that a firm is willing to risk, and is implemented using a franchise. The franchise is the amount that determines which party, of the company or the insurer, is responsible for the loss. For losses below the franchise amount, the firm is responsible for the loss. For losses that exceed the franchise, the insurance company is entirely responsible for the loss. Franchises are often expressed as a percentage of the value of the cargo, such as 3 percent.

- The decision is made based on the types of risks that the firm is willing to take, and those that it would rather transfer to an insurance company. For example, a firm may choose to insure using Coverage B of the Institute Marine Cargo Clauses (see Section 10.5) and retain the risks not covered by this policy, among which are condensation, pilferage, leakage, and breakage. A company may choose to follow this strategy if the goods it sells are resilient.

Any of these strategies can be followed for several reasons. However, while the choice of a monetary deductible is based essentially upon the maximum amount of exposure that a firm is willing to bear, the strategy of splitting risks between the firm and an insurance company is a much more difficult strategy to implement, as it involves identifying risks, determining whether they are significant enough to transfer, and negotiating with an insurance company a specific contract of insurance, taking advantage of the fact that "customized cargo policies are limited only by the imagination of the companies offering them."[55]

10.5   Insurance Policies

An international trading firm—exporter or importer—intent on transferring all or part of its international shipping risks is generally interested only in purchasing marine cargo insurance, because the firm just needs to protect itself from damage to the cargo as well as from its liability toward the ship owners and the rest of the cargo in a general-average case. However, there are a couple of additional insurance coverages available in international shipping that should be mentioned: they pertain mainly to vessel or aircraft owners, but, on rare occasions, those policies matter to an exporter or importer chartering an entire ship for a bulk shipment.

10.5.1 Purchasing Marine Cargo Insurance

Marine cargo insurance can be purchased either under an open ocean-cargo policy or under a special cargo policy.

Open Policy

An open policy is an insurance contract with which a firm insures every international shipment it makes for a fixed period. Such a policy is formally known as an open ocean-cargo policy, and it automatically covers all the shipments of the insured, as long as the firm reports every shipment to the insurance company. This reporting is done using a set of declaration forms, either every time an export shipment is made—or an import shipment is received—or monthly. There is a presumption of goodwill on the part of the firm in that the insurance company will cover damage to an undeclared shipment, as long as the firm intended to notify the insurance company.[56] Because the premiums are based upon the value of the shipments made under such a policy, an open policy presents one great advantage: the firm knows the costs of its insurance coverage and can easily incorporate these costs in its *pro forma* invoices without having to request a quote for each shipment.

open policy
An insurance policy that covers all of the shipments made by a firm.

Special Cargo Policy

The second alternative is for the exporter or importer to purchase an individual policy, called a special cargo policy, for each shipment. A special cargo policy allows a firm to specifically purchase the coverage that pertains best to a shipment. However, it tends to be cumbersome to enter a contract every time the firm gets involved in an international transaction, and thus a special cargo policy is not commonly used, unless the products the firm sells are large capital goods or expensive tailor-made equipment that needs specialized care while in transit.

individual policy
An insurance policy that covers one shipment.

Obtaining Insurance Certificates

On many occasions, the exporter is requested to provide a Certificate of Insurance (see Figure 9.10 on page 308) to the importer and its bank, often because this certificate is required by the issuer of the letter of credit. This requirement is usually not a problem under a special cargo policy, because there is evidence from the insurance company that a specific shipment is insured.

Under an open ocean cargo policy, however, the certificate of insurance requirement used to present some difficulties until recently. The practice used to be that the insurance company would provide the exporter with a Certificate of Open Insurance; however, this certificate did not specifically address the insurance status of a given shipment, and some (few) banks did not accept evidence

certificate of insurance
A certificate, issued by the exporter's insurance company, that attests that a particular shipment is insured.

of an open policy as a proof of insurance for a specific shipment as required in the terms of the letter of credit.[57] Therefore, the insurance company now gives the insured a supply of blank special cargo policy forms, which are then filled out by the exporter to show that a specific shipment is covered. These forms appear—to the issuing bank—as if a special cargo policy has been contracted for the shipment, even though it is covered under an open policy.[58]

Marine Cargo Insurance Intermediaries

Marine cargo insurance can be purchased from two sources:

- An insurance agent, who can assist the firm in obtaining the most appropriate coverage, given its product mix and its risk management strategy. Agents sell most open ocean cargo policies.

- A freight forwarder, who can provide "generic" coverage for a given shipment almost immediately. Freight forwarders sell a lot of special cargo policies.

10.5.2   Marine Cargo Insurance Policy Coverages

There are two major groups of policies that can be purchased to protect cargo during an ocean or air shipment. The first group of policies is governed by British law and was completely rewritten in 1982, mostly to put them into contemporary English. The policies were revised again in 2009 to add greater precision to some terms, and update the remnants of traditional ancient English that had been kept in the 1982 version.[59] This group of insurance policies has become the standard for all other countries as well, except for the United States. These policies are known as the Institute Marine Cargo Clauses, Coverage A, B, or C. They are named after the Institute of London Underwriters, which is also known by its formal name of The International Underwriting Association of London.

The second group of policies is older, with some antiquated clauses and a few modern ones, and these policies are mostly written by U.S.-based insurance companies. These traditional policies are known as all-risks, with-average, and free-of-particular-average policies, and a decreasing number of policies are using these terms. These three types of policies are less standardized than the Institute Marine Cargo Clauses policies.

particular average
A partial loss incurred by a cargo owner on an ocean voyage.

To make things more interesting, these six general policies can be modified to add coverage that is not included in the original contract, such as the risks of strikes and civil unrest, allowing international traders to tailor the coverage they are purchasing to a shipment's specific needs.

However, none of the insurance policies cover five specific risks, against which it is impossible to find insurance:

- **Improper packing**—The goods must be adequately packed for an ocean voyage and be well protected against shocks and water damage, as well as be secured solidly in the container or crate. Chapter 14 discusses this issue in depth.

- **Inherent vice**—The goods shipped have a natural propensity to be affected by time and the elements in a certain way; for example, steel will exhibit surface rust after being exposed for some time to air and moisture, agricultural product shipments will foster insects and rodents, and wood will warp and split. None of these inherent vices are insurable.

- **Ordinary leakage**—Also known as "ordinary loss in weight and volume" and "ordinary wear and tear," this concept states that several products, when shipped, will leak or lose weight; for example, many agricultural products, such as wool, will lose some weight as its moisture content decreases; petroleum oil transported in bulk will partially evaporate; and an automobile carried on a roll-on/roll-off ship will show additional mileage. Again, none of these risks are insurable.

- **Unseaworthy vessel**—This exclusion is not a problem for goods shipped by regularly scheduled container or breakbulk ships; however, it puts a burden of care on the shipper in the case of a shipment going by bulk ship, as the shipper must make certain that the ship is classified by a classification society as seaworthy. In addition, a vessel can depart for a voyage in seaworthy condition and then become unseaworthy due to the perils it encounters. When a ship becomes unseaworthy during a voyage, most policies include a statement that "an unreasonable delay in repairing the ship exonerates the insurer from liability on any loss arising from the defect."

- **Nuclear war**—This risk is always specifically excluded from policies. Note that the risk not covered is the direct result of nuclear war, such as irradiation or destruction. However, should a shipment be damaged by a fire caused by nuclear war, the shipment is covered—if the risk of fire is covered in the policy—because the fire was the peril that caused the loss.

Institute Marine Cargo Clauses—Coverage A

The first general policy is called Coverage A of the Institute Marine Cargo Clauses. Coverage A covers "all risks of loss or damage to the subject-matter insured,"[60] and is based on the traditional all-risks policies that were sold before the Institute Clauses were written. A Coverage A policy is written in plain English, however, which makes it much simpler to decipher. Moreover, unlike traditional all-risks policies, which can be written with U.S. or British clauses—and the different interpretations they imply—and can include or exclude risks at the discretion of the issuer, a policy written with Coverage A of the Institute Marine Cargo Clauses is identical in all countries.

Despite its stated broad scope, a Coverage A policy does not cover literally all risks, as it does not cover the uninsurable perils (improper packing, inherent vice, ordinary leakage, unseaworthy vessel, and nuclear war), as well as several other risks for which specific additional coverage must be purchased separately as endorsements to the main policy: strikes and other civil disturbances (see the Strikes, Riots, and Civil Commotions clause a little further in this Section), acts of war, and seizure by a government (see War and Seizure coverage a little further in this Section).

Nevertheless, Coverage A of the Institute Marine Cargo Clauses is the maximum coverage that an exporter or an importer needs to purchase for a shipment traveling on most trade lanes in the world, specifically from one developed country to another, as long as the route does not cross a particular "hot spot" of the world.

Institute Marine Cargo Clauses—Coverage B

Another general policy is referred to as Coverage B of the Institute Marine Cargo Clauses. Coverage B is called a named-perils policy, as this policy lists specifically the risks that it will cover. A named-perils policy only covers the listed perils and excludes all perils not listed. The list of covered perils in the Institute Marine Cargo Clauses Coverage B includes fire, stranding, sinking, collision, jettisoning, washing overboard, water damage, and total losses during loading and unloading; however, losses due to bad weather are not covered, and neither are partial losses happening during loading and unloading.[61] For a complete list of covered and non-covered perils, refer to Table 10.1, where a comparison is given for all six standard coverages.

Coverage B of the Institute Marine Cargo Clauses is appropriate for goods that have a good tolerance for bad weather, such as bulk raw materials, including coal, iron ore, polymer pellets, and lumber. Coverage B is not appropriate for machinery, paper, and any type of finished goods, unless these goods are particularly resilient.

Institute Marine Cargo Clauses—Coverage C

The last of the general Institute Marine Cargo Clauses is Coverage C. Coverage C is also a named-perils policy, and the policy lists specifically the risks that it will cover. The list of covered perils is limited to fire, stranding, sinking, collision, and jettison; covered perils do not include washing overboard, rough weather damage, water damage, or losses during loading and unloading.[62] For a complete list of covered and non-covered perils, refer to Table 10.5 on page 354, where a comparison is given for all six standard policies.

Coverage C is the minimum coverage required by the CIF and CIP Incoterms® rules. Coverage C is minimal enough as to be inappropriate for most goods, and companies doing business on CIF or CIP terms should extend this coverage to "maximum cover" (*i.e.*, Coverage A of the Institute Marine Cargo Clauses), or, if they are importing under those Incoterms® rules, purchase Difference in Condition coverage (see the explanation of that coverage further in this Section).

Coverage C is insufficient for most containerized goods, except for goods that are unlikely to be affected by an international voyage in any way and, if lost overboard, would not be a major loss. There are few cargoes that fit this description, aside from scrap merchandise, such as scrap metal or recyclable paper. Coverage C is appropriate for bulk cargo, as it is unlikely to experience a loss unless there is major damage to the ship.[63]

Perils Covered by a Specific insurance Policy

Peril	Coverage A	Coverage B	Coverage C	All Risks	With Average	Free of Particular Average
Fire or Explosion	✓	✓	✓	✓	✓	✓
Stranding/Grounding	✓	✓	✓	✓	✓	✓
Sinking	✓	✓	✓	✓	✓	✓
Collision	✓	✓	✓	✓	✓	✓
Jettison	✓	✓	✓	✓	✓	✓
General Average	✓	✓	✓	✓	✓	✓
Overboard Loss	✓	✓		✓	✓	
Boiler Bursting	✓			✓	✓	✓
Seawater Damage	✓	✓		✓	✓	
Condensation	✓			✓		
Heavy Weather	✓			✓	✓	
Rough Handling	✓			✓	✓	
Improper Stowage by Carrier	✓			✓		
Theft	✓			✓		
Pilferage	✓			✓		
Leakage	✓			✓		
Breakage	✓			✓		
Damage while Loading	✓			✓	✓	
Damage while Unloading	✓			✓	✓	

Table 10.1: Marine Insurance Coverage Summary

All-Risks Coverage

An all-risks policy is an older type of policy that is a much less frequently used, except in the United States, where it is still common. Because an all-risks policy can be written as an American contract or as a British contract, it can contain different wordings of the clauses and other minor changes, which makes an American policy differ from a British policy on a few points; therefore, international logisticians should read such policies carefully to ensure that there is a proper match between the risks that the shipper—exporter or importer—is willing to assume and the ones that the policy excludes.

For a U.S. all-risks policy to be enforceable, the goods must be shipped "under deck," which means that the goods must be stowed inside the ship, for the obvious reason that goods inside a ship are exposed to fewer perils than goods stowed on deck. However, this presents a practical problem because the shipper is usually unaware of the way the goods are stowed, and because some containerships no longer have a deck and are instead equipped with stack bars. This problem is solved by requesting that the insurance company cover the goods based upon the Shipper's Letter of Instruction, which requests that the goods be shipped under deck, and not based upon the way the goods are actually stowed. Such coverage can be obtained as an endorsement to the main policy, usually at no additional charge.[64] Once this endorsement has been granted, an all-risks policy is similar to a Coverage A policy, and therefore an all-risks policy is also quite appropriate for shipments of any nature between two developed countries.

With-Average Coverage

A with-average policy is generally written to include coverage that falls between an all-risks policy and a policy with Coverage B of the Institute Marine Cargo Clauses. A with-average policy is a named-perils policy, and it lists specifically the perils that it covers. Again, because a with-average policy can also be written as an American contract or as a British contract, shippers must ensure that they are is not unwillingly accepting a risk that they do not want to retain.

A with-average policy covers risks such as fire, explosion, stranding, collision, and so on (see Table 10.5 on page 354), but also covers damage to cargo from heavy weather, as well as partial losses while loading and unloading the vessel, and the bursting of boilers, none of which Coverage B provides.

A with-average policy insures partial losses using a franchise, which is to say that for partial damage below a certain percentage—say 3 percent—of the value of the merchandise, the goods are not covered. For partial losses greater than this franchise, the entire loss to the insured is covered. A franchise is therefore different from a deductible, where in a loss of 10 percent of the value of the merchandise occurred, the insured is responsible for the first 3 percent and the insurance company is responsible for the remaining 7 percent. Under a with-average policy with a franchise of 3 percent, the insurance company covers the entire 10 percent loss.

A standard with-average policy is appropriate for some of the merchandise shipped internationally; however, because some other coverages such as freshwater damage, condensation, or breakage and pilferage are often added,[65] it seems that shippers use a with-average policy to tailor coverage to include those perils to which the merchandise is sensitive.

Free-of-Particular-Average Coverage

The last general policy is called a free-of-particular-average contract, which is a named-perils policy. A free-of-particular-average policy covers total losses, but covers partial losses in only a few circumstances. The major issue is whether the policy is a free-of-particular-average (English conditions) policy or a free-of-particular-average (American conditions) policy. Under an American-conditions policy, partial losses are covered only if they result directly from a fire, a stranding, a sinking, or a collision. Under an English-conditions policy, the partial losses are covered if they occur on the same voyage that a fire, a stranding, a sinking, or a collision occurs, without these perils having directly caused the loss. These are the types of distinctions that make the field of insurance a complicated one. Shippers would be wise to avoid insurance policies that have not adopted Institute Marine Cargo Clauses, which do not make distinctions of this nature.

A free-of-particular-average policy provides even less coverage than Coverage C of the Institute Marine Cargo Clauses. Such policies do not cover many of the risks associated with an international shipment and a free-of-particular-average policy is rarely sufficient or appropriate for an international shipment of containerized or breakbulk cargo, unless the cargo considered is particularly inexpensive and a loss is not a substantial problem for the shipper. A free-of-particular-average policy is appropriate (with some reservation, because no partial losses are covered) for some bulk cargo of minimal value.

Finally, a free-of-particular-average policy is insufficient to cover the minimum insurance requirements of a shipment conducted on a CIP or CIF Incoterms® rule, which both require the minimum cover of Coverage C of the Institute Marine Cargo Clauses.[66]

Strikes Coverage

All the previous standard policies include a clause, called the "Strikes, Riots, and Civil Commotions" (S.R. & C.C.) clause in the American policies and the "Strikes Exclusion" clause in the Institute Marine Cargo Clauses policies, which exclude coverage of cargo damage due to strikes and other civil disturbances.

Should a shipper be concerned about the possibility of such problems in a specific port or during a specific period, an amendment to include such coverage can always be added, generally called an S.R. & C.C. Endorsement. However, the coverage includes only direct physical damage to the goods or the additional costs of storing the goods during the strike; it does not include incidental damage caused by delay to market, nor the financial losses that accompany a delay in the sale of a cargo.

War and Seizure Coverage

All the previous standard policies also include a clause, called "Free of Capture and Seizure" (F.C. & S.) in the American policies and "War Exclusion" in the Institute Marine Cargo Clauses policies, which excludes coverage of cargo damage due to war and war-like situations, such as the seizure of a ship by a foreign government or the accidental collision of a ship with a mine.

A shipper can insure its cargo against war damages, but this coverage is obtained through an additional policy, called the "War Risks Only" policy, which covers hostile acts by a foreign government or by an organized power. For obvious reasons, a war-risks policy is cancelable by the insurance company with a 48-hour notice; however, the policy cannot be canceled for cargo that is in transit (*i.e.*, merchandise that has already left the port of departure), which is really the coverage that any shipper would want. Most open-cargo policies are accompanied by a separate war-risks policy, according to Cigna Insurance Companies.[67] In times of naval warfare against merchant ships, war risk insurance may be obtainable through only a government-backed policy. This was the case for most Allied vessels and cargoes during World War II.

Lemongate

On July 30, 2004, the United States Coast Guard (USCG), acting upon an "unconfirmed anonymous report" received by e-mail, seized the *Rio Puelo*, a containership bound for Canada that was transporting 120 metric tonnes of lemons from Argentina to Montreal, and was scheduled to stop in Port Elizabeth, New Jersey, to unload some of the remainder of its cargo. The Coast Guard was concerned that the lemons could contain a biological agent that would be released when the ship stopped in the U.S. port.[68]

The ship was ordered to anchor seven nautical miles from shore, and the ship was then boarded by USCG agents. They located the containers aboard the ship and lowered their refrigeration temperature from 4.5 degrees Celsius (40 degrees Fahrenheit) to below 0 degrees Celsius (32 degrees Fahrenheit) to slow down or kill all biological activity in the containers, but also essentially destroying the fruits. After six days,

the ship was allowed to enter the port and unload the containers bound for the United States. The lemon containers were also discharged and immediately isolated. Access holes were cut in the containers and the cargo fumigated with chlorine dioxide gas and eventually incinerated.[69] No biological agent was ever found.

There were many costs associated with this seizure.[70] Cargo aboard the ship was delayed seven days, and the ship had to skip some ports of call to get back on schedule. The shipping line was forced to find other carriers for some of the cargo that it could not load. Finally, the load of lemons, estimated to be worth about U.S.$ 70,000, was completely lost. None of these costs were covered by the insurance companies of the shippers (exporters or importers), unless they had "Free of Capture & Seizure" coverage, which is highly unlikely, as they would not have anticipated such a risk for a shipment from Argentina to Canada.

Warehouse-to-Warehouse Coverage

Another common additional coverage to an open cargo policy is warehouse-to-warehouse coverage, which covers the goods from the time they leave the exporter's warehouse until the time they arrive at the importer's warehouse, or 15 days after they arrive in the port of destination, whichever occurs first.

The warehouse-to-warehouse coverage grew from the demands of shippers who were tired of finding coverage for only the ocean portion of the voyage. First, the all-risks and with-average insurance policies added a shore-perils endorsement to include the perils occurring while loading and unloading ships; this clause was also made part of the Institute Marine Cargo Clauses. Finally, a true warehouse-to-warehouse clause was added to most open-cargo policies, to really cover goods while they transit from one location to another, without interruption in coverage.

In addition, in some policies, there is a marine-extension clause, which expands the warehouse-to-warehouse coverage to ensure unforeseen changes in the voyage and unexpected trans-shipments. Such a clause was developed during World War II to account for unusual and unknown trans-shipments, because all shipping data were classified.[71] It fulfills few practical purposes today.

Warehouse-to-warehouse coverage is an extension of the traditional all-risks, with-average, and free-of-particular-average policies, but it also is an integral part of the Institute Marine Cargo Clauses policies for Coverages A, B, and C, in which it is called the "Transit" clause. A shipper is well advised to consider that point in the purchase of a policy.

Difference in Conditions

Another addition of significance to open cargo policies would be difference-in-conditions coverage. Difference-in-conditions coverage is designed to fill the gap between what an importer wants to have covered under its open-cargo policy and what is covered under its supplier's coverage, which can be the minimum required by the CIP and CIF Incoterms® rules.

difference-in-condition
A clause in an insurance policy that allows an importer to complement the coverage offered by the exporter to the level of coverage that the importer wants.

Because the International Chamber of Commerce requires only Coverage C of the Institute Marine Cargo Clauses for a CIF or CIP shipment, it can be difficult to ensure that a supplier will cover the shipment more thoroughly, even though the importer may request maximum cover (the variants to Incoterms® rules are not part of the rules, and arbitration panels do not rule on these provisions). In those cases, it is simpler for the importer to purchase a difference-in-conditions endorsement on its open-cargo policy and not worry about what coverage the supplier provides.

Difference-in-conditions coverage has the additional benefit of allowing the importer to file a claim with its own insurance company, in its own language, with people with whom it has interacted in the past. Filing a claim this way is far less complicated than having to contact the exporter's insurance company. The provider of the difference-in-conditions policy then contacts the exporter's insurance company to be reimbursed, using subrogation.

Other Clauses of a Marine Insurance Policy

There are many other clauses in a marine insurance policy, either as a part of the general policy or as an endorsement to the general policy. This section will give a brief overview of some of them.

- **General Average Clause**—All insurance policies contain a general-average clause, which specifies that the insurer will cover the general-average responsibilities of a shipper.

- **Constructive-Total-Loss-Coverage Clause**—All insurance policies contain a constructive-total-loss-coverage clause, which specifies that the insurer will reimburse the shipper for goods that have been abandoned after a stranding or a sinking, as long as the costs of recovering the goods and making them marketable is greater than their value. If it is possible to recover the goods at a cost lower than their value, then the insurance company pays for these costs.

- **Sue-and-Labor Clause**—All traditional insurance policies—all-risks, with-average, and free-of-particular-average policies—have a sue-and-labor clause (policies written under the Institute Marine Cargo Clauses have similar wording but do not use this clause name), which directs the shipper to act in the best interest of the insurance company when a loss occurs. The principle is that, after a loss, the insured should protect the cargo from further damage, as it would if it had not been insured, to keep the loss to a minimum.

- *Inchmaree* **Clause**—One of the quaint vestiges of the old marine insurance policies is the *Inchmaree* clause, so named after a lawsuit between the owners of the *Inchmaree*, a vessel, and the insurers of its cargo, which determined that damage caused by a burst boiler (steamship engine) was not covered by the traditional marine insurance policy of the time. Insurers quickly added this coverage to their policy, and it has remained to this day in the all-risks, with-average, and free-of-particular-average policies. The *Inchmaree* clause also covers cargo owners in the event that the ship owner is guilty of errors in navigation and seamanship. Coverages A through C of the Institute Marine Cargo Clauses do not include the *Inchmaree* clause—and do not mention coverage for poor navigation—and do not cover the bursting of boilers, since that technology has long been replaced with diesel engines in international ocean travels.[72]

10.5.3   Other Forms of Marine Insurance

Hull Insurance

hull insurance
A policy contracted by the ship owner to cover damages to the ship.

Hull insurance is contracted by the ship owners to cover the risk of damage to the ship when it is involved in a peril, such as grounding or fire. Hull insurance also covers the owners in case of a complete loss, such as a sinking. This policy also covers the ship owners' liability toward the cargo owners in the case of a general average and damages due to a collision with another ship. An equivalent hull insurance is available to aircraft owners.

Hull insurance rates depend on the ship's seaworthiness, the way it is maintained, and the equipment it has on board, all three of which are appraised by classification societies. Ships are placed in different classes, and hull insurance rates depend on the ship's class. The *Lloyd's Register of Ships* kept classification information on almost all ships in the world from its creation in 1764 until 2009, when Lloyd's sold this business to IHS Fairplay.[73] Hull insurance is paid indirectly by the cargo owners, as the cost of the insurance is included in the freight rates quoted.

classification society
A company whose business is to determine the seaworthiness of a vessel.

Protection and Indemnity

Protection and Indemnity is yet another form of insurance for ship owners; protection and indemnity is a coverage against liability to other parties when a ship sinks or is damaged. In the last few decades, such policies have meant liability for oil spills—specifically cargo spills, but also ship fuel spills—on beaches, and their extensive clean-up costs. However, it also includes the ship owners' liability toward the crew (injury, death) or in repatriating stowaways.

Property and Indemnity Club [P&I Club]
A group of ship owners who agree to mutually share the costs of its members' liabilities to other parties.

Protection and Indemnity insurance is not traditional insurance, but arranged through a mutual P&I club to which ship owners contribute, and which absorbs the costs of one of the owners' mishaps. The liability of a single P&I club is capped, following a liability convention called the Convention on Limitation of Liability for Maritime Claims, originally written in 1976 and revised in 1996, but modified by a European directive that mandates that ships entering EU waters have minimum P&I coverage.[74] The liability is determined by the size of the ship, and also depends on the type of damage (whether it is harm to people or property). For claims that are higher than those limits, the thirteen P&I clubs form an alliance and mutually insure each other. The P&I clubs are then covered by an additional re-insurance policy, to a maximum of U.S. $2.05 billion.[75] Claims involving cargoes of crude oil are covered by a series of international agreements to which 103 countries are signatories, called the International Funds for Oil Pollution Compensation, which has limits that vary in function of the size of the ship. As of June 2013, the maximum cover is U.S. $1,627 million.[76] The United States is not a signatory to this fund.

10.5.4 Elements of an Airfreight Policy

Fortunately, airfreight policies are less complicated than ocean marine cargo insurance policies. All airfreight policies are written as all-risks policies—or Institute Marine Cargo Clauses Coverage A policies—with the exclusions already described in Section 10.5.2:

- **Improper packing**—The goods must be adequately packed for an air shipment and be reasonably protected against shocks and rainwater damage, as well as well secured in the container or the crate. The standards for airfreight packing are less stringent than for an ocean shipment.

- **Inherent vice**—This problem is essentially moot in an air shipment, as the goods are in transit for a much shorter period. Nevertheless inherent vice is specifically excluded from coverage.

- **Ordinary leakage**—Also known as "ordinary loss in weight and volume" and "ordinary wear and tear," ordinary leakage is also much less of a concern for air shipments, as transit times are shorter.

- **Unairworthy aircraft**—This exclusion is not a problem for goods shipped by air; governments oversee the specifications and maintenance requirements of aircraft much more than they do for ships. The absence of "flags of convenience" in air travel is also a positive factor.

- **Nuclear war**—This is a traditional exclusion.

In addition, policies will also exclude war coverage and S.R. & C.C. coverage, like an ocean cargo policy, as well as two risks inherent to air travel: damage caused by cold and changes in atmospheric pressure. These risks can be covered, however, by purchasing additional coverage.

Practically speaking, most air-cargo policies are included as a clause in the open-cargo policy of a firm, which allows the firm to manage its shipping risks with a single document, whether its goods are moving by ocean or by air.

10.6   Filing an Insurance Claim

Unfortunately, any company that engages in international business faces the prospect of cargo loss or damage, and with that occurrence follows the need to file an insurance claim. Proper handling of an insurance claim is paramount to ensuring that the company recovers its loss. There are several steps that must be taken by the insured, including notification of the carrier and the insurance company, protection of the goods from further damage, and the filing of a claim.

10.6.1   Notification

The first and most important step is to promptly notify both the carrier and the insurance company of the loss. The best practice is to notify the carrier or the carrier's agent and the insurance company immediately if the damage is visible at the time the goods are discharged—for instance, if the packaging shows signs of damage, the container seal shows signs of tampering, or the shipment shows some other outward sign of damage. If there is no apparent exterior damage, there are different requirements for the timely notification and eventual filing of a claim, depending on the mode of transportation. If the cargo was transported by ocean, the carrier should be notified within three days. For international air shipments, the carrier must be notified within seven days. For international and domestic land transportation, and for domestic shipments, the notification requirements vary and are outlined in the air waybill or the (intermodal) bill of lading; however, such a notification will likely be within seven days.

It is therefore critical to inspect cargo as quickly as possible after it has been received, even if it shows no sign of damage or pilferage, so that, should the cargo be damaged, a notification and eventual claim can be filed within the contractual time limits.

This notification must be made in writing; the notification should include a description of the damage and a record of the seal number and of its condition. The notification should be sent to the insurance company, to the insurance agent, and to all the carriers involved in the shipment, even if they are only agents of the main carrier; for example, the trucking company hired by the shipping line to make the final delivery should be notified. Notification should be made by certified mail, with return receipt requested, to provide evidence of a timely notification. Even in cases where the damage is apparent, it is not sufficient, although necessary, to make an annotation on the delivery receipt for the goods. In addition, the more precise the annotation on the delivery receipt, the greater the level of protection for the insured.

Once damage is discovered, the insured should hire a surveyor, an independent company that is not affiliated with the insurance company and that can evaluate and assess the damage to the cargo. The insured may use any surveyor that is approved by Lloyd's of London or the American Institute of Marine Underwriters. In most cases, the insurance company can recommend a surveyor. The surveyor is directly paid by the insurance company in most cases, although in some cases, the insured pays the surveyor and is then reimbursed by the insurance company. A surveyor may not be necessary if the damage is minor.

surveyor
An independent company that investigates damage to shipments on behalf of insurance companies.

10.6.2 Protection of the Damaged Cargo

Once an insured has identified that the cargo has been damaged, it has several responsibilities. As much as possible, the insured should stop unloading the goods from the container and leave the cargo as it was found; if that is not possible, an extensive number of photographs should be taken to document the problem. In all cases, the insured should segregate the damaged cargo from other cargo, appropriately mark the damaged cargo so that it is not inadvertently mixed with other shipments, and protect it so that there will be no further damage. There are several reasons for these recommendations.

The first reason, one of the important tenets of insurance, is that the insured must protect the property "as if it were not insured," as the insured has an "onus of good faith" and must protect the interests of the insurance company. For example, further damage, resulting from lack of care after the goods have been damaged, is not covered. If a shipment of cement arrives with several torn bags, the insured must make sure that the cement is protected from rain, even if the torn bags are no longer usable. The damage (tearing) to the cement bags that occurred during the voyage will be paid by the insurance company if it falls within the coverage of the policy, but the water damage after arrival will not be covered, because it was due to the negligence of the insured. In cases where the insured incurs additional costs to prevent further loss, the insurance company will cover such costs under the sue-and-labor clause of the ocean cargo policy.

The second reason is to ensure that the cause of the damage is correctly determined. Such procedures facilitate the work of the surveyor, who is responsible for inspecting the cargo and determining the party responsible for the damage. For example, the surveyor may want to determine the type of bracing that was used in the container. Because improper packing is the responsibility neither of the carrier nor of the insurance company, but of the exporter, the surveyor will want to see how the cargo was stowed in the container. If that evidence is no longer there, it affects the surveyor's ability to assess responsibility accurately. Finally, following these guidelines also allows the carrier(s) to inspect the goods and protect its interests.

10.6.3   Filing of a Claim

Properly filing a claim for recovery of losses has two fundamental requirements. The first requirement is the timeliness of filing the claim, and the second is submitting proper documentation for the claim. The logistics manager should review the insurance policy to ensure that all claim requirements are met.

As mentioned earlier, there are strict time limits for notifying carriers and insurance companies of a claim: three days for ocean cargo, seven days for international air transport, and at most seven days for other forms of transportation. The formal filing of the claim may take somewhat longer, so that the documents required to complete the claim can be collected. Filing of a claim should also be made by certified mail, with return receipt requested.

The claim must be in writing and follow a format that is acceptable to the insurance company. For example, claims filed electronically (by e-mail or Internet) may not be acceptable to some insurance companies and in some jurisdictions. The claim must contain information to identify the shipment, must assert liability against the carrier, and must be for a specific or determinable amount.

Filing an insurance claim also necessitates collecting and copying several documents, most of which should be submitted with the claim; however, the specific documents should be determined from the contractual language on the back of the bills of lading, on the insurance certificate, and in consultation with the insurance company. Generally speaking, the following documents should be included:

- Insurance policy or certificate of insurance

- All bills of lading from origin to final destination

- All invoices (from the exporter and from all carriers and service providers)

- Cargo surveyor's report

- Complete packing lists and manifests

- Seal numbers and reports

- All documents generated during the voyage of the cargo; depending on the type of shipment, the country of origin and the country of destination, and the mode of transportation, a shipment can generate a large number of possible reports, all of which should be included with the claim. Such reports include pre-shipment inspection reports, monitoring tapes and logs (especially for refrigerated cargo), delivery receipts, transportation interchange reports, equipment interchange reports, exception reports, dock receipts, warehouse and container freight station receipts, survey requests, loading surveys, mate's receipts, vessel stowage plan, ship's bridge log, deck reefer log, bilge and engineer's log, vessel hatch survey, discharge survey, and so on.

- Product destroyed or thrown away (such as perishable products) need a certificate of destruction filed with the claim.

- Cargo that can be salvaged at a cost should include salvage bids and receipts.

10.6.4 Carrier Liability Limits

A shipment that is not insured by a specific marine cargo insurance policy may still be covered by the carrier's insurance policy. However, carriers, as noted earlier in this chapter and explained in greater depth in Chapters 11 and 12, have limits on their liability. When a claim is filed against marine cargo insurance, it becomes the responsibility of the insurance company to pursue its own claim against the carrier.

Thus, the controlling law noted in the bill of lading must be reviewed. Usually it is the Carriage of Goods by Sea Act—COGSA—or the so-called Hague, Hague-Visby, Hamburg, or Rotterdam Rules for ocean shipments, and the Warsaw Convention (Montreal Protocol) for international air shipments. However the bill of lading may cite different laws as applicable. Therefore, the contractual portion of the bill of lading should be reviewed for the stated damage limit and the controlling law; that contractual language is usually found on the back of the bill of lading. In the case of an intermodal shipment, because a through or combined bill of lading was issued, the company needs to determine which carrier is "principal" and which carrier is "agent."[77] When filing a claim for an intermodal shipment, the principal carrier should be notified; however, as noted earlier, notifying agent carriers at the same time is prudent.

Freight forwarders, Non-Vessel-Operating Common Carriers, and other third-party logistics providers (called 3PLs in the United States and the United Kingdom) frequently limit their liability, and also set their own statute of limitations on the claim submission. The 3PL may obtain insurance coverage only on specific instructions from the shipper. The 3PLs normally accept claims only for damages from their own actions, not those of carriers, even though the 3PL may have issued a combined or intermodal bill of lading. The 3PLs may be required by regulatory bodies to have a bond for insurance purposes, and there may be additional regulations regarding filing claim against the bond.[78]

Unfortunately, even though a claim may have been filed with all the proper documentation and in the correct time frame, there is no guarantee that the claim will be honored; there is also the possibility that the insurance company will only partially cover the loss. In those cases, it may be necessary for the shipper to file a lawsuit against the carrier; this action should be undertaken by an attorney who practices cargo law and, if appropriate, admiralty law and is licensed to practice in the court that has jurisdiction.

10.7   Lloyd's of London

Lloyd's of London is the oldest insurance market in the history of shipping, having started in Edward Lloyd's coffee house as early as 1688. Although Lloyd's of London is commonly perceived as an insurance company, that perception is incorrect. Since its humble beginnings in Lloyd's coffee shop, the company has acted as an intermediary between people who want insurance and those willing to provide it. Lloyd's does not provide insurance coverage; when one hears of an athlete whose legs are insured "by Lloyd's of London," it is an inaccurate statement: the athlete's legs are insured *through* Lloyd's.

10.7.1   Principles

Before explaining how the functioning of Lloyd's differs from the functioning of an insurance company, it seems relevant to explain how the latter works. An insurance company attempts to strike a balance between the collection of many premiums, each of a moderate monetary amount, and the payment of a few claims, each of a large monetary amount. The correct calculation of a premium relies upon the determination of the expected monetary value of claims (their probability multiplied by their expected costs) divided by the number of policyholders. Over time, the law of (arithmetic) averages allows an insurance company to be profitable. To determine the probability of a loss, insurance companies rely on actuarial tables of statistical data collected over a significant period.

In contrast, Lloyd's of London acts as a market through which unusual risks are insured; unusual risks are those that a traditional insurance company would not consider covering because there is no way to collect many premiums, and therefore the law of averages does not apply. For example, consider a firm that wants to insure the launching of its communication satellite. Although there may be as many as 90 satellite launches[79] worldwide every year, the number of companies launching a satellite—the possible number of premiums to collect—is too small to spread the high expected monetary value of a single loss. Therefore, the insurance company would be faced with a series of years in which it would collect premiums without a loss, and then have one or two losses in a single year, which would have a substantial adverse effect on income.

Lloyd's of London is the place where companies and people wanting to have such risks insured find a group of "members" willing to assume (insure) this risk. These members are either individual persons, who are called "Bespoke Names" in Lloyd's vernacular, or corporations, which are called "corporate members." All members are organized in a syndicate. Each member wagers that the loss will not happen, and collects a portion of the premium that the member shares with the remainder of the syndicate. This share of the premium is therefore income to the member. Should a loss occur, the member is then asked to pay its share of the loss, along with every other member in the syndicate. This payment comes out of the member's income or assets. The members, organized in a syndicate, are the underwriters of the insurance.

Historically, all members of Lloyd's were Names, and very wealthy individuals; this is still the case for the few Names that are left in Lloyd's syndicates. For Names, participation in a syndicate is not truly an investment, because the Name only collects premiums (additional income) while a portion of his or her assets can continue to be invested in other vehicles on which he or she collects market rates. However, because each Name has unlimited liability on his or her personal assets, this can also be an extremely risky venture. Because of this risk, each Name must have substantial personal assets to be allowed to participate in a syndicate. Names cannot ever "retire" from Lloyd's; they can stop underwriting new risks, but they must remain in the syndicate until all of their liabilities have been settled.

In 1994, Lloyd's began allowing corporate members. These members were given the advantage of having limited liability, and joined syndicates in which individual Names retained unlimited liability. This decision, which allowed the syndicates to have more capitalization, also created some friction, as individual Names resented the creation of two classes of members and responsibilities. In 1997, Lloyd's added the possibility of becoming an individual Name with limited liability. Today, most of Lloyd's underwriting capability is provided by corporations and limited-liability individual Names. In 2012, individual unlimited-liability Names had dropped to 3 percent of the underwriting capability of Lloyd's, with the remainder made up of corporate and limited-liability members.[80]

Over the years, insurance coverage provided through Lloyd's has increased to include more traditional risks, such as automobile and home insurance. However, most of the Lloyd's syndicates cover risks that a traditional insurance company will not consider. As of 2015, there were 84 underwriting syndicates.[81]

Some of the risks that Lloyd's syndicates covered in the last few decades included the risk of asbestos product liability. Such was the extent of the liability, though, that many Names were brought to personal bankruptcy, despite efforts by Lloyd's to spread the risk to more syndicates than had originally been involved. The number of Names soared from 14,000 in 1978 to 34,000 by the end of the 1980s. Some of the Names who joined in the 1980s claim to not have been informed of the extent of the liabilities that Lloyd's syndicates faced, and filed lawsuits alleging fraud.[82] In November 2000, Lloyd's was found not guilty of fraud by the British courts, but the language used by the judge in the decision was quite strong, calling Lloyd's "grossly negligent."[83]

10.7.2   Lloyd's in International Logistics

From the perspective of an exporter or importer, the Lloyd's market should only be used for "project cargo," or cargo of exceptional dimensions that does not fit in a traditional container and needs special arrangements with the shipping line. An example of such extraordinary project cargo is a firm shipping several large pieces of equipment to a customer or a subsidiary overseas. Because such cargo may not be insurable by a traditional insurance company, it could be insured through one of Lloyd's syndicates.

Lloyd's is also used extensively by carriers to insure their transportation assets, such as ships, aircrafts, and pipelines.

10.8   Commercial Credit Insurance

Another area where a firm involved in international matters can transfer some of its risks is in commercial credit.

Increasingly, competitive pressures are pushing firms to sell on an open-account basis, as customers try to acquire the best possible payment alternatives. Several countries used to offer subsidized terms on export insurance to their exporters and, although these practices have officially ended with the creation of the World Trade Organization (WTO), which prohibits export subsidies, the mindset was established. In France, for example, more than 25 percent of all new export sales—sales made to a new customer—are insured by the Compagnie Française d'Assurance pour le Commerce Extérieur (COFACE), which insures about €20 billion.[84]

A firm may have to cover several types of transactions with which it feels uncomfortable:

- A sale to a foreign customer on an open-account basis, where the firm is concerned about its exposure, or the amount of money at stake in the sale.

- A sale to a foreign customer on credit terms. The customer has requested that payments be extended over a period of several months. The terms are also open account because the seller's competitors have offered this alternative to the customer. The exporter is concerned about its exposure to this stream of payment.

- A construction firm retained by a foreign customer to build a plant; however, to earn the contract, the firm must post several performance bank guarantees (or performance bonds). The firm is concerned about its exposure in the case of unexpected delays, such as if the customer calls on the bank guarantee. For more information on bank guarantees, refer to Chapter 7.

10.8.1 Risks Involved

In each of these transactions, there are two components to the risk of non-payment:

- **Political risk**—This is the risk presented by the country in which the transaction takes place. Political risk can take many forms. The country's government can decide to increase tariffs on certain imports while the customer refuses delivery; the country's government can decide to freeze accounts held in foreign currencies, and therefore the customer cannot pay; the country's government can decide to prohibit the international purchase of a particular product; the country's government can commit a diplomatic *faux pas* and an embargo is declared by the remainder of the world, which means that no payments can be forwarded by the customer; and so on.

- **Commercial risk**—This is the risk presented by the customer defaulting on its obligation to pay, for whatever reason. Generally, the customer encounters financial difficulties or the customer has a complaint about the product that it cannot resolve any other way—in its management's mind, at least—than by withholding payment.

10.8.2 Risk Management Alternatives

As in the case of international cargo insurance, a firm exposed to these risks has three alternatives available to manage them: it can retain the risks, it can transfer the risks to an insurance company, or it can follow a mixed strategy of retaining some of the risks and transferring others. There are many different reasons for choosing one strategy or another, most of which were covered in Section 10.4.

10.8.3 Insurance Policies Available

Should a company decide to cover its receivable risks with insurance, there are many alternatives, which can be obtained from several insurance companies and governmental or quasi-governmental agencies. Most of these sources have multiple programs, presenting a dizzying array of possible contracts. Most companies interested in commercial-credit insurance policies should contact an insurance agency specializing in these types of policies, as well as contact their banks or governmental export support agencies in their country for further and more specific information.

A quick summary of the programs available in the United States gives an example of what is possible.

Government Programs

There are three government-related organizations in the United States that provide exporters with commercial and political insurance coverage:

- **The Ex-Im Bank**—The Export-Import (Ex-Im) Bank was created as an independent government agency in 1934. Its mission is to help create jobs in the United States by supporting export sales. The Ex-Im Bank has several programs, from political and commercial credit insurance to loan guarantees (for banks lending money to exporters) and loans extended to foreign purchasers of American products. For years, the Ex-Im Bank was the only provider of political risk insurance in the United States. There are two difficulties in dealing with the Ex-Im Bank. The first is the lengthy delays that usually accompany an application—which means that an exporter involved in a negotiation with a foreign customer should attempt to secure coverage very early. The second is that the Ex-Im Bank is an arm of the U.S. government and therefore subject to political pressures, such as abrupt cancellation of coverage for certain countries of the world, or abrupt cancellation of the Ex-Im Bank's very existence, as was threatened in 2015.[85] In addition, the product sold abroad must have at least 50 percent American content. Nevertheless, the Ex-Im Bank provides programs that are extremely popular with exporters and their bankers, such as the Ex-Im Bank Guarantee, which covers loan repayments by foreign purchasers. The Ex-Im Bank's complete program descriptions are available at its website.[86]

- **OPIC**—The Overseas Private Investment Corporation (OPIC) is also a U.S. governmental agency, created in 1971 with the purpose of encouraging private investments in developing countries. Its purpose is quite political, as it seeks to further U.S. values overseas, but it offers several programs of loans, political insurance, and private equity investment funds, all advantageous for corporations interested in investing in developing countries. As of May 2017, there were more than 131 countries eligible for its programs, details of which can be found at the OPIC's website.[87] Unfortunately, OPIC presents the same challenge as the Ex-Im Bank—long processing times—but because the products it offers cover long-term investments owned by U.S. firms, these delays are less critical.

- **SBA**—The Small Business Administration (SBA) has created two programs designed to help exporters finance their sales abroad: working capital loans and long-term loans for capital investments. However, the SBA does not provide any insurance for exporters.

All of these programs, even if not used, present substantial value to an exporter. For example, the Ex-Im Bank has established exposure fees for medium-term and long-term loans. Its cost of guarantees and insurance vary according to, among other factors, the political and commercial risks of non-repayment in a given country and for a particular creditor. The Ex-Im Bank assigns exposure fee levels and transaction risk increments to transactions based on this risk, and calculates them relying upon:[88]

- credit ratings and market spreads,

- credit agency and bank references,

- historical financial statements, and

- the Ex-Im Bank's credit experience with the borrower/guarantor and its industry.

Because banks involved in foreign trade often use a process similar to the Ex-Im Bank's process as their model for establishing transaction risk, this process is also useful to an exporter to assess quickly a risk with which it may be unfamiliar.

Private Insurance Companies

In the United States, there has recently been a substantial increase in the number of programs offered by private insurance companies, but international credit insurance is still a business restricted to a few players, because the practice of insuring a company's foreign receivables is not as well established as it is in many European countries. In the United States, there are few insurance agencies specializing in this field, with approximately 20 of them underwriting most of the business.

The insurance companies that dominate the market are:

- **FCIA**—The Foreign Credit Insurance Association (FCIA) was created in 1961, primarily to offer products that combined the Ex-Im Bank's political insurance coverage and commercial credit insurance products. Today, many of the Ex-Im Bank products that contain credit insurance are using the FCIA for that portion of the coverage. The FCIA, though, is not a government agency but is owned by Great American Insurance Company, a conglomerate of insurance companies. The FCIA products are mostly commercial credit insurance products, ranging from short-term to medium-term coverage for receivables. More information on the company's products can be found on its website.[89]

- **Euler-ACI**—American Credit Indemnity (ACI) is the other large player in the field, offering a similar array of commercial credit insurance products. ACI was purchased by the Allianz Group, a German insurance conglomerate. More information on ACI's products can be found on its website.[90]

- **Lloyd's**—Certain Lloyd's syndicates have added political-risk coverage to their underwriting portfolio and present the advantage of offering insurance for countries for which the U.S. government will not provide any, such as Afghanistan, Albania, and Belarus. Although the U.S. government allows trade with any of these countries, it will not provide political insurance coverage; however, a Lloyd's syndicate will, exemplifying the commitment that the Lloyd's market makes to non-traditional risks.

Review and Discussion Questions

1. Describe some of the risks that an ocean shipment faces.

2. Describe some of the risks that an air shipment faces.

3. Explain the concept of general average, and explain, with a numerical example, how it is utilized.

4. Explain the concept of "insurable interest." Identify who has an insurable interest in three different transactions conducted under three different Incoterms® rules.

5. What risk-management strategies can an exporter/importer follow? Explain each strategy's advantages and disadvantages from the perspective of a small exporter.

6. What insurance coverage is required under CIF or CIP Incoterms® rules? Explain which risks are not covered, and how an importer can still protect itself against them.

7. Choose three possible marine insurance clauses and describe their usefulness.

8. Explain the concept of international credit insurance and explain how it is possible to contract a policy covering commercial and political risks.

Notes

[1] Newell, Ben R., David A. Lagnado, and David R. Shanks, *Straight Choices*, Second Edition, Psychology Press, Taylor and Francis Group, New York, New York, 2015.

[2] "Cargo Theft" https://ucr.fbi.gov/crime-in-the-u.s/2015/crime-in-the-u.s.-2015/additional-reports-/cargo-theft/cargotheft-report_-2015-_final, retrieved March 4, 2017.

[3] "Highway Robbery: Cargo Theft Statistics and Prevention," https://haulhound.com/cargo-theft-statistics/, retrieved March 8, 2017.

[4] McAvoy, Kaitlyn, "Report: Companies Lose Billions Each Year to Cargo Theft," *Spend Matters*, March 31, 2016, http://spendmatters.com/2016/03/31/report-companies-lose-billions-each-year-to-cargo-thieves, retrieved March 4, 2017.

[5] Higgins, Andrew, "Brazen Jewel Robbery at Brussels Airport Nets $50 Million in Diamonds," *The New York Times*, February 19, 2013.

[6] Gooch, Liz, "For Companies, Risk of Cargo Theft in Asia," *The New York Times*, June 22, 2011.

[7] http://www.iumi.com/, requires a login, retrieved March 9, 2017.

[8] Graham, Philip, "Casualty and World Fleet Statistics as of 01.01.2016," International Union of Marine Insurance, http://www.iumi.com/index.cfm?rub=782, accessed March 9, 2017.

[9] Baldwin, Tom, "It's Time to Inspect the Containers . . . (Don't Attempt This One at Home, Folks)," *Journal of Commerce*, November 13, 1997, p. 2B.

[10] Donelan, Mark A. and Anne Karin Magnusson, "The Making of the Andrea Wave and Other Rogues," *Scientific Reports*, March 8, 2017, http://www.nature.com/articles/srep44124, retrieved March 12, 2017.

[11] Baldwin, Tom, "Container Industry Braces for Lawsuits," *Journal of Commerce*, November 12, 1998, p. 1A.

[12] Ford, Peter, "Drifting Rubber Duckies Chart Oceans of Plastic," *The Christian Science Monitor*, July 31, 2003, p.1.

[13] Ebbesmeyer, Curtis, and Eric Scigliano, *Flotsametrics and the Floating World*, 2009, Smithonian Publishing, Washington, D.C.

[14] Holtz, Robert Lee, "The Sober Science of Migrating Rubber Duckies," *The Wall Street Journal*, November 14, 2008, p. A13.

[15] Journal of Commerce Staff, "Complexity, Speed of Modern Ships Increases Risks," *The Journal of Commerce*, November 19, 1999, p. 9.

[16] Schuler, Mike, "Incident Photo of The Week Ű M/V Hyundai Fortune," *G-Captain*, September 12, 2008, http://gcaptain.com/incident-photo-of-the-week-mv-hyundai-fortune/, retrieved March 10, 2017.

[17] Wankhede, Anish, "Details on the Container Ship *MSC Flaminia* Accident, *Marine Insight*, May 6, 2016, http://www.marineinsight.com/case-studies/details-on-the-container-ship-msc-flaminia-accident/, retrieved March 10, 2017.

[18] Graham, Philip, "Casualty and World Fleet Statistics as of 01.01.2016," International Union of Marine Insurance, http://www.iumi.com/index.cfm?rub=782, accessed March 9, 2017.

[19] Marine Accident Investigation Branch, "Report on the investigation into the listing, flooding and grounding of *Hoegh Osaka*," Serious Marine Casualty Report No. 6/2016, March 2016, https://assets.-publishing.service.gov.uk/media/56e9a7afe5274a14d9000000/MAIBInvReport6_2016.pdf, retrieved March 10, 2017.

[20] Baldwin, Tom, "The Case of the Reappearing Rock, and Other Unchartered Navigational Hazards," *Journal of Commerce*, April 30, 1998, p. 2B.

[21] Associated Press, "Cruise Ship Hits Caribbean Reef," December 15, 1998.

[22] Pianigiani, Gaia, "Manslaughter Trial Is Set for Captain of Liner That Capsized Off Italy, Killing 32," *The New York Times*, May 22, 2013.

[23] "Scavengers Take Washed-up Goods," BBC News, January 22, 2007, http://news.bbc.co.uk/2/hi/-uk_news/england/devon/6287457.stm.

[24] "L'impressionnant naufrage du cargo Luno à Anglet," *Mer et Marine*, February 6, 2014, http://-www.meretmarine.com/fr/content/limpressionnant-naufrage-du-cargo-luno-anglet, retrieved March 10, 2017.

[25] Hastings, Warren, *Marine Insurance Compendium*, 1999, General Management Services, Inc., Publisher, 76 Mamaroneck Avenue, Suite 6, White Plains, NY 10601, USA.

[26] *Piracy and Armed Robbery Against Ships: 2016 Annual Report*, ICC International Maritime Bureau, http://www.icc-ccs.org, accessed March 10, 2017.

[27] *Ibid.*

[28] Langewiesche, William, *The Outlaw Sea: A World of Freedom, Chaos and Crime*, New York: North Point Press, 2004.

[29] Burnett, John, *Dangerous Waters: Modern Piracy and Terror on the High Seas*, New York: Penguin Books, 2002.

[30] Cummins, Chip, "Piracy Grips Gulf of Aden," *The Wall Street Journal*, September 8, 2008, A10.

[31] Cummins, Chip, "Oil Tanker Waylaid by Pirates," *The Wall Street Journal*, November 18, 2008, A1.

[32] Gettleman, Jeffrey, and Mohammed Ibrahim, "Somali Pirates Get Ransom and Leave Arms Freighter," *The New York Times*, February 6, 2009.

[33] Cummins, Chip, "Oil Tanker Waylaid By Pirates," *The Wall Street Journal*, November 18, 2008, A1.

[34] McFadden, Robert, and Scott Shane, "In Rescue of Captain, Navy Kills Three Pirates," *The New York Times*, April 13, 2009.

[35] Cowley, Elizabeth, "Tankers Rerouted Away from Pirates," *The Wall Street Journal*, November 11, 2008, B2.

[36] "UK Liner Damaged in Collision," BBC News, August 24, 1999, http://news.bbc.co.uk/2/hi/uk_-news/428545.stm.

[37] "Gas Roman Collision," *Fortunes de Mer*, February 27, 2003, http://www.fortunes-de-mer.com/ru-briques/liens et contacts/detailsactualites/GasRoman2003ru.htm.

[38] Hancock, Paul, "Collision Off Gibraltar," *Shipwreck Log*, May 30, 2014, https://www.shipwrecklog.-com/log/tag/cape-med/, retrieved March 11, 2017.

[39] "Iceberg Table," National Ice Center, http://www.natice.noaa.gov/MainProducts, accessed March 11, 2017.

[40] Associated Press, "Skyway Disaster Lives Remembered," May 8, 2000.

[41] "Casualties," *Cargo Business News*, May 2013, pp.32-33.

[42] Motley, Robert, "Shippers' Case Law," *American Shipper*, February 1999, p. 36.

[43] Motley, Robert, "Shippers' Case Law," *American Shipper*, March 2000, p. 46.

[44] Motley, Robert, "Shippers' Case Law," *American Shipper*, June 1998, p. 40.

[45] Urbina, Ian, "Stowaways and Crimes Aboard a Scofflaw Ship," *the New York Times*, July 17, 2015.

[46] *Ibid.*

[47] Associated Press, "Yugoslav Ship May Be Set Free," *Journal of Commerce*, March 31, 1997, p. 4B.

[48] "Victory and tickets home for *Malaviya* crew," http://www.itfglobal.org/en/news-events/press-releases/2017/february/victory-and-tickets-home-for-malaviya-crew/, retrieved March 11, 2017.

[49] *World Port Source*, http://www.worldportsource.com, retrieved March 11, 2017.

[50] Théobald, Marie, "Pourquoi les Français sont les champions de la grève," *Le Figaro*, July 26, 2016, p. 11.

[51] Crabtree, Thomas, Thomas Hoang, Russell Tom, and Gregg Gildeman, *The World Air Cargo Forecast 2016-2017*, Boeing Corporation, http://www.boeing.com/commercial/market/cargo-forecast/, accessed March 11, 2017.

[52] Vaughan, Emmett J., and Therese M. Vaughan, *Fundamentals of Risk and Insurance*, 11th ed. New York: John Wiley and Sons, 2013.

[53] *Marine Insurance: Notes and Comments on Ocean Cargo Insurance*, undated, Cigna Property and Casualty Specialty Insurance, P.O. Box 7716, Philadelphia, Pennsylvania 19192, USA.

[54] Vaughan, Emmett J., and Therese M. Vaughan, *Fundamentals of Risk and Insurance*, 11th ed. New York: John Wiley and Sons, 2013.

[55] Banham, Russ, "They've Got Them Covered," *The Journal of Commerce*, February 23, 1998, p. 6A.

[56] *Marine Insurance: Notes and Comments on Ocean Cargo Insurance*, undated, Cigna Property and Casualty Specialty Insurance, P.O. Box 7716, Philadelphia, Pennsylvania 19192, USA.

[57] *Ibid.*

[58] *Ocean Cargo Handbook*, undated, Chubb Group of Insurance Companies, Warren, New Jersey 07059, USA.

[59] Cornah, R.R., "A Comparison of the 1982 and 2009 Clauses with additional commentary," undated, Richards-Hogg-Lindley, www.rhlg.com, retrieved May 5, 2013.

[60] "Institute Marine Cargo Clauses (A)," *Marine Cargo Insurance Policies*, www.ms-ins.com/pdf/cargo/MARINECARGOINSURANCECLAUSES.pdf, retrieved June 23, 2013.

[61] "Institute Marine Cargo Clauses (B)," *Marine Cargo Insurance Policies*, www.ms-ins.com/pdf/cargo/MARINECARGOINSURANCECLAUSES.pdf, retrieved June 23, 2013.

[62] "Institute Marine Cargo Clauses (C)," *Marine Cargo Insurance Policies*, www.ms-ins.com/pdf/cargo/MARINECARGOINSURANCECLAUSES.pdf, retrieved June 23, 2013.

[63] Ramberg, Jan, *ICC Guide to Incoterms 2010*, 2011, International Chamber of Commerce Publication No. 720E, ICC Publishing S.A., 38 Cours Albert 1er, 75008 Paris, France and ICC Publishing, Inc., 156 Fifth Avenue, Suite 417, New York, NY 10010, USA.

[64] Bogart, Susan, "Loss to Cargo," *Marine Insurance and General Average*, Maritime Law Association of the United States, January 1, 2001, http://www.mlaus.org/article.ihtml?id=558&committee=160.

[65] *Marine Insurance: Notes and Comments on Ocean Cargo Insurance*, undated, Cigna Property and Casualty Specialty Insurance, P.O. Box 7716, Philadelphia, Pennsylvania 19192, USA.

[66] Ramberg, Jan, *ICC Guide to Incoterms 2010*, 2011, International Chamber of Commerce Publication No. 720E, ICC Publishing S.A., 38 Cours Albert 1er, 75008 Paris, France and ICC Publishing, Inc., 156 Fifth Avenue, Suite 417, New York, NY 10010, USA.

[67] *Marine Insurance: Notes and Comments on Ocean Cargo Insurance*, undated, Cigna Property and Casualty Specialty Insurance, P.O. Box 7716, Philadelphia, Pennsylvania 19192, USA.

[68] Blustein, Paul, and Brian Byrnes, "Lemons Caught in Homeland Security Squeeze," *Washington Post*, September 10, 2004.

[69] Ramirez, Anthony, "Sour Surprise for Officers who Raided Container Ship," *The New York Times*, August 7, 2004.

[70] Jones, Eric, *International Economic Effects of Halting the Voyage of the* CSAV Rio Puelo, Master of Business Administration Thesis, 2005, Massachusetts Institute of Technology, http://dspace.mit.edu/bitstream/handle/1721.1/32115/63201956.pdf, accessed June 22, 2009.

[71] *Ocean Cargo Handbook*, undated, Chubb Group of Insurance Companies, Warren, New Jersey 07059, USA.

[72] Smil, Vaclav, *Prime Movers of Civilization, The History and Impact of Diesel Engines and Gas Turbines*, The MIT Press, 2010, Cambridge, Massachusetts.

[73] "Ship, Ownership, Builder & Company Information," IHS Fairplay, http://www.ihs.com/products/-maritime-information/ships/index.aspx, retrieved June 22, 2013.

[74] "Directive 2009/20/EC of the European Parliament and of the Council of 23 April 2009, on the Insurance of Shipowners for Maritime Claims," *Official Journal of the European Union*, May 28, 2009, pp. 128-131.

[75] "UK P&I Circular Reference 04/09," Thomas Miller, Ltd., February 2009, http://www.ukpandi.com/-ukpandi/infopool.nsf/HTML/ClubCircular0409.

[76] "CLC & Fund Convention," The International Tanker Owners Pollution Federation Limited, http://-www.itopf.com/spill-compensation/clc-fund-convention/, retrieved June 22, 2013.

[77] Faber, Diana, et al., *Multimodal Transport: Avoiding Legal Problems.* London: LLP, 1997.

[78] *Subchapter B—Regulations Affecting Ocean Shipping in Foreign Commerce Part 515—Licensing, Financial Responsibility Requirements, and General Duties for Ocean Transportation Intermediaries*, U.S. Federal Maritime Commission, http://www.fmc.gov/home/515Licensingandsuretyrequirements-foroceantransportationintermediaries.asp, retrieved April 30, 2006.

[79] Clark, Stephen, "2014's launch tally highest in two decades," *Spaceflight Now*, January 4, 2015, https://spaceflightnow.com/2015/01/04/2014s-launch-tally-highest-in-two-decades/, retrieved March 12, 2017.

[80] *2015 Lloyd's Annual Report*, Lloyd's of London, http://www.lloyds.com/annualreport2015/assets/-pdf/lloyds_annual_report_2015.pdf, retrieved March 11, 2017.

[81] *Ibid.*

[82] McClintick, David, "The Decline and Fall of Lloyd's of London," *Time*, European Edition, February 21, 2000.

[83] Redman, Christopher, "For Whom the Bell Tolls," *Time*, European Edition, November 13, 2000, p. 42.

[84] COFACE, *2015 Activity Report*, www.coface.fr/content/download/139307/2181492/file/COFACE-RGP2015-EN.pdf, retrieved March 12, 2017.

[85] Calmes, Jackie, "Ex-Im Bank is Re-Opened, but Big Loans are Stalled," *the New York Times*, December 8, 2015, p. B1.

[86] http://www.exim.gov.

[87] http://www.opic.gov/what-we-offer/where-we-work.

[88] "Exposure Fees," Export-Import Bank of the United States, http://www.exim.gov/tools/exposure-fees/, accessed March 12, 2017.

[89] http://www.fcia.com.

[90] http://www.eulerhermes.com.

Chapter 11

International Ocean Transportation

To manage international logistics, it is fundamental to have a good understanding of the transportation alternatives open to an international shipper. The next three chapters provide an overview of the many options given to an exporter or an importer interested in making transportation arrangements for an international shipment.

The first chapter (Chapter 11) deals with the alternatives available in ocean transportation, and the complexities of the international framework of rules that enable shipping lines to operate. The second chapter (Chapter 12) deals with air transportation and its rules and regulations. The third chapter (Chapter 13) deals with land transportation—rail and road—but also covers multimodal transportation, which is not really a mode of transportation, but a shipping alternative that simplifies the work of the shipper—exporter or importer—by allowing it to send freight with only one carrier (shipping company). Chapter 13 also covers pipelines, which transport a limited range of products, and several other less-frequently used modes of transportation, mostly used in limited domestic markets.

The ocean shipping industry plays a key role in fulfilling world trade. There are more than 50,000 merchant ships operating in the world, registered to more than 150 nations, and operated by more than 1.5 million seafarers of virtually every nationality. Merchant ship operations generate an estimated annual revenue of over U.S.$ 380 billion in freight within the global economy, and transport over 10.1 billion tons of cargo.[1,2] Primarily because it transports all heavy cargoes, the ocean shipping industry is responsible for the carriage of 90 percent of the world's trade when measured by weight. Modern ships are technically sophisticated, high-value assets: large ships have capital costs in excess of U.S.$ 100 million, and the latest very large containerships purchased by several containership lines have estimated building costs of U.S.$ 150 million.[3]

11.1   Types of Service

The first differentiation among ocean vessels is between liner ships and tramp ships.

liner ship
A ship that operates on a regular schedule, traveling from one group of ports to another group of ports.

Liner ships travel on a regular voyage, following a pre-established schedule, and with determined ports of call. A scheduled voyage may include only two ports (Santos, Brazil, to Miami, USA, and back) or, more commonly, a series of ports in one region of the world (e.g., Bremerhaven, Germany; Rotterdam, Netherlands; Felixstowe, Great Britain) to another (e.g., Boston, USA; Baltimore, USA; Nassau, Bahamas). Quite a few liners follow round-the-world (RTW) schedules, either eastbound or westbound, passing through the Panama Canal and/or the Suez Canal. There are many types of liner ships, a large number of which are adapted to specific routes—the ships' size and equipment depend on the ports of call they visit and on the specific types of cargo that their trade route entails. Liners are common carriers as they offer their services to any shipper that pays the freight rate.

Unlike liners, tramp ships operate wherever and whenever the market dictates. Tramp ships do not operate on a regular schedule but travel wherever the company that has contracted (chartered) the vessel wants the cargo delivered. Because of the way tramp ships operate, they usually carry only one type of cargo at a time, for one exporter or importer. Most tramp ships, therefore, are designed for one type of cargo exclusively, even if they carry several dry cargoes or several grades of petroleum products.

tramp ship
A ship that does not operate on a regular schedule and is available for charter for any voyage, from any port to any port.

A possible analogy is that a tramp vessel is a taxicab, whereas a liner ship is a public bus.

11.2   Size of Vessels

The second principal differentiation among ocean vessels is their size. Vessel size dictates trade routes, economies of scale, and ports of call. Ships are often categorized by their size, which is expressed in "tons." Unfortunately, there are several types of tons and several ways of evaluating the tonnage of a vessel, and the tonnage of a vessel can be used for very different purposes, a situation that can lead to some confusion.

Under the English system of measurements, tons are generally used as units of weight and may be "short," or equal to 2,000 pounds (907 kilograms), or "long," equal to 2,240 pounds (1,016 kilograms). However, tons can also be units of volume, equal to 100 cubic feet (2.83 cubic meters), and vessel size can be expressed in those units. Under the metric system, a tonne is only a measure of mass (weight), equal to 1,000 kilograms (2,204.6 pounds).

11.2.1   Deadweight Tonnage and Cubic Capacity

The deadweight tonnage (dwt) is the total weight capacity of the ship (*i.e.*, the maximum cargo weight that a vessel can carry) expressed in long tons (2,240 pounds) or in metric tonnes (2204.6 pounds). Deadweight tonnage is the measurement used by companies interested in shipping cargo and is often just called "tonnage." It is measured using the weight of the difference in water displacement when the ship is empty and when it is fully loaded to its maximum. The deadweight tonnage of a ship includes the fuel that the ship needs to travel—called bunker—and the supplies that the ship needs to function—called stores—and any ballast that the vessel may carry. Therefore, the deadweight tonnage is the theoretical capacity of the ship more than its actual capacity.

deadweight tonnage
The maximum weight that a ship can carry.

bunker
The fuel that a ship carries onboard and that it needs to operate.

stores
All the supplies that a ship needs to carry in order to operate.

grain
An agricultural commodity, such as wheat, corn or sugar, that is loaded directly onboard, without packaging, like a liquid.

bale
The package bundle created by compressing cotton or wool when these commodities are tightly wrapped and bound with string or metal bands.

Vessels also have volumetric capacity for cargo that is called grain or bale cubic capacity. The grain cubic capacity is the cargo space available for loading a flowing cargo such as grain. The bale cubic capacity represents the total volume of space available for loading solid cargoes such as bales or boxes. The grain cubic capacity is always the larger of these two capacity measures. A vessel, when loaded with a very dense material—such as iron ore—can utilize its weight capacity before it reaches its cubic (volume) capacity; conversely, it can reach its volume capacity before it reaches its weight capacity if it is loaded with a light but voluminous cargo, such as timber or corn. A vessel that uses all its cubic capacity and is also loaded down to its maximum draft is said to be "full and down."

11.2.2   Gross and Net Tonnage

gross tonnage
The volume capacity of a ship, expressed in hundreds of cubic feet.

deck
A permanent cover over the ship's hull.

The gross tonnage is the total volume capacity of the ship, expressed in tons, which are equal to hundreds of cubic feet (2.83 cubic meters). The gross tonnage measures only the capacity of the ship below its deck, so this measurement is not appropriate for determining the cargo-carrying capacity of a ship, because many vessels also carry cargo above deck, particularly containerships.

Dimensions of a 35,000-DWT Vessel

Measurements	Metric	U.S.
Length overall (LOA)	186.31 meters	611 feet, 3 inches
Beam (width)	28.40 meters	93 feet, 2 inches
Summer draft (amount of water needed to float)	10.73 meters	35 feet, 2.5 inches
Freeboard (distance between the water line and deck)	4.59 meters	15 feet, 0.75 inches
Winter draft (47/48 of the Summer draft)	10.50 meters	34 feet, 5.75 inches
Freshwater draft	10.96 meters	35 feet, 11.5 inches
Net tonnage (NT)	55,222 cubic meters	19,513 tons
Gross tonnage (GT)	69,007 cubic meters	24,384 tons
Suez gross registered tonnage (GRT)	69,607 cubic meters	24,596 tons
Displacement	44,828 tonnes	44,122 long tons
Light ship displacement	7,768 tonnes	7,646 long tons
Deadweight tonnage (dwt) at summer loadline	37,059 tonnes	36,476 long tons
Bunker (varies with voyage length)	610 tonnes	600 long tons
Potable drinking water (varies with voyage length)	244 tonnes	240 long tons
Constant (allowance for crew and consumable stores)	152 tonnes	150 long tons
Ballast (carried for trim if needed)	102 tonnes	100 long tons
Cargo deadweight (deadweight available for cargo)	35,952 tonnes	35,386 long tons

Table 11.1: Relationships Between the Measurements of a Vessel
Richard Stewart, PhD.

gross registered tonnage[GRT]
The volume capacity of a ship, calculated in a way that meets the requirements of a specific authority, such as the Suez Canal or the Panama Canal Authorities.

The gross-tonnage measurement is used to determine how much a ship owner pays in taxes to the country in which the ship is registered, or tolls to the authorities of the ports it visits or the canals it uses; gross tonnage is also used for regulatory purposes. In that case, gross tonnage is called gross registered tonnage (GRT), which considers the specific way a canal authority (such as Suez or Panama) determines gross tonnage. Once the volume occupied by the engine room, the crew, and other space necessary for the ship's operation is removed, the net tonnage is obtained. Net tonnage is further complicated by the fact that canal authorities calculate net tonnage differently; a ship has a Panama Canal/Universal Measurement System (PC/UMS) net tonnage and a Suez Canal Net Tonnage (SCNT).

Gross tonnage is commonly used when assessing the size of fleets for statistical purposes. Because different organizations set the cutoff for ship size at different gross tonnage levels (for example, in increments of 300 or 1,000 gross tons), this difference in baseline often is the principal cause of fleet size discrepancy between reports.

net tonnage
The volume capacity of a ship, after subtracting the space used for the operation of the ship.

11.2.3   Displacement

The displacement tonnage is the total weight of the ship, when fully loaded, measured by the weight of the volume of water it displaces. The light tonnage is the weight of the ship, measured the same way, but when the vessel is empty, which means that light tonnage is the displacement of the vessel after it was built, but before any ballast, cargo, fuel, or supplies were put aboard. Both displacement and light tonnage are generally measured in long tons and are used for naval architecture purposes to determine the vessel's stability, the stress it endures, and other engineering issues.

The relationship between the different vessel tonnages can be expressed mathematically, and Table 11.1 on the preceding page shows the different measurements of an actual 35,000-dwt (deadweight tonnage) Handysize bulk vessel ready for a 3,500-nautical-mile voyage (6,500 kilometers).

displacement tonnage
The total weight of a fully loaded ship, measured by the weight of the water displaced.

light tonnage
The total weight of an empty ship, measured by the weight of the water displaced.

11.2.4   Plimsoll Mark and Load Lines

One more difficulty arises when one understands that ships are considered fully loaded at different drafts (how deep they sit in the water) due to the season in which they are operating, the latitudes under which they ply their trade, and the density of the water. The deepest salt-water draft a ship can have is called the "tropical line" (T), followed by the "summer line" (S), the "winter line" (W), and the "winter North Atlantic line" (WNA). A "freshwater" line (F) is also present, as well as a "tropical freshwater" line (TF) as freshwater density is lower—a ship sits lower in freshwater than it does in saltwater with the same quantity of cargo. Those load lines are permanently marked on the side of a ship with weld lines and painted with a contrasting color. At the same height as the vessel's summer deadweight draft, there is another diagram called the Plimsoll mark: a circle bisected by a horizontal line, which identifies the classification society that determined the vessel's load lines. Figure 11.1 on the following page shows the Plimsoll mark and load lines for a ship classified by the Bureau Veritas, a Belgian Classification Society.

The deadweight tonnage is generally determined at the summer line or at the line that represents accurately the conditions under which a ship is used. For example, a vessel used consistently in the Caribbean has its deadweight tonnage calculated with the tropical load line. The load lines correspond to geographical regions of the globe, and a vessel must be at the appropriate load line when it

load lines
Marks on the side of the ship that indicate how low a ship can be in the water, depending on the season and conditions.

Plimsoll mark
A mark on the side of the ship that indicates the classification society that inspects the ship.

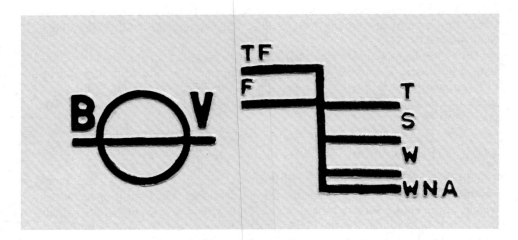

Figure 11.1: Plimsoll Mark and Load Lines on the Side of a Ship

Photo ©J. Quendag/Shutterstock. Used with permission.

arrives in the geographical region. For instance, a vessel that loads in Matadi, Congo, in January and sails for Antwerp will load to the tropical load line (T) but must consume enough fuel to be at the winter North Atlantic load line (WNA) when the vessel arrives in that geographical region. A vessel that exceeds appropriate load lines is subject to heavy fines and may also be considered unseaworthy, a serious issue since insurance companies always deny coverage of cargo loaded on an unseaworthy vessel.

11.2.5   Size Categories

One of the biggest distinctions made in ships' sizes is based on the locks of the Panama Canal, both its original 1914 locks and its new 2016 locks.

Panamax ship
A ship of the maximum size that can enter the original locks of the Panama Canal.

Ships that can travel through the original locks of the Panama Canal are called Panamax ships; such ships can have up to 75,000 long tons of deadweight tonnage, and their outside dimensions allow them to fit within the locks with only a few inches of clearance between the locks' walls and the ship (see Figure 11.2). The locks are 304 meters long (1,000 feet), 33 meters wide (110 feet), and 12.05 meters deep (39.5 feet). The longest ship to cross the Panama Canal is the *Marcona Prospector*, which is 296 meters long (973 feet) and 32 meters wide (106 feet), and the widest is the *USS New Jersey*, which is 32.4 meters wide (106 feet).[4]

neo-Panamax ship
A ship of the maximum size that can enter the new locks of the Panama Canal.

Ships that can travel through the new locks are called Neo-Panamax—or New Panamax—ships. The new locks are 427 meters long (1,400 feet), 55 meters wide (180 feet), and 18.3 meters (60 feet) in depth, and the maximum ships' dimensions are 366 meters (1,200 feet) in length, 49 meters (160.7 feet) in width, and 15.2 meters (49.9 feet) in draft.[5] The dimensions of the Neo-Panamax ships are much smaller than the dimensions of the new locks, because the Panama Canal

Figure 11.2: A Panamax Ship in the Old Panama Locks (13 Containers Abreast)
Photo ©Elena Fernandez Z/Shutterstock. Used with permission.

now uses a system of tugboats to guide the ships through the locks, and room is needed for them to maneuver the ships (see Figure 11.3). The old locks used locomotives—called "mules"—that pulled the ships through the locks (see Figure 11.2).

All ships that are larger than the Neo-Panamax size are called post-Panamax ships. Many of the new very large containerships and crude carriers are too large to fit in either set of Panama Canal locks.

post-Panamax ship
A ship whose size is too large to enter the locks of the Panama Canal.

Other terminologies used are:

- **Handysize ship**—A term commonly used in the dry-bulk trade that refers to ships in the 10,000 to 50,000 deadweight ton range. Such ships tend to be used for tramp service.

- **Suez-Max ships**—This term describes ships sized at roughly 150,000 deadweight tons and which are of the maximum size that can fit through the Suez Canal (about 285 meters long, 35 meters wide, and 23 meters of draft; that is 935 feet long, 115 feet wide, and 75 feet of draft). In 1996, the Suez Canal was deepened and widened, so the Suez-Max terminology is losing some of its validity.

- **Capesize ships**—This term describes large dry-bulk carriers with a capacity greater than 80,000 deadweight tons that cannot transit through the Suez

Figure 11.3: A Ship in the New Panama Canal Locks, with Tugs
Photo ©Adam D. Bowser. Used with permission.

Canal and must pass by the Cape of Good Hope in South Africa.

- **Very large crude carrier (VLCC)**—This term describes an oil tanker of up to 300,000 deadweight tonnage, which is about 350 meters long and 55 meters wide and has 28 meters of draft (see Figure 11.4). These dimensions correspond to 1,150 feet long, 180 feet wide, and 92 feet of draft.

- **Ultra-large crude carrier (ULCC)**—This term describes an oil tanker of more than 300,000 deadweight tonnage. The largest ULCC ever built, the *Knock Nevis*—formerly called the *Seawise Giant* and the *Jahre Viking*—had a deadweight tonnage of 565,000 tonnes, was 458 meters long and 69 meters wide and had a draft of 26.4 meters.[6] Its deck surface was 2.5 hectares. These dimensions translate to 556,000 long tons, 1,527 feet long, 230 feet wide, a draft of 88 feet, and an area of 6.25 acres. The current (2017) largest ULCC, the 441,585-dwt *Hellespont Alhambra* is much smaller: 380 meters long, 68 meters wide, and a draft of 24.5 meters. Such ships generally are unable to go into traditional ports, and they remain in deep sea at all times. Their cargo is removed using a process called lightering, which consists of transferring the cargo onto smaller ships (see Section 11.3.5 on page 397), or using offshore oil terminals.

For comparison purposes, the largest containership in use as of 2017, the MSC *Oscar*, is a much smaller vessel, even though it is gigantic. This ship is 395

Figure 11.4: A Very Large Crude Carrier in the Port of Amsterdam
Photo ©Kevin Nieuwland/Shutterstock. Used with permission.

meters long and 59 meters wide and has a draft of 16 meters (1,296 feet long, 194 feet wide, and a draft of 53 feet). Its deadweight tonnage is 202,470 tonnes (199,273 long tons) and it can carry 19,250 twenty-foot equivalent units (TEUs) (*i.e.*, 20-foot containers).[7] The largest cruise ship in the world, the *Allure of the Seas* is 362 meters long (1,187 feet), 60.5 meters wide (198 feet), and draws 9.3 meters (31 feet). Its displacement is 19,750 tonnes (19,430 long tons).[8]

TEU
Twenty-foot Equivalent Unit. The equivalent of a twenty-foot container. A forty-foot container is two TEUs.

11.3 Types of Vessels

The third principal differentiation among sea-going vessels is made on the type of cargo they carry, which is used to classify merchant ships into many different categories (see Figure 11.5 on the following page).[9] First, a distinction is made between cargo ships that carry wet-bulk (liquid) cargoes and those vessels that carry dry-bulk cargoes. Second, dry cargoes can either be shipped in bulk (where the cargo is loaded as a liquid would be, directly in the hold of a ship) or unitized (shipped in units that are unloaded one at a time, such as boxes, crates, or containers).

hold
In a ship, a portion of the inside volume designed to hold cargo.

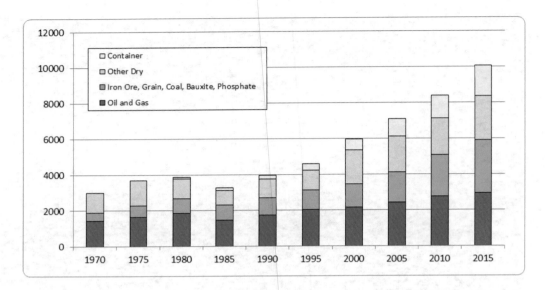

Figure 11.5: Ocean Worldwide Trade by Cargo Type (in millions of tons)
Review of Maritime Transport 2016.

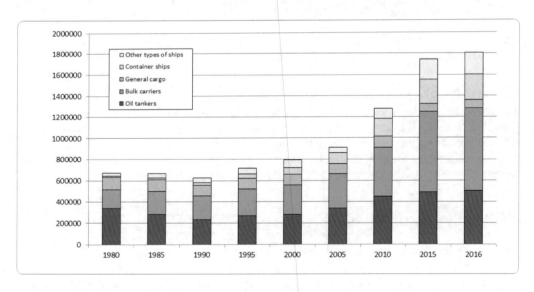

Figure 11.6: Worldwide Vessel Capacity by Cargo Type (in millions of DWTs)
Review of Maritime Transport 2016.

There are more than 50,000 commercial vessels worldwide with an individual capacity greater than 500 gross tonnes. The total cargo carrying capacity of the world's commercial fleet exceeded 1.8 billion deadweight tons in 2016 (see Figure 11.6).[10] Almost every single one of these ships is designed differently. It is therefore difficult to classify them much better than in broad-based groups, with many ships not fitting neatly into one category.

11.3.1 Containerships

The containerized trade is growing rapidly. Approximately 60 percent of world trade (in value) is containerized, and container transportation volume has been growing by 4.7 percent per year since 1996 (see Figure 11.7) based on the number of twenty-foot-equivalent units transported. Even in trade lanes where containers are already solidly implanted, such as Asia-North America or Europe-North America, there is no sign that the growth in the volume of container shipments is slowing. Given the fact that goods that traditionally traveled in bulk are now shipped using containers—for example, forestry products and grain—and given the fact that intermodal transportation is responding well to customer needs, it seems that the container, which was created in 1956, will keep dominating international trade.

Containerships, also known as "box ships," carry containerized cargo on a scheduled voyage. Vessels dedicated to the container trade can carry up to 19,000 TEUs—20-foot equivalent units, or the space equivalent of a 20-foot container—,but there are many mixed-cargo ships that can also carry containers, sometimes

containership
A ship designed to exclusively carry containers, both below its deck and above it. A containership's size is expressed in TEUs.

box ship
Another, more casual, name for containerships.

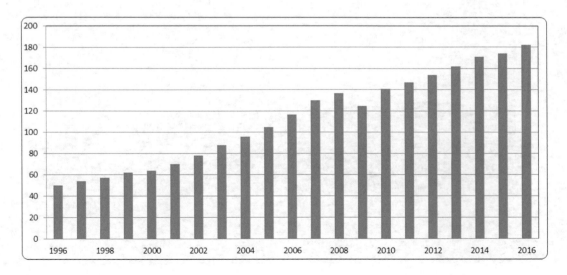

Figure 11.7: Growth in Worldwide Containerized Cargo (in millions of TEUs)
Review of Maritime Transport 2016.

as few as 100 TEUs. Most containerships rely upon the port cranes to unload their cargo, but some containerships do have cranes on board. All containerships used to be capable of going through the Panama Canal and carried around 4,500 TEUs. When the first large containerships were delivered, they carried more than 6,000 TEUs and forced substantial changes in ports. For example, the large container-ships were so wide and high (see Figure 11.8) that some ports had to upgrade their crane equipment. Some ports became entirely inaccessible; for example, some of these ships cannot enter some of the ports on the East Coast of the United States, because their air drafts do not allow them to fit under the bridges that span the port access channels, or their water drafts do not allow them to enter the ports, since they are not deep enough (for example, Port Elizabeth of the Port of New York-New Jersey). The Panama Canal Authority invested \$ 5.5 billion to accommodate these larger ships, but the size of these ships has grown yet further, and many do not fit in the newly built locks.[11]

As larger ships come into service, there will be additional demands made on port infrastructure, and it will reduce the number of ports in which these giant ships can berth to a handful worldwide. The trend in the industry is therefore the creation of a system of large hubs, to and from which the mega-containerships can travel, coupled with many smaller ships, called feeder ships, which would travel between these giant hub ports and smaller ports. Those feeder ships would essentially be the existing fleet of traditional containerships. Although a hub system would cause trans-shipments to occur, it is estimated that it would lower

Figure 11.8: A Post-Panamax Ship: 16,000 TEUs, 22 Containers Abreast
Photo ©Wims-eye-d/Shutterstock. Used with permission.

Figure 11.9: Container Loaded between Slides Below Deck and Containers Held with Metal Bars and Twistlocks Above Deck

Photo ©Prasit Rodphan/Shutterstock. Used with permission.

transportation costs.

Traditional containerships hold containers under deck as well as on deck. Some containers are first loaded in the holds of the ship, then the hatch covers (the deck) are put in place, and the remainder of the containers are placed on top of them. Containers placed under deck are usually held in place by vertical guides, along which the crane operator slides them. On-deck containers are usually stacked on top of each other and latched to each other with metal bars and twistlocks (see Figure 11.9).

Since the early 1990s, several shipping lines have tried to speed up the process of loading containers by equipping their ships with vertical guides for on-deck containers, and some have eliminated the deck hatches altogether, simply choosing to equip the vessel with much larger bilge pumps (the pumps that remove the water from the inside of a ship). Eventually, it is conceivable that the concept of "deck" will no longer exist in the container trade.

11.3.2 Roll-On/Roll-Off Ships

Roll-on/roll-off (RORO) ships were created to accommodate cargo that was self-propelled, such as automobiles or trucks, or cargo that could be wheeled into a ship, such as railroad cars or excavation equipment. RORO ships are essentially

RORO
Roll-On/Roll-Off. A type of ship in which cargo is rolled on board rather than carried by crane.

floating parking garages (see Figure 11.10).

The concept of RORO ships is straightforward. Because it takes a long time to load vehicles over the rail of a ship by using a crane, it is preferable to load them by rolling them onto the ship. RORO ships therefore have a portion of their hulls that opens and acts as a ramp on which the vehicles are driven before being parked on the many decks of the ship and secured with chains. The hull opening is either on the side of the ship or on its stern (rear).

RORO ships have an advantage in that specialized lifting equipment is not required in the port, even for the heaviest of loads, because the cargo rolls under its own power or is pulled by a tractor. A RORO ship therefore needs only some docking space and a substantial number of dock workers to load or unload its cargo. There are distinctions between a pure car-carrier (PCC) ship, which loads only cars and has decks with only 5 feet (1.5 meters) of overhead clearance, and other, more versatile, so-called "true" RORO ships that can accommodate larger cargo. Many RORO ships are equipped with adjustable decks, which allow them to transport any sort of rolling cargo.

Figure 11.10: A Roll-On/Roll-Off Ship Unloading Vehicles
Photo ©James R. Martin/Shutterstock. Used with permission.

As the number of cars manufactured worldwide increases, the future of the RORO concept seems secure. However, several companies now sell specialized equipment that can be used in traditional 40-foot containers to handle six automobiles (on two levels) at once, with equipment that can be collapsed and placed into another container for the return trip. This concept is attractive, as it overcomes some of the drawbacks of RORO ships. First, there is no need to hire expensive stevedore labor to drive the vehicles onto the ship—stevedores are replaced with cheaper inland labor to load and unload the containers—and it makes the loading and unloading faster, as it requires only one cargo movement for every six vehicles. This alternative also eliminates the cost of modifying the configuration of the decks so that regular bulk cargo can be loaded in the now-empty RORO ship on the return trip. The latter issue is significant for trades with countries that import many vehicles but export far fewer, such as the United States.

The concept of RORO has been expanded to another variation, designed for the transport of livestock, which are led aboard the ship rather than hoisted over its rail. Therefore, the ships are given the moniker of trot-on/trot-off (TOTO) ships. Such ships are used mainly to transport sheep between Australia or New Zealand and the Middle East. Some are also used to transport cattle between Argentina or Brazil and the Middle East. The TOTO ships also return empty to their ports of origin.

Trot-On/Trot-Off
A type of ship designed to carry livestock. Animals use a ramp to walk on board and exit the ship.

11.3.3 Breakbulk or General-Merchandise Ships

Breakbulk ships (also called general-merchandise ships) constitute the least homogeneous category of vessels. There are all sorts of breakbulk ships, which are often created for a specialized trade or a specific shipping lane. Altogether, though, breakbulk cargo ships are multipurpose ships that can transport shipments of unusual sizes, unitized on pallets, in bags, or in crates (see Figure 11.11). Because of the increase in the percentage of international cargo shipments that are containerized, including the containerization of some goods that are larger than what can normally fit in a regular container, and because of the increasing role of RORO ships, breakbulk ships' share of international trade is decreasing but they are still the single largest fleet in number of ships.

breakbulk
A type of cargo that is unitized—boxes, crates, or bales—and placed directly in the holds of a ship.

breakbulk ship
A type of ship designed to carry breakbulk cargo.

general-merchandise ship
Another name for a breakbulk ship.

The main problem with general-merchandise ships stems from their labor-intensive loading and unloading; each unitized piece must be handled separately, with several stevedores in the hull of the ship and several stevedores on the quay, in addition to the crane operators. Because the cargo is of different sizes, each piece may require different equipment (a different number of hooks, shorter or longer slings, and so on) and in some cases demand "problem solving," which may involve a few attempts before the cargo is successfully loaded or unloaded. In addition, securing the loads on the decks is just as labor intensive, because pieces of cargo have odd sizes. Consequently, breakbulk ships stay in port much longer, especially because they frequently do not load or unload in the rain, and their schedules can be erratic.

stevedore
A person who loads and unloads goods from a vessel in a port.

Since a large percentage of breakbulk ships are equipped with an onboard crane, which allows them to load and unload without relying on port equipment, they can call at nearly any port to load different kinds of cargo, giving them a flexibility that containerships do not have. Although decreasing in percentage, the breakbulk trade has a significant future in that it will always carry odd-sized shipments and always carry heavy cargoes that cannot be containerized. Nev-

Figure 11.11: A Breakbulk Ship with Cargo in the Lower Hold, a Tweendeck for Lighter Cargo, and an Upper Removable Deck

Photo ©Wathit Kettap/Shutterstock. Used with permission.

ertheless, it is likely that there will be fewer general-merchandise ships in the future—very few breakbulk ships have been built in the last 15 years—although it is likely that there will be a corresponding increase in the number of combination ships, which will carry breakbulk cargo, but also some bulk, some RORO cargo, and a few containers.

11.3.4 Combination Ships

combination ship
A type of ship that is versatile and can carry different types of cargo.

tweendeck
A deck located below the main deck and used to carry smaller cargo.

The ultimate multipurpose ships are combination ships, which are designed to carry all sorts of different loads in a single voyage. A typical combination ship has several holds in which bulk cargo, such as timber or grain, can be placed. Those holds can also be used for breakbulk cargo, especially oversized and heavy cargo, such as machinery and sometimes containers. Combination ships also have a tweendeck, or a deck below the main deck, which accommodates smaller breakbulk cargo as well as vehicles that are loaded through the RORO access door. On its main deck, the typical combination ship can carry several containers (see Figure 11.12).

Figure 11.12: A Combination Ship with RORO Cargo on Deck and Breakbulk Cargo Below Deck

Photo ©Vytautas Kielaitis/Shutterstock. Used with permission.

Finally, a combination ship can have one or more onboard cranes, to increase its versatility and allow it to unload its cargo in any port. Because of their versatility, combination ships thrive in shipping lanes that have a low volume of trade, such as the trade between developed countries and developing countries, or the trade to and from small island nations, such as those in the South Pacific or the Caribbean.

11.3.5   Product, Chemical, and Crude Carriers

Petroleum products transported in bulk by ships are broken down into three principal trades: product, chemical, and crude.

product carrier
A liquid-bulk ship that carries refined oil products.

Product vessels transport refined products such as gasoline, diesel oil, or other refined products. These refined products need to be carefully segregated and kept from contamination. Product vessels range in size from small coastal vessels (about 1,000 dwt) to large product carriers, roughly 60,000 dwt in size. The vessels may carry up to six different products if the vessel's tank and piping system allow segregation.

chemical carrier
A liquid-bulk ship that carries liquid chemicals.

Chemical carriers are specially designed ships in the 1,000 to 40,000 dwt range that carry chemicals (see Figure 11.13). Some chemical carriers may transport as many as 40 different chemicals and are referred to as "drugstore" ships. The hazardous nature of some chemicals, such as benzene, and the handling requirements of other chemicals that require special tanks, dedicated piping systems, and complex safeguards limit these vessels to the chemical trade.

Figure 11.13: A Chemical Carrier with its Network of Tanks and Pipes
Photo ©Joerns/Shutterstock. Used with permission.

crude carrier
A liquid-bulk ship that carries unrefined oil.

Crude carriers are bulk ships dedicated to the transport of unrefined (crude) oil. The largest ships in the world are crude carriers; there is a distinction made between Panamax crude carriers of up to 80,000 dwt, AfraMax tankers with a capacity between 80 and 120,000 dwt, named after the Average Freight Rate Assessment system; very large crude carriers (VLCC), of up to 300,000 dwt; and ultra-large crude carriers (ULCC) beyond this tonnage.

After many oil spills, including the infamous Exxon *Valdez* into Alaskan waters in March 1989, all VLCCs and ULCCs are now equipped with double hulls, which makes them less likely to spill their cargoes if they accidentally run aground. The additional hull (and the space between the hull of the ship and the part of the ship that contains the petroleum oil) provides some protection in the case of groundings, but the design reduces the vessels' carrying capacity by as much as 15 percent and adds to the cost of construction and maintenance.

Masters Unlimited

Maneuvering an ultra-large crude carrier is a job that few people can handle, but it is the daily responsibility of captains who have reached the prestigious title of "Master Unlimited." There are about 3,000 of these captains worldwide and they are the only ones accredited to command ships of more than 5,000 tons GRT.[12] Handling such large ships can be a hair-raising experience. Consider that a ULCC can be as long as four football fields and that, at cruising speed and fully loaded, it stops in a mere six miles if its engine is stopped. If put in full reverse, the distance "shrinks" to two miles. In that case, the ship takes a mere 30 minutes to come to a full stop.[13]

To learn how to pilot these behemoths, captains either practice on computer simulations or travel to the unusual training camp of Port Revel in the foothills of the Alps in France, where they are placed in models of large ships. A similar model training program is operated by the Massachusetts Maritime Academy in Buzzards Bay, Massachusetts. Like their real-life equivalent, these model ships are extremely underpowered, at least relatively speaking. A ship of this size is "like a large lorry [truck] with a moped engine and no brakes," says an instructor at Port Revel, noting that the 40-foot-long model *Europe* weighs 41,000 pounds and has a motor of less than one horsepower.[14] Real-life ULCCs weigh 600,000 tonnes and have engines of 30,000 kW—40,000 HP—which is a higher weight-power ratio than the models.[15]

After a few days on the pond at Port Revel, these gifted sailors are capable of maneuvering these ships so well that they can squeeze a 700-foot behemoth into the 750-foot space left between two other ships in port without the help of a tug. In other words, simple parallel parking.

VLCCs and ULCCs are such large ships (see Figure 11.14) that they can call on only a few ports in the world; because their draft, when loaded, can reach 25 meters (85 feet), they need very deep ports and, because they are so long and wide, a very large docking area. In many cases, the VLCCs and ULCCs do not enter a port but anchor outside of the port in deep waters. The oil cargo of the large crude carrier is then transferred into smaller crude carriers that transport and unload it into the port. This process is called lightering and is also occasionally used for traditional breakbulk or dry-bulk ships. On other occasions, the VLCCs and ULCCs are connected to an artificial island, or a "floating island," which is a pipeline terminal in deep waters. Some countries have transformed natural islands into deep-water oil terminals for such ships, such as in the case of the Mina-al-Bakr oil terminal in Iraq.

Figure 11.14: A Very Large Crude Carrier Unloading in the Port of Hong Kong
Photo ©Lee Yiu Tung/Shutterstock. Used with permission.

11.3.6 Dry-Bulk Carriers

dry-bulk carrier
A dry-bulk ship that carries grain, ores, dry chemicals, or minerals directly in its holds.

Dry-bulk carriers operate like oil tankers in that they are chartered for a whole voyage. Dry-bulk ships (see Figure 13.12) have several holds in their hull, in which non-unitized cargo is loaded through hatches (openings on deck). There are many types of dry-bulk ships, and because of the trade in which they are engaged—the type of merchandise that they carry and the ports on which they call—dry-bulk ships can have specialized configurations or equipment. Generally speaking, dry-bulk ships carry agricultural products, such as cereals, as well as coal, ores, scrap iron, dry chemicals, and other commodities that behave as liquids, since they take the shape of the hold of the ship. Some of those ships, because of the versatility of the cargoes that they can carry, are called oil-bulk-ore (O-B-O) carriers, as they can transport oil during one leg of the voyage and then on the next leg, after cleaning the tanks/holds, carry dry-bulk products.

Dry-bulk ships are generally classified into three types: Capesize, which are ships that are too large to fit through the Suez Canal and must go around the Cape of Good Hope on the southern tip of Africa; Panamax ships, which are small enough to fit through the Panama Canal; and Handysize bulkers, which are from 10,000 to 45,000 deadweight tons. Many of these Handysize tramp bulkers are somewhat older vessels.

A good portion of the world commodities trade transits through a myriad of these Handysize vessels, carrying cargoes of sugar, rice, and other staples from small ports to other small ports. Dry-bulk ships are chartered primarily through

Figure 11.15: A Bulk Carrier in the Port of IJmuiden, the Netherlands
Photo ©Aerovista Luchtfotografie/Shutterstock. Used with permission.

the Baltic Exchange, which is a meeting place for brokers representing the ship owners and the cargo owners to meet and conduct business. The business is initially done verbally, and the word of the brokers is their bond.[16]

As seen in Chapter 9, three types of charters are typically used for bulk vessels. A voyage charter hires the ship with all functions provided by the ship owner, such as crew, management, and fuel, to deliver cargo to one or more ports in the world. A time charter is a vessel hired to deliver cargo with the ship owner providing all services over a fixed period, which may vary from a few months to several years. A bareboat or demise charter is a vessel hired and run by another party. in a bareboat charter, the ship owner provides a vessel that is bare of crew and supplies. The vessel charterer then operates the vessel in all respects and returns the bareboat to the ship owner after the end of the demise charter, which can last months or years. Both dry and wet trade vessels are chartered.

There is a specific group of dry-bulk carriers that serve the Great Lakes ports between the United States and Canada, called lakers (see Figure 11.16). Their characteristics are determined by the size of the canal locks of the Welland Canal, which gives them long and narrow hulls. They are often characterized by a peculiar design; their bridge—the location of the command center of the ship—is in

Baltic Exchange
The world market for maritime cargo transport services, located in London, where ship owners and cargo owners negotiate the cost of moving cargo.

laker
A dry-bulk ship designed to operate on the Great Lakes between the United States and Canada.

the fore of the vessel (see Figure 11.16).

Lakers trade mostly in three commodities: iron ore and iron ore pellets, coal, and finished steel. Lakers are not ocean-going vessels, but they fit the general description of dry-bulk carriers. These vessels have self-unloading gear that allows for the rapid (10,000 short tons per hour) unloading of bulk cargoes. The design of the self-unloading booms allows the vessels to place cargo up to 150 feet (45 meters) off the side of the vessel. Several self-unloading lakers are over 1,000 feet in length (304 meters) and can trade only in four of the five Great Lakes, as they cannot fit through the Welland Canal into Lake Ontario.

Figure 11.16: A Great Lakes Freighter—A Laker in the Welland Canal in St. Catharines, Canada

Photo ©Jon Nicholls/Shutterstock. Used with permission.

Although not the same as dry-bulk carriers, there are also several ships that carry specialized cargoes that can be considered dry-bulk carriers. Examples are refrigerated ships—also called "reefer" ships—which are slowly being replaced by refrigerated containers on containerships with the possible exception of specialized refrigerated ships called banana ships; liquid food carriers, which therefore carry liquid bulk cargoes such as molasses, orange juice, and vegetable oils; lumber carriers; and cement carriers.

The Baltic Exchange

Located in London, the Baltic Exchange was once where traders and ship owners would meet to arrange for the maritime transportation of commodities. The cargo owners and the ship owners negotiated the cost of moving bulk cargo from one port to another.

Today, the Baltic Exchange is the source of maritime market information. Its more than 550 members, representing the majority of the world's shipping companies, help determine the costs of shipping cargo through a series of indices, called the Baltic Exchange Indices, which are published daily. The indices reflect the average cost per day (expressed in U.S. dollars) for a shipper to have a carrier transport a certain commodity in a certain type of ship. The exchange calculates the indices by averaging the daily costs of shipping cargo on several routes.

The most frequently used indices are the Baltic Exchange Capesize Index (BCI), which is the average daily cost of utilizing a vessel capable of carrying 172,000 metric tonnes of cargo, calculated over ten routes; the Baltic Exchange Panamax Index (BPI), which is the daily cost of utilizing a Panamax ship capable of carrying 74,000 metric tonnes of cargo, averaged over four routes; the Baltic Exchange Supramax Index (BSI) for ships capable of carrying 52,454 metric tonnes averaged over six routes; and the Baltic Exchange Handysize Index (BHSI) for ships capable of carrying 28,000 metric tonnes calculated over six routes. These indices are then combined to form the Baltic Exchange Dry Index (BDI).[17]

For oil-related cargoes, the Baltic Exchange publishes the Baltic Exchange Dirty Tanker Index (BDTI), which reflects the costs of shipping unrefined petroleum oil, calculated on the average costs of 17 different routes, and the Baltic Exchange Clean Tanker Index (BCTI), which reflects the cost of shipping oil-based refined products, such as gasoline or naphtha, averaged over seven routes. Both of these indices are combined into the Baltic Exchange International Tanker Route Index (BITR). Finally, there is a Baltic Exchange Palm Oil Route Index (BPOIL) and a Baltic Exchange Liquefied Petroleum Gas Index (BLPG).

The Baltic Exchange Dry Bulk Index is a leading economic indicator. Since ships are hired only when there is cargo to be moved as a result of primary demand, the cost of shipping reflects the derived demand of transportation services. The worldwide demand for raw materials drove the Baltic Exchange Dry Index to reach a record high of 11,793 points on May 20, 2008. On December 5, 2008, less than six months later, the index had dropped by 94 percent, to 663 points, the lowest since 1986.[18] In mid-March 2017, the Baltic Exchange Dry Index had recovered and was at 1,100,[19] still below its long-term average of 1,700.

11.3.7 Gas Carriers

LNG-LPG carrier
A ship designed to
transport liquefied—
compressed—natural gas or
petroleum gas.

Another important bulk trade is the transportation of liquefied natural gas (LNG) and of liquefied petroleum gas (LPG). Gas carriers have a distinctive shape. These ships hold several spheres of compressed gasses, only part of which are visible above their main deck (see Figure 11.17).

The LNG and LPG trades tend to differ slightly from the average bulk transport, as gas carriers are used in a particular trade for long periods, on long-term contracts—called time charter parties (see Chapter 9)—and therefore nearly have a sailing schedule, not unlike liner ships. Gas carriers transport cargo on only half of their voyage and return empty.

Figure 11.17: A Liquefied Natural Gas Carrier with its Characteristic Spherical Tanks

Photo ©Anatoly Menzhiliy/Shutterstock. Used with permission.

The End of the [Shipping] Line

After a mere 20 to 25 years at sea, most ships are so damaged by the sea and the elements that they are no longer economically viable vessels (it costs too much to maintain them). In addition, shipping lines have a surplus of capacity that they are loathe to sell, as they do not want to encourage new competitors.[20]

Where do all of these old ships end their lives?

Many of them end up on the beaches of Pakistan, Bangladesh, or India, where they are dismantled, by hand, into sellable chunks of scrap steel and other metals. At the present time,

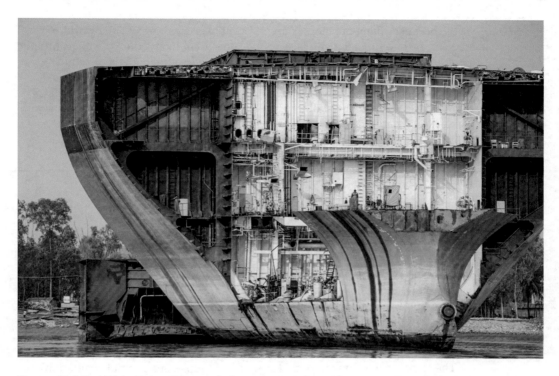

Figure 11.18: A Ship Being Dismantled on the Beach in Chittagong, Bangladesh
Photo ©Katiekk/Shutterstock. Used with permission.

more than three quarters of older ships end their lives in these three countries, and half of them die in Alang, a beach in the Indian state of Gujarat, where 600 or so scrap businesses dismantle 400 old ships and sell their components to scrap yards for recycling.[21] Dismantling ships is dangerous and poorly paid, but such jobs provide direct and indirect employment for thousands of workers.

Despite governmental protests about the impact of this business on India's image and its workers' health, more and more ships are dismantled in the Alang area and, as the world fleet ages and is replaced with more modern and technologically advanced ships, this trend shows no sign of abating. In 2012, the Alang area dismantled a record 365 European ships, and the European Union attempted to ban the practice, arguing that it released toxic materials directly into the environment, and that workers were exposed to dangerous conditions. However, it is also possible that the EU wanted to protect its shipping yards from this foreign competition.

The proposed ban was quickly abandoned, however, for economic and political reasons: ship owners can sell their old ships to the Alang dismantlers for a much higher price per ton than they can to other salvage yards, because Alang businesses are so efficient at recycling all a ship's components, including the dinnerware, tools, and life-jackets. In addition, ship dismantling businesses provide an estimated 1,000,000 low-skill jobs—directly and indirectly—in an impoverished area of the world.[22] More than likely, the EU will eventually achieve its stated goals of reducing pollution and increasing workers' safety by providing guidelines that ship owners will eventually impose on the Alang dismantlers.

11.4 Flag

flag
The flag of the country in which a ship is registered. By extension, the country in which the ship is registered.

By international convention, each vessel engaged in international trade must be registered in a specific country, and therefore fly a specific country's flag. In many ways, a vessel is an extension of a country's territory, and all the country's laws and regulations apply onboard the ship. In exchange, the naval forces of the flag of registry will protect flagged merchant ships in times of conflict. The vessel must pay the taxes that this country imposes. There is one significant *caveat* to this situation: with few exceptions, a ship owner can choose the country in which its ship is registered, or choose the flag that it flies.

The flags of developed countries tend to impose substantial regulations on the way a ship is operated, in such areas as the composition of the crew on board, its minimum training requirement, its nationality (because it is a country's extension of its territory, its immigration rules apply), the work rules on board (such as the number of hours worked per day and per week before overtime pay is earned), the vacation time earned by the crew, and so on. In addition, taxation can be significantly higher. In contrast, regulations and taxes for some developing countries are minimal. It is estimated that flying an American flag rather than a developing country's flag can multiply costs by a factor of 2.7—*i.e.* the operating costs of the U.S. ship are 2.7 times higher than the operating costs of a foreign-flagged vessel. A 2011 Maritime Administration study showed that the operating costs of a cargo ship flying the U.S. flag were U.S.$ 20,053 per day, whereas the same ship flying a developing country's flag were U.S.$ 7,454 per day. The crew sizes were similar (22.9 crew members for U.S.-flagged ships and 21.7 for foreign-flag ships), but the crew costs were considerably different. The U.S.-flagged ships had to pay $ 13,655 per day for labor but the foreign-flag ships only paid $ 2,590.[23]

open registry
A flag—country of registration—that is open to all ship owners, regardless of their nationality.

The National Defense Transportation Administration determined that the taxes that a U.S.-flagged ship is required to pay are approximately U.S.$ 700,000 per year. In contrast, the same vessel, operating under the flag of Panama is required to pay U.S.$ 10,497, and under the flag of the Isle of Man, only U.S.$ 680.[24]

To take advantage of their much lower costs, a few countries have created what is called an open registry, meaning that any ship owner can choose to have its vessel fly this country's flag. There are no requirements regarding the citizen-

Merchandise Fleet by Flag of Registry

Country	Number of Ships	Tonnage (000s dwt)
Panama	8,153	334,368
Liberia	3,185	206,351
Marshall Islands	2,942	200,069
Hong Kong	2,515	161,787
Singapore	3,605	127,193
Malta	2,101	94,992
Bahamas	1,450	79,541
China	4,052	75,850
Greece	1,386	73,568
Cyprus	1,053	33,313
Japan	5,320	31,869
Isle of Man	389	22,539
Norway	1,561	20,697
Indonesia	7,843	18,117
Denmark	671	17,185
Korea	1,906	16,820
Italy	1,376	16,470
India	1,625	16,338
United Kingdom	1,167	15,192
Tanzania	265	13,255
United States	3,570	11,841
Antigua & Barbuda	1,080	11,506
Germany	618	11,402
Bermuda	156	10,610
Malaysia	1,662	9,612

Table 11.2: Twenty Five Largest Merchandise Fleet by Flag of Registry
Review of Maritime Transport 2016.

ship of the ship's owners. Because these countries tend to have minimal onboard requirements and taxes, many ship owners decide to fly such countries' flags, which have been deridingly called "flags of convenience." Most of these open registries emanate from developing countries, but, recently, some developed countries established their own versions of open registries, which are called secondary registries, with much less stringent requirements than their normal registries to prevent their merchant fleets from being entirely registered under flags of convenience. Norway, Denmark, and France are three notorious examples.

Table 11.2[25] shows the 25 largest fleets in the world (by flag), and Table 11.3[26]

flag of convenience
A flag—country of registration—that is open to all ship owners, and imposes few requirements—regulations or taxes—on ship owners. A derogatory term.

Countries' Fleet by Flag of Registry

Country	Bahamas	Cyprus	Liberia	Malta	Marshall Islands	Panama	Other Registry	Own Registry
China	0.1%	0.1%	0.7%	0.4%	0.5%	11.7%	25.1%	61.4%
Denmark	3.0%	0.3%	0.2%	4.7%	2.5%	3.5%	49.4%	36.4%
Germany	0.5%	5.0%	30.1%	5.9%	6.1%	0.9%	44.4%	7.1%
Greece	5.3%	5.8%	19.3%	14.8%	18.8%	10.6%	7.8%	17.6%
Italy	1.5%	1.4%	2.4%	9.9%	0.6%	4.4%	8.1%	71.7%
Japan	2.6%	0.2%	3.5%	0.2%	3.2%	58.0%	11.3%	21.0%
Korea	0.1%	0.0%	0.1%	0.2%	11.8%	33.8%	5.3%	48.7%
Norway	10.4%	1.8%	2.0%	4.6%	6.9%	3.0%	47.9%	23.4%
United Kingdom	13.2%	2.5%	14.9%	8.2%	7.1%	5.9%	23.3%	24.9%
United States	6.4%	0.3%	4.3%	1.6%	15.9%	5.0%	66.4%	0.1%

Table 11.3: Percentage of a Country's Fleet by Flag of Registry
UNCTAD Stat, 2016.

shows the percentage of a country's fleet that is registered in a number of selected registries, mostly flags of convenience.

The choice of flag thus regulates the qualifications of the crew, its compensation, and the amount of taxes that the ship owners pay. The choice of flag does not influence the seaworthiness of the vessel, which is evaluated by classification societies and determines the insurance premiums (hull insurance and P&I insurance) that the vessel owners have to pay (see Chapter 10). A competent crew and a seaworthy vessel are guaranteed if the vessel is registered in a developed country, if it is operated by a reputable shipping company, or if it is classed with one of the major classification societies; however, problems are more likely to arise with vessels registered under a flag of convenience.

Countries attempt to influence, as much as possible, the flags of the ships that enter their ports. Although they cannot ban certain nationalities, they can prevent ships not registered in the country from carrying certain freight. For example, the Cargo Preference Act of the United States requires that at least 50 percent of U.S. government cargo be carried by U.S.-flagged ships. The Jones Act requires that cargo transported from one port in the United States to another port in the United States—a trade called cabotage—must be carried exclusively on U.S.-flagged ships. This is the case for cargo going from the West Coast to Hawaii, for example. Finally, all cargo in trades supported by the Ex-Im Bank must be shipped through U.S.-flagged ships. A study by the Maritime Administration of the United States found that over 50 maritime countries had some form of cabotage or flag protection laws of one form or another.[27]

Flying Flags

The choice of a flag has many consequences beyond the crew's training and the taxes that the ship owners must pay:

• Cabotage rules require that American flags and crews be used for ships traveling from one port in the United States to another port in the United States. Cruise ships, none of which flies the U.S. flag, therefore cannot travel between two U.S. ports. Cruise ships destined for Alaska leave from Vancouver, Canada, and cruise ships destined for Hawaii leave from Ensenada, Mexico.

• Many cruise ships fly flags of convenience, such as that of the Bahamas, or secondary registries, such as that of Norway. Because those registries do not exert much oversight over working conditions on their vessels, working cruise ship crews are generally employed for sub-standard wages and in frequently miserable conditions. Very low wages are common, and so are 12- to 15-hour days. However, U.S. court decisions have determined that because these cruise vessels are based in U.S. ports, select U.S. labor laws can apply.[28].

• When Hong Kong became part of the People's Republic of China (PRC) in July 1997, a flag issue surfaced. Because it is common practice to fly a host port's flag on a ship, it meant that the ships of the Taiwanese shipping company Evergreen would have had to fly the PRC's flag when they called on the port of Hong Kong, and that Hong Kong ships would have had to fly the Taiwanese flag when they were in Taipei. Neither alternative was welcome; the issue was finally resolved when both sides decided not to fly any flag in each other's ports.[29]

• During the conflict between Iran and Iraq in the Persian Gulf, several Kuwaiti ships were temporarily placed under the U.S. flag so that they could gain the protection of the U.S. Navy, a protection refused to U.S. owners of tankers flying flags of convenience. The U.S. Navy finally relented, and all crude carriers were temporarily re-flagged as American while they were in the Persian Gulf.[30]

• When more than a hundred merchant ships were attacked by pirates in the Gulf of Aden in 2008-2009, the U.S. Navy was empowered to intervene to protect only the *Maersk Alabama*, because it was the only ship that was flying the U.S. flag.[31] It was flying the U.S. flag because it was carrying a cargo of relief supplies for USAID, which mandates that its cargo be carried on U.S.-flagged ships.

The United States' situation is yet more complicated. Its government compensates the ship owners that elect to fly the stars-and-stripes flag to the tune of several million dollars per year per vessel,[32] but not just because it is more expensive to run a U.S.-flagged ship. The reason is purely military. Because of its geographical situation, the United States needs a lot of ship transport capacity to ship troops and military materials abroad in the case of a conflict, and the current program was developed in response to military sealift issues.[33] In the event of a conflict, the U.S. government can then requisition all merchant ships registered with the U.S. flag that are under the subsidy program. To ensure that it has some ships to requisition, the U.S. government subsidizes ship owners who choose this alternative, and provides them with preferential treatment when shipping cargoes abroad.

requisition
demand the use of an asset.

Freight Charges

Shipping lines charge for container shipping either by following published tariff rates or by negotiating contract rates with large volume shippers. All tariff rates can be negotiated, and shipping lines will negotiate rates for as few as 12 containers shipped at once. Rates are determined per package or by weight, including cargo shipped in containers on a less-than-container-load (LCL) basis. In addition to the freight rate, there are additional charges of which the international logistics professional must be aware:[34]

• **ARB**—Arbitrary charge. This charge is for added expenses, such as transshipment in an intermediary port, ice-breaking, cleaning returned containers that are not ready for the next cargo, electrical power to refrigerated containers, and monitoring refrigerated containers.

• **BAF or FAF**—Bunker adjustment factor. This charge is also called fuel adjustment factor or surcharge. This is an extra charge applied by shipping companies to reflect fluctuations in the cost of bunker fuel. This surcharge is expressed either as an amount per freight ton or as a percentage of the freight charge.

• **CAF**—Currency adjustment factor.

This is a surcharge applied to freight rates by shipping lines. It ensures that the revenue of the shipping lines is unaffected by movements in the currencies in which transactions are carried out by the lines in relation to the freight rate currency. CAF is normally expressed as a percentage of the freight and may be negative as well as positive.

• **CY/CY**—Container yard to container yard movement of cargo. This is a charge added to the freight rate to reflect the cost of moving cargo from one yard in the port to another yard, a function that is fulfilled by a cartage company.

• **CFS/CY**—Container freight stations to container yard movement of cargo. This is a charge added to the freight rate to reflect the cost of moving cargo from outside of the port to a yard inside the port, a function that is fulfilled by a cartage company.

• **Chassis charge**—This charge is imposed by container shipping lines for providing customers with a truck chassis at the harbor terminals. A chassis is a truck trailer on which the container is placed before it is loaded onto the ship or after it is unloaded from the ship.

• **THC**—Terminal handling charge,

also known as container yard charge. This charge is payable to a shipping line either for receiving a full container load at the container terminal, storing it, and delivering it to the ship at the load port or for receiving it from the ship at the discharge port, storing it, and delivering it to the consignee. Determining the correct charge for a container can be challenging and can amount to much more than the published or negotiated freight rate. Table 11.4 shows an example of the calculation of the cost of a full container shipment from Oakland, California, to Singapore. The container is filled with paper products.

Freight Charges Calculation

Base Container rate		U.S. $2,000
Additional charges:		
· CAF—Currency adjustment factor	5%	
· BAF—Bunker adjustment factor	15%	
· THC—Terminal handling charge	U.S.$ 125	
· ARB—Arbitrary charge: cleaning fee	U.S.$ 40	
Total additional charges:		
[container rate× (CAF+BAF)]+ THC+ARB=		
[$2,000× (0.05+0.15)] + $125 + $40 =		U.S.$ 565
Total Container Charges		**$2,565**

Table 11.4: Calculation of a Container's Freight Charges
NOTE: Container-based rates may at times be calculated by weight or by package, especially if the shipment is less-than-container load (LCL).

11.5   Liability Conventions

In 1924, the International Convention for the Unification of Certain Rules of Law Relating to Bills of Lading was adopted by 26 participating countries. This convention, known as the Hague Rules, limited the ship owner's liability toward the cargo owners to U.S.$ 500 per package or "customary freight unit," and it allowed ship owners to escape liability in 17 specified cases—called the 17 "defenses"—including the infamous nautical fault, or errors of the crew of a ship in its management or navigation; that is, the carrier was not liable if it got "lost." In 1936, the United States adopted the Hague Rules by incorporating them into the Carriage of Goods by Sea Act (COGSA).

Hague Rules
A 1924 international liability convention for ocean cargo that restricts the liability of the carrier to U.S.$ 500 per package or per customary freight unit.

The Hague Rules' U.S.$ 500 limit per package became a problem with the advent of containers, because shipping lines began claiming that containers were "customary freight units" and attempted to limit their liability to U.S.$ 500 per container. Surprisingly, some courts actually agreed with that interpretation, and essentially granted shipping lines immunity from liability.[35] Some countries therefore agreed to revise the Hague Rules in 1968 to clarify the definition of package to the units listed on the bill of lading. The countries also increased the carrier's liability to U.S.$ 666.67 or U.S.$ 2 per kilogram, whichever was higher. These revised rules are known as Hague-Visby Rules. The United States has not ratified this treaty, although it has been ratified by all of its major trading partners. In 1979, the Hague-Visby Rules were amended to reflect the declining value of the U.S. dollar, and the liability limits were expressed in Special Drawing Rights (SDRs), the artificial currency of the International Monetary Fund, and set at SDR 666.67 per package or SDR 2 per kilogram, whichever was higher.

Hague-Visby Rules
A 1968 international liability convention for ocean cargo that restricts the liability of the carrier to SDR 666.67 per package or per customary freight unit.

The advent of better navigational equipment and the annoyance of shippers at the continuous existence of the nautical-fault defense triggered yet another round of international negotiations led by the United Nations Commission on International Trade Law (UNCITRAL), which abolished the 17 defenses of the Hague and Hague-Visby Rules, and replaced them with only three: damage that the carrier took all reasonable steps to avoid, damage by fire, and damage due to an attempt by the carrier to save life or property at sea. These negotiations also increased liability limits to SDR 835 per package and SDR 2.5 per kilogram. These rules are known as the Hamburg Rules and have been ratified by only a few countries, only a handful of which are significant international traders. A complete list of which countries have adopted which rules is available on the internet.[36]

Hamburg Rules
A 1978 international liability convention for ocean cargo that restricts the liability of the carrier to U.S.$ 833 per package or per customary freight unit.

Because the United States has not ratified either the Hague-Visby Rules or the Hamburg Rules, the COGSA is still in effect for goods shipped from the United States, even though it is grossly outdated with its limit of U.S.$ 500 per package. Several efforts have been made to attempt to revise COGSA, but none of them have been successful. In 1999, with the creation of the Ocean Shipping Reform Act (OSRA), the United States brought one additional level of complexity to the conventions regulating the liability of shipping lines by allowing private, confidential contracts between shippers and shipping lines, where traditional liability constraints are replaced by negotiated ones. OSRA allows private contracts between shippers and shipping lines, and it is likely that the carriers' liability limit was lifted in many of these agreements and that all but a handful of defenses have been eliminated. Therefore, the revision of COGSA may not be necessary. Unfortunately, none of these shipper-carrier agreements has been made public.

However, there is still a problem with liability in intermodal freight; that is, freight that is shipped through several means of transportation using only one bill of lading and for which one of the legs is carriage by sea. The liability limits are different for domestic transport in the exporting country, international transport by ocean (and depend further on the nationality of the carrier, which governs which liability convention apply), and domestic transport in the importing country. When cargo is damaged in transit without the possibility of tracing where in the voyage the peril occurred, which liability limit is applicable?

In June 2000, the United Nations Commission on International Trade Law (UNCITRAL) started the process of creating a formal multimodal liability framework. UNCITRAL finished its work in July 2008, and the General Assembly of the United Nations voted to accept the Rotterdam Rules in February 2009. In September 2009, the United States and 15 other countries signed the convention, heeding the recommendations of the International Chamber of Commerce, which had strongly advocated its ratification. Another handful of countries have signed the convention, but only three had ratified it as of March 2017: Spain, Togo, and Congo.[37] The remainder of the signatories have yet to ratify it, and each of the countries still has to complete its own legislation to implement the rules. The Rotterdam Rules will not enter into force until one year after the twentieth country ratifies the treaty;[38] nevertheless, there is optimism that a single liability convention may finally govern international shipments of goods, regardless of the method of transportation. The Rotterdam Rules have their critics, though, who are concerned that the rules are too complex, allow too many exceptions, and are trying to cover too much under one agreement.[39]

Rotterdam Rules
A 2008 international liability convention for intermodal cargo that restricts the liability of the carrier to U.S.$ 875 per package or per customary freight unit.

A main aspect of the Rotterdam Rules is higher liability limits for the carrier: SDR 875 per package and SDR 4 per kilogram for items that are not considered packages, such as automobiles and machinery. The convention eliminates several of the 17 defenses of the Hague Rules, including the navigation-error defense, which has become unsupportable in an era of inexpensive Global Positioning System devices. Finally, the convention applies "door-to-door," which subjects the legs of the voyage that are in the exporting and importing countries to the same liability limits. To mirror the private agreements of the U.S. Ocean Shipping Reform Act, the Rotterdam Rules allow private contracts between shippers and carriers—contracts that could raise or lower the liability limits. While large shippers are likely to negotiate higher liability limits, small shippers are concerned that they will be subjected to lower liability limits by boilerplate bills of lading offered by the carriers.[40]

Not only are these issues of interest to insurance companies, but they also are of interest to any shipper that decides to retain its shipping risks and decline insurance coverage. As the liability of the carrier is difficult to engage, even in the case of navigational errors or negligence, it may make more sense to purchase insurance coverage (see Chapter 10) and let the insurance company interact with the carrier in determining the carrier's responsibility under these international conventions.

11.6   Non-Vessel-Operating Common Carriers

Non-Vessel-Operating Common Carriers (NVOCCs) are another type of shipping company, but with the *caveat* that they do not own and operate ships. Nevertheless, NVOCCs are regulated by the Federal Maritime Commission (FMC). The way an NVOCC operates is by purchasing space on a ship on a given voyage and selling this space to companies that need to ship cargo. The shipping line gets paid for the space—and weight—whether or not the NVOCC fills its allocation.

The NVOCC makes money only by reselling the space at a higher rate than the one at which the space was purchased. In most instances, an NVOCC also acts as a freight consolidator and aggregates less-than-container-load (LCL) freight from several customers into a full container. This allows small shippers to benefit from the protection of a container and allows them to ship without the extra packing protection that breakbulk demands.

The NVOCC system was the basis for the model followed by consolidators in the air passenger business. These consolidators purchase blocks of seats on airplanes and resell them to individuals, through discount travel agencies.

11.7   Security Requirements

After the terrorist attacks that took place in the beginning of the twenty-first century, several measures were taken worldwide to limit the probability of terrorist attacks carried out at sea. The countries that determined they could be targets reasoned that an easy way for a terrorist to smuggle a dangerous weapon was to bring it in using traditional import channels, mixed with traditional ocean cargo. Several initiatives to limit the probability of a terrorist attack through ocean imports were started within a few years, most by the United States and the European Union, but several others by other countries and the International Maritime Organization. More information on these different approaches can be found in Chapter 16, but there are two main measures that affect ocean cargo.

11.7.1   Cargo Inspections

Most countries have a program under which their customs service inspects cargo when it arrives in the port of importation. For example, a percentage of all shipments entering the United States are inspected upon arrival; this percentage varies from 1 to 5 percent, depending on the port. Such inspections have traditionally been conducted to prevent fraud—the import of products that were not correctly identified or valued on the import documentation—but they are now much more focused on terrorism prevention.

For the past decade, inspections have also happened in the port of exportation, either through non-invasive measures, such as a x-rays, or through physical investigation of the contents of a shipment. For example, the United States has implemented a Container Security Initiative, through which Customs and Border Protection (CBP) inspectors are temporarily assigned to foreign ports where they inspect containers bound for the United States. Such containers are either pulled at random or are flagged as suspicious because of their specific characteristics. A World Customs Organization initiative encourages ports abroad to purchase container-scanning equipment and agree to inspect cargo when such inspection is requested by the country of importation. In exchange, cargo shipped from these ports gets preferential treatment when it enters the country that requested the inspection.

11.7.2 Advance Shipping Notifications

Many countries have implemented a process by which shippers must notify the importing country's customs authorities of the particulars of a shipment before cargo is loaded onto the carrier's ship. This notification has to be made at least 24 hours in advance, and must include information on the shipper, the type of cargo, the consignee, and the carrier.

The first program that required such advanced notification was the 24-hour rule implemented by the United States and administered by the CBP of the Department of Homeland Security. That rule required that all importers (and carriers) provide a copy of the manifest of an ocean shipment bound for the United States, including shipments that were just transiting through a U.S. port and were bound for another country, 24 hours before that shipment was loaded onto the vessel bound for the United States.

The U.S. program has been superseded since January 26, 2010, by a program called the Importer Security Filing, which follows the guidelines of the World Customs Organization's SAFE initiative of June 2007 (see Chapter 16), which mandates that importing countries make uniform the information required of shippers. The requirements of the Importer Security Filing expand the number of points of information that the shipper must provide, and it has become better known in the United States as the 10 + 2 rule, which mirrors the number of informational items required.

The purpose of these advanced notification rules is that the importing country's customs authorities are able to inspect the paperwork, and eventually warn the carrier that something may be inappropriate with the shipment. When a shipment is identified as problematic, it is not loaded, and is inspected in the port of departure before it is loaded onto the next available ship. In some cases, the inspection is conducted by customs inspectors from the importing country assigned to the foreign port.

Review and Discussion Questions

1. What are the two different types of ocean cargo services?

2. Describe three different types of ships used in international ocean transportation. What cargoes are they used for?

3. Explain the concept of a flag. Why does a ship need a flag? Why would an owner choose to fly a flag of convenience?

4. What is the Baltic Exchange? What is the purpose of publishing the Baltic Exchange indices?

5. What are the differences between the Hague Rules, the Hague-Visby Rules, the Hamburg Rules, and the Rotterdam Rules?

6. What are the two major initiatives of the world governments in terms of cargo security?

Notes

[1] World Seaborne Trade, International Chamber of Shipping, http://www.ics-shipping.org/shipping-facts/shipping-and-world-trade/world-seaborne-trade, retrieved March 14, 2017.

[2] *Review of Maritime Transport 2016*, UNCTAD, United Nations Conference on Trade and Development, http://unctad.org/en/PublicationsLibrary/rmt2016_en.pdf, retrieved March 14, 2017.

[3] Murray, William, "Economies of Scale in Containership Costs," United States Merchant Marine Academy, http://www.cmashipping2016.com/postprogram/Tuesday/Murray.pdf, retrieved March 14, 2017.

[4] *The Panama Canal*, November 1996, a publication of the Panama Canal Commission Office of Public Affairs, APO Miami 34011-5000.

[5] "Panamax and New Panamax," *Maritime Connector*, http://maritime-connector.com/wiki/panamax/, retrieved March 14, 2017.

[6] "Knock Nevis," http://www.ships-info.info/mer-Knock-nevis.htm, accessed June 24, 2013.

[7] Parkinson, Justin, "On board the world's biggest ship," *BBC News Magazine*, March 11, 2015, http://www.bbc.com/news/magazine-31813045, retrieved March 14, 2017.

[8] "MS Allure of the Seas," Wikipedia, https://en.wikipedia.org/wiki/Oasis-class_cruise_ship, retrieved March 14, 2017.

[9] *Review of Maritime Transport 2016*, UNCTAD, United Nations Conference on Trade and Development, http://unctad.org/en/PublicationsLibrary/rmt2016_en.pdf, retrieved March 14, 2017.

[10] *Ibid.*

[11] Bogdanich, Walt, Jacqueline Williams, and Ana Graciela Méndez, "The New Panama Canal: A Risky Bet," *the New York Times*, June 22, 2016.

[12] Sullivan, Allanna, "A 700-ft Tanker Just Does Not Handle Quite Like a Honda," *The Wall Street Journal*, April 14, 1989, p. 1.

[13] Wells, Ken, "Captain's Course: Life on a Supertanker Mixes Tedium, Stress for Kenneth Campbell," *The Wall Street Journal*, September 11, 1986, p. 1.

[14] McPhee, John, "The Ships of Port Revel," *The Atlantic Monthly*, October 1998, pp. 67-80.

[15] "Propulsion Trends in Tankers," MAN Diesel, mandieselturbo.com/Propulsion trends in tankers.-htm.pdf?, retrieved June 28, 2013.

[16] "The Baltic Code," The Baltic Exchange, http://www.balticexchange.com/default.asp?action=article&ID=4, accessed June 27, 2009.

[17] "A History of Baltic Indices," The Baltic Exchange, June 2013, http://www.balticexchange.com/default.asp?action=article&ID=558, accessed June 25, 2013.

[18] Wright, Robert, "Collapse in Dry Bulk Shipping Rates Unprecedented in Its Severity," *Financial Times*, December 01, 2008.

[19] "Baltic Exchange Dry Index (BDIY)," https://www.bloomberg.com/quote/BDIY:IND, retrieved March 15, 2017.

[20] Knee, Richard, "Many Owners of Aging Vessels Would Rather Scrap than Sell," *The Journal of Commerce*, May 7, 1998, p. 13A.

[21] Langewiesche, William, "The Shipbreakers," *The Atlantic Monthly*, August 2000, pp. 31-49.

[22] Paris, Costas, and Biman Mukherji, "A Scrap over 'Beaching' Old Ships," *The Wall Street Journal*, June 14, 2013, p. B1.

[23] *Comparison of U.S. and Foreign-Flag Operating Costs*, September 2011, United States Maritime Administration, http://www.marad.dot.gov/documents/Comparison_of_US_and_Foreign_Flag_Operat-

ing_Costs.pdf, retrieved June 25, 2013.

[24] Gillis, Chris, "Changing U.S.-Flag Vessel Economics," *American Shipper*, October 2004, pp. 72-76.

[25] *Review of Maritime Transport 2016*, UNCTAD, United Nations Conference on Trade and Development, http://unctad.org/en/PublicationsLibrary/rmt2016_en.pdf, retrieved March 14, 2017.

[26] "Merchant fleet by country of beneficial ownership, annual, 2014 - 2016," UNCTADStat, http://unctadstat.unctad.org/wds/TableViewer/tableView.aspx?ReportId=80100, retrieved March 15, 2017.

[27] *By the Capes Around the World: A Summary of World Cabotage Practices*, U.S. Maritime Administration, 1995.

[28] *Dahingo v. Royal Caribbean Cruises, Ltd.*, 99 CIV 12774, 312 F. Supp. 2d 440 442 S.D.N.Y. 2004, United States District Court Southern District of New York

[29] Bangsberg, P. T., "Shipowners Tackle Asia Flag Question," *The Journal of Commerce*, May 29, 1997, p. 8B.

[30] Carrington, Tim, "U.S. Owners of Foreign-Registry Ships Want Navy to Rally Round the Flag their Vessels Don't Fly," *The Wall Street Journal*, December 29, 1987, p. 44.

[31] McFadden, Robert, and Scott Shane, "In Rescue of Captain, Navy Kills Three Pirates," *The New York Times*, April 13, 2009.

[32] Maritime Administration, "Voluntary Intermodal Sealift Agreement Open Season," Federal Register, July 29, 2016, https://www.federalregister.gov/documents/2016/07/29/2016-17888/voluntary-intermodal-sealift-agreement-open-season, retrieved March 15, 2017.

[33] David G. Harris and Richard D. Stewart, "U.S. Surge Sealift Capabilities: A Question of Sufficiency," Parameters, *U.S. Army War College Quarterly*, Spring 1998.

[34] Brodie, P., *Dictionary of Shipping Terms*. London: Lloyd's of London Press, Ltd. 1994.

[35] Still, Craig, "Thinking Outside the Box: the Application of COGSA's $500 per Package Limitation to Shipping Containers," *Houston Journal of International Law*, Fall 2001, Vol. 24, No. 1.

[36] "International Conventions Membership List," InforMARE, http://www.informare.it/dbase/convuk.htm, accessed March 15, 2017.

[37] "Rotterdam Rules: Introduction," http://www.rotterdamrules.com/content/introduction, retrieved March 15, 2017.

[38] Hooper, Chester, "Ratification of the Rotterdam Rules and their Implications for International Shipping," February 2012, www.skuld.com/Documents/Library/Beacon/Beacon_2_2012_rotterdam_rules.pdf, retrieved June 25, 2013.

[39] Tetley, William, "Summary of Some General Criticisms of the UNCITRAL Convention (The Rotterdam Rules)," McGill University School of Law Internal Document, http://www.mcgill.ca/files/maritime-law/Tetley_Criticism_of_Rotterdam_Rules.pdf, November 5, 2008, accessed June 27, 2009.

[40] Hailey, Roger, "Freight Forwarders Step Up Attacks on Rotterdam Rules," *Lloyd's List*, June 2, 2009, http://www.lloydslist.com/ll/news/freight-forwarders-step-up-attack-on-rotterdam-rules/1243-872041051.htm.

Chapter 12

International Air Transportation

The scale and scope of international air cargo transportation has grown steadily over the past four decades, driven by globalization and the increasing expectations of business and consumers worldwide. Today, even though airfreight represents only 1 percent of world trade by weight, it accounts for more than 35 percent of world trade by value. The demand for airfreight is highly correlated with world GDP, and more than 75 percent of the world's airfreight is carried by non-U.S. airlines.[1] The slow but steady growth in this premium mode of transportation has been driven, in part, by the advent of time-definite shipments, a concept that was implemented with military-like precision by Federal Express in the United States market in the 1970s, and which has been adopted by nearly all cargo airlines in the international arena. Figure 12.1 illustrates the growth in airfreight measured in revenue tonne kilometers (RTKs) from 1997 through 2015.[2] One Revenue Tonne Kilometer is a measurement used by the airfreight industry: it corresponds to one metric tonne of goods transported for one kilometer (One RTK is equal to 0.685 ton-mile).

Prior to 2007, many experts felt that the airfreight industry had no alternative but to grow further, and its annual growth rate was 9 percent per year. However, high fuel prices and financial turmoil took a toll on air cargo traffic in 2008, resulting in a decrease in airfreight in 2008 and 2009, but the industry recovered in 2010. After the downturn, both Boeing and Airbus remained optimistic on the long-term prospects for airfreight, but the prospects for growth were more

time-definite shipments
Cargo or package shipments that must be delivered by a guaranteed, predetermined time and day.

revenue tonne kilometer(RTK)
A unit designed to express total airline activity. It is equal to the number of tonnes of cargo, passengers, baggages and mail shipped multiplied by the number of kilometers they were shipped.

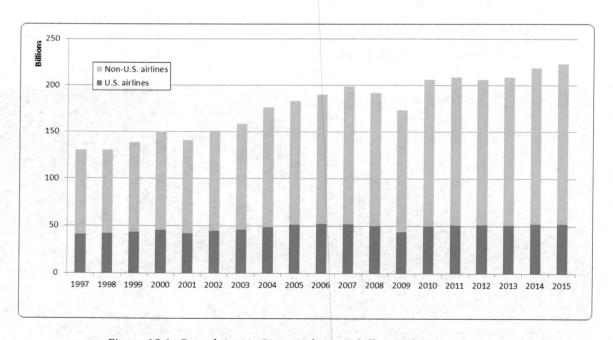

Figure 12.1: Growth in Air Cargo Volume in billions of RTKs 1997-2015
Boeing *World Air Cargo Forecast 2016-17.*

moderate, in the 5 to 7 percent range.[3] By 2017, Boeing still forecasted that worldwide freight traffic would double by 2035, but with a compound annual growth rate of only 1.7 percent.[4]

12.1   Cargo Airlines, Airports, and Markets

FedEx (previously called Federal Express) is the largest airfreight company in the world, serving more than 375 airports worldwide.[5] As seen in Table 12.1, FedEx also earned the top spot for international cargo volume in 2015 with 15.8 billion freight tonne kilometers (FTKs)—10.8 billion freight ton miles—followed by Emirates and UPS (United Parcel Service). Emirates, based in Dubai, is the fastest growing airline in the world, for both cargo and passenger traffic.[6] The top ten cargo carriers in the world account for about 40 percent of the world's freight transportation volume of 223 billion RTKs[7]—153 billion ton-miles.

freight tonne kilometer(FTK)
A unit designed to express cargo volume shipped. It is equal to the number of tonnes of cargo shipped multiplied by the number of kilometers they were shipped.

Top Ten Cargo Airlines, 2015

Rank	Airline	Millions of FTKs
1	FedEx	15,799
2	Emirates	12,157
3	UPS Airlines	10,807
4	Cathay Pacific Airways	9,935
5	Korean Air Lines	7,761
6	Qatar Airways	7,660
7	Lufthansa	6,888
8	Cargolux	6,309
9	Singapore Airlines	6,083
10	Air China	5,718

Table 12.1: The Ten Largest Cargo Airlines in 2015 (in millions of FTKs)
IATA *World Air Transport Statistics.*

The top fifteen cargo airports in the world for 2015 are listed in Table 12.2 on the following page.[8] Each of the largest cargo airports is dominated by one or several large cargo airlines, either because it is headquartered in that city or it uses that airport as a major base for its operations. In the United States, Memphis is FedEx's main hub and headquarters; Anchorage is a major trans-Pacific transit point between the Asian continent and the United States, Canada, and the rest of the Americas; Louisville is the main hub for UPS; and Miami is a major gateway for traffic between the United States and Latin America. In Europe, Frankfurt is the main cargo hub for Lufthansa, and Paris is the main hub for Air France, FedEx, and La Poste. In Asia, Tokyo is the major hub for Japan Airlines; Incheon

(Seoul) is the major hub for Korean Air; Shanghai is a major hub for China Cargo Airlines, China Eastern, and UPS; while Hong Kong is the major Asian hub for DHL and a main hub for Cathay Pacific. Finally, it should be noted that, in that list, only Memphis and Louisville have a significant domestic cargo traffic. All the other cargo airports handle essentially only international cargo.

Top Fifteen Cargo Airports, 2015

Rank	Airport	IATA Code	Metric Tonnes Loaded (in '000s)
1	Hong Kong, China	HKG	4,422
2	Memphis, United States	MEM	4,291
3	Shanghai, China	PVG	3,274
4	Anchorage, United States	ANC	2,624
5	Incheon/Seoul, Korea	ICN	2,596
6	Dubai, U.A.E.	DXB	2,506
7	Louisville, United States	SDF	2,351
8	Tokyo, Japan	NRT	2,122
9	Frankfurt, Germany	FRA	2,076
10	Taipei, Taiwan	TPE	2,025
11	Miami, United States	MIA	2,005
12	Los Angeles, United States	LAX	1,932
13	Beijing, China	PEK	1,890
14	Singapore, Singapore	SIN	1,887
15	Paris, France	CDG	1,861

Table 12.2: Fifteen Largest Cargo Airports in 2015 (metric tonnes loaded)
ACI *World Airport Traffic.*

Regionally, and as illustrated in Figure 12.2,[9] air cargo volume is expected to experience the most growth between Asia and North America, and between Asia and Europe. Other trade lanes in which flows are expected to show substantial growth are in the intra-Asia market, the domestic PRC market, and between South Asia and Europe. All the other markets are expected to grow at a more modest pace.

12.2 Types of Service

The services offered by the airfreight industry are defined by the nature of the demand and type of commodity. Airfreight is well suited for commodities that have a high value-to-weight ratio, or are perishable, quickly obsolete, required on short notice, or expensive to handle or store. Shipping by air is also attractive

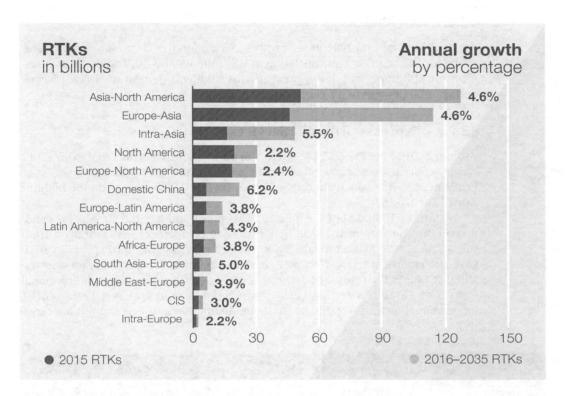

Figure 12.2: Cargo Volume Forecast by Region, in billions of RTKs
Boeing *World Air Cargo Forecast 2016-2035*, used with permission.

when demand is unpredictable, infrequent, exceeds local supply, or is seasonal. Shippers also choose air when the risk of pilferage, breakage, or deterioration is high, when the cost of insurance is high for long periods of transit, when heavy packaging is required for surface transportation, or when there is need for special handling. In some circumstances, shipping by air can avoid warehousing costs that would otherwise be required if other, slower modes of transportation are used, such as ocean transportation.[10] Difficult terrain or the lack of rail, port, or road infrastructure are also valid reasons for shipping by air. Finally, the risk of losing a customer or halting production due to the lack of an urgently-needed repair part can also justify the expense of moving goods by air.

Although the types of products shipped vary by region, air transportation lends itself to the movement of industrial equipment, computers and office machines, consumer products, work-in-process goods, apparel, perishables, small packages, documents, and other manufactured goods. To meet the demand for these products, various services have evolved, including air mail services, express airfreight services, scheduled airfreight services, charter airfreight services, leasing, and airfreight forwarder services.

12.2.1   Air Mail Services

Air mail was the first type of air cargo service offered and "an important factor in the formation of air transportation in the United States."[11] Today, air mail services are still important, but represent a little under 3 percent of airline revenue and about 4 percent of air cargo carried, measured in RTKs.

12.2.2   Express Airfreight Services

express cargo
Cargo shipped with a guaranteed predetermined delivery date.

Although DHL, FedEx, and UPS were not the first carriers to offer express air cargo services, these carriers and their services have continued to grow since FedEx deployed 14 small aircraft to deliver its first 186 packages on the night of April 17, 1973.[12]

Within the United States, FedEx and UPS now dominate the air express cargo market, but outside of the U.S., DHL is a large competitor; DHL withdrew from the U.S. domestic market in late 2008. FedEx's purchase of TNT Express in 2016 gave the company a larger market share in the intra-European market and the Middle East. As the volume of domestic express services has grown, international express air cargo services have also grown and now represent over 13 percent of international air cargo traffic, even as the distinction between express air cargo

Figure 12.3: An Express Carrier Being Loaded in Tel Aviv, Israel (Boeing 747-400)
Photo ©Lerner Vadim/Shutterstock. Used with permission.

and regularly-scheduled air cargo services continues to blur.[13]

Today, FedEx employs over 400,000 people and maintains the world's largest all-cargo airline, operating over 650 aircraft in more than 220 countries and territories. Through its hub in Memphis, Tennessee, FedEx Express operates more than 5,000 flights a month, ships more than 12 million packages and letters every day, and serves 99 percent of the global economy on a 24- to 48-hour basis.[14] In addition to multiple hubs in the United States, FedEx operates major hubs in Paris (France), Subic Bay (The Philippines), Toronto (Canada), Guangzhou (China), and Cologne/Bonn (Germany).

While FedEx entered the market with a new and distinct business model, UPS evolved over time from a messenger service and common carrier into a leader in global supply chain management. Today, UPS owns 237 aircraft (and leases another 420) to provide express airfreight service to over 220 countries and territories.[15] UPS employs 434,000 people, and operates more than 2,500 flights monthly to 313 international airports. In addition to its major hub at Worldport in Louisville, Kentucky, UPS operates major hubs in Cologne/Bonn (Germany), Taipei (Taiwan), Pampanga (The Philippines), Ontario (California), Hong Kong, Singapore, Shanghai (China), and Shenzhen (China). Worldport has been expanded several times and now occupies a 48-hectare distribution center (5.2 million square feet) with the capacity to sort over 300,000 packages per hour.[16]

Outside the United States, Belgium-based DHL, a subsidiary of Deutsche Post, is the leader in many European and Asian markets, claiming 40 percent of the European market for air freight in 2016.[17] DHL has been gaining in the North and South American market, with a new hub in Cincinnati serving international markets only. As of 2016, DHL operated a fleet of 250 aircraft serving over 220 countries and territories. Another Belgium-based airline is TNT Airways, the fourth largest consolidator in the world, and a strong presence in Europe and China. FedEx purchased TNT Airways in 2016, and the company ceased operating as an independent brand in May 2016.

One of the major factors leading to the continued growth and long-term success of the express air cargo industry has been the shift from carrying cargo to providing a bundle of services to meet the needs of customers who are willing to pay for the convenience of one-stop shopping. Over time, FedEx, UPS, DHL, and others have expanded their services to the point of offering supply chain solutions rather than only package delivery. As a result, these firms are often referred to as integrators, where the scope of integrated services has been continuously expanding.

integrator
An air cargo carrier that offers its customers complete door-to-door service.

12.2.3 Scheduled Airfreight Services

As the name implies, scheduled airfreight services are flights that are offered on a published schedule. Scheduled airfreight services have many advantages. Since these services are offered on a routine basis, they tend to be highly reliable and efficient, resulting in relatively low-cost airfreight delivery. Scheduled airfreight services comprise the bulk of international air cargo traffic. However, it is interesting to note that, even though the overall volume of international air cargo has

Figure 12.4: Belly Cargo Being Loaded on a Passenger Aircraft (Airbus A330)
Photo ©Peter Titmuss/Shutterstock, used with permission.

increased over the years, the percentage of world air cargo carried by U.S. carriers has declined as the U.S. domestic market has matured (see Figure 12.1).

Today, passenger airlines, integrators, and airfreight companies offer scheduled airfreight services. Although passenger airliners hold cargo in the belly of the aircraft, such cargo is often considered secondary to their focus on serving passengers. Therefore passenger belly capacity is limited. As a result, many all-cargo airlines and integrators, such as Cargolux and FedEx, operate their airfreighters on a scheduled basis. Some of the leading international scheduled airfreight service providers include Korean Air, Lufthansa, Cathay Pacific, Singapore Airlines, FedEx, China Airlines, Air France, Emirates, Cargolux, JAL, UPS, British Airways, KLM, United Airlines, Qantas, El Al, and DHL. To accommodate changing cargo demand at certain times of the year, these operators will add—or cancel—services between two cities.

12.2.4 Charter Airfreight Services

Charter airfreight services are based on demand and do not operate on a published schedule. Although this alternative can be more expensive than scheduled

Figure 12.5: An Airfreighter, the Boeing 747-F, in Hong Kong
Photo ©EQRoy/Shutterstock. Used with permission.

service, charter airfreight services offer shippers more flexibility. Charter services can be tailored to meet the individual shipper's need for specialized cargo, large volumes of cargo at certain times of the year, emergencies, or delivery to destinations that are not normally served by scheduled airlines or freight carriers. For example, charter aircraft can be used to meet the demands of seasonal traffic, such as the shipment of cherries from the Northwest United States to Japan in July, or roses from Colombia to the United States in February (see Vignette on page 438).[18] A large increase in demand for a new product, such as the shipment of a new Beaujolais Nouveau from France to the United States and Japan in November, can also cause a carrier to supplement its capacity through the use of charter airfreight services. Some of the world's largest air charter cargo providers include Air Charter Services, Lufthansa Cargo Charter, and Polar Air Cargo.

In addition to meeting emergency needs or the demand for products that exceed plans, there are also times when shippers need to ship products that do not fit in the cargo bay of a traditional cargo aircraft. Often referred to as "project cargo" (see Section 13.5), such items exceed the volume or weight restrictions of traditional aircraft and require special handling and carriage by aircraft designed to meet these special needs. Airbus's A-300 *Beluga* (see Figure 12.13), Boeing's

charter airfreight
A type of cargo that can only be shipped on a charter aircraft because it is too heavy, too bulky or its destination is not serviced by a scheduled airfreight service.

747 *Dreamlifter* (see Figure 12.15), and the Antonov 124 *Ruslan* (see Figure 12.11 on page 436) and its even larger cousin, the Antonov 225 *Mriya* (see Figure 12.12 on page 437) fit that category. In at least three of these cases, these aircraft were originally developed to meet the outsize cargo needs of the aviation and aerospace industry itself. For example, the *Beluga* was originally designed to meet the complex logistics challenges of shipping parts across Europe to support the production and assembly of the Airbus series of aircrafts from Hamburg, Germany, to Toulouse, France. Similarly, the *Dreamlifter* was designed to meet the just-in-time assembly needs of Boeing's worldwide network of suppliers for the 787 Dreamliner. Finally, the *Mriya* was originally designed to transport the Russian space shuttle.

12.2.5   Leased Cargo Aircraft Services

As in other industries which involve large capital expenditures, leasing is an option for the major air cargo carriers and other providers of airfreight services. There are several leasing options available, but most leases take the form of a "dry" lease, "damp" lease, "wet" lease, or "aircraft, crew, maintenance, and insurance" (ACMI) lease.

wet lease
A type of leasing contract in which an airplane is leased, along with a crew, maintenance services, insurance and fuel.

ACMI lease
A type of leasing contract in which an airplane is leased, along with a crew, maintenance services, and insurance.

damp lease
A type of leasing contract in which an airplane is leased, along with maintenance services and insurance, but no crew.

dry lease
A type of leasing contract in which only an airplane is leased.

In the past,   a wet lease referred to a short-term lease that usually included the aircraft, crew, maintenance, insurance, and fuel. Today, the most common cargo aircraft leases include only the aircraft, crew, maintenance, and insurance (ACMI) and are therefore called ACMI leases. Damp leasing is similar to ACMI, but without the flight crew. Finally, a dry lease is a form of leasing where the lessor provides an aircraft without any crew, maintenance, insurance, services, or fuel.

According to Boeing's *World Air Cargo Forecast for 2016-2017*, about 5 percent of the world's air cargo is now transported by ACMI providers.[19] Although the demand for ACMI services varies with the economy, the market for large, long-haul international airfreight aircraft has been relatively stable over the years, since the new wide-body airfreighters are more efficient than most conversions—a former passenger aircraft converted into a freighter aircraft—and older airfreight aircraft.

Both UPS and FedEx lease aircraft to supplement their core capacity, especially during the November-December holidays. FedEx, for example, leases almost 100 large jets to supplement its own fleet and approximately 50 smaller piston-driven and turbo-prop aircraft to deliver packages to and from airports served by its larger aircraft.[20]

12.2.6   Airfreight Forwarder Services

Like other modes of transportation, airfreight forwarders provide the link between shippers of airfreight and consignees at the destination. Freight forwarders contract with air carriers, consolidate shipments, buy space on flights, and arrange intermodal surface transportation needs. Some freight forwarders provide a full range of supply chain management services, while others specialize in performing specific tasks. Today, many of the integrators, such as DHL, UPS, and

FedEx, offer international freight forwarding services and compete directly with traditional freight forwarders such as Schenker, Kuehne & Nagel, Panalpina, and numerous others.

12.3 Types of Aircraft

Although many types of aircraft are used to meet the growing demand for fast and efficient air transportation, in general these aircraft can be broken down into four categories: passenger aircraft, combination or "combi" aircraft, quick-change aircraft, and large cargo aircraft that are designed to serve as airfreighters.

12.3.1 Passenger Aircraft

Nearly every passenger aircraft transports cargo in addition to the passengers carried on its main deck. The "belly" of the aircraft is designed to accommodate the passengers' luggage and additional airfreight. Some of this airfreight cargo is loose freight (*i.e.*, not palletized) and is shipped piece by piece; the packages

main deck
The largest deck on an aircraft, the one on which passenger travel in a passenger aircraft.

Figure 12.6: The Largest Passenger Aircraft, Airbus A380, in Frankfurt, Germany
Photo ©Carlos Yudica/Shutterstock, used with permission.

are not secured to the aircraft and are shipped in a manner that is similar to passenger luggage.

In larger, wide-body aircraft, the freight is palletized or containerized (see Figure 12.4) and secured to the aircraft. International cargo services on passenger aircraft are somewhat unreliable, as airlines sometimes "bump" freight, creating more capacity to carry additional passengers and their luggage. Therefore, only the most urgent of cargo makes it on passenger aircraft, and the cargo is often machine or computer parts necessary for repairing a critical piece of equipment, or small shipments of fresh produce, such as vegetables or fish. Such cargo is often shipped on a next-flight-out basis.

The biggest constraint on a shipper when using passenger airplanes for shipping freight is the shipment's maximum weight and volume. The shipper must consider the size of the hold, the weight capacity of the floor of the cargo hold, the overall weight limitations of the aircraft, and the size of the door used to access the cargo hold. Most freight forwarders have a good grasp of the maximum sizes of packages that can be shipped in passenger airplanes and are quite helpful in determining whether the cargo will be allowed on a passenger flight. Another constraint is that some items are not allowed on passenger aircraft and can be transported only on cargo aircraft. Such hazardous material must be labeled Cargo Aircraft Only (CAO) and can be shipped only in airfreighters.

onboard courier (OBC)
A passenger on a regularly scheduled flight who relinquishes his or her baggage allocation to allow cargo in its place.

An alternative way of using passenger airplanes for cargo is to use an onboard courier (OBC) service. A courier is often a student or a retiree who flies to a city and takes cargo as his or her luggage. This is often the fastest way for cargo to get anywhere and is a service used to deliver critical parts and documents. OBC service also presents the advantage of the cargo always making the plane, as passengers' luggage has priority over all other freight. The OBC business is substantial, but unfortunately there are no aggregate statistics for this activity. Onboard couriers can also provide door-to-door shipments if necessary.

Airbus and Boeing

Airbus SAS, the European consortium of aerospace manufacturers, and the Boeing Company, the American manufacturer of commercial airplanes, dominate the aircraft industry. While there are a few other airplane companies, such as Bombardier in Canada, Embraer in Brazil, Tupolev in Russia, and Comac in China, Airbus and Boeing each hold 45 percent of the commercial-airplane market.[21] However, Airbus and Boeing have different perspectives on the way the market for aircrafts is developing.

Airbus observes that there are 55 "mega-city" airports worldwide, and 47 of them are at maximum capacity in terms of the number of flights that they can handle.[22] These airports will not be able to increase the number of flights they handle to accommodate future increased traffic, and therefore the airlines that serve these airports will need airplanes of larger capacity to fly from hub to hub. The Airbus A-380 was designed for that purpose, with the capacity to handle as many as 850 passengers, in addition to much belly cargo.

Boeing makes the same observation, but concludes that airlines will recognize that there is enough demand to justify flights between secondary airports, and replace hub-to-hub flights with smaller-capacity flights between smaller airports

internationally. Boeing therefore designed the 787 with a smaller capacity (fewer than 300 passengers). The belly cargo space is limited as well.

As of 2017, 207 Airbus 380 aircrafts operated in 38 of the mega-city airports (approximately 50 airports in total),[23] and 521 Boeing 787 aircrafts operated in approximately 200 cities.[24]

It looks as if both views are compatible.

12.3.2   Quick-Change Aircraft

As the name implies, quick-change aircraft are those which can be reconfigured from passenger to cargo configurations and vice-versa in a matter of hours. Airlines that operate quick-change aircraft use palletized sections of seats that can be easily added or removed from the main deck. Although limited in demand, the Boeing 737 200/300 series aircraft have had some moderate success as a quick-change aircraft.

12.3.3   Combination Aircraft

Combination aircraft, or combis, are passenger airplanes that are designed to carry freight on the main deck as well as in the belly hold. The main deck is split at some point in the middle of the aircraft, with one portion of the plane reserved for passengers and the other portion reserved for freight. Some aircraft are designed so that this partition is somewhat mobile, depending on the demand for passenger seats (a decision usually based on seasonal fluctuations).

Some of the more common combi aircraft include the Airbus 330 and 340; the DC-10; and the Boeing 737, 747, and 757. Many of the larger wide-body combis, such as the Boeing 747 and DC-10, are used to fly passengers and cargo nonstop to remote areas of the world, such as the islands of the South Pacific, where the volume of passenger traffic by itself is not sufficient to justify such flights. In another example, Alaskan Airlines uses modified Boeing 737-400 combis to meet the needs of the seafood industry, as well as to transport passengers to and from the northern and western parts of Alaska (see Figure 12.7). Canadian North operates similar flights.

For shippers, combis present an advantage over passenger aircraft. The main deck has a greater weight capacity and a much larger door, and can accommodate palletized and containerized cargo. Moreover, the cargo can be secured to the plane to prevent damage caused by movement within the aircraft. However, the restrictions on what may be shipped with passengers aboard remain.

quick-change aircraft
A type of airplane that can be quickly converted from all-cargo service to all-passenger service, with the use of palletized seat sections.

combi aircraft
A type of airplane that is designed to carry both cargo and passengers at the same time on the main deck.

Figure 12.7: An Alaska Airlines Combination Aircraft (Boeing 737)
Photo ©Philip Pilosian/Shutterstock. Used with permission.

12.3.4   Airfreighters

airfreighter
A type of airplane dedicated to carrying cargo.

lower deck
A deck designed to carry cargo and luggage, located underneath the main deck of an aircraft.

Over the past decades, the amount of cargo carried by air has been equally split between airfreighters and the lower decks of passenger aircraft, with only slightly more than half of all air cargo carried by airfreighters. However, both Boeing and Airbus project the demand for new freighters is going to grow. There are several reasons for this, including the increasing demand for air cargo, fewer wide-body passenger aircraft available for conversion, and the fact that older airfreighters are reaching the end of their useful lives. In addition, new airfreighters (see Figure 12.5) are more fuel efficient, larger, and have lower maintenance costs.[25]

Most airfreighters are "liners" (*i.e.*, they operate on a regular schedule) traveling between two airports, one of which is usually a hub, the location at which the cargo will be transferred to another flight. Most airfreighters are also variations of aircraft used for passenger service, with the exception that the freighter is equipped with a roller deck (see Figure 12.8). A roller deck is a main deck equipped with rollers that allows palletized or containerized cargo to be pushed into or off the aircraft, either through an oversize side door or through the nose of the airplane, which, in some cases, can be lifted (see Figure 12.9). The cargo is then secured to the aircraft floor and walls using locks, hooks, and slings.

roller deck
A deck designed to carry cargo, and equipped with rollers and bearings that allow the cargo to be moved in any direction without much friction.

In the past, most airfreighters were older passenger airplanes that were retrofitted for cargo service by specialized firms. Today, passenger-to-freighter conversions are still common, but both Boeing and Airbus now offer freighter versions for almost every aircraft they build. For example, Boeing's 777-200F has sold quite well as a new-built airfreighter, and Airbus offers the popular A330-200F. However, Airbus has canceled the introduction of its A380F, following the

Figure 12.8: The Roller Deck of the Main Deck of an Airbus A300F
Photo ©Tratong/Shutterstock. Used with permission.

withdrawals of pre-orders by FedEx and UPS, with no new introduction date specified by the company. Eventually, some of the A380 passenger aircrafts may eventually be retrofitted as cargo aircrafts, but that unlikely to happen until the aircraft have been in use for more than twenty years (so, not until 2025-2030). The A380-800F would have presented the advantage of having two main decks that can be loaded simultaneously, overcoming one of the pitfalls of a single-deck freighter, for which the loading sequence must be done very carefully, to avoid upsetting the balance of the aircraft on the ground.

Just as the ocean shipping industry has its own way of characterizing vessels, the air cargo industry has its own way of classifying freighters. The airfreighter fleet, for example, is often described in terms of standard body, medium wide-body, and large wide-body.

- The standard body category includes aircraft such as the McDonnell-Douglas DC-8 and DC-9, the Boeing 727, 737, and 757, and the Airbus 320.

- The medium wide-body category includes the McDonnell-Douglas DC-10, the Boeing 767 and 787, and the Airbus 300, 310, 330, and 340.

- The large wide-body category includes aircraft like the McDonnell-Douglas

Figure 12.9: The Boeing 747-F can be Loaded through the Nose
Photo ©Davide Calabresi/Shutterstock. Used with permission.

MD-11, the Boeing 747 and 777, the Airbus 340-600SF, 350, and 380, and the Antonov 124.

Each of these aircraft was designed to meet specific air transportation needs. Figure 12.10 on the next page illustrates how these aircrafts vary by payload and range. As can be seen in this diagram, a Boeing 757-200F freighter is well suited to carry about 40 metric tonnes (66,140 pounds) over 3,100 nautical miles (5,740 kilometers), while a Boeing 777-200F can carry almost 2.5 times that payload, over nearly twice the distance. As of 2017, the largest airline freighter is the Boeing 747-400F, but the possible introduction of the freighter version of the Airbus 380 will jeopardize this standing, since the Airbus 380 was designed to carry 150 metric tonnes (330,693 pounds) over 5,600 nautical miles (10,371 kilometers).[26]

Airfreighters can also be aircraft that do not have passenger versions and are constructed exclusively for moving freight. The Antonov 124 *Ruslan* (see Figure 12.11 on page 436) was built primarily for military use, but has found a niche in the civilian transport of cargo. The Antonov 124 *Ruslan* can take off and land from poorly-maintained and short runways, despite a payload of 150 metric tonnes (330,693 pounds) and a range of 2,900 nautical miles (5,370 kilometers). The Antonov 124 *Ruslan* specializes in delivering project cargo to

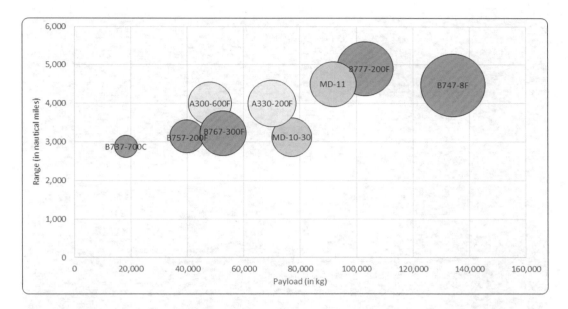

Figure 12.10: Payload, Range, and Cargo Volume of Selected Freighters
Boeing and Airbus.

remote airports. It was the largest aircraft ever built until the Antonov 225 *Mriya* (see Figure 12.12 on page 437) took that distinction, with a payload of 250 metric tonnes and a range of 8,500 nautical miles (15,742 kilometers). The Antonov 225 *Mriya* was designed to transport the Russian Space Shuttle: it now specializes in the transport of very heavy airfreight. There is only one Antonov 225 *Mriya* in operation.

Other aircraft designed exclusively for the transporting freight include the Airbus 300-600 ST *Beluga* (see Figure 12.13 on page 438) and the Boeing 747-400 *Dreamlifter* (see Figure 12.15 on page 441), both of which are transformations of traditional aircraft, originally designed to transport pieces of other aircraft from one assembly plant to another. The *Beluga* is used by Airbus to shuttle fuselage and wings from its plants in the U.K., Spain, and Germany to their final assembly location in Toulouse, France, and the *Dreamlifter* fulfills the same function for Boeing, transporting parts from Japan and Italy to Everett, Washington.

12.4 Airfreight Tariffs

The tariff structure of international air cargo is not nearly as complicated as that of the ocean cargo industry, with its innumerable categories. Airfreight is priced as a function of weight and volume.

To arrive at the freight cost for a particular shipment, airlines calculate two

Figure 12.11: The Antonov *Ruslan* Designed to Handle Project Cargo
Photo ©Vicspacewalker/Shutterstock. Used with permission.

alternatives: the first alternative is based on the actual weight of the shipment, and the other alternative is based on its volume, a computation that uses the volume of the cargo to determine its "equivalent" weight, which is called either the volume-weight of a shipment or its dimensional weight—which many call the "dim weight" of a shipment. The airline will then charge the higher of the volume-weight or the actual weight of the cargo. On international shipments, the volume-weight conversion traditionally used 6,000 cubic centimeters per kilogram (166 cubic inches per pound), although some airlines calculate this ratio slightly differently. FedEx, DHL, and UPS use a different ratio of 5,000 cubic centimeters per kilogram (139 cubic inches per pound).

volume weight (dimensional weight)
An artificial weight, determined in function of the dimensions of a shipment, used by airlines to determine the tariff to be paid for a light shipment.

To illustrate, the cost to fly a cargo of 100 kilograms (220 pounds) with FedEx varies greatly based on its volume. Let's assume that the cost per kilogram is U.S.$ 4 to ship goods from Atlanta to Abu Dhabi. If the shipment is composed of a product that is dense and shipped in five boxes, each measuring $60 \times 30 \times 10$ centimeters ($24 \times 12 \times 4$ inches) and weighing 20 kg, the cost is U.S.$ 400. The dim weight of each of these boxes is 4 kg ($60 \times 30 \times 10/5,000 = 3.6$ rounded up to 4), so the actual weight of the shipment is the value used to calculate the shipping costs. However, the cost to ship a different product of the same weight in five

Figure 12.12: The Antonov 225 *Mriya* in Kuala Lumpur, Malaysia
Photo ©Abdul Hafiz ab Hamid/Shutterstock. Used with permission.

larger containers (five $120 \times 60 \times 20$-centimeter containers [$48 \times 24 \times 8$ inches]) is based on the dim weight of each box ($120 \times 60 \times 20/5,000 = 28.8$ rounded to 29), because their dim weight exceeds their actual weight. The dim weight of the shipment is 145 kg (319 lbs.) and the shipping costs U.S.$ 580.* Thus, one can readily see how the volume of an air shipment vastly affects its shipping costs.

The difficulty for a shipper using airfreight for lightweight products is to ensure that it does not pay too much for shipping by using voluminous packaging. The trade-off is relatively simple. The shipper must decide between using expensive but low-volume packaging that protects the cargo and reduces the overall dimensions of the cargo and therefore its volume-weight, and using more less expensive traditional packaging but increase the freight costs by increasing the volume weight. The decision to decrease packaging should never be made without a thorough analysis, since improper packaging is one of the primary reasons insurance companies deny claims.

---

*These calculations were made using the metric measurements. Traditional measurements will yield slightly different results because of rounding issues.

Figure 12.13: The A300-600ST *Beluga* in Hamburg, Germany
Photo ©Dmitry Finkel/Shutterstock. Used with permission.

Roses and Cherries

In the five weeks that preceded Valentine's Day 2017—February 14—, airfreighters transported 5,000 tonnes of cut flowers from Kenya, Ecuador, and Colombia to the European Union (see Figure 12.14).[27] During the same period, exports of cut flowers from Colombia and Ecuador to the United States amounted to 7,000 tons or roughly 15 million bouquets.[28] To accommodate this enormous spike in cargo volume, UPS used 64 temperature-controlled 767 airfreighters filled with flowers over a two-week period.[29] Almost 90 percent of the flower imports enter the United States through the Miami airport, and the same proportion enters the European market through Schiphol Airport in the Netherlands, Europe's hub for flower shipments.[30]

Outside of the Valentine's Day period, roses account for 33 percent of the business—by value—, carnations 18 percent, and chrysanthemums another 8 percent. A normal day still sees seven to ten flights from Bogotá to Miami, loaded with flowers.[31]

Cut flowers are not the only unusually seasonal business handled by airfreighters, though. From late May until late June, it is "cherry season" on

Figure 12.14: Flowers Arriving at Amsterdam's Schiphol Airport, the Netherlands, from Quito, Ecuador

Photo ©Air France - KLM - Martinair Cargo. Used with permission.

the West Coast of the United States, and cherries utilize much of the worldwide airfreighter capacity during that period. In 2014, more than 1.4 million cartons (cardboard boxes of 8.2 kilograms [18 pounds]) of cherries left the United States for the Japanese market, 2 million cartons went to China, 1 million to South Korea, and 250,000 cartons to Singapore, Malaysia, and Thailand.[32] These cherries all travel by airfreighters or in the bellies of passenger flights, at sometimes prohibitive rates because all West-bound capacity during that period is taken by these fruits (Rates can reach U.S.$ 3.00 per kilogram, whereas cargo normally fetches no more than U.S.$ 1.00 per kilogram on that route). It is the most profitable period of the year for the airlines involved in that trade.

12.5   International Regulations

The international airfreight business is regulated by the International Air Transport Association (IATA) and the International Civil Aviation Organization (ICAO).

Warsaw Convention
A 1929 Convention that established the first liability limits for air carriers.

Montréal Protocol 4
A 1999 protocol that limits the liability of air carriers to SDR 17 per kilogram. There is no limit for death or bodily injury.

International Air Transport Association (IATA)
A trade association comprising almost 230 airlines, representing 93 percent of all scheduled air traffic.

International Civil Aviation Organization (ICAO)
An agency of the United Nations whose mission is to establish safety and security standards for civil aviation.

open-sky agreement
An agreement between two countries, in which the airlines of one country are allowed to serve any of the other country's airports.

International regulation of air traffic started with the Paris Convention of 1919, which established the concept of a country's sovereignty over its airspace. In 1929, the Warsaw Convention was signed, limiting the liability of international airlines toward passengers and freight in case of accidents. Both liability limits were eventually increased in 1955 with the Hague Protocol; in 1966 with the Montréal Agreement; in 1971 with the Guatemala City Protocol; in 1995 with the IATA Intercarrier Agreement on Passenger Liability; and in 1999, the Montréal Convention, which is also known as Montréal Protocol No. 4. As of 2017, for those countries that have ratified the Montréal Protocol, the liability limits for death or bodily injury are removed, and the liability for lost cargo is limited to SDR 17 per kilogram.

Under IATA and ICAO rules, a country can restrict the number of airline flights in and out of its airspace. Generally, the limit is set to favor national airline companies; however, in 1992, the United States and the Netherlands agreed to remove limits on the number of flights that each country's airlines could fly into the other's territory, creating an "open-skies" agreement. Since 1992, numerous additional bilateral agreements have been signed. By early 2017, the United States had more 120 open-skies partners,[33] including agreements with the 27 European countries that are part of the U.S.-European Union Trade Agreement that was signed on April 30, 2007. Open-sky provisions apply to passenger and cargo flights, as well as scheduled and charter air transportation services.

Even though open-skies agreements removed many of the restrictions placed on international routes and carriers, flights in and out of specific airports are still restricted by the number of landing slots available at that airport. For example, the United States and Japan have an open-skies agreement, but Narita Airport had only one international-length runway until 2009[34] and therefore no additional flights could be scheduled until that constraint was lifted.

Both the IATA and ICAO are also starting to assume a more active role in establishing industry standards for environmental protection. In 1983, ICAO established the Committee on Aviation Environmental Protection (CAEP). This committee now includes several groups that focus on both the technical and operational aspects of noise reduction and aircraft emissions.[35] The IATA has been equally aggressive and has established a vision of becoming a carbon-free mode of transportation in the next 50 years.[36]

12.6   Environmental Issues and Sustainability

Over the past ten years, the aviation industry has seen an enormous increase in concern for the environment and the adoption of sustainability practices. This shift is affecting the design and operation of passenger and cargo aircraft, as well as the airports and infrastructure that support them. The IATA, for example, is attempting to reduce greenhouse emissions by focusing on new technologies, changes in operations, infrastructure changes, and various economic incentives to encourage the industry to adopt more environmentally-friendly and sustainable aviation-related standards. Innovations in technology have already

Figure 12.15: The B747-4J6 *Dreamlifter* in Anchorage, United States
Photo ©Rocky Grimes/Shutterstock. Used with permission.

led to more fuel-efficient aircraft engines, lighter airframes, more efficient wing designs, and new biofuels; while changes in operations have led to reduced toxins and waste in ground operations.[37] In fact, today's aircraft are 75 percent cleaner and 70 percent quieter than they were 40 years ago.[38] The new Boeing 787 is particularly noticeable in its remarkably quiet operations.

The major aircraft manufacturers are equally committed to producing eco-friendly and more efficient aircraft. As stated in Airbus's *Global Market Forecast for 2007-2026*, "the need for an increasingly eco-efficient industry, which creates economic and social value with less environmental impact, is well understood by the millions of people involved in aviation. Aircraft manufacturers have an intrinsic requirement to be technological pioneers and to develop increasingly eco-efficient aircraft."[39]

Changes in air traffic control routing and other technology-enabled process changes are also expected to reduce fuel consumption, emissions, and noise pollution. Airfreighters, for example, often operate at off-hours, as their noise can create problems with airport neighbors. Some airports have considered banning night flights altogether. Brussels (Belgium) and the European Union have enacted some stringent noise regulations, mostly aimed at older airfreighters. Frankfurt bans night flights between the hours of 23h00 (11:00 p.m.) and 5h00 (5:00 a.m.).[40] The future is likely to hold more regulations for other heavily-used metropolitan airports, leaving room for the creation of other hubs in less urbanized centers, such as Prestwick in Scotland, Hahn in Germany, and Chateauroux in France.[41] To some extent, this development mirrors that of the Memphis airport, which has become the second largest cargo airport in the world, even though it is not located near a large metropolitan center.

The same motivation was behind the development of the Mid-America Airport near St Louis, Missouri, although it has not been successful. Once believed to be able to become a geographically central hub for many passenger and freight flights in the United States, because of its ideal location and unencumbered airspace, the airport has been essentially unused for the past two decades since its construction, with an average of two passenger flights a day in late 2016.[42]

In addition to the actions noted above, two relatively new approaches have recently been introduced to reduce the impact of aviation carbon emissions on the environment: carbon trading and voluntary carbon offset programs. These two unique programs allow owners and operators to purchase credits in organizations that absorb or offset carbon in an effort to mitigate total carbon emissions.

12.7   International Air Cargo Security

Beyond fuel prices and the overall state of the world's economy, security requirements represent the biggest challenge to the air cargo industry, and the challenge is overwhelming. Within the United States, for example, over 719 million people traveled on commercial aircraft in 2016, and more than 208 million traveled from the United States to foreign destinations.[43] This passenger volume represents more than 800 million pieces of baggage screened for explosives every year. There are also approximately 71 million tons of cargo transported by air domestically, and 5 million shipped internationally.[44] Of the 71 million tons of cargo transported domestically in the United States by air, approximately 7 million are shipped on passenger aircraft and the remaining 64 million are moved on cargo aircraft.[45]

One of the difficulties is that the security requirements differ for cargo shipped on passenger aircraft and cargo shipped on freighters. In addition, because of the evolving state of technology and the dynamic and unpredictable nature of terrorism, the security guidelines and safety processes followed in the air cargo industry are continuously changing.

12.7.1   Transportation Security Administration

Within the United States, the Transportation Security Administration (TSA) has overall responsibility for transportation security for the air cargo industry. To meet this challenge, TSA, with the help of U.S. Customs and Border Protection (CBP), relies on several methods to enhance security. For air cargo transportation, the TSA uses:

- Advance information on shipments by demanding the electronic submission of manifests before a flight can leave the airport of departure or before the flight is allowed to land in the United States.

- An Automated Targeting System (ATS) that screens U.S.-bound shipments prior to their arrival to determine the level of risk they represent, using a risk-analysis algorithm.

- Mandatory security inspections using non-intrusive inspection technology (NII) for all high-risk shipments. These efforts include large-scale imaging and radiation technologies, as well as canine detection teams.

- A partnership with the trade community designed to strengthen air cargo security by giving shippers an incentive to strengthen their internal security systems. One example of such cooperation is the Customs-Trade Partnership against Terrorism (C-TPAT) (see Chapter 16).

12.7.2 Advance Manifest Rules for Air Carriers

The Trade Act of 2002 requires that cargo manifests for all freight shipments that transit the United States be submitted electronically prior to arrival to Customs and Border Protection through its Automated Manifest System (AMS). For flights originating outside North America, electronic manifests must be received at least four hours prior to arrival at their first U.S. airport. For Mexico, Canada, and other locations that are less than four hours away, manifests must be transmitted to CBP prior to the aircraft's departure.

The U.S. Customs and Border Protection has launched a web-based Automated Commercial Environment (ACE) that enables multimodal manifest processing and allows importers, exporters, brokers, and transportation providers to use one integrated system to expedite shipping.

12.7.3 Certified Cargo Screening Program

Another key component in TSA's approach to security is the Certified Cargo Screening Program (CCSP). The CCSP mandates 100 percent screening of all air cargo transported by passenger aircraft, whether shipped within the United States or coming from abroad into the United States. This inspection is conducted at the "piece" level, which means that every item in a shipment must be inspected.[46]

The Certified Cargo Screening Program selects and approves Certified Cargo Screening Facilities (CCSFs) and monitors and maintains the security of shipments throughout the supply chain. The concept is that security is achieved with an inspection at the CCSF and with the continuous monitoring of the goods between the time they are inspected and the time at which they are loaded onto the aircraft. Such efforts are called chain-of-custody security methods. Once approved, a CCSF must adhere to increased TSA-directed security standards, share responsibility for supply chain security, employ chain-of-custody methods, permit onsite validations, submit a facility security plan, and be subject to transportation security inspections.[47]

It should also be noted that the United States built its air cargo Certified Cargo Screening Program based, in part, on best practices adopted from other countries such as the United Kingdom and Ireland.[48] It is also clear that many of the concepts now associated with the CCSP are being adopted by other foreign entities, in partnership with TSA, to validate and maintain the security of airfreight across international boundaries.

12.7.4   Air Carriers and C-TPAT

As is the case for all companies involved in international logistics, the U.S. Customs and Border Protection is looking for air carriers to join the Customs-Trade Partnership Against Terrorism (C-TPAT) to enhance existing security practices and reduce the threat of terrorism to international air shipments. Air carriers enrolled in C-TPAT are required to meet minimum-security criteria to achieve certification. To be eligible, air carriers must meet the following requirements:[49]

- Be an active air carrier transporting cargo shipments to the United States.

- Have an active IATA code.

- Possess a valid continuous international carrier bond registered with CBP.

- Have a designated company officer who will be the primary cargo security officer responsible for C-TPAT.

- Commit to maintaining the C-TPAT security criteria for air carriers.

- Create and provide CBP with a C-TPAT supply chain security profile, which identifies how the air carrier will meet, maintain, and enhance internal policy to meet the C-TPAT security criteria for air carriers.

Air carriers must conduct a comprehensive assessment of their security practices using C-TPAT criteria. These criteria include meeting business partner requirements, as well as the requirements for container or unit load devices (ULD) security, physical access controls, personnel security, procedural security, security training and threat awareness, physical security, and information technology security.

12.7.5   Air Cargo Security Requirements for Other Countries

Numerous countries have developed and implemented air cargo security standards like those established by the United States following the terrorist acts at the beginning of the twenty-first century. The United States and the European Union (EU), for example, signed an agreement in late 2008 to harmonize cargo screening standards for passenger aircraft. This agreement, signed between the TSA and the EU's Directorate General for Energy and Transport, is expected to provide a foundation for other bilateral security agreements based largely on the standards set by the 9/11 Commission Act of 2007. There is still room for greater harmonization between countries, however, and substantial concern among practitioners about multiple conflicting standards. As stated by Harald Zielinski, director of security for Lufthansa Cargo, "It is not possible to have 15 processes for 15 different security standards," and there is much work to be done.[50]

Review and Discussion Questions

1. Briefly describe the different types of air cargo services available.

2. Do you think that demand for air cargo will increase or decrease over the next three years? Why?

3. How does an air carrier determine a shipment costs? What can a shipper do to reduce the costs of shipping a light but voluminous package?

4. What is project cargo? Use the Internet to find and describe at least one example of the use of air transportation to ship project cargo internationally.

5. Using the freighter/payload range chart (Figure 12.10 on page 435), what type of airfreighter would you use to ship 60,000 kilograms over 3,500 nautical miles?

6. What is the purpose of an open-skies agreement?

7. What are some of the environmental challenges facing the air cargo industry today? How is the industry dealing with these issues?

8. What is the purpose of the Certified Cargo Screening Program?

9. What are the Advance Manifest Rules and how do they apply to air shipments bound for the U.S.?

Notes

[1] Crabtree, Thomas, Thomas Hoang, Russell Tom, and Gregg Gildeman, *The World Air Cargo Forecast 2016-2017*, Boeing Corporation, http://www.boeing.com/commercial/market/cargo-forecast/, accessed March 11, 2017.

[2] *Ibid.*

[3] Mecham, Michael, and Guy Norris, "Soft Freighter Market Dampens 747-8 Demand," *Aviation Week & Space Technology*, December 3, 2012.

[4] Crabtree, Thomas, Thomas Hoang, Russell Tom, and Gregg Gildeman, *The World Air Cargo Forecast 2016-2017*, Boeing Corporation, http://www.boeing.com/commercial/market/cargo-forecast/, accessed March 11, 2017.

[5] "About FedEx," http://about.van.fedex.com/our-story/company-structure/express-fact-sheet/, retrieved March 16, 2017.

[6] *World Air Transport Statistics*, International Air Transport Association, 60th Edition (2016), http://www.iata.org/docx/WATS_2016-infographic.pdf, retrieved March 15, 2017.

[7] Crabtree, Thomas, Thomas Hoang, Russell Tom, and Gregg Gildeman, *The World Air Cargo Forecast 2016-2017*, Boeing Corporation, http://www.boeing.com/commercial/market/cargo-forecast/, accessed March 11, 2017.

[8] "Cargo Volume: Loaded and unloaded freight and mail in metric tonnes," Airport Council International, http://www.aci.aero/Data-Centre/Monthly-Traffic-Data/Freight-Summary/Year-to-date, retrieved March 16, 2017.

[9] Crabtree, Thomas, Thomas Hoang, Russell Tom, and Gregg Gildeman, *The World Air Cargo Forecast 2016-2017*, Boeing Corporation, http://www.boeing.com/commercial/market/cargo-forecast/, accessed March 11, 2017.

[10] Wensveen, John, *Air Transportation: A Management Perspective*, Eighth edition, 2015, Routledge Publishing, Abington, United Kingdom.

[11] *Ibid.*

[12] "Connecting People and Possibilities: The History of FedEx," http://about.van.fedex.com/our-story/history-timeline/history/, retrieved March 16, 2017.

[13] Wensveen, John, *Air Transportation: A Management Perspective*, Eighth edition, 2015, Routledge Publishing, Abington, United Kingdom.

[14] "About FedEx," http://about.van.fedex.com/our-story/company-structure/corporate-fact-sheet/, retrieved March 16, 2017.

[15] "UPS Fact Sheet," https://pressroom.ups.com/assets/pdf/pressroom/fact%20sheet/UPS_General_-Fact_Sheet.pdf, accessed March 16, 2017.

[16] *Ibid.*

[17] Deutsche Post - DHL World Net Annual Report 2016, Bonn, Germany: Deutsche Post, http://www.-dpdhl.com/content/dam/dpdhl/Investors/Events/Reporting/2017/FY2016/DPDHL_2016_Annual_Report.pdf, retrieved March 16, 2017.

[18] Solomon, Adina, "Flowers' Fantastic Voyage," *Air Cargo World*, June 2013, pp. 36-40.

[19] Crabtree, Thomas, Thomas Hoang, Russell Tom, and Gregg Gildeman, *The World Air Cargo Forecast 2016-2017*, Boeing Corporation, http://www.boeing.com/commercial/market/cargo-forecast/, accessed March 11, 2017.

[20] *FedEx Corporation Annual Report (10K)*, Item 2. Properties, FedEx Corporation, http://fedex.com/-us/investorrelations/financialinfo/2008annualreport/corp_info.html, accessed February 16, 2009.

[21] Team, Trevis, "Boeing Will Sustain Its Current Market Share In Commercial Airplane Deliveries,"

Forbes, September 8, 2016, https://www.forbes.com/sites/greatspeculations/2015/09/08/boeing-will-sustain-its-current-market-share-in-commercial-airplane-deliveries/#198aeb397dcf, retrieved March 17, 2017.

[22]Leahy, John, *Mapping Demand: 2016-2035,* http://www.airbus.com/company/market/global-market-forecast-2016-2035/, retrieved March 17, 2017.

[23]"Orders and Deliveries," http://www.airbus.com/presscentre/corporate-information/orders-deliveries/, retrieved March 17,2017.

[24]"Orders and Deliveries," http://www.boeing.com/commercial/#/orders-deliveries, retrieved March 17, 2017.

[25]Crabtree, Thomas, Thomas Hoang, Russell Tom, and Gregg Gildeman, *The World Air Cargo Forecast 2016-2017*, Boeing Corporation, http://www.boeing.com/commercial/market/cargo-forecast/, accessed March 11, 2017.

[26]Andriulaitis, Robert. "B747-8F v. A380F," *InterVISTAS*, December 2005, retrieved September 29, 2012.

[27]Roelfzema, Gerard, " 'Flower Power' by Air France - KLM - Martinair Cargo," *Cargo Airport and Airlines Services*, March 9, 2017, http://www.caasint.com/single-post/2017/03/09/"Flower-Power"-by-AIR-FRANCE-KLM-MARTINAIR-Cargo, retrieved March 18, 2017.

[28]Whitefield, Mimi, "Where Did These Valentine's Day Flowers Come From? The Airport, Sweetheart," *MEA Cargo*, February 14, 2017, http://www.meacargo.com/2017/02/14/fl-where-did-these-valentines-day-flowers-come-from-the-airport-sweetheart/, retrieved March 18, 2017.

[29]Ricaurte, Francisco, "From Latin America With Love: The Valentine's Day Challenge," *Longitudes*, February 13, 2017, https://longitudes.ups.com/from-latin-america-with-love-the-valentines-day-challenge/, retrieved March 18, 2017.

[30]*Ibid.*

[31]"Roses are …Brown? Flower Imports Showcase International Logistics," *Compass Online*, UPS, http://compass.ups.com/goingglobal/article.aspx?id=1649, retrieved July 2, 2009.

[32]Karst, Tom, "Cherry exports poised for another strong year," *The Packer*, May 25, 2015, http://www.thepacker.com/news/cherry-exports-poised-another-strong-year, retrieved March 18, 2017.

[33]"Open Skies Partnerships: Expanding the Benefits of Freer Commercial Aviation," United States Department of State, https://www.state.gov/e/eb/rls/fs/2017/267131.htm, retrieved March 19, 2017.

[34]"Runway extension at Narita finally opens," *Japan Times*, October 23, 2009, http://www.japantimes.co.jp/news/2009/10/23/news/runway-extension-at-narita-finally-opens/#.Uc1_Ntjxn4s, retrieved June 28, 2013.

[35]"Committee on Aviation Environmental Protection," International Civil Aviation Organization, http://www.icao.int/env/caep.htm, retrieved March 12, 2009.

[36]*Aviation Carbon Offset Programmes*, International Air Transport Association, May 2008, http://www.iata.org/whatwedo/environment/Documents/carbon-offset-guidelines-may2008.pdf, retrieved May 11, 2017.

[37]Gardner, T., "Aviation Goes Green from the Ground on Up," *Chicago Tribune*, March 9, 2008, p. 2.

[38]*Airbus Global Market Forecast 2007-2026*, Airbus, December 2007, http://www.airbus.com/fileadmin/documents/gmf/PDF_dl/00-all-gmf_2007.pdf, accessed June 29, 2009.

[39]*Airbus Global Market Forecast 2009-2028*, Airbus, September 2009, http://www.airbus.com/en/gmf2009/data/catalogue.pdf, accessed October 29, 2009.

[40]"German Court Nixes Frankfurt Night Flights," *Air Cargo World*, November 2011, pp. 6-7.

[41]Barnard, Bruce, "Night flights to be Banned in Brussels," *Journal of Commerce*, January 5, 2000, p. 3.

[42] Bustos, Joseph, "Allegiant Air to increase flights from MidAmerica this summer," *Belleville News-Democrat*, November 29, 2016, http://www.bnd.com/news/local/article117718058.html, retrieved March 19, 2017.

[43] "Passengers—All Carriers, All Airports," Bureau of Transportation Statistics, https://www.transtats.bts.gov/Data_Elements.aspx?Data=1, retrieved March 19, 2017.

[44] "Passenger Boarding (Enplanement) and All-Cargo Data for U.S. Airports," Federal Aviation Administration, http://www.faa.gov/airports/planning_capacity/passenger_allcargo_stats/passenger/, retrieved March 19, 2017.

[45] Crabtree, Thomas, Thomas Hoang, Russell Tom, and Gregg Gildeman, *The World Air Cargo Forecast 2016-2017*, Boeing Corporation, http://www.boeing.com/commercial/market/cargo-forecast/, accessed March 11, 2017.

[46] "Certified Cargo Screening Program," May 29, 2013, Transportation Security Administration, http://www.tsa.gov/certified-cargo-screening-program, retrieved July 4, 2013.

[47] *Ibid.*

[48] "TSA/CBP Air Cargo Security Workshop," U.S. Customs and Border Protection, http://www.cbp.gov/linkhandler/cgov/trade/trade_outreach/trade_symposium_archive/symposium08/event_materials/air_cargo_ccsp.ctt/air_cargo_ccsp.pdf, retrieved July 4, 2013.

[49] "Air Carrier Eligibility Requirements," U.S. Customs and Border Protection, http://www.cbp.gov/linkhandler/cgov/trade/cargo_security/ctpat/ctpat_application_material/ctpat_security_guidelines/air_carriers/ac_eligibility_requirements.ctt/ac_eligibility_requirements.pdf, retrieved July 2013.

[50] Conway, Peter, "Air Cargo Security Screening Deadline Draw Near," *Airline Business*, October 29, 2008, http://www.flightglobal.com/articles/2008/10/29/318023/air-cargo-security-screening-deadlines-draw-near.html.

Chapter 13

International Land and Multimodal Transportation

This chapter is the last of a series of three chapters covering the different means of transportation available to an international shipper. The preceding two chapters covered ocean and air transportation. This chapter presents the remaining alternatives.

First, this chapter will present the two main land-based shipping methods available to an international shipper: road and rail transportation. Both are more frequently used in Europe for international freight, where they represent more than 80 percent of the total intra-European freight traffic by weight and value,[1] than they are in Asia and North America. However, practices differ, and a savvy international logistics manager should be familiar with the issues presented by road and rail transportation.

The second part of the chapter will cover the specifics of international intermodal transportation, which is not a transportation alternative properly speaking, but is the practice of shipping a product under a single bill of lading that covers more than one mode of transportation. For many shippers, intermodal transportation is often associated with container shipping.

Finally, two additional alternative methods of transportation are covered: inland waterway barges and pipelines. Although both represent a large percentage of the volume of international shipments of some commodities (agricultural raw materials, construction aggregates, coal, and crude oil), they are limited in the types of cargoes they can transport.

Figure 13.1: A North American Semi-Truck (Limited to a 53-foot Trailer (16.1 meter) but with no Limit on the Tractor)

Photo ©Nico Schmedemann/Shutterstock. Used with Permission.

Figure 13.2: A European Semi-Truck, Limited to 18.75 meters overall (61.5 feet) and a Cab-over-Engine Tractor

Photo ©Vytautas Kielaitis/Shutterstock. Used with Permission.

13.1 Truck Transportation

Trucking, from a North American perspective, is primarily a domestic means of transportation, except for the significant amount of trade between Canada and the United States and some limited trade between the United States and Mexico. However, the latter is still mostly trade to and from the U.S.-Mexico border, as a large percentage of the trade between those two countries is conducted on a DAT (Delivered At Terminal) Incoterms® rules 2010 basis (see Chapter 6) and because Mexican trucks are, for all intents and purposes, not yet allowed to operate on American highways, with a few exceptions.[2,3]

For the rest of the world, though, trucking is a vital way of shipping goods internationally. More than half of the merchandise shipped by truck within the European Union is shipped to a destination in a foreign country,[4] and this share is increasing as the countries joining the Union, such as Poland, Slovakia and the Czech Republic, are landlocked and even more reliant on road transport.

Worldwide, trucking is still dominated by a patchwork of domestic rules and regulations, which greatly influence the way the domestic trucking industry is organized. There are limits on the number of axles a truck may have, on the weight it can carry per axle, on its total weight, on its overall length and width, on the overall length of its trailer, as well as requirements regarding its mandatory

semi truck
An articulated truck that is made up of a tractor and a trailer.

tractor
The part of an articulated truck that is in the front and pulls the trailer.

trailer
The part of an articulated truck that is in the rear and pulled by the tractor.

Figure 13.3: The Swiss "Rolling Highway" in the Alps
Photo ©Ralpin AG. Used with Permission.

equipment, and the training of drivers and the number of consecutive hours they can drive. These constraints generate fleets of trucks that differ from country to country. Altogether, however, trucks carrying international cargo tend to be semi-trucks. These are made up of two distinct units: a tractor pulling a trailer, both of which take on characteristics that are country specific (see Figures 13.2 and 13.1); however, in the European Union, if a truck is legal to drive in one of the EU countries, it is legal to drive in all EU countries.

The biggest challenge in shipping goods internationally by trucks is to abide by all these rules and regulations, the complexity of which should not be underestimated. Case in point: European countries, even the smallest ones, like Luxembourg, have driving bans for certain types of trucks and cargo on certain days—generally Sundays or at night—, or change speed limits at night, or on certain days, but none of these bans are coordinated or harmonized. There are hundreds of different driving bans or restrictions in the European Union, if the special holiday restrictions are included,[5] which can create havoc on a company's ability to ship goods just-in-time, or for a shipper to reach a port before a sailing. Poland, for example, prohibits trucks from driving when temperatures reach 30 degrees Celsius (86 degrees Fahrenheit), and Switzerland amended its constitution to prohibit trucks weighing more than 28 metric tonnes from going farther into Switzerland than 10 kilometers (6 miles), relegating all large trucks crossing the country to piggy-back on railroad cars[6] (see Figure 13.3); in 2016, the Rollende Landstrasse (rolling highway) carried a total of 109,000 tractor-trailers through the Alps.[7] The Freight Transport Association publishes an annual *Yearbook of Road Transport Law* to keep its members informed of the different laws and road regulations within the European Union.[8]

piggy-back
A technique that consists of placing semi trucks or trailers on railroad cars.

Such constraints have the effect of having created a large number of rest areas at the entry points into a country and at highway exits, that act as giant parking lots for trucks, while offering amenities to truck drivers. Enforcing this myriad of rules and regulations also creates delays. Although there are officially no longer any border controls for trucks within the European Union, police routinely stop truckers to enforce rules regarding driving times, speed limits, axle loads, cargo manifests and placards, and so on, few of which are the same from one country to the next.

The second challenge regarding shipping by truck is the state of the infrastructure. Load limits, height limits, and speed limits (road conditions) hinder the smooth transportation of goods and have an impact on packing. For example, the

Figure 13.4: An Australian Road Train
Photo ©Inge Hogenbijl/Shutterstock. Used with Permission.

E-30 highway, one of the key links between western Europe (Berlin) and Russia, was so crowded and in such a state of disrepair that traffic was very slow, making it one of the most dangerous highways in Europe. It was not until 2013 that a good percentage of its replacement was completed, but the new road is still a two-lane highway for most of the trip, and was not yet completed as of 2017.[9]

However, that is unfortunately not all: the prohibitive taxation of diesel fuel in some countries influences the power of trucks, the size of the trailers, and the speeds at which cargo moves. In an attempt to save fuel, truck drivers slow down. In addition, the high tolls of some European highways lure truckers into driving on secondary roads that are not as cargo friendly. Some companies are "flagging out" their trucks—registering them in other countries—to take advantage of lower taxation and regulations: as much as 50 percent of trucks operating from Austria have been "flagged out,"[10] bringing the same kind of concerns that flags of convenience have triggered for the marine industry (see Chapter 11).

overloaded
A means of transportation that carries cargo in excess of its stated capacity.

Another factor is the cultural aspect of the industry. While overloaded trucks are rare in developed countries, they are strikingly commonplace in Africa and in some parts of Asia, where, seemingly, a truck is not full until it is no longer possible to add one more piece of cargo (see Figure 13.5).

Finally, the complementary infrastructure of railroads influences the way some

Figure 13.5: An Overloaded Truck in Sudan, Africa
Photo ©Lutz Heckenberger/Shutterstock. Used with Permission.

goods are shipped. In North America, for example, a large fleet of railroad cars capable of carrying truck trailers enables trucking companies to load trailers onto trains rather than drive them across the country. In Australia, however, the complete lack of railroads in some areas, and a mismatch of different gauges, has pushed trucking companies to develop road-trains, which are tractors pulling three to five full-size semi trailers (see Figure 13.4).

road train
An Australian trucking technique, consisting of one tractor pulling three to five semi trailers.

The last challenge regarding trucking, specifically in Europe, is the fact that road transport is often delayed by social unrest. In the first six months of 2016, there were no fewer than ten instances during which some group or another blocked truck traffic somewhere in the European Union.[11] Farmers protesting high gas prices, truckers protesting low wages, ecologists worried about pollution—just about every pretext was used to block entrances to highways, harbors, refineries, Alpine routes, or whatever else, causing lengthy delays up to seven days for truck shipments. Because governments routinely capitulate to these demands, it is unlikely that the number of such protests will diminish in the future.

13.2 Rail Transportation

Another contrast between North America and the rest of the world is the extent to which railroads are used for freight movements. In the United States, for example, 2.86 trillion freight tonne kilometers [FTKs] (1.745 trillion ton-miles) were shipped by rail in 2015, or a market share of more than 40 percent of all ton-miles shipped long-distance in the country.[12,13] The growth of intermodal freight accounted for almost 40 percent of all carloads transported, a total of just under 13.5 million trailers or containers.[14] Although there are no figures available for international freight within North America, it is likely that the percentages are similar.

container
A large metallic box used in international trade that can be loaded directly onto a truck, a railroad car or an ocean-going vessel. The most common dimensions of a container are $8 \times 8.5 \times 20$ feet and $8 \times 8.5 \times 40$ feet.

In contrast, European railroads carried only about 411 billion FTKs of freight traffic (about 250 billion ton-miles) in 2015,[15]—even though the 28 countries of the European Union have a cumulative economy and territorial size that are larger than those of the United States—representing just over 18 percent of all FTKs shipped within the European Union.[16] In addition, only a small percentage of those shipments were intermodal, with a large percentage of cargo transported in traditional railroad cars, each designed for its own specific purpose (see Figure 13.6). Intermodal transport (or co-modality, as it is called within the European Union) can be as high as 60 percent in Norway and as low as 2 percent in Finland, but the average for the entire EU is about 25 percent.[17]

In Australia, of the total 500 billion FTKs carried in the country in 2014—the last year for which data were available—railroads carried 58 percent of freight, and roads 42 percent.[18] Most of the Australian freight traffic is ores and grain shipped over long distances.

The railroad infrastructure in Europe is focused on passenger traffic, and freight traffic is somewhat neglected, with little investment in railroad cars and facilities designed to enable intermodal cargo. In addition, because all railtracks

Figure 13.6: European Railroad Cars, Each Designed for a Type of Merchandise
Photo ©Evlakhov Valeriy/Shutterstock. Used with Permission.

single stack
The practice of placing containers on a railroad car on only one height. It contrasts with the practice of placing them two high.

double-stack
The practice of placing containers on a railroad car on top of one another.

freight corridor
A section of a railroad network dedicated to freight traffic.

are electrified, and therefore catenaries—overhead electric lines—are present on all railways, all European intermodal cargo must be transported on single-stack railroad cars (cars carrying a single container, see Figure 13.7). European practice is also to build short trains of 20-25 cars, mostly because passenger trains are shorter and the signaling equipment has been designed for them. In contrast, most of the United States' infrastructure is not electrified, and has been modified to accommodate double-stack cars (see Figure 13.8), with trains of three or four locomotives and as many as 100 cars.

In the last few years, the European Community has introduced nine "freight corridors" that are designed to carry freight from one part of Europe to another, bypassing the requirements to change to a national locomotive and a national crew at every border crossing and allowing private freight companies to compete with state-owned enterprises.[19] Nevertheless, since these "rail freight freeways" utilize currently existing lines, and because passenger trains have priority over all other traffic, there have been widespread problems with the implementation of this initiative, and "tangible results are not yet visible."[20]

One of these corridors is a double-track rail line from the port of Rotterdam to the Netherlands-Germany border: it is called the Betuweroute. It connects to the network of the Dutch and German railways and relieves congestion in the port. The Betuweroute carries only freight trains and has reached a volume of 111 trains per day, carrying 70 percent of the cargo volume between the Port of Rotterdam and Germany. [21] Although successful, there has been much opposition to the track's expansion, mostly because of the environmental impact of track construction. The other corridors have not created new rail lines, but are long rail connections linking ports in Northern Europe to ports in Southern Europe, or ports in Western Europe to ports and cities in Eastern Europe.[22]

Another attempt at linking ports has been conducted by the Société Nationale des Chemins de Fer Français (SNCF), the French national railroad company. It created a subsidiary, Naviland Cargo,[23] that offers services between the large French ports and the large Belgian ports. There are also inter-modal terminals within the Naviland Cargo network, to facilitate the transfer of cargo from rail to road. The company reports having transported 400,000 TEUs in 2016.[24]

The railroad industry has also experienced a change in the mix of cargo it carries over the past twenty years. In the U.S. particularly, railroads traditionally transported three primary types of cargoes until the 1980s:

- Bulk freight, not only grain, coal, lumber, steel, ores, chemicals, and oil, but also molasses, vegetable oils, and other heavy items. Each of these bulk cargoes tends to have its own type of railroad car.

- Breakbulk freight placed in boxcars, either palletized or simply in its packaging

- Automobile freight, placed on specialized car carriers

Figure 13.7: Single-Stack Container Cars under Electric Catenaries
Photo ©Martin Mojzis/Shutterstock. Used with Permission.

Figure 13.8: North American Double-Stack Container Cars
Photo ©Joseph Sohm/Shutterstock. Used with Permission.

In the last three decades, the advent of intermodal transportation has radically changed this mix of cargo carried by rail and dramatically altered the railroad business. Railroads now carry an increasing number of containers placed on container carriers (see Figure 13.8) and truck trailers on piggy-back cars (see Figure 13.9).

Initially, container carriers were designed to be only one container high, but then double-stacks were introduced, which doubled the capacity of each train but forced railroads to update their infrastructures—tunnels and overhead bridges in particular—so that these double-stack cars would fit. In 2016, U.S. railroads carried a total of 13.5 million trailers or containers,[25] an estimated 25 percent of which were transiting on a land bridge between Asia and Europe (see Section 13.3.2).

land bridge
A term coined to describe the practice of shipping goods from Asia to Europe through the United States by using railroads.

Though the future of rail transportation in the United States was bleak in the 1970s, it has transformed itself into a customer-oriented vibrant industry—despite some serious disturbances when Union Pacific bought Southern Pacific—with substantial expected growth as its focus moves from its traditional cargoes, such as grain and automobiles, to containers and truck trailers. The European railroads appear to have noticed this trend and are attempting to embrace it;

however, the national railroads are such bloated bureaucracies that progress is slow and success is elusive. In November 2000, EU railroad companies passed a resolution that would open their networks to each other's crews and engines; however, as of 2017, little progress had been made. Moreover, France opposes opening its network despite the agreement, so a large, geographically necessary swath of the rail network may not be available. Add to this lack of cooperation the discrepancies of at least two railroad gauges, five electrical systems, and 16 signaling systems, and the task seems daunting. The formation of the European Association for Railway Interoperability in 1996, charged with creating a trans-European network of high-speed passenger trains, has spurred cooperation between the national railroad companies, and these efforts may eventually be extended to freight transport.

Another possible development is the replacement of some ocean trade with rail transportation, notably between the Far East (China, Korea) and Europe; this idea can seriously shorten transit times between the two areas and relieve some of the congestion in southern China's ports. After being extensively studied,[26] such a landbridge was pioneered by DB Schenker, which now offers a daily train from Shanghai to Hamburg and Duisberg.[27,28]

Figure 13.9: North American Piggyback Railcars
Photo ©Richard Thornton/Shutterstock. Used with Permission.

13.3   Intermodal Transportation

intermodal
A shipment that takes more than one mode of transportation under a single bill of lading.

co-modality
A shipment that takes more than one mode of transportation under a single bill of lading.

Probably the best way to introduce intermodal transportation is to define the concept:

> Intermodal describes a shipment that takes several different means of transportation—road, rail, ocean, air—from its point of departure (seller/exporter) to its point of destination (buyer/importer). The meaning of intermodal transport has evolved recently to limit the use of this term to freight for which a single bill of lading covering more than one of these alternatives is issued.

Intermodal transportation is therefore not a means of transportation *per se*, but instead is the practice of utilizing a single bill of lading to cover several means of transportation for a single shipment. For that reason, intermodal transportation is also called multimodal transportation, or co-modality in Europe. To use a recent cliché, the changes in means of transportation are "transparent" to the user, which means that the shipper does not know the specific itinerary and carrier for the cargo. The responsibility of arranging for all of the means of transportation falls onto the shipping company. Nevertheless, the shipper must be aware of the alternatives, so it can pack accordingly.

Shipping companies have had to change their perspectives from simple transportation providers to that of providers of a multiplicity of services, one of which is transportation in their core competency, such as ocean shipping. However, shipping companies also must provide transportation services in other modes, such as trucking or rail in pre-carriage or on-carriage. In addition, shipping companies now interact with their customers directly and offer such ancillary services as tracking shipments online. Most importantly, intermodal service created the possibility for an exporter (or an importer) to have a single interlocutor in a complex international shipment involving more than one mode of transportation. This one-stop shopping is what has made intermodal transportation so popular with shippers.

Because of the ubiquitous use of the seagoing container in multimodal shipments, the term intermodal has also been strongly associated with this transportation concept. Containers are fairly recent. They were created in 1956 by Malcom McLean in an attempt to eliminate the large number of handlings to which ocean cargo was subjected, and to speed up the loading and unloading of ships. Containers have been a smashing success, with more than 10.7 million TEUs (twenty-foot equivalent units) in use worldwide.[29]

Certainly, the use of containers allowed the concept of intermodality to develop, but the two concepts are not entwined. It is possible to have an intermodal shipment that is not packaged in a container, and it is possible to use only one mode of transportation to ship containerized cargo. Nevertheless, the two are strongly connected, and probably 95 percent of all intermodal cargo is shipped in containers, of which there are many different types. In addition, that percentage is growing, as more container types have been created to allow nonstandard cargo to be containerized.

Figure 13.10: 20-foot and 40-foot Containers as well as a Single 45-foot Container (Top Right) on a Containership in the Port of Rotterdam

Photo ©Bjoern Wylezich/Shutterstock. Used with Permission.

13.3.1   Types of Seagoing Containers

Most containers (see Figure 13.10) in the seagoing trade are the standard 20-foot and 40-foot units (6.1 and 12.2 meters, respectively); these containers are 8 feet wide (2.44 meters), 8.5 feet tall (2.59 meters), and fully enclosed in steel. They are equipped with a double door at one end (called the front of the container) and have a wooden floor; some have wooden sides as well. These standard containers are also called ISO boxes, and are named after the International Organization for Standardization.

Seagoing containers can be stacked on top of one another. Below deck, they can be stacked up to nine high, but above deck, it is generally fewer that that. On the largest ships (see Figure 11.8 on page 392), the number of containers in an on-deck stack can be as high as eight. In ports, they generally are not stacked higher than six.

There are several variants that were designed around this common platform. Each of these alternatives is called a "special," and its availability may be limited to certain routes and/or shipping lines. All of these specials possess the same "footprint" as the ISO boxes so that they can be easily stacked aboard a ship, stored in a port, or placed on a truck trailer. Their dimensions are 8 × 40 feet or 8 × 20 feet. The following list represents the most frequently used specials.

standard container
A large metallic box used in international trade that can be loaded directly onto a truck, a railroad car or an ocean-going vessel. The most common dimensions of a container are 8 × 8.5 × 20 feet and 8 × 8.5 × 40 feet.

ISO box
Another term for a standard container.

Figure 13.11: Liquid-Bulk Containers in the Port of Rotterdam
Photo ©VanderWolf Images/Shutterstock. Used with Permission.

high-cube container
A container designed to
hold cargo that is is
voluminous and light. Its
height is 9.5 feet.

- **The high-cube container**—This container is 9.5 feet (2.9 meters) tall and
therefore can hold slightly more cargo. High-cube containers are designed
to hold cargo that "cubes out" before it "weighs out"—*i.e.*, it fills the volume of the container before it reaches the container's maximum weight
limit, which is 24 metric tonnes (52,910 pounds) for a 20-foot container
and 30.5 metric tonnes (67,200 pounds) for a 40-foot container. Several of
the 40-foot containers on Figure 13.10 on the preceding page are high-cube
containers, and they can be placed in the same stack as traditional 40-foot
ISO boxes, without limitations. High-cube containers now represent most
of the containers in use in the world because of their versatility.

extended-length container
A container whose length
extends beyond the
traditional 40-foot length of
standard containers.

- **The extended-length container**—This container is designed to hold cargo
that does not fit in a 40-foot container. The enclosed extended-length containers are 45 feet long (see Figure 13.10). Some other extended-length
containers are designed so that the cargo "sticks out" of the container itself: in those situations, they are more difficult to pack, as the center of
gravity must still be within the box itself. Extended-length containers are
more cumbersome to load aboard ships, and store in ports, as they must be
placed on top of stacks. These containers are utilized for what otherwise

would have been breakbulk cargo. On occasion, extended-length containers must also have the next stacks' top slot empty. Extended-length containers can also present additional challenges when they are placed on trucks, especially in countries where roads are narrow.

- **The liquid-bulk container**—In this 20-foot container (see Figure 13.11), a tank designed to hold liquids is placed inside a frame that has the same outside dimensions as a 20-foot box. Containers holding liquid bulk can have slightly different designs depending on the type of cargo carried and can be made of a variety of materials. Nevertheless, the frame is built to the standards of the International Organization for Standardization (ISO), and liquid-bulk containers can be stacked with traditional containers.

liquid-bulk container
A 20-foot container used to transport liquid loads.

- **The dry-bulk container**—This container is designed to hold dry-bulk products, such as grain or polymer pellets. Using dry-bulk containers to ship dry bulk is becoming more common, as the container allows for fewer handlings than when the cargo is strictly bulk or packaged in drums or bags (see Chapter 14), and therefore there is a lower probability of a portion of the cargo being lost to handling. If the cargo is not too dense, dry-bulk

dry-bulk container
A container used to transport bulk loads that are not unitized.

Figure 13.12: A Dry-Bulk Container with Liner, being Unloaded in Istanbul, Turkey
Photo ©LiquaTrans. Used with Permission.

Figure 13.13: An Open-Top Container in the Port of Cleveland
Photo ©Pierre David. Used with Permission.

can be shipped inside a 40-foot container that is protected with a plastic liner (see Figure 13.12). However, because some bulk cargo is quite heavy (grain, for example), a shorter dry-bulk container exists —about 4 feet tall (1.2 meters)—so that three containers can fit where two traditional 40-foot containers normally do. This design greatly facilitates rail transport, as three containers fit on a double-stack train. However, that design has not gained much popularity.

open-top container
A container designed so that cargo can be loaded from the top, and that is covered by a tarpaulin.

- **The open-top container**—This container (see Figure 13.13) is designed to hold cargo that is too large to be placed in the container through its doors and therefore must be loaded from the top. The container is then covered with a tarpaulin. Open-top containers can also be used to hold cargo that is taller than 8 feet, and the cargo then protrudes through the top of the container. Because it is then impossible to stack another container on top of that tall cargo, open-top containers are always considered "top of stack," whether placed under deck or on deck.

flat-rack container
A container designed to hold cargo whose width does not fit inside a standard container. The width of the cargo should be less than 8 feet.

- **The flat-rack container**—This container (see Figure 13.14 on the next page) is designed to hold cargo that is roughly 8 feet wide but does not fit in a standard container, which has inside dimensions of 92.5 inches (2.35 meters). A flat-rack container may have only four corner posts or two end walls, giving it a shape that allows a flat rack to be part of a stack as long as the cargo is not taller than the corners or walls. When the cargo is too tall or too wide, the flat-rack container must be stowed at the top of a stack. Flat racks are used for shipments of pleasure boats, trucks, and military vehicles, among other large products.

Figure 13.14: A Flat-Rack Container with Oversize Cargo that Must Be Placed Top of Stack
Photo ©Kamonrat/Shutterstock. Used with Permission.

- **The hanger container**—This container is designed to hold garments "on hanger" (*i.e.*, it is equipped with steel bars on which clothes are hung). The hanger container is a relatively new device, but it seems to fulfill the need for a more convenient way to ship hanging clothes, which may be damaged when they are shipped flat in boxes or may be difficult to fold. Garment containers are all high-cube containers as well.

- **The 10-foot container**—When containers were first conceived by Malcom McLean in 1956, one additional size was created, the 10-foot container. This container size has not gained much popularity; most shippers who have a shipment that is small enough to be placed in a 10-foot container use the services of a freight consolidator who places that cargo with other shippers' cargo in a 20- or a 40-foot container.

hanger container
A container designed to hold cargo that cannot be laid flat in a box, and must remain on hangers during the international voyage.

- **The refrigerated container**—These 40-foot containers (see Figure 13.15) are also called "reefers," and can easily be identified as they are always painted white. A refrigerated container is designed to hold cargo at a constant temperature during the voyage. These containers need an outside power source (electricity) to function and must be plugged in during all the legs of the intermodal journey, while they are in port, and while they are being trucked to their final destination. Some refrigerated containers can maintain their temperatures with a refrigeration unit that is independent of shore—or ship—power, but these units must be refueled during their voyage, which can be difficult. Today, most containerships can accommodate many refrigerated container units.

Figure 13.15: A Refrigerated Container on a Truck in Chiangmai, Thailand
Photo ©Nitinut380/Shutterstock. Used with Permission.

A myriad of other specialized containers are available. They have been designed to ship automobiles, livestock, and other cargo that could not otherwise be shipped in a standard ISO box. However, all these modified containers can withstand the rigors of ocean shipping, be stacked with other ISO boxes, and be used in existing ocean-going vessels, railcars, trucks, and port terminals. In that respect, they are still all intermodal containers.

A difficulty with the development of special containers is the fact that they are not multipurpose: while a traditional ISO box that holds a cargo of automobile parts from the United States bound for Malaysia can be used on the way back to ship garments or toys, this is not the case with a livestock container. If it is designed for cattle, it is unlikely that it can be used for anything else but cattle, and will come back empty, forcing the owner to pay for an "empty" return trip before the container can be used to generate income again.

To a lesser extent, a similar problem exists with all ISO boxes because of the imbalance of trade between ports. For example, much more trade arrives in the Ports of Los Angeles and Long Beach in the United States from Asia than leaves these ports for Asian destinations. There is therefore an accumulation of so-called "empties" in the United States (and Europe), while there is a shortage of boxes in most Asian ports. There is also a container imbalance due to the types of products shipped; lower-value products are generally shipped by ocean, and higher-value products are shipped by air, which adds to the problem.

In the United States, the container imbalance is further exacerbated by the fact that most containers are shipped to large population centers, such as New York, Washington, and Chicago, which can be far away from the manufacturing centers that export goods to the Far East.

Figure 13.16: Containers Repurposed as a Retail Store in South Sudan
Photo ©Phototreat/istockphoto. Used with Permission.

Finally, for some trade routes, there is another reason for the shortage of boxes in one direction: a substantial portion of empty containers shipped to some destinations disappear, as they are used for storage or housing. Such is the case in some of the republics of the former Soviet Union and some African countries (see Figure 13.16).

Shippers returning empty containers are charged freight for transport. Empty containers entering the United States are considered "implements of international trade" and do not require a Customs Entry Processing form. However, U.S. Customs and Border Protection requires that empty containers be included on the ship's manifest and clears them as entry-exempt items. Empty containers must be completely empty: no blocking, bracing, or securing equipment, materials, or residual products of any kind can be found inside them. Because they can be inspected by U.S. Customs, the shipper is subject to being fined for illegal entry of goods if they are not completely empty.

Movable Boxes

International commerce was transformed by the arrival of the container. Before containers, the traditional method for loading and unloading a ship was a time-consuming and labor-intensive process. Goods, in boxes small enough to be handled by humans, were loaded by cranes onto breakbulk ships. Gangs of longshoremen were responsible for stowing them into the ship and making sure that they would not be damaged during the ocean voyage. The longshoremen had to make sure that heavy goods were lower in the hold than lighter goods, that the weight of the cargo was distributed evenly through the ship, and that every piece of cargo was wedged solidly against the others. It was back-breaking, dangerous work. Because a ship could not be loaded until it was completely unloaded, it took days to perform both operations. As trade increased, there was ever-more gridlock in the ports, and ocean shipping was agonizingly slow.

Containers revolutionized this system; containers are loaded, once, in the plant that manufactured the product, and unloaded, once, in the plant of the customer. There is no intermediary handling, no chance for pilferage, no possible damage from mishandling. The labor costs are lower, since the laborers are inland and not part of the strong (and costly) longshoremen's unions.

Containers of different sizes had been proposed several times before, but it was Malcom McLean, the owner of a trucking company, who eventually made the first investment in movable boxes of a size similar to a truck trailer and shipped them from Newark to Houston in April 1956. He eventually expanded this concept to other U.S. routes: the West Coast to Hawaii, Miami to Puerto Rico.

McLean's greatest challenges were with the unions of the ports in which he set up his operations; while West Coast ports' unions embraced the container system, the East Coast unions were more reluctant. He also had difficulties convincing port authorities to invest in cranes and docks; in particular the Port of New York was unwilling to invest in docks that were wide enough to allow trucks to come alongside ships. Eventually, the movable container prevailed, as all began to understand the benefits of the concept.

In the late 1950s, containers were of many different sizes. As McLean expanded the concept, others had copied him and chosen different standard sizes. It was eventually determined, after long negotiations between truckers, ship owners, railroads, and port authorities, both in the United States and in Europe, that containers should be 8 feet wide (2.44 meters), 8.5 feet high (2.59 meters) and either 10, 20, or 40 feet long (3.05, 6.10, or 12.19 meters). This standardization effort took the better part of a decade. Today, seagoing containers are only 20 or 40 feet long, so that they can fit in the holds of containerships. A few exceptions to these lengths exist, but they are rare. Since it was possible to modify their height without affecting the compatibility of containers, high-cube containers with a standard height of 9.5 feet high (2.90 meters) were added to the standard.

The composition of the 2015 worldwide fleet of 10.7 million containers is shown in Figure 13.17.

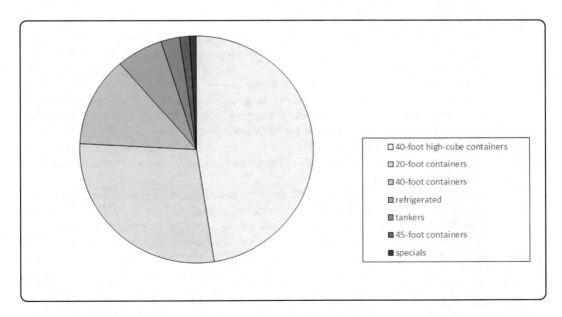

Figure 13.17: Worldwide Fleet of Containers, by Type, in TEUs (One 40-foot Container is 2 TEUs)
Drewry Maritime Research.

13.3.2 Land Bridges

land bridge
A term coined to describe the practice of shipping goods from Asia to Europe through the United States by using railroads.

The intermodal environment created several new ways to ship goods internationally. One of the most striking changes is the concept of land bridges. Via a land bridge, cargo traveling on ocean liners can cross a land obstacle by being unloaded in one port, transferred to a train, carried across the land obstacle by rail, and reloaded onto another ship.

The use of a typical land bridge involves cargo going from the Far East to Europe. A few years ago, breakbulk cargo loaded onto a ship would have crossed the Pacific, gone through the Panama Canal, and crossed the Atlantic before reaching its destination. (It could also have gone westward, through the Suez Canal, but that would be a different story.) Today, the same cargo can be containerized and use a land bridge: the cargo is shipped by ocean from the Far East to the West Coast of the North American Continent—Ports of Prince Rupert, in Canada, Los Angeles/Long Beach in the United States, or Ensenada in Mexico—after which the cargo is unloaded and placed on a train that takes it to the East Coast of the Continent—Ports of Virginia, Halifax, or Baltimore. The cargo is then reloaded onto another ship and sent to its destination in Europe. Using a land bridge is the penultimate in intermodal shipment; such changes in modes of transportation are so transparent to the shipper that it generally has no idea that its international cargo traveled through the Arizona desert on its way from Kobe, Japan, to Rotterdam, the Netherlands.

Such land bridges emerged because of several factors. The first factor is that the time spent by a ship traveling the Panama Canal route was greater than the time necessary to unload the cargo, cross the United States, and reload the cargo. The second factor is that unloading the cargo, traveling by train, and reloading the cargo was either equivalent in costs or cheaper. The third factor was that economies of scale could be achieved with larger ships, which would not fit through the Canal. The fourth factor was the concern, expressed by a few shipping lines, regarding the reliability of the Canal when it became the responsibility of the Panamanian government on December 31, 1999, a concern that fortunately did not materialize.

There are several other possible other locations for land bridges. There is a lot of ocean-going traffic from the Far East to eastern Europe, which can transit faster through Russia than by vessel: the port of Vostochny on the eastern shore of Russia was developed in the mid-1970s using Japanese funds to provide such a service. From conveying a high of 143,000 containers in 1983 to only 66,000 in 2015, this land bridge is but a speck in the transit volume from Japan and Korea to Europe.[30] However, the development of a seriously important land bridge is possible if North Korea were to re-open its railway system, which would allow cargo from South Korea to link with the Russian trans-Siberian railway and Europe. Finally, another ambitious idea has been the possibility of a Eurasian land bridge, which would cross Canada, Alaska, the Bering Strait, and connect the North American continent with Russia and Europe. As of spring 2017, a Eurasian land bridge was only an idea; however, the construction of a bridge spanning the Bering Strait has been considered several times.

There are two trends with land bridge use in the United States that are likely to bring contradictory results:

- **The increased demand for domestic intermodal service**—Domestic intermodal service increasingly competes for resources and capacity with international container service.[31] Specially designed 53-foot-long—16.1 meters—high-capacity containers (they are 8.5 feet wide—2.6 meters—and 9.5 feet tall—2.9 meters—, so wider than ISO containers, but as tall as high-cube boxes) have been put into use by U.S. trucking companies. These containers are intermodal in that they can be placed on a train or a truck, but they are not strong enough to be placed on sea-going ships. These 53-foot containers now account for most of the intermodal domestic traffic of the United States (see Figure 13.18). These domestic intermodal movements add strain to a rail system that is already at or near capacity on key corridors, the primary routes for international intermodal cargo, some of which are still single-track (see Chapter 3).

- **The expansion of the Panama Canal**—The canal locks of the Panama Canal—and its overall capacity—have been the major reasons for some shipments being diverted to land bridges. However, with the completion of the new locks in 2016, and with the Canal's increased capacity, it is likely that more

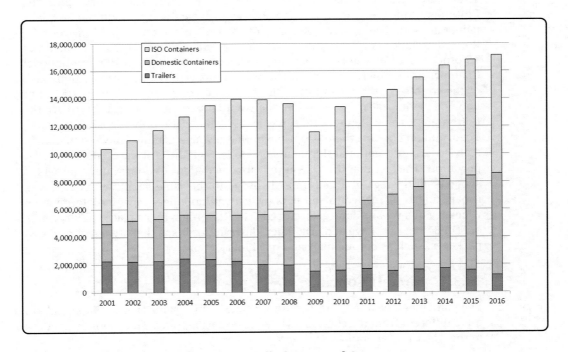

Figure 13.18: United States Intermodal Traffic by Type of Cargo
Adapted from IANA data.

carriers will offer all-water service from East Asia to the East Coast of the United States.

The potential for higher freight rates exists if the capacity of the rail network is strained; however the possible competition with the Panama Canal may also bring some lower rates. It is difficult to predict the outcome of these two trends.

13.3.3   Liability Issues

One aspect of intermodal shipping that has yet to be resolved is the carrier's liability toward the shipper when the goods are damaged while in the carrier's care. As goods travel from one mode of transportation to another, the legal or regulatory liability limits change. The limits are different for the trucking leg of the trip, the rail leg, and the ocean leg. In many cases, the limits are also different from one carrier to another, if such carrier has negotiated a different limit under the U.S. Ocean Shipping Reform Act (OSRA). To add further complexity, the flag under which the ocean carrier operates also matters. This issue is relevant mostly for shippers who elect to not insure their cargoes and for insurance companies. Nevertheless, it is one of the nagging issues left to be determined in intermodal transportation.

Rotterdam Rules
A 2008 international liability convention for intermodal cargo that restricts the liability of the carrier to U.S.\$ 875 per package or per customary freight unit.

As mentioned in Chapter 10, the United Nations Commission on International Trade Law (UNCITRAL) has designed a multimodal liability framework, called the Rotterdam Rules, that governs the liability of carriers when a multimodal bill of lading is used. The General Assembly of the United Nations voted to accept the Rotterdam Rules in February 2009, and in September 2009, the United States and 15 other countries signed it, heeding the recommendations of the International Chamber of Commerce, which had strongly supported the new convention. Each of the countries still has to ratify the treaty and complete its own legislation to implement the rules. A year after the twentieth country ratifies the treaty the Rotterdam Rules will enter into force; as of March 2017, only three had—Congo, Togo, and Spain—but there is optimism that a single liability convention may finally govern international shipments of goods, regardless of the method of transportation. The fact that the Convention applies to door-to-door shipments, which subjects all the legs of a multimodal voyage to the same liability limits, making it particularly attractive to shippers, which will no longer have to determine on which leg of a voyage damage occurred. The Rotterdam Rules place liability limits of SDR 875 per package and SDR 4 per kilogram for items that are not considered packages, such as automobiles and machinery.

13.3.4   Aircraft Containers

unit load device (ULD)
The term used to describe the containers used in airfreight transport.

The containers used in air transport are called Unit Load Devices (ULDs) and are quite different from the containers used in ocean shipping. The major differences in the way ULDs are built and used are:

- Unit Load Devices are used to aggregate small individual packages rather than to form a whole shipment. Freight consolidators and airlines bundle together several different cargo packages going to the same destination and unbundle them at the destination airport, sometimes to re-bundle them in another container for shipment to their final destination. In that regard, air-transport containers are used to speed up the loading and unloading of aircraft by shifting the task of loading and unloading small packages from the airplane to airport facilities. ULDs also allow airfreight companies to use space more efficiently. For example, companies can build shelves in the containers, which allow more freight to be carried.

- Although there have been some attempts to standardize air-transport containers, most are designed to fit a specific aircraft. There are at least 20 different ULD sizes, all identified by a code such as L-2 or EH, and some variants within the same size can be used as well. For example, L-2 can be used only in the belly of a Boeing 767, but EH can be used on any aircraft's main deck. Most aircraft containers, therefore, cannot be conveniently transported from one airplane to the next, and cargo must be de-containerized and re-containerized at airport facilities. This removes the advantage of being able to securely pack a container and leave it undisturbed until it is

Figure 13.19: A Variery of Unit Load Devices [ULD] in the Honolulu Airport
Photo ©Osugi/Shutterstock. Used with Permission.

unpacked by the consignee.

- Aircraft containers are made of lightweight materials and are not designed to protect the cargo in any significant way. Most containers are made of aluminum, Plexiglas, or sometimes plywood, with "doors" that can be made of the same material, or of fabric, or even be nonexistent, with the cargo being simply held by a net. These containers offer little protection against the elements or against theft (see Figure 13.19).

- Aircraft containers are not intermodal by intent. They are designed to be used only in aircraft and, possibly, for very short truck routes to shuttle goods to and from a freight forwarder's facilities. Aircraft containers are rarely used outside of the immediate vicinity of an airport.

13.4   Freight Forwarders

freight forwarder
A company specialized in shipping cargo on behalf of shippers—importers or exporters.

This complex array of shipping alternatives is often bewildering to an occasional shipper; in those cases, it makes sense for the shipper to use the services of a freight forwarder, or a firm that specializes in handling freight, particularly international freight.

A freight forwarder is, in layman's terms, a travel agent for freight. A good freight forwarder knows what alternative routes are available, can determine the cost of shipping goods between two points, and arrange all of the paperwork necessary to ship the goods, from the exporting country's requirements to the importing country's customs clearance.

Freight forwarders differ from customs brokers, who specialize in clearing customs for freight and who must take, at least in the United States, a rigorous examination to be allowed to fulfill this role. Freight forwarders also differ from Non-Vessel-Operating Common Carriers, who buy space on liner ships or airfreighters and resell it to less-than-container-load customers, and are regulated by the Federal Maritime Commission. Nevertheless, it is not uncommon for all three functions to be fulfilled by the same firm.

The business of freight forwarders is highly fragmented and includes many firms. Some are large, with operations in nearly every country. Others are quite small and distinguish themselves by specializing in a specific market, such as moving hazardous cargo, moving live animals, or moving project cargo.

13.5   Project Cargo

project cargo
Cargo that is much larger, heavier, or more complex to handle than regular cargo. Project cargo generally requires specialized means of transport.

Project cargo is cargo that is outside the normal realm of what shipping companies handle, specifically in terms of weight, volume, or destination. Most often, project cargo encompasses all the pieces of machinery or equipment required by a single project, such as the building of a dam or power plant, but also can be an entire plant that is being moved from a developed country, where its technology is outdated, to a developing country, to finish its useful life. Project cargo also includes any cargo that requires extra planning, such as shipping wind-turbine blades and nacelles, locomotives, railroad cars, large trucks, pleasure boats, large engines, electric generators, and so on.

In general, project cargo needs careful planning in order to safely reach its destination. The trucks used to transport project cargo to the port need to trace their itineraries carefully, not only to avoid low bridges and tunnels, but also to make sure that the proper permits can be secured. Port cranes must be checked to make sure they can handle the load, or else floating cranes must be rented. The ship carrying the cargo has to be selected carefully, to ensure it can accommodate the cargo. Roll-on/roll-off and breakbulk ships are the most commonly used means of getting project cargoes to their port of destination. Finally, the final road trip has to be planned thoroughly as well. It is not unusual for project-cargo shipments to be planned more than a year in advance and to cost several million dollars because of their complexity.[32]

Such project cargo also moves quite slowly; it is difficult to make a 250-tonne piece of equipment (550,000-pounds) move quickly, especially when it involves using all lanes of a highway at once, or taking down and replacing all overhanging electric, telephone, and other utility wires.[33] In late 2005, a 1.5-million-pound (680.4 metric tonne) hydro cracker for Canada's oil-sands project in Long Lake, Alberta (Canada), was moved by a heavy-lift ship to the Port of Duluth, Minnesota

Figure 13.20: A Wind-Turbine Blade Transported from Germany to France
Photo ©Volker Schlichting/Shutterstock. Used with Permission.

(U.S.). From the port, the unusual cargo traveled by rail on the world's largest rail car, the 36-axle German-made Schnabel car, that itself had to be shipped in advance to the United States so that it could carry that special load. The planning for the transportation of such a massive piece of equipment took two years. Ed Clarke, the logistician in charge of the move, said, "It's all about pre-planning. At every step along the way you have to check weights, dimensions, clearances. And you have to know everything about the environment in which the equipment will be handled."[34] On a typical oversize, heavy-lift project, the logistics manager has a long list of items to check: the cargo itself, generally where it is manufactured; the docks and cargo-handling equipment (cranes) in the ports in which the cargo will be handled; the vessel on which the oversize piece will be shipped; the rail cars, the rails, and the bridges and tunnels along the trip; and even the rail beds on which the cargo will be hauled.

13.6 Alternative Means of Transportation

Despite the dominance of the traditional means of transportation such as ocean shipping, airfreight, trucking, and railroads for moving cargo internationally, a few alternative means of transportation are also used regularly.

13.6.1 Pipelines

pipeline
A mode of transportation consisting of a long pipe and used for the transportation of liquid cargo.

The most easily overlooked of the alternative means of transportation are pipelines, which carry a substantial percentage of the world's petroleum oil and natural gas. Many of these pipelines are international. For example, Gazprom, the state-owned producer of gas in Russia, ships 525 billion cubic meters (18.5 trillion cubic feet) of gas to Europe in a single pipeline, which meanders through Belarus, Ukraine, Poland, Slovakia, and the Czech Republic before stopping in Germany, and provides fully 20 percent of the European Union's gas needs. A second pipeline is being planned, to serve Southern Europe, and will cross the Black Sea rather than Ukraine. Many other pipelines crisscross the Persian Gulf area and the North American continent.

Pipelines can also be used to replace ships for some areas of the world where it is particularly hazardous to navigate. One such planned pipeline would allow oil shipped from the oil fields of southern Russia to bypass the Bosporus, a particularly congested area located in the middle of a densely populated city, Istanbul. More than 50,000 ships travel its waters every year (see Figure 3.7 on page 78). The people of Istanbul and their government have been advocating such a pipeline, as they cannot control what goes through the strait—it is considered international waters—and they fear a catastrophic accident. Given the condition of some oil tankers, the treacheries of the currents in the narrow passage, and the fact that dozens of ships run aground or collide in the Bosporus every year,[35] it is not an unfounded fear. An oil and gas pipeline would remove some of this hazardous traffic.

Pipelines can be used for transporting coal as well, in the form of "slurry," a mix of water and pulverized coal that is then shipped as a liquid. Such a method can, in some cases, present some economic advantages over traditional railroad and truck transportation.

13.6.2 Barges

River barges are also commonly used to carry international cargo and are significant sources of transportation on certain routes and for certain merchandise. For example, 36 percent of all containers shipped to and from Rotterdam, the eleventh largest container seaport in the world—and the largest in Europe—travel by barge, with 53 percent traveling by truck and 11 percent traveling by rail.[36] The latter is a growing percentage, expected to increase with the European emphasis on low-emission means of transport. However, much of the bulk cargo (ores, agricultural commodities, and petroleum-related products) travels by barge.

In the United States, more than 600 million tons (mostly commodities such as coal, petroleum products, and grain) were carried on U.S. waterways in 2014.[37]

barge
A flat-bottom ship designed to transport cargo on the inland river network. A barge can be pushed or pulled, or be self propelled.

Figure 13.21: A Self-Propelled Chinese Barge on the Yangtse River, in China
Photo ©Claudio Zaccherini/Shutterstock. Used with Permission.

Sixty three percent of that volume was bound for international destinations and traveled mainly on the Mississippi River, the Ohio River, and the Gulf Intracoastal Waterway to the ports of New Orleans, Baton Rouge, Mobile, and Houston. Theses barges can easily be delayed, though, by natural variations in the weather: whenever a river is in flood stage and the currents are too strong, or when there is a drought and the river water level is lower than normal. Although they are much slower, river barges offer a very economical alternative to trucks and railroads.

The barges on the North American rivers are not self-propelled. They are moved in groups of five to ten, pushed by a tugboat, and take considerable skill to maneuver. The European and Asian barges (mostly found in China) are self-propelled, with crews living aboard them (see Figure 13.21 on the preceding page).

Ocean barges are also commonly used for shipping, although it is unclear how much of this mode of transportation is used for international shipping. Nevertheless, most of the traffic between the continental United States and Puerto Rico is done by barge, as is some of the traffic with small Alaskan towns.

13.7 Ground Transportation Security

In the aftermath of the terrorist attacks in the early part of the twenty-first century, additional security efforts in ground transportation primarily involved thorough inspections by customs and immigration officials and other means of increased scrutiny. The strategies were similar in the European Union and in the United States.

At the U.S. border crossings, the early stages of implementation of those increased inspection levels caused substantial additional delays, as there was relatively little capacity to increase the number of inspection stations. As mentioned in Chapter 3, there are only four large border crossings between the United States and Canada: (1) the Ambassador Bridge and a small tunnel between Detroit, Michigan, and Windsor, Ontario, with a combined 10 truck lanes of customs clearance in the United States; (2) the Blue Water Bridge in Port Huron, Michigan and Point Edward, Ontario, with 2 customs clearance truck lanes; (3) the Peace Bridge between Buffalo, New York, and Fort Erie, Ontario, with 3 customs clearance truck lanes; and (4) the Lewiston-Queenston Bridge north of Niagara Falls, with 3 truck lanes. Altogether, these 18 truck lanes must clear about 15,000 trucks each day. That is an average of about two minutes per truck, and therefore any additional inspections beyond a cursory review of paperwork causes delays. While there is a significantly larger number of land border crossings between the European Union and its external trading partners, as well as a smaller volume of international trade, the consequences of increased inspections were similar. Long delays and substantial frustrations were the norm at border crossings between the European Union and Albania, Belarus, Croatia, Macedonia, Russia, Serbia, Turkey, and Ukraine.

The United States and the European Union authorities addressed these issues in similar fashion; to identify the shipments that could present risks, authorities required an advanced shipping notification of the shipment's manifest. In the United States, since May 2008, the notification must be made at least one hour before the expected border crossing, and in electronic form through the Automated Commercial Environment (ACE). For the European Union, since July 2009, the notification must be made two hours in advance and electronically as well.

In addition, the United States implemented the Free and Secure Trade (FAST) program with Canada and Mexico, in which companies that are part of the Customs-Trade Partnership Against Terrorism (C-TPAT) can enroll. To recognize that these firms have implemented security measures in their supply chains, the U.S. Customs and Border Protection agency gives them access to a dedicated FAST lane at border crossings, allowing their trucks to clear customs faster. Being enrolled in FAST also allows companies to send the manifest information as late as 30 minutes before crossing the border. However, in order for a shipment to benefit from the FAST program, all parties involved in the transaction and the logistics of the shipment must be part of the FAST program, including the truck driver, who must possess a FAST card. As of March 2017, more than 78,000 commercial truck drivers had been cleared by U.S. Customs and Border Protection.[38]

Review and Discussion Questions

1. How do ground transport alternatives in various areas of the world differ? What constraints does a shipper face when using ground transport?

2. What is a land bridge? What effect will land bridges have on the frequency of container use in shipping cargo?

3. Choose three different types of ocean containers and explain how they are used.

4. How are ocean-going containers and aircraft containers different?

5. Comment on the opinion that "the number of cargo handling points is not diminished by using aircraft containers."

Notes

[1] *Energy, Transport and Environment Indicators*, European Statistical Agency, http://epp.eurostat-.ec.europa.eu/portal/page/portal/product_details/publication?p_product_code=KS-DK-12-001, retrieved March 20, 2017.

[2] Fritelli, John, "Status of Mexican Trucks in the United States: Frequently Asked Questions," Congressional Research Service, January 3, 2014, https://fas.org/sgp/crs/misc/R41821.pdf, retrieved March 20, 2017.

[3] Dunn, Jill, "As Congress eyes NAFTA rework, FMCSA policy granting Mexican carriers' authority goes to court," *Overdrive*, February 21, 2017, p. 12.

[4] *Energy, Transport and Environment Indicators*, European Statistical Agency, http://epp.eurostat.-ec.europa.eu/portal/page/portal/product_details/publication?p_product_code=KS-DK-12-001, retrieved March 20, 2017.

[5] "Driving Restrictions in Europe on Specific Days and Times," Trans Sib logistics, http://www.trans-sib-logistics.de/en/drivingbans, accessed March 21, 2017.

[6] Mariani, Daniele and Christian Raaflaub, "Shifting Freight Traffic to Rail Proves Daunting," June 24, 2012, Swissinfo.ch, http://www.swissinfo.ch/eng/swiss_news/Shifting_freight_traffic_to_rail_proves_daunting.html?cid=32968240, retrieved June 29, 2013.

[7] "Facts and figures," http://www.ralpin.com/company/factsandfigures/, retrieved March 21, 2017.

[8] *Yearbook of Road Transport Law*, Freight Transport Association, Tunbridge Wells, Kent, UK, http://www.fta.co.uk.

[9] Ciesnowski, Jacek, "Poland's highway overhaul," *Warsaw Business Journal*, July 31, 2014, http://-wbj.pl/polands-highway-overhaul/, retrieved March 21, 2017.

[10] Dieplinger, Maria, Elmar Fürst, and Sabine Lenzbauer, "Flagging Out as a Popular Strategy of Road Freight Transport Companies; Evidence of Three Consecutive Research Projects in Austria," *Association for European Transport*, 2010, abstracts.aetransport.org/paper/download/id/3532, retrieved March 21, 2017.

[11] Osborne, Samuel, "The European countries that strike the most," *Independent*, June 3, 2016.

[12] "Class I Railroad Statistics," Association of American Railroads, May 3, 2016, https://www.aar.org-/Documents/Railroad-Statistics.pdf, retrieved March 21, 2017.

[13] *Freight Rail Today*, Federal Railroad Administration, Department of Transportation, https://www.-fra.dot.gov/Page/P0362, retrieved March 21, 2017.

[14] "Monthly Rail Traffic Data," Association of American Railroads, https://www.aar.org/Pages/Freight-Rail-Traffic-Data.aspx#annualrailtraffic, retrieved March 21, 2017.

[15] *Energy, Transport and Environment Indicators*, European Statistical Agency, http://epp.eurostat-.ec.europa.eu/portal/page/portal/product_details/publication?p_product_code=KS-DK-12-001, retrieved March 20, 2017.

[16] *Ibid.*

[17] Wyman, Oliver, "Assessment of European Railways: Characteristics and Crew-Related Safety," *Association of American Railroads*, June 20, 2016, https://www.aar.org/Documents/Oliver Wyman, Assessment of European Railways (June 2016)[1].pdf, retrieved March 21, 2017.

[18] *Yearbook 2015: Australian Infrastructure Statistics*, 2015, Department of Infrastructure and Regional Development, https://bitre.gov.au/publications/2015/files/BITRE_yearbook_2015_full_report.-pdf, retrieved March 21, 2017.

[19] "The Rail Freight Sector Needs EU Action Now!", *Railway Insider*, June 9, 2009, http://rinsider.club-feroviar.ro/en/afiseaza_stire.php?id=4202.

[20] European Shippers' Council, "ESC position paper on Rail Freight Corridors and Regulation EU

913/2010," April 7, 2016, http://europeanshippers.eu/news/esc-position-paper-on-rail-freight-corridors-regulation-eu-9132010/, retrieved March 21, 2017.

[21] Duursman, Mark, "Betuweroute gaat grens over," *NRC Handelsblad*, April 16, 2016, https://www.nrc.nl/nieuws/2016/04/16/betuweroute-gaat-grens-over-1609267-a122784m, retrieved March 21, 2017.

[22] "Rail Freight Corridors (RFCs)," http://www.rne.eu/rfc-corridors, accessed March 21, 2017.

[23] http://www.naviland-cargo.com/?lang=en

[24] "Naviland Cargo," http://www.sncf.com/en/partners/naviland-cargo, retrieved March 21, 2017.

[25] "Monthly Rail Traffic Data," Association of American Railroads, https://www.aar.org/Pages/Freight-Rail-Traffic-Data.aspx#annualrailtraffic, retrieved March 21, 2017.

[26] "The Northern East-West (N.E.W.) Freight Corridor," International Union of Railways, Executive Project Office, Transportutvikling AS, Narvik, 2004, http://www.transportutvikling.no/NEW_report_-2004.pdf, retrieved October 29, 2009.

[27] "Hitching a Ride on the Eurasian Express," *Inbound Logistics*, October 2008, p. 24.

[28] "DB Schenker to launch daily freight train to China," *Railway Gazette*, September 30, 2011, http://www.railwaygazette.com/news/single-view/view/db-schenker-to-launch-daily-freight-train-to--china.html, retrieved June 30, 2013.

[29] "2010 IICL Annual Leased Container Fleet Survey," Institute of International Container Lessors, April 5, 2010, http://www.iicl.org/news/fleet.cfm, retrieved June 30, 2013.

[30] Russian Railways, "Russia: Trans-Siberian-China transit-container transportation increased 89% in nine months," November 17, 2015, http://uic.org/com/uic-e-news/473/article/russia-trans-siberian-china?page=iframe_enews, retrieved March 23, 2017.

[31] Dupin, Chris, "Intermodal growth engine stalls," February 7, 2017, *American Shipper*, http://www.americanshipper.com/main/news/intermodal-growth-engine-stalls--66677.aspx#hide, retrieved March 23, 2017.

[32] Zeller, Tom, Jr., "Big Loads on a 2-Lane Byway," *The New York Times*, October 22, 2010, p. B1.

[33] Millman, Joel, "Idaho Shortcut Stalls Global Treck," *The Wall Street Journal*, October 22, 2010, p. A6.

[34] Marciniak, Lisa, "Making the Big Jobs Look Easy," *North Star Port*, Duluth Seaway Port Authority, Winter 2005-2006 Issue.

[35] Moore, Molly, "Is the Bosporus Taking On More Than It Can Handle?", *International Herald Tribune*, November 17, 2000, p. 2.

[36] "Modal Split Maritieme Containers," Port of Rotterdam, https://www.portofrotterdam.com/sites/-default/files/Modal split maritieme containers 2014-2011.pdf, retrieved March 24, 2017.

[37] "Inland and Intracoastal Waterways," March 31, 2016, U.S. Army Corps of Engineers, http://www.iwr.usace.army.mil/Portals/70/docs/IWUB/WRRDA_2014_Capital_Investment_Strategy_Final_31Mar-16.pdf, retrieved March 24, 2017.

[38] "FAST Fact Sheet," November 2015, U.S. Customs and Border Protection, https://www.cbp.gov/-sites/default/files/documents/FAST Fact Sheet - FINAL (web ready).pdf, retrieved March 24, 2017.

Chapter 14

Packaging for Export

A challenging practical area of international logistics is packaging goods for international shipment. This responsibility always falls on the exporter, regardless of the terms of trade, or Incoterms® rule, chosen (see Chapter 6). Unfortunately, packaging is oftentimes just left to the shipping department, with few guidelines other than to make sure it gets to the customer without problems, and quite often with pressures to control costs; there is rarely a strategy developed for packaging, even though it is an area that has strategic implications.

This chapter makes distinctions between primary, secondary, and tertiary packaging, as seen in Figure 14.1.

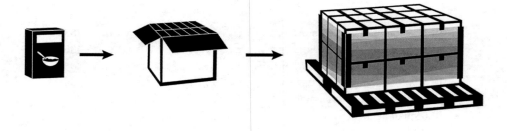

Figure 14.1: Primary, Secondary and Tertiary Packaging
Diagram courtesy of Daisy Krokos. Used with permission.

Primary packaging is consumer packaging, or what the consumers see when they purchase and handle the product. Primary packaging is part of the firm's marketing function and is traditionally covered in marketing management textbooks as part of the firm's promotional efforts; primary packaging is only occasionally mentioned in this chapter. Secondary packaging groups several of the consumer goods into one unit. Secondary packaging is made up of one of two alternatives:

corrugated paper
Two flat sheets of brown paper, in between which a sinusoidally shaped sheet is glued.

- The first alternative is a cardboard box. Since the term used more frequently in the industry is corrugated paperboard box, it will be the one used in this chapter. Paperboard is categorized on several criteria, including thickness, the type of flutes used—the way the layer of paper sandwiched between the faces of the board is folded—and the number of layers: paperboard is available in single-, double-, and triple-wall versions (see Figure 14.2).

- The second alternative is a plastic wrap that is either stretched (stretch-wrap) or heat shrunk (shrink-wrap) over several units of the primary package (see Figure 14.3 on page 489). The purpose of either method is to consolidate multiple units into one unit and to protect them from water. The two techniques differ in the thickness of the wrap, with shrink-wrap generally much thicker than stretch-wrap, and much more resistant to multiple handlings. The term "shrink-wrap," whenever used in this chapter, refers to either of these two techniques.

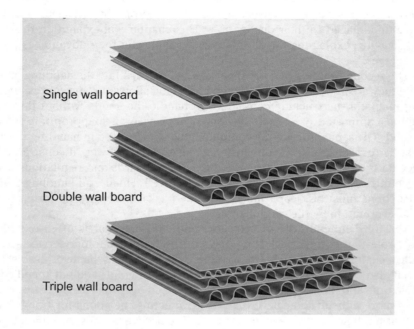

Figure 14.2: Single-Wall, Double-Wall, and Triple-Wall Paperboard
Diagram ©Elgusser/Shutterstock. Used with permission.

Secondary packaging is what the retailer sees and handles before the goods are placed on the shelves. In discount retail stores, this secondary packaging may be seen by the consumer.

Tertiary packaging, or transportation packaging, includes all the additional protection given to the goods to ensure their safe and efficient delivery, in sound condition, at the lowest possible cost, to their foreign purchaser.[1] Tertiary packaging for consumer goods is therefore the packaging placed around the secondary retail packaging units. For industrial goods, because there is generally no primary or secondary packaging of the products, the tertiary packaging encompasses all the packaging activities aimed at protecting them during shipment.

14.1 Packaging Functions

The first function of correct packaging for export is the protection of the goods from the hazards of international shipping by ocean or by air. Proper packag-

improper packing
Packing that is not sufficient
to protect the goods during
their international voyage.
Improperly packed goods
will not be covered under
any insurance policy.

ing has direct cost implications. On one hand, the cost of packaging generally increases as the protection of the goods increases; however, on the other hand, the cost of losing part of the cargo to improper packing is generally much higher and cannot be insured against (Section 10.5.2 on page 356 explained that insurance companies always deny coverage if a surveyor determines that the goods were improperly packaged), and thus no real trade-off exists. It is in the best interest of the exporter to ensure that goods are properly packaged so that they arrive undamaged to their destination. This chapter will expand on this aspect of packaging, explaining the alternatives available and their advantages and disadvantages.

The second function of correct packaging is to facilitate the handling of goods while they are in transit; well-designed packaging allows the stevedores, the shipping line, and the trucking companies to handle the goods without difficulties, but most importantly without having to improvise an inappropriate handling method. The capabilities of the equipment likely to be used in handling the goods must be respected (*i.e.*, the dimensional constraints and weight constraints they place on the package, as well as the different standards and regulations used in the countries through which the goods will travel). Finally, all handling and care instructions must be clearly marked on the package, in pictorial form, to avoid misinterpretation by the cargo handlers.

The third function of correct packaging, and one that is often overlooked, is the role that correct packaging plays in the firm's customer service strategy. While a customer always expects to receive the goods in sellable or usable condition, it also expects to be able to quickly unpack the goods and not spend considerable time and money preparing them to be used or sold. This objective is often much more difficult to achieve than just protecting the goods for transport and facilitating their handling while in transit. The packaging must be simple enough to be opened without using specialized tools or exerting much effort, but most of all, it has to be designed so that it can be opened without damaging the goods. The packaging used by a firm should also reflect the image it is trying to project to customers. A well-conceived and well-constructed package is a positive reflection on the ability of a company to manufacture quality products. Similarly, more and more customers are sensitive to packaging alternatives that are easily reused or placed in the waste stream. In some cases, it is legally mandated.

14.2 Packaging Objectives

The objective of proper packaging is to ensure that goods are protected from the three major losses that can occur in international transit:

- Protecting the goods from mechanical damage: breakage, crushes, nicks, and dents (these perils represent roughly 43 percent of all claims made by shippers to their insurance companies)[2]

- Protecting the goods from water damage: seawater, rain, floods, and container sweat (15 percent of claims made)

- Protecting the goods from theft and pilferage (21 percent of claims made)

The remaining 21 percent of insurance claims are linked to fire, strandings, sinkings, collision, overboard losses, jettison, and other perils of international ocean shipping.

To a great extent, each of these perils can be prevented by properly used packaging techniques and by the correct design of the protective systems around the cargo.

However, that's not all: another objective of packaging is to provide good customer service to the recipient of the goods. This is achieved by paying attention to the details of the packaging process and designing a "smarter" package. While it is difficult to give specific guidance, a few examples may illustrate the concept better:

- Instead of gluing—and then nailing—the plywood panels of a crate, a customer-focused exporter will just nail them or, even better, attach them with screws, so that they can be more easily taken apart by the importer's receiving department. The boards can then be reused internally by the importer or by its employees rather than being discarded. An exporter shipping to countries where packaging materials may end up as housing materials is more empathetic if it considers using a slightly better grade of boards and plywood, and making sure that they have been heat-treated rather than fumigated with chemicals.

- Another way of displaying customer focus is to include a packing list in the recipient's language and to clearly mark all of the packages within a shipment; for example, by color-coding or letter-coding each pallet and its corresponding manifest.

- Yet another way of showing customer concern is to utilize unitized packages that match the size of the ones used by the customer, so that goods can be placed directly in its warehouse, without having to be reloaded onto the pallet size that the customer uses.

While it takes only a few extra minutes (and costs only slightly more) to pack a shipment in a smarter manner, the importer will appreciate the attention; such packaging can become a strategic advantage over a competitor whose shipping department is less attentive to details. In addition, such techniques help prevent claims of shortages when the customer cannot locate items within a shipment.

Finally, packaging should reflect the increasing sensitivity to recycling and energy conservation present in many countries. The focus in this case should be for the exporter to use recyclable and reusable materials rather than disposable materials; for example, it should use starch "peanuts" (packaging pellets) or recycled paper cubes rather than Styrofoam, or inflatable dunnage rather than scrap pallets, and it should load the goods on pallets of the size used by the customer.

14.3   Ocean Cargo

Ocean cargo can be shipped using several packaging alternatives. Because an increasing percentage of cargo shipped by ocean is now containerized, this particular mode will be covered first, followed by breakbulk cargo and its packaging alternatives.

14.3.1   Full-Container-Load (FCL) Cargo

full container load (FCL)
A shipment whose volume or weight is close to the container's limits, or for which the shipper requests that it be the only shipment in the container.

While it is true that containers protect cargo against most damages, the choice of the proper container is important when shipping a full-container-load (FCL) shipment. An FCL shipment utilizes the entire capacity of a container, whether by weight or by volume. A shipper can also elect to use a full container if it wants its cargo to not be exposed to other goods while in transit.

Choice of Container

After determining the correct type of container (see Chapter 13) in which the cargo will be shipped, the exporter should, as much as possible, inspect the container before using it for a shipment. It is a particularly important step if the cargo will not be unitized on pallets or in crates, but will simply be placed in corrugated paperboard boxes or in their retail packaging directly inside the container.

The container should first be inspected from the outside for possible structural damage: a structurally unsound container can collapse under the weight of the several containers that will eventually be placed on top of it. Containers are designed to withstand the weight of up to eight other containers; however, a slight structural problem can weaken it enough to collapse under this kind of weight and a heavy sea. Hundreds of them do every year. The container frame should look straight, the fittings used for lifting it and securing it on the ship or on a truck should be in place and not damaged, the doors should close properly, the repairs—if any—should appear to have been done competently, and there should be no visible structural rust. Surface rust is not pretty, but it usually does not affect the cargo; nevertheless, it may indicate that the container is not well maintained.

The container should also be inspected from the inside, with the doors closed, for possible light leakage, which indicates a water-infiltration risk during shipment. Sometimes, light leakage also indicates a structural problem, as the container could be deformed and not as strong mechanically. The container should have a wooden floor (plywood sheathing) and ideally wooden sides as well, to prevent condensation damage inside the container (container sweat) and protect the cargo from direct contact with the metal sides. The container should also have all its inside hardware in place (tie-down rings and cleats), to allow for good securing of the cargo. The container should be inspected for foul and persistent odors. Several cargoes have been damaged by the content of a preceding shipment. Protruding nails or other fasteners should be removed to prevent accidental punctures. Finally, the container should be clean of grease, dirt, and other foreign material to keep the cargo clean.[3]

Palletization

It is always better for goods in a shipment to be unitized (assembled in a single larger unit) so that they can be manipulated more efficiently using a forklift or other means of material handling. Unitizing goods can be done by placing the goods on pallets, or by building boxes in which they are placed. In either case, the unitized package includes one more layer of protection for the goods, which is better than when they are left in their original secondary package, which is often only some corrugated paperboard boxes.

Goods placed on pallets and shrink-wrapped are better protected from water infiltration (by placing them a few inches above the floor) and from condensation in the container. Palletizing and shrink-wrapping goods also facilitates handling and protects the goods once they have arrived at the importer's warehouse; the lower the likelihood that the goods are manipulated by hand, the greater the

unitized
Cargo in which smaller packaging units are assembled into a single larger unit, to facilitate handling.

pallet
A wooden (plastic) platform on which goods can be placed. A pallet necessitates mechanical equipment to be moved.

shrink/stretch wrap
A polymer film that is stretched over palletized cargo to protect it from water damage.

Figure 14.3: A Well Unitized Pallet of Empty Wine Bottles, Ready for Export
Photo ©Fedor Korolevskiy/Shutterstock. Used with permission.

probability that they will be unloaded in good condition. Unitizing prevents the primary package from being crushed and therefore allows the goods to be immediately sellable; in cases where the boxes have cosmetic damage, it is costly to repackage the goods into a new box, and therefore it is generally much cheaper to properly unitize them. Some shippers include additional (empty) boxes, so that the goods can be re-packaged by the customer if the boxes are damaged. This is a way to overcome the problem, but it is best to prevent it.

Another advantage of a palletized unit is that the secondary packaging of corrugated cardboard may then be sufficient to protect the goods, if the pallets are protected on the corners, and the pallets are properly stacked by adding a rigid support between the lower and upper pallets. This support could be heavy corrugated multi-wall paperboard or plywood.

When unitizing the boxes onto pallets, there is another issue to consider: most pallets are built by employees by alternating the boxes so that they constitute a "brick" pattern, as such patterns are generally believed to be stronger (as in a Lego® building). However, the corners are the stronger parts of the boxes, and therefore corners should support most of the weight of the boxes on top of them. By alternating corners, as in a brick pattern, the weaker part of the box supports the greatest weight. Such a pattern results in a greater likelihood of crushed boxes, and therefore should be avoided. It is better to build pallets in columns, where boxes fit directly on top of one another, as this practice results

Figure 14.4: An Incorrectly Loaded Pallet Can Result in Crushed Boxes
Photo ©Imfoto/Shutterstock. Used with permission.

in fewer crushed or damaged boxes.

Goods that are shipped in corrugated boxes that are not protected with re-inforced corners, placed in a column pattern, or held together with stretch or shrink-wrap are much more likely to be damaged in shipment. The corners and shrink-wrap help keep the boxes together and make the unit much stronger. In the absence of corner protectors, slight damage to one of the lower-level boxes can cause the entire stack to collapse, causing further damage to all the boxes on that pallet. Pallets that are poorly constructed, with boxes of disparate sizes are also very likely to be damaged in transit (see Figure 14.4).

Although unitized cargo is preferable, it can also present challenges. For one, the standardized size of pallets in Europe has been 80×120 centimeters (31.5×47.25 inches) since 1959. Pallet sizes in the United States are, for all intents and purposes, not standardized, even though a great percentage of them are 36×48 inches (91.5×122 centimeters). This presents difficulties, as pallets do not fit neatly into containers that are designed for neither of these sizes: the inside length of a 40-foot container is 12.05 meters (39 feet 6.5 inches), and that of a 20-foot container is 5.92 meters (19 feet 5 inches). Their width is 2.34 meters (7 feet 8 inches). None of these dimensions is a multiple of a pallet size. In addition, there are problems when corrugated-paper boxes that were designed to fit a pallet's footprint do not conveniently fill another size; for example, a European exporter may have boxes that have a base of 40×40 centimeters, and while such boxes fit nicely on a European pallet, they leave a good portion of a U.S. 36-inch pallet unused. Unfortunately, a dimension that is compatible with both standards is a difficult compromise.

Non-unitized Cargo

If the goods inside the container are not unitized, it is preferable that they be somewhat protected from crushing and moisture by being packaged in a higher grade of corrugated paperboard, double- or triple-walled; regular secondary pack-aging is insufficient and its use should be avoided. If the goods are to be stacked, layers of strong corrugated paperboard or sheets of plywood should be used between the layers to protect the lower levels from collapsing and to prevent crushed boxes. If the goods are to be shipped from (or to) a high-humidity area, a layer of plywood on the floor of the container or a layer of pallets should be considered, to insulate the cargo from possible water at the bottom of the con-tainer, due to condensation. In addition, paperboard should be avoided as much as possible, as it loses up to 60 percent of its strength under humid conditions.[4] Figure 10.4 on page 334 illustrates the differences in relative humidity levels for an ocean container shipment from China to the United States—it varied from 15 to 90 percent.

Blocking Materials

When loading a container, it is ideal if the goods can fill out the space as com-pletely as possible, leaving no room for the cargo to shift. Unfortunately, that

Figure 14.5: A Cargo Box Correctly Braced and Blocked in a Container
Photo ©Wathit Kettap/Shutterstock. Used with permission.

is generally not possible. However, there are methods to prevent the cargo from shifting.

The first method is to secure the goods to the container itself, when possible. This is normally done with hooks and straps, or wood braces, a system that is particularly good at keeping the cargo from moving inside the container (see Figure 14.5).

lashing
The process of attaching cargo to the means of transport. On a ship, containers are lashed onto the deck, in a container, goods are lashed to the container walls and floor.

dunnage
Packing material designed to prevent cargo from moving when in transit.

The second method is to insert some sort of spacer between the pallets or the packages. There are several blocking materials used, and they are collectively called dunnage. Some companies use old pallets, some use lumber (in American vernacular, "4×4s," which actually measure 3.5×3.5 inches, or roughly 9×9 centimeters), and some use inflatable bags (see Figure 14.6). Before closing the door of the container, similar bracing material must be inserted between the cargo and the door to prevent shifting. Insurance claim handlers "frequently come across cargo poorly secured in a container, perhaps because void spaces are not filled, or because heavier items are not lashed down."[5] As a reminder, insurance policies do not cover claims for improperly packaged cargo (see Section 10.5.2 on page 356).

The critical part of proper FCL packing is that the entire floor space of the container must be occupied, so that none of the cargo may move. However heavy the cargo may be, it will move and eventually be damaged if it is not braced securely. The cost of replacing damaged cargo will undoubtedly exceed whatever savings were achieved by failing to use proper dunnage. Figure 10.1 on page 331 shows how a poorly secured load can puncture the walls of the container and fall overboard.

Shipping lines have developed substantial container-packing guides that contain further recommendations to assist shippers.[6]

Overall Weight

Truck trailers are limited to a maximum weight that varies from country to country, and sometimes varies within a country (such as the United States, where states have different requirements). Shipping lines recommend that 20-foot containers not exceed 39,500 lbs. (17.9 metric tonnes) and that 40-foot containers not exceed 44,500 lbs. (20.2 tonnes).[7] However, the industry knows that some shippers load containers beyond this limit, and the analysis of two containership casualties, the MOL *Comfort* in June 2013 and the MSC *Napoli* in 2007, determined that the accidents likely happened because 20 percent of the recovered containers had an actual weight higher than their declared weight; that excess

Figure 14.6: An Inflatable Dunnage Bag in a Container Keeps the Goods Tightly Against the Container's Walls

Photo ©Astrid Groeneveld. Used with permission.

weight amounted to 315 tons for 600 containers.[8] If the ratio is extrapolated to an entire 5,000-TEU ship, that translates into an overload of 2,500 tons.

In July 2015, the International Maritime Organization amended the Safety of Life at Sea Convention (SOLAS) to mandate that a container's weight be verified before it can be loaded aboard a ship. Although there was much concern about this new requirement,[9] the new mandate is likely to have several positive consequences on the overall safety of the supply chain, from trucks traveling to the port, to port cranes and containerships.

Stuffing the Container

If there are different types of goods to be placed in the same container, the heavier ones should always be placed on the bottom to lower the load's center of gravity. Similarly, great care should be taken to ensure that the center of gravity is somewhat in the center of the container. This is achieved by loading the goods into the container in a symmetrical fashion and placing the blocking material between the goods, as shown in Figure 14.6 on the preceding page. Many software packages can help exporters load mixed cargoes into containers in the most efficient manner, accounting for their volume and weight.

14.3.2   Less-than-Container-Load (LCL) Cargo

less than container load (LCL)
A shipment that takes less than the full weight and volume capacity of a standard container and is therefore shipped with other LCL cargo in the same container.

consolidated
A shipment that is made up of several small shipments from different shippers.

non-vessel-operating common carrier
A shipment consolidator or freight forwarder that does not own means of transportation, but issues its own bills of lading, and therefore acts as a carrier.

Single shipments that are too small to be shipped as full containers, called less-than-container-load (LCL) shipments, are consolidated by a freight forwarder or a Non-Vessel-Operating Common Carrier (NVOCC) with other freight and then shipped in a full container. Because of the increased number of handlings, it is mandatory that these goods be unitized on a pallet or placed in a crate or box, and be well protected from water damage. Because the nature of the freight with which the shipment is placed is never known, the greatest amount of care should be exercised in packaging such goods. In addition to the risks normally associated with a shipment by ocean, there is also the possibility of damage caused by other cargo in the container; a heavy load can inadvertently be placed on top of the pallet, or another can be poorly braced in the container and move in heavy seas. An LCL shipment can also be subjected to other cargoes' leakage, odors, and other hazards. Although consolidators are quite good at packaging a container properly, with proper dunnage and protection, the owners of other cargo on board the consolidated container may not be as careful and experienced, and that represents a hazard.

14.3.3   Breakbulk Cargo

breakbulk cargo
A type of cargo that is unitized—boxes, crates, or bales—and placed directly in the holds of a ship.

Breakbulk cargo is cargo that cannot be containerized because it is too large and will not fit in a traditional container, or because it exceeds the maximum weight of a container load. Great efforts have been expended to containerize as much cargo as possible, with the creation of special container sizes; however, a substantial proportion of cargo is still shipped as breakbulk.

Breakbulk cargo is placed directly in the hold of the ship (see Figure 14.7) and therefore must be packaged differently than containerized cargo, which enjoys the all-around protection of the metal container. In addition, breakbulk cargo (in its tertiary packaging) is handled more frequently than containerized cargo; for example, at minimum, breakbulk cargo is loaded onto a truck or rail car on its way to the port, then unloaded in the port, loaded onto the ship, unloaded from the ship, and loaded on another truck. However, there can be multiple additional handlings, each presenting its own hazards. Therefore, breakbulk cargo should be well protected by packaging to reflect both the rigors of the journey and the extra handling.

Finally, the company responsible for shipping breakbulk cargo should ensure that the weight and dimensions of the cargo can be handled by all the facilities through which the cargo will travel; if the breakbulk cargo weighs more than the maximum capacity crane in a given port, an alternative shipping route should be found, or arrangements should be made to rent specialized or larger equipment. If the cargo's weight exceeds the port cranes' capacity, there is a great risk that the breakbulk cargo will be taken out of its crate and dismantled so that it can be handled by the port's equipment. There is also the possibility that the port

Figure 14.7: Miscellaneous Cargo Loaded in the Hold of a Breakbulk Ship
Photo ©Wathit Kettap/Shutterstock. Used with permission.

Figure 14.8: Wooden Crates (Left) and Boxes (Right)
Photo ©Kanithar Aiumla-Or/Shutterstock and Sarin Kunthong/Shutterstock. Used with permission.

personnel will try to move the cargo with the existing equipment (using it beyond its rated capacity) and damage the cargo in the process. Heavy and cumbersome cargo, called "project cargo" is usually handled by specialized freight forwarders that have an excellent knowledge of all these limitations and can advise an international shipper accordingly.

Crates and Boxes

box
A wooden container designed to unitize the goods and protect them. The walls are an integral part of a box's structural strength.

crate
A wooden container designed to unitize the goods and protect them. In a crate, the structural strength is provided by a web of wooden cross members.

Boxes and crates—as shown in Figure 14.8—are appropriate containers for either breakbulk cargo or LCL cargo that will be handed to a freight consolidator. The crate or box should be built in a size that accommodates the goods without allowing them to shift. The crate or box should also be solidly built and reinforced at those points where the crate is likely to be lifted. If the cargo needs to be kept in an upright position, the best alternative is to mount the box or crate on a pallet or equip it with hooks or straps that allow the goods to be handled in only one direction. To gather evidence of mishandling, it is often a good idea to include (inside as well as outside of a box or crate) a device that records whether a shipment was handled too roughly or whether it was not kept upright during handling. Such devices are shown on Figure 14.9.[10]

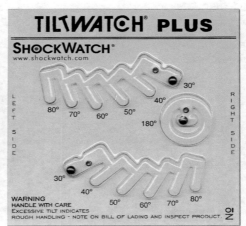

Figure 14.9: Devices that Record Whether a Package was Mishandled
Photo ©ShockWatch. Used with permission.

Figure 14.10: The Three-Way Corner Design is Very Strong
Diagram courtesy of Daisy Krokos. Used with permission.

Figure 14.11: Bags of Wheat Being Loaded in Port Sudan, The Sudan
Photo ©USAID. Used with permission.

Boxes and crates are built somewhat differently. While boxes are containers made of wood where the sides are an integral part of the structure, crates are containers built on a wooden frame that is either open or enclosed with plywood. These walls are not structural; crates rely on the strength of their frame. However, in general terms, well-built crates are stronger than boxes, because the wood used for the frame of the crate is of a larger size. Well-built crates are constructed with three-way corners (see Figure 14.10 on the previous page), which is the strongest possible corner design. Unfortunately, this technique appears to be an "art" that is disappearing, even though it makes a substantial difference in the ability of the crate to resist shocks and crushing. Both crates and boxes should always be reinforced with corner strapping and metallic bands (see Figure 14.8 on page 496).

Open crates are obviously not appropriate for cargo that is not impervious to water. Boxes and enclosed crates protecting a shipment that is sensitive to water or moisture should be lined with a waterproof material such as polyethylene. Some packaging specialists prefer leaving the bottom of the boxes and crates free of waterproof material, while others prefer placing small holes in it to allow drainage should some water infiltration occur. To further protect crated machinery and metallic parts from water damage, it is common to simply spray them with oil before placing them in crates. The drawback to this technique is the time that the importer will have to take to remove the oil from the product.

Since some crates and boxes are light enough to be handled by hand and are likely to be manipulated many times during an international shipment, they are sometimes mishandled despite the shipper's instructions and the markings that they display. It is sometimes wise to determine whether rough handling occurred, and therefore to place devices that monitor whether the goods were subjected to shocks, and whether they were kept upright during the shipment. Two of these devices should be placed on the box; one on the outside of the box, and the other inside.

Bags

Bags can also be used to transport breakbulk merchandise. The multi-wall shipping bag (which can hold around 25 kilograms [50 pounds]) is designed to be used with chemicals, plastics, and other powdered materials that are somewhat unaffected by water and are unlikely to be pilfered.

bag
A paper, plastic, or fabric container designed to unitize dry-bulk cargo and unitize it. A bag can generally be handled by a single stevedore.

The bag is made up of several layers of kraft paper, fabric, and/or light polymers, and is not good at withstanding numerous manipulations. It is recommended to add about 3 percent additional empty, slightly larger bags to contain those bags that may be damaged during an international shipment. Shipping bags are quite sensitive to rough handling by dockhands (see Figure 14.11), including damage by accidental contact with mechanical equipment or other cargo with sharp angles such as boxes, crates, or pallets. The integrity of these bags is increased by palletizing and shrink-wrapping them, because mechanical equipment

Figure 14.12: Tapioca in Flexible Intermediate Bulk Containers
Photo ©Amarin Jitnathum/Shutterstock. Used with permission.

Figure 14.13: Three Different Types of Drums: Steel, Polymer, and Intermediate Bulk Containers

Photo ©Noomcpkstic/Shutterstock. Used with permission.

flexible intermediate bulk containers (FIBC)
A large polymer bag designed to contain dry-bulk cargo and to be handled by mechanized equipment.

must then be used to handle them.

The second type of bag is a very large bag called a flexible intermediate bulk container (FIBC). FIBCs are constructed of woven polymer fibers, such as polyethylene or polypropylene (see Figure 14.12). They usually have a capacity of about 1 cubic meter and can weigh up to 1 metric tonne, but many different sizes and types exist. FIBCs are used to transport granular cargo, such as plastics, grains, and chemicals.

Drums

drum
A cylindrical metal, plastic, or fiber container designed to unitize dry-bulk or liquid-bulk cargo.

Drums are used in three forms: metallic drums (steel drums), polymer drums, and fiber drums. Steel drums, shown in Figure 14.13, can be used for wet or dry cargo, and are resilient containers that can withstand a good amount of abuse. Steel drums present great resistance to water damage and pilferage and have been used for a long time in ocean shipping. They can be handled by a single stevedore (see Figure 2.1 on page 39) but not easily. The main disadvantage of steel drums is their cost and individual weight.

Polymer drums, also shown in Figure 14.13, present the advantage of being able to carry liquid and wet cargo, but they are much less resistant to rough handling. Polymer drums should not be handled manually, but should be placed on pallets and handled mechanically.

Fiber drums can be used for only dry cargo, such as plastic pellets or fertilizers. Fiber drums are usually lined with a polymer bag to contain the cargo. They should be palletized to minimize damage, and should not be handled manually. Fiber drums are slightly more resistant to water damage than bags and are more resistant to pilferage. However, fiber drums are often damaged when port personnel handle them in the same manner as they do steel drums, such as rolling them on their sides, a practice which the drums are not designed to handle. Fiber drums are also sensitive to mechanical damage, such as that caused by careless forklift truck drivers or sharp corners.

Intermediate Bulk Containers, also called pallet totes, are larger than drums and are designed to hold liquids only. They can only be handled by mechanical equipment, as they are too heavy to be moved by hand, unlike drums. They are shown in the back of Figure 14.13.

14.3.4   Wood Requirements

Since March 2005, all wood products used in packaging or dunnage must conform to International Phytosanitary Measure 15, a convention signed by 144 countries and that is designed to further prevent the threat of wood pests, specifically the Asian long-horned beetle that attacked hardwood forests in North America and Europe, and the North American pinewood nematode, which attacked softwood forests in Europe and Asia. All wood products used in international trade must be marked with the International Plant Protection Convention (IPPC) symbol or face heavy fines.

International Plant Protection Convention (IPPC)
An international convention that mandates that wood used in packaging be fumigated or heat-treated against pests.

The IPPC mark identifies the country in which the wood product was treated with the first two letters. Figure 14.14 shows several examples. The marking also identifies the plant at which the process was conducted with an alphanumeric code. Finally, the process used in treating the product is identified; for example, HT indicates that the wood was heat-treated, and MB means that the product was treated with methyl bromide. These are the only two allowable treatments to date, and although MB is a gas that the U.S. Environmental Protection Agency phased out in 2007, it continues to allow its use for IPPC purposes only.[11] Three other abbreviations are used in Figure 14.14: DB stands for "debarked," and KD for "kiln-dried," which are used in many countries. The British IPPC mark also includes the abbreviation FC for the British Forestry Commission. Any wood product that has been marked with the IPPC symbol can be reused indefinitely in the international supply chain.

14.3.5   Markings

There are two reasons to properly mark the cargo as it is shipped: it must be protected from poor handling, and it also must be protected from theft and pil-

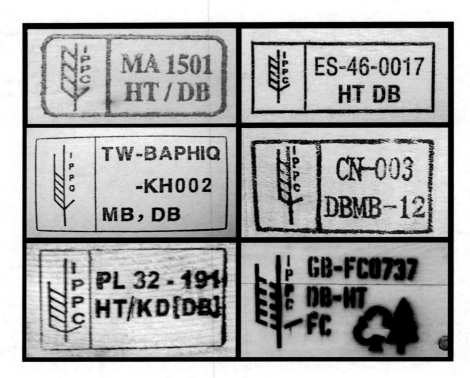

Figure 14.14: International Plant Protection Convention Marks from Morocco, Spain, Taiwan, China, Poland, and Great Britain

Photo ©Pierre David. Used with permission.

ferage.

    To protect the cargo from poor handling, it is necessary to use as many of the international pictorials for cargo handling as apply. Several of these pictorials, as standardized by the International Organization for Standardization (ISO), are shown in Figure 14.15. If possible, the pictorials should be accompanied by their translations in the languages of the ports through which the cargo is expected to transit. Both the net weight (the weight of the cargo alone) and the gross weight (the cargo plus the weight of the packaging) should be clearly displayed in metric units and so-called English units on the outside of the package. The outside dimensions of the goods should also be clearly displayed, both in English and in metric units. This is to prevent, as much as possible, inappropriate equipment from handling the goods.

    To protect breakbulk or LCL cargo from being lost or shipped to the wrong consignee, it should be clearly marked with the consignee's name—the name of the company that will pick it up at the port of the destination—as well as the shipment number. It is always advisable to write that information on several sides of the load; that way, the information is never hidden from view. If possible,

markings
Symbols printed on boxes or crates that help stevedores and terminals determine the proper way to handle, stow, or store a breakbulk shipment.

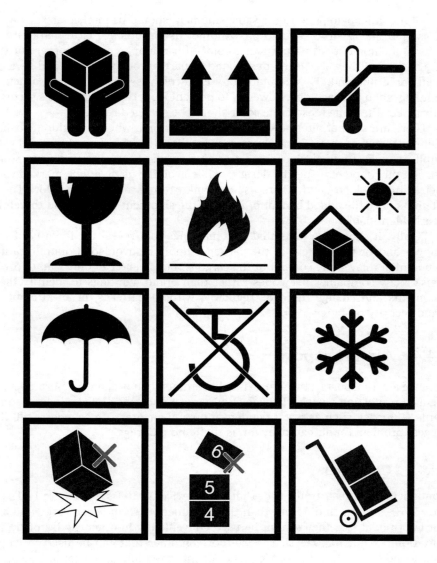

Figure 14.15: International ISO Handling Markings
(From Top Left: Handle with Care, This Way Up, Minimum and Maximum Temperatures, Fragile, Flammable, Keep Indoors, Keep Dry, Use No Hooks, Refrigerated, Do Not Drop, Do not Stack more than 5, Use Handtruck)

Photo ©BankRx, Cool Vector Maker, and SkyExplosion/ all Shutterstock. Used with permission.

the name of the consignee should not include information that could indicate the brand or the type of goods in the shipment, for security reasons. Such markings only increase the probability of theft or pilferage.

All the units belonging to the same shipment should be marked as such, that is, as "1 of 4," "2 of 4," and so on. Another useful practice is to mark all the units in a shipment with a particular color—for example, on the corners of the boxes—so that they are clearly designated as parts of one shipment and none of them are left behind. The temptation to use a color associated with a particular company should be avoided, however, to prevent jeopardizing the firm's security efforts. For the same reason, the color should be changed regularly.

There are several alternatives meant to determine whether a shipment has been the victim of theft. Some shippers paint the outside of their shipments with a uniform color to determine whether a shipment has been tampered with. Some use shipping tape of a specific design—while avoiding using a tape marked with their company logo—and others use a shrink-wrap of a particular color. These attempts have the added benefit of keeping the shipment uniform and therefore clearly identifiable.

Finally, it should be reiterated that markings that reveal the identity of the shipper and/or the content of the package should be avoided. Communicating to potential thieves the content of the cargo is foolish and can only lead to problems. Many companies use codes rather than brand markings to identify their shipments and change the code regularly, without patterns, in an attempt to avoid security problems.

14.4   Air Transport

Because air transport is, by nature, less hazardous than ocean transport, packaging as a protection against damage is of lesser importance. Nevertheless, some perils still exist, such as water condensation and air pressure changes; still, the biggest problem for air cargo, by far, is theft and pilferage.

14.4.1   Containers

unit load device (ULD)
The term used to describe the containers used in airfreight transport.

Containers used in air transport—Unit Load Devices or ULDs (see Figure 13.19 on page 473)—are much different than the containers used in ocean cargo and are not intermodal (*i.e.*, they cannot be used conveniently in other modes of transportation, except for one size: a 20-foot container that can be used in cargo planes and on trucks). The consequence of this situation is that cargo is usually placed (consolidated) in containers at the airport of departure, then manipulated again at the airport of arrival and placed into trucks. This additional handling should be considered when packaging goods for export by air. It is also likely that the goods will be unloaded from one container and reloaded into another at a connecting airport.

Containers used in air transport are lightweight, made of wood, Plexiglas, or aluminum, and are generally clean. As some containers are not fully enclosed, or are enclosed with netting rather than solid walls, some damage may occur in the voyage when cargo shifts. Nevertheless, most damage occurs in the handling before and after the flight; for example, while the container waits on the tarmac, the goods in the container could easily become wet from rain or snow. Such exposure should be considered when deciding on proper packaging.

14.4.2 Packaging Materials

While many air cargo shipments are shipped by air in their secondary packaging, this is generally not an appropriate method for two reasons:

- Secondary packaging is not sufficient to protect the goods from the hazards of manipulation before and after the flight. In many cases, the airline operates on a hub-and-spoke model, and the goods are unloaded and manipulated at one or more hub airports. Goods in secondary packaging can be handled carelessly by hurried airport personnel, and boxes can fall from conveyor belts traveling at high speeds (45 kilometers [30 miles] per hour).

- Secondary packaging often includes markings including the brand name of the goods, as well as model numbers and/or illustrations, which make the goods tempting targets for thieves.

Appropriate shipping packaging would therefore be tertiary in nature and include one additional layer of corrugated paperboard, preferably double-walled, and a shrink-wrap. The United Nations established rules regarding the resistance of air packages to drops and crushes, especially for dangerous goods; these minimum requirements were last updated in 2007.[12] Nevertheless, many shippers still do not follow these rules.

For shipments that are fragile, the best strategy is to use a box within a box; the primary package is placed in a much larger box, which is then filled with packing material around the smaller, fragile product. While this is relatively simple, the cost of packaging this way can be substantial, as airlines charge a shipper on the higher of two alternatives; the actual weight of the product or its volume weight—dimensional weight— which is a weight calculated on the volume of the shipment (see Section 12.4 on page 435). There can therefore be a substantial cost to using a box that is slightly too large.

For cargo sensitive to humidity, a possible way of avoiding condensation damage is to add small packets of desiccant material in the box with the goods, as they are designed to absorb ambient humidity. An additional layer of shrink-wrap is always advisable as well, to protect against other condensation, rain, or leakage caused by other cargo on the plane.

For shipments susceptible to leakage if the primary packaging breaks, such as glass or plastic bottles, the U.S. Federal Aviation Administration regulations (and United Nations rules) require that the secondary or tertiary package be capable of containing an accidental leak. Most secondary packaging is not designed for such a contingency, so adequate additional absorbent material must be packed with the goods. Importantly, the risks associated with improper packaging resulting in a leak in an aircraft are substantial: violations of the U.S. regulations call for up to five years in prison and a U.S.$ 250,000 fine.[13]

14.4.3 Markings

Markings in international air shipments should be handled in much the same way as markings on ocean shipments. The use of the pictorials shown in Figure 14.15 on page 503 is quite appropriate and should be accompanied with written instructions on the boxes, in the languages of the countries in which the cargo is expected to transit.

14.5 Road and Rail Transport

In the case of international road and rail transportation, a policy of protecting the cargo in much the same way as for shipment by ocean container is appropriate. It is always best to unitize the cargo into pallets to facilitate handling when the goods are loaded and unloaded. The cargo pallets should be protected on all four corners, banded with nylon or steel straps, and shrink-wrapped for protection against rain and ambient humidity. As much as possible, the cargo should be blocked and braced in the truck trailer and, if applicable, in the railroad car to avoid damage due to the cargo shifting and sudden accelerations and decelerations. Railroad companies issue specific rules regarding the bracing of cargo in containers or truck trailers that are carried on railroads; in particular, these rules mandate a strong bracing of the cargo[14] to prevent stress against the container or trailer doors.

Large domestic shipments in the United States are almost all by truck or rail. Cargo traveling by truck can be shipped by the full truck load (FTL) or the partial less-than-truck load (LTL), in which case cargo is consolidated by the carrier with other cargo going to the same destination. Domestically and internationally, truck shipments are loaded onto a trailer that is then either driven to its destination or loaded on a railroad car (piggy-backed) to an intermediary destination and then driven to its final destination. LTL cargo can also be shipped to a hub, where it is unloaded from the first truck and reloaded onto a second truck.

Although it may appear that light-weight secondary packaging is sufficient to protect these goods, this is often not the case. In a 2008 study, the Grocery Manufacturers Association determined that the costs of goods damaged in domestic transportation were approximately U.S.$ 4 billion, or approximately 1.1 percent of gross domestic sales before 2004. After 2005-2006, the GMA noticed an improvement, down to less than one percent, which it attributed to "improvements in packaging."[15] Such improvements may include the use of heavier corrugated paper boxes, better pallet loading practices, or the addition of heavy corrugated paperboard between pallets.

In shipping consumer goods, close attention should be paid to the possibility of theft, and the goods should be packed in unmarked boxes to prevent the possibility of pilferage. Goods that are most frequently stolen are too often easily identifiable by their packaging. According to a study of freight theft by Freight Watch International, the most targeted products are food, drinks, and electronics in Asia and North America, but pharmaceuticals in Europe.[16] Anonymous packaging reduces some of that risk.

14.6 Small Packets

Shipments that are not large enough to warrant using a consolidator or a carrier are shipped through small-packet shipping companies, such as the Postal Service, DHL, UPS, or FedEx. Packaging considerations are generally different for small packages as they are handled many more times than cargo that is carried by an ocean shipper or an air carrier.

14.6.1 Considerations

The nature of small shipments is that they are placed in direct contact with hundreds of other small shipments into trucks, railcars, or aircraft cargo areas, without any protection other that the packaging with which they are shipped. Often enough, packages sent by inexperienced consumers are in the mix, with the risk that their packaging is insufficient or inappropriate, and the contents of these packages can damage other shipments. Small packages are also handled many more times, use more means of transportation, and go through several sorting facilities. Automated sorting on high-speed machines subject these packages to shocks, abrasions, and sudden accelerations that take place multiple times during a single sort, as the items are re-directed to different chutes and consolidating areas (see Figure 14.16).

Packaging a small shipment means that the tertiary packaging should be resistant to punctures, abrasions, and present a surface area large enough for the proprietary sorting bar codes of the small-packet company handling the shipment. Any other information on the tertiary packaging, such as a UPC or EAN bar code—Universal Product Code or European Article Number—, can confuse sorting machines and result in a delayed shipment; therefore, the tertiary packaging should be as free of information as possible. To that effect, many of the small-packet companies encourage the use of their own tertiary packaging materials.[17]

14.6.2 Pricing

Small-package carriers traditionally charge based on the weight of the item transported, and its destination.

FedEx, UPS, and DHL have adopted a system of dimensional weight, which has a bearing on the choice of packaging. Dimensional weight is calculated as the length×width×height, divided by a constant to yield an equivalent weight. For a shipment measured in inches, the product is divided by 166 for a United States domestic package or by 139 for an international package. The result is rounded to the next higher integer, and that is the dimensional weight, in pounds, of the package. For shipments measured in centimeters, the division is by 5,000 and the result is in kilograms. For light goods, a tertiary package that is as small as possible while still protecting the product is therefore preferable.[18]

Figure 14.16: A Small-Packet Sorting Facility in Vnukovo, Russia
Photo ©Igor Dolgov/Shutterstock. Used with permission.

The United States Postal Service has adopted a different system, which charges the same amount for pre-set sizes, regardless of weight. It also charges the same amount, regardless of the foreign destination, except for Canada and Mexico, which have lower rates.[19]

Trade in Precious Stones and Other Valuables

Trade in precious goods and valuables is an entire branch of logistics that, although not officially calculated separately from other data, is worth millions of U.S. dollars—in the United States alone, it is estimated at U.S.$ 50 million. There is a substantial business in shipping precious stones internationally, such as diamonds and emeralds, because the stones are often produced, cut, set, and sold in different countries.

Artwork travels from museum collections to museum exhibits (and back). Antiques and collectibles travel to and from dealers and auction houses. Cash travels to where tourists flock.

The crash of Swissair 111 on September 2, 1998, exposed the scale of the international transport of such items: the airplane was carrying 50 kilograms(110 pounds) of cash, 1.8 kilograms (4 pounds) of diamonds, 1.8 kilograms (4 pounds) of watches, 5 kilograms (11 pounds) of jewelry, and an artwork by Picasso entitled "The Painter."[20] Lloyd's of London, through which this cargo was insured, has never disclosed the value of this cargo, although there are speculations that it exceeded U.S.$ 300 million.

Another notable shipment of precious stones was revealed when it resulted in the theft of U.S.$ 350,000,000 of diamonds from a parked airplane at the Brussels airport in February 2013. The thieves, disguised as police officers, were done in "barely five minutes", [21] which indicated a job performed by a well-informed group, which is the greatest threat for shippers of goods with very high value. Altogether, few firms specialize in shipping precious and valuable goods, and these firms emphasize discretion:

they do not advertise, do not display their names on their vehicles, and operate out of anonymous office buildings and warehouses. They also take many additional security measures: they do not ship more than a certain amount on a specific airplane or ship, they use ever-changing consignee names, and they have created a whole series of specialized packaging technologies.

Artex Fine Arts Services is such a firm. Artex is located in Washington, D.C., and specializes in moving artwork, antiques, and jewelry collections. It employs a crew of 75 employees, most of whom are artists or art experts with museum experience. Each piece of work is moved in a crate that is specifically designed for that work of art and fitted with foam to the exact dimensions and shape of the artwork. When Artex was selected to move an African American burial site from New York City to Howard University, it took the firm's employees three months to pack the 20,000 objects this move represented.[22]

In addition, Artex's warehouses and trucks are equipped with air conditioning to keep temperature and humidity to exact pre-set levels. Each of its trucks is tracked with satellite transmitters and Global Positioning System; this way, the firm knows at all times where the art is located. Finally, each of the trucks is driven by a team of at least two drivers equipped with cellular phones and sometimes accompanied by armed guards. Nevertheless, the best security is when no one knows that a move is occurring.

14.7   Security

The issue of theft and pilferage is becoming an increasing problem for cargo shippers. It is estimated that cargo theft represents losses of at least U.S.$ 10 billion per year in the United States,[23] € 8 billion in the European Union,[24] and more than U.S.$ 40 billion worldwide. The problem is that there is little reliable data on the incidence of this type of crime, but it is a substantial concern for international shippers. Many methods have been developed to foil theft of cargo; unfortunately, none has proven completely effective, but a combination of several should cover most shippers and prevent theft and pilferage.

As much as possible, the cargo should not bear the name of the shipper, especially if it is a brand that has street appeal; this issue is crucial for goods that are shipped in their secondary packaging and for which the primary packaging and the secondary packaging are one and the same, as for electronics or appliances. Such a practice jeopardizes the safety of the cargo. A possible way to prevent this problem is to ship exclusively in full container loads (FCLs) or full truck loads (FTLs), to hide the cargo from anyone other than the exporter or the importer. Another is to place the goods in an additional blank paperboard box, which would be recommended for goods shipped as LCL or less-than-truck load (LTL) goods, to protect them from handling damage.

seal
A lock placed on a container door or truck trailer door that must be broken in order to access the cargo.

A plethora of different methods exists to place seals on containers, and all present advantages and disadvantages; however, all show whether the container has been opened. A critical aspect of seals is that the seal number should be written on the bill of lading so that the importer can check, upon arrival, that the seal on the container is the same as the seal with which the container left the exporter's premises.[25] Since October 2008, all containers shipped to the United States must be sealed with a tamper-proof seal, such as the one shown in Figure 16.7 on page 568.

Altogether, though, the aspect that security experts insist is critical when shipping internationally or domestically is the personnel involved. Most thefts seem to take place with some form of insider involvement.[26] All attempts should therefore be made to limit the number of people who know the content of the shipment by making sure that the bill of lading and packaging lists are given to trusted employees only, by keeping track of non-employees on the premises, by making sure that managers are present during loading and unloading operations, and so on. Some companies keep their docks under constant video surveillance to deter crime.

14.8   Hazardous Cargo

Hazardous cargo can be shipped by ocean and by air, but, generally, most dangerous goods that are flammable, explosive, or toxic are shipped by sea, and, if these shipments are containerized, they are shipped on deck rather than under deck.

The shipment of dangerous goods by sea is regulated by the International

Maritime Organization (IMO), which publishes an *International Maritime Dangerous Goods Code* (IMDG) every other year, to keep up with the rapid expansion of the types of hazardous materials created. In April 2016, the IMO's Maritime Safety Committee released its 38th amendment, valid for 2018-2020.[27] The two-volume document is complex; in addition to the two volumes, there is a 2016-2018 IMDG Code Supplement for additional information. Although large, the IMDG Code was significantly reduced in size in 2000; prior to that amendment, it was a four-volume code. As its name indicates, the IMDG Code governs the packaging of all hazardous cargo, as well as their labeling, handling, and emergency responses that carriers are supposed to implement. The IMDG Code is followed by nearly every country in the world, and is a *de facto* world standard.

The shipment of dangerous goods by air is regulated by a similar set of standards published by the International Air Transport Association (IATA). The IATA *Dangerous Goods Regulations* manual was developed in collaboration with the International Civil Aviation Organization (ICAO) and the standard-setting authorities of several countries and is revised every year. As of 2017, the IATA *Dangerous Goods Regulations* are in their 58th edition.[28] As expected, the shipment of hazardous cargo by air is no less complicated and cumbersome than by sea.

In addition to these international requirements, a shipper must also abide by the requirements set by domestic regulatory agencies, as there often are two domestic legs to any international shipment, one in the exporter's country, the other in the importer's country. The complexity of such requirements, and their occasionally contradictory statements, makes it an obligation to contract with a specialized freight forwarder or a specialized consultant before undertaking any international shipment of hazardous goods. Shipments of products containing radioactive components are even more complicated.

14.9   Refrigerated Goods

Goods requiring refrigeration make up another category of cargo that demands particular care and specialized packaging services. It is difficult to generalize about refrigerated goods, as every commodity requires specific handling; therefore, most refrigerated goods travel "alone" (*i.e.*, different refrigerated goods are not mixed with one another, as they require different temperatures and different humidity settings). In addition, some fresh produce simply cannot be mixed together as they emit odors and other gases that would spoil the rest of the cargo. For example, a load of cucumbers should not be mixed with apples, as cucumbers are sensitive to the ethylene that the apples produce,[29] and for obvious reasons, onions and strawberries do not travel well together.

When goods needing refrigeration travel by ocean, they usually travel in a refrigerated container—also known as a reefer (see Figure 13.15 on page 466). Great care should be taken to ensure that the temperature is kept at its correct setting throughout the voyage, which is achieved with temperature-sensitive indicators. Because containers are not very effective at cooling goods—but are effective at keeping them cool—several shippers make sure that the goods are well

refrigerated container (reefer)
A container designed to hold cargo that must be maintained at a constant temperature. It generally needs an outside power supply.

refrigerated before they are loaded to prevent possible damage. It should also be understood that reefers do not have a uniform temperature: temperatures within the box can vary by as much as five degrees Celsius (nine degrees Fahrenheit) just because air circulation cannot be made completely uniform. Finally, another common problem with refrigerated cargo coming in or out of the United States is the confusion between Fahrenheit and Celsius temperature settings and the errors they cause.[30]

With refrigerated cargo, loading the refrigerated container must allow air circulation around the cargo; this requirement means that the goods must be loaded in the center of the container, with sufficient space in between the walls of the container and the cargo for circulation, and that the goods must be braced with a frame rather than with inflatable dunnage, which would prevent air circulation. In addition, some goods need to travel in controlled atmospheres—mixtures of oxygen and nitrogen in different percentages than ambient air—to prevent spoilage. Some experiments are being conducted to determine whether a controlled atmosphere can also be effective against some pests, and whether the right mix of humidity, temperature, and correct gas mix can divert some of the cargo that normally travels by air because of its perishable nature to ocean transport, which is much cheaper.[31]

Fresh produce must also be kept at humidity levels of 95 to 100 percent to maintain its freshness as well as prevent weight loss due to evaporation. Most produce is made up of at least 80 percent water and is quite sensitive to water loss; for example, grapes will wrinkle and soften, and stems will turn brown with a weight loss of only 4 percent, making them more difficult to sell. In addition, because produce is sold by weight, a small weight loss can translate into a substantial decrease in revenue for the importer.

For air shipments of refrigerated cargo, the challenges are different, because the cargo is not placed in refrigerated containers but in cargo holds that have different temperature settings. For example, some cargo carriers offer multiple cargo holds, kept at different temperature settings, to keep perishables in their optimum environments. However, because of the possibility that incompatible cargo might be mixed together—such as the onions and strawberries mentioned earlier—great care should be extended to protect sensitive goods from this eventuality by keeping them in solid-wall corrugated paperboard boxes and possibly in shrink- or stretch-wrap, if applicable.

14.10   Domestic Retail Packaging Issues

For consumer products specifically, several packaging issues are also greatly influenced by primary packaging, or the design of the packaging in which the final consumer purchases the goods, as well as by secondary packaging, or the packaging designed to facilitate handling in the retail environment. Collectively, these constraints tend to be domestic in nature (*i.e.*, they are specific to a single country or possibly a group of countries).

Adapting a firm's strategy to the differing market requirements in a particular country can add substantial costs to manufacturing, as well as to inventory and logistics. A firm must determine whether it makes economic sense to adapt its approach to these different markets and incur those additional costs, or ignore them at the risk of losing potential sales. This is the same strategic dilemma faced by a firm involved in international marketing: should it adapt or standardize?

Some of the factors that may affect primary and secondary packaging decisions are explored in the following sections.

14.10.1 Size

Consumer packages vary by country because of consumer preferences. They are generally smaller in those countries in which retail shopping is done frequently, and larger in those in which consumers shop at greater intervals. However, consumer packaging is complicated; consumers may demand smaller or larger packages based on preferences and customs, as well as packages of different shapes and materials.

For example, sugar is sold in some countries in paper bags weighing five pounds (2.5 kilograms), in others in paperboard boxes weighing 1 kilogram (2.2 pounds), and yet in others in tin cans of 1 pound (0.45 kilograms). Even products that are held to be great examples of international standardization, such as Coca-Cola® soft drinks, are sold in many sizes and therefore require a myriad of primary and secondary packaging units.

Consumer packaging may also be influenced by the layout of store shelves, such as their depth and the linear space allocated, and the design and size of shopping carts, constraining manufacturers to use different retail packaging.

Secondary packaging—the unit that holds several consumer packages—is influenced by the size of the retail stores and their configuration, as well as the size of the delivery trucks; the tertiary packaging unit, such as the pallet; or even the configuration of the storage area. In addition, tertiary packaging is influenced by the frequency and volume of retail sales.

14.10.2 Legal Issues

Consumer packaging is also influenced by legal requirements. Some countries regulate sizes to be a multiple of simple metric units (1 kilogram or 1 liter), while others do not, allowing packages of any size and weight. However, the greatest requirements are in the legal constraints on handling: many countries regulate the maximum weight an employee may carry,[32] which influences the weight of the secondary packaging unit and, consequently, of both consumer packaging and tertiary packaging as well.

The legal constraints placed on distribution channels can also influence consumer packaging. For example, the United States allows retail sales of some medicines over the counter—without a doctor's prescription—which means that consumers can buy them in drugstores, most often in a self-service environment. In France, in contrast, all drugs, including drugs not prescribed by a medical doctor, are sold exclusively through specialized stores called pharmacies. The primary package in a self-service drugstore is often a blister pack or some variation of it, as the goods are sold hanging from aisle racks, and need to attract the attention of the shopper. Primary packages from French pharmacies are usually cardboard boxes, as the pharmacist keeps them on small shelves or in large but shallow drawers. In addition, the drugstore may purchase goods in larger quantities than the pharmacies. In any case, the primary packaging is different and therefore the secondary and tertiary packaging will also be different. Conversely, ethical drugs—drugs dispensed only with a physician's prescription—are pre-packaged in individual boxes in France, and in large containers in the United States, as pharmacists dispense medicines in generic pill containers that the pharmacist fills with the exact count needed.

14.10.3   Storage and Transportation Environment

Finally, there are several environmental influences on packaging, such as the dusty conditions under which transportation takes place. There are similar constraints triggered by high humidity, heat, or cold.

There are also constraints placed by the lack of refrigeration resources. The best example is probably the existence of long-conservation milk, which is sold un-refrigerated with expiration dates six or seven months after its production in many European countries. Not only does this packaging alternative allow the use of non-refrigerated shelving in the store, but it also requires no refrigeration in the remainder of the supply chain, from warehouses to transportation. It can also be transported safely quite far from its production location, including internationally.

All in all, several domestic issues in the importing country will affect the packaging of goods. Companies should develop appropriate strategies to account for the possible diversity of consumer and retail packaging alternatives present in their export markets.

14.11   Packaging as a Marketing Tool

It should be relatively clear by now that an exporter's good handling of packaging requirements will help considerably in the smooth transfer of goods from the exporter to the importer.

The most important way of looking at packaging is to prepare for the worst. The exporter should truly imagine the worst-case scenarios and the roughest possible journey when considering the way in which it will package its goods for export. Only under this premise will the exporter adequately serve the needs of the importer to receive goods in sellable and usable condition.

The exporter should make sure that the goods are protected from physical damage by ensuring that they are packaged in sturdy cartons and loaded correctly on pallets, that the pallets are separated by appropriate dunnage such as plywood and inflatable bags, and that all goods are protected from humidity and rain by protecting them with a plastic film and by outfitting the container with desiccant strips. The container should be cleaned and inspected before it is loaded, and seals used on the container should be of good quality. Shipping procedures should be effective in keeping the paperwork in the hands of appropriate personnel only.

Although such procedures are more expensive than a more casual attitude, the benefits are substantial. Consider a hypothetical case where, where failing to use an inexpensive plywood sheet spread over three pallets (a plywood sheet is 4×8 feet, or 122×244 centimeters), allows several boxes to be slightly crushed, so that the importer has to repackage the goods to make them sellable. The cost of repackaging these few boxes (labor, new boxes, calling the importer to resolve the issue) far exceed the original cost of the plywood sheet. Identical benefits can be drawn from using good pallets that do not break when the goods are unloaded, making sure that the container is watertight, and so on. In addition, because poor packaging can be used by insurance companies to deny a claim, it is to the exporter's advantage to have a track record of stellar packaging.

However, the greatest benefit from a good packaging policy is the goodwill that it generates with the importer and the marketing benefits that can be derived from it. Because the importer is not interested in having to challenge invoices or asking for allowances for goods that were damaged in transit, it welcomes shipments that arrive packaged carefully enough that it does not have to worry about anything. This confidence enhances the relationship between exporter and importer, and builds trust.

Finally, the exporter should ensure that the packaging is friendly to the employees who will unpack the goods: that the packing list is written in their language, that shipments are identified with colors that identify pallets that belong together, that the wood dunnage is assembled so that it can easily be taken apart, and so on. When shipping to countries where the dunnage and packaging materials are likely to be recycled as housing materials, an exporter would be even more empathetic if it considered using a better grade of board and plywood, ensuring that they have been heat-treated rather than fumigated with methyl bromide, so that the importer's employees can recycle or repurpose the wood without harm.

Review and Discussion Questions

1. What are the consequences of improper packaging for the exporter? Does your response depend on the Incoterms® rule used? Does it depend on the insurance policy in force?

2. What are the alternative means of packaging products that are not containerized?

3. What are some issues and risks that international packaging faces that are not present in a domestic shipment?

4. Use a product of your choice and ship it from one country to another in a multimodal shipment. What packaging methods would you use? Why?

Notes

[1] "Packaging Technology and Development," Lund University, Department of Packaging Logistics, Lund, Sweden, http://www.plog.lth.se/about_us/background_and_description/, retrieved July 1, 2013.

[2] *Ports of the World*, 15th ed., Cigna Insurance Corporation, available from Publisher, Ports of the World, Cigna Companies, P.O. Box 7716, Philadelphia, Pennsylvania 19192, USA.

[3] "Container Matters" and "Any Fool Can Stuff a Container," videos published by the Thomas Miller P&I Ltd, International House, 26 Creechurch Lane, London, EC3A 5BA, United Kingdom, available in part on https://www.youtube.com/watch?v=L6zUT55bnJ8 and https://www.youtube.com/watch?v=-XMASnENJ93w.

[4] Mottley, Robert, "Chilling out," *American Shipper*, June 2000, pp. 43-51.

[5] Porter, Janet, "Insurer Warns of the Dangers of Incorrectly Packed Containers," *Journal of Commerce*, August 4, 1997, p. 16A.

[6] Hapag-Lloyd, *Container Packing Brochure - English*, https://www.hapag-lloyd.com/content/dam/-website/downloads/press_and_media/publications/Container_Packing_Broschuere_engl.pdf, retrieved March 26, 2017.

[7] "Operational Restrictions," OOCL, http://www.oocl.com/usa/eng/localinformation/operational-restrictions/Pages/default.aspx, retrieved March 27, 2017.

[8] Fried, Brandon, "Weighty Issues Looming on the High Seas," *Air Cargo World*, March 2016, p. 38.

[9] Chao, Loretta, "Shipping Rule Spurs Outcry," *The Wall Street Journal*, December 7, 2015, p. B3.

[10] ShockWatch, http://shockwatch.com/, accessed March 24, 2017.

[11] Brindley, Chaille, "Fumigation 101," *Pallet Enterprise*, February 2004.

[12] *United Nations Recommendations on the Transport of Dangerous Goods—Model Regulations*, 15th ed., 2007, United Nations Economic Commission for Europe, http://www.unece.org/trans/danger/publi/unrec/rev15/15files_e.html, retrieved July 16, 2009.

[13] "Electronic Code of Federal Regulations," http://ecfr.gpoaccess.gov/cgi/t/text/text-idx?c=ecfr&rgn=div5&view=text&node=49:2.1.1.3.10&idno=49, retrieved July 16, 2009.

[14] AAR-TTCI, *Intermodal Loading Guide for Products in Closed Trailers and Containers*, July 2011, http://www.ns-direct.com/sites/default/files/kcfinder/files/AAR-intermodal-PDF.pdf, accessed March 27, 2017.

[15] Grocery Manufacturers Association, 2008 Joint Industry Unsaleables Report: The Real Causes and Actionable Solutions, written in collaboration with the Food Marketing Institute and Deloitte, September 2008, http://www.gmabrands.com/publications/UnsaleablesFINAL091108.pdf.

[16] "FreightWatch Annual Global Cargo Theft Assessment Shows Theft Rates Climbing in Europe and Asia; No Decline in the Americas," April 29, 2013, Freight Watch International, http://www.freightwatch-intl.com/announcements/04292013-0800/freightwatch-annual-global-cargo-theft-assessment-shows-theft-rates, retrieved July 2, 2013.

[17] *FedEx Small Business Center*, https://smallbusiness.fedex.com/international.html, accessed March 27, 2017.

[18] Walsh, Jack, "Minimizing the Impact of Dimensional Weight Pricing," *Material Handling and Logistics*, July-August 2015, pp. 29-33.

[19] USPS, *Priority Mail International*, https://www.usps.com/international/priority-mail-international.htm, accessed March 27, 2017.

[20] Estrin, Robin, "Swissair 111 Went Down with Millions in Valuables, Including Picasso Painting," Associated Press News Release, September 4, 1998.

[21] Higgins, Andrew, "Brazen Jewel Robbery at Brussels Airport Nets $50 Million in Diamonds," *The New York Times*, February 19, 2013.

[22] Hull, Dana, "How a Moving Company Capitalizes on Valuable Secrets," *Washington Post*, May 5, 1997, p. F12.

[23] "National Commercial Vehicle and Cargo Theft Prevention Initiative," April 16, 2008, National Commercial Vehicle and Cargo Theft Prevention Task Force, https://www.nationalcargothefttaskforce.-org/ncttf/app/doc/Context_preview.action?documentId=NAT.

[24] Cargo Theft Report: Applying the Brakes to Road Cargo Crime in Europe, 2009, Europol, http://-www.europol.europa.eu/publications/Serious_Crime_Overviews/Cargo_Theft_Report.pdf.

[25] "Container Matters" and "Any Fool Can Stuff a Container," videos published by the Thomas Miller P&I Ltd, International House, 26 Creechurch Lane, London, EC3A 5BA, United Kingdom.

[26] Anderson, Bill, "Prevent Cargo Theft," *Logistics Today*, May 23, 2007.

[27] *International Maritime Dangerous Goods Code*, 2016 IMDG Code, Amendment 38-16, International Maritime Organization, available from IMDG Publications/Regulations, ICC Compliance Center, http://imdgpublications.com, retrieved May 3, 2017.

[28] *Dangerous Goods Regulations 2017*, 58th edition, International Air Transport Association, available from http://www.iata.org/publications/dgr/Pages/index.aspx, retrieved May 3, 2017.

[29] Mottley, Robert, "Chilling Out," *American Shipper*, June 2000, pp. 43-51.

[30] *Ibid.*

[31] Seemuth, Mike, "The Ocean Alternative (Transport of Perishable Cargo by Sea)," *Journal of Commerce*, April 16, 2007.

[32] *Hazardous Manual Tasks: Code of Practice*, Safe Work Australia, February 2016, http://www.safe-workaustralia.gov.au/sites/SWA/about/Publications/Documents/640/Hazardous_Manual_TasksV2.pdf, retrieved April 24, 2017.

Chapter 15

International Warehouses and Distribution Centers

warehouse
A building used to store inventory and perform additional inventory-related services.

When a company purchases products from an overseas supplier or ships goods to a foreign subsidiary or a distributor, it can choose among several means of transportation (see Chapters 11, 12, and 13). However, there is one more decision that the logistics manager must make: the optimal point of origin of the goods.

A company can purchase the goods directly from the supplier—or send the goods directly to the customer from its manufacturing facilities—and handle this transaction as a single shipment. Alternatively, the goods can be shipped from a warehouse or distribution center located somewhere else in the world.

Warehouses are an integral part of the supply chain, and they can be used "upstream," that is, in the part of the supply chain encompassing the procurement processes of a firm, and "downstream," in the part of the supply chain relating to the firm's sales activities. Warehouses used in the downstream supply chain are also called distribution centers. This chapter covers the issues that an international-logistics manager needs to review when considering a warehouse for an international distribution channel, whether upstream or downstream. In an international environment, warehouses present challenges that somewhat differ from those presented by warehouses in a strictly domestic supply chain.

For an international logistics manager, using a warehouse located in different country is an option that can present several advantages:

- There are transportation savings: the cost of making many small shipments to a customer located overseas may be much higher than the cost of a single international shipment to a warehouse, even if that shipment is then followed by several smaller domestic shipments.

- There are response time benefits: delivery times for a customer's order may be much lower if the items ordered are physically close to the customer's facilities.

- There are manufacturing savings: it is frequently cheaper to manufacture a larger quantity of certain goods and store them than it is to produce smaller quantities of those goods.

- There are marketing benefits: for some markets, adaptations of the product (packaging, labeling, settings, instructions, . . . etc.) are necessary and better handled in an environment that is close to the customer.

- There may be other reasons that are specific to international trade: for example, the duty rates to import from the country of manufacturing may be higher than the duty rates to import from the country in which the warehouse is located, or there may be quotas that limit imports of a product, and the timing of import has to be carefully determined so that the product is imported before the quota runs out.

Building a warehouse in its international supply chain can provide a company with a strategic advantage over its competition.

15.1 Warehouse Functions

Warehouses fulfill different functions for a company involved in international trade, from the simple storage of goods to the consolidation of orders, as well as other services such as order fulfillment, packaging, after-sale service, and returns.

15.1.1 Inventory Holding

Primarily, warehouses are used to hold inventory. Even though companies operate in an environment of just-in-time shipping and manufacturing,[1] the expectations of customers and the risks inherent to international trade frequently demand that goods be kept in inventory. The inventory can be kept in a warehouse near the manufacturing facility or in a separate location.

Companies hold inventory for several reasons:

- When a raw material is produced seasonally (generally an agricultural product, such as cereal or fruits), but is sold year-round, it is necessary to purchase the raw material when it is available and hold it in inventory before it can be used in production.

- When a raw material's price fluctuates significantly and unpredictably (as with commodities such as sugar, chocolate, copper, or gold), and if the company can purchase the material at a low price, it can store it until the material is used in production.

- When a product is sold only seasonally (a product such as a lawnmower, greeting cards, or snow skis), but the company wants to operate year-round without fluctuations in its manufacturing planning, it needs to accumulate goods in low-sales months and ship them during high-sales months. In the *interim*, goods are warehoused.

- When marketing activities generate a significant increase in sales volume, the company must anticipate that volume change and store additional items to satisfy customer demand.

- Because international supply chains can be affected by significant unforeseen events (such as bad weather, strikes, or natural disasters), firms can absorb these disruptions by storing goods in warehouses beyond the normal safety-stock levels of a manufacturing facility (see Chapter 18).

- When the company anticipates that it will need to fulfill more retail orders, because it operates an online business selling directly to some customers, and these customers expect very short lead times before delivery.[2]

15.1.2 Consolidation

Warehouses can also be used as a location where goods that are produced in different manufacturing facilities, sometimes in different countries, are consolidated so that they can be sold together to customers.

This consolidation function is the primary purpose of a type of warehouse called a distribution center. A distribution center receives full-truck-load or full-container-load shipments of a single product or a few products from a manufacturer, and then builds smaller shipments of multiple products that are then sent to retailers or other members of the downstream supply chain. In some cases, the distribution center can be a fulfillment center for orders that are shipped directly to consumers.

An exporter can use a distribution center or a warehouse to support its distribution channel in foreign countries, whether the distribution channel is an agent, a distributor, a sales subsidiary, a joint venture, or any combination of these in a given region of the world. Chapter 4 provides further details on the differences between these alternatives.

15.1.3 Additional Services

Warehouses can be used to provide specific distribution services to an exporter; goods may need to be packaged differently in different countries, or packaged in different quantities, for legal or other practical reasons. These points are generally well covered in any international-marketing textbook, but an example is the packaging of medical products. The same product may be sold over the counter—without a prescription—in some countries, but require a prescription in others, and therefore is sold in different packaging; a blister pack designed to attract a consumer's eye, or a relatively plain box for the pharmacist to dispense. In some countries, ethical drugs—the ones requiring a prescription—are packaged in bulk because the pharmacist dispenses the quantity required by the prescription, but they are packaged in pre-set quantities in those countries in which the pharmacist only sells pre-packaged medicine.

The labeling requirements, or the instructions that are inserted in the product's package, may also be different in the countries that the warehouse serves, so the warehouse is used to provide this service. Simple language differences can necessitate a change in primary packaging.

The warehouse can also provide value-added services for customers, such as the price-labeling that a retailer requests, or provide after-sale services—small repairs and the sale of parts—as well as process returns and exchanges. In all cases, a warehouse that is geographically close to a market can provide faster and better-tailored services than the shipping department of an exporter. Consumers do not want to deal with a warranty claim that has to be shipped abroad, and would rather deal with a local address.

Any activity that is conducted in a warehouse beyond simple storage is frequently called a value-added process.

15.2 Location Decision

Once a company decides that a warehouse would be useful in its supply chain, management must determine the warehouse's location.[3] It is helpful to breakdown this decision into three levels: the regional—or national—level, which determines the region of the world or the country in which the warehouse is located, then the municipal level, which determines the city or area in which the warehouse will operate, and finally the "parcel" level, which refers to which building or parcel of land will be used.

All these decisions have an impact on the cost of operating the warehouse, as landed costs—the costs of getting goods delivered to the warehouse—and the operating costs are a direct function of the warehouse's location.[4]

15.2.1 Regional Level

At the regional level, choosing the region of the world or the country in which the warehouse is located, requires considering two main factors.

The infrastructure in which the warehouse operates is fundamentally important; a warehouse needs access to the transportation infrastructure, such as ports, canals, railroads, and roads, so it can ship and receive goods. However, it is also important for the country in which the warehouse is located to have a good communication infrastructure, a good utilities infrastructure (reliable access to electricity for example), and a good business support infrastructure, such as banks, third-party logistics providers, and transportation companies.[5]

infrastructure
A term that refers to all the public and private goods that facilitate transportation, communication, and business exchanges.

The overall environment of a country is also critical. A warehouse decision must consider the quality of the labor force, both for entry-level employees and management, the costs of that labor force—from prevailing wages to benefits—, the stability of the government and its openness to foreign investors, the economic policies of the country—from tariff rates to the currency's stability—, the overall cost of operating a business in that country (taxes and interest rates, for example), as well as the business climate.

Companies can also consider the culture of a country, and determine whether the management style of the exporter will be compatible with the way business is traditionally conducted in the country. Sources such as *Culturegrams* provide this type of information.[6]

15.2.2 Municipal Level

At the municipal level, when choosing the city or general area in which the warehouse operates, the exporter needs to consider the same issues, but at the local level. The warehouse must have access to highways, ports, or railroads without problems and without fighting congestion (see Figure 15.1). It must have access to reliable electricity. The warehouse must be able to have access to a high-speed internet connection with a very high uptime percentage. It also must have access to a supply of reliable, clean, freshwater, and to a sewer system. The local authorities must be supportive of a foreign investment in the area, and the labor pool must be sufficiently large, and properly trained. The local schools must be of a quality level that allows the company to hire employees who are willing to move their families to that location. There must be also some form of social infrastructure that allows for recruiting and training young talent.

15.2.3   Parcel Level

At the parcel level, the relevant criteria for choosing an existing building or a parcel of land on which to build a warehouse are more technical. One criterion is the street distance from the warehouse to the points of access to the main means of transportation; the warehouse can be selected by minimizing these distances, using several different algorithms.[7] Another criterion is the cost of the building or land, with potentially substantial differences within the same area. Access to public transportation for employees, proximity of child-care facilities, and other issues of convenience for employees are also important. The impact of the warehouse on the neighborhood should be considered to avoid backlash as operation volume increases.

An existing building must be evaluated on the quality of its construction, from the roof to the foundation, as in any other building. Additional criteria include availability of utilities, quality of the access roads, susceptibility to interruptions in service, possible room for expansion, and similar issues. In selecting a warehouse building, the design of the building matters; issues to consider are whether there are roof-support posts in the middle of the warehouse that will place constraints on the design of the facility, whether the number of docks is

Figure 15.1: Warehouses with Connections to Road, Rail, and Water Transportation in Küçükçekmece, near Istanbul, Turkey

Photo ©Mehmet Çetin/Shutterstock. Used with Permission.

sufficient to allow for trucks to be loaded and unloaded, whether the yard is large enough to accommodate surplus trucks in times of high demand, whether there are constraints that would have a negative impact on security, and so on.

If the company decides to invest in a green-field operation—building the warehouse on a parcel of land—, the number of criteria increase, from the composition of the soil (whether it can handle the weight of the building's contents and the traffic), to drainage, access to utilities, room for expansion, construction costs, and whether local construction companies have the expertise and knowledge to build a warehouse to modern standards.

15.3   Warehouse Ownership

There are three ways to manage the ownership of a warehouse; the exporter can purchase or build the warehouse and handle it as a sales subsidiary, or it can use the services of a third-party logistics provider—a 3PL—, such as a public warehouse or a contract warehouse.[8]

15.3.1   Public Warehouses

Public warehouses are businesses that rent warehousing space to companies that need it, and provide all other services for a pre-determined fee. The space in a public warehouse is shared with many other businesses. A public warehouse has its own employees and equipment, and those costs are spread over multiple tenants.

public warehouse
A warehouse owned by an independent business in which other businesses can rent space as needed.

From the perspective of the exporter, a public warehouse presents the advantage of flexibility. The entire operation is a variable cost; if space is needed, then the exporter incurs the costs of the space that is used, and if services are needed, then the exporter incurs the costs of the services provided. There is no overhead and there are no fixed costs. In most instances, it is easy to request additional space, and easy to reduce the amount of space rented.

One aspect of public warehouses that differs from other alternatives is that their location was determined by the warehouse owner, which can be an advantage and a disadvantage for an exporter. On one hand, the warehouse owner probably selected the best possible site to efficiently serve its customers; however, it is also possible that the warehouse's location is a compromise between its different customers' needs, and it may not be the ideal location from the perspective of the exporter. The analysis conducted to determine the ideal location of a warehouse should not be overlooked prior to contracting with a public warehouse.

15.3.2   Contract Warehouses

A contract warehouse owns and operates a warehouse for an exporter on a long-term contract. In this case, the warehouse company uses its employees and

contract warehouse
A warehouse owned by a company, but managed by another, such as a warehouse-management company.

equipment to provide space and services to a warehouse leased by the exporter. In most instances, a contract warehouse has only one customer in the warehouse.

A contract warehouse is used when the exporter knows that it will need to utilize a warehouse of a pre-determined size, but does not want the responsibility to own it, to manage it, or hire employees for it. The exporter and the contract warehouse have an agreement, and the warehouse is a monthly, recurring expense for the exporter. While this arrangement provides less flexibility than a public warehouse, some exporters choose contract warehouses when they feel that they do not have the managerial expertise to optimally manage a warehouse, and when they want to reduce their exposure to labor contracts in foreign countries.

An additional advantage of a contract warehouse is that the exporter benefits from the expertise of the third-party logistics provider running the warehouse; its expertise in site selection, size, and operational design can allow the exporter to reach an optimal decision faster.[9]

15.3.3   Private Warehouses

private warehouse
A warehouse owned and operated by a business to store its own goods and perform other services.

In a private warehouse, the exporter owns and operates the warehouse in the foreign country, using its own employees and assets. This arrangement is similar to the sales subsidiary alternative that was described in Chapter 4, and the exporter has some risks and exposure in this investment. In addition to the capital investment, the exporter must hire management and labor to operate the warehouse.

A private warehouse is used when the exporter has acquired the skills to manage a warehouse, and when it considers that the services that it provides to its customers, and the quality of the services it can provide, justify the costs incurred. A private warehouse is also supported when the exporter anticipates that there will be substantial market growth, and that the exporter does not think that a public warehouse or a contract warehouse can match that growth. In rare cases, an exporter will use a private warehouse if there is no other alternative, that is, there are no public warehouses available, or the skills of the contract warehouse providers are not to its standards.

15.4   Warehouse Activities

Once a warehouse is selected, its operations can be divided into five broad categories.

15.4.1   Receiving

receiving
A warehouse activity that consists of unloading the goods shipped by a supplier and verifying all aspects of the shipment.

Chronologically, the first warehousing activity is receiving the goods so that they can be placed in storage.

To facilitate the receiving process, the warehouse must ensure that, prior to receiving the goods, some elements are communicated to the supplier:

- **The acceptable pallet sizes**—A pallet necessitates mechanical equipment to be moved. While pallet sizes are somewhat standardized in some industries and countries, they are not universally uniform. European pallets are 1.2 meters by 0.8 meters (approximately 48 inches by 32 inches), but other sizes exist in those countries.[10] U.S. pallets are more varied, with the most common pallet size being the one used by the Grocery Manufacturer Association, which is 40 inches by 48 inches (approximately 1.01 meters by 1.22 meters), but many other options exist.[11] Australian pallets are completely standardized domestically, but are a size that is not used anywhere else in the world, as they are square, 1.16 meters (approximately 46 inches).[12] It is important that the pallets be the correct size so that goods are not moved from one pallet to another as they are received.

pallet
A wooden (plastic) platform on which goods can be placed.

- **The markings and other labeling requirements of the warehouse**—Proper labeling prevents delays in accepting the goods. Most warehouse operate with a barcode system that must be able to read whatever information is on the received goods.

- **The time at which the goods should arrive**—While it is sometimes difficult to enforce in an international environment, a time of arrival allows the warehouse to plan for proper receipt of the goods with the appropriate personnel and equipment, so that there are no delays for the delivery driver.

Receiving the goods takes place on a dock, generally from a truck trailer or a container placed on a truck. Containers that originate abroad should be opened cautiously. First the seal should be inspected and its number checked to determine that it matches the documents sent by the shipper. This ensures that the integrity of the shipment was not compromised. Once the seal is cut, it is important to secure a chain that ties the doors together before opening them. Goods may have shifted during transit and be wedged against the doors; it is dangerous to open them without that simple precaution.[13]

Once the goods have been received, and the quantities and types checked against the purchase order and transport documents, they are placed in storage.

15.4.2 Storage

After the goods are received, they must be placed in storage. There are many ways in which goods can be stored in a warehouse.

Some warehouses, such as e-commerce warehouses, hold the goods in their primary packaging—consumer packaging, see Figure 14.1 on page 484— on low shelves so that they can be accessed by warehouse personnel without the help of mechanized equipment. However, most warehouses hold goods in their secondary or tertiary packaging. Secondary packaging refers to corrugated paperboard boxes in which primary-package goods are placed, and tertiary packaging refers to pallets of secondary-packaging boxes.

storage
A warehouse activity that consists of placing the goods that were shipped by a supplier on shelves or other means of storage.

Warehouses can simply place the pallets of goods on the floor of the warehouse and stack them on top of one another. This method is used when the warehouse has a low ceiling, and it is acceptable if the stacks are of the same type of products, so that there is not an excessive number of handlings to reach a product: obviously, it is time consuming to have to move the two upper pallets to reach the bottom one, so it is preferable to have stacks of the same goods. Due to weight constraints, the stacks generally do not exceed three, possibly four, pallets (see Figure 15.2); otherwise, there is the risk of crushing the secondary packages of the bottom pallet.

Alternatively, the goods can be placed on metallic racks. The racks can be designed to hold pallets or to hold merchandise in their secondary packaging on shelves. Pallet racks can hold one or two pallets in depth, and one or two pallets in height. Most pallet racks are utilized with only one pallet in height to simplify retrieval.

The racks can be of low height, or approximately 7.5 meters high (25 feet), for warehouses in which the ceiling is low. Warehouses in which the ceiling is as high as 15 meters (or 50 feet) can install high-bay racks. The aisles between the racks can be wide, so that traditional-size fork-lift trucks can load and unload the goods (see Figure 15.3), or they can be narrow, as shown in Figure 15.4 on page 530, in

pallet stacking
A method used to store pallets, in which pallets are placed on the floor of the warehouse and on top of one another.

rack
A metallic storage area in a warehouse used for storing pallets or boxes.

Figure 15.2: Stacked Pallets in a Low-Ceiling Warehouse in Rayong, Thailand
Photo ©Sarawuth Wannasathit/Shutterstock. Used with Permission.

Figure 15.3: Palletized Goods on Wide-Aisle Low-Height Racks in a Warehouse in Torino, Italy

Photo ©Champiofoto/Shutterstock. Used with Permission.

which case the warehouse must use more compact mechanized equipment.

Higher racks and narrower aisles are used in warehouses in regions where the costs of land are high. Because the warehouse floors must be able to withstand greater loads, they cost more to install, and because of the specialized equipment the warehouses need, they cost more to operate; however, they use much less land. Lower racks and wider aisles are cheaper to build and cheaper to operate, but they demand much more land. There is a clear trade-off between the height of the racks and the area used by the warehouse.

A wide variety of racking systems has been developed in the past twenty-five years, designed to be utilized in warehouses located in areas where land is very expensive, or in situations where the warehouse cannot be expanded. All these alternatives are much more expensive than wide-aisle low-height racking systems, but they allow better utilization of existing space, and companies are implementing them to avoid building larger warehouses.[14,15]

- **Pallet-flow racks** or **gravity-fed racks** are designed to store pallets on rollers rather than fixed shelves (see Figure 15.5). The bays are inclined so that the pallets or boxes can be loaded in the back of the racks and flow

Figure 15.4: Non-Palletized Goods on Narrow-Aisle High-Bay Racks in a Warehouse in St. Petersburg, Russia
Photo ©Petinov Sergey Mihilovich/Shutterstock. Used with Permission.

automatically to the front of the rack when a pallet is removed. These racks allow for a greater density of goods in the warehouse, but each bay can only store one type of item. Rollers are more expensive than fixed shelves and demand more maintenance.

- **Mobile racks** are wheeled racks that can move on rails, so that the aisles between racks can be eliminated. Whenever an item needs to be stored or retrieved, the racks are moved to create an aisle. Even heavy-duty racks for pallets can operate on this basis. The racks move using electric motors or human power. The cost of installing and operating mobile racks is higher than static racks, but the capacity of the warehouse can increase by as much as 100 percent without a change in its size.

- **Very-High-Bay racks** can be as high as 60 meters high (180 feet), and are built as part of the structure of the warehouse; that is, unlike traditional racks that are built inside a warehouse, the very-high-bay racks are built before the roof of the warehouse is installed, and they help hold the roof in place. It also gives the racks more rigidity. Therefore existing warehouses cannot be retrofitted to use very-high-bay racks. These warehouses utilize their space very well, but the high costs of construction and operation make this option only attractive in areas in which land is very expensive.

- **Automated Storage and Retrieval Systems** or **ASRS** operate in warehouses that use conveyor belts, lifts, and other automated devices to place full pallets in high-bay or very-high-bay racks.[16] Their speed and ability to work concurrently (each aisle has its own devices) allows ASRS to be very quick and accurate. Automated Storage and Retrieval Systems must utilize uniform pallet sizes that are all in perfect condition; any deviation from the standard makes it a challenge for the system to handle. ASRS warehouses are very expensive to build and operate, and they are only built in areas where land is limited and labor prices are high. The Mansueto Library of the University of Chicago holds its collection in an ASRS warehouse that handles the books in identically sized bins and stores them in a 50-foot-deep (15 meters) underground area.[17] This system allows the library to keep its entire collection on-site rather than keep the less frequently used books off-site, as other libraries must do to save shelf space. Books can be retrieved in minutes.

automated storage and retrieval system
A computerized system that uses conveyor belts, lifts, and robots to store and retrieve goods in a warehouse.

Figure 15.5: Roller Racks in a Warehouse in the United Kingdom
Photo ©Baloncici/Shutterstock. Used with Permission.

- **Robots** have become more common in warehouses, especially since Amazon purchased Kiva, a manufacturer of robots, in March 2012. Since then, Amazon has purchased more than 45,000 robots for its warehouses.[18] In a robotic warehouse, the goods are kept in their primary packaging in small "pods," which are metallic racks with three to five shelves, with a footprint of approximately 2 feet by 2 feet (50 centimeters). When a product has to be stored or retrieved, the robots retrieve the pod on which the product is kept. The robots are small enough to fit under the pods and therefore circulate under them. When it is time to pick up a pod, the robot "unscrews" itself below the selected pod, which allows the pod to be lifted off the ground and be carried away. When robots carry pods, they travel in the aisles—the company calls them streets and boulevards—and taking them to the front of the warehouse, where a human worker picks the product to fulfill the order. The robot then returns the pod to an empty space in the warehouse, "screws" itself so that the pod now rests on its feet, and the robot then travels to its next assigned pod. When the robots are low on battery power, they pull themselves out of the available pool of robots and travel to an area where they recharge their battery.

A wide variety of companies offer products that are based on the concepts presented in this section, although many of them have added features and attributes that are specific to that manufacturer and which they promote as more cost-effective or presenting significant advantages. Since the design of storage systems depends on the type of products handled by the warehouse and on the characteristics of the warehouse, an exporter should look into multiple design alternatives and multiple suppliers before making a decision.

15.4.3   Picking

picking
A warehouse activity that consists of retrieving from storage goods that were ordered by a customer.

Once the goods have been received and placed in storage, the next activity in a warehouse is picking the items to fulfill customer orders. The picking activity consumes most of the labor costs of a warehouse or distribution center.

There are two main points to consider in determining the best picking alternative for a warehouse; the overall strategy, which includes selecting a method to fulfill the strategy, and the technique utilized to support that combination of strategy and method.[19,20]

Picking Strategies

Picking strategies are best determined by looking at the type of orders that the warehouse fulfills. The picking strategy will differ if the orders are for full pallets, for several secondary-packaging boxes on that pallet— called a pallet layer—, for single boxes, for several consumer items to be taken from a box, or for single items. The order size is also relevant; orders that include several different products, such as the order placed by a distributor seeking to replenish its inventory

Figure 15.6: A Kiva Robot carrying a Pod in an Amazon.com Warehouse
Photo ©Amazon Robotics. Used with Permission.

every week, will be picked differently than orders that are mostly for one or two items, as are orders placed by consumers.

The least commonly used strategy is a **goods to picker** strategy. In that case, the goods are sent to the picker through an automated system. The Kiva robots in the Amazon warehouses are an example of a method that can be used to fulfill such a strategy, as the pods are carried by the robots to the picker. That is also the way in which an Automated Storage and Retrieval System works; in that method, the pallets are brought to the picker by a conveyor belt managed by the ASRS. However, several other methods exist as well; warehouses that handle products that are physically small use carousel storage systems on which all of the products are kept, and the carousels will turn until the appropriate item is in front of the picker. This is common in a pharmaceutical warehouse, for example, since it handles small products. As the use of robots increases in warehouses, the goods-to-picker strategy is likely to become used more frequently.[21]

Alternatively, a warehouse can use a **picker to goods** strategy, in which the employee is sent to retrieve the goods from the storage system. This is the most commonly used picking strategy, but it presents the great disadvantage that a large percentage of the employees' time is spent traveling from one area of the warehouse to another. As much as 50 percent of the picker's time can be spent on travel.[22] The rest of the time, the picker is determining which item to select for the order, and in which quantity. The location at which a picker is stationary and making a selection is called a pick face; this is an area of the storage shelving that is approximately the width of a pallet.

The simplest way to implement a picker-to-goods strategy is to fill orders like a shopper in a supermarket; the employee is given a list of the items on the order, and the quantity needed, and the employee then retrieves all the items in the order and places them in a cart or on a pallet. The picker is said to "pick by order." However, this method tends to be least effective until the orders are large and the goods for each order tend to be in close proximity. The employee in Figure 15.8 is picking a pallet of only two different items, so the "pick by order" method is appropriate. He retrieved them from the rack located at a pick face labeled B-36.

However, it is frequently more efficient to ask the picker to fill multiple orders at the same time. In that case, the picker is following a "cluster picking" method. The employee is given several orders at once, generally two to ten different orders, and the employee goes around the warehouse filling these orders at the

Figure 15.7: A Picker Retrieving Goods for an Order in a Thai Warehouse
Photo ©MooNoi Amphol/Shutterstock. Used with Permission.

same time. The picker places the orders in different boxes—called totes—on a cart, or in separate carts. It is the responsibility of the picker to ensure that the correct goods go into the correct tote or cart. After the picking is over, the orders are brought to the shipping area where they are packaged and shipped.

Another alternative is a "batch picking" method, which is somewhat similar; the employee picks several orders at the same time, but the orders are commingled on a single list. The picker does not need to identify which goods go to which order; they are gathered together on a single cart or pallet. After the picker has completed the task, that person or another employee separates the orders so that they can be packaged and shipped.

Another alternative method is "zone picking." When a warehouse uses that method, employees are assigned a zone in the warehouse from which they pick items for an order. The size of the zone can be a few aisles, or a single aisle, depending on the volume of business that the warehouse experiences. Each employee then sends the goods to a central area, either by cart or some other mechanical system, such as a conveyor belt, where goods from different zones are assembled into complete orders and then shipped. Under a "zone picking" method, there are two types of employees; the pickers, who remain in their zone, and order assemblers, who put the goods of a single order together. That second group of employees functions in a fashion similar to their counterparts in a goods-to-picker warehouse.

Picking Techniques

In addition to the picking strategy and the method used to implement that strategy, warehouse managers must implement a picking technique to help employees pick the correct goods, in the right quantity, for the correct order.

While it is considered old technology, many warehouses still use a simple **paper list** picking technique; each order is printed on a sheet of paper that is given to the picker. The picker manually checks the list and marks the items that were placed in the cart at every stop in the warehouse. The picker is responsible for selecting the correct item and for counting the correct number of items to be placed in the cart. If there are multiple orders, the picker is also responsible to place the correct items in the correct tote.

To increase productivity and reduce errors, especially in warehouses in which the orders are somewhat complex, or in environments in which employees may not be well educated, many warehouses have implemented techniques that rely less on the abilities of the picker and more on technology.[23]

A small improvement over a simple paper list is the **label picking** technique. Instead of printing the pick list on paper, it is printed on a sheet of labels. As the picker finds items on the list, the employee places the label on the item. That allows the picker to check for accuracy—the label must match the item—and quantity—the number of labels must match the number of items; there cannot be any product in the cart without a label, and there should be no labels left on the order sheet at the end of the pick.

Another alternative is the **barcode picking** technique. In warehouses that employ this technology, every item is labeled with a barcode, and every pick face (location in the warehouse where a pallet can be stored) has a barcode. The picker is given a barcode reader and a screen, mounted on the forklift truck, on the cart, or even on the forearm, that lists the next item to pick, in which quantity, and at what location. When retrieving items from storage, the employee scans the barcode of the pick face, then the barcode of the items picked, multiple times if necessary. The system does not move on to the next item to pick until the picker has scanned the correct product in the correct quantity. The barcode technique is the most frequently used technique used in warehouses.

One of the drawbacks of the barcode technique is that the picker must refer to the screen frequently to identify the next pick, and that slows productivity. To improve the efficiency of the barcode picking technique, companies have implemented a **voice picking** technique. Voice picking allows the warehouse computer to instruct the picker of the next item to select and its location. The picker wears a headset through which the next pick is communicated by an artificial voice. Earlier voice-picking headphones simply had instructions and the picker confirmed every pick with a hand-held barcode scanner, but more recent systems

Figure 15.8: A Warehouse Employee Using a Voice-Picking Headset
Photo ©Monkey Business Images/Shutterstock. Used with Permission.

are equipped with voice-recognition software, and the picker simply repeats the item number or the barcode number in the headset for confirmation. That has the advantage of allowing the picker to work with two hands (one hand is no longer holding the barcode reader). Voice recognition technology was particularly welcome in warehouses that are cold (such as for refrigerated or frozen goods), as the picker did not have to remove gloves all the time, and in warehouses where the picker needs both hands to retrieve boxes of goods.

In warehouses where a zone picking method is followed, picking can be conducted with a technique called **light picking**. Each pick face is equipped with a series of lights and a small display with numbers (called a seven-segment display). The picker is directed to the pick face that is lit. There the employee picks the products in the quantities marked on the display and places them in totes or on a conveyor belt to be taken to the order-assembly area. The picker has free hands and no headset, but the costs of equipping the warehouse with lights and displays is much higher than other techniques. It is therefore implemented only in warehouses that conduct a high number of transactions.

15.4.4 Packaging and Shipping

Once orders are picked, they must be consolidated into packages going to customers. This can be a pallet shipped LTL or FTL, or a corrugated paperboard box shipped with a small-packet carrier.

packaging
A warehouse activity that consists of assembling the goods that were ordered by a customer into packages so that they can be shipped.

shipping
A warehouse activity that consists of organizing the transport of goods that were ordered by a customer.

The goods shipped by the warehouse frequently must meet national requirements in size, weight, and labeling, which can be different from country to country, and can be different than the sizes of the packages used in the warehouse. Goods shipped within the European countries must be packaged in boxes that meet maximum criteria for weight and size, so that they can be safely handled by manual labor, and many countries have similar requirements.[24] The pallet sizes must meet the customer's requirements, as well as the requirements of the trucking or railroad company. The responsibility for these decisions falls on the shipping manager, and a good execution of all these requirements makes for more satisfied customers.

In addition to these legal constraints, the shipping activities in the warehouse must attempt to minimize the costs of shipping the goods, from reducing the size of packages if they are subject to shipping costs based on dimensional weight, to selecting the best mode of transportation and carrier. These operational constraints must also be weighed against the imperative of ensuring that the goods arrive at their destination with no damage. Although Chapter 14 focused on international shipping, much of its information is also valid for domestic shipments originating in a warehouse.

15.4.5 Other Operations

Some warehouses also handle additional services for their customers.

The warehouse may handle **returns** for goods that are not of the quality that the customer expected, or that are returned by customers for other reasons (unsold items). Frequently, to meet managerial quality standards such as QS-9000 (see Section 19.7.3 on page 661), returns must be segregated from the remainder of the goods in the warehouse until they are inspected, and then placed back in storage, repaired, re-packaged, given away to charitable organizations,[25] or simply discarded.

Warehouses may also handle **after-sales services** for manufacturers, with an area dedicated to warranty claims processing, spare parts, inspections, and repairs of defective or damaged products. The after-sale-service area of the warehouse generally acts as a separate "business," with its own receiving, storage area, and shipping, and is rarely commingled with the other warehouse operations.

Finally, some warehouses provide additional **value-added services** such as labeling goods for resale, inserting instruction booklets in packages, assembling kits of different parts for customers, placing goods in retail packages, or providing some other small services for their customers. Warehouses can charge for these services separately or provide them as a goodwill gesture to their customers.

15.5   Warehouse Layout Options

To accomplish these functions, warehouses must be designed so that they can fulfill them efficiently.[26] The overall layout of a warehouse is constrained by many factors:

- The physical size of the building and its other characteristics (age, construction, height, floor characteristics).

- The cost of land and other environmental constraints (maximum height, road access, utilities, location).

- The physical characteristics (weight and volume) of the products.

- The manner in which goods are packaged when they are received (pallets, secondary packages) and when they are shipped out (pallets, secondary packages, or single units).

- The variety of products.

- The velocity of products (how long they stay in the warehouse, from receiving to shipping).

- The number of shipments, both incoming and outgoing.

- The average size of shipments.

- The additional services that the warehouse provides.

- The possible expansion of the warehouse.

However, there are some general guidelines that are useful in determining the best layout for a warehouse.

15.5.1 Fixed Areas

Each warehouse must include some areas that are essential to its functioning and these do not vary.

The warehouse needs loading docks for receiving and for shipping. Ideally, the loading docks for receiving are separate from the loading docks for shipping, so that pallets of products that are being received do not interfere or get confused with pallets of products that are being shipped.

There should be an inspection area at the receiving dock, so that goods can be inspected and counted. Even though most of the goods may not need to be inspected and counted because the goods are received from a trusted vendor, or one who holds the quality certification that the warehouse prefers—QS9000 for example—there are instances where there are issues; a new vendor, a shipment that was damaged in a road accident or by bad weather, a bill of lading that does not match the purchase order, or some other irregularity in a shipment that requires more effort than a routine shipment. Therefore, some area needs to exist to isolate the shipment while it is inspected, so that it is not commingled with other acceptable shipments.

There should be a staging area near the shipping dock, where the goods that are being shipped are assembled before they are loaded onto the shipping trucks or rail cars, so that the loading proceeds as quickly as possible. Most frequently, staging takes place in the warehouse for full truckloads and full containerloads, so that each pallet can be weighed. The loading software can then optimize the load by ensuring that the center of gravity is in the middle of the load and at its lowest possible point.

staging
Prior to shipment, assembling the goods to be shipped on the floor of the warehouse, so that they can be loaded as quickly as possible.

There should be some service space allocated for ancillary warehouse activities, such as returns and repairs. That space should be isolated from the remainder of the warehouse so that none of these activities interfere with its main operations.

There must also be some maintenance space where forklift trucks are recharged or refueled, where they are repaired, and where other materials, such as racks, barcode readers, headsets, and even pallets, are repaired and maintained.

Finally, there should be some office space for management. Frequently this office space is located on a mezzanine, or a second-floor area above the part of the warehouse that holds goods in low-height storage. Such a layout presents little inconvenience for the management team, but saves space at the floor level.

However, most of a warehouse's layout is dedicated to storage space. That storage space can be arranged in many different ways.

15.5.2 A-B-C Rules

Most warehouses are organized using some variation of an A-B-C rule. An A-B-C rule is an extension of Pareto's Law, first articulated by Joseph Juran,[27], but attributed to the Italian economist Vilfredo Pareto, who had observed that 80 percent of land in Italy was owned by 20 percent of the population. In business, Juran extended it to mean that "80 percent of a company's sales come from 20

A-B-C classification
A method used to separate inventory items into three categories in function of their costs or other characteristics.

percent of its customers." This observation is believed to be empirically accurate, and it has been extended to many different aspects of a business; inventory managers have derived the A-B-C rule from it (see Section 18.5 on page 624).

The A-B-C rule states that inventory can be divided into three classes: the A-class represents approximately 80 percent of a company's inventory costs and about 20 percent of a company's product mix; the B-class represents approximately 15 percent of a company's inventory costs and 30 percent of its product mix; and the C-class represents the remaining 5 percent of costs and 50 percent of products.[28]

Warehouse managers use a similar A-B-C rule to determine the optimal layout of their storage space. In some warehouses, the A-B-C classification is used to segregate storage between A-class items that represent 80 percent of the warehouse's sales, and that area is located close to the loading docks, to decrease the length of trips for employees placing items in storage or retrieving them. The B-class items are further from the docks, and the C-class furthest.

Warehouse managers can use a different A-B-C rule to layout the warehouse's storage space, applied to the physical volume of goods. The larger A-class goods are in a high-bay, wide-aisle area of the warehouse, whereas the C-class goods are in a low-bay narrow-aisle area, and the B-class goods are in some intermediary location. The differentiation can also be made on value, with the goods with high value near the loading dock and the managerial offices, so that they can be more closely monitored, and the goods with lower value further away. Finally, the classification can be made on the velocity of goods, or the speed at which they move from receiving to shipping. The A-class goods that move frequently are placed near the shipping docks, the B-class further away, and the C-class, which are received and shipped infrequently, are furthest away. The number of different interpretations of the A-B-C concept is almost endless.

In all cases, warehouse layout design is frequently determined with input from consulting firms that specialize in that field, and a new warehouse will benefit from the accumulated experience and wisdom of warehouses that handle a similar product mix.[29]

15.6   Security

There are two primary concerns for a warehouse in terms of security; protecting the goods from theft, and protecting them from damage.

As first mentioned in Chapter 10, theft can take three forms:

- Pilferage happens when individuals opportunistically steal goods in the warehouse; such crimes are not planned and usually happen at random. They are more frequent for goods that are kept at the individual level, because these goods make a more tempting target. Pallets and secondary-package boxes make the cargo more difficult to identify and more difficult to steal in small quantities. However, it is possible to place a box in a doorway or aisle to be retrieved later with an employee's car.

- Organized theft refers to planned operations that are directed at a higher quantity of goods. Organized theft usually targets a pallet that is "left" in a truck rather than unloaded, or one "misplaced" in the warehouse, to be placed with another outgoing shipment.

- System's theft uses the information system of the warehouse to change paperwork, substitute paperwork, or delete files so that goods can be removed without immediate detection. This type of theft requires either inside accomplices or the ability to gain access to a company's computer system.

The best method for preventing any type of theft is screening employees carefully and monitoring visitors to the warehouse; however, this can be challenging and cannot be implemented in some situations, as the data may not be available. Other complementary alternatives include creating processes that make one employee responsible for one aspect of warehousing and another employee responsible for a complementary aspect of the task; for example, one employee is responsible for unloading a truck and another for counting the goods, with frequent rotations to eliminate the possibility of collusion. Companies have also successfully implemented a reward system that benefits the entire employee group if theft is kept to a minimum, since all have a vested interest in preventing it.

For damage prevention, such as damage due to careless driving of a forklift truck or other equipment, or due to products not placed in storage carefully (too many products on top of one another, for example), workforce training is of primary importance; when employees feel that management is committed to a damage-free environment, and when there is a reward system in place for good work, they take fewer short cuts and engage in more careful behaviors. Damage can also be caused by a poorly maintained warehouse (rain damage because of a leaky roof, products that cannot be sold because they are dirty, products that can no longer be sold because they could not be found in the warehouse and are now obsolete). Good processes and procedures can prevent this type of damage quite well.

Although there is the possibility that a warehouse could be used to commit terrorist acts (by substituting products with explosives, for example), the methods used to prevent theft are generally sufficient to prevent this type of activity. The processes in place in the international supply chain (described in Chapter 16) are designed to reduce the possibility of terrorism.

15.7 Warehousing as a Marketing Tool

For an exporter, warehouses can play a major role in gaining a competitive advantage.[30]

A warehouse that is in close proximity to customers means that the exporter can offer lead times similar to those offered by domestic competitors; in some cases, that simple possibility can make a difference to a potential customer who may not have had the option to wait for an international shipment.

A warehouse can also provide great service to a distributor or customer who had not anticipated the sales success of the exporter's products; by being able to provide the product quickly because it is in inventory, the exporter can avoid a dissatisfied customer and potentially lost sales.

In addition, a warehouse can also provide value-added services that are important to the customer, and the warehouse's proximity to the market allows those services to be added just prior to delivery. Similarly, after-market services can be provided in customer-friendly way: no need to return goods internationally for warranty work or repairs.

Overall, a warehouse is an integral and strategic component of an international supply chain.

Review and Discussion Questions

1. What are five criteria that can be used to determine the location of a warehouse?

2. What are the two primary picking strategies in a warehouse?

3. Describe three techniques that can be used to increase the productivity of a picker. What additional costs do they have over a simple paper list?

4. What are some of the value-added services that a warehouse can fulfill for an exporter?

5. Watch a Youtube video about the way Kiva robots operate in an Amazon warehouse. What advantages are there to operating a warehouse with such robots?

Notes

[1] Frazelle, Edward H., *World-Class Warehousing and Material Handling*, 2016, Second Edition, McGraw-Hill, New York, New York.

[2] O'Reilly, Joseph, "Site Selection: Follow the Signs to Competitive Advantage," *Inbound Logistics*, January 2014, pp. 215-221.

[3] Lewis, Chris, "The Science Behind Site Selection," *Inbound Logistics*, January 2016, pp. 227-234.

[4] Wisser, John, "Four Things to Consider when Choosing Warehouse Locations," *Digital Supply Chain*, August 14, 2014, http://www.supplychaindigital.com/warehousing/four-things-consider-when-choosing-warehouse-locations, retrieved April 21, 2017.

[5] Trunik, Perry, "Site Selection Decisions: A Matter of Data," *Inbound Logistics*, July 2011, pp. 23-31.

[6] Culturegrams, Pro-Quest and Brigham Young University, http://www.culturegrams.com.

[7] Huifeng, Ji and Xu Aigon, "The Method of Warehouse Location Selection Based on GIS and Remote Sensing Images," *The International Archives of the Photogrammetry, Remote Sensing and Spatial Information Sciences*, 37, B2, 2008, www.isprs.org/proceedings/XXXVII/congress/2_pdf/4_WG-II-4/07.pdf, retrieved April 21, 2017.

[8] Keller, Scott B., and Brian C. Keller, *The Definitive Guide to Warehousing*, Council of Supply Chain Management Professionals, 2014, Pearson Education, Upper Saddle River, New Jersey, USA.

[9] Buxbaum, Peter, "Global Logistics: Setting your Sites Overseas," *Inbound Logistics*, May 1998, pp. 41-46.

[10] ISO 6780:2003, Flat Pallets for Intercontinental Materials Handling—Principal Dimensions and Tolerances, https://www.iso.org/standard/30524.html, accessed April 21, 2017.

[11] Clarke, John, "Pallets 101: Industry Overview and Wood, Plastic, Paper & Metal Options," *International Safe Transit Association*, https://secure.ista.org/emarket/category/Technical-Library/Pallets, accessed April 21, 2017.

[12] Pallet Sizes—Pallet Dimensions, Commonwealth Handling Equipment Pool, http://www.chep.com-/pallets/pallet_sizes, accessed April 21, 2017.

[13] TT Talk - Be careful when opening container doors, Through Transport Mutual Insurance Association Limited, May 29, 2008, https://www.ttclub.com/loss-prevention/tt-talk/article/tt-talk-be-careful-when-opening-container-doors-3056/, retrieved April 21, 2017.

[14] Richards, Gwynne, *Warehouse Management: A Complete Guide to Improving Efficiency and Minimizing Costs in the Modern Warehouse*, 2014, Second Edition, Kogan-Page, London, United Kingdom.

[15] Frazelle, Edward H., *World-Class Warehousing and Material Handling*, 2016, Second Edition, McGraw-Hill, New York, New York.

[16] Fiveash, Charlie, "Warehouse Automation: the Next Generation," *Inbound Logistics*, January 2016, pp. 237-246.

[17] Automated Storage and Retrieval System, the Joe and Rika Mansueto Library, the University of Chicago, https://www.lib.uchicago.edu/mansueto/tech/asrs/, retrieved April 22, 2017.

[18] Bhasin, Kim, and Patrick Clark, "How Amazon Triggered a Robot Arms Race," *Bloomberg Technology*, June 29, 2016, https://www.bloomberg.com/news/articles/2016-06-29/how-amazon-triggered-a-robot-arms-race, retrieved April 22, 2017.

[19] Richards, Gwynne, *Warehouse Management: A Complete Guide to Improving Efficiency and Minimizing Costs in the Modern Warehouse*, 2014, Second Edition, Kogan-Page, London, United Kingdom.

[20] Frazelle, Edward H., *World-Class Warehousing and Material Handling*, 2016, Second Edition, McGraw-Hill, New York, New York.

[21] Graves, Jeffrey, "Bring the Work to the Worker," *World Trade 100*, October 2012, pp. 38-40.

[22] Tompkins, James A., and Jerry D. Smith, *The Warehouse Management Handbook*, Second Edition, 1998, Tompkins Press, Raleigh, North Carolina, USA.

[23] Muller, Robert, *Piece Picking: Which Method is Best?*, 2007 white paper, www.OPSdesign.com, http://www.distributiongroup.com/articles/piecepickingwhichmethod.pdf, retrieved April 20, 2017.

[24] *Hazardous Manual Tasks: Code of Practice*, Safe Work Australia, February 2016, http://www.safe-workaustralia.gov.au/sites/SWA/about/Publications/Documents/640/Hazardous_Manual_TasksV2.pdf, retrieved April 24, 2017.

[25] Smith, Gary, "Product Philanthropy," *Inbound Logistics*, October 2015, p. 36.

[26] Fiveash, Charlie, "Warehouse Makeover: Blueprint for Change," *Inbound Logistics*, May 2016, pp. 48-53.

[27] Bunkley, Nick, "Joseph Juran, 103, Pioneer in Quality Control, Dies," *The New York Times*, March 3, 2008, p. B7.

[28] Pyke, David F., Edward A. Silver, and Rein Peterson, *Inventory Management and Production Planning and Scheduling*, Third Edition, 1998, John Wiley and Sons, New York, New York.

[29] *Capabilities Presentation*, St. Onge Company, undated document.

[30] Dutton, Gail, "Can Warehousing Really, Truly Be Strategic?," *World Trade*, October 2008, pp. 36-38.

Chapter 16

International Logistics Security

The terrorist attacks of September 11, 2001 in New York and Washington tragically illustrated the vulnerability of open economies to acts of terrorism. While many terrorist attacks had preceded the destruction of the New York World Trade Center towers, the scale and symbolism of their destruction made it a turning point in the way governments addressed terrorist threats. Strategies shifted from mostly reactive to a decidedly preventive and systematic approach. The response to the September 11 attacks was therefore unprecedented; within a few years, the United States, its trading partners, and many international organizations implemented measures designed to prevent further occurrences of acts of international terrorism. These measures have greatly influenced the way international business is now conducted.

The creation of these security measures, as well as efforts by corporations to reduce the vulnerability of their international supply chain to more traditional criminal activities, have triggered the creation of several corporate management functions, collectively called security management. This chapter outlines the way security measures imposed by governments and international organizations can be integrated with the security activities of a firm involved in international trade.

security management
A corporate function that manages all of a security efforts of a company.

While none of these security measures taken in isolation can be considered significantly effective in reducing the threat of terrorist activities, their collective implementation has resulted in a much higher level of security in international logistics, and certainly a greater focus on these efforts.

The Fallacy of One-Hundred-Percent Inspections

Whenever the topic of international security is debated, there are always proponents of a one-hundred-percent inspection alternative, in which all imported cargo is inspected—regardless of its origin, destination, or means of transportation. A one-hundred-percent inspection is often touted as the safest method: since all cargo is inspected, nothing dangerous can be shipped into the country. The proponents of one-hundred-percent inspection support their position with two logical reasons: the first is that everything that is dangerous will be caught by the inspection process, and the other is that the fear of being caught will act as a deterrent for criminals.

While a one-hundred-percent inspection process may act as a deterrent, and can therefore be considered partially effective for that reason, it is an ineffective way to increase the security of a country's borders, for several reasons.

First, such an inspection process consumes an extraordinary amount of resources. Considering that to physically inspect each container, the container must be opened and its

Figure 16.1: Passenger and Cabin Luggage Screening at the Beijing Airport
Photo ©Tony Vingerhoets/Shutterstock. Used with permission.

cargo unloaded, inspected, and then reloaded, it is safe to assume that it takes about three hours to ensure that a container is carrying safe cargo. Assuming that paperwork must be completed for each inspection and that the officer conducting the inspection is particularly efficient and can work alone, an average of three containers can be inspected by a single inspector every day. Given a work-year of 250 days, a single inspector would be able to handle 750 containers in a year. In 2016, more than 12 million ocean containers crossed the borders of the United States, and a similar number crossed into the European Union. Just for these two economic entities, and just for ocean cargo, 25 million containers would need to be inspected, and therefore a total of 32,000 inspectors would need to be hired. Add air and road cargo, the remainder of the world's economies, and the number of inspectors would easily reach 100,000, at a cost of many billions of dollars.

Second, such an inspection process would result in incredible delays in ports. A single port crane can handle between 15 and 40 container movements per hour. There are often three or four cranes unloading a containership. There is therefore a need for a space sufficiently large to store and inspect approximately 120 newly unloaded containers every hour. Meanwhile, the containers from the preceding two hours are still being inspected, since it takes about three hours for each, assuming that none are isolated because they are believed to be carrying dangerous goods. Ports would then need to have enough room to inspect all the containers that are unloaded in addition to the space needed to accommodate container movements from the ship to the inspection area, and from the inspection area to the secondary means of transportation (truck or rail). This lack of infrastructure would force ships to wait to unload their cargoes. Shifting the inspection process to the port of departure does not alleviate the problem; it just displaces it to a different location.

Finally, a one-hundred-percent inspection program is a fallacy. Since it is not possible to hire the required number of inspectors, nor to find the necessary room in the ports of the world, the inspection process would have to be much less thorough; possibly reduced to checking the paperwork and opening the doors before resealing them, which would take 10 minutes. Each container would be inspected, but in such a rushed fashion that it would not be inspected very well. There would be a perception that the system works (after all, all containers are inspected), but inspection would never uncover carefully hidden dangerous goods. Even then, this cursory system would still need 2,500 inspectors (assuming 5 containers inspected every day for 250 days a year), and its costs are staggering for a small decrease in risk.

There is strong empirical evidence that one-hundred-percent inspection does not work effectively; the TSA—Transportation Safety Administration—in the United States operates a system that is based on one-hundred-percent inspection of all passengers and all pieces of cabin luggage. In reviews of the TSA's progress toward its interdiction mission, the U.S. Government Accountability Office (GAO) found that TSA employees "missed 95 percent of the mock explosives and banned weapons" brought by screeners testing the system[1] and "did not have the ability to perform'"[2] its mission well. These reports document that GAO's testers were able to bring all sorts of unauthorized items onboard aircraft, undetected.[3]

16.1   The Impact of a Significant Disruption in International Logistics

The extent to which world trade can be seriously disrupted by a single catastrophe should not be underestimated. The closing of the U.S. ports located on the Gulf of Mexico after Hurricane Katrina delayed shipments of grain and other commodities for months.[4] The fires around Los Angeles in 2003 and the three-day power outage of August 2003 in the Midwest and Northeast of the United States cost billions of dollars in manufacturing delays and shipment disruptions.[5] The 2010 eruption of the Eyjafjallajökull volcano in Iceland essentially stopped all air traffic in Europe for six days, and disrupted it for a month thereafter.[6]

However, the greatest impact to international trade is that of a terrorist act. All North American international and domestic airline traffic was completely stopped after September 11, 2001, for three days; it took one complete day to reposition all the aircraft and a couple of weeks to clear the logjam of air cargo shipments. Thirteen months later, in October 2002, the Booz-Allen-Hamilton firm conducted a "war game" simulation in which the players were told that a dirty bomb—a bomb containing radioactive materials that are spread by the force of the explosion—had been found in the Port of Los Angeles; they were then told that another bomb had been found in Minneapolis and that a third one had exploded in Chicago. The initial response of the 85 game participants (all from the U.S. government) was to shut down two ports for 3 days and, as the crisis worsened, to shut down all U.S. ports for 12 days.[7] The Booz-Allen-Hamilton report estimated that this single decision would have engendered a backlog of containers in U.S. ports that would have taken three months to clear. In addition, the delays would have cost the U.S. economy U.S.\$ 58 billion in 2002.[8] The corresponding costs in 2017 are likely much higher, probably closer to U.S.\$ 75 to 80 billion.

Similar disruptions can be anticipated in other parts of the world, whether due to natural or man-made catastrophes. To prevent those occurrences, governments and international agencies have collaborated to establish security measures that address possible weaknesses in the international supply chain.

16.2 International Organizations

The first groups to implement large-scale security efforts were the international organizations that monitor agreements and treaties, such as the International Maritime Organization (IMO) and the Customs Cooperation Council.

16.2.1 International Maritime Organization

One of the first international organizations to implement enhanced security measures was the International Maritime Organization (IMO), when it voted to create the International Ship and Port Facility Security (ISPS) Code in December 2002. To implement this code quickly, the IMO made the ISPS code a part of the International Convention for the Safety of Life at Sea (SOLAS), in a section that addresses "Special Measures to Enhance Maritime Security." Since the SOLAS code had already been signed by 148 countries, the ISPS changes had to be implemented by all signatory countries, and they did so relatively quickly, with most ports and ships in compliance with the ISPS Code less than two years later.

To enhance port security, the ISPS code contains two sections: the first specifies the required measures that a port must put in place (Part A), and the second is a series of recommendations for the implementation of these measures (Part

International Maritime Organization (IMO)
A United Nations agency responsible for improving maritime safety and preventing pollution from ships.

International Ship and Port Facility Security (ISPS) Code
A series of security requirements placed by the International Maritime Organization upon ports and ships.

B). Because ports face different threats due to their location, the types of cargo they handle, and their physical layout, the implementation of the ISPS Code has differed from port to port, and the costs of implementation have also varied widely.[9,10] This discrepancy is also caused by the mandatory requirements being worded mostly in terms of questions that need to be addressed rather than specific requirements.[11] Nevertheless, the consensus of the research reports is that implementing the ISPS Code has improved the security situation everywhere and that there have been many benefits in addition to the increased security levels. The implementation of the ISPS code has led to a decrease in the incidence of theft and pilferage, a substantial decline in the number of stowaways, and much smoother operations in loading and unloading ships—all at a cost of a few cents to a few dollars per container handled.[12]

Ports have implemented the ISPS Code in three specific ways. First, the port authorities tightly monitor who has access to the port facilities. This is achieved by mandating that workers carry identification cards, allowing access only to authorized persons, and requiring visitors to provide identification. Second, the ports record all port activities on video cameras (see Figure 16.2) and keep these recordings for a few weeks. Finally, the ports have secure communication systems, designed to raise the alarm whenever a threat is detected. The alarm systems must be redundant, so that they cannot be easily rendered ineffective by an intruder. Each port also must nominate a port security officer to supervise all these activities.

The United States Coast Guard also participates in a program with 47 other countries through which International Port Security Liaison Officers collaborate with their foreign counterparts through port visits and the discussion and sharing of port security's best practices.[13] Such dissemination of information will likely lead to better outcomes and practices that may become more uniform worldwide.

As it applies to ships, the ISPS Code involves creating a company security officer for each carrier and a ship security officer for each ship. These individuals must then develop a Ship Security Assessment, as well as several ship security plans to respond to possible threats against the ship, all of which dependent on the type of ship and the type of cargo it carries. Ships are also required to possess certain types of equipment and to restrict onboard access. Ship owners must adhere to additional standards, such as conducting background checks before hiring crew members, ensuring the security of paperwork on board, training employees in security procedures, and so on.

Unfortunately, since the research on ISPS has concentrated mainly on port facilities and since the ships' implementations of the ISPS Code are private corporate decisions, little is known about the ways these measures were enacted. Nevertheless, the IMO has issued countless International Ship Security Certificates, which indicates that most ships are in compliance with the ISPS Code requirements.

Figure 16.2: Monitoring of Port Facilities by Video Cameras

Photo ©Volodymyr Kyrylyuk/Shutterstock. Used with permission.

16.2.2   World Customs Organization

Another international institution involved in security improvements in the international shipping of goods is the Customs Cooperation Council, better known as the World Customs Organization (WCO). Despite the fact that the primary role of the WCO has traditionally been the "simplification and harmonization of customs' procedures,"[14] it has been involved in several initiatives designed to enhance security.

World Customs Organization (WCO) An international body whose mission is to improve the administration of Customs. Its members are the national Customs administrations.

Early on, the WCO saw its role as complementing the efforts of the IMO by helping importing countries and importers identify, before the goods leave the country of export, the cargoes that should be scrutinized before being allowed on their international trip. The WCO achieved that objective by encouraging the standardization of documents, identifying the data characteristics of high-risk shipments, and by establishing guidelines that allowed customs authorities to have access to the documents of a shipment before it is loaded on board the carrier's vessel or aircraft. This particular emphasis is called the Advanced Cargo

Information guidelines,[15] which mirrors one of the initiatives of the U.S. Customs and Border Protection agency.

Security and Facilitation in a Global Environment (SAFE)
A set of guidelines to increase the cooperation of national Customs administrations in fighting security threats.

In June 2005, the WCO implemented its Security and Facilitation in a Global Environment (SAFE) initiative, a program it revised in June 2007. The SAFE initiative further coordinates the efforts of customs authorities worldwide in their efforts to combat terrorism. The SAFE requirements are fourfold:

- All customs authorities must adhere to a set of advance electronic information standards for all international shipments. What is required of shippers should be identical, regardless of country of export and country of import.

- Each country must have consistent risk management approaches to address security threats.

- Exporting countries' customs authorities must comply with a reasonable request from the importing country's customs authorities to inspect outgoing cargo, preferably using non-intrusive technology (x-rays) if possible (see Figure 16.3).

Figure 16.3: Mobile X-Ray Scanner for Cargo Containers in New Zealand
Photo ©Rafael Ben-Ari/Shutterstock. Used with permission.

- All customs authorities must provide benefits to companies that demonstrate that they meet minimum standards of security. Such companies are called Authorized Economic Operators, and benefit from faster processing of customs clearance and lower inspection rates.[16]

16.2.3   International Chamber of Commerce

The International Chamber of Commerce (ICC) also weighed in on security initiatives in the domain of international logistics, in a policy statement dated November 2002;[17] in it, the ICC emphasized that security initiatives should be the domain of international agreements between countries, rather than initiatives imposed unilaterally by some governments. The ICC also emphasized that businesses involved in international trade have already invested considerable sums in security initiatives and that, therefore, the rules and regulations imposed by international agreements should capitalize on these investments.

The recommendations made by the ICC reflect the organization's goals of facilitating international trade; its concerns were that country-specific requirements would place undue burdens on businesses and hamper trade. The ICC also was concerned about the widespread dissemination of information among several law enforcement authorities and counseled that great care should be taken in handling of business information collected by security initiatives, so that no "sensitive confidential company information" is released.[18]

International Chamber of Commerce (ICC) The largest business organization in the world. Its goal is to champion international business growth and its members are the national chambers of commerce.

16.2.4   National Governments' Involvement

Despite the efforts undertaken by international organizations to make international trade more secure, and the admonitions of the ICC that unilateral security requirements would hinder trade, as well as the efforts of the WCO toward a common set of requirements, many governments unilaterally implemented several different security measures in the wake of the terrorist attacks of the past two decades. While the attacks on the World Trade Center and the Pentagon in 2001 tend to be at the forefront of most Americans' consciousness, the list of tragedies is unfortunately much longer, as shown in Table 16.1. The frequency of terrorist attacks, as well as the increasing diversity of groups intent on disrupting democratic societies—and their "creativity" in creating harm to civilian populations—, led many governments to create and enforce several security measures, many of which have had a substantial impact on international trade.

Each government implemented those security measures because they felt that their country was specifically targeted. Unfortunately, this is not the case, as is shown in Table 16.1 on the next page; terrorists, from groups to individuals, are indiscriminate in their activities, attacking multiple targets in many different countries. Terrorism has truly become a worldwide concern, and very few countries have escaped this plague. Some terrorists are foreign, but most are citizens of the countries they target.

Major Terrorist Attacks 1990-2017

Terrorist Act	Date	Location
World Trade Center bombing	February 26, 1993	New York, United States
Sarin gas subway attack	March 20, 1995	Tokyo, Japan
Oklahoma City bombing	April 19, 1995	Oklahoma City, United States
Métro bombings	Summer-Fall 1995	Paris, France
Omagh bombings	August 15, 1998	Omagh, Northern Ireland
World Trade Center attacks	September 11, 2001	New York, United States
Anthrax mailings	September-October 2001	United States
Bali bombings	October 12, 2002	Bali, Indonesia
Istanbul bombings	November 15 and 20, 2003	Istanbul, Turkey
Moscow Metro bombing	February 6, 2004	Moscow, Russia
Madrid train bombings	March 11, 2004	Madrid, Spain
Beslan School Hostages	September 2004	Beslan, Russia
London subway bombings	July 7, 2005	London, United Kingdom
Mumbai train bombings	July 11, 2006	Mumbai, India
Mumbai hotel attacks	November 26, 2008	Mumbai, India
Peshawar bombings	October 28, 2009	Peshawar, Pakistan
Lahore bombings	March 8 & 12, 2010	Lahore, Pakistan
Kampala attacks	July 11, 2011	Kampala, Uganda
Utoya Island massacre	July 22, 2011	Utoya Island and Oslo, Norway
Monterrey Casino attack	August 25, 2011	Monterrey, Mexico
Borno State church attacks	January 2012	Nigeria
Sana'a bombings	May 21, 2012	Sana'a, Yemen
Boston Marathon bombing	April 15, 2013	Boston, United States
Village market	March 16, 2014	Kaduna, Nigeria
Village markets	May 7, 2014	Gamboru Ngala, Nigeria
College campus attacks	April 2, 2015	Garissa, Kenya
Russian Airbus bombing	October 31, 2015	Sinai, Egypt
Bataclan theater	November 13, 2015	Paris, France
Chemical attack on rebels	April 7, 2016	Aleppo, Syria
Bombings	May 23, 2016	Jableh and Tartus, Syria
Truck rampage	July 14, 2016	Nice, France
Car rampage	March 23, 2017	London, United Kingdom

Table 16.1: Worldwide Terrorist Attacks 1990-2017 (Chronologically)
Multiple sources.

16.3 The United States' Approach

The United States government implemented several security measures to limit the country's vulnerability to terrorist attacks, focusing initially on interdiction, a strategy that the country had already been pursuing in its war against contraband street drugs and illegal immigration, and eventually moving to a system of partnership with importers.

16.3.1 Interdiction

Interdiction attempts to eliminate all imports of a particular type of good and all entries of a specific group of persons into a country. The reasoning is relatively simple: if no terrorist can enter the country, and if no materials that can be used to cause widespread harm can be imported, then no terrorist acts are possible. The United States started to follow this approach almost immediately after the terrorist attacks of September 11, 2001, with strict monitoring of the flying public and the luggage transported on airliners. In early 2017, the United States extended its interdiction efforts to certain groups of foreigners who were denied visas to visit the United States, whether for immigration, tourism, or business.[19]

interdiction
A security strategy that consists of preventing all imports of potentially dangerous goods and potentially dangerous persons.

The Transportation Security Administration (TSA) was created in November 2001 by consolidating many small private security firms, a move that was controversial at the time, as many employees of these firms did not meet federal hiring standards.[20] The interdiction policy implemented by the TSA involves systematically inspecting all passengers and their checked luggage, a policy which is plagued with several failings (see Vignette on page 546). Because of these issues, TSA policies have increasingly been characterized as "theater," ineffective at achieving their stated goals, but presenting a reassuring presence in airports that demonstrates that "something is being done" to combat terrorism.[21,22]

The United States further formalized its interdiction strategy on November 25, 2002, by creating the Department of Homeland Security (DHS), consolidating 22 services that had, until that point, operated somewhat independently. The idea was that these departments could be more effective if they were able to cooperate around a shared mission. The DHS reinforced the visibility of its mission of interdiction by renaming or regrouping many of these agencies to reflect their role in terrorism prevention: The U.S. Customs Service became Customs and Border Protection (CBP), and the investigative bureaus of the former Immigration and Naturalization Service and Customs became Immigration and Customs Enforcement (ICE). This DHS now has more than 200,000 employees, is third in size to the Department of Defense and the Department of Veterans Affairs, and is three times larger than the Social Security Administration.

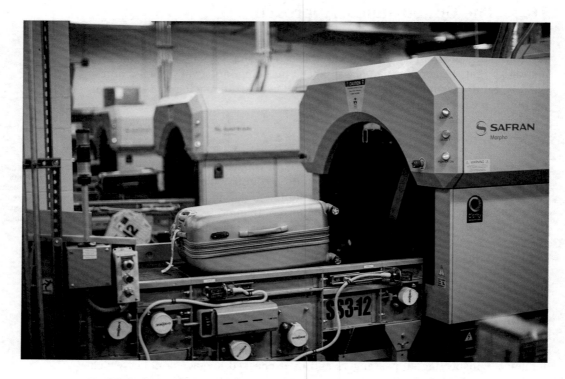

Figure 16.4: An Explosive Detection Machine at the Mexico City Airport
Photo ©Piotr Redlinski/Safran. Used with permission.

Understanding Type I and Type II Errors

Implementing security measures is predicated on correctly understanding the two types of errors that can be made in statistics, called a Type I error and a Type II error. Although these concepts are relatively complex mathematically, they can be understood relatively easily through an illustration using airport procedures for handling passenger luggage.

Suppose that there is a machine, such as the one depicted in Figure 16.6 designed to determine whether an explosive device (a bomb) is present in a piece of luggage. Although this machine can be well made, because it must process hundreds of pieces of luggage a day means that it cannot investigate thoroughly each and every piece that is loaded onto an aircraft. It thus must rely on some method that is less time-consuming and less invasive. Most of these machines take a sample of the air that surrounds a bag and analyze it to detect the presence of certain chemical molecules.[23] If a particular molecule is present in a minimum concentration, the machine alerts the operator that there is the possibility of a bomb. At that time, the operator then opens the luggage and conducts a more thorough, physical investigation.

However, the machine can commit two types of errors, as illustrated in Figure 16.5:

• The machine can erroneously detect a bomb where there is none; this can happen because it must be calibrated to be extremely sensitive. After all, the machine must detect minute levels of certain chemicals in a fraction of a second. Since some of these chemical molecules can be on the luggage for other reasons, the machine sounds the alarm even though there is actually no bomb in the luggage. Further investigation by the operator confirms that the bag is fine, and the piece of luggage is then cleared. This is called a Type I error. Another terminology, more commonly used in medicine, calls this type of error a "false positive:" The medical device concludes that the patient has a certain disease when in reality that patient does not have it.

• The machine can erroneously clear a piece of luggage when it actually contains a bomb; this may be because the terrorist has done a particularly good job of packaging the bomb or because the sample that the machine used did not contain, by chance alone, enough of the trace chemicals it needed to sound an alarm. In that case, the machine does not ring the alarm even though the piece of luggage is dangerous. This is called a Type II error. In medicine, it is called a "false negative:" the medical device concludes that the patient does not have a particular disease when in reality the patient does have it. Suppose that the bomb-sniffing machine in this example is designed and calibrated so that it experiences a five-percent error rate for both Type I and Type II errors. Which of the two error rates is most worrisome?

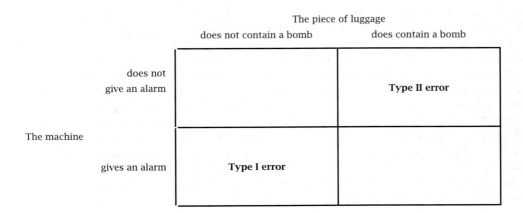

Figure 16.5: Type I and Type II Errors

When asked to evaluate a bomb-sniffing machine with equal Type I and Type II error rates of five percent, most people conclude that the Type II error rate is most worrisome; after all, a machine that misses five percent of all bombs is very scary indeed. However, this is an incorrect position; the Type I error rate is the problem. This is known as the paradox of Type I and Type II errors.

Suppose that there is an incidence of one bomb per one million pieces of luggage. For simplicity's sake, suppose that the total volume of luggage that the system processes every year is also one million pieces of luggage. In this example, the "bomb rate" is 0.0001 percent, which is much higher than the actual rate. There are, thankfully, far fewer bombs and far many more pieces of luggage; however, restricting the analysis to one million pieces of luggage, inspected at the rate of approximately 2,750 pieces a day, makes the paradox more understandable.

Let's assume that a terrorist places a bomb in a piece of luggage. With a Type II error rate of five percent, there is a 95 percent chance that the machine will correctly detect the bomb and sound the alarm, which makes it a quasi-certainty. However, over the past year, the machine also inspected 999,999 other pieces of luggage, none of which contained a bomb; nevertheless, for approximately 50,000 of them, the machine rang the alarm (because it committed a Type I error) and the operator had to manually inspect the luggage.

Out of the 50,000 pieces of luggage that the operator has inspected to this point, none contained a bomb. The operator has been vigilant, looking for all possible ways a bomb could be hidden in someone's belongings, but has not found one. However, the operator has only a few minutes to do the work, since the luggage must be sent to its destination with the plane on which the passenger is ticketed. The single piece of luggage that does contain a well-concealed bomb will not escape scrutiny; the operator will handle it with much care. However, it is also likely that the operator will assume that the machine has given—once more—a false alarm; after all, 100 percent of the ones inspected so far were. The dangerous piece of luggage will then be cleared, even though the bomb-sniffing machine correctly identified it as dangerous. Consider that only 0.002 percent of the luggage physically inspected by the operator (1 out of 50,000) will contain a bomb; 99.998 percent of the inspected bags are perfectly fine. Human nature prevents most of us from paying much attention to a phenomenon that is that infrequent;[24] facing a probability of 0.002 percent is equivalent to meeting a U.S. national for the first time and assuming that this person is an undergraduate student at the University of Chicago (the ratio is roughly identical: 6,000 students in a population of 300 million); we know it's possible, but that is certainly not our first assumption.

16.3.2 Customs-Trade Partnership Against Terrorism

The United States complemented its interdiction approach with the creation of the Customs-Trade Partnership Against Terrorism (C-TPAT) in 2001; however, only a handful of companies were involved in this program in 2001 and 2002. By 2003, 137 companies had joined, and in 2016, there were over 11,500 importers and logistics services providers enrolled in the program.[25] About 55 percent of the shipments entering the United States—by value—were entered by C-TPAT participants, and 100 percent of the shipments made by C-TPAT participants complied with U.S. Customs and Border Protection security guidelines.

The C-TPAT program is a shift away from interdiction and one-hundred-percent inspection; it recognizes that the immense majority of international shipments are innocuous and, therefore, that they should not be the targets of law enforcement. The only concern with these shipments should be the possibility that they are intercepted by criminals and the merchandise that they contain is substituted for dangerous goods. The goal of the C-TPAT program is therefore to encourage corporations involved in international trade to enact security measures that prevent tampering with the shipments at any point in the supply chain; corporations are asked to evaluate their levels of security in the supply chain, determine their vulnerability, and remedy any issues.

The C-TPAT program is a voluntary program in which companies elect to participate. Corporations must first apply to participate in the C-TPAT program, and after their application is accepted, they become "Tier I" members. Tier I members are also called certified corporations. After their supply-chain security has been analyzed by U.S. Customs and Border Protection and the firms' security measures have been found to be "reliable, accurate, and effective,"[26] the firms' applications are validated, and the firms become "Tier II" members. In 2014, U.S. Customs and Border Protection validated or re-validated 2,131 companies.[27] (Data for 2015 and 2016 were not available, as the CBP implemented a new portal that had difficulties compiling the data.[28]) Corporations that go beyond the minimum requirements of Customs can become "Tier III" members. As of March 2017, there were about 10,500 corporations that had Tier II status, and almost 350 had reached Tier III status.

To encourage corporations to participate in the C-TPAT program, Customs and Border Protection offers companies several advantages:

- **A lower inspection probability**. At the port of entry, U.S. Customs and Border Protection assigns a security score to a shipment. If a shipment's score falls below a specified threshold, an inspection is deemed necessary. For C-TPAT participating companies, the threshold is lowered. Tier I companies have an inspection rate that is 15 to 20 percent of the inspection rate of non-C-TPAT companies. The threshold is lowered further for Tier II companies, and Tier III companies' shipments are not subjected to security inspections, only random compliance inspections.[29]

- **Priority inspections**. For Tier II companies, if an inspection is deemed necessary, the shipment receives priority, and is moved to the front of the

Customs-Trade Partnership Against Terrorism (C-TPAT)
A voluntary partnership program of the U.S. CPB. Participating companies obtain priority processing and reduced inspection rates.

one-hundred-percent inspection
A security strategy that consists of inspecting every single shipment.

line.

- **Priority processing**. Both Tier I and Tier II companies have access to the FAST lane at the land borders of the United States, allowing them to process shipments faster. Tier III companies have access to a true "green lane," which speeds up the processing on an import considerably.[30] That "green lane" was what had been promised in the beginning of the implementation of the C-TPAT program, and what Tier II companies had hoped to obtain. As of 2013, it is not anticipated that this benefit will be extended to companies that have not achieved Tier III.

- **Customs assistance**. All C-TPAT participating companies can obtain assistance from Customs' supply-chain security specialists to resolve security challenges.

Although C-TPAT was originally instituted as a voluntary program for companies involved in international trade, it has evolved into a mandatory program for all importers, carriers, and third-party logistics providers; participation is not encouraged, it is expected.

The C-TPAT program operates within the guidelines established by the SAFE initiative enacted by the WCO. In addition, by concentrating on the analysis of shipments that can be presumed to present some level of risk (determined by their characteristics, often the fact that they are unusual in some fashion), the C-TPAT program also meets the requirements of the ICC to be least disruptive to international commerce.

In May 2012, the United States and the European Union signed an agreement that grants mutual recognition to each other's program of security compliance. A U.S.-validated (Tier II) C-TPAT company is recognized as an Authorized Economic Operator (see Section 16.4.1 on page 565) in the European Union, and *vice versa*.[31] Similar agreements were signed with New Zealand, Canada, the Dominican Republic, Israel, Jordan, Japan, Korea, Mexico, Singapore, and Taiwan.[32]

Another U.S. Customs and Border Protection program is the Importer Self-Assessment (ISA) program, to which companies that have been C-TPAT Tier II certified for more than two years can apply. Those companies agree to undertake a self assessment of their supply-chain security and demonstrate they can monitor their compliance with CBP requirements. ISA members are removed from the "audit pool" for C-TPAT compliance. The electronics industry and the oil industry are the two most-represented groups of companies participating in the ISA program.[33]

As of early 2017, U.S. Customs and Border Protection was developing yet another program, called the Trusted Trader Program (TTP), for companies that face regulatory requirements beyond those of CPB, such as from the U.S. Department of Agriculture, the Consumer Product Safety Commission, or the Federal Drug Administration. These companies will be eligible to participate in the TTP and will then only face one regulatory hurdle. TTP participants will be expected to manage their trade compliance on a self-assessment basis, and the ISA program will eventually be replaced by the TTP.[34]

16.3.3 Maritime Transportation Security Act

In addition to the C-TPAT program, the United States has also created several other initiatives, all designed to improve security: in 2002, the U.S. Congress passed the Maritime Transportation Security Act (MTSA), which has been made part of the Code of Federal Regulations, 33-CFR-101 through 107.

The MTSA is the U.S. implementation of the IMO's International Ship and Port Facility Security Code (ISPS), although there are minor differences. The MTSA is slightly more encompassing: it applies to cargo vessels of more than 100 dwt, and to "any structure of any kind located in, on, under, or adjacent to any waters subject to the jurisdiction of the United States," both of which are more encompassing than the ISPS, which only covers vessels of more than 500 dwt and port facilities. The MTSA also differs from the ISPS in that it applies to passenger vessels of more than 150 passengers, whereas the ISPS applies to all passenger ships.[35]

The MTSA requires ports to have a security plan, monitored by a Port Security Officer. It mandates that the port security plan be approved by the U.S. Coast Guard Captain of the Port before the port can operate. The port-security plan must contain information on port access, training programs, drills, record keeping, and the existence and maintenance of emergency communication equipment.[36]

The MTSA also requires a security plan for vessels. Vessel security plans are managed by a Vessel Security Officer, and the plan must be submitted and approved by the U.S. Coast Guard Marine Safety Center. This requirement applies to all vessels calling on a U.S. port, whether the ship flies a U.S. or foreign flag.

Marine Transportation Security Act (MTSA)
The U.S. legislation that implemented the recommendations of the International Maritime Organization's International Ship and Port Facility Security Code.

16.3.4 Security and Accountability for Every Port

In 2006, the U.S. Congress passed an additional piece of legislation called the Security and Accountability For Every Port (SAFE Port) Act, which modified some aspects of the Container Security Initiative (CSI), and of the Customs-Trade Partnership Against Terrorism (C-TPAT), and created the Transportation Workers' Identification Credential (TWIC) program. The primary effect of the SAFE Port Act legislation was to empower the U.S. Coast Guard to enforce the implementation of the MTSA.

The Act's existence was mostly a reaction to the Dubai Ports World's purchase of the P&O company, that was under contract to manage several terminals in the United States ports, including New York, Miami and New Orleans. Since the Dubai company was state-owned, several politicians objected to the possibility of a Middle-Eastern company running a United States port, and passed the SAFE Port Act. Because of this opposition, Dubai Ports World relinquished the management of the terminals to a U.S. company.

Although the SAFE Port Act shares the same acronym as the WCO's initiative, the two are not related.

The SAFE Port Act mandated that, by 2012, 100 percent of all cargo (not just containers) entering the United States had to be checked for possible weapons of

Security and Accountability For Every Port (SAFE)
A U.S. piece of legislation that created a number of security-related programs.

mass destruction through a non-invasive process, such as x-rays. The mandate was subsequently extended to 2014, 2016, and finally May 2018.[37] The U.S. DHS Secretary Jeh Johnson told Congress in May 2014 that the department's "ability to fully comply with this mandate of 100-per-cent scanning, even in the long term, is highly improbable, hugely expensive and, in our judgment, not the best use of taxpayer resources to meet this country's port security and homeland security needs."[38]

16.3.5   The Transportation Workers' Identification Credential

Transportation Workers' Identification Credential (TWIC)
A U.S. program designed to limit access to ports to persons without a serious criminal background.

The Transportation Workers' Identification Credential (TWIC) program requires that all persons who have access to U.S. ports must carry an identification card. The identification card is based on biometric information and is obtained after the worker has completed a background check. There are approximately 3 million transportation workers who have acquired their TWIC credentials.

Few criminal offenses disqualify workers from obtaining a TWIC card (espionage, sedition, treason, or terrorism), and many criticisms regarding the reliability of the cards, the ease with which they might be counterfeit, and their overall ability to prevent terrorist acts have been expressed. The TWIC program has been branded as essentially ineffective,[39] a position that was confirmed by a scathing Government Accounting Office report.[40] As of March 2017, no further analysis has been conducted, and no changes have been made to the program, although it is still in place.

Originally, the TWIC program was conceived to be extended to other transportation modes—beyond truck drivers having access to ports—including airports and public transportation. As of July 2013, these plans were on hold, and no progress had been made as of March 2017.

16.3.6   Container Security Initiative

Container Security Initiative (CSI)
A U.S. Customs and Border Protection program that consists of inspecting overseas the shipments that are bound for the United States.

The Container Security Initiative (CSI) addresses the threat posed by the terrorist use of a container to deliver a weapon. The CSI attempts to identify containers before they are placed onboard vessels headed for the United States. U.S. Customs and Border Protection has stationed teams of U.S. officers from both U.S. Customs and Border Protection (CBP) and Immigration and Customs Enforcement (ICE) in foreign ports to identify, target, screen, and eventually inspect containers before they are loaded. The CSI requirements demand cooperation from foreign officials, since U.S. Customs and Border Protection does not have the authority to conduct searches in non-U.S. territories.

CSI is the United States' implementation of the World Customs Organization's SAFE (Security and Facilitation in a Global Environment) initiative, and it is careful to operate within the constraints of this program; containers are screened through a non-invasive method, such as x-rays, and the process does not delay the shipping of goods.

As of 2014, CSI was operational in 58 ports in North America, Europe, Asia, Africa, the Middle East, and Latin America, and screened over 80 percent of all maritime containerized cargo imported into the United States.[41]

16.3.7 Free and Secure Trade

The Free and Secure Trade (FAST) program is a joint initiative between the Canada Border Services Agency (CBSA) and U.S. Customs and Border Protection (CBP), and between Mexican Customs and CBP. FAST is designed to allow cargo and carriers to cross borders between the U.S. and Canada, and between the U.S. and Mexico more expeditiously. Three entities must be cleared to obtain the benefits of the program: the exporter/importer, the carrier of the goods, and the driver. The clearance process involves a background check for the driver, and a review of the security measures used at the importer's facilities, and those used by the carrier.

If all three entities are FAST members, they can gain access to dedicated lanes at border crossings, for faster and more efficient border clearance. At the crossing, the driver presents three bar-coded documents to the border services officer (one for each of the participating parties: the driver, the carrier and the importer). The officer can quickly scan the bar codes while all trade data declarations and

Free And Secure Trade (FAST)
A joint Canada-U.S.-Mexico voluntary program. Participating companies enjoy dedicated fast lanes when crossing the Canada-U.S. border or the Mexico-U.S. border.

Figure 16.6: Detroit's Blue-Water Bridge Border Crossing: The FAST Lane is on the Right of the Building and Trucks Line Up in the Center Lane on the Bridge
Photo ©Donna Burton/U.S. CBP. Used with permission.

verifications are done later, away from the border. If there is no dedicated FAST lane, the process is the same, but the driver does not enjoy priority handling.

FAST is a voluntary program that customs officials in all three countries are encouraging shippers to join. As of 2016, there were 78,000 drivers enrolled in the program.[42]

16.3.8 Importer Security Filing

Importer Security Filing
A U.S. program that
implements the Security
and Facilitation in a Global
Environment (SAFE)
guidelines of the World
Customs Organization.

In 2002, the United States implemented a program called the "24-hour rule" that required all importers (and carriers) to provide a copy of the manifest of an ocean shipment bound for the United States, including shipments that were just transiting through a U.S. port and were bound for another country, 24 hours before that shipment was loaded onto the vessel bound for the United States.

This program has been superseded since January 26, 2010, by a program called the Importer Security Filing, which follows the guidelines of the World Customs Organization's SAFE initiative, which mandates that importing countries make uniform the information required from shippers. The requirements of the Importer Security Filing expand the number of points of information that the shipper must provide, and it has become better known in the United States as the 10 + 2 rule, which mirrors the number of items required.

The Importer Security Filing requires that the importer provide U.S. Customs and Border Protection with the following ten items of data:

1. The identification number of the importer of record (Employer Identification Number [EIN] or Social Security Number [SSN])

2. The identification number of the consignee (EIN or SSN)

3. The manufacturer (name and address)

4. The seller of the goods (name and address)

5. The buyer of the goods (name and address)

6. The name and address of the business to which the shipment is going

7. The stuffer's name and address (the party that filled the container)

8. The location where the container was stuffed

9. The country of origin of the goods

10. The six-digit Harmonized System number for the goods

In addition, the Importer Security Filing requires the following 2 items from the carrier:

1. The vessel stow plan (the way the containers are organized onboard the vessel)

2. The container status message (container number, location, condition—full or empty—, events—loading or unloading—, and event times)

The importer must provide U.S. CBP with the data contained in the Importer Security Filing at least 24 hours prior to the goods arriving in the United States port.

16.4   The European Union's Programs

The European Union has approached security in a significantly different way: while the EU recognizes that there are new security issues with the increase in terrorism and the availability of weapons of mass destruction, its primary focus has been prevention. In a paper outlining its security strategy, the European Union emphasized that reducing poverty, enforcing international agreements against arms proliferation, restoring democratic governments in areas of regional conflicts, and increasing international cooperation for criminal investigations would be most effective in dealing with security threats.[43]

Nevertheless, the European Union has implemented several programs in response to international organizations' guidelines, first the International Ship and Port Facilities Security Code of the IMO, and then the SAFE framework of the WCO. Although there were some unilateral interpretations of these guidelines, the European Union, by and large, has responded to security threats in a relatively uniform fashion.

16.4.1   Authorized Economic Operator

The Authorized Economic Operator (AEO) program is designed to respond to the WCO mandate that customs organizations provide benefits to businesses that meet minimal supply chain security standards and best practices.

A company involved in the international movement of goods—importer, exporter, carrier, port, airport, or other trade intermediary—can become an AEO after demonstrating that it has several security measures in place, and these measures have been reviewed and approved by a national customs administration. AEO is a standard similar to Tier II of the United States C-TPAT; however, the EAO has requirements regarding financial viability[44] that are not found in the C-TPAT requirements.

An Authorized Economic Operator benefits from simplifications in customs procedures and reductions in customs controls,[45] but those benefits tend to be country specific rather than apply in all European countries.

The AEO status is granted by one of the customs authorities of the European Union, and the other customs authorities "should grant" the same simplified processes that their own AEOs are given.[46] Similarly, the status of AEO is granted to companies that have been validated (Tier II) under the Customs-Trade Partnership Against Terrorism (see Section 16.3.2 on page 559).

Authorized Economic Operator (AEO) An E.U. program that implements the Security and Facilitation in a Global Environment (SAFE) guidelines of the World Customs Organization.

16.4.2　Customs Security Programme

The European Union's Customs Security Programme (CSP) was designed to develop and implement measures that enhance border security. CSP achieves this through improved customs controls. Importers are required to provide customs authorities with information on goods prior to their arrival in the European Union (pre-arrival declaration), and customs use this advance electronic information to perform a risk analysis of every shipment, which enables customs to identify high risk cargo bound for Europe.

In a way that is encouraged by the WCO, European customs cooperate with other customs authorities worldwide to identify cargo that may present a threat, and inspect cargo prior to shipment when requested.

16.5　Other Countries' Approach

Countries outside of Europe and North America have implemented policies that mirror those of the European Union, by implementing the ISPS Code and SAFE framework, mostly in the spirit of international cooperation rather than as a response to a perceived threat of terrorism. The prevalent viewpoint was that terrorists target mostly the United States and possibly the European Union and therefore terrorism was a U.S. problem, from which other countries could remove themselves.

This attitude was reinforced by actions of the United States that imposed additional measures on its trade partners, who were asked to implement them under the scrutiny of U.S. enforcement agencies, whether Customs and Border Protection, Immigration and Customs Enforcement, or the Coast Guard.

Many countries engaged in these changes reluctantly, as they had more significant domestic problems and did not want to spend resources on a "foreign" problem. The subsequent bombings in Bali, Istanbul, Moscow, and Mumbai changed this perspective relatively quickly, and most countries now agree that terrorism is a worldwide problem, although they often see it as a less significant risk than widespread poverty and its associated significant criminal activity and potential social unrest.

16.6　Corporate Efforts

Although governments frame the issue of supply chain security in terms of the risk of terrorism, most companies see security in a narrower way, focusing principally on the risk of theft and other criminal activities, such as tampering, vandalism, and counterfeit products. Companies participate in governmental programs and other efforts to secure the international logistics' environment, but they see the benefits of increased security in terms of reduced cargo losses, and participate in security-related programs to prevent delays in customs clearance.

Nevertheless, the surge in government programs designed to eliminate terrorism was the impetus for many companies to engage in Total Security Management (TSM), a management philosophy based on the Total Quality Management concepts developed by W. Edwards Deming in the 1970s,[47] which encourages every employee, at every level, to recognize the importance of security and suggest improvements in processes and procedures. By having a commitment to security that permeates all levels of responsibility within the company, security is increased and becomes an essential part of the firm's culture. Even though there are costs to making security improvements, the idea behind TSM is that these costs will be offset by the corresponding reductions in theft, damaged goods, and lost productivity, in the same way Crosby once determined that "quality is free."[48]

Total Security Management (TSM)
A management philosophy that posits that security is better achieved if every member of the organization is vigilant and pro-active in identifying security issues.

To be comprehensive in their security efforts, companies must secure four areas in their supply chains: (1) their fixed assets (plants, warehouses, distribution centers), (2) their inbound and outbound shipments while they are in transit, (3) the information on which they rely to manage their operations, and (4) their workforce, to ensure that it is reliable and trustworthy.

To protect their fixed assets, companies install physical barriers designed to prevent entry by unauthorized persons. Fences are built along the facilities' perimeter, the building doors are locked (emergency exit doors are locked from the inside so that they cannot be opened from the outside), all other points of building access (*e.g.*, roof hatches) are secured, the number of outside lights is increased, a backup electric generator is added to prevent interruptions to lights and communication systems, and a public-address and alarm system are installed. Companies also build gates at facility entrances, with a security guard ensuring that no unauthorized person may enter. Companies install security cameras to monitor all activities on the premises, and the videos are monitored by trained security personnel. Finally, emergency security procedures are established and training is provided for all employees, so that they know what their responsibilities are in the event of a security breach. These measures mirror the requirements of the ISPS Code for port facilities.

To protect their shipments while they are in transit, companies implement a different set of measures. They ensure that all cargo containers are sealed before they leave any facility, with a seal that is a good deterrent to a potential thief (see Figure 16.7), and that the seal numbers are carefully monitored. They make sure that the information on the identity of the cargo is released to as few people as possible. Companies also instruct truck drivers to continuously monitor their surroundings and ensure that they do not stop at a rest area soon after leaving a plant, as most cargo thefts occur within a few miles of the cargo's point of origin.

seal
A lock placed on a container door or truck trailer door that must be broken in order to access the cargo.

Many U.S. companies have implemented a "geo-fencing" system, which alerts security personnel when the cargo departs from a pre-determined itinerary. Geo-fencing is based on the Global Positioning System (GPS) and allows only slight variations in itinerary (such as a detour for construction or an accident), but sends a warning if the cargo strays more than 25 miles (40 kilometers) from the highway that the truck is supposed to take. The truck driver is then immediately contacted for further information, and the local police authorities are dispatched if there is a problem. Finally, an emergency plan should be developed and all employees should be trained in its application.

geo-fencing
A technique based on Global Positioning System that alerts management when a shipment is diverted from its intended itinerary.

Figure 16.7: Two Container Seals: A Bolt Seal (Top) and a Wire Seal (Bottom). Only the Bolt Seal is Accepted in International Shipments
Photo ©Pierre David. Used with permission.

It is also critical for companies to guard corporate information. While the techniques used to safeguard electronic data are quite complex, and the subjects of many books,[49] a good system of procedures must ensure that information reaches only those people who need to know what is transported or what is currently in inventory. Procedures should be in place to monitor the dissemination of information (electronic and paper) within the firm.

Finally, good security measures are fundamentally predicated on good human resources practices. For instance, if employees are intent on violating a corporation's security measures, they likely will achieve their goals, as it is impossible to defend against all possibilities without affecting the normal conduct of business. It is therefore crucial to verify employees' backgrounds, monitor their activities, train them to recognize security violations, and provide an anonymous system to report their concerns.

Review and Discussion Questions

1. What are the different main international logistics security programs implemented either by international agencies or national governments?

2. What are the main differences between the alternative approaches to security taken by the United States and the European Union?

3. What problems arise in a security policy that is based on one-hundred-percent inspection?

4. What are the four areas in which a corporation must enact security measures to protect itself against theft and terrorism?

5. Suppose a disease has an incidence of one percent in the population. The test used to detect this disease has a five percent Type I error rate; there is no Type II error rate. A physician sees test results from a patient indicating that the patient has the disease; the probability that the patient actually has that disease is 0.01/0.0595, or about 17 percent. Explain this result.

Notes

[1] Elliott, Christopher, "The TSA has Never Kept You Safe: Hereŝs Why," *Fortune*, June 2, 2015, http://fortune.com/2015/06/02/the-tea-airport-security-problems/, retrieved March 27, 2017.

[2] Roth, John, "Statement of John Roth, Inspector General - Department of Homeland Security," Committee on Oversight and Government Reform, U.S. House of Representatives, November 3, 12015.

[3] "What GAO Found," U.S. Government Accountability Office, June 7, 2016, http://www.gao.gov/products/GAO-16-707T, retrieved March 27, 2017.

[4] Peige, John, "Gulf Coast Hurricanes Have Huge Impact on Shipping Flows," *MM&P Wheelhouse Weekly*, October 27, 2005, p.43.

[5] Ritter, Luke, J. Michael Barrett, and Rosalyn Wilson, *Securing Global Transportation Networks*, 2007, McGraw-Hill, New York, New York.

[6] Bye, Bente Lilja, "Volcanic Eruptions: Science And Risk Management," *Science 2.0*, May 27, 2011, http://www.science20.com/planetbye/volcanic_eruptions_science_and_risk_management-79456, retrieved March 27, 2017.

[7] Gerencser, Mark, Jim Weinberg, and Don Vincent, "Port Security War Game: Implications for U.S. Supply Chains," Booz-Allen-Hamilton, 2003, http://www.boozallen.com/media/file/128648.pdf, retrieved September 21, 2009.

[8] *Ibid.*

[9] *Maritime Security: ISPS Code Implementation, Costs and Related Financing*, Report by the UNCTAD Secretariat, March 14, 2007, United Nations Conference on Trade and Development, http://www.unctad.org/en/docs/sdtetlb20071_en.pdf.

[10] Boske, Leigh, *Port and Supply-Chain Security Initiatives in the United States and Abroad*, Lyndon B. Johnson School of Public Affairs, University of Texas at Austin, Policy Research Project Report 150, 2006, http://www.utexas.edu/lbj/pubs/pdf/prp_150.pdf, retrieved September 22, 2009.

[11] Kruk, C. Burt, and Michel Luc Donner, *Review of Cost of Compliance with the New International Freight Transport Security Requirements: Consolidated Report of the Investigations Carried Out in Ports in the Africa, Europe and Central Asia, and Latin America and the Caribbean Regions*, World Bank, Transport Paper 16, February 2008, http://siteresources.worldbank.org/INTTRANSPORT/Resources/tp_16_ISPS.pdf.

[12] *Ibid.*

[13] International Port Security Program, U.S. Coast Guard, http://www.uscg.mil/d14/feact/Maritime_Security.asp, accessed March 27, 2017.

[14] "About Us," World Customs Organization, http://www.wcoomd.org/home_about_us.htm, accessed September 22, 2009.

[15] "The Role of Customs and the World Customs Organization in Border Management," United Nations Counter-Terrorism Committee, March 2004, http://www.osce.org/documents/sg/2004/03/2196-_en.pdf.

[16] "WCO SAFE Framework of Standards," June 2007, World Customs Organization, http://www.wcoomd.org/files/1. Public files/PDFandDocuments/SAFE Framework_EN_2007_for_publication.pdf.

[17] "Supply Chain Security," November 18, 2002, Policy Statement, International Chamber of Commerce's Commission on Transport and Logistics, http://www.iccwbo.org/policy/transport/id518/index.html, retrieved March 12, 2015.

[18] *Ibid.*

[19] Shear, Michael, "Trump Administration Orders Tougher Screening of Visa Applicants," *The New York Times*, March 24, 2017, p. A13.

[20] Roots, Roger, "Terrorized into Absurdity: the Creation of the Transportation Security Adminis-

tration," *Independent Review*, March 22, 2003.

[21] Stross, Randall, "Theater of the Absurd at the T.S.A.," *The New York Times*, December 17, 2006.

[22] Goldberg, Jeffrey, "The Things He Carried," *Atlantic Monthly*, November 2008.

[23] Caygill, J. Sarah, Frank Davis, and Seamus P.J. Higson, "Current Trends in Explosive Detection Techniques," *Talenta*, **88**:14-29, January 15, 2012, http://dx.doi.org/10.1016/j.talanta.2011.11.043, retrieved March 28, 2017.

[24] Johnson, Eric, John Hershey, Jacqueline Meszaros, and Howard Kunreuther, "Framing, Probability Distortions, and Insurance Decisions," *Journal of Risk and Uncertainty*, August 1993, pp. 35-51.

[25] *Performance and Accountability Report—Fiscal Year 2016*, March 6, 2017, U.S. Customs and Border Protection, https://www.cbp.gov/newsroom/publications/performance-accountability-financial, retrieved March 28, 2017.

[26] Boske, Leigh, "Port and Supply-Chain Security Initiatives in the United States and Abroad," Lyndon B. Johnson School of Public Affairs, University of Texas at Austin, Policy Research Project Report 150, 2006, http://www.utexas.edu/lbj/publications/3986, retrieved July 3, 2013.

[27] *Partnering in Supply Chain Security and Facilitation for the 21st Century*, July 18, 2015, U.S. Customs and Border Protection, http://www.cosco-usa.com/omd/2014/2014-State.pdf, retrieved March 28, 2017.

[28] *Supply Chain Security*, Government Accounting Office, February 2017, http://www.gao.gov/assets-/690/682620.pdf, retrieved March 28, 2017.

[29] "Customs-Trade Partnership Against Terrorism (C-TPAT)," Samuel Shapiro and Company, Inc., http://www.shapiro.com/html/ctpat.html, retrieved July 3, 2013.

[30] *Ibid.*

[31] "Customs-Trade Partnership Against Terrorism Mutual Recognition," August 23, 2016, U.S. Customs and Border Protection, https://www.cbp.gov/border-security/ports-entry/cargo-security/c-tpat-customs-trade-partnership-against-terrorism/mutual-recognition, retrieved March 28, 2017.

[32] *Ibid.*

[33] Importer Self-Assessment, U.S. Customs and Border Protection, https://www.cbp.gov/sites/default/files/documents/isa_factsheet_2.pdf, retrieved March 28, 2017.

[34] *Trusted Trader Framework Strategy Draft*, U.S. Customs and Border Protection, July 2016, https://-www.cbp.gov/sites/default/files/assets/documents/2016-Aug/Trusted Trader Title Page.pdf, retrieved March 28, 2017.

[35] "Introduction to The Maritime Transportation Security Act (MTSA) and The International Ship and Port Facility Security Code (ISPS)," February 1, 2013, U.S. Coast Guard, Office of Port and Facility Compliance, https://homeport.uscg.mil/mycg/portal/ep/home.do, retrieved July 4, 2013.

[36] *Ibid.*

[37] Gallagher, John, "US looks to private sector for 100 percent scanning help," *the Journal of Commerce*, May 13, 2016.

[38] "Feds Seeking New Ideas to Achieve 100 Percent Cargo Container Scanning," Sandler, Travis & Rosenberg Trade Report, May 31, 2016, https://www.strtrade.com/news-publications-100-percent-scanning-cargo-containers-waiver-request-053116.html, retrieved March 27, 2017.

[39] Bryant, Dennis, "Maritime Security and the Useless TWIC," *Maritime Reporter & Engineering News*, May 2012.

[40] *Transportation Workers' Identification Credential: Card Reader Pilot Results Are Unreliable; Security Benefits Need to Be Reassessed*, May 8, 2013, Government Accounting Office report GAO-13-198, www.gao.gov/assets/660/654431.pdf, retrieved July 4, 2013.

[41] "CSI: Container Security Initiative," U.S. Customs and Border Protection, June 26, 2014, https://-www.cbp.gov/border-security/ports-entry/cargo-security/csi/csi-brief, retrieved March 28, 2017.

[42] "FAST Fact Sheet," U.S. Customs and Border Protection, http://wwwcbp.gov/xp/cgov/travel/trusted_traveler/fast/fast_driver/, retrieved March 28, 2017.

[43] Solana, Javier, "A Secure Europe in a Better World: European Security Strategy," December 12, 2003, http://www.consilium.europa.eu/uedocs/cmsUpload/78367.pdf.

[44] "Authorised Economic Operator (AEO)," Taxation and Customs Union, http://ec.europa.eu/taxation_customs/customs/policy_issues/customs_security/aeo, retrieved July 4, 2013.

[45] "Customs-related security initiatives of the EU," Taxation and Customs Union, http://ec.europa.eu/taxation_customs/customs/policy_issues/customs_security/security_initiatives/index_en.htm, retrieved July 4, 2013.

[46] *Ibid.*

[47] Ritter, Luke, J. Michael Barrett, and Rosalyn Wilson, *Securing Global Transportation Networks*, 2007, McGraw-Hill, New York, New York.

[48] Crosby, Philip, *Quality Is Free*, 1980, Mentor/Penguin-Putnam, New York, New York.

[49] Merkow, Mark, and James Breithaupt, *Information Security: Principles and Practices*, 2005, Prentice-Hall, Englewood Cliffs, New Jersey.

Chapter 17

Customs Clearance

Another aspect of international trade is the process that an importer must follow when it brings goods into a country. This process is dictated by customs authorities, the government office in charge of collecting taxes on imports and of enforcing rules and regulations regarding what can and cannot be admitted into the country. Clearing customs is generally a complex process, fraught with pitfalls and loaded with paperwork. Most countries—if there are any exceptions—do not like to import goods, and they act accordingly. This chapter explains how the customs system works in general but draws most of its examples from the process followed to import goods into the United States.

17.1   Duty

duty
The amount of tax paid to the importing country on an imported good.

Duty is the tax that an importer must pay to bring goods into a country. Such duty is calculated in several different ways, generally based upon three criteria:

1. The type of goods imported, which is determined according to several rules of classification that essentially have been standardized worldwide.

2. The value of the goods imported, which is determined not only by the invoice value, but also according to many rules that differ from country to country, collectively called valuation rules.

3. The country from which the goods are imported; this determination is made according to the rules of origin, a process recently simplified but still quite cumbersome for manufactured products with components made in multiple countries.

From these three elements, customs calculates what tariff will be charged on the import, or the tax that the importer must pay on the imported goods. The tariff is generally a percentage of the goods' value, but it can also be calculated with other methods, based on the number of units shipped or their weight, for example.

17.1.1   Classification

classification
The process of determining what is the correct Harmonized System number for an import.

Harmonized System of classification
A system of classification for goods, developed by the World Customs Organization, and followed by 179 countries.

The classification of goods follows a coding scheme that is the same worldwide, as most countries have adopted the Harmonized Commodity Description and Coding System—also called the Harmonized System (HS) of classification—developed by the Customs Cooperation Council (also known as the World Customs Organization [WCO]).

The Harmonized System is used by 181 countries, representing 98 percent or more of world trade, to classify both exports and imports.[1] The first country to have adopted the system was Denmark in 1951, and the latest is Kosovo, on January 25, 2017; the United States joined in 1970.[2] The fact that a trader can use the same code when it is exporting a product from one country and importing it into another is a great process simplification. At one time, almost every country had its own classification and coding system, a situation that made coding cumbersome.

According to the Harmonized Commodity Description and Coding System, each product can have a code that uses up to ten digits. An example, taken from the tariff schedule of the United States, is:

6402.19.05		**golf shoes**
	30	for men
	60	for women
	90	for other persons

where the first six digits represent the "root" of the international coding (*i.e.*, the code that will be identical in all the countries that have adopted the Harmonized System for this product). Since "golf shoes" are not specifically listed in the six-digit system, they fall under "other" types of shoes, which is the six-digit code 6402.19. The last four digits are country specific (*i.e.*, every country can use them to differentiate between different sub-categories of the main product, as the United States does). For the United States, the 8-digit code 6402.19.05 represents golf shoes, and a further differentiation is made between golf shoes for men, for women, and for "other persons" (presumably children rather than aliens).

Details on the Classification of Golf Shoes

The Harmonized System is divided into 21 sections, logically determined by the type of product and material, each divided into one or more chapters, with a total of 97 chapters for the entire HS nomenclature.[3] The chapter in which golf shoes are classified is Chapter 64, entitled "Footwear, gaiters, and the like; parts of such articles."

Each chapter is then divided into headings, which make up the first four digits of the HS number.

The heading 6401 is *Waterproof footwear with outer soles and uppers of rubber or plastics, where the uppers of which are not assembled to the sole by means of stitching, riveting, nailing, screwing, plugging or similar process.* That remark means that the soles and the uppers are "one" or welded together, like rubber boots and downhill ski boots.

Each heading is then divided into subheadings, and this six-digit code is common to all countries that have adopted the Harmonized System. For example, heading 6401 has these two subheadings (among others):

∘ 6401.10 is *footwear [of the type defined in 6401] that includes a protective metal toe-cap.*

∘ 6401.92 is *other footwear [of the type defined in 6401] covering the ankle but not the knee.* (for example, downhill ski boots).

The next heading is 6402, *Other footwear with outer soles and uppers of rubber or plastics.* Since it is a different heading than 6401, it is easy to conclude that shoes whose uppers are stitched, riveted, nailed, or screwed to the soles would be classified under this heading. They would not be considered waterproof either. Heading 6402 has five subheadings:

- 6402.12 is *ski-boots and cross-country ski footwear and snowboard boots.* This classification would apply to boots that are not considered waterproof and for which the uppers are stitched or glued to the soles.
- 6402.19 is *other footwear [of the type defined in 6402] where 90 percent or more of the external surface area is rubber or plastics*, where most golf shoes are classified.
- 6402.20 is *footwear with upper straps or thongs assembled to the sole by means of plugs (zoris)*, which are likely to be thongs, flip-flops or zoris.
- 6402.91 is *other footwear [defined in 6402] that covers the ankle.*
- 6402.99 is *other footwear [defined in 6402] and that does not cover the ankles.*

Worldwide, golf shoes are classified as 6402.19, since they are made with rubber soles, their uppers are attached to the soles by some mechanical method, and 90 percent of the external surface area is rubber or plastics. The United States defines golf shoes yet further, with a specific subheading for golf shoes, 6402.19.05, and then a differentiation made between men's, women's, and children's shoes.

---

rules of interpretation
A series of six rules developed to help importers and Customs determine the correct HS classification of a good.

The Harmonized System of classification is accompanied by a series of six General Rules of Interpretation, which detail how an importer should determine the correct HS code for an entry:[4]

1. The section, chapter, and heading serve only as guides, and the correct classification may be in a different section, chapter, and heading altogether.

2. The classification of an incomplete or unfinished product is that of the finished product. For example, shipments that contain all the subassemblies for a final product should be classified as the final product, rather than as individual parts. This is also true of chemical compounds.

3. When in doubt between two classifications, the one with the most specific description is the correct one. However, if the product is made up of several parts, each of which would lead to a different classification, then the classification that lends it its "essential character" is the correct one.

4. When there is no category under which a specific product can be classified, then the classification that should be used is that of a product that would be most like it.

5. Containers and packaging materials are classified with the products with which they enter. Such is the case for camera cases, for example. However,

if the container has usage beyond the product itself, then it must be entered and classified separately.

6. When comparing classifications, only descriptions at the same level should be compared; it is not appropriate to compare a heading to a subheading, for example.

Nevertheless, the correct classification is always subject to interpretation on the part of the importer and customs officers. Because the classification of a specific article determines its tariff rate and whether it will be subjected to numerical quotas (as are some articles in developed countries, such as the United States; see Section 17.2.1), classification can be a critical issue. If a U.S. importer is in doubt about a correct classification, the Customs Office will issue, prior to the entry of the goods, a binding ruling where it determines the correct classification of a specific product, a decision that is binding on both parties.[5]

Although it is no longer printed, the Harmonized Tariff Schedule of the United States (2017) that lists all possible classification categories, is a pdf document that is 3,707 pages long. In the early 2000s, there were efforts to simplify the ten-digit classification used by the United States and model it after some other countries' systems, which use only the six-digit subheadings of the HS. However, as of 2017, the U.S. Customs tariff schedule was still using a ten-digit-based classification system, and there were no plans to change that method.

The correct classification of an imported good is generally made by the importer and then verified by the Customs Office; however, each country has different standards, and a few put the entire classification responsibility on customs. In any case, it is critical to have a complete and accurate description of the goods on the commercial invoice, and not just a part number or an item number. When in doubt, customs may ask to see the merchandise before it is released, and this inspection can create substantial delays.

binding ruling
A determination, made by Customs prior to the importation of a good, of the correct classification of a good. The ruling is binding on the Customs administration of the country that issued it.

tariff schedule
A document listing all the possible Harmonized System categories and their associated duty rates for different countries.

17.1.2 Valuation

Because most duty is collected *ad valorem* (on the value of the goods imported in a country), a correct valuation amount must be determined by the importer, following several valuation rules governed by the Customs Office of the country in which the goods are imported.

For all member countries of the World Trade Organization (WTO), the valuation of goods is based on the transaction value of the sale. Therefore, the valuation of the goods must start with the value presented on the invoice sent by the exporter to the importer. For most countries, the value used is the "landed" value, or the CIF/CIP value of the goods (see Chapter 6), that is, the invoice value including packaging costs, transportation costs in the exporting country—pre-carriage—international transportation costs to the country of destination—main carriage—and international insurance costs. For other countries, including the United States, the value used is the FCA or FAS value (see Chapter 6), that is, the invoice value of the goods, as well as packaging costs and transportation costs

valuation
The process of determining the value of an import, specifically the amount on which the duty is calculated.

***ad valorem* duty rate**
A duty rate based on the value of the imported item.

in the exporting country, but excluding the costs of international shipping and insurance.

There are obvious difficulties in reaching the correct valuation unless the commercial invoice is detailed enough to include these different costs in a clear, itemized fashion, regardless of the terms of trade (Incoterms® rule) used in the transaction. For example, a CIF sale to an American importer should spell out the costs of international freight and international insurance, so that they can be deducted from the invoice value for customs purposes.

The valuation process can be much more complicated than what has been outlined so far. Some countries used to determine value based upon the Brussels Definition of Value (BDV), or the "usual" price of a commodity, based on the price at which a product would sell in a free market between an unrelated buyer and seller. However, since 1994 and the conclusion of the Uruguay Round of the General Agreement on Tariffs and Trade, BDV has slowly been replaced by the transaction value.[6] In those cases where customs suspects that valuation based on the invoice would result in undervaluation—or, possibly, overvaluation—it can legitimately decide that valuation can be determined through other methods:

- **Comparative method**—Customs determines the value of the goods based upon the value of identical or similar goods imported in similar quantity into the same country. Note that the determination of the value of the goods is made based upon importing data and that differences in exporting countries' costs are not taken into consideration.

- **Deductive method**—Customs determines at what price identical or similar goods are sold within 90 days of importation into the importing country, and determines an entry value based upon normal markups in the distribution channel.

- **Computed or reconstructed value method**—Customs determines the value of the goods by computing their manufacturing costs and adding "an amount for profit and general expenses equal to that usually reflected in the sales of goods of the same class or kind."[7]

- **Method of last resort**—Customs uses well-trained and well-informed customs officials to determine the value of the goods imported. No specific guidelines are given, other than the valuation cannot be "arbitrary." It is unlikely to be anything else, though.

assist
An item provided by the importer to the exporter so that the exporter could manufacture the imported goods. The value of the assist should be included in the valuation of the imported goods.

The valuation of the imported goods can be increased by some items not included on the invoice: for example, a royalty paid by the importer to the exporter, a commission paid by the importer to a purchasing agent in the exporting country, or a percentage of the price at which the importer sells the goods to their final purchaser. The valuation can also be affected by the presence of what customs calls an assist, or an item that the importer provided to the exporter to produce the goods: for example, a mold or a die that the exporter used in manufacturing the product. The value of such an assist must be added, on a per-item basis, to the value of the imported goods.

Finally, the issue of exchange rates is relevant. Customs must determine the value of the goods in the importing country's currency, even though the invoice may be written in a different currency. Each national Customs Office therefore has rules to determine what exchange rate will be used to convert an invoice issued in a foreign currency. U.S. Customs and Border Protection uses the exchange rate of the date of export of the merchandise.

17.1.3 Rules of Origin

The third element necessary to determine the duty that will be applied to a specific import is the goods' country of origin. Goods are given a country of origin based upon the rules of origin, which follow one or the other of two methods, neither of which has been adopted universally, despite the fact that the WTO has had a committee working on this project since 1995. So far, the committee has agreed that countries must make their rules of origin "transparent" and unbiased to importers,[8] and provide a ruling on a country of origin within 150 days.

rules of origin
The rules used to determine the country of origin of an imported product.

- **Substantial transformation**—A product's country of origin is the country in which it acquired its most substantial transformation. The determination of "substantial transformation" is fraught with pitfalls and can lead to widely different interpretations. For example, consider a computer assembled in Mexico from parts originating in Taiwan (memory chips), the United States (CPU), China (board and hard drive), Brazil (monitor), and so on. Where did the substantial transformation take place, and what is the country of origin of the product? Although vague, this is still the method followed by the United States—except for textiles—and it can lead to complex decisions.

- **Change in HS classification**—The country of origin is the country in which the last change in Harmonized System classification occurred. This method is the one currently followed by the United States for textile products, and it has proven to be easier to implement. Nevertheless, the decision can sometimes lead to a product's country of origin being a country in which an inconsequential transformation took place and where little value was added. Already several exceptions have been made to this rule.

Unfortunately, there seems to be no easy way to determine a complex product's country of origin. The determination of a country of origin—and the markings that are associated with it—is one of the most difficult issues facing firms engaged in international trade today, as different duty rates are used for different countries and numerical quotas exist for some countries but not others. An importer can be charged very different duty rates and, in some cases, be fined for having mis-represented the country of origin: in 2015, the U.S. Department of Justice and U.S. Customs and Border Protection fined Medtronic U.S.$ 4.1 million for having sold medical devices in violation of the country-of-origin rules of the United States' Buy American Act (1933), which mandates that products sold to the U.S. government be made in the United States. In 2014, the U.S. arm of

U.K. medical device manufacturer Smith & Nephew settled a dispute for U.S.$ 8.3 million.[9]

In addition, a good's country of origin can have substantial marketing consequences, as most countries require that the goods be marked with their country of origin. For obvious reasons, importers of luxury clothing items prefer to mark them *Made in Italy* rather than mark them as made in a country not known for its designers. However, this issue is of consequence for many products, as consumers are sensitive to what international marketers call country-of-origin effects,[10] the perceptions that the country of origin imparts on the product.

The rules of origin can also be affected by bilateral or multilateral agreements. For example, the North American Free Trade Agreement (NAFTA) between Canada, the United States, and Mexico has its own rules of origin, and its rules differ from commodity to commodity. In general, a product qualifies to enter duty free into any of the three NAFTA countries if its regional content (the percentage of its value that it acquired in any of the three countries) is at least 50 percent. For some goods, though, the maximum percentage of their value that can be outside of NAFTA is 7 percent.[11] Other free-trade agreements have their own rules of origin: the Canada-Chile Free Trade Agreement has its own rules, and so does the European Union in those agreements designed to provide EU market access to developing countries.[12] Because there are over 300 free-trade agreements worldwide, most of which have their own rules of origin, a uniform system is sorely needed.[13]

Finally, the markings for a product's origin can be different if the product is sold in different countries. A product imported in Canada from the United States can be marked "made in the United States" if its content is at least 50 percent from the United States. The same product cannot be sold in the United States with that marking, because a product with this marking requires that it be "all or virtually all" made in the U.S.

17.1.4 Tariffs

tariff rate
The rate at which an import is taxed. The rate depends on classification and origin. Also called the duty rate.

An importing country usually manages its imports under an n-column tariff system, with n, the number of columns, corresponding to the number of different classes of countries that the importing country considers. The tariff rates are the same for all the countries in a given class. Most tariff schedules are known as two-, three-, or four-column schedules. For example, the United States operates under a two-column tariff schedule, with the countries with which the United States has normal trade relations (NTR) subject to Column 1 tariffs, and others to Column 2 tariffs. In 2000, what had been the "most favored nation" (MFN) designation was officially changed to the NTR classification.

Annotated for Statistical Reporting Purposes

XVIII
91-34

Heading/ Subheading	Stat. Suf- fix	Article Description	Unit of Quantity	Rates of Duty		
				1		2
				General	Special	
9114		Other clock or watch parts:				
9114.10		Springs, including hairsprings:				
9114.10.40	00	For watches..................................	No............	7.3%	Free (A+, AU, BH, CA, CL, CO, D, E, IL, JO, KR, MA, MX, OM, P, PA, PE, R, SG)	65%
9114.10.80	00	Other..	No............	4.2%	Free (A+, AU, B, BH, CA, CL, CO, D, E, IL, JO, KR, MA, MX, OM, P, PA, PE, SG)	65%
9114.30		Dials:				
9114.30.40	00	Not exceeding 50 mm in width.......................	No............	0.4¢ each + 7.2%	Free (A+, AU, B, BH, CA, CL, CO, D, E, IL, JO, KR, MA, MX, OM, P, PA, PE, R, SG)	5¢ each + 45%
9114.30.80	00	Exceeding 50 mm in width...............	No............	4.4%	Free (A+, AU, B, BH, CA, CL, CO, D, E, IL, JO, KR, MA, MX, OM, P, PA, PE, R, SG)	50%
9114.40		Plates and bridges:				
9114.40.20	00	Watch movement bottom or pillar plates or their equivalent...................	No............	12¢ each	Free (A+, AU, BH, CA, CL, CO, D, E, IL, JO, KR, MA, MX, OM, P, PA, PE, R, SG)	75¢ each
9114.40.40	00	Any plate, or set of plates, suitable for assembling thereon a clock movement...............	No............	10¢ each	Free (A+, AU, B, BH, CA, CL, CO, D, E, IL, JO, KR, MA, MX, OM, P, PA, PE, SG)	38¢ each
		Other:				
9114.40.60	00	For watches...............	X............	7.3%	Free (A+, AU, BH, CA, CL, CO, D, E, IL, JO, KR, MA, MX, OM, P, PA, PE, R, SG)	65%
9114.40.80	00	Other...............	X............	4.2%	Free (A+, AU, B, BH, CA, CL, CO, D, E, IL, JO, KR, MA, MX, OM, P, PA, PE, SG)	65%

Legend:

A+: Generalized System of Preference
AU: United States – Australia Free Trade Agreement
B: Automotive Product Trade Act
BH: Bahrain Free Trade Agreement
CA: NAFTA Agreement with Canada
CO: United States – Colombia Free Trade Agreement
CL: United States Chile Free Trade Agreement
D: African Growth and Opportunity Act
E: Caribbean Basin Economic Recovery Act
IL: United States – Israel Free Trade Area
J: Andean Trade Preference Act

J+: Andean Drug Eradication Act
JO: United States – Jordan Free Trade Area Implementation Act
KR: United States – Korea Free Trade Agreement
MA: United States- Morocco Freee Trade Agreement
MX: NAFTA Agreement with Mexico
OM: Oman Free Tree Agreement
P: Dominican Republic – Central America US Free Trade Agreement
PE: Peru Free Trade Agreement
R: United States - Carribean Basin trade Partnership Act
SG: United States – Singapore Free Trade Agreement

Figure 17.1: United States Tariff Schedule (2017)

United States International Trade Commission.

However, the number of columns is often an oversimplification of the actual tariff system. Because the number and complexity of multilateral trade agreements has increased, this terminology can sometimes be confusing, as there can be many more than n classes. Nevertheless, the terminology has remained.

For the United States, there are only two trading partners that do not have NTR status, both of which are, at best, minor trading partners: Cuba and North Korea.[14] However, among the NTRs, there are trading partners with which the United States has free-trade relations (Canada, Mexico, Israel, Chile, Colombia, Jordan, Korea, Singapore, Australia, New Zealand, as well as all Caribbean countries, all Central American countries, and all sub-Saharan African countries), and several that have a special status on specific products. Add to these several bilateral agreements on specific products, and the system is much more than a two-column system. Therefore, in the United States, the first column is split into two sub-columns, one labeled "General" for all NTR countries, and the other "Special" for all countries for which, for a given HS number, there is a special negotiated rate (see Figure 17.1).

The United States also grants most developing countries duty-free access to the U.S. market under the Generalized System of Preference (GSP).[15] However, the GSP legislation has become a source of political disagreements in the United States. The GSP expired on July 31, 2013, and it was only renewed on June 29, 2015 for a period of 2.5 years (until December 31, 2018).[16] In future versions, the GSP may be changed to exclude countries that have made much economic progress—such as Brazil, India, and Thailand—but maintained for countries that are less developed.[17]

Figure 17.1[18] shows the layout of the Tariff Schedule of the United States, with a total of 21 special tariffs. (Only three are not present in the table: the codes **C** for the Agreement on Trade in Civil Aircraft, **K** for the Agreement on Trade in Pharmaceutical Products, and **L** for the Uruguay Round Concessions on Intermediate Chemicals and Dyes.) Each product category has its own negotiated specific treatment, and the Harmonized Tariff Schedule of the United States is replete with these types of exceptions.

Tariffs are generally calculated *ad valorem* or as a percentage tax on the value of the goods imported. Nevertheless, other methods exist, such as a fixed amount per unit imported. Some others are calculated with a mixed system, such as a fixed amount per unit in addition to a percentage of the value of the goods imported; such a tariff is called a compound duty rate. Figure 17.1 illustrates all these alternatives:

compound duty rate
A duty rate based on a combination of value, number, or some other measurement of the imported item (weight, dimensions,...).

- A company importing springs for watches (classified as 9114.10.4000) would have to pay 7.3 percent duty on the FCA value of the goods if they came from an NTR country—for example, Japan. If the springs came from one of the eighteen different countries for which imports would be duty-free, such as India (Generalized System of Preference), Australia (U.S.-Australia Free Trade Agreement), Canada (NAFTA), Haiti (Caribbean Basin Initiative), Israel (U.S.-Israel Free Trade Agreement), Peru (U.S.-Peru Trade Promotion Agreement Implementation Act), or Mexico (NAFTA), the importer would have no duty to pay. If the springs came from North Korea, the duty rate would be 65 percent.

- A company importing small watch movement bottoms (classified as 9114.-40.2000) from an NTR country, like Germany, would have to pay U.S.$ 0.12 per movement, regardless of the FCA value of the movements. The same product coming from countries such as Korea or Singapore could be imported duty free. An importer obtaining the bottoms from Cuba would be saddled with a U.S.$ 0.75 duty per movement.

- A company importing watch dials whose size is inferior to 50mm (1.97 in) (classified as 9114.30.4000) would have to pay U.S.$ 0.004 per dial and 7.2 percent of the FCA value of the goods if they are imported from Switzerland or Great Britain, would pay nothing if the dials came from Morocco or Peru, and would pay U.S.$ 0.05 per dial and 45 percent duty if they came from Cuba.

The complexity of the tariff rate schedule in most countries is baffling, and the level of detail that is imparted to duty impossible to justify. Figure 17.1 shows that the U.S. duty rate for watch springs (classified as 9114.10.4000) is reduced from 7.3 percent to zero if the country of export is in the Caribbean [code R] or in sub-Saharan Africa [code D]. However, for other clock parts (items classified as 9114.10.8000, and not springs, jewels, or plates), those coming from a Caribbean country would have to pay the 7.3 percent duty rate, and the African country's products would be imported duty free. Similarly, it is hard to explain why dials smaller than 50 millimeters pay a compound duty rate of $0.004 per dial in addition to 7.2 percent duty, when those larger than 50 millimeters pay a duty of 4.4 percent. It is highly unlikely that it was the intent of the U.S. Congress to tax small dials at roughly twice the rate of larger ones. Many other examples exist for this level of detail in the Harmonized Schedule of the United States and most countries. Such a level of differentiation cannot be defended, and makes the work of international traders particularly complex.

Several importers of clothing products have filed lawsuits against the U.S. government, accusing it of engaging in gender discrimination. The companies are fighting the fact that bathing suits are taxed at 27.8 percent for men (classified as 6211.11.1010) and 11.8 percent for women (classified as 6211.12.1010), that artificial-fiber overalls (classified as 6103.49.2000) for men are taxed at 13.6 percent, and 14.9 percent for women (classified as 6014.63.1020), and that wool suits for men (classified as 6103.10.1000) are taxed at 10 percent and a fee of U.S.$ 0.388 per kg, but can come in duty free for women (classified as 6104.13.1000) as long as the wool content is at least 23 percent.[19] The first complainant to file a lawsuit was Totes-Isotoner, an importer of gloves, which charged that the government was discriminating by charging 14 percent duty for men's gloves and 12.6 percent for "other persons." In July 2008, Totes-Isotoner's lawsuit was dismissed by the Court of International Trade. A similar lawsuit was filed, and lost, by Forever 21, an apparel chain. The February 2012 decision stated that the company needed to "connect the tariff provisions and congressional action in a way to suggest with plausibility the existence of a governmental intent to discriminate."[20] In May 2014, the U.S. Supreme Court refused to hear appeals from these importers. However, "there is little doubt that gender-based tariffs have a discriminatory impact, since the burden of tariffs falls almost exclusively on consumers."[21] Since most of the tariff differentiations between genders in made at the 10-digit level, a move by the United States to keep the complexity of the Harmonized Tariff Schedule to a 6-digit classification system would eliminate that problem.

Figure 17.2: A U.S. CBP Agent Ensuring Correct Classification of an Import
Photo ©James Tourtellotte/United States CBP. Used with permission.

17.1.5 Dumping

dumping
A strategy, followed by some exporters, that consists of selling the goods at a price considered "too low" by the importing country's Customs authorities.

In some cases, customs can determine that the invoice value is lower (in some rare cases, higher) than the actual value of the goods. This is generally uncovered by comparing the value of an invoice with a database of import entries with the same Harmonized System number made in preceding years. For example, in the United States, the invoice value is systematically compared to previous valuations. This is one of the purposes of the column labeled "unit of quantity" in Figure 17.1 that represents the units under which the customs computer database keeps the values of other entries under a specific HS number to determine whether an entry is within the bounds of "normal." Should the invoice give a value outside of these bounds, a Customs and Border Protection's import specialist will scrutinize the entry before liquidating it.

When the invoice's value is below what customs has historically accepted and when a much higher valuation is reached with one of the alternative valuation methods (see Section 17.1.2), customs can determine that the exporter is dumping the goods in the importing country, *i.e.*, selling the goods at a price that is below their commercial value. The exact definition of "dumping" varies from country to country, but the prevailing definition is that a price is set below the wholesale price in the exporting country, and that this low price causes injury to competitors (or some other group, such as a labor union) located in the importing country. For some countries, such as the United States, there must be a complaint from an injured party before customs considers that the under-valuation is a case of dumping. In addition, an organization independent of customs—in the United States, the International Trade Commission—is asked to determine whether there is actual injury to competitors and to ascertain whether the goods are sold below their commercial value before an exporter is found guilty of dumping.

In cases of dumping, customs can add an additional duty to the regular duty rate of the commodity, and this duty rate is called an anti-dumping duty, which can range from one percent to several times the value of the imported goods. Unfortunately, dumping accusations are one of the most commonly used tools of certain countries to restrict imports, and it is still one of the most commonly used methods of protectionism. In addition, customs can use a countervailing duty to tax products that the exporting government is found to have subsidized. In that case again, it only acts after an allegation of injury by an affected competitor. However, although there is strong support for such countervailing duties in some industries, the U.S. Commerce Department has declined to impose them on products coming from countries in which non-market economies prevail.

In the United States, there was a rash of anti-dumping duty requests in the early and mid-2000s, due to the Byrd Amendment, named for Senator Robert Byrd of West Virginia. The Byrd Amendment directed customs to give the anti-dumping duty it collected from importers to the U.S. companies that were harmed by the dumping. In 2003, U.S. Customs and Border Protection distributed U.S.$ 190 million to U.S. companies, U.S.$ 885 million in 2004, and an estimated U.S.$ 3.85 billion after 2005.[22] The Timken Company, one of the largest beneficiaries of the Byrd Amendment, reported anti-dumping income of U.S.$ 66 million in 2003, which was equal to 67 percent of its operating income of $ 98 million.[23] Although the WTO ruled against the Byrd Amendment by finding that it violated the rules of international trade in August 2004,[24] the U.S. Congress did not repeal the amendment until October 2007.

17.1.6 Value-Added Tax

In some countries, an additional tax is collected in addition to the duty, but is generally considered to have no bearing on importers—even if it adds up to a

value-added tax
A tax collected by many countries that is very similar to a sales tax, but is based on the increase in the value of the product at each step of the manufacturing process.

significant amount—because it is collected from domestic producers as well as from importers, and is eventually paid by consumers: the Value-Added Tax (VAT). The idea of VAT is simple in its concept: the tax is collected on the value added by each firm involved in adding value to a good, from the first firm in the production chain to the last. The implementation of a VAT is somewhat complex, though.

It is best to explain the VAT concept and its implementation—as it is practiced in the European Union countries, at least—with a simplified example:

1. A farmer purchases seeds, fertilizer, pesticides, and fuel to produce corn. On each production-related purchase, the farmer pays the VAT. The farmer keeps track of the VAT paid in a special bookkeeping account, as a debit. The farmer then sells the corn she has produced and collects the VAT from her customer, which is recorded in the special bookkeeping account as a credit. At the end of the quarter, the farmer deducts the VAT she has paid from the VAT she has collected, and sends the difference to the government.

2. The corn is purchased by a mill that transforms it into several products, including corn syrup. On all the products the mill sells to wholesalers and retailers, it collects VAT, an amount it records in a special bookkeeping account. At the end of the quarter, the mill deducts the VAT it has paid to farmers and for its other purchases from the VAT it has collected from its customers and sends the difference to the government.

3. The corn syrup is purchased by a consumer who uses it in his kitchen. The consumer pays the VAT, but has no way to collect any, so the consumer bears the tax's entire burden.

For imports, the concept is the same. The VAT is collected from the importer, but the importer can deduct the value of the VAT it has paid from the VAT it eventually collects from its customers; therefore, the tax is not an actual cost to the importer. However, in reality, there are substantial accounting and cash-flow costs associated with the VAT method of garnering taxes. Nevertheless, because both domestic and imported products are taxed the same way, there are no advantages garnered by either in their final costs to the consumer. The cost is substantial for the ultimate consumer, though, as the VAT rate in the European Union is approximately 20 percent.

In the E.U., the VAT is computed on the sum of the value of the imported goods and the duty levied at importation.

17.2 Non-tariff Barriers

Some countries use high tariffs to limit the import of certain goods. However, steady pressure from the General Agreement on Tariffs and Trade, and now the World Trade Organization, has reduced the duty paid by most goods in most countries. The average tariff rate for goods imported in developed countries is just above four percent, and the average tariff rate for goods imported in developing countries is 10 percent.[25] While there are some exceptions, the trend is toward ever-lower duty rates, with rates dropping an average of 0.5 percent per year.[26]

At the same time, the WTO has also been active in attempting to decrease the number of non-tariff trade barriers that countries place on imports. Nevertheless, several of those alternatives are still in place, which effectively limit exporters' access to certain markets. Non-tariff trade barriers are policies and actions that have the effect of reducing the number of items imported in a specific country. Often, not surprisingly, what is perceived as a trade barrier by an international trader is presented as an innocuous requirement by the importing country's government.

17.2.1 Quotas

The primary method used by countries to limit imports is a system of quotas, which limit the quantity of goods that can enter a country. A quota can take two forms:

quota
A limit, set by the importing country's government, on the quantity of a commodity that can be imported in a given year.

- **An absolute quota**, which places a yearly limit on the number of items entering a country under a specific Harmonized-System (HS) number. On occasion, the quota can be implemented using the value of the goods imported by placing a ceiling on the total value of goods imported under a specific HS number. Once the quota is reached, goods in that category can no longer be imported. Some countries, whose products are subject to quotas, have established a system of visas to monitor how much of a given quota has been filled by its exporters (see Section 17.3.7).

- **A tariff-rate quota**, which places a two-tiered tariff rate on a category of products. Until a specific number of goods are entered, the tariff is low, but once the quota is reached, the tariff rate changes to a much higher percentage. Nevertheless, the goods can still be legally imported.

Quotas are usually placed on specific items coming from a specific country of origin. As of 2013, the United States no longer has absolute quotas, but it did until January 1, 2009. Until then, a complex system of quotas for textiles and apparel was followed by the United States and other developed countries for products originating in some developing countries, which was outlined in an international treaty called the Multi-Fiber Agreement (MFA). Those quotas restricted the number of textile items imported from many developing countries. The WTO negotiated the Agreement on Textiles and Clothing to eliminate these quotas, and all developed countries' textile quotas were supposed to have been lifted by January 1, 2005. However, practical considerations made the United States and China negotiate three one-year agreements under which there was a limit on the number of certain textile items exported from China into the United States, called the "safeguard quotas."[27] This had been anticipated, should the elimination of quotas be harmful to the economies of the importing countries.

However, the elimination of quotas was particularly harmful to the developing countries that were competing with China. Under the MFA quota system, many countries gained access to the large markets of Europe and the United States because Chinese firms were limited in the number of products they could sell. After the quotas were lifted, the Chinese firms, being the world's chief low-cost producers of textile apparel and having seemingly unlimited capacity, displaced these other countries' products and created economic hardship there.

As of March 2017, the United States had many tariff-rate quotas on an array of more than fifty products, including brooms, ethyl alcohol, milk and cream, olives, mandarins, tuna, upland cotton, worsted wool, infant formula, peanut butter, tobacco, cocoa powder, and others.[28]

Quotas can also be "voluntary." Under pressure from the importing government, exporters may agree to limit their exports "voluntarily" to a certain quantity. Such was the case during the early 1980s in the United States when Japanese automobile manufacturers agreed to absolute quotas for automobiles and light trucks.

Finally, quotas can come in the form of export quotas, when an exporting country limits the quantity of a certain type of good that firms can export from its territory (see Chapter 9).

17.2.2   Adherence to National Standards

Unfortunately, quotas are hardly the only non-tariff trade barriers placed by countries to restrict imports. In many instances, countries enact "safety measures" designed to ostensibly protect their populations from defective, dangerous, or unhealthy products from abroad. While most of these restrictions are justified and necessary, some of them are based on dubious data and are a form of undisguised protectionism for less efficient domestic producers.

Countries can demand that products sold within their borders meet the standards that their governments have enacted—for example, there are many requirements regarding the quality of consumer products in developed countries. The most prominent ones are the *Deutsche Industrie Normen* (DIN) in Germany, the Japanese Industry Standards (JIS) in Japan, the *Normes Françaises* (NF) in France, and the American National Standard Institute (ANSI) standards in the United States. A few international standards exist as well, such as those defined by the International Organization for Standardization in its ISO requirements. Most of these requirements are legitimate in that they reflect national preferences and sentiment toward consumer protection, health standards, and safety. For example, the European Union requires that vehicles be equipped with rear turn signals that are distinct from the brake lights, and the United States requires that automobiles be equipped with airbags. Both are obviously worthy requirements.

The Sugar Quotas

The United States has had a tariff-rate quota on sugar for many years. The total amount of raw sugar that could be imported in 2017 at the low tariff rate of U.S.$ 0.014606 per kilogram is 1,117,195 metric tonnes,[29] and any amount above that is charged U.S.$ 0.3387 per kilogram.[30] The world market price for sugar fluctuates between U.S.$ 0.11 and U.S.$ 0.24 per kilogram,[31] so the tariff can more than triple the cost of sugar for U.S. importers.

Several powerful groups of sugar producers in the United States are vocal supporters of this tariff-rate quota and are substantial financial backers of both political parties, so it has never been abolished, even though the WTO has ruled against it. This group is so powerful that when the United States negotiated its free-trade agreement with Australia, it covered all products, but specifically excluded sugar.[32]

Under this tariff-rate quota system, each producing country is allocated a portion of the quota; in 2017, for example, India's share of the quota is 8,424 metric tonnes, and Brazil, the world's largest producer, is allowed 152,691 tonnes.[33] These quotas are very low. Consider that a Handysize ship can hold 35,000 tonnes. Essentially, Brazil, the largest producer of sugar in the world (37,780,000 metric tonnes)[34] can ship only about five small boatloads of sugar (0.4 percent of its production) to the United States, the fourth largest market in the world, which has an annual consumption of 10,719,000 metric tonnes.[35] Brazilian sugar imports represent about 1.4 percent of the total U.S. consumption. India, the second largest producer of sugar in the world at 23,945,000 tonnes, can only export about one fourth of a Handysize ship, representing 0.03 percent of its production and 0.08 percent of the total U.S. market. The Indian share represents less than a third of what the United States consumes in a day.

The quota has an impact on the sugar market in the United States. Although consumers are largely unaffected by the high price of sugar because it represents a small portion of people's expenses, the overall market size is much smaller than it would be if there were no sugar quota; many industrial users of sugar have substituted corn syrup (soft drink manufacturers) or moved abroad (candy manufacturers are producing in Mexico and Canada to ship to the U.S. market) to circumvent the artificially high cost of sugar. This restriction also distorts the export market for American products: Mexico has a retaliatory 20 percent tax on soft drinks made with corn syrup, for example.[36]

However, the impact of the sugar quota is greatest on the economies of the Caribbean and Central American countries that cannot export one of their largest agricultural crops to the United States. Table 17.1 shows the quota allocations for these countries. Note the disparities between the quotas of Haiti and the Dominican Republic, which have about the same size population; whether it is a cause or a consequence, the gross domestic product of the Dominican Republic is roughly 8.5 times that of Haiti.[37] As of March 2017, there were no signs that ending the quota was even being considered.

Selected Sugar Quota Quantities in metric tonnes

Country	Quota
Argentina	45,281
Barbados	7,371
Belize	11,584
Brazil	152,691
Costa Rica	15,796
Dominican Republic	185,335
El Salvador	27,379
Guyana	12,636
Haiti	7,258
India	8,424
Jamaica	11,584
Mexico	7,258
Panama	30,538
Peru	43,175
Swaziland	16,849
Uruguay	7,258

Table 17.1: Selected Sugar Quota Allocations for 2017 (in tonnes)
United States Trade Representative.

The point at which these requirements become non-tariff barriers is unclear. An exporter may be unwilling to incorporate an additional product feature that is costly or that it deems unnecessary, and claims that the requirement is a non-tariff barrier, when it may just be an unwillingness to deal with one of the differences and difficulties of selling a product in a foreign country. General Motors publicly complains that it cannot sell its vehicles to Japanese consumers because of unfair trade barriers; however, the company makes no effort to sell automobiles in that market.[38] In March 2017, GM was still selling Corvettes—a vehicle with a 6.2-liter engine—with the driving wheel on the left, speedometers labeled in miles per hour, and temperatures in degrees Fahrenheit.[39]

In a parallel fashion, such a requirement may not be a non-tariff barrier, even if it is required only of imported products and not of domestic manufacturers, if it is to protect a country from importing a disease that has not yet been observed domestically. Such was the case when non-European countries (Japan, the United States, Brazil) tried to protect themselves against the threat of mad-cow disease.

Nevertheless, countries' efforts to make imports adhere to national standards are often considered to be trade barriers. There have been lengthy spats over the safety of Mexican avocados in the United States,[40] of U.S. cherries in Mexico,[41] of New Zealand apples in Japan,[42] and of U.S. hormone-treated beef[43] and genetically-modified cereals[44] in the European Union. The dispute with Japan over the safety of U.S. tomatoes lasted 46 years before being resolved in favor of U.S. exporters.[45]

17.2.3   Other Non-tariff Barriers

Countries have enacted creative means to slow or restrict imports without having recourse to high tariffs, quotas, or standardization requirements. Here are several examples, which certainly do not constitute an exhaustive list:

- In the early 1980s, France decided that it needed to protect its nascent industry in videocassette recorders (VCRs). It achieved this goal by requiring that every VCR entering the country be inspected, that a sticker be placed on every machine, and that the inspection take place in Poitiers, a landlocked small town about 250 miles from the port of Le Havre, through which most VCRs were shipped. Moreover, the inspection station was a one-man operation.[46] Countless countries have enacted similar "slow" customs clearance processes, to deter imports by increasing costs to importers for additional storage, and creating potential marketing delays.

- Another tactic is to require a mind-numbing number of documents and approvals. For example, in the late 1990s, in India, "an exporter has to complete and process fifty-four documents [...]: twenty-seven pre-shipment documents, fourteen for customs clearance, and thirteen for post-shipment realization of bills. As many as 16 approvals are needed from departments of the central government."[47] The process has been largely simplified since: as of 2013, there were eleven documents necessary to import in India, which is still twice the average for countries that are members of the Organisation for Economic Co-operation and Development (OECD).[48]

- Another way to slow customs entries is to request additional papers that are not readily available or that are close to impossible to gather. The United States requests the "sewing tickets" for some garments, an internal work document of the garment factory, as well as the time cards of the employees working there, to ascertain the country of origin of textile products and prevent diversions—the shipping of goods from a country other than the country of manufacture.[49]

- South Korea has been tremendously effective at keeping foreign cars out of its domestic market. In 2016, there were 1,216,000 Korean-made automobiles sold on the U.S. market, but fewer than 20,000 U.S.-made automobiles sold in Korea, and only 225,279 foreign-made cars.[50] This was achieved, despite relatively low tariffs of 8 percent, with a systematic campaign designed to portray the purchase of a foreign car as unpatriotic. To bolster this perception, the South Korean government has all but threatened all purchasers of foreign cars with an income-tax audit.[51]

- Russia asked U.S. exporters of chicken parts (legs and wings) to individually inspect every bird for specific diseases before they can enter the country, effectively preventing all U.S. imports of such parts.[52]

17.2.4   Pre-shipment Inspections

pre-shipment inspection
The inspection, conducted by an independent company, that allows the determination that the goods conform to the description contained in the exporter's invoice.

Pre-shipment inspections (PSIs) are performed by independent companies at the point of departure of goods destined to be exported. The company determines that the goods shipped are the ones the importer ordered, in the correct quantity, and sufficiently well packed for an international shipment. When the independent firm has ascertained that all these aspects conform to the invoice, it issues a Certificate of Inspection (see Section 9.4.3 on page 299) to the importer. Inspection companies have representatives in most ports and can handle nearly any shipment; on many occasions, though, the exporter experiences delays with PSIs as the workload of inspectors can be substantial, and the expertise needed for a specific shipment may not be available.

Pre-shipment inspections are sometimes requested by importers to ensure that exporters are shipping the correct product in the correct quantity; they are used when the importer is purchasing on a cash-in-advance basis or on a letter of credit. However, many PSIs are required by countries as part of their import process. There are several reasons for this requirement:

- The country wants an expert opinion on the classification and the value of the products that are about to enter its territory.

- The country wants to fight corruption in its own ports of entry. By having a foreign, independent firm determine the classification and value of imported goods, its own customs authorities have lost the ability to change their classifications and valuations for a bribe. Such was the motivation when Indonesia demanded that any good shipped into Indonesia had to be pre-inspected by the Société Générale de Surveillance.[53]

- The country wants an estimate of the currency requirements it will face in the short term, and uses the value of the shipments, as determined by the PSIs, to forecast its foreign currency needs.

- The country wants to generate some revenues in addition to the tariff it charges. Most of the countries requiring PSIs have long-term contracts giving an exclusive right to a single inspection company to inspect all the goods about to enter its territory. Although it is pure speculation, it is likely that inspection companies compensate the country for this exclusive right by transferring a portion of the revenues generated by inspections to the national treasury.

Banana Wars

In 1993, the European Union, in an effort to support the economies of some of its members' former colonies in the Caribbean and Africa, devised a complex system of quotas, preferential tariffs, and import licenses to favor bananas imported from these countries. Even though it is not an exporter of bananas, the United States was drawn in this dispute because two of the companies affected by these restrictions were Dole Foods and Chiquita Brands, two American firms exporting bananas grown in Central America to Europe.[54]

Even after three rulings against this practice by the WTO, the European Union maintained this convoluted system of preferential treatment, and the United States eventually retaliated with higher tariffs on products from Europe. The "banana wars" escalated to a point where it involved the highest levels of government, and it took years to be resolved, despite the efforts of

WTO panels to ease the tension and resolve the issue.[55]

In early 2001, Chiquita Brands took the unusual step of suing the European Union for U.S.$ 525 million, which the company claims were lost profits the company incurred because of the restrictions, and which caused it to default on its bond payments.[56]

The spat between the United States and the European Union is now over, and European consumers pay slightly less for bananas today than they did when the trade barrier was in place. However, there were additional conflicts between the European Union and some of the countries in which bananas are produced; in 2012, the WTO ruled in favor of ten Latin American countries in a dispute that alleged that the European Union's trade policies favored Caribbean and African producers of bananas. In 2009, the EU had agreed to reduce its tariffs on Latin American bananas from € 176 per tonne to € 114 per tonne over an eight-year period.[57]

17.3   Customs Clearing Process

The customs clearing process differs from country to country. In some countries, the process tends to be arcane and cumbersome; in others, it's a relatively simple process. The World Bank records the number of hours that it takes to clear goods through customs: the worst offender is Venezuela, requiring an estimated 1330 hours of work to import goods, and the best performers are the countries of the European Union, with only one hour of work required. The United States requires about 10 hours of work for each entry.[58] In most countries, because of the complexity of the task, only certified customs brokers or customs agents can file the paperwork necessary to clear customs. This section will give only a brief overview of the processes generally followed by customs authorities worldwide and give examples based upon the U.S. system.

17.3.1   General Process

In some countries, the customs-clearing process starts with an application for an import license, a request for the express authorization to import a certain product. Import licenses are granted according to several criteria, most of which are based on the availability of foreign currency to pay for the import and on the availability of domestic substitutes. Countries with scarce foreign-currency resources generally attempt to limit import licenses to those companies that have generated export revenues, and to those companies purchasing goods for which no close domestic substitute is available.

entry
The process by which an importer notifies Customs that it has imported a product.

cleared
The term used to indicate that the goods were imported in the country and that the importer paid the correct amount of duty.

For most countries, however, the customs-clearing process simply starts when an importer files an entry (*i.e.*, notifies the customs authorities that it will import—or has imported—a product). There is usually an electronic or paper form (see Figure 17.3 on page 596) that must be filed and which must be accompanied by all the documents associated with the import: the exporter's invoice, a Certificate of Origin, a Certificate of Inspection (when required), a Certificate of Insurance, and other forms as required by the customs rules of the importing country.

In most developed countries, the importer is usually responsible for classifying the goods according to the tariff schedule of the importing country, and for determining the amount of duty. In many developing countries, this task is still left to the customs authorities, a requirement which often delays the process of clearance. In most instances, the goods are not released to the importer (cleared) until after the duty is paid or after there is evidence that the importer will pay, a requirement often met with a customs bond (see Section 17.3.3). Generally, customs authorities review a percentage of the entries made by importers after the goods have been cleared and have a few months to a couple of years to challenge them. If an entry is reviewed satisfactorily, the entry is deemed liquidated. In some countries, such as the United States, an importer dissatisfied with the final decision of customs authorities has a brief period to protest a liquidated entry and request a review before the entry is settled.

liquidated entry
An entry that has been successfully reviewed by Customs authorities, and for which duty has been paid.

protest
A process by which an importer can file a grievance after an entry is liquidated, so that Customs reviews classification, valuation, and country of origin.

Customs broker
A person authorized by Customs authorities to file entries.

17.3.2 Customs Brokers

Because of the complexity and time-consuming nature of filling out customs entries, many countries demand that importers delegate the task of interacting with customs to a customs broker. A customs broker is a representative of the importer who has acquired the knowledge and experience required to deal effectively and efficiently with customs. In many countries, customs brokers are the only entities qualified to enter goods (*i.e.*, fill out the paperwork necessary to import goods). This is not the case in the United States, though, where importers can complete their own entries, as long as they have posted a customs bond. Customs brokers are usually compensated on a fee basis for each entry they handle. In the United States, customs brokers are highly qualified individuals who must take a grueling test on issues of classification, duty computation, and quotas, before being allowed to manage importers' entries.

17.3.3 Customs Bonds

In most countries, the importer must pay the duty to customs before the shipment can be legally released. However, this can be extremely unwieldy, especially in those cases where the shipment is an express package or is time sensitive (*e.g.*, perishable produce). Therefore, customs authorities allow importers (or customs brokers entering goods on their behalf) to post a surety bond, which guarantees that the importer or the customs broker will eventually pay the duty. A surety bond is generally a sum of money deposited with customs, from which any unpaid duty can be withdrawn, or an insurance policy with a surety company that acts as a guarantor of the importer or the customs broker, which is required to pay if the importer or the broker does not pay the duty on time. This process allows goods to be entered before the duty is paid. In some cases, the goods are sold long before the entry is liquidated.

Customs bond
A sum of money collected by Customs from Customs brokers, that is held as a guarantee that duty will be paid in the correct amount.

In the United States, the bond is not just a guarantee that the duty will be paid on time; it is also a contract that obligates the importer or the customs broker to perform all customs-related functions in a timely manner, such as filing entries that are complete and accurate, as well as presenting customs with the goods after they have physically entered the country, generally for inspection purposes.

Canadian Food Inspection Agency **Agence canadienne d'inspection des aliments**

IMPORT DECLARATION   **DÉCLARATION D'IMPORTATION**

1			
☐ Dairy Products / Produits laitiers	☐ Processed Fruits and Vegetables / Fruits et légumes transfrmés	☐ Honey / Miel	☐ Maple Products / Produits de l'érable
☐ Pesticides / Semences	☐ Seeds / Semences	☐ Feed / Aliments du bétail	☐ Fertilizer * / Engrais *

* Registrable / Sujets à l'enregistrement

2. Name and Address of Manufacturer / Nom et adresse du febricant	3. Name and Address of Exporter / Nom et adresse de l'exportateur
4. Name and Canadian Address of Importer / Nom et adresse canadienne de l'importateur	5. Name and Address of Destination (consignee) / Nom et adresse du destinataire
Telephone Number / Numéro de téléphone ➡	Telephone Number / Numéro de téléphone ➡
6. Transaction No. / N° de transaction	7. Carrier / Transporteur
	9. Container No. / N° de conteneur
8. Flight No. / N° de vol	10. Trailer No. / N° de remorque

PRODUCT DESCRIPTION AND PACKAGING (ATTACH LIST IF NECESSARY)
DESCRIPTION DU PRODUIT ET DE L'EMBALLAGE (ANNEXER UNE LISTE AU BESOIN)

11. Common Name / Nom usuel	12. Brand Name / Marque	13. Grade / Catégorie	14. No. of Shipping Containers / Nbre de contenants

15. No., Type and Net Contents of Individual Containers per Shipping Container / Nbre, type et contenu net des contenants individuels par contenant d'expédition	16. Total Net Quantity / Quantité totale nette	17. Label Approval No. / N°. d'approbation de l'étiquette	18. Registration No. / N° d'enregistrement	19. Purpose of Importation / Motif de l'importation	20. Additional documentation and other references / Documents additionnels et autres références

21. Declaration / Déclaration

I, _____ the importer of the products described on this form do hereby certify that the information provided on this form is complete, correct and accurately describes the products contained in the shipment.

By signing this declaration in the case of the food products used for human consumption, I affirm that I have read the "Regulatory Requirements for Food Products Imported into Canada" set forth in the instructions to fill out this form and that the products described on this form meet those requirements.

Je, _____, l'importateur des Produits décrits sur ce formulaire, certifie que l'information fournie sur ce formulaire est complète et qu'elle décrit avec précision les produits contenues dans cechargement.

En signant cette déclaration, dans le cas de produits alimentaires utilisés pour consommation humaine, j'affirme que j'ai lu les "Exigences réglementaires pour les produits alimentaires importés au Canada" inscrites dans les instructions pour remplir ce formulaire et que les produits décrits sur ce formulaire satisfont ces exigences.

_____   _____
Signature   Date

GOVERNMENT USE ONLY / RÉSERVÉ A L'ADMINISTRATION

22. Stamp / Estampe	23. Instructions to Customs and Importers /Directives aux douaniers et importateurs
	☐ Release to the control of AAFC (i.e. inspection at destination) at the time of importation / Au moment de l'importation, main levée et remise sous le contrôle d'AAC (pour l'inspection à l'arrivée à destination)
	Further action to be conducted on the shipment at the following place:
	☐ Autres mesures à prendre à l'égard du chargement à l'endroit suivant :
	☐ Other instruction / Instruction particulière

The information is collected by the Canadian Food Inspection Agency for the purpose of administering all Agriculture Acts. Information may be accessible or protected as required under the provisions of the Access to Information Act.

L'information est recueillie par l'Agence canadienne d'inspection des aliments aux fins d'application de la législation agricole. L'information peut être accessible ou protégée en vertu des exigences de la Loi sur l'accès à l'information.

Canadä

CFIA / ACIA 4560 (1999/06)

Figure 17.3: Canadian Import Form for Food Products
Canadian Food Inspection Agency.

17.3.4 Informed Compliance and Reasonable Care

The U.S. Customs Modification Act of 1993 created the concepts of informed compliance and reasonable care, neither of which can be easily defined, but both of which have become pivotal to the efforts of Customs and Border Protection in the United States.

The idea behind informed compliance is that, if an importer has been trained in classifying and valuing goods for import purposes, it is more likely to perform these tasks correctly. If the importer has been found to exert reasonable care in the past, the likelihood that one of its shipments is going to be inspected is minimal, thereby minimizing entry delays and allowing the importer to organize its supply chain more predictably. This also lowers costs, as merchandise is cleared quickly and does not languish in some bonded warehouse while the importer and customs argue about its correct classification, valuation, or country of origin.

For an importer to be found compliant, it must show that it exercised reasonable care when filing its customs entries. To demonstrate reasonable care, the importer must follow a long list of obligations that the U.S. Customs and Border Protection Office provides.[59] These obligations ensure that the importer employs a customs specialist, who in turn ensures that all—including the most recent—customs regulations are followed and that the importer has a process by which it correctly determines the valuation, classification, and country of origin of an import. Reasonable care is monitored through a system of compliance audits organized by U.S. Customs.[60]

informed compliance
A standard of behavior, enforced by U.S. Customs, that is expected of importers if they want their entries to be cleared quickly and inspections kept to a minimum.

reasonable care
A standard of behavior, enforced by U.S. Customs, that is expected of importers if they want their entries to be cleared quickly and inspections kept to a minimum.

17.3.5 Required Documentation

The documentation required by any customs authority can be extensive. Ideally, there should be only three documents required in every country to make an entry:

- A form designated for entry (specific to the record-keeping requirements of the importing country)

- A Certificate of Origin to ascertain the goods' country of origin

- A commercial invoice with enough information to determine the goods' valuation and classification

However, many more forms can be required, from an import license to a series of certificates or other documents (most of these documents were introduced and explained in Chapter 9). Many countries' requirements are available online; many of the forms for many countries can be accessed through the export.gov website, maintained by the U.S. Department of Commerce's International Trade Administration.[61]

The critical element of import documentation is that it is established on a per-transaction basis. Every import, however small, must have its own specific entry, which can lead to an inordinate amount of paperwork, under which both the importer and the customs authorities are drowning. The United States has implemented an International Trade Data System, which is also called the Automated Commercial Environment and the "single window" system, through which all entries can be completed electronically, and with which entries can be entered monthly rather than one by one. Payment of duty can also be completed monthly.[62]

17.3.6 Required Markings

Products imported into a country often require a marking—*made in [country]* or *product of [country]*—printed on or affixed to the product or its packaging. Rules differ from country to country on the location of the marking, its size, and whether it needs to be permanently attached to the product. The country placed on the marking is also determined by rules put into place by the country of importation. However, there are no known instances of a country on the marking being different from the country of origin for customs duty purposes.

In the United States, markings are required for most products, although the U.S. Customs and Border Protection maintains a list of exceptions, mostly products on which it is difficult or impossible to place a marking. All markings must be legible, conspicuous, and durable. However, the United States has an additional, unusual requirement. No product imported into the United States can have a name or package that may mislead the public as to its country of origin. It is therefore prohibited to include words such as "American," "United States," or "U.S.A." on the package that may lead consumers into thinking that the product is of U.S. origin. Inappropriate or missing markings are subject to penalties, liquidated damages, and seizures by U.S. Customs.

Finally, there is the issue of the *made in the USA* label, which is often a marketing advantage for U.S. companies in the U.S. market. Although the Federal Trade Commission considered lowering the minimum United States content to 75 percent of a product's value, it has maintained this content at "all or virtually all" of a product for the foreseeable future, making it all but impossible to mark a product as made in the United States unless it is entirely domestically produced.[63]

17.3.7 Merchandise Visas

merchandise visa
A document, provided by the exporting country, that allows an exporter to ship goods subject to a quota in the importing country.

For products whose importation is limited by quotas, and particularly for textile products, a bilateral monitoring system is sometimes implemented by the importing and exporting countries.

Because there is a maximum quantity of goods that can be imported into a country in a calendar year, the government of the exporting country will grant the right to export a set quantity of a specific good to the country with the import quota. Such authorization is a merchandise visa. The exporting country's government can grant the merchandise visa through a lottery, through a determination made upon prior sales, or simply sell the merchandise visa to an exporting firm. The visa specifies the type of good (by Harmonized System number), the quantity, and the destination country to which the exporter can sell.

For products for which such a system is in place, the visa is added to the required documents that must be presented to the customs authorities of the importing countries, and often to the customs authorities of the exporting country as well. As quotas are slowly eliminated, so should be the visa requirements. Nevertheless, although merchandise visas were once predicted to become obsolete, they have not disappeared, and they are often required as part of the documentation package for an import.

17.3.8 Duty Drawbacks

Several countries, including the United States, grant a substantial tax break to exporters who use imported parts in the products they export. Such a tax break is called a duty drawback.

duty drawback
A process by which an exporter can be reimbursed for duty that it paid on products that it imported but which products it eventually exported.

In the United States, U.S. Customs and Border Protection will refund 99 percent of the duty paid by an importer in one of three cases:

- For merchandise that is rejected by the importer as non-conforming to the original purchase order

- For imported products that are re-exported unused

- For imported parts that are used—without substantial transformation—in the assembly or manufacturing of products that are eventually re-exported

Note that this duty drawback is not available for products exported to NAFTA countries.

This drawback can often represent a considerable savings. However, few U.S. firms take advantage of this duty drawback opportunity, either because they do not know about it or because they fear the paperwork requirements that accompany this program. Actually, the paperwork requirements used to be mind-boggling: for example, to take advantage of the "unused" drawback, customs required importers to track individual items from their time of import to the time at which they were leaving the country. However, the requirements have been relaxed, allowing "commercially interchangeable goods" to qualify as exports for the drawback.[64] In exchange for this flexibility, customs has substantially stiffened penalties for illegitimate drawbacks.

Duty drawbacks can be used by some countries to bolster exports. Historically, Korea and Taiwan supported their exporters by allowing them to engage in aggressive duty drawbacks, for example.[65] In other cases, countries have been accused of using drawbacks to engage in protectionism. Since exporters using imported goods get reimbursed for the duty that they pay upon importing them, the tariff rates can be high, and the companies do not complain. However, these high duty rates prevent other importers, who would sell the goods in the country, from being competitive.[66]

17.4   Foreign Trade Zones

Foreign Trade Zones (FTZs) are locations of a country that have a special customs status. Foreign Trade Zones—sometimes called Free Trade Zones—are areas of a country that, for customs purposes, still are located "outside" of a country. Practically, that means that goods can be shipped to the FTZ without being subject to the duties, quotas, and customs regulations of the host country. In most countries, however, including the United States, goods admitted into an FTZ must be legal in the country in which the zone is located; the exemption applies only for customs purposes, not to other legal requirements. For example, medical devices not yet approved in the country in which the FTZ is located would not be acceptable in that FTZ, even though the devices may be perfectly legal in other countries.

Once in the FTZ, the goods can be warehoused until they are sent to their final destination, either in the host or in a foreign country. If the goods are sold in the host country, they are dutiable only at the time of sale. If they are sold abroad, they are dutiable only in the importing country; the country in which the FTZ is located will never collect any duty on the value of that merchandise. The country of origin used for customs purposes remains the country from which the goods originated, rather than the country in which the FTZ is located.

Foreign Trade Zones exist in one form or another in nearly every country. The most common form of FTZ is a location through which cargo transits. For example, most ports are FTZs, so that cargo can be unloaded from a ship, temporarily stored in a warehouse, and then loaded onto another vessel to its final destination. Such cargo, although physically present in the country in which the port is located, never enters the country from a Customs' Office perspective, and is therefore never assessed duty. Because shipping companies are moving toward a system of very large containerships serving very large hub ports, from which smaller, so-called feeder ships are serving smaller ports, the importance of FTZs is expected to increase. Airports, which often operate on the same concept of "hub and spoke," also often possess a few warehouses in an FTZ. Because such FTZs are available to all companies involved in international trade, the United States calls them General Purpose (Foreign Trade) Zones.

Foreign Trade Zones

Another type of FTZ is not located in a port or cargo area, but at a corporation's place of business, such as a plant or a refinery. In most of these types of trade zones, some economic activity beyond simple warehousing is conducted, such as manufacturing, assembly, repackaging, and refining. The FTZ is created with the purpose of creating jobs in the host country by providing a lower cost structure to the businesses using them, because the business does not have to pay duty on the goods that are being processed and are eventually re-exported.

Another way a business can save money by obtaining FTZ status is when the host country has an "inverted" tariff structure (*i.e.*, the tariffs charged on parts are higher than the tariffs charged on the final product). Such FTZ locations are called "subzones" in the United States, affiliated for legal purposes with a General Purpose Foreign Trade Zone, because these locations are available to only a specific company and not to others. An interesting issue arises when a substantial transformation takes place in an FTZ and the goods change from one Harmonized System (HS) classification to another. Even though the rules of origin call for the goods to be "made" in the country in which this change of HS number took place—the country in which the FTZ is located, in this case—negotiations between customs and the company determine the country of origin that is used for duty purposes, be it the country of origin of the parts used, or that of the main component, or yet some other alternative. In any case, it is never the country in which the change in HS took place.

Foreign Trade Zones can be quite advantageous to hold goods in inventory until they are sold, improving the cash flow of their owners, to wait for a numerical quota to open, or for an inspection by the host country's government. However, in view of the progress made in the last few years by the WTO to lead countries toward lower tariffs and increased trade, FTZs created for other purposes than cargo transfers may have a limited future because their advantages are dwindling.

Review and Discussion Questions

1. What is a Harmonized System number? How is it used? What are the advantages of such a system?

2. Explain the concept of valuation from the perspective of customs. Why is it important to have a detailed commercial invoice for valuation?

3. Explain the concept of classification from the perspective of customs. Why is it important to have a detailed commercial invoice for classification?

4. Explain the concept of country of origin. How is it currently determined? Why is it such a difficult concept? Why is it important?

5. What are non-tariff barriers? Why are they used? Give a few examples.

6. What are the types of quotas in existence? How does the United States enforce the quotas it imposes? What is a merchandise visa?

Notes

[1]"Membership," World Customs Organization, http://www.wcoomd.org/en/about-us/wco-members/membership.aspx, retrieved March 29, 2017.

[2]*Ibid.*

[3]Harmonized Tariff Schedule (2017 HTSA Basic Edition), United States International Trade Commission, https://hts.usitc.gov/current, retrieved March 29, 2017.

[4]"General Rules for the Interpretation of the Harmonized System," World Customs Organization, http://www.wcoomd.org/en/faq/7/media/B7BC612CEB3B417BB5183841DA7413CB.ashx, retrieved March 29, 2017.

[5]"Requirements for Electronic Ruling Requests," November 17, 2016, United States Customs and Border Protection, https://www.cbp.gov/trade/rulings/eruling-requirements, retrieved March 29, 2017.

[6]"Technical Information on Customs Valuation," World Trade Organization, http://www.wto.org/english/tratop_e/cusval_e/cusval_info_e.htm, retrieved July 5, 2013.

[7]*Ibid.*

[8]"Understanding the Agreements," World Trade Organization, http://www.wto.org/english/thewto_e/whatis_e/tif_e/agrm9_e.htm#origin, retrieved March 30, 2017.

[9]Manatt, Phelps, and Phillipps, LLP, "So...Where you from? The Use of 'Country of Origin' violations as the basis for False Claims Act *qui tam*s Spreads to the Medical Device Industry," April 21, 2015, http://www.lexology.com/library/detail.aspx?g=c66c2094-f4a8-49a4-bb62-d63c7c1edd0f, retrieved March 30, 2017.

[10]Roth, Martin S., and Jean B. Romeo, "Matching Product Category and Country Image Perceptions: A Framework for Managing Country-of-Origin Effects," *Journal of International Business Studies*, third quarter 1992, pp. 477-497.

[11]"Rules of Origin (Preference Criteria)," North American Free Trade Agreement, U.S. Customs and Border Protection, http://www.cbp.gov/xp/cgov/trade/trade_programs/international_agreements/free_trade/nafta/rules_of_origin/, accessed March 30, 2017.

[12]"General Aspects of Preferential Origin," Taxation and Customs Union, http://ec.europa.eu/taxation_customs/customs/customs_duties/rules_origin/preferential/index_en.htm, retrieved March 30, 2017.

[13]Gillis, Chris, "Origin Compliance Challenges Shippers," *American Shipper*, March 2004, pp. 36-37.

[14]General Note 3: Rates of Duty, "Harmonized Tariff Schedule Online Reference Tool," 2017, United States International Trade Commission, http://hts.usitc.gov, retrieved March 30, 2017.

[15]"Generalized System of Preferences (GSP)," Office of the United States Trade Representative, http://www.ustr.gov/trade-topics/trade-development/preference-programs/generalized-system-preference-gsp, retrieved March 30, 2017.

[16]"Generalized System of Preferences (GSP)," United States Customs and Border Protection, https://help.cbp.gov/app/answers/detail/a_id/266/7/generalized-system-of-preferences-(gsp), retrieved March 30, 2017.

[17]Jones, Vivian, "Generalized System of Preferences: Background and Renewal Debate," January 9, 2013, Congressional Research Service, www.fas.org/sgp/crs/misc/RL33663.pdf, retrieved July 5, 2013.

[18]"Harmonized Tariff Schedule Online Reference Tool," 2017, United States International Trade Commission, http://hts.usitc.gov, retrieved March 30, 2017.

[19]"Harmonized Tariff Schedule Online Reference Tool," 2017, United States International Trade Commission, http://hts.usitc.gov, retrieved March 30, 2017.

[20]Donahue, Bill, "Ann Taylor Latest To Sue Over Gender-Based Tariffs," *Law360*, http://www.law360-

.com/articles/440379/ann-taylor-latest-to-sue-over-gender-based-tariffs, retrieved July 5, 2013.

[21] Taylor, Lori, and Jawad Dar, "Fairer Trade: Removing Gender Bias in U.S. Import Taxes," *The Takeaway*, March 2015, **6**:3, http://bush.tamu.edu/mosbacher/takeaway/V6-3 Tariff Discrimination Takeaway.pdf, retrieved March 30, 2017.

[22] Kulish, Eric, "Dumped On," *American Shipper*, July 2004, pp. 7-16.

[23] *2004 Annual Report*, The Timken Company, Canton, Ohio.

[24] Meller, Paul, and Elizabeth Becker, "U.S. Loses Trade Cases and Faces Penalties," *The New York Times*, September 1, 2004.

[25] David, Bob, and Jon Hilsenrath, "Globalization Backers Face End of an Era," *The Wall Street Journal*, March 30, 2017, p.A1.

[26] *Ibid.*

[27] *Office of International Trade Textile and Quota Newsletter*, January 2012, http://www.cbp.gov/-linkhandler/cgov/trade/trade_outreach/trade_newsletter/textile_jan.ctt/textile_jan.pdf, retrieved July 5, 2013.

[28] "Commodities Subject to Import Quotas," U.S. Customs and Border Protection, January 12, 2016, https://www.cbp.gov/trade/quota/guide-import-goods/commodities, retrieved March 30, 2017.

[29] "Ambassador Froman Announces FY 2017 WTO Tariff-Rate Quota Allocations for Raw Cane Sugar, Refined and Specialty Sugar and Sugar-Containing Products," Office of the United States Trade Representative, May 6, 2016, https://ustr.gov/about-us/policy-offices/press-office/press-releases/-2016/may/USTR-Froman-announces-FY-2017-WTO-TRQ-Allocations-Sugar, retrieved March 30, 2017.

[30] Chapter 17, "Harmonized Tariff Schedule Online Reference Tool," 2017, United States International Trade Commission, http://hts.usitc.gov, retrieved March 30, 2017.

[31] "Sugar Monthly Price—US cents per Pound," Index Mundi, http://www.indexmundi.com/commodities/?commodity=sugar&months=60, retrieved March 30, 2017.

[32] Lukas, Aaron, "A Sticky State of Affairs: Sugar and the U.S.-Australia Free-Trade Agreement," *CATO Institute*, February 9, 2004, https://www.cato.org/publications/free-trade-bulletin/sticky-state-affairs-sugar-us-australia-free-trade-agreement, retrieved March 30, 2017.

[33] "Ambassador Froman Announces FY 2017 WTO Tariff-Rate Quota Allocations for Raw Cane Sugar, Refined and Specialty Sugar and Sugar-Containing Products," Office of the United States Trade Representative, May 6, 2016, https://ustr.gov/about-us/policy-offices/press-office/press-releases/-2016/may/USTR-Froman-announces-FY-2017-WTO-TRQ-Allocations-Sugar, retrieved March 30, 2017.

[34] "Centrifugal Sugar Production by Country," http://www.indexmundi.com/AGRICULTURE/?commodity=centrifugal-sugar&graph=PRODUCTION, retrieved March 30, 2017.

[35] "U.S. sugar deliveries," U.S. Department of Agriculture, March 16, 2017, https://www.ers.usda.gov/data-products/sugar-and-sweeteners-yearbook-tables/sugar-and-sweeteners-yearbook-tables/#U.S. Sugar Supply and Use, retrieved March 30, 2017.

[36] Malkin, Elisabeth, "In Mexico, Sugar vs. Corn Syrup," *The New York Times*, June 9, 2004.

[37] Dominican Republic, "The World Fact Book," and Haiti, "The World Fact Book," Central Intelligence Agency, https://www.cia.gov/library/publications/the-world-factbook, accessed March 30, 2017.

[38] Flicking, David, "The Land that GM Forgot," *Bloomberg News*, February 1, 2017, https://www.bloomberg.com/gadfly/articles/2017-02-01/the-land-that-gm-forgot, retrieved March 30, 2017.

[39] chevroletjapan.com, accessed March 30, 2017.

[40] "U.S.-Mexico Avocado Trade Dispute," American University in Washington, http://www1.american.edu/ted/avocado.htm, retrieved July 5, 2013.

[41] Riley, Kate, "Finally! Mexico ends its tariffs on Washington's apples and cherries and pears and ...," *The Seattle Times*, July 6, 2011.

[42]"WTO disputes with New Zealand a third party complainant," New Zealand Ministry of Foreign Affairs and Trade, April 7, 2011, http://www.mfat.govt.nz/Treaties-and-International-Law/02-Trade-law-and-free-trade-agreements/0-Japan-Apples.php, retrieved July 5, 2013.

[43]"Win-win ending to the 'hormone beef trade war'," *European Parliament News*, March 14, 2011, http://www.europarl.europa.eu/news/en/pressroom/content/20120314IPR40752/html/Win-win-end-ing-to-the-hormone-beef-trade-war, retrieved July 5, 2013.

[44]Harmon, Amy, and Andrew Pollack, "Battle Brewing Over Labeling of Genetically Modified Food," *The New York Times*, May 24, 2012.

[45]Linn, Gene, "U.S. Renews Attack on Asian Barriers to Food Exports," *The Journal of Commerce*, April 23, 1998, p. 1A.

[46]"The Second Battle of Poitiers," *Time*, December 6, 1982, p. 31.

[47]Rao, N. Vasuki, "India to Introduce EDI to Cut Paperwork," *Journal of Commerce*, November 24, 1998, p. 3A.

[48]Trade Across Borders, The World Bank, http://www.doingbusiness.org/data/exploretopics/trad-ing-across-borders, accessed March 31, 2017.

[49]"Customs Law Advisory—Court Decision Details The Costs of Failure to Maintain Records To Support Import Declaration," Steptoe and Johnson, LLP, January 30, 2007, http://www.steptoe.com/publi-cations-4183.html, retrieved July 5, 2013.

[50]"225,279 Imported Cars were Newly Registered in 2016," Korea Automobile Importers and Distributors Association, January 5, 2017, http://www.kaida.co.kr/en/kaida/bbsView.do?boardSeq=17-&articleSeq=49599, retrieved March 31, 2017.

[51]"What are these Korean non-tariff barriers to U.S. cars and trucks?", Korea-U.S. FTA, July 2, 2010, http://benmuse.typepad.com/koreaus_fta/2010/07/what-are-these-korean-nontariff-barriers-to-us-auto-imports.html, retrieved July 5, 2013.

[52]Banerjee, Neela, and Helene Cooper, "Are Russians Playing a Game of Chicken with . . . Chickens?", *The Wall Street Journal*, March 18, 1996, p. B1.

[53]Borsuk, Richard, "Changing of the Port Guards: Some Importers Fear a Return to Corruption," *Asian Wall Street Journal*, April 7, 1997, p. 14.

[54]Weinstein, Michael M., "Banana Spat Could Have Serious Consequences for World Trade," *The New York Times*, December 29, 1998.

[55]Zaroscostas, John, "EU Officials Reject Plan to Ease Banana Gridlock," *Journal of Commerce*, January 27, 1999, p. 3A.

[56]DePalma, Anthony, "Chiquita Sues Europeans, Citing Banana-Quota Losses," *The New York Times*, January 26, 2001.

[57]"Banana war ends after 20 years," *BBC News*, November 8, 2012, http://www.bbc.com/news/bus-iness-20263308, retrieved March 30, 2017.

[58]Trade Across Borders, The World Bank, http://www.doingbusiness.org/data/exploretopics/trad-ing-across-borders, accessed March 31, 2017.

[59]"What Every Member of the Trade Community Should Know About: Reasonable Care," February 2004, U.S. Customs and Border Protection, http://www.cbp.gov/linkhandler/cgov/trade/legal/inform-ed_compliance_pubs/icp021.ctt/icp021.pdf, retrieved July 6, 2013.

[60]"Customs Compliance and Reasonable Care under the Mod Act," Samuel Shapiro and Company, Inc., http://www.shapiro.com/html/Compliance1.html, retrieved July 6, 2013.

[61]http://export.gov/logistics, retrieved March 31, 2017.

[62]"ACE and Automated Systems," U.S. Customs and Border Protection, https://www.cbp.gov/trade/-automated#, retrieved March 31, 2017.

[63]"Complying with the Made in USA Standard," Federal Trade Commission, https://www.ftc.gov/tips-

advice/business-center/guidance/complying-made-usa-standard, retrieved March 31, 2017.

[64]MacCausland, Shawn, "CBP Eases Process for Claiming Drawback on Unused Merchandise," Sandler, Travis & Rosenberg Trade Report, http://www.strtrade.com/publications-cbp-unused-merchandise-drawback-040913.html, retrieved July 6, 2013.

[65]"Export Competitiveness and Duty Drawback," The World Bank, http://go.worldbank.org/KV8U1-ULIT0, retrieved July 5, 2013.

[66]Cadot, Olivier, Jaime de Melo, and Marcelo Olarreaga, "Can duty-drawbacks have a protectionist bias? Evidence from MERCOSUR," January 31, 2010, The World Bank, http://go.worldbank.org/70G3A-9ZRB0, retrieved July 6, 2013.

Chapter 18

Supply Chain
Operations—Inventory

An international logistics manager must make sure that the goods that the company offers for sale are available. This goal is usually more difficult to achieve for a company selling abroad, as the number of "things that can wrong" in the global environment is much greater. Therefore, ensuring item availability usually means that the company must have a good, comprehensive inventory policy, that covers both the warehouses it owns or operates and the facilities of its distributors abroad.

In an international environment, some inventory problems are exacerbated, as companies experience higher costs and longer transit times that can be affected by many uncontrollable variables, such as weather, customs clearance delays, or simply time zones. This environment makes providing good service much more challenging.

Unlike in domestic markets, it is challenging to provide Just-in-Time (JIT) deliveries to international customers, because transit times are longer and are affected by several uncontrollable variables.

The techniques shown in this chapter form the bases of a good inventory management for a company doing business internationally.

18.1   Aspects of Inventory Management

There are two types of demand to consider when approaching inventory management, and the techniques used to manage them are different.

dependent demand
A product has a dependent demand if its sales are based on the sales of another product.

A **dependent demand** item is one for which sales depend on the sales of another product; for example, sales of parts to an Original Equipment Manufacturer (OEM) are considered dependent upon the sales of the final product. The sales of the final product are forecasted, and the ones on which sales efforts are focused. Examples of such parts are tires sold to an automobile company, hydraulic hoses sold to a manufacturer of heavy earth-moving equipment, and memory chips sold to a computer assembly plant. The sales of these parts are "dependent" on the sales of automobiles, bulldozers and computers, as the quantity ordered flows from the final product's sales. The techniques used for this situation are described in Section 18.6.

independent demand
A product has an independent demand if it is sold directly to consumers or customers.

An **independent demand** item is one for which sales do not depend on the sales of another item. In general, the product is sold directly to an end-user organization or to another reseller. Examples of independent demand items are tires sold to a retail chain of mass-merchandisers, hydraulic hoses sold to heavy equipment repair shops, and memory chips sold directly to a company repairing or updating computer systems. The sales of these parts are "independent" in that the quantity sold is not dependent on the sales of another product, but only on the company's marketing efforts. The techniques shown in Sections 18.2 to 18.4 relate mostly to items that have an independent demand, but they are also used for dependent-demand items.

An important aspect of the efficient management of independent-demand items is that their sales volume must be forecasted as accurately as possible.

There are many forecasting techniques, from simple-moving-average techniques to neural-network algorithms, all of which can be used to help forecast the demand for independent demand items. There are also many textbooks focused on forecasting techniques.[1,2,3,4,5]

18.1.1 Management Alternatives

There are only a few ways to approach the management of inventories: the periodic re-order model and the fixed-order-quantity model are relevant to managing independent-demand and dependent-demand products. Materials Requirement Planning (MRP) applies only to dependent-demand products.

Periodic Re-order Model

In a periodic re-order model, the inventory is checked at a given set interval, such as weekly or monthly, and an order quantity is calculated to replenish the inventory to a certain level; this order quantity is variable, changing based on the product sales during the period.

periodic re-order model
An inventory-management technique in which inventory levels are checked at intervals, and the re-order quantity is variable.

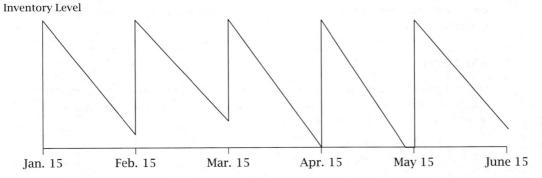

Figure 18.1: Periodic Re-order Model

The periodic re-order method of inventory management can be employed for some goods, but it presents several disadvantages; the varying order quantity is more difficult to manage (different purchase orders, different freight costs), but most importantly, it is possible to experience a stock-out situation (*i.e.* the inventory is completely depleted before the next shipment comes in, and therefore it is impossible to deliver to the customer on time). Such a stock-out occurred just before May 15 in Figure 18.1.

fixed-order-quantity model
An inventory-management technique in which inventory levels are checked continuously, and the re-order quantity is fixed.

Fixed-order-quantity Model

In a fixed-order-quantity model, the level of inventory is monitored continuously, and when the inventory reaches a certain level, an order is placed. The order quantity purchased is constant, but the intervals between replenishment orders varies. The fixed-order-quantity model is the inventory model that is most commonly followed.

Inventory Level

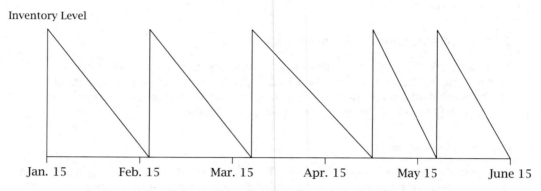

| Jan. 15 | Feb. 15 | Mar. 15 | Apr. 15 | May 15 | June 15 |

Figure 18.2: Fixed Order Quantity Model

Modern technology facilitates the use of this method. The electronic tracking systems in place in most organizations monitor inventory on a continuous basis, and automatically re-order the products when inventory reaches a pre-determined level.

MRP Models

Materials Requirement Planning (MRP)
A management tool that allows a manufacturer to determine what to produce and in which quantity, in function of what it sells to its customers.

Dependent-demand products are managed using computer-based processes that are collectively known as Materials Requirement Planning. These models will be described in Section 18.6 on page 625.

18.1.2   Inventory Costs

Inventory costs can be divided into two categories; those that are related to holding the item in inventory, and those costs related to the activities involved in replenishing the inventory.

Holding Costs

holding costs
The costs of having inventory on hand. Holding costs increase as the number of goods in inventory increases.

carrying costs
Another term used for holding costs.

Holding costs—also called carrying costs or inventory-carrying costs—are dominated by the cost of the capital immobilized in inventory; the inventory is either financed through stock, bonds or bank loans, which all have a cost. This major component of the inventory-carrying costs can be approximated by the firm's cost of capital.

Additional inventory holding costs include warehousing costs, such as space (especially in a public warehouse, in which space is rented), insurance, and utilities. In addition, the larger the inventory, the greater the labor costs and amount of equipment necessary to manage and handle this inventory. In addition, in some countries, taxes are sometimes collected on the value of the facility's assets, including the inventory.

Carrying costs also include other costs, such as what is commonly called "shrinkage:" pilferage, theft, damage due to poor handling, misplaced items, or items lost to mistakes in labeling and marking. Other costs may be industry-specific, such as product obsolescence; either the arrival of a new model—what to do with the 2018 models once the 2019 models are available for sale—or the emergence of a new technology.

Inventory holding costs are directly proportional to the size of the inventory; the larger the inventory, the higher the inventory carrying costs.

In an international setting, inventory carrying costs are generally higher than in a domestic setting; the costs of land, labor, taxes, and management may be higher. However, simply because it is more difficult to control costs and manage a facility located away from the home office, carrying costs are assumed to be higher than domestically.

Ordering Costs

Ordering costs are the costs associated with replenishing inventory. Ordering costs include the costs of writing the purchase order, receiving the merchandise, unpacking it, stocking it, processing the invoice, paying the invoice, and other transaction-related costs. Ordering costs are independent of the size of the shipment, *i.e.* they are the same from shipment to shipment.

ordering costs
The costs of placing an inventory-replenishment order. Ordering costs are unaffected by the size of the order.

In an international environment, ordering costs tend to be higher, as the transactions are more complex and involve more steps:

- **Transaction Costs**—The transaction costs for an international transaction are higher than for a domestic shipment; for example, the costs of opening a letter of credit (or paying through documentary credit) are higher than paying with an open account. Packing and unpacking costs are also higher, since shipping materials are more abundant to protect the merchandise during its international transit. The banking fees associated with an international payment are greater (exchange rate commissions, SWIFT charges, wire-transfer fees). Even staple items such as phone calls, faxes, and postage used to monitor orders are more expensive.

- **Paperwork**—Sending a shipment internationally involves much additional paperwork, and therefore, greater costs.

- **Time:** The time involved in performing the tasks associated with an international shipment is much greater than with a domestic purchase: it takes employees longer to fill out additional paperwork, clear the merchandise through customs, manage the currency exposure, arrange for shipment, purchase insurance, and manage receivables and payables. These additional efforts translate into higher costs.

Set-Up Costs

set-up costs
The costs of starting a new production run. Set-up costs are unaffected by the size of the run.

Ordering costs refer to expenses associated with the purchase of goods. However, in many cases, a company manufactures the products it puts in inventory before offering them for sale. The set-up costs are the costs associated with starting the manufacturing process, and they are conceptually similar to ordering costs; the company incurs set-up costs every time it makes a product, and the quantity of goods produced does not affect theses costs.

Set-up costs are all the costs associated with starting up the production process for manufacturing a product: they include the cost of the changes that must be made to the process settings to switch from one process to another, the cost of down-time while the process is being prepared, the cost of the personnel who complete these tasks, and other associated costs, such as moving raw materials.

Figure 18.3: A Printer Setting Up a Four-Color Offset Press in India.
Photo ©Paul Prescott/Shutterstock. Used with permission.

Shortage Costs

shortage costs
The costs of having run out of inventory.

Shortage costs are incurred when the company is unable to meet customer demand because the requested item is not in inventory. There are three ways to handle shortage costs:[6]

- The shortage can be a single cost, regardless of the duration of the shortage and regardless of the number of units that are "short." This situation occurs when a company anticipates a shortage—for example, by noticing that demand outpaces the forecast and that a shortage is likely before the next inventory replenishment takes place—and asks the supplier to expedite ("rush") the order, by shipping a portion of it by air for example.

- The shortage cost can be an additional cost per unit "short :" for example, it is common practice in some industries to pay the freight for an item that is back-ordered (the item that was not available in inventory is shipped after the remainder of the order has already been shipped), and there are obvious direct costs such as invoices, packing, tracking incomplete orders, and other related charges.

- The shortage cost can be a cost per unit per period: this means that the stock-out costs increase proportionally with the number of units "short" increase, and that the stock-out costs increase proportionally to the length of time during which the inventory is in a stock-out situation. This occurs, for example, when the item which is short is a part for a piece of machinery which is idle until the part is available. The machinery costs money while it is not producing.

However, the main cost of a shortage is the loss of good-will; while a customer is unlikely to switch to another supplier after one or two incomplete orders, the probability of a switch increases with their frequency. Shortage costs then become quite high, as they equate the loss of business (and profit) from a customer. Another way of measuring this shortage cost is to consider the costs associated with finding a customer whose business will replace the lost customer. Finally, there are yet additional costs, which are difficult to evaluate, such as the possibility of a reputation for poor reliability or service.

In an international environment, shortage costs are higher, as business is often competitive and expensive to obtain; it is much cheaper to maintain an existing customer base by providing good service than it is to seek out new customers.

Transportation Costs

In international transactions, direct transportation costs (freight, insurance and duties) tend to be much higher. However, these costs are absorbed as direct costs and added to the cost of goods sold. In this respect, transportation costs influence inventory management decisions: however, they are not considered inventory costs *per se*.

18.2   Economic Order Quantity Model

In 1912, Ford W. Harris[7] developed the first mathematical model designed to minimize inventory costs, and it remains the basis for modern inventory models.

economic order quantity
The size of an order that allows a company to minimize its holding costs and its ordering costs.

Harris used a fixed-order-quantity model and determined mathematically that total inventory costs are minimized at the point where yearly ordering costs and yearly holding costs are equal. He called the order quantity that corresponds to this point the economic order quantity (EOQ).

In Harris's model, total inventory costs include two components: ordering costs that decrease as the quantity ordered decreases, and inventory carrying costs, that increase as the quantity ordered increases. The trade-off between these two components is evident in Figure 18.4, where the minimum costs are reached at $Q^\star$.

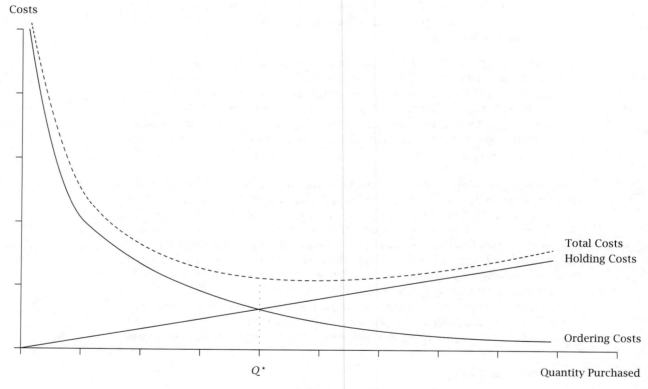

Figure 18.4: Annual Inventory Costs

18.2.1 General Model

The general formula for the economic order quantity [EOQ] model is as follows:

$$Q^\star = \text{EOQ} = \sqrt{\frac{2 \times D \times C_o}{C_h}}$$

where:

- D is the demand for the item, expressed in units per year

- C_o is the cost of placing an order

- C_h is the cost of holding one unit in inventory per year

The units in which these terms are expressed must be carefully handled; the reference units used in D and in C_h must be the same, *i.e.* if the demand is expressed in pounds, then the holding costs must also be expressed per pound and if the demand or the holding costs per unit are not expressed per year, they need to be computed per year.

The economic order quantity is the quantity of goods that the company should order every time it is necessary to replenish the inventory. By ordering that quantity, the company will minimize its annual inventory costs.

18.2.2 Annual Costs

The annual inventory costs of the economic-order-quantity model can be calculated in two ways:

- The following formula is the most commonly used: it is somewhat easy to comprehend, and is particularly useful when the EOQ is rounded up or down—for example, because the EOQ does not fit in a single container.

$$\text{Annual Costs} = \text{AC} = \left[\frac{D}{\text{EOQ}} \times C_o \right] + \left[\frac{\text{EOQ}}{2} \times C_h \right]$$

where:

- $\dfrac{D}{\text{EOQ}}$ is the number of orders placed per year and

- $\dfrac{\text{EOQ}}{2}$ is the average inventory level over the year.

This formula also allows a quick arithmetic check, as both the ordering costs (first bracket) and the carrying costs (second bracket) should approximately be equal (see Figure 18.4).

- If the EOQ is not rounded (or not far from its calculated value), the annual costs can be calculated with a faster formula:

$$\text{Annual Costs} = \text{AC} = \sqrt{2 \times D \times C_o \times C_h}$$

Numerical Example: Economic Order Quantity

A company has a distribution center in Singapore, serving Singapore and its neighboring countries; Malaysia, Indonesia, Thailand, Brunei, and the Philippines. The product for which the company wants to design an inventory management system is a brake pad for passenger automobiles. Brake pads are sold to small distributors in these countries that, in turn, sell to retailers, such as repair shops, automotive part stores, and a few large superstores. The brake pads sell for S$ 30.00 per pair, and demand for the product is 57,000 pairs annually. The company's inventory holding costs are its cost of capital (at 15 percent *per annum*) and an overhead accounting charge of 14 percent *per annum* that covers rent, utilities, insurance, taxes, and other inventory holding costs. The cost of placing and processing a shipment from the parent company in the U.S. to the warehouse in Singapore is estimated at U.S.$ 320.

Since the data are expressed in more than one currency, the company makes its calculations in Singapore dollars. The following data can be derived from the information above:

- $D = 57,000$ pairs per year

- C_o = U.S.$ 320 or S$ 450 per order (exchange rate of U.S.$ 1.00 = S$ 1.406)

- $C_h = 30 \times (0.15 + 0.14) =$ S$ 8.70 per pair per year

The number of brake pads that the company should ship, every time that the inventory needs to be replenished at the Singapore distribution center (the economic order quantity), is then:

$$\text{EOQ} = \sqrt{\frac{2 \times 57,000 \times 450}{8.70}}$$
$$= 2,428.28 \sim 2,400 \quad \text{pairs per shipment}$$

The annual costs (AC) of this inventory policy are:

$$\left[\frac{57,000}{2,400} \times 450\right] \quad \text{(Ordering Costs)} +$$
$$\left[\frac{2,400}{2} \times 8.70\right] \quad \text{(Holding Costs)} =$$
$$\text{AC} = 10,687.50 + 10,440$$
$$= \text{S\$ } 21,127.50 \quad \text{per year}$$

Note that the annual ordering costs (S$ 10,687.50) and annual carrying costs (S$ 10,440.00) are approximately the same and that the total annual costs calculated with the "non-rounding" formula are S$ 21,126.05, a minor difference.

18.3   Economic Lot Size Model

The economic lot size (ELS) model is similar to the EOQ model in concept, but deals with gradual inventory replenishments:

economic lot size
The size of a production run that allows a company to minimize its holding costs and its set-up costs.

Inventory Level

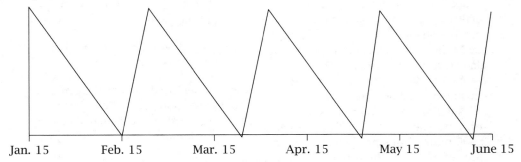

Figure 18.5: Gradual Replenishment

Gradual replenishment of inventory occurs when the goods are manufactured (or assembled) on site and are put in inventory as they are produced. The inventory is therefore not replenished at once, but gradually, as the goods are manufactured.

18.3.1   General Model

The general formula for the economic lot size [ELS]—sometimes also called the economic production lot size [EPLS]—model is as follows:

$$\text{ELS} = \sqrt{\frac{2 \times D \times C_s}{C_h} \times \frac{P}{P - D}}$$

where:

- D is the demand for the item, expressed in units per year
- C_s is the cost of setting up the production process
- C_h is the cost of holding one unit in inventory per year
- P is the production rate for the item, expressed in units per year

The units in which these terms are expressed must be carefully handled; the reference units used in D, P and C_h must be the same, *i.e.* if the demand is expressed in dozens, then the production rate must also be expressed in dozens, and so should the holding costs. If the demand is expressed per quarter, then it needs to be converted to a yearly number, and so should the production rate and the holding costs per unit.

The economic lot size is the quantity of goods that the company should manufacture every time it needs to replenish the inventory.

Numerical Example: Economic Lot Size

A Japanese company has an assembly facility in Luxembourg, serving not only the Benelux countries (Belgium, the Netherlands, Luxembourg), but also France and Germany. The company sells a multi-system DVR, capable of reading and recording SECAM, PAL and NTSC television formats. The company sells about 3,600 units of this product a year at a price of € 1,350. The product is assembled from standard parts in the plant and then sold to small distributors who order them directly for customers.

The inventory holding costs are 22 percent *per annum*. The costs of setting up the assembly process that manufactures this product are calculated by headquarters' accounting department at ¥ 500,000. The capacity of the assembly area is theoretically 4,000 units per month, but it has never been able to operate at full capacity; the company estimates its actual capacity as 87 percent of the rated capacity.

In this example, the company uses the data after converting the information to euros.

Here is a summary of the information:

- $D = 3,600$ units per year

- $C_s = $ ¥ $500,000$ or € $4,115$ per set-up (exchange rate of € $1.00 =$ ¥ 121.51)

- $C_h = 1,350 \times (0.22) = $ € 297 per unit per year

- $P = 4,000 \times 12 \times 0.87 = 41,760$ units per year

The number of DVRs that the company should assemble, every time that the inventory needs to be replenished (the economic lot size), is:

$$
\begin{aligned}
\text{ELS} &= \sqrt{\frac{2 \times 3,600 \times 4,115}{297} \times \frac{41,760}{41,760 - 3,600}} = \\
&= \sqrt{99,757.57 \times 1.09434} \\
&= 330.4 \sim 330 \quad \text{DVRs}
\end{aligned}
$$

The annual costs (AC) of this inventory policy is the sum of the set-up costs and holding costs:

$$
\begin{aligned}
&\left[\frac{3,600}{330} \times 4,115 \right] \\
&\qquad + \\
&\left[\frac{330}{2} \times 297 \times \frac{41,760 - 3,600}{41,760} \right] = \\
\text{AC} &= 44,890.91 + 44,780.43 \\
&= \text{€ } 89,671.34
\end{aligned}
$$

Note that the set-up costs (€ 44,890.91) and the carrying costs (€ 44,780.43) are approximately the same and that the total annual costs calculated with the "speedy" formula give the same annual amount: € 89,671.27.

18.3.2 Annual Costs

The total annual inventory costs of the ELS model can be calculated in two ways:

- If there is some rounding involved, for whatever reason, then the annual costs must be calculated as:

$$\text{Annual Costs} = \text{AC} = \left[\frac{D}{\text{ELS}} \times C_s \right] + \left[\frac{\text{ELS}}{2} \times C_h \times \frac{P - D}{P} \right]$$

where:

- $\dfrac{D}{\text{ELS}}$ is the number of times per year that the company sets up the machinery to manufacture this product and

- $\dfrac{\text{ELS}}{2} \times \dfrac{P - D}{P}$ is the average inventory level over the year.

This formula also provides a quick arithmetic check, as both the set-up costs (first bracket) and the holding-carrying costs (second bracket) should approximately be equal.

- If the ELS is not rounded very far from its calculated value, the annual costs can be calculated with this "faster" formula:

$$\text{Annual Costs} = \text{AC} = \sqrt{2 \times D \times C_s \times C_h \times \frac{P - D}{P}}$$

18.4 Safety Stock

The preceding sections deal with the quantity that should be ordered every time an order is placed. So far, the *timing* of the order placement has been overlooked. In this section, the concepts of re-order point, safety stock and service level will be presented.

safety stock
Additional inventory used to prevent inventory shortages of a product.

18.4.1 Lead Time

The lead time is the time between the moment an order is placed and the time the order arrives to be put in inventory. As inventory is depleted by customer demand, the proper inventory procedure is to re-order the goods at least n days before the inventory is expected to be exhausted. Those n days correspond to the expected delay due to transit time. The level of inventory at which it is necessary to place an order—*i.e.* the level of inventory that corresponds to n days of demand—is called the re-order point, marked $R^\star$ in Figure 18.6 on the following page.

lead time
The time between the moment an order is placed and the time the order arrives.

In international inventory management, lead times tend to be long, for reasons explained earlier. Lead times, however, are not difficult to manage if their durations are known ahead of time and if the demand stays constant during these

Inventory Level

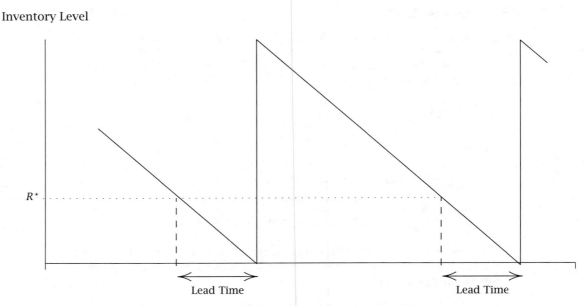

Figure 18.6: Lead Time

periods. Unfortunately, however, lead times vary in duration from one order to another and the demand during the lead time tends to fluctuate as well.

The first techniques presented in this section deal with managing the variability in demand during the lead time: for simplification purposes, it will be assumed that the lead time duration remains constant. Later in this section, the assumption of a fixed-length lead time will be removed and managing the combination of variations in lead time's duration and in demand during the lead-time will be explained.

18.4.2   Safety Stock

The idea of safety stock is almost self-explanatory; since there is variation in demand during the lead time, it makes sense to carry a buffer of additional inventory to cover unexpected requests from customers during the lead time—requests beyond what is expected to be sold during that period. This concept is best explained with an illustration:

In Figure 18.7, the solid demand line corresponds to the expected (average) demand during the lead time. However, demand may vary, and two examples are provided. In example ①, the demand is lower than expected and the inventory is obviously sufficient to cover the customer orders. In example ②, the demand is higher than expected, and the company needs to "dip" into its safety stock to cover these orders.

It is generally assumed—mostly for simplification purposes—that demand

Inventory Level

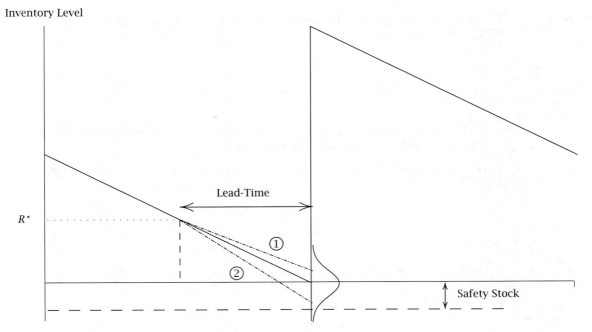

Figure 18.7: Safety Stock

during the lead time is normally distributed: the expected (average) demand during the lead time is noted D_{LT} and the standard deviation of the demand during the lead time is noted σ_{LT}. The hypothesized distribution of the demand during the lead-time is shown by the normal curve in Figure 18.7.

18.4.3   Safety Stock Determination

There are several factors that must be used to decide how much safety stock a firm should carry:

Service Level

The service level in an inventory management situation is the probability that the firm will have the item in inventory if the customer places an order during the lead time. The relationship between the service level and the safety stock is simply calculated using a normal-distribution table (see the Appendix on page 686).

The following formulas can be used to determine the proper safety stock level for a given service level:

- The average demand during the lead time, $D_L = n \times \overline{d}$ where n is the number of days during the lead time and $\overline{d}$ is the average daily demand.

service level
The probability that the firm will have an item in inventory if a customer places an order during the lead time.

- The standard deviation of the demand during the day, σ_d, is calculated with the following formula:

$$\sigma_d = \sqrt{\sum_{i=1}^{N} (d_i - \overline{d})^2}$$

where d_i is the demand on any given day i and where N is the number of days over which daily demand data is available.

- The standard deviation of the demand during the lead time σ_{LT} is calculated with:

$$\sigma_{LT} = \sqrt{\sum_{i=1}^{n} (\sigma_d)^2}$$

- The safety stock is quickly calculated as:

$$SS = z_{\text{Service Level}} \times \sigma_{LT}$$

where $z_{\text{Service Level}}$ is the z-score corresponding to the chosen service level. It can easily be found from the table in Appendix on page 686 by searching for the service level in the table and its corresponding z-score.

- The re-order point $R^\star = D_{LT} + SS$.

18.4.4　Variability in the Lead-Time

In international inventory management, there is another variation to account for when calculating the safety stock: the variability of the lead time. This variability is due to the number of intermediaries involved and due to the great number of possible delays; weather, strikes, customs clearance, shipping delays, and so on.

The standard deviation of the demand during the lead time (σ_{LT}) is therefore a function of two random variables which are assumed to be independent, *i.e.* to not affect each other. The first variable is the standard deviation of the daily demand (σ_d) and the second is the standard deviation of the duration of the lead time σ_L. Both random variables are assumed normally distributed, for computational simplicity purposes.

The following formulas apply to the determination of the cumulative variations in demand during the lead time and in lead time duration:

$$D_{LT} = \overline{d} \times L \quad \text{and} \quad \sigma_{LT} = \sqrt{L \times (\sigma_d)^2 + (\overline{d} \times \sigma_L)^2}$$

The calculations of the safety stock and the re-order point are completed using the formulas presented earlier.

Numerical Example: Safety Stock

The inventory manager of a dental supply wholesaler in Brazil has a product for which the demand is 36,000 cases per year. The standard deviation of the demand per day is 6 cases. The company wants to offer good service and has chosen a service level of 95 percent during the lead time, which lasts 8 days. The company obtains this product from a supplier in Switzerland.

The following data can be calculated from the data above (assuming 360 days per year):

- $D_d = 36,000/360 = 100$ cases per day

- $\sigma_d = 6$

- $D_{LT} = 100 \times 8 = 800$ cases

- $\sigma_{LT} = \sqrt{8 \times 6^2} = \sqrt{288} = 16.97 \sim$ 17 cases

- The service level is 95 percent

- $z_{0.95} = 1.645$ *i.e.* $P(z \leq 1.645) = 0.95$ (from the Table on page 686)

- The safety stock is $SS = 1.645 \times 17 = 27.96 \sim 28$ cases

- The re-order point is $R^\star = 800 + 28 = 828$ units

The wholesaler therefore reorders from its supplier whenever the inventory falls to 828 cases, which corresponds to a safety stock of 28 cases.

The manager knows that there is some variability in the lead time. Although the goods usually arrive in 8 days, there are times when they arrive in 6 days, and there have been occasions where they took 18 days. The manager estimates the standard deviation of the lead time's duration by using a simple calculation:

$$\sigma_L = \frac{\text{Highest value} - \text{Lowest value}}{6}$$

$$= \frac{18 - 6}{6} = 2$$

The manager re-calculates the safety stock using this additional information. The standard deviation of the demand during the lead time is now:

$$\sigma_{LT} = \sqrt{L \times (\sigma_d)^2 + (\bar{d} \times \sigma_L)^2}$$
$$= \sqrt{8 \times 6^2 + 100 \times 2^2}$$
$$= \sqrt{288 + 400} = \sqrt{688}$$
$$= = 26.23 \text{ cases}$$

The safety stock then becomes $SS = 1.645 \times 26.23 = 43.15 \sim 44$ cases, and the reorder point is now $R^\star = 800 + 44 = 844$ cases.

18.5 A-B-C Classification

The models presented earlier in this chapter help international logistics managers develop effective and efficient inventory management policies. However, each of these models requires substantial effort; the tasks associated with accurately determining demand from past invoices, forecasting demand using mathematical models, determining holding costs, and determining ordering costs are time consuming and difficult to update regularly.

It is for this reason that inventory managers often use an A-B-C classification in inventory management; the A-B-C classification is based on Pareto's Law, first articulated by Joseph Juran,[8], but attributed to the Italian economist Vilfredo Pareto, who had observed that 80 percent of land in Italy was owned by 20 percent of the population. Pareto's law is also known as the 80-20 rule, and it extends to many concepts in business: for example, 80 percent of a business's sales are likely to come from 20 percent of its products or 20 percent of its customers. Similarly, 80 percent of a company's costs are likely to come from 20 percent of its inputs.

This relationship applies to inventory as well: 80 percent of inventory costs come from 20 percent of the products carried. Therefore, the following classification is often utilized by practicing inventory managers:

Inventory Class	Percentage of Products	Percentage of Inventory Costs
A	20	80
B	30	15
C	50	5

Table 18.1: Percentage of Goods and Costs in an A-B-C Classification

Although this classification is arbitrary, it holds true in almost all situations; however, the percentages may vary by a few points. However, the idea of classifying of products into an A-B-C taxonomy is helpful as it makes sense to treat these products differently:

- The products classified as "A Products" should be carefully monitored, with frequent forecast revisions and adjustments to the economic order quantities—possibly as frequently as yearly. Similarly, safety stocks should be determined as accurately as possible, to maintain good customer service while keeping costs under control.

- The products classified as "B Products" should be monitored, but much less frequently; for example, the EOQs could be revised every three to five years, rather than yearly. A similar policy can be followed for safety stocks, which can be determined more arbitrarily.

- The products classified as "C Products" probably do not deserve much time and attention from the inventory manager. A simplistic re-order policy—such as re-ordering twenty cases when inventory is down to one case—and an arbitrary safety stock suffice and do not affect overall inventory costs much, even if they are far from optimal.

18.6   Material Requirements Planning

There are two types of demand to be considered when approaching inventory management. A dependent-demand item is one for which sales depend on the sales of another product; for example, sales of parts to an original equipment manufacturer (OEM) depend on the sales of the final product. An independent-demand item is one for which sales do not depend on the sales of another item. Material requirement planning can only be used for dependent-demand products.

Materials requirements planning (MRP) was developed by Joseph Orlicky in 1964,[9] and first implemented by the Black & Decker corporation that same year. By 1975, Orlicky had written the definitive book for this technique,[10] and by the early 1980s, Oliver Wight had extended the concept to Manufacturing Resource Planning (MRP II).[11] In the late 1980s, the same principles were used to create Enterprise Resource Planning (ERP)[12] and Distribution Resources Planning (DRP).[13]

Materials Requirement Planning (MRP)
A management tool that allows a manufacturer to determine what to produce and in which quantity, in function of what it sells to its customers.

Today, almost all companies that manufacture finished goods use an MRP system or one of its derivatives: MRP II, ERP, and DRP. The differences between MRP and these products will be explained later in this section.

18.6.1   Principles

Material requirements planning is a computer-based system (see Figure 18.8) that utilizes four main input files:

- **Bill of Materials**—The bill of materials file must list all of the components of a finished product in minute detail.

- **Inventory File**—The inventory file must contain an accurate record of the inventory quantities of all the product's components.

- **Orders Received**—A sales file that contains all orders already received for the product.

- **Forecasted Sales**—A sales file that contains forecasted sales for the product.

From this information, the MRP system creates a master production schedule which tells the company what to make, in which quantity to make it, when to make it, as well as what to purchase, in what quantity, and when. If necessary, the system determines which scheduled production runs—or purchases—must be expedited (moved to an earlier date) or de-expedited (moved to a later date).

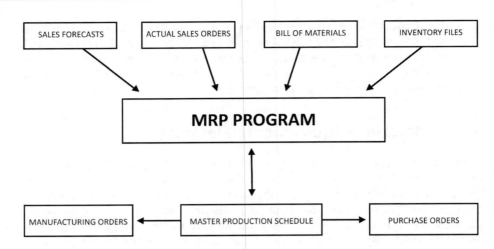

Figure 18.8: The File Interactions in a MRP System.

An MRP system follows a pull principle. Dependent-demand items—the components of a final product—are manufactured based upon the actual or planned demand for the finished product. As demand for the finished product increases, demand for its components also increases, and the MRP system adjusts the manufacturing schedule. If the demand for the finished product decreases, the MRP system curtails production and the purchase of component parts.

Bill of Materials Files

bill of materials
An electronic file containing a hierarchical list of all the components of a final product.

A product's bill of materials is the precise list of all the parts that constitute that product (see Figure 18.9 on the next page).

The bill of materials is separated by level, with level 0 being the final product and level 1 being the sub-assemblies and parts that are put together to make the final product. Each of the level-1 items are assembled from parts that are listed in level 2, and level-2 items are assembled from parts listed in level 3, and so on. For a simple product like the wagon in Figure 18.9, there are only four levels, but for complicated products, there can be many more levels.

Figure 18.9 shows that the wagon (level 0) is assembled from a tray, a rear wheel assembly, and a front wheel assembly, all of which are joined together by 10 bolts, washers, and nuts (all level-1 sub-assemblies or parts).

Each of the sub-assemblies is made with level-2 parts; the rear wheel assembly is made with a rear frame and two wheels; the front wheel assembly is made with a front frame and two wheels. In turn, the rear frame is made with 3 feet of tubing and welded using 2 welding rods, the front frame is made with a casting, a roller bearing, a handle, and assembled with a bolt & cotter pin (all level-3 parts).

The bill of materials in Figure 18.9 is a simplified example because the level of detail for many parts is insufficient: the wheel sub-assemblies are more complex than represented, for example.

| | Level | | | Part No. | Description | Quantity | Units | Unit Cost | Lot Size | Lead Time | Units |
A	B	C	D	E	F	G	H	I	J	K	L
0				100-001	Wagon, Assembled	1	EA		L4L	1	WK
	1			101-025	1/4-in Bolts	10	EA	$0.008	5,000	2	WK
	1			101-026	1/4-in Nuts	10	EA	$0.006	5,000	2	WK
	1			101-027	1/4-in Washers	10	EA	$0.001	10,000	2	WK
	1			101-050	Wagon, Tray	1	EA	$4.850	75	3	WK
	1			101-051	Wheel Assy, Rear	1	EA		200	1	WK
		2		102-101	Rear Frame	1	EA		150	1	WK
			3	103-000	Tube	3	FT	$0.350	1,000	3	WK
			3	103-001	Welding Rod	2	EA	$0.153	50	2	WK
		2		102-150	Wheel	2	EA		2,500	1	WK
			3	103-001	Tire	1	EA	$0.580	8,000	5	WK
			3	103-001	Plastic Rim	1	EA	$0.720	10,000	5	WK
	1			101-052	Wheel Assy, Front	1	EA		250	1	WK
		2		102-501	Front Frame	1	EA		180	1	WK
			3	103-020	Stamping	1	EA	$0.240	1,000	4	WK
			3	103-021	Roller Bearing	1	EA	$0.780	4,000	3	WK
			3	103-022	Handle	1	EA	$0.250	1,500	2	WK
			3	103-070	Bolt + Cotter Pin	1	EA	$0.030	5,000	2	WK
		2		102-150	Wheel	2	EA		2,500	1	WK
			3	103-001	Tire	1	EA	$0.580	8,000	5	WK
			3	103-001	Plastic Rim	1	EA	$0.720	10,000	5	WK

Figure 18.9: A Toy Wagon and its Simplified Bill of Materials.
Photo ©Paul Prescott/Shutterstock. Used with permission.

The bill of materials also includes information on lot sizes. The lot size is the number of items that the company produces or purchases at one time. Lot sizes are calculated using the formulas and information presented earlier in this chapter; if the company manufactures a product, the lot size is the economic lot size. If the company purchases the part, the lot size is the economic order quantity. In the example on Figure 18.9, the lot sizes are shown for all products purchased and assembled, but they have been simplified. The lot size for the wagon trays (part 101-050) is 75 units, which means that the company purchases 75 wagon trays at a time. The lot size for the rear-wheel sub-assemblies (part 101-051) is 200 units; this is the quantity that the company makes every time it produces them. The lot size for the finished wagons (part 100-101) is marked as L4L, which stands for "lot for lot:" in that case, the company assembles as many wagons as requested, with no minimum quantity.

The bill of materials also includes information on lead times for each of the parts that the company produces or purchases. The lead times for parts that are manufactured by the company reflect the time that it takes to assemble them once all components are available: as shown in Figure 18.9, it takes the company one week to assemble 2,500 wheels (part 102-150) once it has 2,500 tires and 2,500 plastic hubs. It takes the company one week to assemble 200 rear-wheel sub-assemblies (part 101-051) once it has 200 rear frames (part 102-101) and 400 wheels (part 102-150). These lead times are clearly simplified in this example, as they are all expressed in weeks. The lead times for purchased parts reflect the time that it takes to obtain the goods, from the time the order is placed to the time at which the parts arrive. For domestic purchases, the time on the bill of materials is reasonably close to the actual procurement time, but for international purchases, most companies use a longer lead time to avoid having manufacturing delays if a part is not received on schedule. In Figure 18.9, the lead time for tires (part 103-001) is 5 weeks, and the lead times for the 1/4-in bolts, nuts, and washers (parts 101-025 through 101-027) is 2 weeks.

Finally, the bill of materials also includes the costs for purchased products. For most parts, the cost is on a per-unit basis; such is the case for wagon trays (part 101-050) that cost $ 4.85 per unit, or roller bearings (part 103-021) that cost $ 0.78 each. For some parts, the price can be expressed in other units: for example, the tube (part 103-000) used to make the rear-wheel frames (part 102-101), is purchased per linear foot.

Forecasts and Sales Order

The MRP system must have sales-forecasts files and actual-orders files as its inputs. The actual and forecasted sales data is used by the system to create the master production schedule.

The files and their linkage to the MRP system have benefits for the company's sales force; as the sales force interacts with a customer considering placing an order, they can query the MRP system to determine whether the anticipated or requested delivery window is feasible. The MRP can immediately include the potential order in its planning, and calculate whether the company will have the resources and parts to manufacture the products. From a sales person's stand-point, this is a useful tool; customers are more likely to place an order if they know that the delivery schedule is possible. If it's not, the customers would rather know that as well, so that plans can be adjusted accordingly.

Inventory Files

The MRP system must also know what is available in inventory. Inventory ac-curacy is a fundamental requirement, as the system determines the production schedule based on what is in inventory. The inventory files should be as close to 100-percent accurate as possible.

Master Production Schedule

Once the MRP system has collected information from the actual-sales file, from the sales-forecast file, from the bill-of-materials file, and from the inventory file, it creates a master production schedule.

master production schedule
An electronic file created by an MRP system that specifies what products to make, in which quantity, and when.

Figure 18.10 shows the master production schedule for an order of 24 fin-ished wagons in week 8.

Part Number: Wagons 100-101   Lot Size: L4L   Lead-Time: 1

WEEK	1	2	3	4	5	6	7	8	9	10
Gross Requirements								24		
Units On Hand	0	0	0	0	0	0	0	0	0	0
Net Requirements								24		
Planned Order Receipts								24		
Planned Order Releases							24			

Figure 18.10: Master Production Schedule for an Order of 24 Wagons in Week 8.

The gross-requirements line refers to the number of units ordered. Since the MRP system recorded an order for 24 wagons in week 8, the master production schedule shows 24 units required in week 8. The units-on-hand line refers to the number of units in inventory. In this example, there were no wagons in inventory. The net-requirement line is calculated by subtracting the number of units on hand from the gross requirements; in this example, there was a net requirement of 24 wagons in week 8.

The planned-order-receipts line refers to the number of units that will be produced and received from production; since the lot size for finished wagons is

L4L, the company will make exactly what it needs, or 24 units. The planned-order-releases line shows the week at which the wagon production must start, which is determined by the lead time for this process. In this example, the company will start assembling 24 wagons in week 7, since the lead time is 1 week. Since it makes exactly as many as it needs, there will still be no inventory in week 9.

The order then "cascades" down to the next level, the parts that are needed to make the finished wagons: the wagon trays (part 101-050), the rear-wheel sub-assembly (part 101-051), and the front-wheel sub-assembly (part 101-052). The master production schedules for these parts are shown in Figure 18.11 on the facing page, but the MPSs for the nuts and bolts are omitted.

- The master production schedule for the trays shows a demand for 24 trays in week 7, because the company needs 24 trays at that time to start assembling them into finished wagons. There were 10 trays left in inventory, so the net requirements in week 7 are for 14 trays.

  The lot size for trays is 75, so this is the quantity that the firm will purchase from its supplier, and therefore it will receive 75 trays in week 7. Since the lead time for ordering trays is 3 weeks, the system will place a purchase order for 75 trays in week 4.

- The second master production schedule shows the number of rear-wheel sub-assemblies needed to make 24 wagons. Since there is one sub-assembly per wagon, there is a gross requirement of 24 rear-wheel sub-assemblies in week 7. There are 18 in inventory, so the net requirements in week 7 are for 6 rear-wheel sub-assemblies.

  Since the lot size is 200, the company will plan to receive 200 in week 7, and since the lead time is one week, it will start working on these 200 rear-wheel sub-assemblies in week 6. With 200 produced rear-wheel sub-assemblies, and only 6 needed, the remainder (194) will be placed in inventory. That number appears in week 8.

- The master production schedule for the front-wheel sub-assemblies also shows a demand of 24 for week 7. However, there are still 52 left in inventory, so the net requirements in week 7 are 0.

  The number of front-wheel sub-assemblies is reduced in week 7 by the number that are used to make the 24 wagons, and therefore there are 28 front-wheel sub-assemblies in inventory in week 8.

- The master production schedules for the bolts, nuts, and washers would show gross requirements of 240 units for each part. Depending on whether there are some of these in inventory, the MRP system would place a purchase order with the company's supplier for these parts. Since the lead time for these parts is 2 weeks, the orders would be placed in week 5.

After completing this level of the master production schedule, the MRP system then moves down to the next level.

Part Number: Trays 101-050   Lot Size: 75   Lead-Time: 3

WEEK	1	2	3	4	5	6	7	8	9	10
Gross Requirements							24			
Units On Hand	10	10	10	10	10	10	10	61	61	61
Net Requirements							14			
Planned Order Receipts							75			
Planned Order Releases				75						

Part Number: RW S-Assy 101-051   Lot Size: 200   Lead-Time: 1

WEEK	1	2	3	4	5	6	7	8	9	10
Gross Requirements							24			
Units On Hand	18	18	18	18	18	18	18	194	194	194
Net Requirements							6			
Planned Order Receipts							200			
Planned Order Releases						200				

Part Number: FW S-Assy 101-052   Lot Size: 250   Lead-Time: 1

WEEK	1	2	3	4	5	6	7	8	9	10
Gross Requirements							24			
Units On Hand	52	52	52	52	52	52	52	28	28	28
Net Requirements							0			
Planned Order Receipts										
Planned Order Releases										

Figure 18.11: Master Production Schedules for Trays and Wheel Sub-assemblies.

Part Number: R. Frame 102-101   Lot Size: 150   Lead-Time: 1

WEEK	1	2	3	4	5	6	7	8	9	10
Gross Requirements						200				
Units On Hand	70	70	70	70	70	70	20	20	20	20
Net Requirements						130				
Planned Order Receipts						150				
Planned Order Releases					150					

Part Number: Wheel 102-150   Lot Size: 2,500   Lead-Time: 1

WEEK	1	2	3	4	5	6	7	8	9	10
Gross Requirements						400				
Units On Hand	450	450	450	450	450	450	50	50	50	50
Net Requirements						0				
Planned Order Receipts										
Planned Order Releases										

Figure 18.12: Master Production Schedules for Parts of the Rear-Wheel Sub-Assembly.

Figure 18.12 shows the master production schedules for the parts needed to produce the rear-wheel sub-assemblies: the rear frames and the wheels. Since the MRP system calls for the manufacture of 200 rear-wheel sub-assemblies starting in week 6, then the parts that are needed for this sub-assembly will have gross requirements of 200 in that week.

- The master production schedule for the rear frames shows a demand for 200 frames in week 6. Assuming there are 70 in inventory, the net requirements in week 6 are for 130 frames. Since the lot size for frames is 150 units and the lead time is 1 week, the MRP system determines that the manufacturing of 150 frames will need to start in week 5.

- The second master production schedule shows the number of wheels needed for the rear-wheel sub-assemblies is 400 in week 6, since there are two wheels for each sub-assembly. Since there are 450 wheels in inventory, the net requirements are for 0 in week 6. The inventory level drops to 50 wheels in week 7.

The master production schedule for the wheels has no gross requirements for the other part for which wheels are necessary, the front-wheel sub-assembly. However, if the MRP called for 200 front-wheel sub-assemblies to be produced in week 6, then the gross requirements for wheels would increase to 800 (400 for the rear-wheel sub-assemblies and 400 for the front-wheel sub-assemblies), and the net requirements would become 350, triggering a planned order receipt for 2,500 wheels in week 6 and a production order for 2,500 wheels to be made in week 5.

At soon as the master production schedules that are internal to the company are completed, the data can be transmitted to suppliers, so that the suppliers can integrate the data into their MRP system. The manufacturer of the trays, for example, would be notified that it should anticipate an order for 75 trays in week 4, and it would incorporate that information into its own MRP system, so that it can order the raw materials for this production run, and plan accordingly.

18.6.2 Just-in-Time Inventory Systems

As MRP systems became widely used, they provided another benefit: they allowed companies to implement just-in-time product-replenishment processes.

Just-in-time (JIT) processes were first created by Toyota Manufacturing in Japan in the late 1970s.[14] Theses processes involved a system of cards (called *kanban* in Japanese) that accompanied each batch of manufactured parts; as a batch was starting to be utilized on the assembly line, the card was sent back to the area of the plant that manufactured that part, and another batch was started. This allowed the company to manufacture "just in time" for production.

Few companies implemented the Toyota *kanban* system, but two elements favored the development of a system based on MRP software that allowed companies to adopt just-in-time processes:

- A greater understanding of the effect of improvements in set-up costs; as the ELS model shows, the production lot size increases as the set-up costs increase (see the ELS formula on page 617). By reducing set-up costs, companies also decreased lot sizes and therefore produced only what was needed. Such decreases were achieved using clever ways to switch from one type of product to another, or by avoiding "big changes" in the types of products manufactured.[15] They were also achieved because of better technology; a numerically controlled machine has essentially no set-up costs between production runs. This textbook is produced using digital printing, which has no set-up costs, a significant improvement over offset printing (see Figure 18.3), which was itself a big improvement over the set-up costs of letter-press technology.[16]

just in time (JIT)
A management philosophy that consists of planning the manufacturing of goods in such a way that they are produced just before they are needed in the next step of the assembly process.

- At the same time as MRP systems became more common, computing power and the means of transmitting large amounts of data quickly became readily available and affordable. The first MRP systems were processed in "batch mode," *i.e.* at the end of the day, only once a day. However, starting in the early 1990s, they were run in real time, so that every input created a recalculation of the master production schedule. In addition, companies started to link their MRP systems to those of their suppliers. That is, an OEM would produce a master production schedule for its factory, and the information from that schedule became the information used as input for its suppliers' MRP systems. Such developments allowed suppliers to have immediate information regarding production schedule changes, to which they could react quickly.

With lower set-up costs and information that allowed them to adapt quickly to changes in demand, suppliers became able to make just-in-time deliveries to their customers. Although not yet well developed in an international context, JIT shipments have become the norm between U.S. suppliers and OEMs. Large OEMs actually give their suppliers delivery windows of two to four hours only; if the delivery happens at a different time than the one assigned, the supplier is penalized.

18.6.3   MRP, MRP II, ERP, and DRP

Materials requirement planning is the simplest technique used to manage the production of dependent-demand products. Originally, MRP only included the materials needed to manufacture a product; its parts, their lead time, and their lot size.

Manufacturing Resource Planning (MRP II)
A materials requirement planning tool that includes additional information, such as manufacturing costs.

As the benefits of MRP became evident, a significant drawback also started to appear: MRP did not include cost information, even though it was a fundamental aspect of manufacturing, and it did not include how much labor was needed to manufacture or assemble each component. Oliver Wight proposed to add this information on the bill of materials, as well as many other aspects of a manufacturing environment on the master production schedule. He included the possibility of having reduced-time shifts (a day on which employees do not work a full eight-hour day), reduced-personnel shifts (when an employee is off), or scheduled maintenance on certain shifts, all of which affected a plant's production capability. By adding these factors and others, he changed the name of the product to manufacturing resource planning, which was later shortened to MRP II.

Enterprise Resource Planning (ERP)
A software package, based on an MRP system, that integrates all the functions of a company.

Enterprise resource planning (ERP) is another tool based on MRP. Two factors triggered the creation of ERP:

- The first factor was the fact that the benefits of MRP II systems had become very clear to top management. MRP II systems were providing great information about the manufacturing costs of products and had eliminated many manufacturing issues, such as stock-outs and manufacturing delays. MRP II systems had also provided great information for planning purposes.

- The second factor was the looming concern about what was known in the 1990s as the "Y2K" problem; legacy computer programs written in the 1960s, 1970s, and 1980s, had been coded when computer memory was scarce, so every effort was made to use as little memory as possible. Variable fields that held dates had been using two digits; so, a 1985 date had only been kept as "85." There was concern that computations such as the number of years between two dates would become incorrect after the year 2000. While it was obvious that 1999-1985 was unaffected, 2000-1985 would be −85 if the computer program was not "patched." However, many of these programs had been patched multiple times since they had been written, and much of the documentation had been lost. Many had also been written in COBOL which few programmers knew.

  As the deadline of January 1, 2000 became imminent, many companies decided to jettison their legacy computer programs and move to an integrated system that would run the entire company.

The first enterprise resource planning (ERP) systems included not only an MRP II module, but also a finance module and an accounting module. Within a few years, ERP software suppliers added modules to handle marketing management, warehouse management, human resource management, and eventually global trade management (see Section 2.1.5 on page 45).

The leader in providing ERP software is a German company named SAP, and its ERP product is called R/3. There are several other ERP suppliers, notably Microsoft and Oracle, but as of 2017, more than 80 percent of Fortune-500 companies used SAP R/3 systems.[17]

Distribution resource planning (DRP) was created by retailers after they saw the success of MRP programs in manufacturing environments. Retail is also driven by a pull principle; the end consumer in the store purchases a product, and the entire supply chain depends on that retail sale. As the retailer records a sale in its system, it can communicate with the systems of its suppliers, from wholesaler to manufacturer, so that they immediately see whether a product is successful. Manufacturers can then use that information to increase production in anticipation of additional sales, or curtail it to avoid surpluses when sales are lagging.

18.7 Inventory Management as a Marketing Tool

There are several reasons for good inventory management practices to be associated with a strong competitive advantage.

It is critical for a company to be able to deliver goods to customers when they are needed, and not postpone or lose sales because an item is not in inventory. Good planning, appropriate inventory levels (determined by using EOQ and ELS formulas), and satisfactory safety stocks allow a company to provide customers with goods when they request them, and ensure good service levels. Customers become repeat customers when they are satisfied that the goods they purchase will arrive on time.

However, good inventory management practices also reduce costs, providing companies with higher profits: if inventory levels are adequate, there is no need to "rush" production and pay for employees to manufacture on overtime pay. There is no need to expedite purchases or shipments and pay for air transport when good planning would have allowed products to be transported more economically by ocean. A company that understands its inventory costs can reduce them by implementing manufacturing solutions that lower set-up costs, ordering costs, and holding costs. A company can also reduce inventory costs significantly by adopting just-in-time deliveries. If the associated cost savings are not used to increase profitability, they can allow a company to sell goods at a lower price, which is likely to translate into higher sales.

An MRP system allows a company to provide customers with information that specifies when they should expect the goods they order. A company can avoid "over promising and under delivering," which is very valuable: customers like to know when they should expect the products they have purchased. Reliability is a substantial competitive advantage.

Review and Discussion Questions

1. What are the differences between dependent-demand and independent-demand products?

2. Explain the different elements of inventory holding costs.

3. Explain the similarities between ordering costs and set-up costs.

4. Why is it important for a company to determine its stock-out costs?

5. How are lead times more uncertain in an international environment than they are in a domestic environment?

6. How can an MRP system help a company implement a just-in-time production process?

Notes

[1] Makridakis, Spyros G., Steven C. Wheelwright, and Rob J. Hyndman, *Forecasting: Methods and Applications*, Third Edition, 1997, John Wiley and Sons, New York, New York.

[2] Bowerman, Bruce, L., Richard O'Connell, and Anne Koehler, *Forecasting, Time Series, and Regression*, Fourth Edition, 2004, Cengage Learning, Mason, Ohio.

[3] Box, George E.P., Gwilym M. Jenkins, Gregory C. Reinsel, and Greta M. Ljung, *Time Series Analysis: Forecasting and Control*, Fifth Edition, 2015, John Wiley and Sons, New York, New York.

[4] Lewis, Nigel D., *Neural, Novel, and Hybrid Algorithms for Time Series Predictions*, First Edition, 1995, John Wiley and Sons, New York, New York.

[5] Neter, John, Michael Kutner, William Wasserman, and Christopher Nachtsheim, *Applied Linear Statistical Models*, Fourth Edition, 1996, McGraw-Hill, New York, New York.

[6] Pyke, David F., Edward A. Silver, and Rein Peterson, *Inventory Management and Production Planning and Scheduling*, Third Edition, 1998, John Wiley and Sons, New York, New York.

[7] Harris, Ford W., "How Many Parts to Make at Once," *Factory, the Magazine of Management*, February 1913, **10**, 2, pp. 135-136, 152, reproduced in *Operations Research*, December 1, 1990, pp. 947-950, http://dx.doi.org/10.1287/opre.38.6.947, retrieved April 25, 2017.

[8] Bunkley, Nick, "Joseph Juran, 103, Pioneer in Quality Control, Dies," *The New York Times*, March 3, 2008, p. B7.

[9] Ptak, Carol, and Chad Smith, *Orlicky's Material Requirements Planning*, Third Edition, 2011, McGraw-Hill, New York, New York.

[10] Orlicky, Joseph, *Material Requirements Planning: The New Way of Life in Production and Inventory Management*, First Edition, 1975, McGraw-Hill, New York, New York.

[11] Wight, Oliver, *Manufacturing Resource Planning: MRP II: Unlocking America's Productivity Potential*, First Edition, 1995, John Wiley and Sons, New York, New York.

[12] Wagner, Brett, and Ellen Monk, *Concepts in Enterprise Resource Planning*, Third Edition, 2008, Cengage Learning, Mason, Ohio.

[13] Martin, André, *DRP: Distribution Resource Planning: The Gateway to True Quick Response and Continuous Replenishment*, Third Edition, 1992, John Wiley and Sons, New York, New York.

[14] Emiliani, Michael L. "Origins of lean management in America: The role of Connecticut businesses," *Journal of Management History*, 2006, **12**-2, pp.167-184.

[15] Flowers, A. Dale, "The Modernization of Merit Brass," *Interfaces*, February 1993, pp. 97-108.

[16] Leeper, Don, "Print Positive: Letterpress, Offset, and the Inexorable Rise of Digital," *Bookmobile*, October 3, 2014, http://www.bookmobile.com/uncategorized/print-positive-offset-digital-printing-compared/, retrieved April 27, 2017.

[17] "SAP Customer List," https://www.salesinsideinc.com/services-details/sap-customer-list, accessed April 27, 2017.

Chapter 19

Supply Chain Operations—Quality

One of the concerns of a company involved in international commerce is to ensure that the goods it purchases are of good quality and that the goods it sells meet the performance requirements of its customers.

The techniques shown in this chapter form the bases of good quality-control management.

19.1   Quality Assurance

quality assurance
A statistical process followed by purchasers to ensure that a shipment of parts meets quality requirements.

Until the 1980s, quality assurance was the responsibility of the buyer; there were processes in place, called quality-assurance processes, that had been created by statisticians in military procurement, that the buyer used to determine whether a shipment of a particular product was of acceptable quality.

Quality-assurance departments followed military standards (MIL STD 105E and MIL STD 414) to determine whether goods provided by the seller were conform to the buyer's requirements. They took random samples from a shipment, evaluated or measured the goods that had been selected, and either accepted a shipment as conform, or rejected it based on the information they had obtained. Literally, companies refused shipments because the random-testing procedures they had put in place had determined that the entire shipment did not meet their requirements.[1]

Starting in the 1980s—earlier in Japan—, quality assurance on the buyer's side was replaced with quality control on the supplier's side. Once the buyer had confidence that the supplier was following appropriate statistical quality control methods, there was no longer a need for checking parts upon their delivery.

19.2   Statistical Quality Control Concepts

statistical quality control
A statistical process followed by manufacturers to ensure that a manufacturing process is working correctly.

Statistical quality control tools were created by Walter Shewhart before World War II,[2] but were not implemented in industry until after the war. It was W. Edwards Deming, who had studied under Ronald Fisher and Jerzy Neyman, who made Shewhart's work better known by authoring the seminal book on this topic and publishing it with Shewhart.[3] In 1950, Deming went to Japan and taught these techniques to several Japanese manufacturers such as Toyota, Honda, Mitsubishi Motors, Pioneer, and Sony, whose goals were to rebuild their company and generate exports. "Using these concepts, the Japanese set the quality standards for the rest of the world to follow."[4] Joseph Juran, another disciple of Shewhart's work, went to Japan in 1954, and advocated the viewpoint that management—not simply manufacturing and engineering—was responsible for the quality of the products that their firms were making, a notion that was not widely accepted at the time.

By the early 1980s, several large United States and European companies had adopted the principles of statistical quality control, and by the 1990s, essentially all manufacturing firms were using statistical process control tools to monitor the manufacturing of their products.

Statistical Quality Control is based on the observation that processes used in the production of goods have a certain amount of natural fluctuations, which yield products that exhibit some level of "normal" variation. The issue is to identify, while products are manufactured, the ones that vary too much from the norm, as they may not be manufactured within the specifications demanded by the customer.

It is therefore fundamental to determine the level of normal variations in a process used to manufacture a product. This is done in four steps:

1. Collection of Historical Data

In the first step, historical data must be collected. This is done after the process has been confirmed to be working correctly: the machine is operating at its normal setting and it has been serviced recently so that no problem is likely to be present. During the historical-data collection, the process must be "left alone." The machine operator should not change any setting on the machine or adjust or replace anything. The goal is to gather data that reflect the natural fluctuations of the process. The historical data should include a minimum of 30 samples. The size of these samples is determined by the type of data collected, and that point will be explained later in this section.

historical data
The initial manufacturing data collected to create a statistical quality control system.

2. Calculation of Statistics

From these samples of data, statistics, such as the mean and a measure of deviation, should be calculated for each of the samples, and other statistics calculated for the entire set of samples.

3. Creation of Control Charts

These statistics should then be used to create statistical process control charts. They are visual tools that help the operator determine whether the process is working "normally," that is, whether it is producing parts that have the normal amount of variation, or whether it is producing parts that have too much variation.

control charts
A visual tool used to determine whether a manufacturing process is working correctly.

4. Plotting of New Data

In the last step, and once the control charts are built, samples are collected again as the process runs, and the data plotted on the control charts. In most instances, the data will show that the process is working normally, but on occasion, the operator is alerted if something "out of normal" is happening and the process is not working correctly. Once a process is found to not be working properly, the process operator can take remedial action.

These four steps are identical for all the different types of control charts that can be used in statistical process control. The next two Sections will show how this methodology is followed for statistical process control charts for attributes (called p-charts) and for variables (called $\overline{X}$ and R charts). There are other forms of statistical process control charts, but they are omitted in this textbook.

19.3   SPC With Attributes

attribute
A binary variable that indicates whether a manufacturing part is conform or non-conform.

SPC with attributes
A statistical quality control method used to determine whether a manufacturing process is working correctly.

In Statistical Quality Control, attributes are binary variables—0-1 variables—that cannot be measured. A product is either conforming (built the way the manufacturer intended) or it is not. Examples of attribute data include whether a molded plastic part is free of bubbles (conforming) or has some surface defect (non-conforming), whether a door is of the same color as the remainder of a refrigerator, whether a part fits into another part, or whether a piece of cloth has a surface defect. Attributes take only two values: 0 when the product is conforming, 1 if the product is non-conforming. A non-conforming product is not defective to the point that it will not work, but it is not of acceptable quality.[5]

19.3.1   Collection of Historical Data

The historical data is made up of a minimum of 30 samples. The number of samples collected is denoted as m. In the case of attribute data, the samples must be relatively large; this is data for which the sample size must be at least 50. The size of each sample collected is denoted as n. The operator is therefore collecting information for 30 samples of 50 items each: $m = 30$ and $n = 50$.

For each sample, the process operator determines the percentage p of products that are non-conforming. For each sample, the number of items that are non-conforming (d) is determined and divided by n to find the proportion of defectives p.

Historical data therefore consists of m data points: p_1 for the first sample, p_2 for the second sample, ..., and p_m for the mth sample.

19.3.2   Calculation of Statistics

Once the historical data are collected, the operator can calculate two statistics:

- The average proportion of defectives, noted $\overline{p}$

$$\overline{p} = \frac{p_1 + p_2 + p_3 + \cdots + p_m}{m}$$

- The standard deviation of the proportion of defectives, noted σ

$$\sigma = \sqrt{\frac{\overline{p}(1 - \overline{p})}{n}}$$

19.3.3   Creation of Control Charts

Attribute data follow a binomial distribution; when the sample size n is sufficiently large, the distribution of a binomial variable approximates a normal distribution. A normal distribution has specific properties that are the foundations on which Statistical Process Control charts are built.

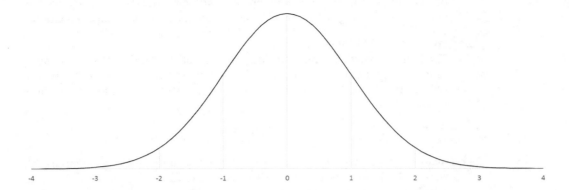

Figure 19.1: The Normal Distribution.

In a normal distribution, the area under the curve represents the distribution all of the possible values of a statistic calculated from samples taken from a population. In SPC with attributes, the normal distribution represents the distribution of all of the possible values of the percentage of defectives that can be found in samples taken from the process that is being evaluated. There are very few samples for which the percentage of defectives is very low, and very few samples for which the percentage of defectives is very high, and most of the samples will have percentages of defectives that are "close" to average.

Figure 19.1 shows a standardized normal distribution, which is a distribution for which the mean is 0 and the standard deviation is 1. It is a simple way of representing all normal distributions. In statistical process control, the normal curve approximates the distribution of the proportion of defectives in samples taken from a given population.

- The proportion of the samples for which the percentage of defectives fall between the mean minus one standard deviation and the mean plus one standard deviation (the interval on the horizontal axis between −1 and +1) is 68.26 percent of all samples. That is, the area under the curve between −1 and 1 is 68.26 percent of the entire area under the curve.

- The proportion of the samples for which the percentage of defectives fall between the mean minus two standard deviations and the mean plus two standard deviations (the interval between −2 and +2 on the horizontal axis) is 95.44 percent. The proportion of the samples for which the percentage of defectives fall between ± three standard deviations from the mean is 99.73 percent.

- Only 0.13 percent of the samples will have percentages of defectives to the left of −3 and 0.13 percent of the samples will have percentages of defectives to the right of +3; that is, very few of them will have percentages of defectives that are below the mean -3 standard deviations, and very few will have percentages of defectives above the mean $+3$ standard deviations.

The Upper Control Limit (UCL)
The control chart assumes that few samples fall "naturally" above the mean plus three standard deviations, and it considers that number to be the upper control limit, beyond which no more than 0.13 percent of all sample statistics fall. Its value is:

$$UCL = \overline{p} + 3 \times \sigma$$

The Lower Control Limit (LCL) The control chart assumes that few samples fall "naturally" below the mean minus three standard deviations, and it considers that number to be the lower control limit, below which no more than 0.13 percent of all sample statistics fall. Its value is:

$$UCL = \overline{p} - 3 \times \sigma$$

Figure 19.2 shows the control chart that is built with these data. It is called a p-chart.

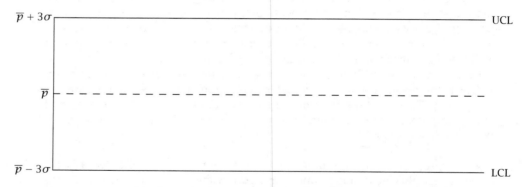

Figure 19.2: Control Chart for SPC with Attributes—p-Chart

19.3.4 Plotting of New Data

New data consists of additional samples of n items collected after the control chart is created. For each of these samples, the operator calculates p, the proportion of defectives for that sample, and places that value on the control chart. As the process continues working, the operator places additional points on the chart, and connects them.

Figure 19.3 on the facing page shows the end result of having collected 20 new samples. All of the newly collected samples' proportions of defectives fall between the lower control limit and the upper control limit, and therefore the operator can conclude that the process is "in control." It is not operating differently that it did in the past: it is not yielding a percentage of defectives that is statistically different from the proportions of defectives that were observed during the historical-data collection.

Everything is going well, and the operator should be unconcerned. This should be the case most of the time; the process is working as it is intended to work, without issues.

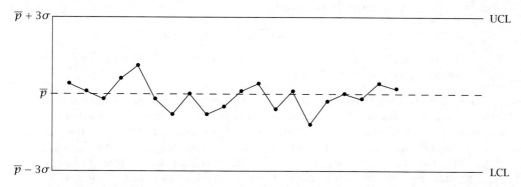

Figure 19.3: New Data on Control Chart for SPC with Attributes

19.3.5 Identification of Out-of-Control Situations

However, there are times when the process is not working as it is intended; the process is said to be "out of control."

The operator notices these situations because the process is yielding percentages of defectives that are not within the "normal" range.

There are several cases that will lead the operator to consider that the process is out of control:

out-of-control situation
An observation on a control chart that indicates that the manufacturing process may not be working correctly.

- A single value above the Upper Control Limit (UCL), as shown in example① on Figure 19.4

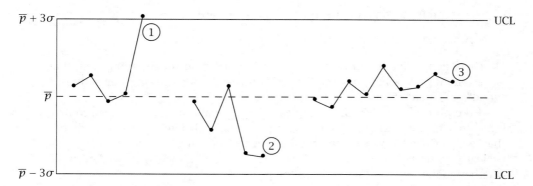

Figure 19.4: Out-of-Control Situations on Chart for SPC with Attributes

- A single value below the Lower Control Limit (LCL)

In either of these cases, the probability that a sample yields a statistic outside of the control limit is 0.13 percent, so it is not likely that such an even happened by chance; something may have caused it. It is therefore important for the operator to stop the process and investigate what happened, because it is possible that the process is not working correctly.

- Two consecutive values "near" the Upper Control Limit (UCL)

- Two consecutive values "near" the Lower Control Limit (LCL), as shown in example ② on Figure 19.4

Operators will sometimes color their control charts in green for the area between -1 and 1 standard deviation, in yellow between -2 and -1 standard deviations as well as between 1 and 2 standard deviations, and in red between the LCL and -2 standard deviations, and between 2 standard deviations and the UCL. They will then interpret being "near" the UCL or LCL as being in the red area. The probability that two consecutive samples yield proportions of defectives that are between 2 and 3 standard deviations from the mean is $\dfrac{99.73 - 95.44}{2} \times \dfrac{99.73 - 95.44}{2}$ or 0.046 percent, which is unlikely. Therefore, something may have caused it, and the process should be investigated.

- Seven consecutive values above the mean $\overline{p}$, as shown in example ③ on Figure 19.4

- Seven consecutive values below the mean $\overline{p}$

The probability that seven consecutive samples are above the mean is 0.5^7 or 0.78 percent. Since this is unlikely, the operator should investigate the process. to determine whether it is working correctly.

Two other cases are associated with out-of-control situations, but they are less frequently used, because they are more difficult to identify:

- A trend in the data points, upward or downward

- A process that behaves erratically

There is one final point that is relevant in out-of-control situations, and that is determining whether the fact that the process is not working normally is a "good" or a "bad" thing.

If the process is generating samples that yield values near the upper control limit, that means that it is producing a percentage of defectives that is higher than what was observed during the historical-data collection, so that situation is clearly an undesirable outcome. The operator should investigate to determine whether something went wrong with the process.

However, if the process is generating percentages of defectives that are lower than the ones collected during the historical-data collection, then it is a desirable outcome, and if the process is working differently than during the historical-data collection period, this is an improvement. The operator should investigate what happened, and find a way to reproduce those conditions, so that the process improves. If it is possible to duplicate the effect, then a new process has been identified, and a new set of historical data should be collected and new process-control charts created.

Figure 19.5: An Operator Checking an SPC Chart in Hanoi, Vietnam
Photo ©Vietnam Stock Photos/Shutterstock. Used with Permission.

Numerical Example: SPC With Attributes

Gascuel is a French company that produces bolts of denim cloth. The company considers that a bolt of fabric is conforming if there are no defects in the fabric, and non-conforming if there is a defect, such as a knot in the thread, a discoloration in the dye, or some other surface imperfection. Non-conforming bolts are still acceptable to Gascuel's customers, but they prefer defect-free fabric.

The table on the next page shows the historical data for the 30 samples that the company collected over a period of a month. Each of these samples included the inspection of 50 bolts of fabric.

0.01	0.03	0.01	0.02	0.01	0.03	0.02	0.01	0.03	0.02
0.02	0.01	0.03	0.02	0.01	0.01	0.02	0.03	0.01	0.02
0.01	0.01	0.02	0.02	0.02	0.02	0.03	0.01	0.02	0.01

$$\Sigma = 0.54$$

For the fabric manufacturer, $\overline{p}$, the average proportion of defectives, is $\frac{0.54}{30} = 0.018$ and σ, the standard deviation of the proportion of defectives is
$$\sqrt{\frac{0.018 \times 0.982}{50}} = 0.0188.$$
The company then calculates the values needed to create the control charts. The value of the upper control limit UCL is

$0.018 + 3 \times 0.0188 = 0.0744$ and the value of the lower control limit LCL is $0.018 - 3 \times 0.0188 = -0.0384$. Since the proportion of defectives cannot possibly be less than zero, the LCL is simply changed to 0.

The following table shows new data for 20 samples that the company collected after having created its control chart. The operator places these data on the p-chart.

| 0.02 | 0.01 | 0.01 | 0.03 | 0.01 | 0.02 | 0.01 | 0.01 | 0.04 | 0.02 |
| 0.03 | 0.01 | 0.01 | 0.02 | 0.03 | 0.01 | 0.01 | 0.02 | 0.02 | 0.01 |

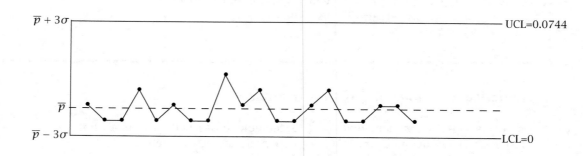

None of the samples collected show an "out-of-control" situation, and therefore the company is confident that the process is working correctly, as it has worked in the past.

19.4   SPC With Variables

In Statistical Quality Control, variables refer to continuous measurements. Examples of variable data include the length of a part, its thickness, or its diameter, the resistance of an electric motor, the temperature of an oven, or the frequency at which a tuning fork vibrates. Variables can take an infinite number of values.[6]

variable
On a manufactured product, a measurement that can take an infinite number of values.

SPC with variables
A statistics quality control method used to determine whether a manufacturing process is working correctly.

19.4.1   Collection of Historical Data

The historical data is made up of a minimum of 30 samples. The number of samples collected is denoted as m. In the case of statistical process control with variable data, the samples are relatively small; the sample size must be at least 4, but in most cases, it is less than 10. The size of the samples collected is denoted as n. The operator is therefore collecting information for 30 samples of between 4 and 10 items each: $m = 30$ and $n = 4$ to 10.

For each sample, the process operator measures each of the items in the sample, and obtains n measurements, from X_1 for the first observation in the sample to X_n for the nth observation. Two statistics are then calculated for each sample: the first is the average measurement in the sample, $\overline{X}$, and the second is the range of measurements in the sample, which is the difference between the largest observation X_{max} and the smallest observation X_{min} in the sample.

Their values are:

$$\overline{X} = \frac{X_1 + X_2 + X_3 + \cdots + X_n}{n}$$

and

$$R = X_{max} - X_{min}$$

19.4.2   Calculation of Statistics

Once the historical data are collected, the operator can calculate two statistics for the entire historical-data set:

- The average average measurement, noted $\overline{\overline{X}}$, and called either grand average or simply X-bar-bar:

$$\overline{\overline{X}} = \frac{\overline{X}_1 + \overline{X}_2 + \overline{X}_3 + \cdots + \overline{X}_m}{m}$$

- The average range, noted $\overline{R}$

$$\overline{R} = \frac{R_1 + R_2 + R_3 + \cdots + R_m}{m}$$

19.4.3 Creation of Control Charts

There are two control charts that must be built for SPC with variables; one for the values of the mean, called the $\overline{X}$-chart, and another for the values of the range, called the R-chart.

As for SPC with attributes, the control charts are built so that the Upper Control Limit and the Lower Control Limit represent the mean plus three standard deviations and the mean minus three standard deviations. That way. the control limits show the interval in which 99.73 percent of the sample statistics will fall.

However, in the statistics that were computed during the historical-data collection, the operator did not calculate a standard deviation, but simply took the range of measurements in the observations. The standard deviation therefore needs to be estimated based on the range.

Sample Size	Factor for $\overline{X}$-Chart	Factors for R-Chart	
n	A_2	D_3	D_4
4	0.73	0	2.28
5	0.58	0	2.11
6	0.48	0	2.00
7	0.42	0.08	1.92
8	0.37	0.14	1.86
9	0.34	0.18	1.82
10	0.31	0.22	1.78
11	0.29	0.26	1.74
12	0.27	0.28	1.72
13	0.25	0.31	1.69
14	0.24	0.33	1.67
15	0.22	0.35	1.65
16	0.21	0.36	1.64
17	0.20	0.38	1.62
18	0.19	0.39	1.61
19	0.19	0.40	1.60
20	0.18	0.41	1.59

Table 19.1: Coefficients A_2, D_3 and D_4 for SPC Charts with Variables
Grant and Leavenworth.

Table 19.1 shows the coefficient A_2 by which the range must be multiplied to estimate the value of three standard deviations above the $\overline{X}$ mean, and the coefficients D_3 and D_4 by which the range must be multiplied to estimate the values of the upper control limit and lower control limit for the R-chart.

The values of the control limits for the control charts are:

$$UCL_{\overline{X}} = \overline{\overline{X}} + A_2\overline{R} \qquad\qquad LCL_{\overline{X}} = \overline{\overline{X}} - A_2\overline{R}$$
$$UCL_R = D_4\overline{R} \qquad\qquad LCL_R = D_3\overline{R}$$

19.4.4 Plotting of New Data

Once the $\overline{X}$-chart and the R-chart are built, the operator can start the process of collecting new data and plotting these data onto the control charts.

The operator collects the data from samples of the same size as the ones used in the historical-data collection: the sample size must be at least 4, but in most cases, it is less than 10.

For each sample, the process operator calculates the mean $\overline{X}$ and plots it on the $\overline{X}$-chart, and the range of measurements in the sample, R, and plots it on the R-chart.

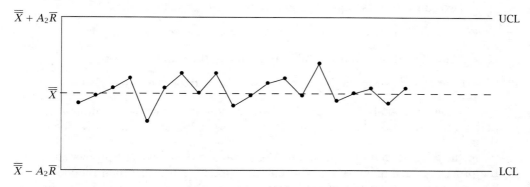

Figure 19.6: Control Chart for SPC with Variables—$\overline{X}$-Chart

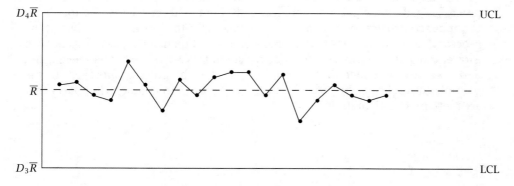

Figure 19.7: Control Chart for SPC with Variables—R-Chart

Both of the charts show that the process is in control. However, the two charts show different aspects of the process.

- The $\overline{X}$-chart shows the average measurement of the parts in the sample, and it monitors whether the process manufactures parts that are close to the expected measurement. It is a tool used to monitor accuracy.

- The R-chart measures the range of measurements, or the variations of the parts in the same sample. If the range of measurements is low, the products are made more consistently. It is a tool used to monitor precision.

19.4.5 Identification of Out-of-Control Situations

Out-of-control situations for $\overline{X}$-charts and R-charts are determined in the same manner as out-of-control situations for p-charts. The operator needs to investigate what may have caused, whether on the $\overline{X}$-chart or the R-chart:

- A sample statistic to be above the UCL or below the LCL,

- Two consecutive sample statistics to be "near" the UCL or the LCL,

- Seven consecutive sample statistics being above or below the mean,

- A downward or upward trend in the value of the sample statistics,

- Erratic behavior in the values of the sample statistics collected.

However, the analysis of out-of-control situations is somewhat different in determining whether the cause of the unusual results is a "good" or a "bad" thing.

In the $\overline{X}$-chart, out-of-control situations are always considered problematic; the process is manufacturing parts that are lighter (or heavier) than they have been in the past, or parts that are longer (or shorter) than they have been in the past, ... and so on.

The analysis is different in out-of-control situations for the R-chart. If the process is generating parts that are less consistent (two consecutive samples near the upper control limit), that should be a concern for the operator. However, if the process is generating parts that are more consistent than in the past—that is, with a lower range than normal—, the operator should investigate what happened, and find a way to reproduce those conditions, so that the process improves. If it is possible to duplicate the effect, then the company is manufacturing parts that are more precise than in the past.

Numerical Example: SPC With Variables

Ling-Sun Co. in Taipei, Taiwan is a manufacturer of piezzo-electric polymers, a type of plastic that vibrates (gives a sound) when subjected to an electric current. It produces them on a VanLorn-Lemag press from the United States: the company collected the following historical data on samples of size $n = 6$.

Sample	Mean	Range	Sample	Mean	Range	Sample	Mean	Range
1	201	8	13	201	6	25	199	6
2	198	5	14	200	7	26	199	8
3	199	3	15	197	3	27	201	6
4	201	7	16	199	9	28	202	6
5	198	5	17	201	7	29	200	4
6	200	7	18	202	4	30	200	7
7	202	6	19	198	5	31	200	5
8	201	6	20	201	2	32	201	5
9	197	7	21	198	9	33	197	4
10	197	3	22	200	4	34	196	7
11	198	6	23	198	7	35	199	6
12	199	4	24	199	4	36	197	7

$$\Sigma[\overline{X}] = 7{,}176 \qquad \Sigma(R) = 205$$

For the manufacturer, the grand average measurement is:

- $\overline{\overline{X}} = \dfrac{7,176}{36} = 199.333$

and the average range is:

- $\overline{R} = \dfrac{205}{36} = 5.694.$

The values of the coefficients for the upper and lower control limits for the charts can be found in Table 19.1 on page 650: $A_2 = 0.48$, $D_3 = 0$ and $D_4 = 2$.

The control limits are therefore:

$$
\begin{aligned}
UCL_{\overline{X}} &= 199.333 + 0.48 \times 5.694 \\
&= 202.07 \\
LCL_{\overline{X}} &= 199.333 - 0.48 \times 5.694 \\
&= 196.60 \\
UCL_R &= 2 \times 5.694 = 11.39 \\
LCL_R &= 0
\end{aligned}
$$

The Table on the next page shows data for 18 new samples that the company collected.

Sample	Mean	Range	Sample	Mean	Range	Sample	Mean	Range
1	201	6	7	200	4	13	200	6
2	198	8	8	200	6	14	199	7
3	199	7	9	198	6	15	200	4
4	201	5	10	199	5	16	197	4
5	201	6	11	201	3	17	199	5
6	199	13	12	200	7	18	200	6

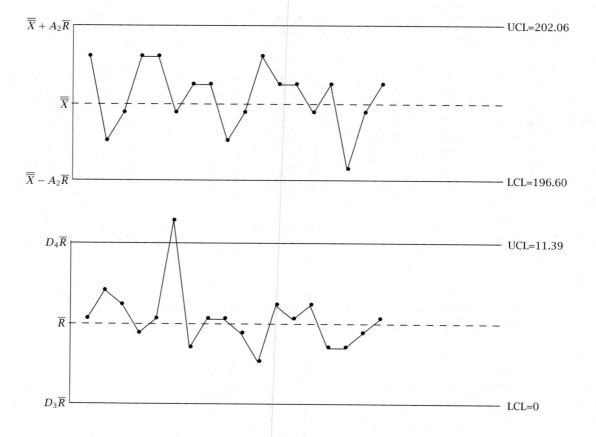

The $\overline{X}$-chart shows that the process is in control. However, in the R-chart, sample 6 was out of control. It is likely that the process operator noticed the problem, stopped the process, and corrected the issue, as the remainder of the samples are in control.

19.5   Process Capability

Statistical process control tools are put in place to monitor that processes are working correctly. They allow the operator to determine when the process is out of control, and to remedy the situation before parts are manufactured with a process that is not working correctly.

However, a process that is in control may still not be producing parts that are within the specifications of the customer. A process-capability study allows a company to determine whether the process is producing parts that are acceptable to the customer.

The customer's engineering department determines what a part's characteristics should be. The supplier is given specifications: a part's diameter must be 200mm ± 0.3mm, or its resistance must be 15 Ω ± 0.01 Ω.

The upper limit of this range is called the upper specification—called almost invariably "upper spec"—and the lower limit is the lower specification—or "lower spec." Whether a process is capable of producing parts within the specifications is determined by computing the C_{pk}, the coefficient of capability of a process for a set of specifications.

The coefficient is:

$$C_{pk} = \frac{\dfrac{\min\left[US - \overline{\overline{X}} \; ; \; \overline{\overline{X}} - LS\right]}{\sqrt{n}}}{\dfrac{\left(UCL_{\overline{X}} - LCL_{\overline{X}}\right)}{2}}$$

where:

- US is the upper specification

- LS is the lower specification

- $\overline{\overline{X}}$ is the grand average of the $\overline{X}$-chart for the process

- n is the sample size used in the statistical process control

- UCL is the upper control limit for the $\overline{X}$-chart

- LCL is the lower control limit for the $\overline{X}$-chart

- the function "min" returns the lowest of two values; in this case, the lowest number between $US - \overline{\overline{X}}$ and $\overline{\overline{X}} - LS$

The value of the C_{pk} determines the extent to which the process is capable of producing parts within the specifications outlined by the customer. Table 19.2 shows the value of C_{pk} and the corresponding number of parts (per million) that will be non-conforming.

The way many companies refer to their processes' capabilities is often expressed in "sigmas," i.e. their processes are five-sigma capable or four-sigma capable.

process capability
A measurement of the ability of a manufacturing process to produce parts that meet customer's specifications.

C_{pk}
A coefficient measuring the ability of a manufacturing process to produce parts that meet customer's specifications.

C_{pk}	Percentage of population Within Limits	Number of defects per million	Number of σ
1.00	99.7300204	2,700	± 3.0
1.10	99.9033152	967	± 3.3
1.20	99.9681783	318	± 3.6
1.30	99.9903807	96.2	± 3.9
1.33	99.9936658	63.3	± 4.0
1.40	99.9973309	26.7	± 4.2
1.50	99.9993205	6.80	± 4.5
1.60	99.9998413	1.59	± 4.8
1.67	99.9999427	0.573	± 5.0
1.70	99.9999660	0.340	± 5.1
1.80	99.9998933	0.067	± 5.4
1.90	99.9999988	0.012	± 5.7
2.00	99.9999998	0.002	± 6.0

Table 19.2: Coefficient of Capability and Number of Defects per Million.

Numerical Example: Capability Study

Ling-Sun Co. has received an order for 500,000 sheets of a certain plastic which is used in an application where the plastic must vibrate at 200 Hz. The tolerances are ± 10 Hz.

The company wants to determine whether its process is capable of manufacturing parts within these specifications. It therefore calculates the C_{pk} for this process:

$$C_{pk} = \frac{\dfrac{\min\left[US - \overline{\overline{X}} \; ; \; \overline{\overline{X}} - LS\right]}{\sqrt{n}}}{\dfrac{\left(UCL_{\overline{X}} - LCL_{\overline{X}}\right)}{2}} = \frac{\dfrac{\min\left[210 - 199.333 \; ; \; 199.333 - 190\right]}{\sqrt{6}}}{\dfrac{\left(202.07 - 196.60\right)}{2}} = \frac{3.81}{2.73} = 1.39$$

Ling-Sun Co. considers that a C_{pk} of 1.39 is acceptable. From Table 19.2, it determined that the number of parts that would fall out of the specification range would be approximately 30 parts per million. The company simply communicated to the customer that there would be "fewer than 50" out-of-specifications parts. The customer was satisfied with this answer and placed the order.

19.6 Continuous Improvement

The Motorola company created the position of Corporate Quality Officer in 1980,[7] with the goal of improving the quality of its products to match or surpass the quality of its Japanese competitors, widely considered the worldwide quality leaders in electronics manufacturing. Its intent was to achieve that goal by continuously improving its operations.

continuous improvement
A method used by manufacturers to reduce the natural variability in a manufacturing process.

19.6.1 Motorola's Six Sigma

Bill Smith, an engineer at Motorola, is considered the father of Six-Sigma,[8] which he created in 1981. By 1987, Motorola had implemented the six-sigma quality system on all its internal manufacturing operations, and had required it of its suppliers by the early 1990s.

six sigma
A measurement of the ability of a manufacturing process to produce parts that meet customer's specifications.

The company was not looking for its manufacturing operations to produce only 0.002 defects per million parts, however. The reason behind the six-sigma requirement is that Motorola's engineers allowed for the possibility that the process would "shift" over time, and deviate from its historical-data mean: the parts would change in some way. They accounted for a possible shift as large as 1.5 sigmas, which would render the process only 4.5-sigma capable.[9]

This 4.5-sigma capability—after the worst-case scenario of a 1.5-sigma shift to the right or left of the distribution—would yield 3.4 defective parts per million: that is the case because the shift caused the entire distribution to move left or right, and therefore there is only one tail of the distribution that generates defective parts. The other tail is well within the specifications. The number of defects in Table 19.2 includes both tails (a symmetric distribution), but that is lost when the entire distribution shifts; therefore, the number of defects per million is $\frac{6.8}{2} = 3.4$ defects per million.

Numerical Example: A Second Look at the Capability Study

Ling-Sun's analysis would have been more thorough if it had considered the difference between the mean of the specifications (200 Hz) and the mean of its process (199.33 Hz), which should considered a "shift." The $UCL_{\overline{X}}$ of the process is 202.07 and its mean is 199.33, so its standard deviation is:

- $\dfrac{202.07 - 199.33}{3} = 0.9133.$

The shift is therefore equal to:

- $\dfrac{200 - 199.33}{0.913} = 0.73$

standard deviations.

The shift places the distribution of the parts made by Ling-Sun to the left of the specifications by 0.73 standard deviations. A calculation of the C_{pk} yielded 30 parts per million outside of the specifications, but the calculation was made on a symmetric distribution. In this case, though, that calculation only holds true for the left tail of the distribution, so there are 15 parts per million that are out of specifications in that tail. On the right tail, because of the shift, the number of defectives is essentially nil (< 0.002 per million). The number of out-of-specifications parts that Ling-Sun should anticipate in a production run of 500,000 parts is approximately 8, which is much lower than what the customer considered acceptable.

19.6.2 Black Belts

black belt
The name given to an individual whose responsibilities include quality control and process improvements.

The effort to get manufacturing operations at Motorola to become six-sigma capable created a significant need for employees who were well versed in the design of processes and quality-control systems. Motorola first relied on a handful of employees for implementing this change, and they eventually became known as "black belts" within the company.[10] They were the ones who took the leadership roles in implementing this system. Eventually, the martial-arts analogy was extended with the creation of "green belts," who helped black belts in designing processes, and "yellow belts," who were the novices in the six-sigma quality system, and the "master black belts," who were the trainers and coaches for black belts. The black-belt terminology had significant appeal—black belts led the "fight" in increasing quality and making companies competitive—, and after Jack Welch made its use mandatory at General Electric in 1995,[11] the terminology became widely accepted, beyond quality management.

Even though the trend had started at Motorola, it was at General Electric that the six-sigma concept was significantly enlarged to mean much more than a capability study's results. It was first understood as a managerial commitment to quality; black belts had the support of top management when they designed improvements for manufacturing processes, analyzed them, and implemented changes based on the controls they had put in place. Six-sigma eventually became a managerial philosophy focused on eliminating errors and defects in all processes, with a focus on customer satisfaction.[12] General Electric claimed to have saved US$ 12 billion in the first five years of six-sigma implementation.[13]

19.6.3 Taguchi Methods

Taguchi methods
A set of methods used to reduce the variability in a manufacturing process.

The six-sigma-capability push by Motorola was imitated by several other companies. Many suppliers realized that they had no choice but to improve their processes if they wanted to be able to sell to these customers.

Genichi Taguchi was the first to create a methodology, which became known as Taguchi methods, to improve manufacturing processes. These methods are based on his own ideas and the ones developed by Ronald Fisher on designs of experiments and analysis of variance—ANOVA—. His point was that much of the variation of manufactured parts was due to controllable variations in manufacturing inputs, and that, by analyzing and isolating the elements that created that variation, parts could be made reliably more consistent.[14]

Continuous improvement uses experiments that are designed to determine what factors in a process cause variations in a product's characteristics. By trying multiple combinations and levels of factors, through a careful experimental design, quality managers can ascertain which combination reduces variation the most. By reducing variation, they reduce the standard deviation of the process, narrow the difference between the upper control limit and the lower control limit, and make the process more capable.

Continuous improvements are incremental, not revolutionary; most of them reduce variation by a few percentage points of the total, but, in the end, variation can be reduced to a bare minimum.

19.7 Quality Standards

Industry quality standards were first created by the craftsmen of medieval Europe, who organized in craft guilds.[15] Guilds were organizations created by artisans engaged in the same occupation, such as cobblers, cabinet makers, stone masons, or carpenters. The guilds were created for protection and mutual aid, but they also served to maintain a monopoly of a particular craft especially against outsiders. In protecting its own members, the guilds protected the consumer as well. Many guild regulations prevented poor workmanship, and articles had to be examined by a board of the guild, and stamped as approved, before they could be sold. The most important processes were considered trade secrets that the guild protected.[16]

quality standards
A set of industry standards that dictate the minimum performance attributes of a product.

19.7.1 Industry Standards

Starting with the industrial revolution, many industries created standards of performance, so that parts could be made to fit one another; a finished-product manufacturer could use bolts made by one company and nuts from another, and they would work together. An electric switch would function with a certain amperage and voltage. A plumbing fixture could be connected to supply lines.

Industry standards of performance are still needed in the twenty-fist century to make sure that items made by one company are compatible with complementary items made by another company, and that products perform to customers' expectations. Standards are "requirements for products, services and/or processes, [including] their required characteristics. They help ensure the free movement of goods and encourage exports. They serve to safeguard people and goods and to improve quality in all areas of life."[17]

These standards of performance are mostly organized by industry, especially in the United States, or by country. However, in 1947, the International Organization for Standardization (ISO) was created "to facilitate the international coordination and unification of industrial standards." Its membership today consists of the national standards bodies of more than 160 countries, such as the American National Standard Institute (ANSI) in the United States, the Deutsches Institut für Normung (DIN) in Germany, the Japanese Industrial Standards Committee (JISC)

International Organization for Standardization (ISO)
An international standard-setting body whose membership is made up of national standard-setting bodies.

in Japan, the Associação Brasileira de Normas Técnicas (ABNT) in Brazil, the Association Française de Normalisation (AFNOR) in France, the British Standard Institute (BSI) in the United Kingdom, ... and so on.[18] The ISO has published more than 20,000 standards, such as ISO 4217, the standard for currency abbreviations (the U.S. dollar is USD, the British pound is GBP, the Japanese yen is JPY, so that there are no possible confusions on the currency being mentioned), or ISO 3166, which spells out country codes: LTU is Lithuania, GTM is Guatemala, and CHE is Switzerland (Confédération Helvétique).[19]

19.7.2   ISO 9000

ISO 9000
A standard of quality procedures developed by the International Organization for Standardization.

ISO 9000 is a set of international standards on quality management developed and published in 1987 by the International Organization for Standardization (ISO). It was one of the first standards that was not a standard of performance. ISO 9000 is a standard of procedures: any process that a company is using to make its product has to be described, and the employees trained in that process.

The ISO 9000 standards are based on standards that were first published by the British Standards Institute (BSI) in 1971 and called BS 9000, which had been developed for the electronics industry. in the 1970s, BSI convinced other industries to adopt the same standard, and it was published as the BS 5750 standard in 1979. The standard formally shifted the responsibility for the inspection and quality of manufactured goods from the customer to the supplier, eliminating quality-assurance processes,[20] a fundamental shift in the way quality was managed.

The original ISO 9000 standards included three different types of certification (9001, 9002, and 9003). A company would select the correct one based on the type of processes in which it was engaged. The standards were implemented as "standards of procedures:" companies would create documents that explained every procedure that could have an impact on quality, perform training to make sure that employees knew them, and then audited plants to ensure the standards were followed. These standards were very useful because they forced companies to formally identify the best way to perform certain tasks, and then make sure that all employees performed them correctly. However, many companies became certified by creating "shelf-loads of procedure manuals and became burdened with ISO bureaucracy. [They had created] a 'system of documents' "[21] rather than a quality system: one of the derisive criticisms of ISO 9000 was that a firm could meet the standards by manufacturing life jackets made with concrete— and therefore utterly ineffective—, as long as it had documented all aspects of its manufacturing processes.

The International Organization for Standardization felt that processes improvements were particularly difficult in such an environment, and it revised the ISO 9000 standards in 2000, in 2008, and again in September 2015.[22] The standards are therefore known as ISO 9000:2015. Today, they include only one certification (ISO 9001 certification), and it emphasizes that companies should have a system in place to improve their manufacturing processes. They are still required to document them—still a fundamental aspect of ISO 9000—, but the emphasis is now on enforcing a system of process-improvement management.

19.7.3 QS 9000 and IATF 16949

The QS 9000 standard was developed by the "big three" automotive manufacturers (General Motors, Ford, and Daimler-Chrysler) in 1994. It was written because their suppliers had to deal with the quality standards of each of these three manufacturers (GM had one for North America called *Targets For Excellence*, and one for Europe called *General Quality Standard*, Ford had named its program *Q101 Quality System Standard*, and Chrysler had its *Supplier Quality Assurance Manual*). These standards were mostly based on manufacturing capabilities (C_{pk} studies and control charts).

QS 9000
A quality standard created by the three largest North American automobile manufacturers.

When the ISO 9000 standards appeared, the auto makers appreciated that another dimension of quality had been introduced (standardization and documentation of processes), and they decided to create a single standard for the North American auto industry that would incorporate all of the elements of ISO 9000 as well as additional process-capability and performance standards. Tier-

Figure 19.8: An IATF-16949 Certified Truck-Engine Plant (Skoda) in Mlada Boleslav, Czech Republic.

Photo ©Nataliya Hora/Shutterstock. Used with Permission.

one suppliers (companies selling directly to the auto makers) would have to be QS 9000-certified before they could ship parts, and, over time, the tier-two suppliers (companies selling to the tier-one suppliers), and eventually the tier-three suppliers became certified. In many instances, the certification of suppliers was conducted by the automotive manufacturers.

Problems were still present in the auto industry, because suppliers in countries outside of the United States had to comply to QS 9000 as well as to standards designed by their own country's automotive manufacturers. It was possible for a manufacturer of parts to have to follow the manufacturing requirements for Toyota, Honda, Mitsubishi, Volkswagen, PSA, Fiat, Volvo, in addition to the QS 9000 standards of the North American market. The International Organization for Standardization created the ISO 16949 standard in 1999 to attempt to supplant all of these standards, and by 2006, QS 9000 had been formally replaced by ISO 16949.

In 2016, the ISO 16949 standard had become the only standard that was acceptable in the automobile industry, and it changed its name to IATF 16949, after the International Automobile Task Force, a consortium of automobile manufacturers that had created it under the umbrella of the International Organization for Standardization.

19.8   Quality as a Marketing Tool

Providing customers with products that meet their specifications is not a competitive advantage; this is the minimum that a customer would expect. However, it is possible to use a quality-management program as a marketing tool and create a competitive advantage.

First, an exporter can gain a competitive advantage by providing customers with a detailed capability study that demonstrates that the process that the manufacturer is using is capable of producing the parts within the specifications. By providing a C_{pk} or a n-sigma—4 or 5 sigma—capability analysis, the exporter can ensure that the customer receives parts that meet the specifications, with no defects.

Second, the supplier may include the SPC charts that were produced during the production run that produced the products the customer purchases. That way, the customer can confirm that the process was working as it was designed, and that therefore the parts are within specifications without issue.

Review and Discussion Questions

1. What does it mean when a process is "in control"?

2. Why would a customer want evidence that a supplier's manufacturing process is in control and capable?

3. Explain the similarities and differences between quality standards and ISO 9000.

4. Why is it important for an OEM to have tier-one, tier-two, and tier-three suppliers that are QS 9000 or IATF 16949 certified?

5. How can an exporter gain a competitive advantage with quality-control tools?

Notes

[1] *Military Standard 105E*, May 10, 1989, superseding MIL-STD-105D, April 29, 1963, http://www.barringer1.com/mil_files/MIL-STD-105.pdf, retrieved May 3, 2017.

[2] Grant, Eugene L., and Richard S. Leavenworth, *Statistical Quality Control*, Seventh Edition, 2004, McGraw-Hill, New York, New York.

[3] Shewhart, Walter A., and W. Edwards Deming, *Statistical Method from the Viewpoint of Quality Control*, First Edition, 1939, reprinted (1986) by Dover Publications, Mineola, New York.

[4] Besterfield, Dale H., *Quality Control*, Fourth Edition, 1994, Prentice-Hall, Englewood Cliffs, New Jersey.

[5] Grant, Eugene L., and Richard S. Leavenworth, *Statistical Quality Control*, Seventh Edition, 2004, McGraw-Hill, New York, New York.

[6] *Ibid.*

[7] "Motorola: A Tradition of Quality," *Quality Magazine*, May 16, 2003, http://www.qualitymag.com/articles/84187-motorola-a-tradition-of-quality, retrieved May 3, 2017.

[8] "Remembering Bill Smith, Father of Six Sigma," Inside Six Sigmas, https://www.isixsigma.com/new-to-six-sigma/history/remembering-bill-smith-father-six-sigma/, retrieved May 3, 2017.

[9] Pyzdek, Thomas, and Paul Keller, *The Six Sigma Handbook*, Fourth Edition, 2014, McGraw-Hill, New York, New York.

[10] "History of the Six Sigma Black Belt Naming Convention," Inside Six Sigma, https://www.isixsigma.com/new-to-six-sigma/history/history-six-sigma-black-belt-naming-convention/, retrieved May 3, 2017.

[11] Trainer, Andy, "Jack Welch and the History of Six Sigma," Silicon Beach Training's Blog, September 26, 2013, https://www.siliconbeachtraining.co.uk/blog/jack-welch-history-of-six-sigma, retrieved May 3, 2017.

[12] Welch, Jack, "Six-Sigma," unknown date, https://www.youtube.com/watch?v=aNMULFcLuIM, retrieved May 3, 2017.

[13] Trainer, Andy, "Jack Welch and the History of Six Sigma," Silicon Beach Training's Blog, September 26, 2013, https://www.siliconbeachtraining.co.uk/blog/jack-welch-history-of-six-sigma, retrieved May 3, 2017.

[14] Taguchi, Genichi, Subir Chowdhury, and Yuin Wu, *Taguchi's Quality Engineering Handbook*, First Edition, 2004, John Wiley and Sons, New York, New York.

[15] "History of Quality," American Society for Quality, http://asq.org/learn-about-quality/history-of-quality/overview/overview.html, retrieved May 3, 2017.

[16] Betcher, Gloria J., "Medieval Guilds," http://www.public.iastate.edu/gbetcher/373/guilds.htm, retrieved May 3, 2017.

[17] "A Brief Introduction to Standards," Deutsches Institute für Normung, http://www.din.de/en/about-standards/a-brief-introduction-to-standards, retrieved May 3, 2017.

[18] "ISO: a Global Network of National Standards Bodies," https://www.iso.org/members.html, accessed April 28, 2017.

[19] "Popular Standards," International Organization for Standardization, https://www.iso.org/popular-standards.html, accessed May 3, 2017.

[20] "ISO History," British Assessment Bureau, http://www.british-assessment.co.uk/iso-9001-history/, retrieved April 28, 2017.

[21] *Ibid.*

[22] "What is the ISO 9000 Standards Series," American Society for Quality, http://asq.org/learn-about-quality/iso-9000/overview/overview.html, retrieved April 28, 2017.

Chapter 20

Developing a Competitive Advantage

The preceding chapters outlined many of the challenges that an international logistics manager faces in an international business environment. They covered
the infrastructure of international business, the management of financial and
transportation risks, and the choices related to international transportation and
packaging, all of which are eminently more complex than for domestic transactions.

However, a good export manager should not see these challenges as obstacles,
but as opportunities to offer a higher level of service than competitors. This
can be done by following several elementary points. The recommendations that
follow may not be sufficient to clinch the sale; however, they will help in all
circumstances.

Consider that an importer, in most situations, is getting several quotes from
several exporters located in different countries. Although the alternative bids are
likely to be evaluated on many criteria (price, support, after-sale service, delivery
terms, and so on), one of the most important issues will be the ease with which
the purchase transaction will take place. From the importer's perspective, the
easiest alternative is to purchase from a supplier who communicates clearly, who
has a flexible approach, who offers convenient terms of sale, who is careful in
handling paperwork and transportation, who keeps sufficient inventory on hand,
who ensures that goods meet quality requirements, and who packages the goods
carefully. When all else is the same, the well prepared exporter will earn the sale
by being better prepared on those logistical details.

Thus, the good management of international logistics can be a competitive
advantage.

20.1   Communication Challenges

One of the most challenging aspects of international business is effective communication. Conducting business with people in foreign countries is often ham-
pered by language barriers. It can be quite difficult to conduct business when two
people from different languages and cultures are communicating. An additional
challenge for the international logistics manager is that most communications
with foreign counterparts are conducted in an impersonal fashion, through e-
mail, fax, and letters. This detached contact does not allow for the subtleties of
in-person communication, such as tone of voice or gestures, which comprise a
large portion of communications and often help make communications more in-
telligible. There is also no opportunity to ask for immediate clarification, as there
is in verbal communication, and the possibility of errors or misunderstandings is
greatly increased.

The U.S. Department of State classifies languages by the degree of difficulty
that they present for a native English speaker learning that language. Table 20.1[1]
outlines these categories and languages. The greater the differences between two
persons' languages, the greater the communication difficulties are likely to be.
Sentences can often be interpreted differently, and both parties will then be left

---

Group I: Languages closest to English, Easiest to Learn

(Roman alphabet, similar grammar, similar syntax)

Spanish, French, Italian, Dutch, German, Norwegian, Swedish, Romanian

---

Group II: Languages Difficulty to Learn

(Roman alphabet, different grammar, different syntax)

Turkish, Indonesian, Icelandic, Czech, Hungarian, Polish, Vietnamese, Finnish

---

Group III: Languages Very Difficult to Learn

(Different alphabet, different grammar, very different syntax)

Hebrew, Russian, Greek, Hindi, Thai

Group IV: Languages Extremely Difficult to Learn

(Complex alphabet, multiple alphabets, different grammar, different syntax)

Mandarin Chinese, Cantonese Chinese, Arabic, Korean, Japanese

---

Table 20.1: Classification of Languages, by Difficulty, for an English Speaker
Effective Language Learning and U.S. Department of State.

to wonder what the other person meant by a certain word, phrase, or sentence.

To the international logistician, the diversity of languages and associated possible misunderstandings means that extreme care should be taken with communication, to ensure that the correct meaning is conveyed every time.

20.1.1 English in International Logistics

Conveniently for the native speaker of English, most international communication takes place in that language. English has become everybody's second language, not only because it is the easiest language to learn,* but also because it is the language of most countries' largest trading partners. However, the advantage of being able to communicate in one's own language means that there are significant responsibilities attached to doing so.

International English

International logistics professionals engage mostly in written communications with their counterparts abroad using e-mail, fax, or other written documents, and therefore it is critical that they communicate clearly in writing. A specific style of writing for native English speakers has developed to increase the probability that non-native speakers of English can clearly understand what is written.

international English
A technique of written communication that attempts to remove all ambiguities, so that a person with limited knowledge of English can understand it.

---

*Contrary to a commonly held belief in the United States and Britain, English is one of the easiest languages to learn because of its relatively simple grammar, its lack of gender forms, and its smaller number of tenses.

This technique, dubbed International English by Edmond Weiss, is outlined in his outstanding book *The Elements of International English Style*.[2]

Writing in International English means following several rules (Weiss lists 57 of them), but the most important one is that the native English speaker should strive to make the meaning of the communication absolutely clear to the non-native speaker: "Business and technical documents intended for those who read English as their second language must be unusually simple, unambiguous, and literal. Ideally, they should be edited for ease of translation."[3] The most important rules are:

- Always assume that the person for whom English is a second language is relying on a dictionary. That means that the word definition used should preferably be the first one in the dictionary and should always be unambiguous. For example: "The company's sales took off 25 percent last year" should be replaced with "The company's sales increased 25 percent last year," for several reasons. First, "to take" has a very long entry in the English dictionary, and the meaning of "to take off" is listed toward the end of that entry. Another reason is that one of the first meanings listed for "to take off" is "to remove (one's clothes);" therefore there is a strong possibility that the sentence will be understood as "sales [removed] decreased 25 percent." A convenience sample of foreign students in the author's classes reinforced this point; about 30 percent of them thought "sales took off" meant a decrease. By using a precise and accurate verb, "to increase," no confusion is possible. This recommendation can be contrary to the caution to write in "simple words" that is often advocated by native-English teachers everywhere. In practicality, more complex words tend to be more precise and have the smallest number of alternative meanings, and therefore are far better for International-English communication.

- Always proofread carefully and avoid grammatical and spelling errors. There is a strong possibility of confusion in a sentence that reads, "The customer purchases products from company A and it's marketing services form company B." The reader is left to determine whether there are two typos (*it's* rather than *its* and *form* rather than *from*) or just one (*form*). Is the sentence communicating that the customer purchases products from company A and marketing services from company B, or that it is purchasing products from company A and providing marketing services to (for) company B? Actually, a non-native speaker will probably not understand that there are typos in that sentence and not grasp its meaning at all.

Other common misspellings result from the confusion between *there, they're*, and *their*; between *accept* and *except*; between *too, two* and *to*; and between *effect* and *affect*. There is also the frequently found "should of done" instead of "should have done," which is only understandable to a native speaker who "hears" English rather than reads it. For example, it is very likely that a foreign reader will not comprehend the sentence "Our company would like to except your company's proposal," as the reader will not understand that the word "except" was used instead of "accept." Actually, it is more likely that the foreign reader will understand the opposite of what was meant, and believe that the company rejected the proposal.

Another issue for native English speakers is the correct usage of the final *s* in forming the plural and possessive. It is important to make sure that documents are proofread so that *shipments* does not appear as *shipment's*, an error that can create confusion. Is the document referring to all shipments or just one?

- Always ensure that quantitative information will be understood without question. A date of 12/11/18 can be understood three different ways: A U.S. reader will understand 12/11/18 to mean December 11, 2018; a French, British or German reader will understand 12/11/18 to mean 12 November 2018; and a Chinese reader will understand 12/11/18 to mean 18 November 2012. It is best to follow the practice of spelling all dates fully: "11 December 2018" is unambiguous.

  The number 10^9 is 1 billion to a North American reader, but 1,000 million (or 1 milliard) to a British or German reader, for whom a billion is 10^{12}; meanwhile, 10^9 is 100 crore (or 10,000 lakhs) to an Indian, Pakistani, or Nepalese. Writing the number (1,000,000,000) in its entirety leaves no doubt and is always the best strategy. In some countries, though, that is still insufficient; an Indian, Pakistani, or Nepalese writer will write that number as 100,00,00,000. To a Western reader, that notation will be misunderstood as a typo, and the issue would be to determine what the actual number should be. If necessary, use scientific notation to avoid any misunderstanding.

  It is common in some countries to abbreviate 35,000 to 35k, and 23,000,000 to 23M, but it is certainly not common in all. Therefore the preference is to spell out the entire number rather than cause doubt in the reader's mind.

- Always use simple and short sentences. As much as possible, sentences should contain only one main idea. If there are possible writing shortcuts, they should be avoided—for example, "The company requests the report be sent early in the month" should be changed to "The company requests that the report should be sent between the first and the fifth day of the month." When in doubt, punctuation should be added to enhance clarification, even if it seems too heavily punctuated to a native speaker.

- Never use idioms that are related to sports or the military, as they are rarely, if ever, understood properly. Writing that a salesperson "struck out" on a deal or that she "hit a home run" will confuse a foreigner, who, in looking for "hit a home run" in the dictionary will read that she "ran around the bases with one hit."[4] A correct sentence conveying the same meaning would say that she was "unsuccessful" or "successful beyond our expectations."

Military terminology should also be avoided. Terms such as "plan of attack" or "price war" tend to be difficult to translate or offensive to some cultures.[5]

If there is any doubt that foreign sport terminology is incomprehensible to the uninitiated, a quick visit to a British newspaper, such as *The Guardian,*[6] or an Indian newspaper, such as *The Telegraph,*[7] and a glance at the cricket page will quickly dispel it (see the Vignette below).

The concept behind International English is that communication should be easy to understand and devoid of cultural references. One of the most effective ways to determine whether a message is written clearly enough to be understood by a foreign reader is to translate it using machine-translation software into another language (preferably not a European language) and translate it back into English. It will rarely, if ever, be the same as the original text; however, if its original meaning is still understandable, then the text was written in an English that can be properly understood by a non-native speaker.

Culturally Laden English

Here are three article excerpts, taken on April 28, 2017, from three newspapers: one British, one Indian, and one American. All of them tell a story about a national pastime: football (soccer), cricket, and football. For all three of them, these are the opening paragraphs:

- "If the howls of anguish coming from the Soccer Saturday presenter's chair are a little louder than normal this weekend there may be a justifiable reason for it. Hartlepool United's 96-year grip on a Football League place is in grave peril and a defeat at Cheltenham Town, two places and four points above them in League Two, may be enough to apply the final wound with a game to spare. The club's plight should be familiar to anybody who has regularly seen Jeff Stelling, their most visible fan, in action this season and

  should the worst happen at 4.50pm it is reasonable to assume the nation will soon be well apprised."[8]

- "Rahul Dravid shone brightly among the selfie-hunters in the fading daylight of the Eden on Thursday. Dravid is everything that T20 is not, but the stalwart, it seems, remains in demand among the T20-addicts of this generation. Fact is, had he not retired, the Delhi DareDevils mentor would also have been in demand on the 22-yard strip that is to be used for Friday's IPL X game.

  With a fair sprinkling of grass, the pitch at the Eden in all probability would be loved as much by the fast bowlers as it would be dreaded by the batsmen. The memories of the famed Royal Challengers

Bangalore batting line-up being embarrassingly stripped naked in the last match here are still fresh."[9]

- "Everybody's mock draft was dead by 8:15 ET on Thursday night, which is fine. As it should be, really. Mock drafts are fun things we do to pass the time in the months ahead of the actual draft. And as Thursday night showed, the actual draft is a heck of a lot more entertaining.

  Not even the mock draft of San Francisco 49ers brain trust John Lynch and Kyle Shanahan's wildest dreams featured the Chicago Bears trading them three picks to move up one spot so they could take North Carolina quarterback Mitchell Trubisky. That move was a no-brainer for the 49ers, who weren't going to take Trubisky and were happy to get Solomon Thomas one spot later."[10]

To the uninitiated, it is difficult to comprehend what is expressed in these articles. Using similar vocabulary and cultural references in international correspondence will ensure that the meaning of the message is lost.

Special English

For oral or spoken communications, the challenge is much greater, as there is less time to refine sentences used and ensure that the meaning is clear. It is important to realize that one of the greatest difficulties experienced by a non-native speaker—of any language—is to talk on the telephone. There are no visual cues that help communication and, on occasion, there are technical difficulties that hamper good communication.

To communicate clearly in English with foreigners, it is useful to become familiar with Special English, a reduced-vocabulary English developed by the Voice of America, the U.S. government-sponsored news organization that broadcasts worldwide. While the Voice of America is prohibited from broadcasting in the United States,[11] it is possible to hear its broadcast on the Internet.[12] Here are the main characteristics of Special English:

special English
A technique of oral communication that uses a limited vocabulary and short sentences, so that a person with limited knowledge of English can understand it.

- Sentences should be short and contain only one idea. It is more effective to use two sentences ("Sentences should be short. Sentences should contain only one idea.") than to confuse the listener. The listener is often trying to understand a particular word or sentence structure and may not remember how the sentence started, due to spending so much energy concentrating on understanding. It takes a little practice, but it is certainly easy for a native speaker to learn to speak in this way.

- Vocabulary should be limited to correct and accurate terms. Much sports-related imagery exists in American English, but such imagery should be avoided; stating that a contract negotiation is still "in the first inning" (it is in the very first stages, with only one of the two parties having made its points), or that the companies competing for a particular sale are "not on a level-playing field" (one of the competitors has an unfair advantage over the other) is unlikely to be understood correctly by a non-native speaker. The same is true of terms such as "stand up to" or "roll over," which should be replaced with their precise equivalents: "confront" or "reinvest." Even expressions that are clearly understood in one English-speaking country can be difficult for others: "carrying coals to Newcastle" makes as little sense to U.S. English speakers as "selling refrigerators to Eskimos" makes to Australians.

- The speed at which sentences are spoken should be slower. The broadcasts of the Voice of America aim for two-thirds of the speed of normal speech. From the author's personal experience, people from the southern part of the United States are much more easily understood than people from the north because they tend to speak at a slower pace. The U.S. southern accent is much less of an issue for foreigners, who tend to visualize the words as they are spoken.

- Finally, if a foreigner asks a native speaker to repeat a sentence, the native speaker should not repeat the sentence louder, as if the person had difficulty hearing. The issue is generally about a word that the listener did not understand or a sentence that was too complicated. It is best to just repeat the sentence using slightly different vocabulary or repeat the sentence and offer an alternative word. For example, "Our company would like to sleep on that proposal for a few days" (a sentence that violates the principles listed above, and is likely to be misunderstood) can be repeated as "Our company would like to sleep on that proposal, think about it, for a few days." In this manner, the non-native speaker better understands the sentence and gains new vocabulary.

20.1.2 Translations

Communications between the exporter and the importer frequently take place in English. However, exporters should not expect consumers to be able to understand the language of the exporter, and therefore an exporter of consumer products should make every effort to communicate accurately with its end customers. Although it is mostly the responsibility of the marketing department rather than that of the logistics manager, well-designed packaging, accurate instruction manuals, and precise other communications are important to provide responsible customer service.

translation
A conversion of words or text from one language into another.

Translation is frequently not sufficient. It is necessary to adapt the language to the target audience, so that the communication takes into consideration consumer preferences and product-usage conditions. Consider Westmark, the manufacturer and exporter of a small kitchen utensil (see Figure 20.1 on the next page). It sells its products not only in a consumer package that includes a description of

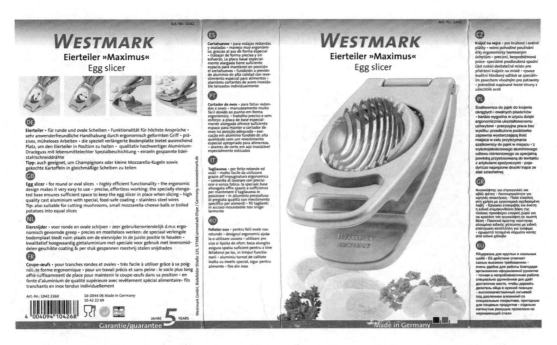

Figure 20.1: Westmark's Packaging of a Kitchen Tool, with Export in Mind

Photo ©Westmark GmbH. Used with permission.

the product in twelve different languages—taking three of the four sides of the packaging—,but each translation is adapted to its audience. Although the photograph clearly depicts that the device can slice eggs and mushrooms, the English and German versions also mention that the device can slice mozzarella balls and cooked potatoes. However, the French, Spanish, and Italian versions do not. The English and Romanian versions do not mention that the wires are individually tensioned, but most of the others do—at least the ones that the author can decipher. What is not clear is whether these differences in translation have much importance; nevertheless, these variations were approved by the company.

adaptation
A translation that accounts for cultural differences and contexts.

A good exporter has packaging that uses good translations. Unfortunately, it is frequent to see packaging from some exporters that use approximate translations, possibly done by machine or by employees with a marginal command of the language, and those translations reflect poorly on the exporter. Good translations are more likely to engender confidence in the exporter's products than poor ones.

Ikea solved the problem in a different manner. Although its instruction manuals include safety warnings in 35 languages (Ikea is present in 38 countries),[13] they are identical otherwise in all countries. The company makes them understandable to all its customers by using directions that use only pictorials (see Figure 20.2). In many ways, the drawings are easier to understand than written

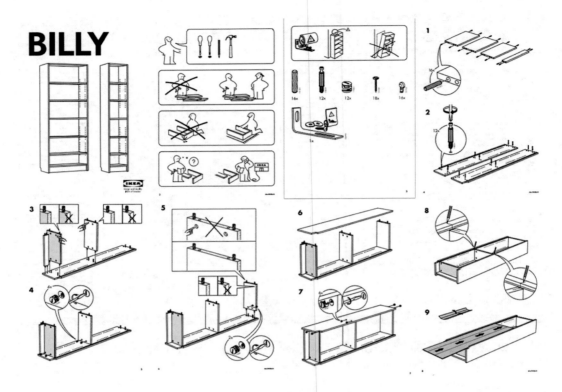

Figure 20.2: The First Eight Pages of Assembly Instruction for an Ikea Bookshelf
Photo ©Inter IKEA Systems B.V. Used with permission.

instructions; they start with the tools needed for assembly, the number of people needed, and the surface area on which the assembly must take place. The parts are clearly identified, including the hardware needed to assemble them. Each step is clearly explained and many assembly details are included; these directions are easy to follow, and they even include diagrams of commonly made errors.

20.2   Metric System

metric system
A decimal system of measurements, part of the International System of Units, that is widely adopted worldwide.

English system
A system of measurements used almost exclusively in the United States.

Communication is also better served by using what is familiar. Unfortunately, U.S. exporters and importers do not use the system of measures—the metric system—that every other country in the world uses (except for Liberia and Myanmar, which also do not use the metric system) but instead uses a system called the English system that even its everyday users find difficult to understand. Foreigners, thus, tend to be entirely baffled by the U.S. system of measurement.

For example, within the so-called English system of measures, there are at least four types of tons: (1) the short ton, which is a measure of weight and weighs 2,000 pounds; (2) the long ton, which is also a measure of weight at 2,240 pounds; and (3) the gross (registered) or net ton, which is a measure of volume and equals 100 cubic feet; (4) the refrigeration ton, which is the capacity of a refrigeration system, measured by its ability to freeze one ton (short, long, metric?) of water in 24 hours. In addition, there is often no indication of which ton is the one mentioned in the message: only tradition and context dictate which "ton" is the one that is intended.

Measurement units can get much more complicated. There are five types of ounces: (1) an *avoirdupois* weight unit of 437.5 grains; (2) an apothecary or Troy weight unit of 480 grains; (3) a U.S. fluid ounce, which is a measure of volume worth six teaspoons; (4) its "equivalent" regulatory fluid ounce, which is defined as 30 milliliters or 1.5 percent more than a U.S. fluid ounce; and (5) an imperial fluid ounce, which is 4 percent smaller than the U.S. unit. There is generally no indication of which unit is the correct one in a document or regulation, including guidelines for the nutrition labeling of foods.[14] As if this were not difficult enough, there are traditional units in some industries that use the same terminology very differently. For example, leather is measured in the United States in ounces, which, in this case, is a measure not of weight nor of volume, but of thickness: "Two-ounce leather such as calf or goat skin is about 1/32 inches thick, while eight-ounce leather is a full 1/8 inches."[15]

Another peculiarity of the English measurement system is that a measurement may not refer to actual product dimensions, but to a nominal measurement whose origins may be only loosely linked to its actual dimensions. If a measurement is given as $\frac{1}{2}$ inch, there are countless instances in which the actual measurement is **not** 0.5 inches:

- A 1/2-in copper pipe has an external diameter of 0.625 inches, and an internal diameter that depends on the thickness of the pipe's wall, but none of them is equal to 0.5 inches (they are between 0.527 and 0.569 inches).[16]

- A 1/2-in electrical conduit pipe made of polyvinyl chloride (PVC) has an inside diameter of 0.622 inches, and an external diameter of 0.84 inches. If it is made of galvanized metal, its inside diameter is 0.660 inches and outside diameter is 0.815 inches.[17]

- A 1/2-in piece of plywood is generally only 15/32 inches thick, but can be between 7/16 inches and 31/64 inches thick.[18]

This problem extends to other measurements as well:

- A piece of lumber to which every American refers as a 2-by-4 stud (2 × 4) measures actually 1.5 × 3.5 inches. A 2 × 6 piece of lumber is 1.5 × 5.5 inches, but a 2 × 8 is 1.5 × 7.25 inches.

A few more peculiarities of the English measurement system make it difficult for non-Americans. U.S. measurements are often given as a fraction, rather than a decimal; for example a measurement will be given as $2\frac{5}{16}$ inches rather than

2.3125 in, a preference which is disconcerting to people who are used to a metric system that is entirely decimal.

This mathematical notation can also be confusing as it is an unconventional way to display a quantity without an operator (whether $\times$, $+$, $\hat{}$, $-$, or $\div$). What is meant by $2^{\frac{5}{16}}$ (sometimes noted as $2\frac{5}{16}$), is determined by context.

In the absence of the operator, the quantity $2^{\frac{5}{16}}$ can be read three different ways:

- $2 + \dfrac{5}{16}$ is generally meant,

- but it can also mean $2 \times \dfrac{5}{16}$,

- or possibly $2^{\frac{5}{16}}$, that is, 2 to the power of $\dfrac{5}{16}$

Because of the issues presented by communications made in English measurements, it is to the advantage of everyone involved in a transaction to use the metric system, which has a well defined set of measures, all of which are clearly and accurately established. A kilogram is a measure of mass, a liter is a measure of volume, and a meter is a measure of distance. There are convenient ways to move from one unit set to the next: one liter is exactly equal to a cube of side 0.1 meter (10^{-3} cubic meters), and a kilogram is equal to the mass of water contained in a liter. There are conventions for the names of multiples (kilo, hecto, deka) and for the names of fractions (deci, centi, and milli), all of which are decimal. More importantly, there are no ambiguous usages.

While utilizing the metric system may represent a challenge for a U.S. exporter or importer, its customers or suppliers will understand metric communications much better, and this effort will result in a greater probability of making a sale.

Converting to the metric system, though, is more than just multiplying by the correct coefficient. Selling a product in 3.785-liter bottles (equivalent to one U.S. gallon bottle), in 1.13-kg bags (equivalent to 2.5 lbs. or 40 oz), or in 3.05 meter increments (equivalent to 10 feet), does not satisfy the admonition to use the metric system; while it is a convenient conversion of common English units, these quantities are unusual for customers used to the metric system, for whom products are generally sold in one- or two-liter bottles, one-kilo bags, and one-meter lengths. A correct conversion would therefore use round units of measurement rather than direct translations of round units in the English system into awkward decimal quantities in the metric system.

Calculating a Shipment's Weight and Volume

There are substantial differences between the effort extended by a shipper using the metric system and that of a shipper using the English system. Consider two juice manufacturers, one American, the other European, who need to decide whether an identical shipment of juice boxes can fit in a 40-foot container. Will the shipment weigh less than the maximum allowable weight? Will it physically fit inside the box? The American will use the so-called traditional English system, and the European will use the metric system. Both shipments contain 5,000 cartons of 24 juice boxes of the same size.

• The American shipper

The American shipper must first determine the weight of this shipment of juice boxes. Each juice box contains 7 fluid ounces of apple juice. Ignoring the fact that apple juice has a slightly higher density than water, and having found that 1 fluid ounce weighs 1.04 avoirdupois ounce, the American shipper determines that each juice box weighs 7.28 ounces. The total weight of the shipment is therefore $5,000 \times 24 \times 7.28 = 873,600$ ounces. Because one pound is 16 ounces, the shipper then divides that result by 16 to obtain the total shipment's weight of 54,600 pounds. Will that shipment fit in a container whose maximum capacity is 26.29 long tons? The shipper needs now to divide 54,600 pounds by 2,240 and ends up with 24.375 long tons. Even accounting for the additional weight of packaging and

dunnage, the shipment is well within the container's weight limit.

Each juice box measures $1\frac{5}{8}$ inches by $2\frac{1}{2}$ inches by $3\frac{1}{2}$ inches. Will this shipment fit in a regular 40-foot container whose inside measurements are 39 feet 6 inches long by 7 feet $8\frac{1}{8}$ inches wide by 7 feet $5\frac{3}{4}$ inches high? The shipper must first determine the volume of each juice box: $1.625 \times 2.5 \times 3.5 = 14.22$ cubic inches. Then, the shipper determines the volume of the entire shipment: $5,000 \times 24 \times 14.22 = 1,706,400$ cubic inches. Finally the shipper needs to determine the volume of the container and, for that, needs to calculate how many inches there are in each dimension: 39 feet 6 inches is $(39 \times 12) + 6$ inches or 474 inches in length, 7 feet $8\frac{1}{8}$ inches is $(7 \times 12) + 8.125$ inches or 92.125 inches in width, and 7 feet $5\frac{3}{4}$ inches is $(7 \times 12) + 5.75$ inches or 89.75 inches in height. The entire volume of the container is therefore $474 \times 89.75 \times 92.125 = 3,919,136$ cubic inches. The shipment of 1,680,000 cubic inches fits without problem, even accounting for the space taken by packaging and dunnage. Converting the dimensions to feet and calculating in cubic feet would not have simplified the task at all.

• The European shipper

Using a similar shipment, the European shipper can make the same calculations much faster in the metric system. The capacity of each juice box is 205 milliliters and therefore it weighs 205 grams, if the slightly higher density of juice is ignored. The total shipment weighs $5,000 \times 24 \times 205$ grams $= 24,600,000$ grams or 24.6 tonnes. Because the capacity of the container is 26.72 tonnes, there is no issue, even after packaging and dunnage are added. The dimensions of each juice box are $4.1 \times 6.3 \times 8.9$ centimeters. Each box therefore has a volume of 230 cubic centimeters or 230 milliliters. (This is more than the volume of the juice itself, which is 205 cubic centimeters, and that is because the juice boxes tend to have sides that are slightly concave. This was also the case for the American juice boxes but it was unnoticeable because of the units used.) The entire shipment is therefore 27,600,000 cubic centimeters or 27.6 cubic meters. The container is the same, with inside dimensions of 1,204 centimeters long by 234 centimeters wide by 228 centimeters high. Its total volume is $1,204 \times 234 \times 228 = 64,235,808$ cubic centimeters or 64.23 cubic meters, and therefore the shipment fits without difficulty, even after the packaging and dunnage are added.

Unless the American shipper knew it by heart, a dictionary was needed to find out that a fluid ounce weighs 1.04 ounces and that a long ton is 2,240 pounds. The shipper may have had to glance at a decimal-equivalence table to know that $\frac{1}{8} = 0.125$. The American shipper certainly needed a piece of paper to keep it all straight, as well as a calculator. The European shipper only needed a calculator.

20.3   Cultural Sensitivity

Although communicating information clearly is fundamental to becoming a better international logistician, it is also valuable to become savvy about others' cultures. Unfortunately, if there is one aspect of international business about which it is difficult to generalize, it is culture. There is little about culture that can be summarized in a few sentences, and when such an attempt is made, exceptions abound. In the long term, the best that an international logistician can do is to study intercultural communication. In the meantime, a few of these pointers can help.

One aspect of communication that is shaped by culture is the way people address each other in person, in the mail, or over the telephone. In some cultures, the forms of address are quite formal (France), and in others (Australia) quite informal. In some cultures, people are very sensitive to titles (Germany), in others much less so (Canada). U.S. culture is among those that care the least about titles and formalities, although there are a few notable exceptions to that rule. In all cases, because it is difficult to offend someone by being too formal, an astute international logistics manager will therefore always err on the side of formality, and communicate as politely and formally as possible until there is evidence that it is appropriate to adopt a less formal tone.

Another area in which it is easy to make quick progress is in understanding a country's work culture. First, the international logistician should consider the separation between work and private life. In some countries, there is a considerable divide between work and family, and the two never or rarely intersect (Japan). In others, the two are closely tied to one another (Indonesia). When in doubt, it is generally better to consider that personal life and work life are separate, unless there is evidence on the part of the foreign interlocutor that it is appropriate to mention family and private life in business communications.

Another area in which there are culturally determined differences is the speed at which people operate in the workplace. In some countries, it is expected of business persons to answer an inquiry very quickly, in order to show that the inquiry is important and that it commands their full attention (Germany). A delay implies a lack of interest. In others, it is impolite to answer too quickly, as a response should be given careful thought (Saudi Arabia). There is no ideal way to handle these discrepancies, but the advice for international logisticians is, again, to learn the appropriate response time from what their foreign counterparts do and mirror that behavior.

Finally, culture influences the way people spend their workday; the time at which they arrive at work, leave work in the evening, and eat during the day. Culture also influences the amount of time that they spend at each meal and the days of the week that they work. Finally, it influences the holidays that are celebrated. Countries have different holidays, and different customs during identical holidays. Sometimes it is appropriate for an exporter or importer to send a card or a greeting, in others it is not. In those cases, the CultureGrams[19] mentioned in Chapter 1 are most useful. In any case, for the international logistician, a delayed response to a request on a certain day may simply be due to a holiday rather than a lack of interest. Considering that India, due to its multiplicity of religions, has a total of 43 official holidays, it is more likely than not that there is some celebration during a given week.

20.4 Specific Advice

In addition to the general advice presented so far, the international logistician has multiple opportunities to gain a competitive advantage by following several strategies in specific areas. Some of these strategies were presented in earlier chapters, but they bear repeating.

20.4.1 Terms of Payment

Although the choice of the term of sale depends on the level of experience of both the exporter and the importer, and on the level of confidence that the exporter has in the ability of the importer to make the payment, there are some alternatives that are preferable and will increase an exporter's probability to close a sale.

An importer, in most situations, is getting several quotes from exporters located in different countries. Alternative bids are evaluated on many criteria (price, specific capabilities, after-sale service, delivery terms, and so on), and on the ease with which the purchase transaction will take place. From the importer's perspective, the easiest term of payment is to purchase on an open-account basis. It is likely that at least one of the potential suppliers will offer such terms, and that others will ask for a letter of credit or documentary collection. Therefore, the supplier offering an open-account transaction has an advantage over the others. If that supplier has purchased credit insurance, offering the option to purchase on an open-account basis does not affect its probability of getting paid.

Therefore, an exporter intent on increasing its sales should choose to display confidence in the importer's ability to pay for the goods by using an open account. If the exporter is unsure about the importer's ability to pay, it should consider purchasing a credit insurance policy.

20.4.2 Currency of Payment

In an international transaction, the currency of payment exposes the exporter (or the importer) to the risk of currency exchange rate fluctuation. Rather than view this risk as a drawback in an international sale, a good exporter should consider it an opportunity and take advantage of the several alternatives it has to reduce its risk of currency fluctuation.

Because of the intense competition that an exporter faces in international markets, a significant percentage of the companies competing for the importer's business will offer quotes in the importer's currency. Because it is easier for the importer to handle a purchase in its own currency, an exporter that does not offer to conduct the transaction in the importer's currency is at a strategic disadvantage.

An exporter intent on increasing its sales abroad should therefore offer all of its quotes in the importer's currency and discuss with its banker the most appropriate hedging strategy for each transaction.

20.4.3 Incoterms® Rule Choice

In some cases, an exporter can facilitate the sale of its products and gain a strategic advantage by assisting a novice importer in handling an international shipment. In other cases, an experienced importer may gain a price advantage by performing all or most of the tasks involved in the shipment.

Most exporters do not like to determine which Incoterms® rule to use on a case-by-case basis. Instead, an exporter adopts a policy to include in international quotes those services that it feels competent providing. It is difficult for an exporter to adapt its Incoterms® strategy to accommodate an importer's requirements, as it may require the exporter to be responsible for tasks that it would rather not perform. However, if the importer wants to perform more tasks than the exporter prefers, it is certainly possible for the exporter to do less than it expected, and use a different Incoterms® rule on that transaction, so that it is responsible for less.

An exporter intent on increasing sales should therefore offer the importer the most customer-friendly Incoterms® rule quotes (either DAP or DDP) and, if necessary, use the services of a competent freight forwarder. If the importer wants to assume more responsibilities, the exporter can always reduce its involvement and quote FCA or even EXW. The best quote is one in which the exporter lists different prices for different Incoterms® rules, allowing the importer to choose which option is best for its specific case.

For example, an exporter can submit a quote that reads:

FCA · 2500 Industrial Parkway, Cleveland, OH 44114, USA _____ $10,000

FCA · Terminal 5, Cincinnati Airport, Covington, KY 41048, USA ___ $11,000

CIP · CDG Cargo, route des badaux, 95700 Roissy-en-France, France $15,500

DAP · 114 rue de Prat, 63100 Clermont-Ferrand, France _____ $16,500

DDP · 114 rue de Prat, 63100 Clermont-Ferrand, France _____ $17,800

and leave the customer to decide which Incoterms® rule it wants to use. The *pro forma* invoice is then created after that decision has been reached.

20.4.4 Document Preparation

Accurate and timely document preparation and delivery are an essential part of international logistics and of the smooth transfer of goods from an exporter to an importer.

Any failure to provide complete documents in a timely manner is likely to delay a shipment, generate additional costs by requiring last-minute mailings of critical documents, or create difficulties for one or more of the parties involved in the transaction. Because proper document preparation falls mostly on the exporter, regardless of the Incoterms® rule used in a transaction, an exporter can turn its ability to do a good and thorough job in preparing documents for international trasactions into a marketing advantage.

An exporter intent on increasing sales should, therefore, be thorough and meticulous in the way it prepares the documents that it provides to the importer. This approach should be reflected in the first contact, the *pro forma* invoice, and be communicated to the importer by emphasizing the exporter's experience in providing accurate and thorough documents.

20.4.5 Packaging

An exporter's good handling of packaging requirements will also facilitate the smooth transfer of goods from the exporter to the importer.

The most crucial way of looking at packaging is to prepare for the worst. The exporter should imagine the worst-case scenario and the roughest possible journey for the goods when packaging them for export. It is only under this premise that the exporter will adequately serve the importer's need to receive goods in sellable and usable conditions.

Although good packaging procedures are expensive, the benefits are substantial. First, good packaging procedures allow the goods to arrive at their destination in perfect shape and be immediately sellable or usable by the importer. Good packaging also reduces the costs of repackaging or the costs of damaged goods. In addition, because insurance companies can always deny a claim based on poor packaging, it pays to have a track record of stellar packaging.

However, the greatest benefits from a good packaging policy are the goodwill that it generates between the importer and the exporter, and the marketing benefits that can be derived from it. Because the importer is not interested in challenging invoices or asking for allowances for damaged goods, it welcomes shipments that arrive carefully packaged and in good condition.

20.4.6 Warehousing and Inventory Management

For an exporter, warehouses and inventory management tools can play a major role in gaining a competitive advantage.

A warehouse in close proximity to customers means that the exporter can offer lead times similar to those of domestic competitors; in some cases, that simple possibility can make a difference to a potential customer who may not have had the option to wait for an international shipment. A warehouse can also provide value-added services that are important to the customer, and its proximity to the market allows those services to be added just prior to delivery. Similarly, after-market services can be provided in a customer-friendly way: no need to return goods internationally for warranty work or repairs.

Good inventory management practices are critical to ensure goods can be delivered to customers when they are needed, and avoid postponing or losing sales because an item is not in inventory. Good planning, appropriate inventory levels, and satisfactory safety stocks allow an exporter to provide customers with goods when they request them, and ensure good service levels. Customers become repeat customers when they are satisfied that the goods they purchase will arrive on time.

However, good inventory management practices also reduce costs, providing exporters with higher profits or more competitive prices. An MRP system allows a company to provide customers with clear information on delivery dates and ensure that it can deliver reliably, on the dates to which it committed.

20.4.7 Quality

Good quality-control processes provide customers with assurances that the products they are purchasing were manufactured within the customer's specifications and within industry norms. The exporter can provide the customer with a detailed capability study that demonstrates that the process is capable of producing the parts within the specifications. By using a manufacturing process that has a C_{pk} of at least 1.33—a process that is at least 4-sigma capable—, the exporter can ensure that the customer receives parts meet the specifications.

20.4.8 An Integrated Effort

Careful packaging, meticulous document preparation, considerate choices in terms of payment and Incoterms® rule selection, good quality controls, good inventory practices, and clear communications will enhance the relationship between exporter and importer through goodwill and trust. Learning and understanding these skills will help an international logistician gain a substantial competitive advantage.

Review and Discussion Questions

1. What are the advantages of learning to use International English and Special English in communicating with non-native speakers of English?

2. What are the advantages of using the metric system in international commerce?

3. What are the trade-offs exist for an exporter when choosing between a standardized policy and remaining flexible? You can choose either terms of payment or Incoterms® rules to illustrate your points.

4. In your opinion, why is it important for an exporter to sell in the importer country's currency?

5. What advantages exist for exporters to have an "environmentally friendly" packaging policy?

Notes

[1] Adapted from "Language Difficulty Ranking," Effective Language Learning, http://www.effective-languagelearning.com/language-guide/language-difficulty, retrieved April 27, 2017.

[2] Weiss, Edmond H., *The Elements of International English Style: A Guide to Writing Correspondence, Reports, Technical Documents, Internet Pages for a Global Audience*, 2005, Armonk, NY.

[3] *Ibid.*

[4] *New College German Dictionary: German-English, English-German*, Duncan, SC: Langenscheidt, 1973.

[5] Beamer, Linda, and Iris Varner, *Intercultural Communication in the Global Workplace*, Fifth Edition, 2010, McGraw-Hill-Irwin, New York, New York.

[6] http://www.guardian.co.uk

[7] http://www.telegraphindia.com

[8] Ames, Nick, "Hartlepool need to kickstart great escape with or without Jeff Stelling's help," *The Guardian*, April 28, 2017, https://www.theguardian.com/football/blog/2017/apr/28/hartlepool-jeff-stelling-sky-league-two-relegation, retrieved April 28, 2017.

[9] Staff Reporter, "KKR aim to pile on DareDevils' agony," *The Telegraph*, April 28, 2017, https://www.telegraphindia.com/1170428/jsp/sports/story_148782.jsp, retrieved April 28, 2017.

[10] Graziano, Dan, "Day 1's Biggest Head-Scratchers: Bama Prospects Drop; the Bears did What?," *ESPN*, http://www.espn.com/blog/nflnation/post/_/id/236225/the-bears-did-what-nfl-draft-first-round-head-scratchers, retrieved April 28, 2017.

[11] Chmela, Holli, "A Language to Air News of America to the World," *The New York Times*, July 31, 2006.

[12] "Special English News," Voice of America, http://www.voanews.com/specialenglish.

[13] "This is Ikea," http://www.ikea.com/ms/en_SG/about_ikea/facts_and_figures/ikea_group_stores/-index.html, retrieved May 14, 2017.

[14] "Nutrition Labeling of Food," *Code of Federal Regulations*, Title 21, Volume 2, Section 101.9, Food and Drug Administration, 21 CFR 101.9, April 1, 2004, U.S. Government Printing Office, http://edocket.-access.gpo.gov/cfr_2004/aprqtr/21cfr101.9.htm, retrieved April 28, 2017.

[15] "Leather and Leatherworking Tips," *Legio XX Online Handbook*, May 6, 2003, http://www.larp.com-/legioxx/leather.html, retrieved April 28, 2017.

[16] Standard Copper Tubing Dimensional Reference, https://www.petersenproducts.com/category-s/1979.htm, retrieved April 28, 2017.

[17] Electrical Pipe and Conduit Dimensions from 1/2"-6", http://www.mrelectrician.tv/conversionch-arts/pipeconduit.html, retrieved April 28, 2017.

[18] Plywood Thickness, http://theplywood.com/thickness, retrieved April 28, 2017.

[19] CultureGrams, http://www.proquest.com/products-services/culturegrams.html, accessed April 28, 2017.

Appendix—Cumulative Normal Distribution

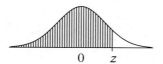

z	0.00	0.01	0.02	0.03	0.04	0.05	0.06	0.07	0.08	0.09
0.0	0.5000	0.5040	0.5080	0.5120	0.5160	0.5199	0.5239	0.5279	0.5319	0.5359
0.1	0.5398	0.5438	0.5478	0.5517	0.5557	0.5596	0.5636	0.5675	0.5714	0.5753
0.2	0.5793	0.5832	0.5871	0.5910	0.5948	0.5987	0.6026	0.6064	0.6103	0.6141
0.3	0.6179	0.6217	0.6255	0.6293	0.6331	0.6368	0.6406	0.6443	0.6480	0.6517
0.4	0.6554	0.6591	0.6628	0.6664	0.6700	0.6736	0.6772	0.6808	0.6844	0.6879
0.5	0.6915	0.6950	0.6985	0.7019	0.7054	0.7088	0.7123	0.7157	0.7190	0.7224
0.6	0.7257	0.7291	0.7324	0.7357	0.7389	0.7422	0.7454	0.7486	0.7517	0.7549
0.7	0.7580	0.7611	0.7642	0.7673	0.7704	0.7734	0.7764	0.7794	0.7823	0.7852
0.8	0.7881	0.7910	0.7939	0.7967	0.7995	0.8023	0.8051	0.8078	0.8106	0.8133
0.9	0.8159	0.8186	0.8212	0.8238	0.8264	0.8289	0.8315	0.8340	0.8365	0.8389
1.0	0.8413	0.8438	0.8461	0.8485	0.8508	0.8531	0.8554	0.8577	0.8599	0.8621
1.1	0.8643	0.8665	0.8686	0.8708	0.8729	0.8749	0.8770	0.8790	0.8810	0.8830
1.2	0.8849	0.8869	0.8888	0.8907	0.8925	0.8944	0.8962	0.8980	0.8997	0.9015
1.3	0.9032	0.9049	0.9066	0.9082	0.9099	0.9115	0.9131	0.9147	0.9162	0.9177
1.4	0.9192	0.9207	0.9222	0.9236	0.9251	0.9265	0.9279	0.9292	0.9306	0.9319
1.5	0.9332	0.9345	0.9357	0.9370	0.9382	0.9394	0.9406	0.9418	0.9429	0.9441
1.6	0.9452	0.9463	0.9474	0.9484	0.9495	0.9505	0.9515	0.9525	0.9535	0.9545
1.7	0.9554	0.9564	0.9573	0.9582	0.9591	0.9599	0.9608	0.9616	0.9625	0.9633
1.8	0.9641	0.9649	0.9656	0.9664	0.9671	0.9678	0.9686	0.9693	0.9699	0.9706
1.9	0.9713	0.9719	0.9726	0.9732	0.9738	0.9744	0.9750	0.9756	0.9761	0.9767
2.0	0.9772	0.9778	0.9783	0.9788	0.9793	0.9798	0.9803	0.9808	0.9812	0.9817
2.1	0.9821	0.9826	0.9830	0.9834	0.9838	0.9842	0.9846	0.9850	0.9854	0.9857
2.2	0.9861	0.9864	0.9868	0.9871	0.9875	0.9878	0.9881	0.9884	0.9887	0.9890
2.3	0.9893	0.9896	0.9898	0.9901	0.9904	0.9906	0.9909	0.9911	0.9913	0.9916
2.4	0.9918	0.9920	0.9922	0.9925	0.9927	0.9929	0.9931	0.9932	0.9934	0.9936
2.5	0.9938	0.9940	0.9941	0.9943	0.9945	0.9946	0.9948	0.9949	0.9951	0.9952
2.6	0.9953	0.9955	0.9956	0.9957	0.9959	0.9960	0.9961	0.9962	0.9963	0.9964
2.7	0.9965	0.9966	0.9967	0.9968	0.9969	0.9970	0.9971	0.9972	0.9973	0.9974
2.8	0.9974	0.9975	0.9976	0.9977	0.9977	0.9978	0.9979	0.9979	0.9980	0.9981
2.9	0.9981	0.9982	0.9982	0.9983	0.9984	0.9984	0.9985	0.9985	0.9986	0.9986
3.0	0.9987	0.9987	0.9987	0.9988	0.9988	0.9989	0.9989	0.9989	0.9990	0.9990

Glossary

A-B-C classification A method used to separate inventory items into three categories in function of their costs or other characteristics.

absolute advantage An economic theory that holds that when a nation can produce a certain type of product more efficiently than other countries, it will trade with countries that produce other goods more efficiently.

absolute quota A limit, set by the importing country's government, on the quantity of a commodity that can be imported in a given year. Once that limit is reached, it is not possible to import that product.

acceptance The second step in the formation of the contract. After the offer is made, the other party accepts the terms offered.

ACMI lease A type of leasing contract in which an airplane is leased, along with a crew, maintenance services, and insurance.

ad valorem **duty rate** A duty rate based on the value of the imported item.

adaptation A text translation that accounts for cultural differences and contexts.

advertising The promotional activities that each party to a contract is committing to pursue.

advising bank A bank that reviews the letter of credit on behalf of the beneficiary.

agent The overseas representative of a manufacturer. The agent represents the manufacturer in sales negotiations.

air draft The minimum amount of space between the water and the lowest point on a bridge that a ship needs in order to enter a port.

air waybill A bill of lading used for transportation by air, domestically or internationally.

airfreighter A type of airplane dedicated to carrying cargo.

all-risks policy A marine cargo insurance policy that covers all risks, except those specifically mentioned in the policy. The broadest coverage available under U.S.-based insurance policies.

amendment A change to a letter of credit to which all parties have agreed, from the applicant to the beneficiary.

Anti-Bribery Convention An OECD convention that requires countries to penalize companies engaging in bribery.

applicant The firm whose payment is supported by the letter of credit, the importer.

arbitration A process by which parties to a contract choose to settle a dispute. An arbitration decision is binding on both parties.

arbitration panel A group of arbitrators who are empowered by both parties to resolve a contract dispute. Their decision is binding on both parties.

artificial currency A currency that does not circulate. After the euro was changed into a circulating currency in 2002, the only artificial currency in the world is the Special Drawing Rights of the International Monetary Fund.

assist An item provided by the importer to the exporter so that the exporter could manufacture the imported goods. The value of the assist should be included in the valuation of the imported goods.

attribute A binary variable used in statistical quality control to indicate whether a manufacturing part is conform or non-conform.

Authorized Economic Operator (AEO) An E.U. program that implements the Security and Facilitation in a Global Environment (SAFE) guidelines of the World Customs Organization.

aval In a documentary collection, the promise by the presenting bank that the importer will honor the draft and that, should the importer default, the bank will make the payment.

average A loss incurred by a cargo owner on an ocean voyage.

average (general) A loss incurred by multiple cargo owners on an ocean voyage. A general loss.

average (particular) A partial loss incurred by a cargo owner on an ocean voyage.

back-to-back letter of credit A letter of credit issued using another letter of credit as a payment guarantee.

bag A paper, plastic, or fabric container designed to unitize dry-bulk cargo and unitize it. A bag can generally be handled by a single stevedore.

bale The package bundle created by compressing cotton or wool when these commodities are tightly wrapped and bound with string or metal bands.

Baltic Exchange The world market for maritime cargo transport services, located in London, where ship owners and cargo owners negotiate the cost of moving cargo.

Bank for International Settlements The bank that advises central banks and provides a clearinghouse for exchanges between central banks.

bank guarantee A contract from a bank in which the bank guarantees that the exporter will perform as required by the importer.

banker's acceptance In a documentary collection, banker's acceptance takes place when the bank signs the draft on behalf of the importer.

barge A flat-bottom ship designed to transport cargo on the inland river network. A barge can be pushed or pulled, or be self propelled.

barratry Willful misconduct on the part of the captain of a ship or the crew.

beneficiary The party for the benefit of which the letter of credit was open, the party that will be paid by the letter of credit, the exporter.

berth In a port, the location at which a ship can load and unload its cargo.

bill of exchange Another term for a draft. A promissory note with which the importer formally recognizes it debt to the exporter.

bill of lading The contract of carriage between a carrier and the shipper.

bill of materials An electronic file containing a hierarchical list of all the components of a final product.

binding agent An agent who is allowed to make decisions that are binding on the principal. The principal must abide by whatever statements the agent has made.

binding ruling A determination, made by Customs prior to the importation of a good, of the correct classification of a good. The ruling is binding on the Customs administration of the country that issued it.

black belt The name given to an individual whose responsibilities include quality control and process improvements.

box A wooden container designed to unitize the goods and protect them. In a box, the walls are an integral part of its structural strength.

box Another, more casual, name for containers.

box ship Another, more casual, name for containerships.

breach In the event that one of the parties to a contract does not meet its obligation, that is in *breach* of the contract.

breakbulk A type of cargo that is unitized—boxes, crates, or bales—and placed directly in the holds of a ship.

breakbulk ship A type of ship designed to carry breakbulk cargo.

Bretton-Woods A 1944 conference at which many of the international institutions were created.

bunker The fuel that a ship carries onboard and that it needs to operate.

C_{pk} A coefficient measuring the ability of a manufacturing process to produce parts that meet customer's specifications.

cabotage An ocean trade consisting of shipping goods between two ports located in the same country.

call option A currency option with which a firm buys the right to buy a currency at a given price some time in the future.

canal A man-made waterway connecting two natural bodies of water.

cargo movement The fact that cargo transported internationally will be subjected to several changes of mode of transportation, and to vibrations, jolts, drops, and side-to-side movements during an ocean voyage.

carrier The company that transports the goods on its vessel, truck, or train.

carrying costs The costs of having inventory on hand. Carrying costs increase as the number of goods in inventory increases.

cash in advance A method of payment in which an importer has to pay the exporter before the exporter ships the goods.

central bank The entity that countrols the money supply of a nation and functions as a clearinghouse for inter-bank exchanges.

certificate of analysis A certificate, provided by an independent company, that attests that the goods conform to the physical description contained in the exporter's invoice.

certificate of certification A certificate, issued by an independent company, that attests that the goods conform to the industrial standards of the importing country.

certificate of conformity Another name for a certificate of certification.

certificate of free sale A certificate, issued by the exporter, that attests that the goods can be legally sold in the exporting country.

certificate of inspection A certificate, provided by an independent company, that attests that the goods conform to the description contained in the exporter's invoice.

certificate of insurance A certificate, issued by the exporter's insurance company, that attests that a particular shipment is insured.

certificate of manufacture A certificate, signed by the exporter's chamber of commerce, that attests that the goods were manufactured in the country in which the exporter is located.

certificate of origin A certificate, signed by the exporter's chamber of commerce, that attests that the goods originated in the country in which the exporter is located.

charter airfreight A type of cargo that can only be shipped on a charter aircraft because it is too heavy, too bulky or its destination is not serviced by a scheduled airfreight service.

charter party A type of contract of carriage, in which the shipper uses all or most of the carrying capacity of the ship to transport commodities.

chemical carrier A liquid-bulk ship that carries liquid chemicals.

choice of forum The court in which disputes regarding the contracts will be resolved.

choice of law The national laws that govern the terms of the contract.

choice of venue The court in which disputes regarding the contracts will be resolved.

classification The process of determining what is the correct Harmonized System number for an import.

classification society A company whose business is to determine the seaworthiness of a vessel.

clean bill of lading A bill of lading that reflects the fact that the carrier received the goods in good condition.

cleared The term used to indicate that the goods were imported in the country and that the importer paid the correct amount of duty.

cluster An observation that a firm can develop a substantial competitive advantage in manufacturing certain goods when a large number of its competitors and suppliers are located in close proximity.

co-modality A shipment that takes more than one mode of transportation under a single bill of lading.

combi aircraft A type of airplane that is designed to carry both cargo and passengers at the same time on the main deck.

combination ship A type of ship that is versatile and can carry different types of cargo.

Commerce Control List (CCL) A list of products that cannot be exported from the United States without an export license.

commercial invoice The document sent by the seller to the buyer that lists the goods purchased and the amount due.

commercial risk The probability of not being paid by a creditor, either because the creditor does not have the funds, or because it refuses to recognize the debt.

comparative advantage An economic theory that holds that nations will trade with one another as long as they can produce certain goods relatively more efficiently than one another.

competing lines Products manufactured by a company other than the principal that compete directly with the principal's products.

competition driver One reason a firm may go international is to compete more aggressively against its foreign competitors.

compound duty rate A duty rate based on a combination of value, number, or some other measurement of the imported item (weight, dimensions,...).

confidentiality A promise by both parties to a contract to not disclose what they have learned about each other's business to other parties.

confirmed letter of credit When a letter of credit is confirmed, should the issuing bank not pay, the confirming bank does.

confirming bank The bank that confirms a letter of credit. Should the issuing bank not pay, the confirming bank does.

consignee The party to whom the goods should be surrendered at destination.

consolidated A shipment that is made up of several small shipments from different shippers.

constant dollars Dollars adjusted for inflation so that it is possible to compare dollar values from one period to another.

consular invoice An invoice printed on stationery provided by the importing country's Consulate.

container A large metallic box used in international trade that can be loaded directly onto a truck, a railroad car or an ocean-going vessel. The most common dimensions of a container are $8 \times 8.5 \times 20$ feet and $8 \times 8.5 \times 40$ feet.

Container Security Initiative (CSI) A U.S. Customs and Border Protection program that consists of inspecting overseas the shipments that are bound for the United States.

container sweat The humidity that condenses on the inside walls of a container and on its cargo.

container terminal A location where containerized cargo changes mode of transportation.

containership A ship designed to exclusively carry containers, both below its deck and above it. A containership's size is expressed in TEUs.

continuous improvement A method used by manufacturers to reduce the natural variability in a manufacturing process.

contract language The language in which a contract is written. If the contract exists in other languages, those versions are considered translations, and not the original contract.

contract law A set of laws that govern relationships established by contracts between two parties.

contract manufacturing An arrangement between two companies where one manufactures goods for the other.

control charts A statistical-process-control tool used to determine whether a manufacturing process is working correctly.

Convention on Contracts for the International Sale of Goods A United Nations' treaty that acts as international sales law.

convertible currency A currency that can be converted into an other currency.

copyright An intellectual property item that refers to a musical piece, a piece of art, or a written product.

corporate accounts The customers to which the agent or distributor is not allowed to sell. These accounts are handled directly by the exporter.

correspondent bank A foreign bank with which a domestic bank has a preferred business relationship.

corrugated paper Two flat sheets of brown paper, in between which a sinusoidally shaped sheet is glued.

cost driver One reason a firm may go international is to spread its costs over a large number of units.

counterfeit goods Goods manufactured to look like original products, but whose manufacturing was not approved by the brand owners.

counter-offer An intermediary step in the formation of the contract. After the offer is made, the other party does not accept the terms offered, and proposes modifications ot the terms of the contract.

country risk The probability of not being paid by a creditor, because the importer's country does not have the foreign currency or does not allow the creditor to pay—political embargo.

Coverage A policy A marine cargo insurance policy that covers all risks, except those specifically mentioned in the policy. The broadest coverage available under Marine Cargo Clauses policies.

Coverage B policy A marine cargo insurance policy that covers only the risks listed in the policy. The second broadest coverage available, but not suitable for many cargoes because of its restrictions.

Coverage C policy A marine cargo insurance policy that covers only the risks listed in the policy. The narrowest coverage available, not suitable for most cargoes because of its restrictions. The coverage required by CIP and CIF Incoterms® rules.

crate A wooden container designed to unitize the goods and protect them. In a crate, the structural strength is provided by a web of wooden cross members.

credit insurance An insurance policy that the exporter can purchase to protect itself against the risk of non-payment by the importer.

crude carrier A liquid-bulk ship that carries unrefined oil.

currency The monetary unit used to settle economic transactions in a given country.

currency bloc A group of currencies whose values fluctuate in a parallel fashion with other currencies and whose values vary within a small percentage among themselves.

currency future The value of a fixed quantity of a foreign currency, to be delivered at a fixed date in the future.

currency option The right—but not the obligation—to purchase (or sell) a currency at a certain price some time in the future.

current dollars Dollars not adjusted for inflation. Their value is determined by the year they were actually received or paid.

customers' list The list of the customers to which the agent or distributor sells the principal's products.

Customs bond A sum of money collected by Customs from Customs brokers, that is held as a guarantee that duty will be paid in the correct amount.

Customs broker A person authorized by Customs authorities to file entries.

Customs Security Programme (CSP) An E.U. program that implements the Security and Facilitation in a Global Environment (SAFE) guidelines of the World Customs Organization.

Customs-Trade Partnership Against Terrorism (C-TPAT) A voluntary partnership program of the U.S. CPB. Participating companies obtain priority processing and reduced inspection rates.

damp lease A type of leasing contract in which an airplane is leased, with maintenance and insurance, but no crew.

date draft A draft in which the importer promises to pay the exporter 30, 60 or 90 days after the shipment date of the goods, regardless of the date on which importer has signed the draft.

deadweight tonnage The maximum weight that a ship can carry.

deck A permanent cover over the ship's hull.

deck stow collapse A stack of containers placed on deck that collapses in heavy seas.

deemed export A product sold in the United States to a non-U.S. citizen.

delivery In an international voyage, the point at which the responsibility for the goods switches from the exporter to the importer.

dependent demand A product has a dependent demand if its sales are based on the sales of another product.

difference-in-condition A clause in an insurance policy that allows an importer to complement the coverage offered by the exporter to the level of coverage that the importer wants.

dimensional weight (volume weight) An artificial weight, determined in function of the dimensions of a shipment, used by airlines to determine the tariff to be paid for a light shipment.

direct quote The value of a foreign currency expressed in units of the domestic currency.

discrepancy A difference between the documents required by the letter of credit and the documents provided or obtained by the exporter.

displacement tonnage The total weight of a fully loaded ship, measured by the weight of the water displaced.

distribution contract A contract between an exporter and an overseas intermediary, whether an agent or a distributor.

Distribution Resources Planning (DRP) A management tool that allows a retail firm to determine what to order from its suppliers and in which quantity, in function of what it sells to its customers.

distributor An overseas company that purchases a manufacturer's products with the goal of reselling them at a profit.

documentary credit Another term for letter of credit. A method of payment in which a bank promises to pay the beneficiary (the exporter) on behalf of the applicant (the importer), as long as the exporter has provided the documents requested in the documentary credit.

documentary collection A method of payment in which an exporter enlists the help of a bank in the importer's country to collect payment from the importer.

dollarization The decision by a country to replace its domestic currency with the dollar.

double-stack The practice of placing containers on a railroad car on top of one another.

draft The minimum depth of water that a ship needs in order to float.

draft A promissory note in which the importer formally recognizes its debt to the exporter. A draft can be a date draft, a sight draft, or a time draft.

dredging The removal of sediments or soil from the bottom of a water channel to increase its depth.

drum A cylindrical metal, plastic, or fiber container designed to unitize dry-bulk or liquid-bulk cargo.

dry-bulk container A container used to transport bulk loads that are not unitized.

dry-bulk carrier A dry-bulk ship that carries grain, ores, dry chemicals, or minerals directly in its holds.

dry lease A type of leasing contract in which only the airplane is leased.

dumping A strategy, followed by some exporters, that consists of selling the goods at a price considered "too low" by the importing country's Customs authorities.

dunnage Packing material designed to prevent cargo from moving when in transit.

duty The amount of tax paid to Customs authorities in the importing country on imported goods.

duty drawback A process by which an exporter can be reimbursed for duty that it paid on products that it imported but which products it eventually exported.

economic order quantity The size of an inventory re-order that allows a company to minimize its inventory holding costs and its ordering costs.

economic lot size The size of a production run that allows a company to minimize its inventory holding costs and its set-up costs.

electronic data interchange (EDI) A method to send documents from one company to another, using electronic means.

electronic export information A set of data collected by U.S. Customs detailing the type and value of goods exported, as well as their destination.

end-use certificate A certificate, required by the exporting country, that attests that the goods are purchased for a legitimate purpose.

English system A system of measurements used almost exclusively in the United States.

Enterprise Resources Planning (ERP) A software package, based on an MRP system, that integrates all the functions of a company.

entry The process by which an importer notifies Customs that it has imported a product.

euro The common currency of 19 of the 28 countries of the European Union.

Eurozone The nineteen countries of Europe in which the euro is the currency.

evergreen contract A contract that, by design or by default, does not have a specified duration.

Ex-Im Bank An agency of the U.S. federal government that provides financial assistance to U.S. exporters.

exchange rate risk The risk presented by the fluctuations in exchange rates between the time at which the sale is made and the time at which it is paid.

exclusive representative An agent or a distributor that has been granted the right to be the sole representative of the exporter in a given territory.

export license The express authorization, granted by the exporting country's government to the exporter, to export a particular product.

export management corporation A company that puts suppliers in touch with potential buyers, and earns a commission if a sale is completed.

export quota A limit on the quantity of a particular commodity that can be legally exported.

export tax A tax collected on the value of the goods exported.

export trading company A company that purchases goods in one country for the purpose of reselling them in another country at a profit.

exposure The impact of an unpaid receivable for an exporter. Its effect on the exporter's financial well-being.

express cargo Cargo shipped with a guaranteed predetermined delivery date. em[FCL shipment] An international shipment that uses, by weight or volume, the entire capacity of a container.

extended-length container A container whose length extends beyond the traditional 40-foot length of standard containers.

facilities and activities The specific facilities and activities that each party to a contract is committing to maintaining.

factor endowment An economic theory that holds that a nation will have a comparative advantage over other countries if it is naturally endowed with a greater abundance of one of the factors of economic production.

factoring A means of financing international receivable accounts, by which a firm asks a factoring company to advance funds on the receivable.

FCL (full container load) A shipment whose volume or weight is close to the container's limits, or for which the shipper requests that it be the only shipment in the container.

Fisher effect An economic theory that holds that interest rates that businesses pay should be uniform throughout the world.

fixed-order-quantity model An inventory-management technique in which inventory levels are checked continuously, and the re-order quantity is fixed.

flag The flag of the country in which a ship is registered. By extension, the country in which the ship is registered.

flag of convenience A flag—country of registration—that is open to all ship owners, and imposes few requirements—regulations or taxes—on ship owners. A derogatory term.

flat-rack container A container designed to hold cargo whose width does not fit inside a standard container. The width of the cargo should be less than 8 feet.

flexible intermediate bulk containers (FIBC) A large polymer bag designed to contain dry-bulk cargo and to be handled by mechanized equipment.

floating currency A currency whose value is determined by market forces. A floating currency's value changes frequently.

force majeure An event beyond the control if any of the parties in an agreement that prevents one of the parties from fulfilling its obligations.

Foreign Corrupt Practices Act A U.S. law that punishes severely U.S. companies engaging in bribery outside of the borders of the United States.

foreign sales corporation A subsidiary, created for tax-reduction purposes only, that handles an exporter's overseas sales.

foreign trade zone An area that is physically within the borders of a country, but that is considered outside of its borders for Customs' purposes.

forfaiting A means of financing an international sale in which an exporter collects a series of drafts from the importer, and then sells them.

forward exchange rate The exchange rate of a foreign currency for delivery in 30, 60 or 180 days from the day of the quote.

forward-market hedge A technique to reduce exchange rate fluctuation risk that uses forward market exchange rates.

foul bill of lading A bill of lading that reflects the fact that the carrier did not receive the goods in good condition.

franchisee The company granted the right to use an array of related intellectual property items owned by the franchisor in exchange for a royalty.

franchising An arrangement between two companies where one licenses an array of related intellectual property items.

franchisor The company that owns an array of related intellectual property items and lets another firm use them in exchange for a royalty.

Free And Secure Trade (FAST) A joint Canada-U.S.-Mexico voluntary program. Participating companies enjoy dedicated fast lanes when crossing the Canada-U.S. border or the Mexico-U.S. border.

free-of-particular-average policy A marine cargo insurance policy that covers only the risks listed in the policy. The narrowest coverage available under U.S.-based policies. Not suitable for most cargoes because of its restrictions.

freight corridor A section of a railroad network dedicated to freight traffic.

freight forwarder A company specialized in shipping cargo on behalf of shippers—importers or exporters.

freight tonne kilometer(RTK) A unit designed to express cargo volume shipped. It is equal to the number of tonnes of cargo shipped multiplied by the number of kilometers they were shipped.

full container load (FCL) A shipment whose volume or weight is close to the container's limits, or for which the shipper requests that it be the only shipment in the container.

General Agreement on Tariffs and Trade An agreement between countries to lower tariffs and trade barriers.

general average A loss incurred by multiple cargo owners on an ocean voyage. A general loss.

general-merchandise ship Another name for a breakbulk ship.

geo-fencing A technique based on Global Positioning System that alerts management when a shipment is diverted from its intended itinerary.

good faith The assumption that both parties entering a contract do not have ulterior, undisclosed, motives.

grain An agricultural commodity, such as wheat, corn or sugar, that is loaded directly onboard, without packaging, like a liquid.

gray market goods Goods purchased in one country by unauthorized intermediaries and sold to unauthorized retailers in another country.

gross tonnage The volume capacity of a ship, expressed in hundreds of cubic feet.

gross registered tonnage (GRT) The volume capacity of a ship, calculated in a way that meets the requirements of a specific authority, such as the Suez Canal or the Panama Canal Authorities.

guarantor The bank that provides the bank guarantee.

Hague Rules A 1924 international liability convention for ocean cargo that restricts the liability of the carrier to U.S.$ 500 per package or per customary freight unit.

Hague-Visby Rules A 1968 international liability convention for ocean cargo that restricts the liability of the carrier to SDR 666.67 per package or per customary freight unit.

Hamburg Rules A 1978 international liability convention for ocean cargo that restricts the liability of the carrier to U.S.$ 833 per package or per customary freight unit.

hanger container A container designed to hold cargo that cannot be laid flat in a box, and must remain on hangers during the international voyage.

hard currency A currency that can be easily converted into an other currency.

Harmonized System of classification A system of classification for goods, developed by the World Customs Organization, and followed by 179 countries.

hold In a ship, a portion of the inside volume designed to hold cargo.

holding costs The costs of having inventory on hand. Holding costs increase as the number of goods in inventory increases.

high-cube container A container designed to hold cargo that is is voluminous and light. Its height is 9.5 feet.

historical data The initial manufacturing data collected to create a statistical quality control system.

hull insurance A policy contracted by the ship owner to cover damages to the ship.

import license The express authorization, granted by the importing country's government to the importer, to import a certain product.

Importer Security Filing A U.S. program that implements the Security and Facilitation in a Global Environment (SAFE) guidelines of the World Customs Organization.

improper packing Packing that is not sufficient to protect the goods during their international voyage. Improperly packed goods will not be covered under any insurance policy.

inconvertible currency A currency that cannot be converted into an other currency.

Incoterms® Rules A series of eleven international terms of trade standardized by the International Chamber of Commerce that delineate the responsibilities of the exporter and those of the importer in an international transaction.

Incoterm® rule variant A modification to an Incoterm® rule, not sanctioned by the ICC, that changes one or more of its parameters.

independent demand A product has an independent demand if it is sold directly to consumers or customers.

indirect quote The value of the domestic currency expressed in units of a foreign currency.

individual policy An insurance policy that covers one shipment.

Individual Validated Export License The express authorization, given by the U.S government, to export a particular commodity.

infrastructure A term that refers to all the public and private goods that facilitate transportation, communication, and business exchanges.

informed compliance A standard of behavior, enforced by U.S. Customs, that is expected of importers if they want their entries to be cleared quickly and inspections kept to a minimum.

inherent vice The fact that some goods are inherently changing appearance during their international voyage. They experience shrinkage, they rust, they warp. Inherent vice is never covered by an insurance policy.

instruction letter In a documentary collection, a document prepared by the exporter that instructs the presenting bank on the steps to take before releasing the documents to the importer.

insurable interest A party who would experience a financial loss in the case of a peril is said to have an insurable interest.

integrator An air cargo carrier that offers its customers complete door-to-door service.

interdiction A security strategy that consists of preventing all imports of potentially dangerous goods and potentially dangerous persons.

interest rate parity An economic theory that holds that the forward exchange rate between two currencies should reflect the differences in nominal interest rates between these two countries.

intermodal A shipment that takes more than one mode of transportation under a single bill of lading.

intermodal bill of lading A bill of lading used for transportation that uses more than one mode of transportation, domestically or internationally.

International Air Transport Association (IATA) A trade association comprising almost 230 airlines, representing 93 percent of all scheduled air traffic.

International Chamber of Commerce (ICC) The largest business organization in the world. Its goal is to champion international business growth and its members are the national chambers of commerce.

International Civil Aviation Organization (ICAO) An agency of the United Nations whose mission is to establish safety and security standards for civil aviation.

international English A technique of written communication that attempts to remove all ambiguities, so that a person with limited knowledge of English can understand it.

international Fisher effect An economic theory that holds that spot exchange rates between two currencies should reflect the differences in nominal interest rates between these two countries.

International Maritime Organization (IMO) A United Nations agency responsible for improving maritime safety and preventing pollution from ships.

International Monetary Fund (IMF) The international organization created in 1945 to oversee exchange rates and develop an international system of payments.

International Organization for Standardization (ISO) An international standard-setting body whose membership is made up of national standard-setting bodies.

International Plant Protection Convention (IPPC) An international convention that mandates that wood used in packaging be fumigated or heat-treated against pests.

international product life cycle An economic theory that holds that, over its life cycle, a product will be manufactured in different countries.

International Ship and Port Facility Security (ISPS) Code A series of security requirements placed by the International Maritime Organization upon ports and ships.

international trade The sale of goods and services across international borders.

irrevocable letter of credit A letter of credit that cannot be altered without the consent of the issuing bank and the beneficiary.

ISO 9000 A standard of quality procedures developed by the International Organization for Standardization.

ISO box Another term for a standard container.

issuing bank The bank that opens the letter of credit on behalf of the importer and pays the exporter if the exporter provides the documents requested in the letter of credit.

jettison The act of throwing cargo overboard to save the ship and the remainder of the cargo.

joint venture An overseas company that is jointly owned by two or more companies.

just-in-time A management philosophy that consists of planning the manufacturing of goods in such a way that they are produced just before they are needed in the next step of the assembly process.

LCL shipment An international shipment that is combined with other shipments in a single container.

labor law A set of laws that govern relationships between employees and employers.

land bridge A term coined to describe the practice of shipping goods from Asia to Europe through the United States by using railroads.

laker A dry-bulk ship designed to operate on the Great Lakes between the United States and Canada.

lash bar The bars used to tie the containers to the deck of a ship.

lashing The process of attaching cargo to the means of transport. On a ship, containers are lashed onto the deck, in a container, goods are lashed to the container walls and floor.

LCL less than container load.

lead time The time between the moment an inventory-replenishment order is placed and the time the order arrives.

leap frogging The idea that some countries will "skip" a technology to adopt the most recent one available.

less than container load (LCL) A shipment that takes less than the full weight and volume capacity of a standard container and is therefore shipped with other LCL cargo in the same container.

letter of credit A method of payment in which a bank promises to pay the beneficiary (the exporter) on behalf of the applicant (the importer), as long as the exporter has provided the documents requested in the letter of credit.

Lex Mercatoria The body of laws and international agreements that govern the relationships and contracts between international parties.

light tonnage The total weight of an empty ship, measured by the weight of the water displaced.

liner ship A ship that operates on a regular schedule, traveling from one group of ports to another group of ports.

liquid-bulk container A 20-foot container used to transport liquid loads.

list A ship that leans to one side is said to *list*.

licensee The company that obtains the right to use the licensor's intellectual property.

licensing An arrangement between two companies where one uses the other's intellectual property in exchange for a royalty.

licensor The company that grants to another company, the licensee, the right to use its intellectual property.

liquidated entry An entry that has been successfully reviewed by Customs authorities, and for which duty has been paid.

litigation The final process by which parties to a contract have to settle a dispute, in a court of law.

LNG-LPG carrier A ship designed to transport liquefied—compressed—natural gas or petroleum gas.

load lines Marks on the side of the ship that indicate how low a ship can be in the water, depending on the season and conditions.

longshoreman A person who performs manual labor in a port.

lower deck A deck designed to carry cargo and luggage, located underneath the main deck of an aircraft.

Maastricht Treaty A 1992 Treaty between the European Union countries in which a number of standards were adopted, including a standard currency.

main carriage The portion of an international shipment that takes place between the exporting country and the importing country.

main deck The largest deck on an aircraft, the one on which passenger travel in a passenger aircraft.

manifest A document, internal to the shipping company (carrier), that lists all cargoes onboard the transportation vehicle.

maquiladora A plant located in Mexico that have the same status as a foreign trade zone located both in the United States and Mexico.

Marine Transportation Security Act (MTSA) The U.S. legislation that implemented the recommendations of the International Maritime Organization's International Ship and Port Facility Security Code.

market driver One reason a firm may go international is to follow its customers when they travel abroad.

marketing subsidiary An overseas firm owned by an exporter that is responsible for selling the exporter's products in a foreign market.

markings Symbols printed on boxes or crates that help stevedores and terminals determine the proper way to handle, stow, or store a breakbulk shipment.

master production schedule An electronic file created by an MRP system that specifies what products to make, in which quantity, and when.

Manufacturing Resources Planning (MRP II) A materials requirement planning tool that includes additional information, such as manufacturing costs.

Materials Requirement Planning (MRP) A management tool that allows a manufacturer to determine what to produce and in which quantity, in function of what it sells to its customers.

mediation A process by which parties to a contract choose to find a compromise in a dispute. A mediation recommendation is not binding.

merchandise visa A document, provided by the exporting country, that allows an exporter to ship goods subject to a quota in the importing country.

metric system A decimal system of measurements, part of the International System of Units, that is widely adopted worldwide.

money-market hedge A technique to reduce exchange rate fluctuation risk that uses the banking institutions of the foreign currency's country.

Montréal Protocol 4 A 1999 protocol that limits the liability of air carriers to SDR 17 per kilogram. There is no limit for death or bodily injury.

negotiable bill of lading A bill of lading on which the name of the consignee has been left blank.

net tonnage The volume capacity of a ship, after subtracting the space used for the operation of the ship.

non-vessel-operating common carrier A shipment consolidator or freight forwarder that does not own means of transportation, but issues its own bills of lading, and therefore acts as a carrier.

objective risk A risk whose probability can be calculated.

ocean bill of lading The contract of carriage between an ocean carrier and the shipper.

open account A method of payment in which the exporter sends an invoice to the importer along with the goods and expects the importer to pay within a reasonable amount of time.

offer The first step in the formation of a contract. The contract is initiated when one of the parties makes an offer to the other.

onboard courier (OBC) A passenger on a regularly scheduled flight who relinquishes his or her baggage allocation to allow cargo in its place.

on-carriage The portion of an international shipment that takes place in the importing country.

one-hundred-percent inspection A security strategy that consists of inspecting every single shipment.

open registry A flag—country of registration—that is open to all ship owners, regardless of their nationality.

open policy An insurance policy that covers all of the shipments made by a firm.

open-sky agreement An agreement between two countries, in which the airlines of one country are allowed to serve any of the other country's airports.

open-top container A container designed so that cargo can be loaded from the top, and that is covered by a tarpaulin.

options-market hedge A technique to reduce exchange rate fluctuation risk that uses options for a particular currency.

ordering costs The costs of placing an inventory-replenishment order. Ordering costs are unaffected by the size of the order.

ordinary leakage The fact that some goods will weigh less after their international voyage because of evaporation. Ordinary leakage cannot be insured against.

Organisation for Economic Cooperation and Development An international economic organization that promotes policies designed to improve the economic and social well-being of people around the world.

organized theft Theft of a cargo shipment by a group of organized criminals.

outsourcing A practice that consists of a business contracting with other businesses to have them perform some of the operations it used to handle in-house.

overloaded A means of transportation that carries cargo in excess of its stated capacity.

out-of-control situation An observation on a statistical control chart that indicates that the manufacturing process may not be working correctly.

packing list A detailed list of the contents of a shipment.

pallet A wooden (plastic) platform on which goods can be placed. A pallet necessitates mechanical equipment to be moved.

Panamax ship A ship of the maximum size that can enter the locks of the Panama Canal.

parallel imports Goods purchased in one country by unauthorized intermediaries and sold to unauthorized retailers in another country.

particular average A partial loss incurred by a cargo owner on an ocean voyage.

patent An intellectual property item that refers to a process, material, or design.

pegged currency A currency whose value is determined by a fixed exchange rate with a more widely traded currency, such as the dollar or the euro.

permanent establishment A fixed place of business abroad that subjects the exporter to tax liability in the importing country.

periodic re-order model An inventory-management technique in which inventory levels are checked at intervals, and the re-order quantity is variable.

phyto-sanitary certificate A certificate, provided by the agricultural authorities of the exporting country, that attests that the agricultural products exported are free of disease and pests.

piggy-back A technique that consists of placing semi trucks or trailers on railroad cars.

piggy-backing When a manufacturer goes overseas and asks its suppliers to continue doing business abroad with him, the suppliers are said to be *piggy backing* on that customer's efforts.

pilferage An opportunity theft of part of a cargo shipment.

pipeline A mode of transportation consisting of a long pipe and used for the transportation of liquid cargo.

piracy A violent overtaking of a ship and its crew.

Plimsoll mark A mark on the side of the ship that indicates the classification society that inspects the ship.

post-Panamax ship A ship whose size is too large to enter the locks of the Panama Canal.

pre-carriage The portion of an international shipment that takes place in the exporting country.

pre-shipment inspection The inspection, conducted by an independent company, that allows the determination that the goods conform to the description contained in the exporter's invoice.

presenting bank In a documentary collection, the presenting bank interacts with the importer and withholds the documents until payment is received or a draft signed.

principal The manufacturer represented by an agent.

pro forma **invoice** A quote provided by the exporter to the importer for the purpose of obtaining a letter of credit or an import license.

process capability A measurement of the ability of a manufacturing process to produce parts that meet customer's specifications.

product carrier A liquid-bulk ship that carries refined oil products.

project cargo Cargo that is much larger, heavier, or more complex to handle than regular cargo. Project cargo generally requires specialized means of transport.

Property and Indemnity Club (P&I Club) A group of ship owners who agree to mutually share the costs of its members' liabilities to other parties.

protest A process by which an importer can file a grievance after an entry is liquidated, so that Customs reviews classification, valuation, and country of origin.

purchasing cards Credit cards used by companies to make small purchases, and that can be used in international transactions.

purchasing power parity An economic theory that holds that exchange rates should reflect the price differences paid by consumers.

pure risk A risk that can only generate a loss.

put option A currency option with which a firm buys the right to sell a currency at a given price some time in the future.

quality assurance A statistical process followed by purchasers to ensure that a shipment of parts meets quality requirements.

quality standards A set of industry standards that dictate the minimum performance attributes of a product.

quick-change aircraft A type of airplane that can be quickly converted from all-cargo service to all-passenger service, with the use of palletized seat sections.

quota A limit, set by the importing country's government, on the quantity of a commodity that can be imported in a given year. A quota can be an absolute quota or a tariff-rate quota.

QS 9000 A quality standard created by the three largest North American automobile manufacturers.

ratification The process by which a state fully accepts to be bound by an international treaty. It makes it part of its national legislation by having its Congress vote on it.

reefer Another (casual) term for refrigerated container.

refrigerated container (reefer) A container designed to hold cargo that must be maintained at a constant temperature. It generally needs an outside power supply.

registration For an agent or a distributor, the process of notifying the importing country's government that it is entering a distribution agreement with an exporter.

rejection An intermediary step in the formation of the contract. After the offer is made, the other party rejects the terms offered and makes a counter-offer.

remitting bank In a documentary collection, the remitting bank collects the documents from the exporter and sends them to the presenting bank. It has no other involvement.

reasonable care A standard of behavior, enforced by U.S. Customs, that is expected of importers if they want their entries to be cleared quickly and inspections kept to a minimum.

red-clause letter of credit A letter of credit that allows the beneficiary to obtain funds from the applicant before the goods are shipped.

reshoring The practice of returning to the home country the manufacturing processes that had been outsourced abroad.

revenue tonne kilometer(RTK) A unit designed to express total airline activity. It is equal to the number of tonnes of cargo, passengers, baggages and mail shipped multiplied by the number of kilometers they were shipped.

risk The probability of a peril.

risk (objective) A risk whose probability can be calculated.

risk (pure) A risk that can only generate a loss.

risk (speculative) A risk that can generate a loss or a gain.

risk (subjective) A risk whose probability cannot be relied upon.

risk retention A risk management strategy in which a company decides to retain a risk and not insure or hedge against it.

risk transfer A risk management strategy in which the company decides to insure against its risks.

road train An Australian trucking technique, consisting of one tractor pulling three to five semi trailers.

Roll-On/Roll-Off (RORO) . A type of ship in which cargo is rolled on board rather than carried by crane.

roller deck A deck designed to carry cargo, and equipped with rollers and bearings that allow the cargo to be moved in any direction without much friction.

Rotterdam Rules A 2008 international liability convention for intermodal cargo that restricts the liability of the carrier to U.S.$ 875 per package or per customary freight unit.

royalty The fee paid by a company so that it can use another party's intellectual property.

rules of interpretation A series of six rules developed to help importers and Customs determine the correct HS classification of a good.

rules of origin The rules used to determine the country of origin of an imported product.

runway The strip of concrete in an airport from which airplanes take off and land.

scope of appointment The scope [products, territory, customers] to the contract applies.

seal A lock placed on a container door or truck trailer door that must be broken in order to access the cargo.

secured Once goods are stowed and the vessel trimmed, the goods are tied to the vessel by means of ropes or chains.

SAFE Either the Security and Accountability For Every Port of the United States, or the Security and Facilitation in a Global Environment of the World Customs Organization.

safety stock Additional inventory used to prevent inventory shortages of a product.

Security and Accountability For Every Port (SAFE) A U.S. piece of legislation that created a number of security-related programs.

Security and Facilitation in a Global Environment (SAFE) A set of guidelines to increase the cooperation of national Customs administrations in fighting security threats.

security management A corporate function that manages all of a security efforts of a company.

seizure An action, taken by a legitimate government, to stop and detain a ship for safety or other reasons.

semi truck An articulated truck that is made up of a tractor and a trailer.

service level The probability that the firm will have an item in inventory if a customer places an order during the lead time.

set-up costs The costs of starting a new production run. Set-up costs are unaffected by the size of the run.

shipper The party in an international transaction–exporter or importer—that is responsible for arranging the main carriage.

shipper's letter of instruction A document in which the shipper spells out how it wants the carrier to handle the goods while they are in transit.

shrink/stretch wrap A polymer film that is stretched over palletized cargo to protect it from water damage.

shortage costs The costs of having run out of inventory.

signatory (full) The acceptance of a treaty by a state. It signs it to indicate that it agrees with its premises, without further ratification.

signatory (simple) The first step in the acceptance of a treaty by a state. It signs it to indicate that it agrees with its premises, but it will need to ratify it before it is bound by it.

sight draft A draft in which the importer promises to pay the exporter immediately, "at sight."

single-stack The practice of placing containers on a railroad car on only one height. It contrasts with the practice of placing them two high.

sinking In a sinking, a ship is damaged, no longer floats, and goes to the bottom of the sea.

six sigma A measurement of the ability of a manufacturing process to produce parts that meet customer's specifications.

soft currency A currency that cannot always be converted into an other currency.

sogo shosha The Japanese term for a trading company.

soiled bill of lading A bill of lading that reflects the fact that the carrier did not receive the goods in good condition.

Special Drawing Rights An artificial currency whose value is determined by the the value of a basket of currencies.

special English A technique of oral communication that uses a limited vocabulary and short sentences, so that a person with limited knowledge of English can understand it.

speculative risk A risk that can generate a loss or a gain.

spot exchange rate The exchange rate of a foreign currency for immediate delivery (within 48 hours).

standard container A large metallic box used in international trade that can be loaded directly onto a truck, a railroad car or an ocean-going vessel. The most common dimensions of a container are $8 \times 8.5 \times 20$ feet and $8 \times 8.5 \times 40$ feet.

stand-by letter of credit A letter of credit that is valid for multiple shipments and allows for bills of lading issued on multiple dates.

statistical process control A statistical process followed by manufacturers to ensure that a manufacturing process is working correctly.

statistical quality control A statistical process followed by manufacturers to ensure that a manufacturing process is working correctly.

SPC with attributes A statistical quality control method used to determine whether a manufacturing process is working correctly.

SPC with variables A statistical quality control method used to determine whether a manufacturing process is working correctly.

stevedore Historically, an individual, and today a company, that loads and unloads goods from a vessel.

straight bill of lading A bill of lading on which the name of the consignee has been entered.

stranding In a stranding, a ship runs into high ground and can no longer move.

strike price The price at which a currency option is exercised.

stores All the supplies that a ship needs to carry in order to operate.

stowed Goods are considered stowed when they are aboard the ship and placed in the position in which they will be transported.

stretch/shrink wrap A polymer film that is stretched over palletized cargo to protect it from water damage.

subjective risk A risk whose probability cannot be relied upon.

subsidiary A company entirely owned by another company.

surveyor An independent company that investigates damage to shipments on behalf of insurance companies.

SWIFT-Society for Worldwide Interbank Financial Telecommunications An interbank electronic network for the secure transfer of funds and documents.

system's theft Theft perpetrated by someone with access to the shipper's or carrier's computers.

Taguchi methods A set of methods used to reduce the variability in a manufacturing process.

tariff A tax collected by an importing country on the value of imported goods.

tariff rate The rate at which an import is taxed. The rate depends on classification and origin. Also called the duty rate.

tariff-rate quota A limit, set by the importing country's government, on the quantity of a commodity that can be imported at a certain tariff rate in a given year. Once that limit has been reached, the tariff rate is higher.

tariff schedule A document listing all the possible Harmonized System categories and their associated duty rates for different countries.

technology driver One reason a firm may go international is to respond to technologically savvy customers who buy products worldwide.

term of appointment The initial duration of the distribution contract, and the duration of its eventual renewal periods.

term of sale An element of the contract of sale that specifies the method of payment used in an international transaction.

term of trade An element of the contract of sale that specifies the responsibilities of the exporter and those of the importer in the shipment of the goods.

termination for "convenience" The unilateral decision, by one of the parties to a contract, to terminate the contract for reasons unrelated to the performance of the contract by the other party.

termination for "just cause" The unilateral decision, by one of the parties to a contract, to terminate the contract because the other party has not met the terms of the agreement.

territory The geographical area in which the agent or distributor is restricted/expected to sell.

TEU Twenty-foot Equivalent Unit. The equivalent of a twenty-foot container. A forty-foot container is two TEUs.

time-definite shipments Cargo or package shipments that must be delivered by a guaranteed, predetermined time and day.

time draft A draft in which the importer promises to pay the exporter 30, 60 or 90 days after the importer has signed the draft.

to-order bill of lading A bill of lading on which the name of the consignee is marked "to order." A negotiable bill of lading.

Total Security Management (TSM) A management philosophy that posits that security is better achieved if every member of the organization is vigilant and pro-active in identifying security issues.

tractor The part of an articulated truck that is in the front and pulls the trailer.

trailer The part of an articulated truck that is in the rear and pulled by the tractor.

trade acceptance In a documentary collection, trade acceptance takes place when the importer signs the draft.

trade deficit A situation where the total exports of a country are worth less than its total imports.

trade surplus A situation where the total exports of a country are worth more than its total imports.

TradeCard A proprietary process that combines payment and documents and facilitates international transactions.

trademark An intellectual property item that refers to a brand, a commercial name, or a slogan.

tramp ship A ship that does not operate on a regular schedule and is available for charter for any voyage, from any port to any port.

transaction exposure The impact of a change in a currency exchange rate for a company involved in international trade. Its effect on the company's financial well-being.

transferable letter of credit A letter of credit that the beneficiary can use as a means to insure its creditors that they will be paid.

translation A conversion of words or text from one language into another.

transfer of responsibility In an international voyage, the point at which the exporter ceases to be responsible for the goods.

transfer of title The point in time at which the ownership of the goods changes from the exporter to the importer.

transferable letter of credit A letter of credit that the beneficiary can use as a means to insure its creditors that they will be paid.

Transportation Workers' Identification Credential (TWIC) A U.S. program designed to limit access to ports to persons without a serious criminal background.

Treaty of Rome The treaty between six European countries that created the European Union.

trimmed A ship is considered trimmed when the cargo aboard the ship is balanced side-to-side and front-to-back.

Trot-On/Trot-Off A type of ship designed to carry livestock. Animals use a ramp to walk on board and exit the ship.

tweendeck A deck located below the main deck and used to carry smaller cargo.

Type I error A statistical error; although the null hypothesis is true, the test concludes erroneously that the alternative hypothesis is true.

Type II error A statistical error; although the alternative hypothesis is true, the test concludes erroneously that the null hypothesis is true.

unairworthy aircraft An aircraft not capable to safely fly and carry cargo.

uniform bill of lading A bill of lading used for transportation by truck or train, domestically or internationally.

Uniform Commercial Code The set of federal laws that govern commercial contracts in the United States.

unit load device (ULD) The term used to describe the containers used in airfreight transport.

unitized Cargo in which smaller packaging units are assembled into a single larger unit, to facilitate handling.

unseaworthy vessel A vessel not capable to safely travel and carry cargo.

valuation The process of determining the value of an import, specifically the amount on which the duty is calculated.

value-added tax A tax collected by many countries that is very similar to a sales tax, but is based on the increase in the value of the product at each step of the manufacturing process.

variable In statistical quality control, a measurement on a manufactured product that can take an infinite number of values.

Vienna Convention Another name for the Convention on Contracts for the International Sale of Goods.

volume weight (dimensional weight) An artificial weight, determined in function of the dimensions of a shipment, used by airlines to determine the tariff to be paid for a light shipment.

Warsaw Convention A 1929 Convention that established the first liability limits for air carriers.

wet lease A type of leasing contract in which an airplane is leased, along with a crew, maintenance services, insurance, and fuel.

wholly-owned foreign enterprise Another term for a subsidiary.

with-average policy A marine cargo insurance policy that covers only the risks listed in the policy. The second broadest coverage available under U.S.-based policies, but not suitable for many cargoes because of its restrictions.

World Bank The bank that was created at Bretton-Woods in 1944 and finances large-scale infrastructure projects in the world.

World Customs Organization (WCO) An international body whose mission is to improve the administration of Customs. Its members are the national Customs administrations.

World Trade Organization The international organization responsible for enforcing international trade agreements and for ensuring that countries deal fairly with one another.

Index